Financial Management
for Decision Makers

Visit the *Financial Management for Decision Makers, fifth edition*, Companion Website at **www.pearsoned.co.uk/atrillmclaney** to find valuable **student** learning material including:

- Learning outcomes for each chapter
- Multiple choice questions to test your learning
- Solutions to end of chapter review questions
- Revision questions to help you check your understanding
- Extensive links to valuable resources on the web
- An online glossary to explain key terms
- Flashcards to test your knowledge of key terms and definitions

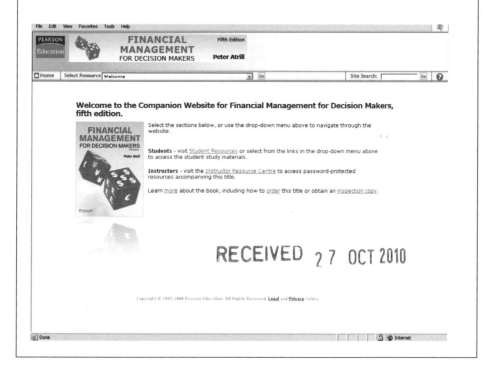

5th Edition

Financial Management
for Decision Makers

Peter Atrill

FT **Prentice Hall**
FINANCIAL TIMES

An imprint of **Pearson Education**
Harlow, England • London • New York • Boston • San Francisco • Toronto
Sydney • Tokyo • Singapore • Hong Kong • Seoul • Taipei • New Delhi
Cape Town • Madrid • Mexico City • Amsterdam • Munich • Paris • Milan

Pearson Education Limited
Edinburgh Gate
Harlow
Essex CM20 2JE
England

and Associated Companies throughout the world

Visit us on the World Wide Web at:
www.pearsoned.co.uk

First published 1997
Second edition published 2000
Third edition published 2003
Fourth edition published 2006
Fifth edition published 2009

ISBN: 978-0-273-71764-5

British Library Cataloguing-in-Publication Data
A catalogue record for this book is available from the British Library

Library of Congress Cataloging-in-Publication Data
Atrill, Peter.
  Financial management for decision makers / Peter Atrill. — 5th ed.
     p. cm.
  Includes bibliographical references and index.
  ISBN 978-0-273-71764-5 (pbk. : alk. paper)   1. Accounting.   2. Decision making.
I. Title.
  HF5635.A8846 2009
  658.15—dc22

                                                            2008037205

10 9   8   7   6   5   4   3   2
12 11 10 09

Typeset in 9.5/12.5pt Stone Serif by 35
Printed and bound by Graficas Estella, Navarra, Spain

The publisher's policy is to use paper manufactured from sustainable forests.

For Simon and Helen

Contents

Supporting resources

Visit **www.pearsoned.co.uk/atrillmclaney** to find valuable online resources

Companion Website for students

- Learning outcomes for each chapter
- Multiple choice questions to test your learning
- Solutions to end of chapter review questions
- Revision questions to help you check your understanding
- Extensive links to valuable resources on the web
- An online glossary to explain key terms
- Flashcards to test your knowledge of key terms and definitions

For instructors

- Complete, downloadable Instructor's manual
- PowerPoint slides that can be downloaded and used as OHTs
- Progress tests, consisting of various questions and exercise material with solutions
- Tutorial/seminar questions and solutions
- Solutions to individual chapter exercises

Also: The Companion Website provides the following features:

- Search tool to help locate specific items of content
- E-mail results and profile tools to send results of quizzes to instructors
- Online help and support to assist with website usage and troubleshooting

For more information please contact your local Pearson Education sales representative or visit **www.pearsoned.co.uk/atrillmclaney**

Preface

This book has been written for those who wish to achieve a broad understanding of financial management at either undergraduate or postgraduate/post-experience level. It is aimed primarily at students who are not majoring in financial management but who, nevertheless, are studying introductory-level financial management as part of their course in business, management, economics, computing, engineering or some other area. Students who are majoring in financial management should, however, find the book useful as an introduction to the main principles which can serve as a foundation for further study. The book should also be suitable for those who are not following a particular course but nevertheless need an understanding of financial management to help them manage their business.

As there are several excellent books on financial management already published, you may wonder why another book is needed in this area. A problem with many books is that they are too detailed and demanding to provide a suitable introduction to the subject. They are often around a thousand pages in length and contain mathematical formulae that many find daunting. This book assumes no previous knowledge of financial management (although a basic understanding of financial statements is required) and is written in an accessible style. Each topic is introduced carefully and there is a gradual building of knowledge. In addition, mathematical formulae have been kept to a minimum.

The book rests on a solid foundation of theory but the main focus throughout is its practical value. It is assumed that readers are primarily concerned with understanding financial management in order to make better financial decisions. The title of the book reflects this decision-making focus.

The book is written in an 'open learning' style. That is, it tries to involve you in a way not traditionally found in textbooks. Throughout each chapter there are activities and self-assessment questions for you to attempt. The purpose of these is to help check understanding of the points that are being made and to encourage you to think around particular topics. More detail concerning the nature and use of these activities and self-assessment questions is given in the 'How to use this book' section following this preface. The open learning style has been adopted because, I believe, it is more 'user friendly'. Irrespective of whether you are using the book as part of a taught course or for independent study, the interactive approach employed makes it easier for you to learn.

I recognise that most of you will not have studied financial management before and so I have tried to minimise the use of technical jargon. Where technical terminology is unavoidable, I try to provide clear explanations. To help you further, all the key terms are highlighted in the book and then listed at the end of each chapter with a page reference to help you rapidly revise the main concepts. All these key terms are listed alphabetically with a short definition in the glossary, which can be found towards the end of the book.

In writing the fifth edition, I have taken account of helpful comments and suggestions made by lecturers, students and other readers. Many areas have been revised to improve the clarity of the writing and I have introduced more diagrams and graphs to aid understanding. The number of real world exhibits has been increased to help illustrate the practical application and importance of the topics discussed.

I do hope that you will find the book readable and helpful.

Peter Atrill
April 2008

Acknowledgements

I wish to acknowledge the generosity of the ACCA for allowing me to use extracts from articles that I wrote for *Finance Matters* magazine.

Publisher's acknowledgements

We are grateful to the following for permission to reproduce copyright material:

Figure 3.5 from Beaver, W.H. (1966) Financial ratios as predictors of failure, Empirical Research in Accounting: Selected Studies, supplement to *Journal of Accounting Research*, Blackwell Publishers Limited; Real World 3.9 from Marks and Spencer Group plc *Annual Report 2007*; Real World 5.1 from Arnold, G.C. and Hatzopoulos, P.D. (2000) The theory practice gap in capital budgeting: evidence from the United Kingdom, *Journal of Business Finance and Accounting*, 27(5) and (6), Blackwell Publishers Limited; Real World 6.5 from *Corporate Finance: A valuation approach*, Benninga, S.Z. and Sarig, O.H. (1997) © The McGraw Hill Companies, Inc.; Figure 7.3 from Reading the signs, *The Independent* © The Independent 2004; Figure 7.6 from The venture capital vacuum in *Management Today*, (Van der Wayer, M. 1995); Real World 7.14 from *Angel Investing: Matching Start-up Funds with Start-up Companies – A Guide for Entrepreneurs and Individual Investors*, Jossey Bass, Inc., (Van Osnabrugge, M. and Robinson, R. J. 2000); Figure 8.6 from Graham, J. and Harvey, C. (2002) How do CFOs make capital budgeting and capital structure decisions?, *Journal of Applied Corporate Finance*, Vol. 15, No. 1, Blackwell Publishers Limited; Figures 8.7 and 8.8 from McLaney, E., Pointon, J., Thomas, M. and Tucker, J. (2004) Practitioner's perspectives on the UK cost of capital, *European Journal of Finance*, 10, pp. 123–138, April; Figure 9.4 from Revisiting managerial perspectives on dividend policy in *Journal of Economics and Finance*, Springer, (Baker, H., Powell, G. and Veit, E. Theodore 2002); Figure 11.7 from Tesco plc, *Annual Report and Financial Statements* 2007; Figure 12.4 from *Creating Long-term Value through Mergers and Acquisitions*, PA Consulting Group, PA Knowledge Ltd, 2003.

Real World 1.1 Assessing the Rate of Return, Financial Times Mastering Management Series, 1995, Supplement No. 1, © Elroy Dimson; Real World 1.8 from *Code of Ethics*, www.shell.com; Real World 1.9 from *The Combined Code*, www.frc.org.uk © The Financial Reporting Council – adapted and reproduced with the kind permission of the FRC. All rights reserved; extracts (pp. 29 and 31) from *Annual Report to Shareholders*, Berkshire Hathaway Inc., Buffett, W.E. (1985); Real World 1.13 from *Corporate Governance and Voting Policy* (www.jupiteronline.co.uk); Real World 3.10 from Dirty laundry: how companies fudge the numbers, *The Times*, © NI Syndication Limited, 22 September 2002; Real World 4.12 from Rolls-Royce plc *Annual Report and Accounts 2006*, © Rolls-Royce Group plc; Real World 4.13 from Artisan (UK) plc, www.artisan-plc.co.uk and Tesco plc *Corporate Governance Report*, www.tescocorporate.com; Real World 5.4 from Proposed Disposal of Hard Rock and Related Special Dividend and Share Consolidation, *Notice of Extraordinary Meeting*, The Rank Group plc, December 2006, www.rank.com; Real World 6.1 from Ryanair blunted by Buzz takeover, *Daily Telegraph*, (Osborne, A. 2004); Real World 6.8 from Temperature falls to freezing for junk bonds, www.telegraph.co.uk, (Evans-Pritchard, Ambrose 2007); Real World 6.9 from Wolseley plc *Annual Report 2007*, www.wolseleyplc.com and Barratt Developments plc *Annual Report and Accounts 2007*; Real World 6.14 from Holidaybreak plc *Annual Report and Financial Statements 2007*; Real World 7.4 from Internet FD is in the money after floatation, *Accountancy Age*, (Jetuah, David 2007); Real World 7.12 from bbc.co.uk/news; Real World 9.1 *Financial calendar 2008*, www.admiralgroup.co.uk; Real World 9.2 from Press release, 19 June 2007, www.cadburyschweppes.com; Real World 10.10 from *Accountancy Magazine* (2000); Real World 11.3 from Hanson PLC *Annual Report and Form 20-F 2006*, www.hanson.biz; Real World 12.5 and 12.11 from Warren Buffett's letter to Berkshire Hathaway Inc. shareholders, 1981, www.berkshirehathaway.com.

We are grateful to the Financial Times Limited for permission to reprint the following material:

Text: Real World 1.2 Profit without honour, © *Financial Times*, 29–30 June 2002; Real World 1.4 Forget how the crow flies, © *Financial Times*, 17 January 2004; Real World 1.5 Appetite for risk drives industry, © *FT.com*, 27 June 2007; page 12 Tasks of the Finance Function, Rose, H., Financial Times Mastering Management Series, supplement issue no. 1, p. 11., © *Financial Times*, 1995; Real World 1.11 Move to oust SkyePharma chairman, © *FT.com*, 20 January 2006; Real World 1.12 UBM investors in bonus revolt, © *FT.com*, 4 May 2005; Real World 2.3 Vanco's shares fall on profit warning, © *FT.com*, 21 August, 2007; Real World 2.5 Everything in the millennium garden is far from rosy, © *FT.com*, 24 November 2005; Real World 3.4 Investing in Bollywood, © *Financial Times*, 26 June 2007; Real World 3.5 Adapted from 'Small companies surprise on lending, © *Financial Times*, 25 April 2003; Real World 4.6 Adapted from Bond seeks funds in London to mine African diamonds, © *FT.com*, 23 April 2007; Real World 4.7 A hot topic, but poor returns, © *FT.com*, 27 August 2005; Real World 4.11 Satellites need space to earn, © *FT.com*, 14 July 2003; Real World 6.6 BA regains investment-grade status, © *FT.com*, 20 June 2007; Real World 6.7 EDS warns of a dividend cut, © *Financial Times*, 11 May 2004; Real World 6.13 Sale and leasebacks, © *FT.com*, 1 March 2005; Real World 7.3 What a difference a delay makes for Moneysupermarket.com, © *FT.com*, 27 July 2007; Real World 7.6 Pundit warns of 'incipient bubble' in mainland equities, © *Financial Times*, 30 October 2007; Real World 7.7 Rights issue to cut SMG debt by £91m, © *FT.com*, 7 November 2007; Real World 7.8 Rise possible following bonus issue adjustment, © *FT.com*, 24 March 2007; Real World 7.9 Ultimate outlines £25m share placing plan, © *FT.com*, 23 January 2007; Real World 8.7 Gearing levels fall amid fears over risks, © *FT.com*, 29 April 2005; Real World 8.10 BAA's finances, © *FT.com*, 9 November 2007; Real World 9.2 Dividends to rise at National Grid, © *FT.com*, 1 February 2008; Real World 9.4 Focus on dividend payments, © *FT.com*, 18 February 2008; Real World 9.5 Samsung and the joys of middle age: sharing out the cash, © *FT.com*, 27 September 2004; Real World 9.6 Premier Foods reaches its nadir, © *FT.com*, 26 February 2008; Real World 9.7 SSE to raise dividend 18 per cent in new pay-out policy, © *FT.com*, 6 March 2007; Real World 9.10 Dividend hike marks shift in investor rewards, © *FT.com*, 5 February 2008; Real World 10.8 Late payment hits small companies, © *FT.com*, 29 January 2007; Real World 10.12 NHS paying bills late in struggle to balance books, say suppliers, © *FT.com*, 13 February 2007; Real World 11.2 Siemens chief finds himself in a difficult balancing act, © *FT.com*, 6 November 2006; Real World 12.4 Decline of the conglomerates, © *FT.com*, 4 February 2007; Real World 12.9 Safeway directors' £5.5m compensation, © *Financial Times*, 10 June 2003; Real World 12.10 MITTA/ARCELOR: $100m payday for advisers, © *FT.com*, 27 June, 2006; Real World 12.12 Take-Two's severance plan puts EA on notice, © *FT.com*, 10 March 2008; Real World 12.14 Airline shareholders look for spin-off plans, © *FT.com*, 30 October 2007; Real World 12.15 Trying to put a price on a promise, © *Financial Times*, 9 March 2004.

Tables: Real World 12.8 Money section, © *Financial Times*, 15–16 March 2008.

In some instances we have been unable to trace the owners of copyright material, and we would appreciate any information that would enable us to do so.

How to use this book

The contents of the book have been ordered in what I believe is a logical sequence and, for this reason, I suggest that you work through the book in the order in which it is presented. Every effort has been made to ensure that earlier chapters do not refer to concepts or terms that are not explained until a later chapter. If you work through the chapters in the 'wrong' order, you will probably encounter concepts and points that were explained previously but which you have missed.

Irrespective of whether you are using the book as part of a lecture/tutorial-based course or as the basis for a more independent form of study, I recommend you follow broadly the same approach.

Integrated assessment material

Interspersed throughout each chapter are numerous **Activities**. You are strongly advised to attempt all these questions. They are designed to stimulate the sort of 'quick-fire' questions that a good lecturer might throw at you during a lecture or tutorial. Activities seek to serve two purposes:

- To give you the opportunity to check that you understand what has been covered so far.
- To encourage you to think about the topic just covered, either to see a link between that topic and others with which you are already familiar, or to link the topic just covered to the next.

The answer to each Activity is provided immediately after the question. This answer should be covered up until you have deduced your solution, which can then be compared to the one given.

Towards the end of most chapters, there is a **Self-assessment question**. This is rather more demanding and comprehensive than any of the Activities and is designed to give you an opportunity to see whether you understand the core material in the chapter. The solution to each of the Self-assessment questions is provided at the end of the book. As with the Activities, it is very important that you attempt each question thoroughly before referring to the solution. If you have difficulty with a Self-assessment question, you should go over the relevant chapter again.

End-of-chapter assessment material

At the end of each chapter, there are four **Review questions**. These are short questions requiring a narrative answer or discussion within a tutorial group. They are intended to enable you to assess how well you can recall and critically evaluate the core terms and concepts covered in each chapter. Suggested answers to these questions are included at the end of the book. Again, a real attempt should be made to answer these questions before referring to the solutions.

At the end of a chapter, there are normally seven **Exercises**. (However, Chapter 1 has none, Chapter 9 has six and Chapter 11 has five.) These are mostly computational and are designed to reinforce your knowledge and understanding. Exercises are of varying complexity, with the more advanced ones clearly identified. Although the less advanced Exercises are fairly straightforward, the more advanced ones can be quite demanding. Nevertheless, they are capable of being successfully completed if you have worked conscientiously through the chapter and have attempted the less advanced Exercises beforehand.

Answers to those Exercises marked with a coloured number are provided at the end of the book. Three out of the seven Exercises normally found in a chapter are marked with a coloured number to enable you to check progress. The marked Exercises will be a mixture of less advanced and more advanced Exercises. Solutions to the Exercises that are not marked with a coloured number are given in a separate lecturer's Solutions Manual. Yet again, a thorough attempt should be made to answer these Exercises before referring to the solutions.

Guided tour of the book

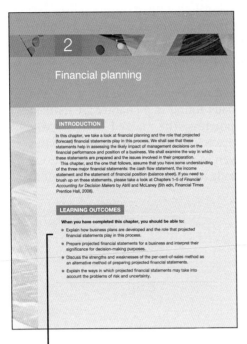

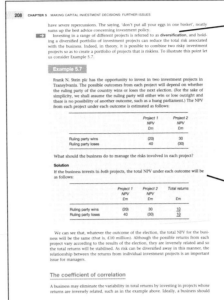

Learning outcomes Bullet points at the start of each chapter show what you can expect to learn from that chapter, and highlight the core coverage.

Key terms The key concepts and techniques in each chapter are highlighted in colour where they are first introduced, with an adjacent icon in the margin to help you refer back to the most important points.

Examples At frequent intervals, throughout most chapters, there are numerical examples that give you step-by-step workings to follow through to the solution.

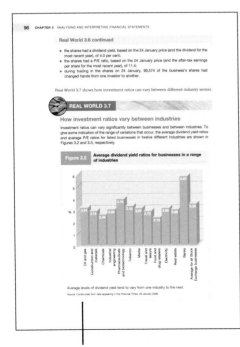

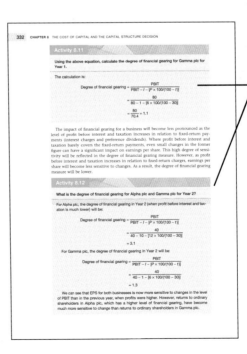

Activities These short questions, integrated throughout each chapter, allow you to check your understanding as you progress through the text. They comprise either a narrative question requiring you to review or critically consider topics, or a numerical problem requiring you to deduce a solution. A suggested answer is given immediately after each activity.

'Real World' illustrations Integrated throughout the text, these illustrative examples highlight the practical application of accounting concepts and techniques by real businesses, including extracts from company reports and financial statements, survey data and other interesting insights from business.

Self-assessment questions Towards the end of most chapters you will encounter one of these questions, allowing you to attempt a comprehensive question before tackling the end-of-chapter assessment material. To check your understanding and progress, solutions are provided in Appendix C.

Bullet point chapter summary Each chapter ends with a 'bullet point' summary. This highlights the material covered in the chapter and can be used as a quick reminder of the main issues.

Key terms summary At the end of each chapter, there is a listing (with page reference) of all the key terms, allowing you to easily refer back to the most important points.

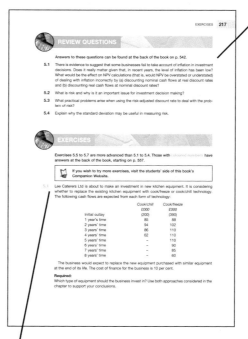

Review questions These short questions encourage you to review and/or critically discuss your understanding of the main topics covered in each chapter, either individually or in a group. Solutions to these questions can be found on the Companion Website at **www.pearsoned.co.uk/ atrillmclaney**

Further reading This section comprises a listing of relevant chapters in other textbooks that you might refer to in order to pursue a topic in more depth or gain an alternative perspective.

References Provides full details of sources of information referred to in the chapter.

Exercises These comprehensive questions appear at the end of most chapters. The more advanced questions are separately identified. Solutions to some of the questions (those with coloured numbers) are provided in Appendix D, enabling you to assess your progress. Solutions to the remaining questions are available for lecturers only. Additional exercises can be found on the Companion Website at **www.pearsoned.co.uk/atrillmclaney**

Guided tour of the Companion Website

Extra material has been prepared to help you study using *Financial Management for Decision Makers*. This material can be found on the book's Companion Website at **www.pearsoned.co.uk/atrillmclaney**. You will find links to websites of interest, as well as a range of material including:

Interactive quizzes

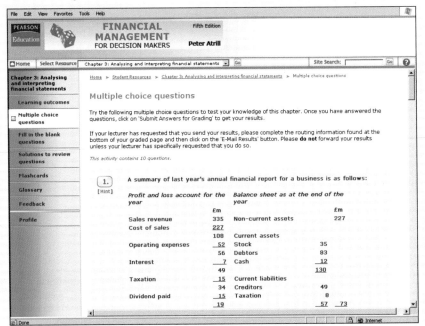

For each chapter there is a set of interactive multiple choice questions, plus a set of fill-in-the blanks questions and an extra exercise. Test your learning and get automatic grading on your answers.

Revision questions

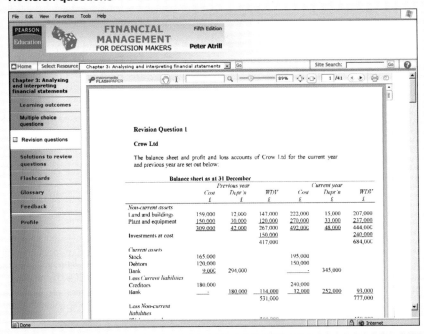

Sets of questions covering the whole book are designed to help you check your overall learning whilst you are revising.

Solutions to review questions

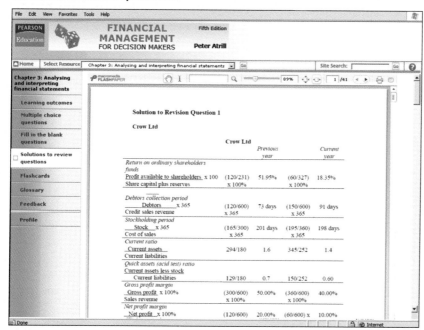

Answers to end-of-chapter review questions that appear in the book are to be found on the website, so you can check your progress.

Glossary and flashcards

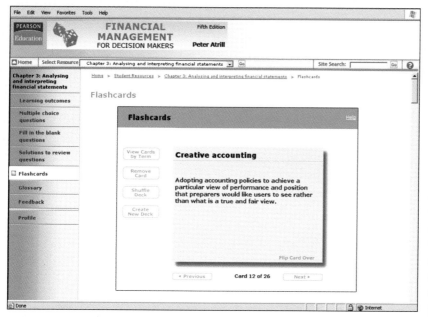

Full version of the book's glossary to help you check definitions while you are online. Flashcards help you to learn and test yourself on definitions of key terms. A term is displayed on each card: 'flip over' for the definition, 'shuffle' the cards to randomly test your knowledge.

The world of financial management

INTRODUCTION

In this first chapter, we consider the role of the finance function within a business and the context within which financial decisions are made. We begin by identifying the tasks of the finance function and their relation to the tasks of managers. We then go on to consider the objectives that a business may pursue.

Modern financial management theory assumes that the primary objective of a business is to maximise the wealth of its owners (shareholders). We examine this and other possible objectives for a business and discuss reasons why the shareholder wealth maximisation objective is considered to be the most appropriate. This objective, however, cannot be pursued to the exclusion of everything else. We shall see that the level of risk, the need to act ethically and the interests of other groups associated with a business must be taken into consideration.

Adopting a commitment to shareholder wealth maximisation does not automatically mean that it will be carried out. There is always a risk that managers will pursue their own interests at the expense of shareholders' interests. This is often referred to as the 'agency problem' and the ways in which it may be managed, through regulation and through the active involvement of shareholders, will be considered.

LEARNING OUTCOMES

When you have completed this chapter, you should be able to:

● Discuss the role of the finance function within a business.

● Identify and discuss possible objectives for a business and explain why shareholder wealth maximisation is considered to be the most appropriate.

● Explain how risk and ethical considerations influence the pursuit of shareholder wealth maximisation.

● Describe the agency problem and explain how this problem may be dealt with.

The finance function

Put simply, the finance function within a business exists to help managers to manage. To understand how the finance function can do this, we must first be clear about what managers do. One way of describing the role of managers is to classify their activities into the following categories:

- *Strategic management.* This involves developing objectives for the business and then formulating long-term plans to achieve them. When making long-term plans, possible options (strategies) must be identified and evaluated. The one chosen should offer the greatest potential for achieving the agreed objectives.
- *Operations management.* This refers to the day-to-day decision making and control that managers undertake. Actual events must conform to the plans that were made and action must be taken to see that this occurs.
- *Risk management.* This involves identifying the risks faced by the business and then ensuring that they are properly managed. Risks arise from the nature of the business operations and/or the way in which the business is financed.

As we can see from Figure 1.1, these three categories are not separate and distinct. They are interrelated and overlaps arise between them. When considering a particular strategy, for example, managers must also make a careful assessment of the risks involved and how these risks may be managed. Similarly, when making operational decisions, managers must try to ensure they fit within the strategic (long-term) plans that have been formulated.

Figure 1.1	**The role of managers**

The figure shows the three overlapping roles of management.

The finance function is concerned with helping managers in each of the three areas identified. The key tasks undertaken by the finance function are set out in Figure 1.2 and described below.

- *Financial planning.* The likely effect of proposals on the financial performance and position of the business is a vitally important input to the overall planning process. By developing projected financial statements (such as cash flow statements and income statements), as well as other financial estimates, the viability of proposed courses of action can be evaluated.

● *Investment project appraisal.* Assessing the profitability and riskiness of proposed investment projects is another important input to the overall planning process. By appraising projects in this way, managers can make more informed decisions concerning either their acceptance or rejection. They can also prioritise those projects that are expected to be profitable.

● *Financing decisions* Future strategies and investment projects have to be financed. It is important, therefore, to be able to identify and assess possible sources of finance available. When choosing among different financing options, consideration must be given to the overall financial structure of a business. This involves achieving the appropriate balance between long-term and short-term finance and between the financing contribution of shareholders and that of lenders. Not all financing requirements are derived from external sources: some funds may be internally generated. An important source of internally generated funds is profits, and the extent to which a business reinvests profits, rather than distributing them in the form of dividend, is another important decision.

● *Capital market operations.* A business may try to raise funds from the capital markets and so finance staff should understand how these markets work. In particular, they need to know how finance can be raised through the markets, how securities (shares and loan capital) are priced and how the markets may react to proposed investment and financing plans.

● *Financial control.* Once plans are put into action, managers must try to ensure that things stay on course. Information is required on matters such as the profitability of investment projects, levels of working capital and cash flows, which can be used as a basis for monitoring performance and, where necessary, taking corrective action.

Figure 1.2	The tasks of the finance function

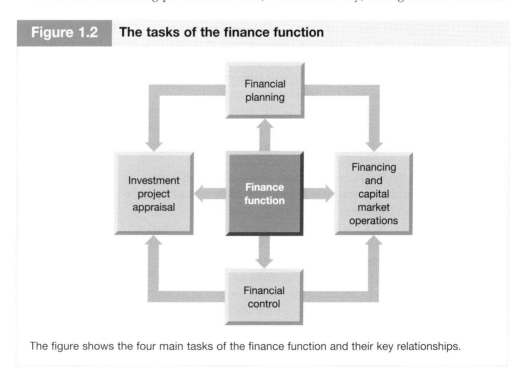

The figure shows the four main tasks of the finance function and their key relationships.

The links between the tasks of managers, which were identified earlier, and the tasks of the finance function are many and varied. Strategic management decisions, for example, may require an input from the finance function on issues relating to financial planning, investment project appraisal, financing and capital market operations.

Operations management may require an input on issues relating to financial planning, investment project appraisal, financing and financial control. Risk management may require an input from the finance function on issues relating to all of the tasks identified above.

Structure of the book

In this book, each of the tasks of the finance function described above will be considered. We begin, in Chapter 2, by examining the way in which financial plans are prepared and the role of projected financial statements in helping managers to assess likely future outcomes.

In Chapter 3 we go on to consider how financial statements can be analysed and interpreted. The financial techniques examined in this chapter are important both for the evaluation of projected financial statements and for other areas such as long-term financing decisions and the control of working capital, which are discussed later in the book.

Chapters 4 and 5 are concerned with investment decision making. In these two chapters, we take a look at various methods used to assess investment proposals. We also consider how risk may be taken into account and how investment projects, once implemented, may be monitored.

Chapters 6 to 9 are concerned with various aspects of the financing decision. We first consider the various sources of finance available and then go on to consider the role and efficiency of capital markets. We also examine the issues surrounding the appropriate mix of finance that a business should have within its capital structure. We shall see that the level of borrowing that a business takes on can have a significant effect on future risks and returns. Finally, we consider the dividend decision and the factors to be taken into account when deciding upon the appropriate balance between the retention and distribution of profits.

In Chapter 10, we look at the ways in which managers can exert financial control over the working capital of a business. We examine each element of working capital (inventories, receivables, cash and payables) and discuss the various techniques available for controlling each of these elements.

In Chapter 11, we consider some of the key methods for measuring and managing shareholder wealth. We shall assess their potential value and explore their links to the strategic objectives and plans of a business.

Finally, in Chapter 12, we take a look at mergers and takeovers. When examining this area, we draw on our understanding of a number of topics that were covered earlier, particularly those relating to investment appraisal, financing and capital market operations. We consider the effect of mergers on shareholder wealth and the ways in which merger proposals may be financed. We end the book by examining how shares may be valued for mergers, or for other purposes.

Modern financial management

In the early years of its development, financial management was really an offshoot of accounting. Much of the early work was descriptive, and arguments were based on casual observation rather than any clear theoretical framework. However, over the years, financial management became increasingly influenced by economic theories and the reasoning applied to particular issues has become more rigorous and analytical. Indeed, such is the influence of economic theory that modern financial management is often viewed as a branch of applied economics.

Economic theories concerning the efficient allocation of scarce resources have been taken and developed into decision-making tools for management. This development of economic theories for practical business use has usually involved taking account of both the time dimension and the risks associated with management decision making. An investment decision, for example, must look at both the time period over which the investment extends and the degree of risk associated with the investment. This fact has led to financial management being described as the *economics of time and risk*. Certainly time and risk will be recurring themes throughout this text.

Economic theories have also helped us to understand the importance of **capital markets**, such as stock markets and banks, to a business. Capital markets have a vital role to play in bringing together borrowers and lenders, in allowing investors to select the type of investment that best meets their risk requirements and in helping to evaluate the performance of businesses through the prices assigned to their shares.

Real World 1.1 is an extract from an article by Professor Dimson of London Business School. It neatly sums up how time, risk and capital markets are at the centre of modern financial management.

REAL WORLD 1.1

Finance on the back of a postage stamp   **FT**

The leading textbooks in finance are nearly 1,000 pages long. Many students learn by making notes on each topic. They then summarise their notes. Here is one student's summary of his Finance course . . . Time is money . . . Don't put all your eggs in one basket . . . You can't fool all the people all of the time.

● The idea that time is money refers to the fact that a sum of money received now is worth more than the same sum paid in the future. This gives rise to the principle that future cash flows should be discounted, in order to calculate their present value.

● You can reduce the risk of an investment if you don't put all your eggs in one basket. In other words, a diversified portfolio of investments is less risky than putting all your money in a single asset. Risks that cannot be diversified away should be accepted only if they are offset by a higher expected return.

● The idea that you can't fool all of the people all of the time refers to the efficiency of financial markets. An efficient market is one in which information is widely and cheaply available to everyone and relevant information is therefore incorporated into security prices. Because new information is reflected in prices immediately, investors should expect to receive only a normal rate of return. Possession of information about a company will not enable an investor to outperform. The only way to expect a higher expected return is to be exposed to greater risk.

These three themes of discounted cash flow, risk and diversification, and market efficiency lie at the very heart of most introductory finance courses.

Each of these themes will be considered in this book.

Source: E. Dimson, *Assessing the Rate of Return*, Financial Times Mastering Management Series, supplement issue, no. 1, 1995, p. 13.

Why do businesses exist?

A key idea underpinning modern financial management is that businesses exist to make money for their owners (shareholders). To be more precise, it is assumed that the primary objective of a business is **shareholder wealth maximisation**. Within a market economy, shareholders provide funds to a business in the expectation that they will receive the maximum possible increase in wealth for the level of risk that must be faced. When we use the term 'wealth' in this context, we are referring to the *market value of the ordinary shares*. The market value of these shares will, in turn, reflect the future returns the shareholders will expect to receive *over time* from the shares and the level of risk involved. Note that we are concerned not with maximising shareholders' returns over the short term, but rather with providing the highest possible returns over the long term.

Wealth maximisation or profit maximisation?

Wealth maximisation is not the only financial objective that a business can pursue: profit maximisation provides an alternative objective for a business. Profit maximisation differs from wealth maximisation in a number of important respects, as we shall see. Before considering these differences, however, we must first decide what is meant by the term 'profit'. There are various measures of both profit, and profitability, which could be maximised, including the following:

● operating profit (that is, profit before interest and tax)
● profit before tax
● profit after tax
● profit available to shareholders per ordinary share
● profit available to shareholders as a percentage of ordinary shareholders' funds invested, and so on.

The availability of different measures means that the evaluation of an investment opportunity may be influenced by the particular measure used. This point is illustrated in Activity 1.1.

Activity 1.1

Pointon Ltd has the following long-term capital and annual profits:

Capital invested (£1 ordinary shares)	£100,000
Profit available to ordinary shareholders	£ 15,000

The business is considering the issue of 20,000 new £1 ordinary shares and investing the amount raised in an opportunity that provides an additional profit of £2,000 for ordinary shareholders.

What should be done if the objective of the business is to maximise:

(a) profit available to ordinary shareholders?
(b) profit available to ordinary shareholders per ordinary share?

....

The profits available to ordinary shareholders will be increased by the investment to £17,000 (£15,000 + £2,000).

The profit per ordinary share, however, will be decreased. The current profit per ordinary share is 15 per cent (£15,000/£100,000) whereas the expected profit per ordinary share on the investment is 10 per cent (£2,000/£20,000). The effect of taking the opportunity will, therefore, be to lower the overall profit per ordinary share to 14.2 per cent (£17,000/£120,000).

We can see that an objective of maximising profit available to shareholders would lead to a decision to invest, whereas an objective of maximising profit available to shareholders per ordinary share would lead to a decision to reject the opportunity.

Profit maximisation, however measured, is usually seen as a short-term objective whereas wealth maximisation is a long-term objective. There can be a conflict between short-term and long-term performance. It would be quite possible, for example, to maximise short-term profits at the expense of long-term profits, as explained in Activity 1.2.

Activity 1.2

How might the managers of a business increase short-term profits at the expense of long-term profits?

The managers may reduce operating expenses, and so increase short-term profits, by:

- cutting research and development expenditure
- cutting staff training and development
- buying lower quality materials
- cutting quality control mechanisms.

Whilst these policies may all have a beneficial effect on short-term profits, they may undermine the long-term competitiveness and performance of a business.

In recent years, many businesses have been criticised for failing to consider the long-term implications of their policies on the wealth of the owners. Real World 1.2 gives some examples of how an emphasis on short-term profits can have a damaging effect.

 **REAL WORLD 1.2**

Short-term gains, long-term problems   **FT**

John Kay argues that some businesses have achieved growth in short-term increases in profits by sacrificing their longer-term prosperity. He points out that:

> The business of Marks and Spencer, the retailer, was unparalleled in reputation but mature. To achieve earnings growth consistent with a glamour rating the company squeezed suppliers, gave less value for money, spent less on stores. In 1998, it achieved the highest (profit) margin in sales in the history of the business. It had also compromised its position to the point where sales and profits plummeted.
>
> Banks and insurance companies have taken staff out of branches and retrained those that remain as sales people. The pharmaceuticals industry has taken advantage of mergers to consolidate its research and development facilities. Energy companies have cut back on exploration.
>
> We know that these actions increased corporate earnings. We do not know what effect they have on the long-run strength of the business – and this is the key point – do the companies themselves know? Some rationalisations will genuinely lead to more productive businesses. Other companies will suffer the fate of Marks and Spencer.

Source: John Kay, 'Profit without honour', *Financial Times*, Weekend section, 29–30 June 2002.

A final problem with the use of profit maximisation as an objective is that it fails to take account of risk. We shall see a little later that, the higher the level of risk associated with a particular investment, the higher the expected return required by shareholders. This means that, logically, a profit maximisation policy should lead managers to invest in high-risk projects. Such a policy, however, may not reflect the needs of the shareholders. When considering an investment, shareholders are concerned with both risk and the *long-run returns* that they expect to receive. Only a wealth maximisation objective takes both of these factors into account. Managers who pursue this objective will choose investments that provide the highest returns in relation to the risks involved.

To maximise or to satisfy?

Even if we reject the use of profit and accept shareholder wealth as an appropriate financial objective, we may still question whether the *maximisation* of shareholder wealth is appropriate. Accepting this objective implies that the needs of the shareholders are paramount. Shareholders are not the only ones, however, that have a financial interest in a business. A business can be viewed more broadly as a coalition of various interest groups, with each group having a 'stake' in the business.

Activity 1.3

Identify the main 'stakeholder' groups that have a financial interest in a business.

The following groups may be seen as stakeholders:

- shareholders
- employees
- managers
- suppliers
- customers
- the community.

This is not an exhaustive list. You may have thought of others.

If we adopt this broader view of a business, shareholders become simply one of a number of stakeholder groups whose needs have to be satisfied. It may therefore be argued that, rather than seeking to maximise shareholder returns, managers should try to provide each stakeholder group with a *satisfactory return*. The term **satisficing** has been used to describe this particular business objective.

Although a satisficing approach may sound appealing, there are practical problems associated with its use. By taking this broader approach, each of the various stakeholder groups must be considered when deciding on a particular course of action. This will make matters more complex and will greatly add to the difficulties of decision making. It will also obscure the accountability of managers, who may find it easier to pursue their own interests behind a fog of multiple objectives. Shareholder wealth maximisation, on the other hand, provides a single objective for managers to pursue, and for which to account.

Within a market economy there are strong competitive forces at work that ensure that failure to maximise shareholder wealth will not be tolerated for long. Competition for the funds provided by shareholders and competition for managers' jobs should ensure that the interests of the shareholders prevail. If the managers of a business do not provide the expected increase in shareholder wealth, the shareholders have the power to replace the existing management team with a new team that is more responsive to their needs. Alternatively, the shareholders may decide to sell their shares in the business (and reinvest in other businesses that provide better returns in relation to the risks involved). The sale of shares in the business is likely to depress the market price of the shares, which management will have to rectify in order to avoid the risk of takeover. This can only be done by pursuing policies that are consistent with the needs of shareholders.

Do the above arguments mean that the interests of shareholders are all that managers must consider and that the interests of other stakeholders are irrelevant? The answer is almost certainly no. Satisfying the needs of the other stakeholder groups will often be consistent with the need to maximise shareholder wealth. A dissatisfied workforce, for example, may result in low productivity, strikes and so forth, which will in turn have an adverse effect on the shareholders' investment in the business. This kind of interdependence has led to the argument that the needs of other stakeholder groups must be viewed as constraints within which shareholder wealth should be maximised.

Viewing the needs of the other stakeholders as constraints that must be satisfied is a rather neat way of reconciling the shareholder wealth maximisation objective with the interests of other stakeholders. It assumes, however, that a business should *maximise* the wealth of shareholders but provide only a *satisfactory return* to other stakeholders. Whether or not this assumption is considered valid will involve a value judgement being made. It is important to recognise, however, the implications of ignoring the needs of shareholders in a competitive market economy. It is likely that all other stakeholder groups will suffer if the share price performance of the business falls below the expectations of the shareholders.

A final argument made in support of the wealth maximisation objective is that, even if we accept the view that wealth maximisation is not necessarily appropriate, the models that are based on this objective may still be useful for management decision making. By employing these models, managers can identify the most appropriate course of action from the shareholders' viewpoint and can see the costs borne by shareholders if a different (that is, non-wealth maximising) course of action is decided upon. The managers would then have to account to shareholders for their decision.

Wealth maximisation in practice

There is evidence that businesses pursue shareholder wealth as their primary objective, or at least claim to do so. A business will often produce a **mission statement**. This statement is a concise attempt to capture the essence of a particular business and will frequently adorn a business's annual reports and websites. **Real World 1.3** provides a few examples of mission statements that proclaim a commitment to maximising shareholder wealth (or value as it is often called).

REAL WORLD 1.3

On a mission

Stagecoach plc is a large transport business that is focused on applying:

> entrepreneurial vision to local transport operations in core geographic markets. Through a combination of organic growth and complementary acquisitions, we are committed to maximising shareholder value.

Dana Petroleum plc is a leading British independent oil business that is:

> committed to maximising shareholder value through the creation and execution of high impact opportunities.

Diamond Corp plc is a diamond producer focused on:

> maximising shareholder value through the development of high margin diamond production assets.

Sources: www.stagecoachgroup.com, www.dana-petroleum.com, www.diamondcorp.plc.uk.

A paradox. . . .

How should a business go about maximising shareholder wealth? Many appear to believe that this primarily involves controlling costs, increasing revenues and ensuring that only opportunities offering clear wealth-maximising outcomes are undertaken. John Kay, however, argues that such a narrow focus may prove to be self-defeating and that shareholder wealth maximisation is more likely to be achieved when pursued indirectly. He points out that those individuals and businesses which are most successful in generating wealth are often seized by a passion to develop the best possible product or to provide the best possible service for their customers. If a business concentrates its efforts on the challenges that this entails, the financial rewards will usually follow. In other words, to maximise shareholder wealth, it may be best to concentrate on something else.

Real World 1.4 is an extract from an article written by John Kay in which he points out that the richest individuals are often not driven by the need for wealth or material gain.

REAL WORLD 1.4

How to make real money   **FT**

Sam Walton, founder and principal shareholder of Wal-Mart, the world's largest retailer, drove himself around in a pick-up truck. 'I have concentrated all along on building the finest retailing company that we possibly could. Period. Creating a huge personal fortune was never particularly a goal of mine', Walton said. Still, five of the top ten places in the Forbes rich list are occupied by members of the Walton family . . .

Warren Buffett, the most successful investor in history, still lives in the Omaha bungalow he bought almost fifty years ago and continues to take pleasure in a Nebraskan steak washed down with cherry Coke. For Buffett, 'It's not that I want money. It's the fun of making money and watching it grow.'

The individuals who are most successful in making money are not those who are most interested in making money. This is not surprising, the principal route to great wealth is the creation of a successful business, and building a successful business demands exceptional talents and hard work. There is no reason to think that these characteristics are associated with greed and materialism: rather the opposite. People who are obsessively interested in money are drawn to get-rich-quick schemes rather than to business opportunities, and when these schemes come off, as occasionally they do, they retire to their villas in the sun . . .

Source: John Kay, 'Forget how the crow flies', *Financial Times*, 17 January 2004, p. 21.

The above arguments do not undermine the role of financial management in delivering wealth to shareholders. Rather, it suggests that it must be attuned to the challenges and aspirations of the business.

Balancing risk and return

All decision making is an attempt to influence future outcomes and financial decision making is no exception. The only thing certain about the future, however, is that we cannot be sure what is going to happen. There is a risk that things will not turn out as planned, and this possibility should be carefully considered when making financial decisions.

As in other aspects of life, risk and return tend to be related. Evidence shows that returns relate to risk in something like the way shown in Figure 1.3.

Figure 1.3   **Relationship between risk and return**

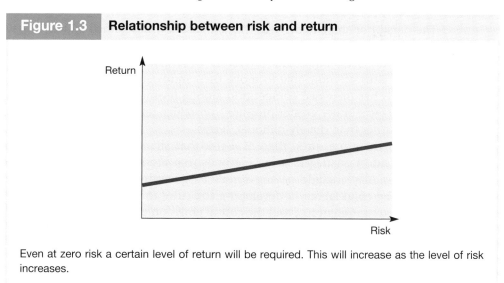

Even at zero risk a certain level of return will be required. This will increase as the level of risk increases.

This relationship between risk and return has important implications for the owners (shareholders) of a business. They will require a minimum return to induce them to invest at all, but will require an additional return to compensate for taking risks; the higher the risk, the higher the required return. Thus, future returns from an investment must be assessed in relation to the likely risks involved. As stated earlier, managers who pursue the shareholder wealth maximisation objective will choose investments that provide the highest returns in relation to the risks involved.

Real World 1.5 below describes how some businesses have recently been making higher-risk investments in pursuit of higher returns.

REAL WORLD 1.5

Appetite for risk drives businesses   **FT**

Over the last few years, companies from the US and western Europe, joined increasingly by competitors from China and India, have looked to new markets abroad both to source and sell their products.

Driven by intensifying competition at home, companies have been drawn into direct investment in markets that not long ago were considered beyond the pale. But in the drive to increase returns, they have also been forced to accept higher risks.

Over time, the balance between risk and reward changes. For example, companies flooded into Russia early in the decade. But recently returns have fallen, largely due to booming raw materials prices. Meanwhile the apparent risk of investing in Russia has grown significantly.

As the risk-reward calculation has changed in Russia, companies have looked to other countries such as Libya and Vietnam where the rewards may be substantial, and the threats, though high, may be more manageable.

Source: Adapted from Stephen Fidler, 'Appetite for risk drives industry', www.ft.com, 27 June 2007.

Behaving ethically

The pursuit of shareholder wealth maximisation has gained added impetus in recent years. One of the effects of the global deregulation of markets and of technological change has been to provide investors with greater opportunities to increase their returns. They are now able to move their funds around the world with comparative ease. This has increased competition among businesses for investment funds and has put managers under greater pressure to produce returns that are attractive in international, rather than merely national, terms.

Given these pressures, there is a risk that shareholder wealth maximisation may be pursued by managers using methods that are not acceptable to the community. Examples may include paying bribes to government officials to secure contracts, employing child labour in developing countries to minimise production costs, polluting the environment to avoid the cost of emission controls, and so on. Some managers may feel such behaviour is acceptable because 'all is fair in business'. Professor Rose, however, points out that responsibility to maximise the wealth of shareholders 'does not mean that managers are being asked to act in a manner which absolves them from the considerations of morality and simple decency that they would readily acknowledge in other walks of life' (see reference 1 at the end of the chapter).

Thus, when considering a particular course of action, managers should ask themselves whether it conforms to accepted moral standards, whether it treats people unfairly and whether it has the potential for harm.

Nowadays, large businesses often publicly proclaim their commitment to high standards of ethical behaviour and social responsibility. Appropriate codes of practice may also be developed. **Real World 1.6** provides an example of how one business sets out its position on these issues.

REAL WORLD 1.6

Playing the game

SCi Entertainment Group plc is the UK's leading publisher of computer games and one of the world's leading developers and publishers of entertainment software. Its website sets out in some detail the business's attitude to ethical standards and social responsibility. An extract from this website is set out below:

> SCi has a strong commitment to its customers, shareholders, employees and, in a wider context, to local communities and the environment generally. The Board also recognises that in today's business world, corporate social responsibility (CSR) and the maximisation of long-term shareholder value are not incompatible but increasingly interdependent. Accordingly, and in taking ultimate responsibility for enhancing its good corporate citizenship status with all stakeholders, the Board is committed to developing and implementing CSR policies and best conduct practices which are targeted at
>
> ● complying with local laws and regulations;
> ● providing safe and healthy working conditions;
> ● promoting equality, fairness and ethical behaviour;
> ● maintaining corporate integrity and reputation;
> ● caring for the environment and participating in the community.

The website also states:

> SCi strives to observe high standards of moral, legal and ethical behaviour. The key message to all employees (and other interested parties) is that they must observe a code of conduct based on honesty, integrity and fair dealing at all times.

Source: SCi Entertainment Group (http://corporate.sci.co.uk).

In Real World 1.6, it is suggested that wealth maximisation and ethical behaviour need not conflict. Indeed, some believe that high ethical standards may be a necessary condition for wealth maximisation. A business that treats customers, suppliers and employees fairly and with integrity is more likely to flourish over the longer term.

In recent years, attempts have been made to demonstrate a link between high ethical standards and superior financial performance over time. **Real World 1.7** briefly describes two of these.

REAL WORLD 1.7

Profiting from ethics?

In 2003 the Institute for Business Ethics produced a report which suggested that businesses with a code of ethics produced superior financial performance than those without a code. It compared a group of companies in the FTSE 250 index over a period of four years, divided into those that had codes of ethics for five years or more and those that explicitly said they did not. It found that on three measures – economic value added, market value added and stability of price/earnings ratios – the ethical companies outperformed, though on a fourth measure – return on capital employed – the figures were more mixed.*

Some caveats are perhaps in order. The time period for the study is not that long. And taking the existence of ethical codes as a proxy for ethical behaviour could be stretching

Real World 1.7 continued

reality. After all, even Enron had a code of ethical behaviour. So while indicative, this is not likely to be the last word. As the study admits, it is not clear why an ethical stance should mean better results. Maybe it is simply that good managers, who produce good results, tend to view ethical codes as part of good business. (1)

In 2007 the Institute of Business Ethics published a follow-up research study. The majority of large businesses now have a code of ethics and so it is not really possible to use the existence of a code as evidence that a business is 'more ethical'. Instead, 'more ethical' businesses were identified as those that attempted to embed ethical business practice through staff training programmes. A group of 50 large businesses, selected from the FTSE 350 index, were divided into two equal-size groups based on this criterion. Using four measures (return on capital employed, return on assets, total return and market value added*) over a five-year period, the study found that those with training programmes had significantly better financial performance than those without. (2)

Again, the results are not conclusive. It is not clear why there should be a link between ethical training and financial performance. It may be that ethical training of employees instils confidence among stakeholders and this makes the business more able to deal with setbacks and change. On the other hand, it may simply be that profitable businesses can afford to spend money on ethical training programmes.

* Each of these measures is discussed later in the book.

Source: (1) Adapted from Martin Dickson, 'Ethics', *Financial Times*, 3 April 2003. (2) Ugoji K., Dando N., and Moir L., *Does Business ethics pay? – Revisited: The value of ethics training*, Institute of Business Ethics, 2007.

Ethics and the finance function

Integrity and ethical behaviour are particularly important within the finance function, where many opportunities for sharp practice exist. To demonstrate their commitment to integrity and ethical behaviour, some businesses provide a code of standards for their finance staff. **Real World 1.8** provides an example of one such code.

REAL WORLD 1.8

Shell's ethical code

Shell plc, the oil and energy business, has a code of ethics for its executive directors and senior financial officers. The key elements of this code are that these individuals should:

- adhere to the highest standards of honesty, integrity and fairness, whilst maintaining a work climate that fosters these standards;
- comply with any codes of conduct or rules concerning dealing in securities;
- avoid involvement in any decisions that could involve a conflict of interest;
- avoid any financial interest in contracts awarded by the company;
- not seek or accept favours from third parties;
- not hold positions in outside businesses that might adversely affect their performance;
- avoid any relationship with contractors or suppliers that might compromise their ability to act impartially;
- ensure full, fair, timely, accurate and understandable disclosure of information that the business communicates to the public or publicly files.

Source: Code of Ethics (www.shell.com).

Although there may be rules in place to try to prevent sharp practice, these will only provide a partial answer. The finance staff themselves must appreciate the importance of fair play in building long-term relationships for the benefit of all those connected with the business.

Protecting shareholders' interests

→ In recent years, the issue of **corporate governance** has generated much debate. The term is used to describe the ways in which businesses are directed and controlled. The issue of corporate governance is important because, in businesses of any size, those who own the company (that is, the shareholders) are usually divorced from the day-to-day control of the business. The shareholders employ professional managers (known as directors) to manage the business for them. These directors may, therefore, be viewed as *agents* of the shareholders (who are the *principals*).

Given this agent–principal relationship, it may seem reasonable to assume that the best interests of shareholders will guide the directors' decisions. In other words, the directors will seek to maximise the wealth of the shareholders. However, in practice this does not always occur. The directors may be more concerned with pursuing their own interests, such as increasing their pay and perks (such as expensive cars, overseas visits and so on) and improving their job security and status. As a result, a conflict can occur between the interests of shareholders and the interests of directors.

→ It can be argued that in a competitive market economy, this **agency problem**, as it is termed, should not persist over time. The competition for the funds provided by shareholders, and competition for directors' jobs referred to earlier, should ensure that the interests of the shareholders will prevail. However, if competitive forces are weak, or if information concerning the directors' activities is not available to shareholders, the risk of agency problems will be increased. Shareholders must be alert to such risks and should take steps to ensure that the directors operate the business in a manner that is consistent with shareholder needs.

Protecting through rules

Where directors pursue their own interests at the expense of the shareholders, it is clearly a problem for the shareholders. However, it may also be a problem for society as a whole. If investors feel that their funds are likely to be mismanaged, they will be reluctant to commit those funds. A shortage of funds will mean that businesses can make fewer investments. Also, the costs of finance will increase as businesses compete for what funds are available. Thus, a lack of concern for shareholders can have a profound effect on the performance of individual businesses and, with this, the health of the economy. To avoid these problems, most competitive market economies have a framework of rules to help monitor and control the behaviour of directors.

These rules are usually based around three guiding principles:

● *Disclosure*. This lies at the heart of good corporate governance. An OECD report (see reference 2 at the end of the chapter for details) summed up the benefits of disclosure as follows:

> Adequate and timely information about corporate performance enables investors to make informed buy-and-sell decisions and thereby helps the market reflect the value of a corporation under present management. If the market determines that present management is not performing, a decrease in stock [share] price will sanction management's failure and open the way to management change.

● *Accountability*. This involves defining the roles and duties of the directors and establishing an adequate monitoring process. In the UK, the law requires that the directors of a business act in the best interests of the shareholders. This means, among other things, that they must not try to use their position and knowledge to make gains at the expense of the shareholders. The law also requires larger businesses to have their annual financial statements independently audited. The purpose of an independent audit is to lend credibility to the financial statements prepared by the directors.

● *Fairness*. Directors should not be able to benefit from access to 'inside' information that is not available to shareholders. As a result, both the law and the London Stock Exchange place restrictions on the ability of directors to buy and sell the shares of the business. One example of these restrictions is that the directors cannot buy or sell shares immediately before the announcement of the annual trading results of the business or before the announcement of a significant event such as a planned merger or the loss of the chief executive.

Strengthening the framework of rules

The number of rules designed to safeguard shareholders has increased considerably over the years. This has been in response to weaknesses in corporate governance procedures, which have been exposed through well-publicised business failures and frauds, excessive pay increases to directors and evidence that some financial reports were being 'massaged' so as to mislead shareholders.

 The most important development has been the introduction of the **Combined Code** which sets out best practice on corporate governance matters for large businesses. The Combined Code has the backing of the London Stock Exchange, which means that all businesses listed on this exchange must 'comply or explain'. That is, they must comply with the requirements of the Code or must give their shareholders good reason why they do not. Failure to do one or other of these can lead to the business's shares being suspended from listing. This is an important sanction as the exchange offers a means of raising new finance and provides a market for existing shareholders to sell their shares.

The Combined Code sets out a number of principles relating to such matters as the role of the directors, their relations with shareholders, and their accountability. **Real World 1.9** outlines some of the more important of these.

REAL WORLD 1.9

The Combined Code

Some of the key elements of the Combined Code are as follows:

● Every listed company should have a board of directors to lead and control the company.
● There should be a clear division of responsibilities between the chairman and the chief executive officer of the company to ensure that a single person does not have unbridled power.
● There should be a balance between executive and non-executive (who are often part-time and independent) members of the board, to ensure that small groups of individuals cannot dominate proceedings.

- The board should receive timely information that is of sufficient quality to enable them to carry out their duties.
- Appointments to the board should be the subject of rigorous, formal and transparent procedures.
- All directors should submit themselves for re-election at regular intervals, subject to satisfactory performance.
- Remuneration levels should be sufficient to attract, retain and motivate directors of the quality required to run the company.
- There should be formal and transparent procedures for developing policy on directors' remuneration.
- The board should ensure that a satisfactory dialogue with shareholders occurs.
- Boards should use the annual general meeting to communicate with private investors and encourage their participation.
- Institutional shareholders should ensure that they use their votes and enter into a dialogue with the company based on a mutual understanding of objectives.
- The board should publish a balanced and understandable assessment of the company's position and future prospects.
- Internal controls should be in place to protect the shareholders' wealth.
- Formal and transparent arrangements for applying financial reporting and internal control principles and for maintaining an appropriate relationship with auditors should be in place.
- The board should undertake a formal and rigorous examination of its own performance each year.

Source: www.frc.org.uk.

Strengthening the framework of rules in this way has been generally agreed to have improved the quality of information available to shareholders, resulted in better checks on the powers of directors, and provided greater transparency in corporate affairs. However, rules can only be a partial answer. A balance must be struck between the need to protect shareholders and the need to encourage the entrepreneurial spirit of directors – which could be stifled under a welter of rules. This implies that rules should not be too tight and so unscrupulous directors may still find ways around them.

Shareholder involvement

Improving corporate governance has focused mainly on developing a framework of rules for managing businesses listed on the London Stock Exchange. Whilst rules are important, there are many who take the view that it is also important for those who own the businesses to play their part by actively monitoring and controlling the behaviour of directors. In this section, we identify the main shareholders of listed businesses and discuss their role in establishing good corporate governance. We also consider why there has been greater shareholder activism in recent years.

Who are the main shareholders?

Real World 1.10 provides some impression of the ownership of London Stock Exchange listed shares.

REAL WORLD 1.10

Becoming institutionalised

At 31 December 2006, 40 per cent (by market value) of London Stock Exchange listed shares were owned by investors (individuals and institutions) that are based overseas. Of those that are owned by UK investors (individuals and institutions), the breakdown of ownership is as shown in Figure 1.4.

Figure 1.4	**Beneficial ownership of UK shares owned by UK investors, end 2006**

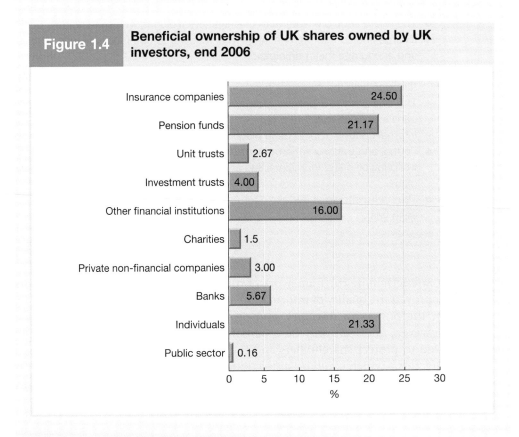

Large financial institutions such as insurance businesses, banks, pension funds, unit trusts and investment trusts are now the most important investors in shares listed on the London Stock Exchange. These institutions have increased their hold on the ownership of Stock Exchange listed shares over time, whilst the proportion of listed shares held directly by individuals has decreased.

Looking at the changes in the ownership of listed shares over the past four decades shows two striking features:

1 The value of listed shares owned by overseas investors has gone up progressively (from just 7 per cent in 1963 to 40 per cent in 2006); and
2 Of those held by UK residents, the value of listed shares held by individuals has fallen fairly steadily (from 58 per cent in 1963 to 21 per cent in 2006).

Source: Office for National Statistics (www.statistics.gov.uk).

This concentration of ownership of listed shares means that financial institutions have enormous voting power and, as a result, the potential to exercise significant influence over the way in which Stock Exchange listed businesses are directed and controlled. In the past, however, they have been reluctant to exercise this power and have been criticised for being too passive and for allowing the directors of businesses too much independence.

What can shareholders do?

There are two main ways in which shareholders try to control the behaviour of directors. These are by:

- introducing incentive plans for directors that link their remuneration to the share performance of the business. In this way, the interests of directors and shareholders should become more closely aligned.
- closely monitoring the actions of the directors and exerting influence over the way in which they use business resources.

We shall see, however, that neither offers a perfect solution.

Rewarding directors

Incentive plans based on share performance are in widespread use. A common form of incentive plan is to give directors **share options**. These options give them the right, but not the obligation, to purchase shares in the business at an agreed price at some future date. If the current market value exceeds the agreed price at that due date, the directors will make a gain by taking up the options. Advocates of share options argue that they give directors a direct financial incentive to increase the value of the shares of the business and thereby increase shareholder wealth. It is claimed that, where share options form a significant part of the total remuneration package of directors, they are placed in a similar position to that of shareholders. This, in turn, helps them to 'think like shareholders'.

Warren Buffett, one of the world's shrewdest and most successful investors, has, however, made clear his opposition to the use of options. One problem that concerns him is that share option schemes cannot differentiate between the performances achieved by individual directors. He argues:

> Of course stock [share] options often go to talented, value-adding managers and sometimes deliver them rewards that are perfectly appropriate. (Indeed, managers who are really exceptional almost always get far less than they should.) But when the result is equitable, it is accidental. Once granted, the option is blind to individual performance. Because it is irrevocable and unconditional (so long as a manager stays in the company), the sluggard receives rewards from his options precisely as does the star. A managerial Rip Van Winkle, ready to doze for ten years, could not wish for a better 'incentive' system. (See reference 3 at the end of the chapter.)

A further problem concerning the incentive value of share options, to which Buffet refers, is that, where the share price falls significantly below the exercise price, the prospects of receiving benefits from the share options may become remote and any incentive value will be lost.

It is worth remembering that both rises and falls in share price may be beyond the control of the directors. Any incentive scheme that is subject to the vagaries of the stock market is, therefore, likely to present problems. There is always a risk that directors will be either under-compensated or over-compensated for their achievements.

Activity 1.4

Try to identify four factors that may influence the price of a share but which are beyond the control of the directors.

These may include:

- changes in interest rates
- changes in taxation policy
- economic recession
- changes in legislation affecting the industry
- a takeover bid.

You may have thought of others.

Buffett's criticism of share options is not confined to their dubious incentive value. He also challenges the view that share options place directors in the same position as that of shareholders. He argues:

> the rhetoric about options frequently describes them as desirable because they put owners and managers in the same financial boat. In reality, the boats are far different. No owner has ever escaped the burden of capital costs, whereas a holder of a fixed-price option bears no capital costs at all. An owner must weigh upside potential against downside risk: an option holder has no downside. In fact, the business project in which you would wish to have an option frequently is a project in which you would reject ownership. (I'll be happy to accept a lottery ticket as a gift – but I'll never buy one.) (See reference 3 at the end of the chapter.)

Share options are not the only way of trying to align the interests of directors with those of shareholders. Other methods exist, but bring their own problems. For this reason, businesses may base an incentive plan on a combination of methods to mitigate the weaknesses of each.

Getting active

In the past, financial institutions have chosen to take a non-interventionist approach to the affairs of a business. Instead, they have confined their investment activities to determining whether to buy, hold or sell shares in a particular business. They appear to have taken the view that the costs of actively engaging with directors and trying to influence their decisions are too high in relation to the likely benefits. It is also worth pointing out that these costs are borne by the particular financial institution that becomes actively involved, whereas the benefits are spread across all shareholders. (This phenomenon is often referred to as the 'free-rider' problem.)

Waking the sleeping giants

In recent years, financial institutions have begun to play a more active role in corporate governance. More time is being invested in monitoring the actions of directors and in engaging with the directors over key decisions. This change of heart has occurred for a variety of reasons. One important reason is that the increasing concentration of share ownership has made it more difficult for financial institutions to simply walk away from an investment in a poorly performing business by selling its shares. A substantial number of shares are often held and so a decision to sell can have a significant impact on the market price, perhaps leading to heavy losses.

A further reason why it may be difficult to disinvest is that a business's shares may be included in a stock market index (such as the FTSE 100 or FTSE 250). Certain types of financial institution, such as investment trusts or unit trusts, may offer investments that are designed to 'track' the particular index and so they become locked into a business's shares in order to reflect the index. In both situations outlined, therefore, a financial institution may have little choice but to stick with the shares held and try to improve performance by seeking to influence the actions and decisions of the directors.

It is also worth mentioning that financial institutions have experienced much greater competitive pressures in recent years. There have been increasing demands from clients for them to demonstrate their investment skills, and thereby justify their fees, by either outperforming benchmarks or beating the performance of similar financial institutions. These increased competitive pressures may be due, at least in part, to the fact that economic conditions have not favoured investors in the recent past; they have experienced a period of relatively low stock market returns. Whatever the reason, the increased pressure to enhance the wealth of their clients has led financial institutions, in turn, to become less tolerant towards underperforming boards of directors.

The regulatory environment has also favoured greater activism on the part of financial institutions. The Combined Code, for example, urges institutional shareholders to use their votes and to enter into a dialogue with businesses.

Forms of activism

It is important to be clear what is meant by the term 'shareholder activism' as it can take various forms. In its simplest form it involves taking a more active role in voting for or against the resolutions put before the annual general meeting or any extraordinary general meeting of the business. This form of activism is seen by the government as being vital to good corporate governance. The government is keen to see much higher levels of participation than currently exists and expects institutional shareholders to exercise their right to vote. In the past, financial institutions have often indicated their dissent by abstaining from a vote rather than by outright opposition to a resolution. There is some evidence, however, that they are now more prepared to use their vote to oppose resolutions of the board of directors.

Much of the evidence available remains anecdotal rather than based on systematic research. One such example concerns the merger of two large media businesses – Carlton and Granada. The chairman of Carlton, Mr Michael Green, was nominated as independent chairman of the combined business but some financial institutions felt he was unsuitable and succeeded in opposing his appointment by voting against the resolution. **Real World 1.11** provides a more recent example of a situation where shareholders have acted to try to make changes to the board.

REAL WORLD 1.11

Revolting shareholders   **FT**

Dissident investors in SkyePharma have finally run out of patience with the board of the drug delivery company and launched a coup attempt to oust Ian Gowrie-Smith, chairman, and replace him with industry heavyweight Bob Thian.

North Atlantic Value [NAV], the shareholder activist group, joined forces with Insight Investment and Morley Fund Management and other investors to call for an extraordinary meeting to vote on the proposed management change.

It is believed that the final trigger for the revolt was SkyePharma's plan to announce the appointment of two executives, including a chief executive, without consulting investors.

NAV said: 'We did not intend to do this but rushing out two executives is not negotiating in good faith.'

The dissident group, which has named itself the Requisitionists, said SkyePharma had repeatedly failed to listen to the concerns of large shareholders.

Investors have increasingly become frustrated with the lack of progress in finding a buyer for all or part of the business, following SkyePharma's announcement in November that it had appointed Lehman Brothers to conduct a strategic review.

The Requisitionists, who have a combined 13.15 per cent stake, firmly placed the blame for what they described as a corporate strategy of over-promising on performance but under-delivering on the shoulders of Mr Gowrie-Smith.

'Their entire strategy has been delay, delay, delay and time just ran out for them,' said one large shareholder.

Other shareholders, including Legal and General and Fidelity, who between them have a 12 per cent holding in SkyePharma, are also believed to be prepared to support the move to change the management.

Source: 'Move to oust SkyePharma chairman', www.ft.com, 20 January 2006.

A particularly rich source of contention between shareholders and directors concerns directors' remuneration and there have been several shareholder revolts over this issue. Shareholders are often upset by what they regard as the setting of undemanding performance targets or unjustified, 'one-off' payments to directors. **Real World 1.12** provides an example of a fairly recent falling out.

REAL WORLD 1.12

Easy money   **FT**

Lord Hollick, outgoing chief executive of United Business Media [UBM], is facing an embarrassing shareholder revolt at the company's annual meeting next week over plans to award him a special £250,000 bonus.

The chance of UBM's remuneration report being voted down at the meeting increased on Wednesday when the Association of British Insurers [ABI], a powerful investor group, issued 'red-top' guidance to members, indicating its highest level of concern.

The National Association of Pension Funds [NAPF] is urging its members to rebel against the report. The Research, Recommendations and Electronic Voting advisory service, which is half-owned by the NAPF, says investors should also vote against the re-election of Chris Powell as a non-executive director because he chairs the committee that approved the bonus.

Investor anger was sparked last month when the company revealed in its annual report that Lord Hollick would receive the unusual bonus for helping to ensure a 'successful handover' to David Levin, the incoming chief executive.

Most of the company's largest institutional investors plan to register their fury by voting against the company's remuneration report. Few expect UBM to win the vote; a loss would force the company to back down or ignore its leading investors.

One shareholder said: 'I predict UBM will lose this vote. We simply cannot allow these types of payments. Why should Lord Hollick be paid extra simply to hand over to a successor?'

Peter Montagnon, ABI's head of investment affairs, said: 'We have reached our decision after careful discussion with members and their view is firm. These payments are not appropriate.'

Companies work hard to avoid losing the remuneration vote. The last high-profile casualty was GlaxoSmithKline in May 2003, when shareholders voted down the pay package of Jean-Pierre Garnier, chief executive.

UBM on Wednesday refused to say whether it would withdraw the bonus if it lost the vote. The company said: 'It is too early to pre-judge the outcome of the annual meeting but UBM takes all representations from shareholders seriously.'

Source: 'UBM investors in bonus revolt', www.ft.com, 4 May 2005.

Although the examples mentioned above are widely reported and catch the newspaper headlines, they do not happen very often. Nevertheless, the benefits for shareholders of flexing their muscles and voting against resolutions put forward by the directors may go beyond their immediate, intended objective: other boards of directors may take note of shareholder dissatisfaction and adjust their behaviour in order to avoid a similar fate. The cost of voting need not be high as there are specialist agencies which offer research and advice to financial institutions on how their votes should be cast.

Another form of activism involves meetings and discussions between representatives of a particular financial institution and the board of directors of a business. At such meetings, a wide range of issues affecting the business may be discussed.

Activity 1.5

Can you think of five topics that an institutional shareholder may wish to discuss with the directors of a business?

Some of the more important issues that are likely to attract their attention include:

- Objectives and strategies adopted
- Trading performance
- Internal controls
- Policies regarding mergers and acquisition
- Major investments and disinvestments
- Adherence to the recommendations of the Combined Code
- Corporate social responsibilities
- Directors' incentive schemes and remuneration.

This is not an exhaustive list. For shareholders, and therefore owners, of a business, anything that might have an impact on their wealth should be a matter of concern.

This form of activism requires a fairly high degree of involvement with the business and some of the larger financial institutions have dedicated teams for this purpose. This can be, therefore, a costly exercise. **Real World 1.13** is an extract from the website of one major financial institution that is committed to a dialogue with directors and gives an insight to the approach taken.

REAL WORLD 1.13

Active investing

Jupiter Asset Management Limited, manager of unit trusts and investments trusts, believes that, when monitoring investments:

> An important part of the process is the dialogue (usually private) between institutional shareholders and the companies in which they invest. As such, its fund managers and analysts host and attend regular meetings with the management of companies, with a high percentage of companies being seen twice a year where corporate strategy, performance and other management issues are discussed.

Source: Corporate governance and voting policy, p. 14 (www.jupiteronline.co.uk).

Such meetings can be useful for exchanging views and for gaining a greater understanding of the needs and motivations of each party. This may help to pre-empt public spats between the board of directors and financial institutions, which is rarely the best way to resolve issues.

The final form of activism involves intervention in the affairs of the business. This, however, can be very costly, depending on the nature of the problem. Where strategic and operational issues raise concerns, intervention can be very costly indeed. Identifying the weaknesses and problems relating to these issues requires a detailed understanding of the nature of its business. This implies close monitoring by relevant experts who are able to analyse the issues and then propose feasible solutions. The costs associated with such an exercise would normally be prohibitive, although the costs may be mitigated through some kind of collective action by financial institutions.

Not all forms of intervention in the affairs of a business, however, need be costly. Where, for example, there are corporate governance issues to be addressed, such as a failure to adhere to the recommendations of the Combined Code, a financial institution may nominate individuals for appointment as non-executive directors who can be relied upon to ensure that necessary changes are made. This should involve relatively little cost for the financial institution.

The future of shareholder activism

The rise of shareholder activism raises two important questions that have yet to be answered. First, is it simply a passing phenomenon? It is no coincidence that shareholder activism took root during a period when stock market returns were fairly low. There is a risk that financial institutions will become less active and less vigilant in monitoring businesses when stock market returns improve. Secondly, does shareholder activism really make a difference to corporate performance? The research on this topic so far has been fairly sparse but early research in the USA is not encouraging for those who urge financial institutions to take a more active approach. We may have to wait some while, however, for clear answers to these questions.

SUMMARY

The main points in this chapter may be summarised as follows:

The finance function

- Helps managers in carrying out their tasks of strategic management, operations management and risk management.
- Helps managers in each of these tasks through financial planning, investment appraisal, financing decisions, capital market operations and financial control.

Modern financial management

- Is influenced by economic theory.
- Has been described as the economics of time and risk.

Shareholder wealth maximisation

- Is assumed to be the primary objective of a business.
- Is a long-term rather than a short-term objective.
- Takes account of both risk and the long-run returns that investors expect to receive.
- Must take account of the needs of other stakeholders.
- Is often proclaimed in the mission statements of businesses.
- May be best achieved through a commitment to developing the best possible product or service.

Risk and return

- Risk and return are related.
- Investors normally require additional return to compensate for additional risk.
- Wealth maximisation involves selecting investments that provide the highest returns in relation to the risks involved.

Ethical behaviour

- Need not conflict with the maximisation of shareholder wealth objective.
- May be set out in policies and codes.
- Is particularly important in the finance function.

Protecting shareholders

- An agency problem may exist between shareholders and the directors.
- This has led to rules, set out in the Combined Code, to help monitor and control the behaviour of directors.

Shareholder involvement

- Financial institutions are now the most important group of UK shareholders in London Stock Exchange listed businesses.
- Shareholder involvement may take the form of introducing incentive plans for directors and/or monitoring and controlling their actions.
- Incentive plans based on share performance can be difficult to implement and costly.
- Shareholder activism may involve taking a more active role in voting, meetings and discussions with directors and direct intervention in the affairs of the business.

→ **Key terms**

Capital markets   p. 5   **Corporate governance**   p. 15
Shareholder wealth maximisation   p. 6   **Agency problem**   p. 15
Satisficing   p. 8   **Combined Code**   p. 16
Mission statement   p. 9   **Share options**   p. 19

For definitions of these terms see the Glossary, pp. 574–583

References

1 **Tasks of the Finance Function**, *Rose, H.*, Financial Times Mastering Management Series, supplement issue no. 1, 1995, p. 11.

2 **Corporate Governance: Improving competitiveness and access to capital in global markets**, OECD Report by Business Sector Advisory Group on Corporate Governance, Organisation for Economic Co-operation and Development, 1998.

3 **Annual report to shareholders**, *Buffet W.*, Berkshire Hathaway Inc., 1985, p. 12.

Further reading

If you wish to explore the topics discussed in this chapter in more depth, try the following books:

Boards at Work, *Stiles, P. and Taylor, B.*, Oxford University Press, 2001, chapter 1.

Corporate Finance and Investment, *Pike, R. and Neale, B.*, 5th edn, Financial Times Prentice Hall, 2006, chapters 1 and 2.

Corporate Financial Management, *Arnold, G.*, 3rd edn, Financial Times Prentice Hall, 2005, chapter 1.

Corporate Governance, *Monks, R. and Minnow, N.*, 3rd edn, Blackwell, 2004, chapters 1–3.

Reading the *Financial Times and Investors' Chronicle* on a regular basis can help you to keep up to date on financial management topics.

REVIEW QUESTIONS

Answers to these questions can be found at the back of the book on p. 539.

1.1 What are the main functions of the finance function within a business?

1.2 Why is the maximisation of wealth viewed as superior to profit maximisation as a business objective?

1.3 Some managers, if asked what the main objective of their business is, may simply state, 'To survival' What do you think of this as a primary objective?

1.4 Some businesses try to overcome the agency problem referred to in the chapter by using an incentive scheme that is based on the growth of profits over a period. What are the drawbacks of this type of scheme?

2

Financial planning

INTRODUCTION

In this chapter, we take a look at financial planning and the role that projected (forecast) financial statements play in this process. We shall see that these statements help in assessing the likely impact of management decisions on the financial performance and position of a business. We shall examine the way in which these statements are prepared and the issues involved in their preparation.

This chapter, and the one that follows, assume that you have some understanding of the three major financial statements: the cash flow statement, the income statement and the statement of financial position (balance sheet). If you need to brush up on these statements, please take a look at Chapters 1–5 of *Financial Accounting for Decision Makers* by Atrill and McLaney (5th edn, Financial Times Prentice Hall, 2008).

LEARNING OUTCOMES

When you have completed this chapter, you should be able to:

● Explain how business plans are developed and the role that projected financial statements play in this process.

● Prepare projected financial statements for a business and interpret their significance for decision-making purposes.

● Discuss the strengths and weaknesses of the per-cent-of-sales method as an alternative method of preparing projected financial statements.

● Explain the ways in which projected financial statements may take into account the problems of risk and uncertainty.

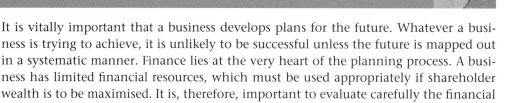

Planning for the future

It is vitally important that a business develops plans for the future. Whatever a business is trying to achieve, it is unlikely to be successful unless the future is mapped out in a systematic manner. Finance lies at the very heart of the planning process. A business has limited financial resources, which must be used appropriately if shareholder wealth is to be maximised. It is, therefore, important to evaluate carefully the financial implications of each proposed course of action. In this section, we briefly examine the planning process within a business and then, in later sections, go on to consider the ways in which those plans are expressed in financial terms.

Developing plans for a business involves the following key steps:

1 *Setting the aims and objectives of the business.* The starting point in the planning process is to establish the aims and objectives of the business. These will set out what the business is basically trying to achieve and should provide a clear sense of direction.

2 *Identifying the options available.* To achieve the aims and objectives set for the business, a number of possible options (strategies) may be available to the business. Each option must be clearly identified, which will usually involve collecting a wide range of information. The process can be extremely time consuming, particularly when the business is considering entering new markets or investing in new technology.

3 *Evaluating the options and making a selection.* Each option must be examined in the context of the objectives that have been set and the resources available. The effect of each option on future financial performance and position must also be considered. It is in this final part – the financial evaluation of the various options – that projected financial statements have a valuable role to play.

Figure 2.1 sets out this process diagrammatically.

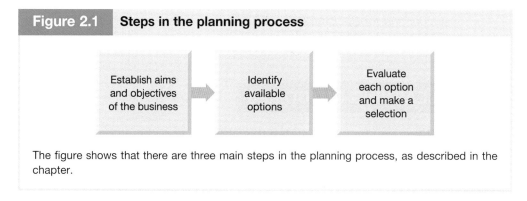

Figure 2.1	Steps in the planning process

The figure shows that there are three main steps in the planning process, as described in the chapter.

The role of projected financial statements

Projected (forecast) financial statements reveal the likely financial effect from pursuing particular courses of action. Their ultimate purpose is to provide information that will help managers to make informed decisions. The statements will normally comprise a:

● projected income statement
● projected statement of financial position (balance sheet)
● projected cash flow statement.

When taken together, they provide a comprehensive picture of likely future performance and position. Where a number of competing options are being considered, projected statements can be prepared for each option. A comparison can then be made of the impact of each option on future profitability, liquidity and financial position. Where only a single new option is being considered, a comparison can still be made with the option to do nothing.

When managers are developing plans for the future, a forecast horizon of three to five years is typically employed and projected financial statements for each year of the forecast period can be prepared for each option being considered. These statements may be updated during the planning period to take account of changes in circumstances. When we examine the preparation of projected statements later in the chapter, we shall deal with fairly short time periods for the sake of simplicity. The main principles of preparation are not affected by the particular forecast horizon.

Real World 2.1 briefly describes the main elements of the planning process for one business.

REAL WORLD 2.1

Acal plc is a major distributor providing sales and marketing services to suppliers of electronic components. In its annual corporate governance report, the company states that it undertakes:

- a comprehensive planning process which starts with a strategic plan and culminates in an annual budget;
- regular forecasting throughout the year of orders, sales, profitability, cash flow and balance sheets;

Source: Corporate governance report for year ended 31 March 2007 Acal plc (www.acalplc.co.uk).

Projected financial statements are prepared for internal management purposes and only on rare occasions, such as seeking new finance or takeovers, will external parties see these statements. Businesses tend to avoid publishing any forecast information for fear that it may damage competitiveness or may be misunderstood by investors. Nevertheless, some large businesses do publish key projections, such as the likely sales and profit figures for a financial year. This may be done, however, at some advanced point in that year. Where projected figures enter the public domain, managers become accountable for any divergence between the forecast and actual figures. If the projected figures ultimately prove to have been over-optimistic, an adverse reaction is likely from shareholders.

Real World 2.2 sets out the forecast information made available by one well-known fashion retailer.

REAL WORLD 2.2

What next?

Next PLC, the high street and catalogue fashion retailer, has forecast a year to Jan 26 2008 pre-tax profit 'slightly ahead' of market expectations following respectable Christmas trading but said it is 'extremely cautious' about the new year and now does not expect the retail chain to return to underlying sales growth in 2008, sending its shares nearly 6 pct lower.

Real World 2.2 continued

The Leicester-based group said it expects to report a current year pre-tax profit in the region of £492–502m, up from £478m last time.

It anticipates an operating profit up 4–6 pct on the previous year's £507.5m and earnings per share (EPS) up 14–17 pct on the previous year's 146.1 pence, the higher EPS forecast reflecting share buybacks and a lower tax rate.

The profit guidance came as Next published its Christmas trading statement.

Combined sales of Next Retail and Next Directory for the 21 weeks to Dec 24 increased 0.3 pct compared to the same period last year.

Next Retail sales were down 0.3 pct in the period, with mainline like-for-like sales in the 309 stores unaffected by new openings down 3.2 pct. Next Directory sales were up 2.2 pct.

'Our like-for-like sales performance was in line with the guidance we gave in September and is an improvement on our performance in spring summer,' the group said.

'This was despite a worsening consumer environment and significant markdown activity on the high street.'

Next plc maintained its policy of trading full price in the run up to Christmas. It said stocks were well controlled going into the end of season Sale, which started on Dec 27. So far clearance in the Sale is in line with internal hopes.

However, the retailer is very concerned about the outlook for the year ahead (the year to end-Jan 2009) with consumers continuing to face increasing demands on their finances.

Many consumers will experience year on year increases in mortgage charges for much of the coming year as a result of favourable fixed rate mortgage terms expiring, it noted.

Next is not forecasting a return to like-for-like growth in the UK in 2008 for Next Retail. In September the group had said it was hopeful of achieving positive territory.

'We are more cautious now than we were in September,' finance director David Keens told Thomson Financial News.

'When we announced in September, various headlines that we've seen over September, October, November weren't in our thinking – what happened to sub-prime, interest rates, the economy,' he said.

'We've seen a lot of negative headlines come out for the economy . . . so you've got to be more cautious that you would have been three months ago.'

'I think anybody who is not in our industry is not looking at what is going on out there.'

Source: 'Next sees FY profit ahead of market hopes but cautious on 2008', AFX UK Focus, 3 January 2008; and Interactive Investor (www.iii.co.uk).

Preparing projected financial statements

In the sections that follow, we look at the process of developing projected financial statements. The emphasis of this chapter is on the preparation of projected statements and their usefulness, and so we shall deal only briefly with forecasting issues.

Preparing projected financial statements involves four main steps, which are as follows.

Step 1: Identify the key variables affecting future financial performance

The likely effect of each key variable on future financial performance must be identified and assessed. These variables fall into two broad categories: external and internal.

External variables

These usually relate to government policies and economic conditions, and include:

- the rate of tax
- interest rates for borrowings
- the rate of inflation.

There is often a great deal of published information available to help identify future rates and movements for each of the variables mentioned. Care must be taken, however, to ensure that their particular impact on the business is properly assessed. When estimating the likely rate of inflation, for example, each major category of item affected by inflation should be considered separately. Using an average rate of inflation for all items is often inappropriate as levels of inflation can vary significantly between items.

Internal variables

These cover the policies and agreements to which the business is committed. Examples include:

- capital expenditure commitments
- financing agreements
- inventory holding policies
- credit period allowed to customers
- payment policies for trade payables
- accounting policies (for example, depreciation rates and methods)
- dividend policy.

The last item listed may require some clarification. For large businesses at least, a target level of dividends is often established and managers are usually reluctant to deviate from this target. The target may be linked to the level of profits for the particular year and/or to dividends paid in previous years. (This issue is discussed in more detail in Chapter 9.)

Step 2: Forecast the sales for the period

Once the key variables influencing future performance and position have been identified, we can begin to forecast the items included in the projected financial statements. We have to make a start somewhere and the usual starting point is to forecast sales. It is sales that normally sets a limit to business growth and determines the level of operating activity. The influence of sales on other items appearing in the financial statements, such as cost of goods sold, overheads, inventories, receivables and so on, makes a reliable sales forecast essential. If this forecast is wrong, other forecasts will also be wrong.

Producing a reliable sales forecast requires an understanding of general economic conditions, industry conditions and the threat posed by major competitors.

General economic conditions. Most businesses are affected by economic cycles. During an upturn in a cycle, sales and profits will increase and businesses will increase their scale of operations. During a downturn in a cycle, the reverse will happen. The particular phase of the economic cycle can, therefore, exert a significant influence on sales.

Industry conditions. A careful examination of industry variables that can influence sales should be carried out. These factors include:

- market size and growth prospects
- level of competition within the industry

- bargaining power of customers
- threat of substitute products or services.

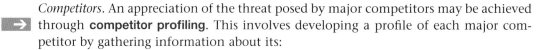 *Competitors.* An appreciation of the threat posed by major competitors may be achieved through **competitor profiling**. This involves developing a profile of each major competitor by gathering information about its:

- goals and strategies
- resources, including financial, technological and human resources
- products and/or services being developed
- alliances and joint ventures with other businesses that affect market power
- cost structures, profits and sales.

This can help assess the ability of a major competitor to upset sales plans and initiatives.

Competitor information is not always easy to obtain as businesses are reluctant to release information that may damage their competitive position. Nevertheless, there are sources of information that can be used to help build a picture of competitors, such as their published accounts (which are obligatory for limited companies) press reports, industry reports, physical observation, information gathered from customers and suppliers and so on.

Forecasting approaches

Two main approaches to forecasting sales can be found in practice: the subjective approach and the objective approach.

Subjective approach. This approach normally relies on the views of the sales force or sales managers. It is a 'bottom-up' approach which involves aggregating forecasts from those with specialist knowledge of particular products, services or market segments. It is often useful for fairly short forecasting horizons; however, care must be taken to ensure that there is no bias, particularly towards optimism, in the forecasts developed.

Objective approach. This approach relies on statistical techniques or, in the case of very large businesses, such as multinational motor-car manufacturers, econometric models. These techniques and models can range from simple extrapolation of past trends to extremely sophisticated models which incorporate a large number of variables with complex interrelationships.

There are no hard and fast rules concerning the most appropriate approach to use. Each business must assess the benefits of the various approaches in terms of reliability, and then weigh these benefits against the associated costs. Where a business wishes to carry out a cross-check on the reliability of the forecast figures, both approaches may be used.

The sales forecast, however derived, may be modified if senior managers believe that proper account has not been taken of the competitive environment or planned initiatives.

Step 3: Forecast remaining elements of financial statements

Having forecast the level of sales, all other items appearing in the projected financial statements can then be forecast.

Forecasting income statement items

It was mentioned earlier that the level of sales will have an influence on many other items in the financial statements, including certain operating costs. However, not all operating costs relating to a business will vary with the level of sales. Although some vary in direct proportion to the level of sales, others are unaffected by the level of sales during a period.

Try to identify two operating costs that are likely to vary in direct proportion to the level of sales and two that are likely to stay constant irrespective of the level of sales.

Cost of sales, royalty payments and sales force commission are examples of costs that vary in direct proportion to sales output. These are referred to as **variable costs**. Other operating costs, such as depreciation, rent, rates, insurance and salaries, may stay fixed during a period, irrespective of the level of sales generated. These are referred to as **fixed costs**.

Some operating costs have both a variable and a fixed element and so may vary partially with sales output. These are referred to as **semi-variable** (or semi-fixed) **costs**. These costs may be identified by examining past records of the business. Heat and light costs may be an example of a semi-variable cost. A certain amount of heating and lighting will be incurred irrespective of the level of sales. If, however, overtime is being worked due to heavy demand, this cost will increase. Semi-variable costs can be broken down into their fixed and variable elements (perhaps using a statistical technique such as regression analysis). Once this has been done, the total variable costs and total fixed costs can be established. By splitting costs into their fixed and variable elements it is possible to forecast the likely impact of a particular level of sales output much more reliably.

As the total operating costs of a business have both a variable and a fixed element, they will rise directly, but not proportionately, with the level of output. Their behaviour in relation to the level of activity is shown in Figure 2.2.

Figure 2.2 Graph of total cost against the level of activity

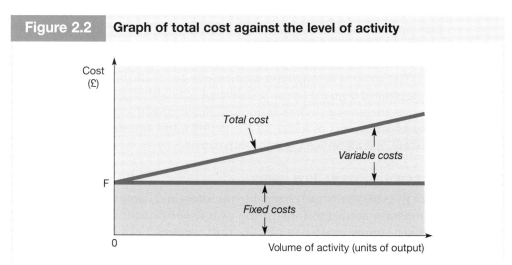

The bottom part of the graph represents the fixed cost element. To this is added the wedge-shaped top portion, which represents the variable costs. The two parts together represent total costs. At zero level of output, the variable costs are zero so total costs equal fixed costs. As activity increases so do the total costs, but only because variable costs increase.

The forecast of sales and operating costs along with forecasts of tax rates, interest rates and dividend policy, which were considered in Step 1, provide the basis for preparing the projected income statement for the period.

Forecasting items for the statement of financial position

The level of sales has an effect on the level of particular assets and liabilities held. When sales increase, there will be a 'spontaneous' increase in these items.

Activity 2.2

Can you think of two items (either assets or liabilities) that will increase 'spontaneously' as a result of an increase in the level of sales?

An increase in the level of sales is likely to lead to:

- an increase in trade receivables, and
- an increase in inventories to meet the increase in demand.

An increase in the level of sales should also lead to:

- an increase in trade payables as a result of increased purchases, and
- an increase in accrued expenses as a result of increased overhead costs.

The policies adopted by the business (for example, to offer customers a one-month credit period or to hold inventory equivalent to two months' sales) also influence the amounts of 'spontaneous' assets and liabilities held at the end of the forecast period. These policies, which were identified in Step 1, must also be taken into account.

An increase in sales may also lead to an increase in non-current (fixed) assets if they are already being operated at full capacity. If this is not the case, an increase in sales may simply absorb excess capacity. A temporary decrease in sales will probably have no effect on the level of non-current assets.

Long-term borrowings and share capital do not increase in line with increases in sales. The amount of long-term finance invested at the beginning of the period, which can be gleaned from the opening statement of financial position, will remain unchanged unless management decides otherwise. Retained earnings, however, will change as a result of any profits or losses for the period (after adjusting for dividends). This item, therefore, has an indirect relationship to sales.

Forecasting cash flow items

Once the sales, costs and changes to the assets and liabilities have been forecast, all the information needed to forecast the cash flow items for the period is available. It is a relatively simple matter to identify cash received from customers, payments to suppliers, payments for operating costs and the cash flow effects of changes in assets and liabilities. All that is needed is to adjust each item to take account of its opening and closing balances.

Example 2.1 provides an illustration of how the amount of cash to be received from the sales generated during a period is forecast.

Example 2.1

Assume that:

1 The opening balance of receivables (receivables) is £200,000 (representing the previous month's sales).
2 Sales revenue for the month is forecast to be £300,000, of which 80 per cent are on credit.
3 The business allows one month's credit to its credit customers.

What is the cash received from customers during the month?

Solution

The cash received will be:

	£000
Opening receivables	200
Sales for the month	300
Total amount due	500
Closing receivables (80% × £300,000)	(240)
Cash received from customers	260

A broadly similar approach can be taken for other cash flow items mentioned.

Activity 2.3

A business has £150,000 in trade payables outstanding at the beginning of the month. During the month, purchases of £760,000 are forecast, 50 per cent of which are on credit. The business pays all credit suppliers in the month following the month of purchase.
  How much will be paid to suppliers during the month?

The amount paid to suppliers can be calculated as follows:

	£000
Opening payables	150
Purchases for the month	760
Total amount owing	910
Closing payables (50% × £760,000)	(380)
Cash paid to suppliers	530

Step 4: Prepare the projected financial statements

Having prepared forecasts for the various elements of the financial statements, the final step is to include them in the projected financial statements. The way in which we prepare these statements will be considered in some detail in the following section.
  Figure 2.3 illustrates the steps in the planning process just described.

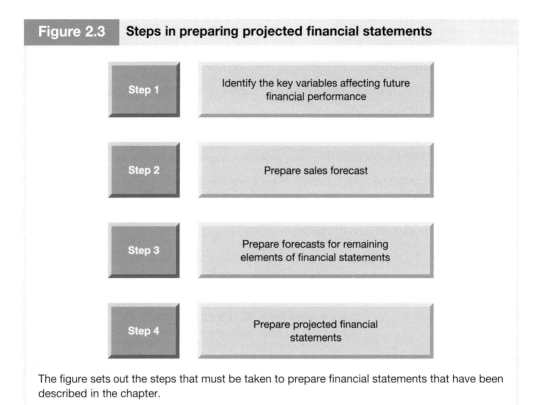

Figure 2.3   Steps in preparing projected financial statements

Step 1   Identify the key variables affecting future financial performance

Step 2   Prepare sales forecast

Step 3   Prepare forecasts for remaining elements of financial statements

Step 4   Prepare projected financial statements

The figure sets out the steps that must be taken to prepare financial statements that have been described in the chapter.

Preparing the projected statements: a worked example

It was mentioned earlier that these financial statements consist of a:

● projected cash flow statement
● projected income statement
● projected statement of financial position (balance sheet).

If you already have some background in accounting, the following sections should pose few problems. This is because the methods and principles employed for projected financial statements are the same as those employed for historic financial statements. The only real difference lies in the fact that the statements are prepared using forecast information rather than *actual* information.

To illustrate the preparation of projected financial statements let us consider Example 2.2.

Example 2.2

Designer Dresses Ltd is a small business to be formed by James and William Clark to sell an exclusive range of dresses from a boutique in a fashionable suburb of London. On 1 January, they plan to invest £50,000 cash to acquire 25,000 £1 shares each in the business. Of this, £30,000 is to be invested in new fittings in January. These fittings are to be depreciated over three years on the straight-line basis (their scrap value is assumed to be zero at the end of their lives). The straight-line basis of depreciation allocates the total amount to be depreciated evenly over the life of the asset. In this case, a half-year's depreciation is to be charged in the first six months. The sales and purchases projections for the business are as follows:

	Jan	Feb	Mar	Apr	May	June	Total
Sales revenue (£000)	10.2	30.6	30.6	40.8	40.8	51.0	204.0
Purchases (£000)	20.0	30.0	25.0	25.0	30.0	30.0	160.0
Other costs* (£000)	9.0	9.0	9.0	9.0	9.0	9.0	54.0

* 'Other costs' includes wages but excludes depreciation.

The sales will all be made by credit card. The credit card business will take one month to pay and will deduct its fee of 2 per cent of gross sales before paying amounts due to Designer Dresses. One month's credit is allowed by suppliers. Other costs shown above do not include rent and rates of £10,000 per quarter, payable on 1 January and 1 April. All other costs will be paid in cash. Closing inventory at the end of June is expected to be £58,000.

You should ignore taxation. For your convenience, you are advised to work to the nearest £000.

Required:
(a) Prepare a projected cash flow statement for the six months to 30 June.
(b) Prepare a projected income statement for the same period.
(c) Prepare a projected statement of financial position (balance sheet) at 30 June.

(Note that, for the sake of simplicity, the example considers only one course of action and all the forecast figures are provided for use in preparing the projected financial statements. This should help in getting to grips with the main principles of preparation.)

Projected cash flow statement

Cash has been described as the 'lifeblood' of a business. It is vital for a business to have sufficient liquid resources to meet its maturing obligations, as failure to do so can have disastrous consequences. The projected cash flow statement monitors future changes in liquidity and helps managers to assess the impact of expected future events on the cash balance. It can identify periods where there are cash surpluses and cash deficits, which will allow managers to plan for these occurrences. Where there is a cash surplus, managers should consider the profitable investment of the cash. Where there is a cash deficit, managers should consider the ways in which this can be financed.

The cash flow statement is fairly easy to prepare. It simply records the cash inflows and outflows of the business. The main sources of cash inflows and outflows can be identified as follows:

- issue and redemption of shares
- purchase and sale of non-current assets
- operating activities (sales and expenses)
- tax and dividends.

These are set out in Figure 2.4.

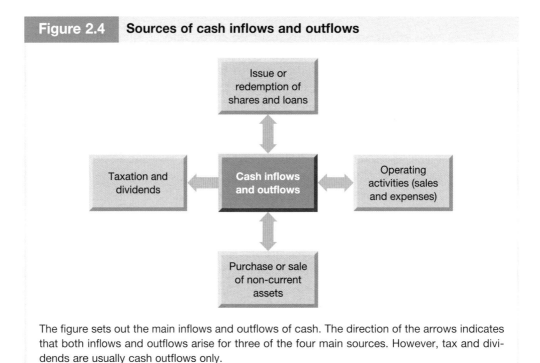

Figure 2.4   Sources of cash inflows and outflows

The figure sets out the main inflows and outflows of cash. The direction of the arrows indicates that both inflows and outflows arise for three of the four main sources. However, tax and dividends are usually cash outflows only.

When preparing the cash flow statement for a fairly short period, such as six months, it is often useful to provide a monthly breakdown of the cash inflows and outflows. This helps managers to monitor closely changes in the cash position of the business. The further the business projects its cash flow statements into the future, however, the more difficult it becomes to provide a monthly breakdown.

There is no set format for the projected cash flow statement as it is normally used for internal purposes only. Managers are free to decide on the form of presentation that best suits their needs. Set out below is an outline projected cash flow statement for Designer Dresses Ltd for the six months to 30 June. This format seems to be widely used and is as good as any format proposed. It is recommended, therefore, that this format be used when preparing projected cash flow statements.

Projected cash flow statement for the year to 30 June

	Jan £000	Feb £000	Mar £000	Apr £000	May £000	June £000
Cash inflows						
Issue of shares						
Credit sales	____	____	____	____	____	____
	____	____	____	____	____	____
Cash outflows						
Credit purchases						
Other costs						
Rent and rates	____	____	____	____	____	____
	____	____	____	____	____	____
Net cash flow						
Opening balance	____	____	____	____	____	____
Closing balance	____	____	____	____	____	____

We can see from this outline that:

● Each column represents a monthly period.
● At the top of each column the cash inflows are set out and a total for each month's inflows is shown.
● Immediately below the monthly total for cash inflows, the cash outflows are set out and a monthly total for these is also shown.
● The difference between the monthly totals of cash inflows and outflows is the net *cash flow* for the month.
● If we add this net cash flow to the opening cash balance, which has been brought forward from the previous month, we derive the closing cash balance. (This will become the opening cash balance in the next month.)

When preparing a projected cash flow statement, there are really two questions to be asked concerning each item of information presented. The first question is: does the item of information concern a cash transaction (that is, does it involve cash inflows or outflows)? If the answer to this question is no, then the information should be ignored when preparing this statement. There are various items of information relating to a particular period, such as depreciation charges, that do not involve cash movements.

If the answer to the question above is yes, then a second question must be asked, which is: when did the cash transaction take place? When providing a monthly breakdown of cash flows, it is important to identify the particular month in which the cash movement takes place. Where sales and purchases are made on credit, the cash movement will often take place after the month in which the sale or purchase takes place. (We return to this point later when discussing the projected income statement.)

Problems in preparing cash flow statements usually arise because these two questions above have not been properly addressed.

Activity 2.4

Fill in the outline cash flow statement for Designer Dresses Ltd for the six months to 30 June using the information contained in Example 2.2 above.

The completed statement will be as follows:

Projected cash flow statement for the six months to 30 June

	Jan £000	Feb £000	Mar £000	Apr £000	May £000	June £000
Cash inflows						
Issue of shares	50					
Credit sales	–	10	30	30	40	40
	50	10	30	30	40	40
Cash outflows						
Credit purchases	–	20	30	25	25	30
Other costs	9	9	9	9	9	9
Rent and rates	10			10		
Fittings	30					
	49	29	39	44	34	39
Net cash flow	1	(19)	(9)	(14)	6	1
Opening balance	–	1	(18)	(27)	(41)	(35)
Closing balance	1	(18)	(27)	(41)	(35)	(34)

→

Activity 2.4 continued

Notes
1 The receipts from credit sales will arise one month after the sale has taken place. Hence, January's sales will be received in February, and so on. Similarly, trade payables are paid one month after the goods have been purchased.
2 The closing cash balance for each month is deduced by adding to (or subtracting from) the opening balance, the cash flow for the month.

It is worth noting that the format used above is for internal reporting purposes only. When a (historic) cash flow statement is prepared for external reporting purposes, a summary of the cash flows for the year rather than a monthly breakdown of cash flows is provided. Furthermore, a particular format for presenting the information must be followed.

Accurate cash flow projections are particularly important for businesses that are growing rapidly. Failure to generate sufficient cash to meet growing commitments can have dire consequences. Where a growing business publishes cash flow projections, which it then fails to meet, there is a risk that shareholders will view this as a sign of weakness and react by selling shares. **Real World 2.3** provides an example of one growing business that suffered from this problem.

REAL WORLD 2.3

Vanco's shares fall on target warning   **FT**

Shares in Vanco, the virtual telecoms network operator, yesterday slumped to their lowest level in two years after warning it would miss its interim cash flow targets because of delays to the signings of three contracts.

The group forecast a cash outflow of around £20m for the six months to July 31. The figure was about double the company's expectations, although Vanco said one contract had since been signed.

The group, which does not own a physical network but buys capacity from telecommunications groups, manages data networks on behalf of large organisations.

The shares, which have dropped 25 per cent in the last three months on fears about its cash flow, yesterday fell 38p to 318p.

Vanco said total order intake between February 1 and July 31 rose from £49.5m to £120m, although only £16m would be receivable in cash in the current year.

However, it retained its full-year forecast to January 31 that revenue would be about £227m and operating profit about £27m. Interim net debt is expected to be about £37m, compared with £24.4m a year ago.

Source: Philip Stafford, 'Vanco's shares fall on profit warning', www.ft.com, 21 August 2007.

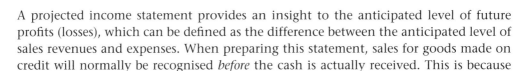

Projected income statement

A projected income statement provides an insight to the anticipated level of future profits (losses), which can be defined as the difference between the anticipated level of sales revenues and expenses. When preparing this statement, sales for goods made on credit will normally be recognised *before* the cash is actually received. This is because revenue is usually recognised when goods have been passed to, and accepted by, the customer. Expenses are matched to the sales they help to generate and are included in the same income statement. This means that expenses may be reported in an income statement for a period occurring either before or after they are actually paid. The purpose of the income statement, however, is to show the wealth generated during a particular period, which may bear little relation to the cash generated during that period. The timing of the cash inflows from credit sales and cash outflows for expenses is, therefore, irrelevant for this statement.

The format of the projected income statement for Designer Dresses Ltd will be as follows:

Projected income statement for the six months to 30 June

	£000	£000
Credit sales revenue		
Less Cost of sales		
Opening inventory		
Add Purchases	____	
Less Closing inventory	____	____
Gross profit		
Less		
Credit card discounts		
Rent and rates		
Other costs		
Depreciation of fittings	____	
Profit for the period		____

Activity 2.5

Fill in the outline projected income statement for Designer Dresses Ltd for the six months to 30 June, using the information contained in Example 2.2 above.

The statement will be as follows:

Projected income statement for the six months to 30 June

	£000	£000
Credit sales revenue		204
Cost of sales		
Opening inventory	–	
Purchases	(160)	
	(160)	
Closing inventory	58	(102)
Gross profit		102
Credit card discounts		(4)
Rent and rates		(20)
Other costs		(54)
Depreciation of fittings		(5)
Profit for the period		19

Notes
1 There was no opening inventory in this case.
2 The credit card discount is shown as a separate expense and not deducted from the sales figure. This approach is more informative than simply netting off the amount of the discount against sales.

Projected statement of financial position (balance sheet)

The projected statement of financial position reveals the end-of-period balances for assets, liabilities and equity (capital) and is the last statement to be prepared. This is because the other two statements will produce information needed to prepare the projected statement of financial position. The projected cash flow statement provides the end-of-period cash balance for inclusion under 'current assets' (or where there is a negative balance, for inclusion under 'current liabilities'). The projected income statement provides the projected profit (loss) for the period for inclusion under the 'equity' section of the statement of financial position (after adjustment for dividends). The projected income statement also provides the depreciation charge for the period, which is used to adjust 'non-current assets'.

The format of the projected statement of financial position for Designer Dresses Ltd will be as follows:

Projected statement of financial position (balance sheet) as at 30 June

	£000
Non-current assets	
Fittings	
Accumulated depreciation	_____
	_____
Current assets	
Inventory	
Trade receivables	_____
	_____
Total assets	_____
Equity	
Share capital	
Retained earnings	_____
	_____
Current liabilities	
Trade payables	
Bank overdraft	_____
Total equity and liabilities	_____
Total equity and liabilities	_____

Activity 2.6

Fill in the outline projected statement of financial position for Designer Dresses Ltd as at 30 June using the information contained in Example 2.2 and in the answers to Activities 2.4 and 2.5.

The completed statement will be as follows:

Projected statement of financial position (balance sheet) as at 30 June

	£000
Non-current assets	
Fittings	30
Accumulated depreciation	(5)
	25
Current assets	
Inventory	58
Trade receivables	50
	108
Total assets	133
Equity	
Share capital	5U
Retained earnings	19
	69
Current liabilities	
Trade payables	30
Bank overdraft	34
	64
Total equity and liabilities	133

Note: The trade receivables figure represents June credit sales (less the credit card discount). Similarly, the trade payables figure represents June purchases.

Projected financial statements and decision making

The projected financial statements should be examined with a critical eye. There is always a danger that the figures will be too readily accepted. Forecast figures are rarely completely accurate and some assessment must be made of the extent to which they can be relied upon. Thus, managers should ask such questions as:

- How were the projections developed?
- What underlying assumptions have been made and are they valid?
- Have all relevant items been included?

Only when the managers have received satisfactory answers to these questions should they use the statements for making decisions.

Unfortunately, projected financial statements do not come with clear decision rules to indicate whether a proposed course of action should go ahead. Judgement is required. In order to form a judgement, answers to the following questions should be sought:

- Are the cash flows satisfactory? Can they be improved by changing policies or plans (for example, delaying capital expenditure decisions, requiring receivables to pay more quickly and so on)?
- Is there a need for additional financing? Is it feasible to obtain the amount required?
- Can any surplus funds be profitably reinvested?
- Is the level of projected profit satisfactory in relation to the risks involved? If not, what could be done to improve matters?
- Are the sales and individual expense items at a satisfactory level?
- Is the financial position at the end of the period acceptable?
- Is the level of borrowing acceptable? Is the business too dependent on borrowing?

Activity 2.7

Evaluate the projected financial statements of Designer Dresses Ltd. Pay particular attention to the projected profitability and liquidity of the business.

The projected cash flow statement reveals that the business will have a bank overdraft throughout most of the period under review. The maximum overdraft requirement will be £41,000 in April. Although the business will be heavily dependent on bank finance in the early months, this situation should not last for too long provided the business achieves, and then maintains, the level of projected profit and provided it does not invest heavily in further assets.

The business is expected to generate a profit of 9.3p for every £1 of sales. The profit of £19,000 on the original outlay of £50,000 by the owners seems high. However, the business may be of a high-risk nature and therefore the owners will be looking to make high returns. As this is a new business, it may be very difficult to project into the future with any accuracy. Thus, the basis on which the projections have been made requires careful investigation.

Some further points regarding profitability can be made. It is not clear from the question whether the wages (under 'other costs' in the income statement) include any remuneration for James and William Clark. If no remuneration for their efforts has been included, the level of profit shown may be overstated. It may not be possible to extrapolate the projected revenues and expenses for the six-month period in order to obtain a projected profit for the year. It is likely that the business is seasonal in nature and, therefore, the following six-month period may be quite different.

Activity 2.8

Dalgleish Ltd is a wholesale supplier of stationery. In recent months, the business has experienced liquidity problems. It has an overdraft at the end of November 2008 and the bank has been pressing for a reduction in this overdraft over the next six months. The business is owned by the Dalgleish family, who are unwilling to raise finance through long-term borrowing. The most recent statement of the financial position of the business is as follows:

Statement of financial position (balance sheet) as at 30 November 2008

	£000	£000
Non-current assets		
Land and premises	250	
Accumulated depreciation	(24)	226
Fixtures and fittings	130	
Accumulated depreciation	(38)	92
		318
Current assets		
Inventory		142
Trade receivables		120
		262
Total assets		580

	£000
Equity	
£1 ordinary shares	200
Retained earnings	109
	309
Current liabilities	
Trade payables	145
Bank overdraft	126
	271
Total equity and liabilities	580

The following projections for the six months ended 31 May 2009 are available:

1 Sales revenue and purchases for the six months ended 31 May 2009 will be as follows:

	Sales	Purchases
	£000	£000
December	160	150
January	220	140
February	240	170
March	150	110
April	160	120
May	200	160

2 Seventy per cent of sales are on credit and 30 per cent are cash sales. Credit sales are received in the following month. All purchases are on one month's credit.

3 Wages are £40,000 for each of the first three months. However, this will increase by 10 per cent as from March 2009. All wages are paid in the month they are incurred.

4 The gross profit percentage on goods sold is 30 per cent.

5 Administration expenses are expected to be £12,000 in each of the first four months and £14,000 in subsequent months. These figures include a monthly charge of £4,000 in respect of depreciation of non-current assets. Administration expenses are paid in the month they are incurred.

6 Selling expenses are expected to be £8,000 per month except for May 2009 when an advertising campaign costing £12,000 will be paid for. The advertising campaign will commence at the beginning of June 2009. Selling expenses are paid for in the month they are incurred.

7 A dividend of £20,000 will be proposed and paid in December 2008.

8 The business intends to purchase, and pay for, new fixtures and fittings at the end of April 2009 for £28,000. These will be delivered in June 2009.

Required:

(a) Prepare a projected cash flow statement for Dalgleish Ltd for each of the six months to 31 May 2009.

(b) Prepare a projected income statement for the six months to 31 May 2009.

(c) Briefly discuss ways in which the business might reduce the bank overdraft as required by the bank.

(a) The cash flow projection will be as follows:

Projected cash flow statement for the six months to 31 May 2009

	Dec £000	Jan £000	Feb £000	Mar £000	April £000	May £000
Cash inflows						
Credit sales	120	112	154	168	105	112
Cash sales	48	66	72	45	48	60
	168	178	226	213	153	172
Cash outflows						
Purchases	145	150	140	170	110	120
Admin. Expenses	8	8	8	8	10	10
Wages	40	40	40	44	44	44
Selling expenses	8	8	8	8	8	20
Fixtures					28	
Dividend	20					
	221	206	196	230	200	194
Cash flow	(53)	(28)	30	(17)	(47)	(22)
Opening balance	(126)	(179)	(207)	(177)	(194)	(241)
Closing balance	(179)	(207)	(177)	(194)	(241)	(263)

(b) The projected income statement will be as follows:

Projected income statement for the six months to 31 May 2009

	£000
Sales revenue	1,130
Cost of sales (balancing figure)	(791)
Gross profit (30% of sales)	339
Wages	(252)
Selling expenses (exc. ad. campaign)	(48)
Administration expenses (inc. depreciation)	(76)
Loss for the period	(37)

Note: The advertising campaign relates to the next financial period and will therefore be charged to the income statement of that period.

(c) You may have thought of a number of possible options. The following (or perhaps some combination of these) might be feasible:

- an injection of new share capital by the Dalgleish family or others
- reduce inventory levels
- delay purchase of/payment for fixtures
- sell non-current assets
- increase the proportion of cash sales
- delay payment of trade payables.

Each of the above options has advantages and disadvantages and these must be carefully assessed before a final decision is made. (Note that the Dalgleish family has ruled out the possibility of raising a loan.)

Per-cent-of-sales method

An alternative approach to preparing a projected income statement and statement of financial position (balance sheet) is the **per-cent-of-sales method**. This is a simpler approach to forecasting, which assumes that most items appearing in the income statement and statement of financial position vary with the level of sales. Hence, these statements can be prepared by expressing most items as a percentage of the sales for the forecast period.

To use this method, an examination of past records needs to be undertaken to see by how much items vary with sales. It may be found, for example, that inventory levels have been around 30 per cent of sales in previous periods. If the sales for the forecast period are, say, £10 million, the level of inventories will be forecast as £3 million (that is, 30% × £10 million). The same approach will be used for other items.

Shown below is a brief summary of how key items appearing in the income statement and statement of financial position are derived.

Income statement

The per-cent-of-sales method assumes that the following income statement items can be expressed as a percentage of sales:

- operating expenses
- profit before tax, which is the difference between sales revenues and expenses.

However:

- Tax is assumed to vary with the level of profit before tax and so is expressed as a percentage of this figure. It has, therefore, an indirect relationship with sales.

Statement of financial position (balance sheet)

The per-cent-of-sales method assumes that the following items in the statement of financial position can be expressed as a percentage of sales:

- current assets that increase spontaneously with sales, such as inventory and trade receivables;
- current liabilities that increase spontaneously with sales, such as trade payables and accrued expenses;
- cash (as a projected cash flow statement is not available to provide a more accurate measure of cash).

However:

- non-current assets will only be expressed as a percentage of sales if they are already operating at full capacity – otherwise they will not usually change;
- non-current liabilities and share capital will not be expressed as a percentage of sales but will be based on figures at the beginning of the forecast period (unless changes are made as a result of management decisions).

Identifying the financing gap

When sales revenue increases, there is a risk that a business will outgrow the finance that has been committed. The forecast increase in assets may exceed the forecast increase in equity (in the form of retained earnings) and liabilities and so a financing gap may arise. This gap is easily identified under the per-cent-of-sales method because the statement of financial position will not balance. The additional finance required by the business will be the amount necessary to make the statement of financial position balance.

The way in which a business decides to fill the financing gap is referred to as the **plug**. There are various forms of finance that may be used as a plug, including borrowings and share capital. We shall, however, leave a discussion of the different forms of finance available until Chapter 6.

A worked example

Let us go through a simple example to show how the per-cent-of-sales method works.

Example 2.3

The financial statements of Burrator plc for the year that has just ended are as follows:

Income statement for Year 8

	£000
Credit sales revenue	800
Cost of sales	(600)
Gross profit	200
Selling expenses	(80)
Distribution expenses	(20)
Other expenses	(20)
Profit before taxation	80
Tax (25%)	20
Profit for the year	60

Statement of financial position (balance sheet) at the end of Year 8

	£000
Non-current assets	160
Current assets	
Inventory	320
Trade receivables	200
Cash	20
	540
Total assets	700
Equity	
Share capital – 25p ordinary shares	60
Retained earnings	380
	440
Current liabilities	
Trade payables	240
Tax due	20
	260
Total equity and liabilities	700

A dividend of 50% of the profit for the year was proposed and paid during the year.

The following information is relevant for Year 9:

1 Sales revenue is expected to be 10 per cent higher than in Year 8.
2 The non-current assets of the business are currently operating at full capacity.
3 The tax rate will be the same as in Year 8 and 50% of the tax due will be outstanding at the year end.
4 The business intends to maintain the same dividend policy as for Year 8.
5 Half of the tax relating to Year 9 will be outstanding at the year end. Tax due at the end of Year 8 will be paid during Year 9.
6 Any financing gap will be filled by an issue of long-term loan notes.

Required:

Prepare a projected income statement and statement of financial position (balance sheet) using the per-cent-of-sales method. (Assume that Year 8 provides a useful guide to past experience.)

Solution

To prepare the projected income statement, we calculate each expense as a percentage of sales for Year 8 and then use this percentage to forecast the equivalent expense in Year 9. Tax is calculated as a percentage of the profit before tax for Year 9, using percentages from Year 8.

The statement is therefore as follows:

Projected income statement for the year ended 31 December Year 9

	£000
Credit sales revenue (800 + (10% × 800))	880
Cost of sales (75% sales)	(660)
Gross profit (25% sales)	220
Selling expenses (10% sales)	(88)
Distribution expenses ($2\frac{1}{2}$% sales)	(22)
Other expenses ($2\frac{1}{2}$% sales)	(22)
Profit before taxation (10% sales)	88
Tax (25% of profit before tax)	(22)
Profit for the year	66

We apply the same broad principles when preparing the projected statement of financial position (balance sheet) for Year 9.

Activity 2.9

Prepare a projected statement of financial position for Burrator plc at the end of Year 9.

Activity 2.9 continued

This will be as follows:

Projected statement of financial position (balance sheet) as at 31 December Year 9

	£000
Non-current assets (20% sales)	176
Current assets	
Inventory (40% sales)	352
Trade receivables (25% sales)	220
Cash ($2\frac{1}{2}$% sales)	22
	594
Total assets	770
Equity	
Share capital – 25p ordinary shares	60
Retained earnings [380 + (66 – 33*)]	413
	473
Non-current liabilities	
Loan notes (balancing figure)	22
Current liabilities	
Trade payables (30% sales)	264
Tax due (50% tax due)	11
	275
Total equity and liabilities	770

* The dividend is 50% of the profit for the year and is deducted in deriving the retained profit for the year.

The advantage of the per-cent-of-sales method is that the task of preparing the projected financial statements becomes much more manageable. It can provide an approximate figure for the finance required without having to prepare a projected cash flow statement. It can also help reduce the time and cost of forecasting every single item appearing in the projected income statement and statement of financial position (balance sheet). These can be of real benefit, particularly for large businesses.

The problem, however, is that this method uses relationships between particular items and sales that are based on those that have existed in the past. These relationships may change over time because of changes in strategic direction (for example, launching completely new products) or because of changes in management policies (for example, liberalising credit facilities to customers).

Taking account of risk

When making estimates concerning the future, there is always a chance that things will not turn out as expected. The likelihood that what is estimated to occur will not actually occur is referred to as **risk** and this will be considered in some detail in Chapter 5. However, it is worth taking a little time at this point to consider the ways in which managers may deal with the problem of risk in the context of projected financial statements. In practice, there are various methods available to help managers deal with any uncertainty surrounding the reliability of the projected financial statements. Below we consider three possible methods.

Sensitivity analysis

Sensitivity analysis is a useful technique to employ when evaluating the contents of projected financial statements. This involves taking a single variable (for example, volume of sales) and examining the effect of changes in the chosen variable on the likely performance and position of the business. By examining the shifts that occur, it is possible to arrive at some assessment of how sensitive changes are for the projected outcomes. Although only one variable is examined at a time, a number of variables, which are considered to be important to the performance of a business, may be examined consecutively.

One form of sensitivity analysis is to pose a series of 'what if?' questions. If we take sales as an example, the following 'what if?' questions may be asked:

● What if sales volume is 5 per cent higher than expected?
● What if sales volume is 10 per cent lower than expected?
● What if sales price is reduced by 15 per cent?
● What if sales price could be increased by 20 per cent?

In answering these questions, it is possible to develop a better 'feel' for the effect of forecast inaccuracies on the final outcomes. However, this technique does not assign probabilities to each possible change nor does it consider the effect on projected outcomes of more than one variable at a time.

Scenario analysis

Another approach to helping managers gain a feel for the effect of forecast inaccuracies is to prepare projected financial statements according to different possible 'states of the world'. For example, managers may wish to examine projected financial statements prepared on the following bases:

● an optimistic view of likely future events
● a pessimistic view of likely future events
● a 'most likely' view of future events.

This approach is referred to as **scenario analysis** and, unlike sensitivity analysis, it will involve changing a number of variables simultaneously in order to portray a possible state of the world. To help in assessing the level of risk involved, knowing the likelihood of each state of the world occurring, however, would also be useful.

The pessimistic scenario is usually referred to as the 'worst-case scenario'. **Real World 2.4** mentions the worst-case scenario for a well-known football club, which is, apparently, not particularly bad.

REAL WORLD 2.4

Worst case scenario

Celtic PLC reported a profit of £15.04m for the year ending 30 June 2007 (2006: £4.22m loss), its first profit since 1999.

Sales were up 31% to £75.237m (2006: £57.859m), largely due to participation in the UEFA Champions League; the previous season Celtic failed to reach the first round proper of either European tournament.

Real World 2.4 continued

The £15.04m profit was considerably influenced by the sale of Stilyan Petrov, Stephen Pearson, Ross Wallace and Stanislav Varga, which earned the club £9.40m during the period.

In the year, £14.4m was spent on new player acquisition, including those purchased over the summer. While most of this cash will have been paid during the period, the effects of the expenditure on the income statement will be amortised over each player's contract period.

The club was still in debt at the year end, but only to the tune of £4.99m.

A key underlying indicator for the club is the relationship between operating expenses, which were £59.283m (2006: £53.674m) and the previous year's sales, £57.859m, achieved with only £0.75m European income.

Operating expenses do not include debt servicing or player acquisition charges, but are a reasonable indicator of non-variable running costs. With the previous year's sales so close to this figure with very little European income, the potential for damaging losses is marginal.

Celtic is in excellent financial shape. Champions League income is clearly crucial to the club's development plans, but the worst case scenario should not present too many challenges.

Source: Adapted from 'Celtic Profit Alfie Conn', www.bbc.co.uk, 20 August 2007.

Simulations

The **simulation** approach is really a development of sensitivity analysis that we discussed earlier. The approach creates a distribution of possible values to key variables in the projected financial statements and a probability of occurrence is attached to each value. A computer is used to select one of the possible values from each distribution on a random basis. It then generates projected statements on the basis of the selected values for each variable. This process represents a single trial. The process is then repeated using other values for each variable until many possible combinations of values for the key variables have been considered. This may, in practice, mean that thousands of trials are carried out.

From the huge amount of information produced, a range of likely outcomes may be deduced and the probability of each outcome identified. For example, a business may carry out 4,000 trials based on key variables in the projected income statement. These trials may indicate that the expected profit for the following period will fall within the range £100,000–£500,000. There may be 20 per cent of the trials producing an expected profit between £100,000 and £200,000; 30 per cent of the trials producing a profit between £200,001 and £300,000; 35 per cent of the trials producing an expected profit between £300,001 and £400,000; and 15 per cent of the trials producing a profit between £400,001 and £500,000. This information may help managers decide whether the expected level of performance is satisfactory.

This approach is claimed to make managers think carefully about the relationships between the key variables in the projected statements. In practice, however, there is a danger that carrying out simulations will lead to a rather mechanical approach to dealing with risk. Undue emphasis may be placed on carrying out trials and producing their results, and insufficient emphasis may be given to a more critical evaluation of the underlying assumptions and issues.

Real World 2.5 highlights the need for risk assessment to be taken more seriously in certain parts of the public sector.

REAL WORLD 2.5

Everything in the millennium garden is far from rosy   **FT**

The £43m National Botanic Garden of Wales, a millennium project funded partly by the public, was built without applying common commercial disciplines and in breach of Treasury guidelines, according to Jeromy Colman, auditor-general for Wales.

Mr Colman's highly critical report, published today, has implications for future landmark schemes funded from the public purse, suggesting they should be more tightly controlled.

The creation of the gardens was part of a frenzy of building to mark the millennium. The typical project was a visitor attraction combining education and entertainment, as exemplified by the crisis-hit Millennium Dome in Greenwich. Subsidies generally covered only capital costs, leaving some projects struggling to attract enough visitors to pay running expenses.

The National Botanic Garden, in contrast to the hugely successful Eden Project in Cornwall, was worthy rather than inspiring in content and had problems luring visitors to its rural site on the periphery of the south Wales conurbation. Its backers included the Millennium Commission, the Welsh assembly and the Welsh Development Agency. The garden faced financial collapse in late 2003 and early 2004. It was bailed out last March by the Millennium Commission, the Welsh assembly and a local council. The project has since hit targets set under a recovery plan.

The failure of several of the garden's backers to request or produce comprehensive sensitivity analysis – forecast cashflows under good and bad scenarios – was a glaring omission. Even entrepreneurs seeking small bank loans often produced these. Mr Colman said: 'It is surprising sensitivity analysis was only done on one occasion. If you look at Treasury advice on the approval of investment in public projects it is clear [more] sensitivities should have been done.'

Mr Colman said insufficient allowance had been made for the well-known fact that visitor numbers to attractions such as the garden were highly unpredictable. He also found there had been a lack of co-ordination between the project's publicly funded backers.

He said: 'Each body focused on their own investments but no one formed a view of collective exposure.'

Source: Jonathan Guthrie, 'Everything in the millennium garden is far from rosy', www.ft.com, 24 November 2005.

Self-assessment question 2.1

Quardis Ltd is an importer of high quality laser printers, which can be used with a range of microcomputers. The most recent statement of financial position of Quardis Ltd is as follows:

Self-assessment question 2.1 continued

Statement of financial position (balance sheet) as at 31 May 2008

	£000	£000
Non-current assets		
Premises	460	
Accumulated depreciation	(30)	430
Fixtures and fittings	35	
Accumulated depreciation	(10)	25
		455
Current assets		
Inventory		24
Trade receivables		34
Cash at bank		2
		60
Total assets		515
Equity		
£1 ordinary shares		200
Retained earnings		144
		344
Non-current liabilities		
Borrowings – Loan		125
Current liabilities		
Trade payables		22
Tax due		24
		46
Total equity and liabilities		515

The following forecast information is available for the year ended 31 May 2009:

1   Sales are expected to be £280,000 for the year. Sixty per cent of sales are on credit and it is expected that, at the year end, three months' credit sales will be outstanding. Sales revenues accrue evenly over the year.

2   Purchases of inventory during the year will be £186,000 and will accrue evenly over the year. All purchases are on credit and at the year end it is expected that two months' purchases will remain unpaid.

3   Fixtures and fittings costing £25,000 will be purchased and paid for during the year. Depreciation is charged at 10 per cent on the cost of fixtures and fittings held at the year end.

4   Depreciation is charged on premises at 2 per cent on cost.

5   On 1 June 2008, £30,000 of the loan from the Highland Bank is to be repaid. Interest is at the rate of 13 per cent per annum and all interest accrued to 31 May 2009 will be paid on that day.

6   Inventories at the year end are expected to be 25 per cent higher than at the beginning of the year.

7   Wages for the year will be £34,000. It is estimated that £4,000 of this total will remain unpaid at the year end.

8   Other overhead expenses for the year (excluding those mentioned above) are expected to be £21,000. It is expected that £3,000 of this total will still be unpaid at the year end.

9   A dividend of 5p per share will be announced and paid during the year.

10 Tax is payable at the rate of 35 per cent. Tax outstanding at the beginning of the year will be paid during the year. Half of the tax relating to the year will also be paid during the year.

All workings should be shown to the nearest £000.

Required:

(a) Prepare a projected income statement for the year ended 31 May 2009.

(b) Prepare a projected statement of financial position (balance sheet) as at 31 May 2009.

(c) Comment on the significant features revealed by these statements.

Note: A projected cash flow statement is not required. The cash figure in the projected statement of financial position will be a balancing figure.

The answer to this question may be found at the back of the book on p. 529.

SUMMARY

The main points in this chapter may be summarised as follows:

Planning for the future

- Developing plans involves:
  - setting aims and objectives
  - identifying the options available
  - evaluating the options and making a selection.
- Projected financial statements help in evaluating the options available.

Preparing projected financial statements

- Involves a four-stage process:
  - identifying the key variables that affect future financial performance
  - forecasting sales for the period, as many other items vary in relation to sales
  - forecasting the remaining elements of the financial statements
  - preparing the projected financial statements.
- The projected financial statements normally prepared are:
  - a projected cash flow statement
  - a projected income statement
  - a projected statement of financial position (balance sheet).
- The projected cash flow statement is usually broken down into monthly periods.

Projected financial statements and decision making

- Projected statements should be checked for reliability before using them for decision-making purposes.
- They do not provide clear decision rules for managers, who must employ judgement.

Per-cent-of-sales method

- Assumes that most items on the income statement and statement of financial position (balance sheet) vary with sales.
- Calculates any financing gap by reference to the amount required to make the statement of financial position (balance sheet) balance.

● Makes the preparation of forecast statements easier and less costly but assumes that relationships between individual items and sales that held in the past will also hold in the future.

Taking account of risk

● Three methods of dealing with risk are:
  – sensitivity analysis
  – scenario analysis
  – simulations.

 Key terms

Projected financial statements p. 30	**Plug** p. 50
Competitor profiling p. 34	**Risk** p. 52
Variable costs p. 35	**Sensitivity analysis** p. 53
Fixed costs p. 35	**Scenario analysis** p. 53
Semi-variable costs p. 35	**Simulation** p. 54
Per-cent-of-sales method p. 49	

For definitions of these terms see the Glossary, pp. 574–583.

Further reading

If you wish to explore the topics discussed in this chapter in more depth, try the following books:

Financial Management, *Brigham, E. and Ehrhardt, M.*, 12th edn, Harcourt, 2007, chapter 4.

How to Forecast: A guide for business, *Morrell, J.*, Gower, 2002.

Principles of Corporate Finance, *Brealey, R., Myers, S. and Allen, F.*, 9th edn, McGraw-Hill, 2007, chapter 29.

Cash Flow Forecasting (Essential Capital Markets), *Fight, A.*, Butterworths, 2005, chapters 1–4.

REVIEW QUESTIONS

Answers to these questions can be found at the back of the book on p. 540.

2.1 In what ways might projected financial statements help a business that is growing fast?

2.2 'The future is uncertain and so projected financial statements will almost certainly prove to be inaccurate. It is, therefore, a waste of time to prepare them.' Comment.

2.3 Why would it normally be easier for an existing business than for a new one to prepare projected financial statements?

2.4 Why is the sales forecast normally of critical importance to the preparation of projected financial statements?

EXERCISES

Exercises 2.5 to 2.7 are more advanced than 2.1 to 2.4. Those with a coloured number have answers at the back of the book starting on p. 549.

 If you wish to try more exercises, visit the students' side of this book's Companion Website.

2.1 Choice Designs Ltd operates a small group of wholesale/retail carpet stores in the north of England. The statement of financial position (balance sheet) of the business as at 31 May 2008 is as follows:

Statement of financial position as at 31 May 2008

	£000	£000
Non-current assets		
Premises	600	
Accumulated depreciation	(100)	500
Fixtures and fittings	140	
Accumulated depreciation	(80)	60
		560
Current assets		
Inventory		240
Trade receivables		220
Bank		165
		625
Total assets		1,185
Equity		
£1 ordinary shares		500
Retained earnings		251
		751
Current liabilities		
Trade payables		268
Tax due		166
		434
Total equity and liabilities		1,185

As a result of falling profits the directors of the business would like to completely refurbish each store during June 2008 at a total cost of £300,000. However, before making such a large capital expenditure commitment, they require projections of performance and position for the forthcoming year.

The following information is available concerning the year to 31 May 2009:

- The forecast sales for the year are £1,400,000 and the gross profit is expected to be 30 per cent of sales. Eighty per cent of all sales are on credit. At present the average credit period is six weeks but it is likely that this will change to eight weeks in the forthcoming year.
- At the year end inventories are expected to be 25 per cent higher than at the beginning of the year.
- During the year the directors intend to pay £40,000 for a fleet of delivery vans.
- Administration expenses for the year are expected to be £225,000 (including £12,000 for depreciation of premises and £38,000 depreciation of fixtures and fittings). Selling expenses are expected to be £85,000 (including £10,000 for depreciation of motor vans).
- All purchases are on credit. It has been estimated that the average credit period taken will be 12 weeks during the forthcoming year.
- Tax for the year is expected to be £34,000. Half of this will be paid during the year and the remaining half will be outstanding at the year end.
- Dividends proposed and paid for the year are expected to be 6.0p per share.

All workings should be made to the nearest £000.

Required:
(a) Prepare a projected income statement for the year ended 31 May 2009.
(b) Prepare a projected statement of financial position (balance sheet) as at 31 May 2009.

Note: The cash balance will be the balancing figure.

2.2 Prolog Ltd is a small wholesaler of powerful microcomputers. It has in recent months been selling 50 machines a month at a price of £2,000 each. These machines cost £1,600 each. A new model has just been launched and this is expected to offer greatly enhanced performance. Its selling price and cost will be the same as for the old model. From the beginning of January Year 6, sales are expected to increase at a rate of 20 machines each month until the end of June Year 6 when sales will amount to 170 units per month. They are expected to continue at that level thereafter. Operating costs, including depreciation of £2,000 a month, are forecast as follows:

	Jan	Feb	Mar	Apr	May	June
Operating costs (£000)	6	8	10	12	12	12

Prolog expects to receive no credit for operating costs. Additional shelving for storage will be bought, installed and paid for in April costing £12,000. Tax of £25,000 is due at the end of March. Prolog expects that receivables will take two months to pay. To give its customers a good level of service, Prolog plans to hold enough inventory at the end of each period to fulfil anticipated demand from customers in the following month. The computer manufacturer, however, grants one month's credit to Prolog. Prolog Ltd's statement of financial position (balance sheet) appears below.

Statement of financial position (balance sheet) at 31 December Year 5

	£000
Non-current assets	80
Current assets	
Inventory	112
Receivables	200
Cash	–
	312
Total assets	392

	£000
Equity	
Share capital – 25p ordinary shares	10
Retained earnings	177
	187
Current liabilities	
Trade payables	112
Tax due	25
Borrowings – bank overdraft	68
	205
Total equity and liabilities	392

Required:

(a) Prepare a projected cash flow statement for Prolog Ltd showing the cash balance or required overdraft for the six months ending 30 June Year 6.

(b) State briefly what further information a banker would require from Prolog before granting additional overdraft facilities for the anticipated expansion of sales.

2.3 Davis Travel Ltd specialises in the provision of winter sports holidays but it also organises out-door activity holidays in the summer. You are given the following information:

Abbreviated statement of financial position (balance sheet) as at 30 September 2008

	£000
Non-current assets	560
Current assets	
Cash	30
Total assets	590
Equity	
Share capital	100
Retained earnings	200
	300
Non-current liabilities	
Borrowings – loans	110
Current liabilities	
Trade payables	180
Total equity and liabilities	590

Its sales estimates for the next six months are:

	Number of bookings received	Number of holidays taken	Promotion expenditure (£000)
October	1,000		100
November	3,000		150
December	3,000	1,000	150
January	3,000	4,000	50
February		3,000	
March		2,000	
Total	10,000	10,000	450

1 Holidays sell for £300 each. Ten per cent is payable when the holiday is booked, and the remainder after two months.

2 Travel agents are paid a commission of 10 per cent of the price of the holiday one month after the booking is made.

3 The cost of a flight is £50 per holiday and a hotel £100 per holiday. Flights and hotels must be paid for in the month when the holidays are taken.

4 Other variable costs are £20 per holiday and are paid in the month of the holiday.

5 Administration costs, including depreciation of non-current assets of £42,000, amount to £402,000 for the six months. Administration costs can be spread evenly over the period.

6 Loan interest of £10,000 is payable on 31 March 2009 and a loan repayment of £20,000 is due on that date. For your calculations you should ignore any interest on the overdraft.

7 The payables of £180,000 at 30 September are to be paid in October.

8 A payment of £50,000 for non-current assets is to be made in March 2009.

9 The airline and the hotel chain base their charges on Davis Travel's forecast requirements and hold capacity to meet those requirements. If Davis is unable to fill this reserved capacity a charge of 50 per cent of those published above is made.

Required:

(a) Prepare:
   (i)   A projected cash flow statement for the six months to 31 March 2009.
   (ii) A projected income statement for the six months ended on that date.
   (iii) A projected statement of financial position (balance sheet) at 31 March 2009.

(b) Discuss the main financial problems confronting Davis Travel Ltd.

Ignore taxation in your calculations.

2.4 Changes Ltd owns a chain of eight shops selling fashion goods. In the past the business maintained a healthy cash balance. However, this has fallen in recent months and at the end of September 2008 the company had an overdraft of £70,000. In view of this, Changes Ltd's managing director has asked you to prepare a cash flow projection for the next six months. You have collected the following data:

	Oct £000	Nov £000	Dec £000	Jan £000	Feb £000	Mar £000
Sales forecast	140	180	260	60	100	120
Purchases	160	180	140	50	50	50
Wages and salaries	30	30	40	30	30	32
Rent			60			
Rates						40
Other expenses	20	20	20	20	20	20
Refurbishing shops				80		

Inventory at 1 October amounted to £170,000 and payables were £70,000. The purchases in October, November and December are contractually committed, and those in January, February and March are the minimum necessary to restock with spring fashions. Cost of sales is 50 per cent of sales and suppliers allow one month's credit on purchases. Tax of £90,000 is due on 1 January. The rates payment is a charge for a whole year and other expenses include depreciation of £10,000 per month.

Required:

(a) Compute the projected cash balance at the end of each month, for the six months to 31 March 2009.

(b) Compute the projected inventory levels at the end of each month for the six months to 31 March 2009.

(c) Prepare a projected income statement for the six months ended 31 March 2009.

(d) What problems might Changes Ltd face in the next six months and how would you attempt to overcome them?

(*Hint*: A forecast of inventory flows is required to answer part (b). This will be based on the same principles as a cash flow statement, that is, inflows and outflows with opening and closing balances.)

2.5   Kwaysar Ltd sells television satellite dishes both to retail outlets and direct to the public. Its most recent statement of financial position is as follows:

Statement of financial position (balance sheet) as at 31 May 2008

	£000	£000
Non-current assets		
Premises	350	
Accumulated depreciation	(60)	290
Fixtures and fittings	80	
Accumulated depreciation	(42)	38
		328
Current assets		
Inventory at cost		44
Receivables		52
Cash at bank		120
		216
Total assets		544
Equity		
£1 ordinary shares		200
Retained earnings		252
		452
Non-current liabilities		
Borrowings – loan		48
Current liabilities		
Trade payables		32
Accrued overheads		12
		44
Total equity and liabilities		544

In the second half of the financial year to 31 May 2008, the business generated a profit of £62,400 and sales of £525,000. It is believed that this level of performance will be repeated in the forthcoming six-month period provided the business does not implement any changes to its marketing strategy. The business, however, is determined to increase its market share and is considering the adoption of a new marketing strategy that has been developed by the marketing department. The main elements of the new strategy are as follows:

1   The selling price of each satellite dish will be reduced to £90. At present each dish is sold for £120.
2   There will be an increase in the amount of advertising costs incurred by the business. Advertising costs will increase from £6,500 per month to £12,000 per month.
3   Retail outlets will be allowed to pay for satellite dishes three months after delivery. At present, trade receivables are allowed one month's credit. Those retail outlets that continue to pay within one month will, for future sales, be given a 2 per cent discount.

The marketing department believes that, by adopting the new strategy, sales in each of the first three months to retail outlets will rise to 1,000 units and sales to the public will rise to 300 units. Thereafter, sales each month will be 1,200 units and 400 units respectively.

Assuming the strategy is adopted, the following forecast information is available:

1   The purchase of satellite dishes will be made at the beginning of each month and will be sufficient to meet that month's sales. Each satellite dish costs £50. Trade payables are paid one month after the month of purchase.
2   Depreciation will be charged on premises at 2 per cent per year on cost and for fixtures and fittings at 15 per cent per year on cost.

3 Motor vans costing £80,000 will be acquired and paid for immediately. These are required to implement the new strategy and will be depreciated at 30 per cent per year on cost.

4 Wages will be £18,000 per month and will be paid in the month in which they are incurred.

5 Advertising costs will be paid for in the month incurred.

6 Other overheads (excluding those mentioned above) will be £14,000 per month and will continue to be paid for one month after the month in which they are incurred.

7 The loan of £48,000 will be repaid in July 2008.

8 Sales direct to the public will continue to be paid for in cash. No credit will be allowed.

9 It is estimated that 50 per cent of retail sales will continue to be on one month's credit and 50 per cent will be on three months' credit.

Ignore taxation.

Required:

Assuming that the new marketing strategy is adopted:

(a) Prepare a projected income statement for the six-month period to 30 November 2008. (A monthly breakdown of profit is not required.)

(b) Prepare a projected cash flow statement for the six-month period to 30 November 2008. (A monthly breakdown of cash flows is not required.)

(c) Comment on the financial results of Kwaysar Ltd for the six-month period to 30 November 2008.

2.6 Newtake Records Ltd owns a chain of 14 shops selling CDs and DVDs. At the beginning of June, the business had an overdraft of £35,000 and the bank has asked for this to be eliminated by the end of November of the same year. As a result, the directors of the business have recently decided to review their plans for the next six months in order to comply with this requirement.

The following forecast information was prepared for the business some months earlier:

	May	June	July	Aug	Sept	Oct	Nov
	£000	£000	£000	£000	£000	£000	£000
Expected sales	180	230	320	250	140	120	110
Purchases	135	180	142	94	75	66	57
Admin. expenses	52	55	56	53	48	46	45
Selling expenses	22	24	28	26	21	19	18
Tax payment				22			
Finance payments	5	5	5	5	5	5	5
Shop refurbishment	–	–	14	18	6	–	–

Notes

1 Inventory held at 1 June was £112,000. The business believes it is necessary to maintain a minimum inventory level of £40,000 over the period to 30 November of the same year.

2 Suppliers allow one month's credit. The first three months' purchases are subject to a contractual agreement that must be honoured.

3 The gross profit margin is 40 per cent.

4 All sales income is received in the month of sale. However, 50 per cent of customers pay with a credit card. The charge made by the credit card business to Newtake Records Ltd is 3 per cent of the sales value. These charges are in addition to the selling expenses identified above. The credit card business pays Newtake Records Ltd in the month of sale.

5 The business has a bank loan that it is paying off in monthly instalments of £5,000 per month. The interest element represents 20 per cent of each instalment.

6 Administration expenses are paid when incurred. This item includes a charge of £15,000 each month in respect of depreciation.

7 Selling expenses are payable in the following month.

Required:

(a) Prepare a projected cash flow statement for the six months ended 30 November that shows the cash balance at the end of each month.

(b) Compute the projected inventory levels at the end of each month for the six months to 30 November.

(c) Prepare a projected income statement for the six months ended 30 November. (A monthly breakdown of profit is not required.)

(d) What problems is Newtake Records Ltd likely to face in the next six months? Can you suggest how the business might deal with these problems?

2.7 Goya Music Direct Ltd operates a mail order business offering classical music CDs to the general public. Its most recent statement of financial position is as follows:

Statement of financial position (balance sheet) as at 31 May 2008

	£	£
Non ourront asscts		
Fixtures and fittings	72,000	
Accumulated depreciation	(24,000)	48,000
Motor vehicles	46,000	
Accumulated depreciation	(28,000)	18,000
		66,000
Current assets		
Inventory		80,000
Trade receivables		107,000
Cash at bank		27,000
		214,000
Total assets		280,000
Equity		
£1 ordinary shares		10,000
General reserve		60,000
Retained earnings		40,000
		110,000
Non-current liabilities		
Borrowings – 10% loan notes 2010/11		60,000
Current liabilities		
Trade payables		93,000
Accrued overheads		17,000
		110,000
Total equity and liabilities		280,000

The following forecast information for the six months ended 30 November 2008 is available:

1 Sales revenue and purchases for the six months ended 30 November 2008 are estimated as follows:

	Sales revenue £	Purchases £
June	130,000	102,000
July	140,000	118,000
August	150,000	115,000
September	110,000	88,000
October	90,000	67,000
November	105,000	110,000

2 The gross profit margin on goods sold is 40 per cent.

3 Customers are allowed one month's credit.

4 Salaries and wages are expected to be £30,000 each month. In addition, an annual staff bonus of £12,000 is due for payment in October 2008. All salaries and wages are paid in the month incurred.

5 Selling and administration expenses are expected to be £20,000 per month, which is payable one month in arrears. This figure includes a monthly charge of £3,000 per month in respect of depreciation of non-current assets. In addition to these expenses, the business is committed to a large advertising campaign. This is not due to commence until December 2008 although advance payments of £60,000 must be made to newspapers and magazines in November 2008.

6 The only finance expense incurred by the business is loan note interest which is not payable until the year end.

7 £10,000 of the loan note will be repaid in August 2008.

The business has agreed with the bank an overdraft limit of £100,000 to cover the next 12 months, which both parties are anxious should not be exceeded.

Ignore taxation.

Required:

(a) Prepare a projected cash flow statement for each of the six months to 30 November 2008.

(b) Prepare a projected income statement for the six months to 30 November 2008. (A monthly breakdown is not required.)

(c) Discuss the problems, if any, the business is likely to face in the next six months and how these might be resolved.

3

Analysing and interpreting financial statements

INTRODUCTION

In this chapter we consider the analysis and interpretation of financial statements. We shall see how financial (or accounting) ratios can help in assessing the financial health of a business. We shall also discuss the problems that are encountered when applying this technique.

Financial ratios can be used to examine various aspects of a financial position and performance and are widely used for planning and control purposes. As we shall see in later chapters, they can be very helpful to managers in a wide variety of decision areas, such as profit planning, working-capital management, financial structure and dividend policy.

LEARNING OUTCOMES

When you have completed this chapter, you should be able to:

● Identify the major categories of ratios that can be used for analysis purposes.

● Calculate important ratios for assessing the financial performance and position of a business, and explain the significance of the ratios calculated.

● Discuss the limitations of ratios as a tool of financial analysis.

● Discuss the use of ratios in helping to predict financial failure.

Financial ratios

Financial ratios provide a quick and relatively simple means of assessing the financial health of a business. A ratio simply relates one figure appearing in the financial statements to some other figure appearing there (for example, operating profit in relation to capital employed) or, perhaps, to some resource of the business (for example, operating profit per employee, sales revenue per square metre of selling space, and so on).

Ratios can be very helpful when comparing the financial health of different businesses. Differences may exist between businesses in the scale of operations, and so a direct comparison of, say, the operating profit generated by each business may be misleading. By expressing operating profit in relation to some other measure (for example, capital (or funds) employed), the problem of scale is eliminated. A business with an operating profit of, say, £10,000 and capital employed of £100,000 can be compared with a much larger business with an operating profit of, say, £80,000 and sales revenue of £1,000,000 by the use of a simple ratio. The operating profit to capital employed ratio for the smaller business is 10 per cent (that is, (10,000/100,000) × 100%) and the same ratio for the larger business is 8 per cent (that is, (80,000/1,000,000) × 100%). These ratios can be directly compared whereas comparison of the absolute operating profit figures would be less meaningful. The need to eliminate differences in scale through the use of ratios can also apply when comparing the performance of the same business over time.

By calculating a small number of ratios it is often possible to build up a good picture of the position and performance of a business. It is not surprising, therefore, that ratios are widely used by those who have an interest in businesses and business performance. Although ratios are not difficult to calculate, they can be difficult to interpret, and so it is important to appreciate that they are really only the starting point for further analysis.

Ratios help to highlight the financial strengths and weaknesses of a business, but they cannot, by themselves, explain why those strengths or weaknesses exist or why certain changes have occurred. Only a detailed investigation will reveal these underlying reasons. Ratios enable us to know which questions to ask, rather than provide the answers.

Ratios can be expressed in various forms, for example as a percentage or as a proportion. The way that a particular ratio is presented will depend on the needs of those who will use the information. Although it is possible to calculate a large number of ratios, only a few, based on key relationships, tend to be helpful to a particular user. Many ratios that could be calculated from the financial statements (for example, rent payable in relation to current assets) may not be considered because there is no clear or meaningful relationship between the two items.

There is no generally accepted list of ratios that can be applied to the financial statements, nor is there a standard method of calculating many ratios. Variations in both the choice of ratios and their calculation will be found in practice. However, it is important to be consistent in the way in which ratios are calculated for comparison purposes. The ratios that we shall discuss here are those that are widely used. They are popular because many consider them to be among the more important for decision-making purposes.

Financial ratio classifications

Ratios can be grouped into categories, each of which relates to a particular aspect of financial performance or position. The following broad categories provide a useful basis for explaining the nature of the financial ratios to be dealt with. There are five of them:

- *Profitability*. We saw in Chapter 1 that businesses are concerned with creating wealth for their owners. Profitability ratios provide an insight to the degree of success in achieving this purpose. They express the profit made (or figures bearing on profit, such as sales revenue or overheads) in relation to other key figures in the financial statements or to some business resource.

- *Efficiency*. Ratios may be used to measure the efficiency with which particular resources have been used within the business. These ratios are also referred to as *activity* ratios.

- *Liquidity*. It is vital to the survival of a business that there are sufficient liquid resources available to meet maturing obligations (that is, amounts owing that must be paid in the near future). Some liquidity ratios examine the relationship between liquid resources held and amounts due for payment in the near future.

- *Financial gearing*. This is the relationship between the contribution to financing the business made by the owners of the business and the amount contributed by others, in the form of loans. The level of gearing has an important effect on the degree of risk associated with a business and is, therefore, something that managers must consider when making financing decisions. Gearing ratios tend to highlight the extent to which the business uses borrowings.

- *Investment*. Certain ratios are concerned with assessing the returns and performance of shares in a particular business from the perspective of shareholders who are not involved with the management of the business.

The analyst must be clear *who* the target users are and *why* they need the information. Different users of financial information are likely to have different information needs, which will in turn determine the ratios that they find useful. For example, shareholders are likely to be interested in their returns in relation to the level of risk associated with their investment. Profitability, investment and gearing ratios will, therefore, be of particular interest. Long-term lenders are concerned with the long-term viability of the business and, to help them to assess this, the profitability and gearing ratios of the business are also likely to be of particular interest. Short-term lenders, such as suppliers of goods and services on credit, may be interested in the ability of the business to repay the amounts owing in the short term. As a result, the liquidity ratios should be of interest.

We shall consider ratios falling into each of the five categories (profitability, efficiency, liquidity, gearing and investment) a little later in the chapter.

The need for comparison

Merely calculating a ratio will not tell us very much about the position or performance of a business. For example, if a ratio revealed that the business was generating £100 in sales revenue per square metre of counter space, it would not be possible to deduce from this information alone whether this particular level of performance was good, bad or indifferent. It is only when we compare this ratio with some 'benchmark' that the information can be interpreted and evaluated.

Activity 3.1

Can you think of any bases that could be used to compare a ratio you have calculated from the financial statements of a particular period? There are three main possibilities.

We shall now take a closer look at these three in turn.

Past periods

By comparing the ratio we have calculated with the same ratio, but for a previous period, it is possible to detect whether there has been an improvement or deterioration in performance. Indeed, it is often useful to track particular ratios over time (say, five or ten years) to see whether it is possible to detect trends. The comparison of ratios from different periods brings certain problems, however. In particular, there is always the possibility that trading conditions were quite different in the periods being compared. There is the further problem that, when comparing the performance of a single business over time, operating inefficiencies may not be clearly exposed. For example, the fact that sales revenue per employee has risen by 10 per cent over the previous period may at first sight appear to be satisfactory. This may not be the case, however, if similar businesses have shown an improvement of 50 per cent for the same period. Finally, there is the problem that inflation may have distorted the figures on which the ratios are based. Inflation can lead to an overstatement of profit and an understatement of asset values.

Similar businesses

In a competitive environment, a business must consider its performance in relation to that of other businesses operating in the same industry. Survival may depend on the ability to achieve comparable levels of performance. A useful basis for comparing a particular ratio, therefore, is the ratio achieved by similar businesses during the same period. This basis is not, however, without its problems. Competitors may have different year ends, and therefore trading conditions may not be identical. They may also have different accounting policies, which can have a significant effect on reported profits and asset values (for example, different methods of calculating depreciation or valuing inventories). Finally, it may be difficult to obtain the financial statements of competitor businesses. Sole proprietorships and partnerships, for example, are not obliged to make their financial statements available to the public. In the case of limited companies, there is a legal obligation to do so. However, a diversified business may not provide a breakdown of activities that is sufficiently detailed to enable analysts to compare the activities with those of other businesses.

Planned performance

Ratios may be compared with the targets that management developed before the start of the period under review. The comparison of planned performance with actual performance may therefore be a useful way of revealing the level of achievement attained. However, the planned levels of performance must be based on realistic assumptions if they are to be useful for comparison purposes.

Planned performance is likely to be the most valuable benchmark for the managers to assess their own business. Businesses tend to develop planned ratios for each aspect of their activities. When formulating its plans, a business may usefully take account of its own past performance and that of other businesses. There is no reason, however, why a particular business should seek to achieve either its own previous performance or that of other businesses. Neither of these may be seen as an appropriate target.

Analysts outside the business do not normally have access to the business's plans. For these people, past performance and the performances of other, similar, businesses may be the only practical benchmarks.

Calculating the ratios

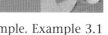

Probably the best way to explain financial ratios is through an example. Example 3.1 provides a set of financial statements from which we can calculate important ratios.

Example 3.1

The following financial statements relate to Alexis plc, which operates a wholesale carpet business:

Balance sheets as at 31 March

	2007 £m	2008 £m
Non-current assets		
Property, plant and equipment (at cost less depreciation)		
Land and buildings	381	427
Fixtures and fittings	129	160
	510	587
Current assets		
Inventories at cost	300	406
Trade receivables	240	273
Cash at bank	4	–
	544	679
Total assets	1,054	1,266
Equity		
£0.50 ordinary shares (Note 1)	300	300
Retained earnings	263	234
	563	534
Non-current liabilities		
Borrowings – 9% loan notes (secured)	200	300
Current liabilities		
Trade payables	261	354
Tax due	30	2
Short-term borrowings (all bank overdraft)	–	76
	291	432
Total equity and liabilities	1,054	1,266

Example 3.1 continued

Income statements for the year ended 31 March

	2007	2008
	£m	£m
Revenue (Note 2)	2,240	2,681
Cost of sales (Note 3)	(1,745)	(2,272)
Gross profit	495	409
Operating expenses	(252)	(362)
Operating profit	243	47
Interest payable	(18)	(32)
Profit before taxation	225	15
Tax	(60)	(4)
Profit for the year	165	11

Notes:
1   The market value of the shares of the business at the end of the year was £2.50 for 2007 and £1.50 for 2008.
2   All sales and purchases are made on credit.
3   The cost of sales figure can be analysed as follows:

	2007	2008
	£m	£m
Opening inventories	241	300
Purchases (Note 2)	1,804	2,378
	2,045	2,678
Closing inventories	(300)	(406)
Cost of sales	1,745	2,272

4   A dividend of £40m had been paid to the shareholders in respect of each of the years.
5   The business employed 13,995 staff at 31 March 2007 and 18,623 at 31 March 2008.
6   The business expanded its capacity during 2008 by setting up a new warehouse and distribution centre in the north of England.
7   At 1 April 2006, the total of equity stood at £438m and the total of equity and non-current liabilities stood at £638m.

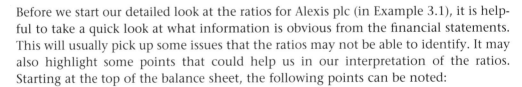

A brief overview

Before we start our detailed look at the ratios for Alexis plc (in Example 3.1), it is helpful to take a quick look at what information is obvious from the financial statements. This will usually pick up some issues that the ratios may not be able to identify. It may also highlight some points that could help us in our interpretation of the ratios. Starting at the top of the balance sheet, the following points can be noted:

- *Expansion of non-current assets.* These have increased by about 15 per cent (from £510m to £587m). Note 6 mentions a new warehouse and distribution centre, which may account for much of the additional investment in non-current assets. We are not told when this new facility was established, but it is quite possible that it was well into the year. This could mean that not much benefit was reflected in terms of additional sales revenue or cost saving during 2008. Sales revenue, in fact, expanded by about 20 per cent (from £2,240m to £2,681m), greater than the expansion in non-current assets.
- *Major expansion in the elements of working capital.* Inventories increased by about 35 per cent, trade receivables by about 14 per cent and trade payables by about 36 per

cent between 2007 and 2008. These are major increases, particularly in inventories and payables (which are linked because the inventories are all bought on credit – see Note 2).

- *Reduction in the cash balance.* The cash balance fell from £4m (in funds) to a £76m overdraft, between 2007 and 2008. The bank may be putting the business under pressure to reverse this, which could raise difficulties.
- *Apparent debt capacity.* Comparing the non-current assets with the long-term borrowings implies that the business may well be able to offer security on further borrowing. This is because potential lenders usually look at the value of assets that can be offered as security when assessing loan requests. Lenders seem particularly attracted to land and, to a lesser extent, buildings as security. For example, at 31 March 2008, non-current assets had a balance sheet value of £587m, but long-term borrowing was only £300m (though there was also an overdraft of £76m). Balance sheet values are not normally, of course, market values. On the other hand, land and buildings tend to have a market value higher than their balance sheet value due to inflation in property values.
- *Lower operating profit.* Though sales revenue expanded by 20 per cent between 2007 and 2008, both cost of sales and operating expenses rose by a greater percentage, leaving both gross profit and, particularly, operating profit (profit before interest and tax) massively reduced. The level of staffing, which increased by about 33 per cent (from 13,995 to 18,623 employees), may have greatly affected the operating expenses. (Without knowing when the additional employees were recruited during 2008, we cannot be sure of the effect on operating expenses.) Increasing staffing by 33 per cent must put an enormous strain on management, at least in the short term. It is not surprising, therefore that 2008 was not successful for the business.

Having had a quick look at what is fairly obvious without calculating the normal ratios, we shall now go on to calculate and interpret them.

Profitability

The following ratios may be used to evaluate the profitability of the business:

- return on ordinary shareholders' funds
- return on capital employed
- operating profit margin
- gross profit margin.

We shall now look at each of these in turn.

Return on ordinary shareholders' funds (ROSF)

The **return on ordinary shareholders' funds ratio** compares the amount of profit for the period available to the owners, with the owners' average stake in the business during that same period. The ratio (which is normally expressed in percentage terms) is as follows:

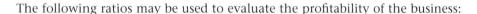

$$\text{ROSF} = \frac{\text{Profit for the year (net profit) less any preference dividend}}{\text{Ordinary share capital} + \text{Reserves}} \times 100$$

The profit for the year (less preference dividend (if any)) is used in calculating the ratio, as this figure represents the amount of profit that is left for the owners.

In the case of Alexis plc, the ratio for the year ended 31 March 2007 is:

$$\text{ROSF} = \frac{165}{(438 + 563)/2} \times 100 = 33.0\%$$

Note that, when calculating the ROSF, the average of the figures for ordinary shareholders' funds as at the beginning and at the end of the year has been used. It is preferable to use an average figure as this is likely to be more representative. This is because the shareholders' funds did not have the same total throughout the year, yet we want to compare it with the profit earned during the whole period. We know, from Note 7, that the total of the shareholders' funds at 1 April 2006 was £438m. By a year later, however, it had risen to £563m, according to the balance sheet as at 31 March 2007.

The easiest approach to calculating the average amount of shareholders' funds is to take a simple average based on the opening and closing figures for the year. This is often the only information available, as is the case with Example 3.1. Averaging in this way is generally valid for all ratios that combine a figure for a period (such as profit for the year) with one taken at a point in time (such as shareholders' funds).

Where not even the beginning-of-year figure is available, it is usually acceptable to use just the year-end figure, provided that this approach is consistently adopted.

Activity 3.2

Calculate the ROSF for Alexis plc for the year to 31 March 2008.

The ratio for 2008 is:

$$\text{ROSF} = \frac{11}{(563 + 534)/2} \times 100 = 2.0\%$$

Broadly, businesses seek to generate as high a value as possible for this ratio, provided that it is not achieved at the expense of potential future returns by, for example, taking on more risky activities. In view of this, the 2008 ratio is very poor by any standards; a bank deposit account will yield a better return than this. We need to try to find out why things went so badly wrong in 2008. As we look at other ratios, we should find some clues.

Return on capital employed (ROCE)

The **return on capital employed ratio** is a fundamental measure of business performance. This ratio expresses the relationship between the operating profit generated during a period and the average long-term capital invested in the business during that period.

The ratio is expressed in percentage terms and is as follows:

$$\text{ROCE} = \frac{\text{Operating profit}}{\text{Share capital} + \text{Reserves} + \text{Non-current liabilities}} \times 100$$

Note, in this case, that the profit figure used is the operating profit (that is, the profit *before* interest and taxation), because the ratio attempts to measure the returns to all suppliers of long-term finance before any deductions for interest payable on borrowings, or payments of dividends to shareholders, are made.

For the year to 31 March 2007, the ratio for Alexis plc is:

$$\text{ROCE} = \frac{243}{(638 + 763)/2} \times 100 = 34.7\%$$

ROCE is considered by many to be a primary measure of profitability. It compares inputs (capital invested) with outputs (operating profit). This comparison is vital in assessing the effectiveness with which funds have been deployed. Once again, an average figure for capital employed may be used where the information is available.

Activity 3.3

Calculate the ROCE for Alexis plc for the year to 31 March 2008.

For 2008, the ratio is:

$$\text{ROCE} = \frac{47}{(763 + 834)/2} \times 100 = 5.9\%$$

This ratio tells much the same story as ROSF; namely a poor performance, with the return on the assets being less than the rate that the business has to pay for most of its borrowed funds (that is, 10 per cent for the loan notes).

Real World 3.1 shows how financial ratios are used by businesses as a basis for setting profitability targets.

REAL WORLD 3.1

Targeting profitability

The ROCE ratio is widely used by businesses when establishing targets for profitability. These targets are sometimes made public and here are some examples:

● BMW, the German car maker, has a target ROCE of 26 per cent for 2012 onwards.
● BSkyB plc, the satelite broadcaster, has a target ROCE of 15 per cent by 2011 for its broadband operation.
● AirFrance-KLM, the world's largest airline operator, has a target ROCE of 8.5 per cent by 2009/10.
● Siemens, Europe's largest engineering group, has a target ROCE of 14–16 per cent.

Sources: John Reed, 'Higher currency costs dent BMW figures', www.FT.com, 6 November 2007; 'BSkyB/triple play', www.FT.com, 12 July 2006; Kevin Done, 'Air France-KLM raises targets', www.FT.com, 24 May 2007; 'Siemens post-Kleinfeld', www.FT.com, 26 April 2007.

Real World 3.2 provides some insight to the levels of ROCE achieved by UK businesses.

REAL WORLD 3.2

Achieving profitability

UK businesses reported an average ROCE of 15.1 per cent for the first quarter of 2007, improving on the 2006 rate of 14.5 per cent. This was the highest level of ROCE since the Office for National Statistics first kept records.

Service sector businesses were much the more successful with an average ROCE of 21.1 per cent, compared with 5.3 per cent among manufacturers. In fact, manufacturers' average ROCE had fallen from 7.7 per cent in 2006.

Source: Information taken from 'Corporate profitability', *Office for National Statistics* (www.statistics.gov.uk), 3 July 2007, *Financial Times*, 5 July 2006.

Operating profit margin

The **operating profit margin ratio** relates the operating profit for the period to the sales revenue during that period. The ratio is expressed as follows:

$$\text{Operating profit margin} = \frac{\text{Operating profit}}{\text{Sales revenue}} \times 100$$

The operating profit (that is, profit before interest and taxation) is used in this ratio as it represents the profit from trading operations before the interest payable expense is taken into account. This is often regarded as the most appropriate measure of operational performance, when used as a basis of comparison, because differences arising from the way in which the business is financed will not influence the measure.

For the year ended 31 March 2007, Alexis plc's operating profit margin ratio is:

$$\text{Operating profit margin} = \frac{243}{2,240} \times 100 = 10.8\%$$

This ratio compares one output of the business (operating profit) with another output (sales revenue). The ratio can vary considerably between types of business. For example, supermarkets tend to operate on low prices and, therefore, low operating profit margins. This is done in an attempt to stimulate sales and thereby increase the total amount of operating profit generated. Jewellers, on the other hand, tend to have high operating profit margins but have much lower levels of sales volume. Factors such as the degree of competition, the type of customer, the economic climate and industry characteristics (such as the level of risk) will influence the operating profit margin of a business. This point is picked up again later in the chapter.

Activity 3.4

Calculate the operating profit margin for Alexis plc for the year to 31 March 2008.

The ratio for 2008 is:

$$\text{Operating profit margin} = \frac{47}{2,681} \times 100 = 1.8\%$$

Once again, this is a very weak performance compared with that of 2007. Whereas in 2007 for every £1 of sales revenue an average of 10.8p (that is, 10.8 per cent) was left as operating profit, after paying the cost of the carpets sold and other expenses of operating the business, for 2008 this had fallen to only 1.8p for every £1. It seems that the reason for the poor ROSF and ROCE ratios was partially, perhaps wholly, a high level of expenses relative to sales revenue. The next ratio should provide us with a clue as to how the sharp decline in this ratio occurred.

Operating profit margins are often used as a basis for setting performance targets. **Real World 3.3** sets out the target operating profit margins for some well-known car-makers.

REAL WORLD 3.3

Driving in the same direction

The leading car makers below have all set similar targets for their operating profit margins:

- Renault, the French car maker, has a target operating profit margin of 9 per cent for 2009.
- Toyota, the Japanese car maker, is targeting a 10 per cent operating profit margin.
- Daimler, the German car maker, has a target operating profit margin of 10 per cent for 2010.

Source: J. Reed, 'Renault hits profitability targets', www.ft.com, 8 February 2007; M. Sanchanta, 'Nissan's empty product pipeline', *Financial Times*, 6 November 2006; J. Reed, 'Daimler roars ahead with 4% leap in profits', www.ft.com, 26 October 2007.

Gross profit margin

The **gross profit margin ratio** relates the gross profit of the business to the sales revenue generated for the same period. Gross profit represents the difference between sales revenue and the cost of sales. The ratio is therefore a measure of profitability in buying (or producing) and selling goods before any other expenses are taken into account. As cost of sales represents a major expense for many businesses, a change in this ratio can have a significant effect on the 'bottom line' (that is, the profit for the year). The gross profit margin ratio is calculated as follows:

$$\text{Gross profit margin} = \frac{\text{Gross profit}}{\text{Sales revenue}} \times 100$$

For the year to 31 March 2007, the ratio for Alexis plc is:

$$\text{Gross profit margin} = \frac{495}{2,240} \times 100 = 22.1\%$$

Activity 3.5

Calculate the gross profit margin for Alexis plc for the year to 31 March 2008.

The ratio for 2008 is:

$$\text{Gross profit margin} = \frac{409}{2,681} \times 100 = 15.3\%$$

The decline in this ratio means that gross profit was lower *relative* to sales revenue in 2008 than it had been in 2007. Bearing in mind that:

Gross profit = Sales revenue − Cost of sales (or cost of goods sold)

this means that cost of sales was higher *relative* to sales revenue in 2008 than in 2007. This could mean that sales prices were lower and/or that the purchase cost of goods sold had increased. It is possible that both sales prices and goods sold prices had reduced, but the former at a greater rate than the latter. Similarly they may both have increased, but with sales prices having increased at a lesser rate than the cost of the goods sold.

Clearly, part of the decline in the operating profit margin ratio is linked to the dramatic decline in the gross profit margin ratio. Whereas, after paying for the carpets sold, for each £1 of sales revenue 22.1p was left to cover other operating expenses and leave an operating profit in 2007, this was only 15.3p in 2008.

The profitability ratios for the business over the two years can be set out as follows:

	2007	2008
	%	%
ROSF	33.0	2.0
ROCE	34.7	5.9
Operating profit margin	10.8	1.8
Gross profit margin	22.1	15.3

Activity 3.6

What do you deduce from a comparison of the declines in the operating profit and gross profit margin ratios?

We can see that the decline in the operating profit margin was 9 per cent (that is, from 10.8 per cent to 1.8 per cent), whereas that of the gross profit margin was only 6.8 per cent (that is, from 22.1 per cent to 15.3 per cent). This can only mean that operating expenses were greater, compared with sales revenue, in 2008 than they had been in 2007. The declines in both ROSF and ROCE were caused partly, therefore, by the business incurring higher inventories purchasing costs relative to sales revenue and partly through higher operating expenses to sales revenue. We would need to compare these ratios with the planned levels for them before we could usefully assess the business's success.

The analyst must now carry out some investigation to discover what caused the increases in both cost of sales and operating expenses, relative to sales revenue, from 2007 to 2008. This will involve checking on what has happened with sales and inventories prices over the two years. Similarly, it will involve looking at each of the individual areas that make up operating expenses to discover which ones were responsible for the increase, relative to sales revenue. Here, further ratios, for example staff expenses (wages and salaries) to sales revenue, could be calculated in an attempt to isolate the cause of the change from 2007 to 2008. In fact, as we discussed when we took an overview of the financial statements, the increase in staffing may well account for most of the increase in operating expenses.

Real World 3.4 is a *Financial Times* article that discusses the reasons for improving profitability in 'Bollywood'.

REAL WORLD 3.4

Investing in Bollywood

FT

Alas for investors, the economics of Bollywood have long been about as predictable as, but rather less uplifting than, the plotline of the average Hindi movie. The world's biggest movie market in terms of number of tickets sold – a massive 3.7bn – has traditionally offered miserable returns to its backers. Instead, revenues were swallowed up by a blend of piracy, taxes and inefficiencies.

Now the script appears to be changing. Big backers – in the shape of international entertainment giants such as Walt Disney and Viacom, and venture capitalists are starting to enter Bollywood. With a brace of Indian film production companies listed on London's Alternative Investment Market and a third due to follow shortly, smaller investors are also getting in on the act. That is testament to improving industry dynamics. Digital technology and tougher regulation is helping reduce piracy while tax strains are being mitigated either by new rules at home – such as scrapping entertainment tax for multiplexes – or shifting production abroad.

Entertainment companies are also sharpening up their acts and evolving from one-stop shops to specialists in, say, production or distribution. Cleaner corporate structures enable them to access a broader range of financing. The economics of movie-making are improving too. Perhaps 40 per cent of Indian movies are now shot overseas, benefiting from tax breaks, 'captive' actors and producers and – in Europe – longer working days. As a result, a movie may be in the can in perhaps a quarter of the time it would normally take in India.

Evolution in other parts of the media world also plays into the hands of Bollywood moguls; for example, the growth in satellite TV means more channels to bid on movie licensing rights. Industry analysts reckon Bollywood now offers a return on capital employed of about 30–35 per cent, not too dissimilar from Hollywood. Years of tears followed by a happy ending? How Bollywood.

Source: 'Investing in Bollywood', Lex column, *Financial Times*, 26 June 2007.

Efficiency

Efficiency ratios examine the ways in which various resources of the business are managed. The following ratios consider some of the more important aspects of resource management:

- average inventories turnover period
- average settlement period for trade receivables
- average settlement period for trade payables
- sales revenue to capital employed
- sales revenue per employee.

We shall now look at each of these in turn.

Average inventories turnover period

Inventories often represent a significant investment for a business. For some types of business (for example, manufacturers), inventories may account for a substantial proportion of the total assets held (see Real World 10.1, p. 396). The **average inventories turnover period ratio** measures the average period for which inventories are being held. The ratio is calculated as follows:

$$\text{Average inventories turnover period} = \frac{\text{Average inventories held}}{\text{Cost of sales}} \times 365$$

The average inventories for the period can be calculated as a simple average of the opening and closing inventories levels for the year. However, in the case of a highly seasonal business, where inventories levels may vary considerably over the year, a monthly average may be more appropriate.

In the case of Alexis plc, the inventories turnover period for the year ended 31 March 2007 is:

$$\text{Average inventories turnover period} = \frac{(241 + 300)/2}{1{,}745} \times 365 = 56.6 \text{ days}$$

This means that, on average, the inventories held are being 'turned over' every 56.6 days. So, a carpet bought by the business on a particular day would, on average, have been sold about eight weeks later. A business will normally prefer a short inventories turnover period to a long one, because holding inventories has a cost, for example the opportunity cost of the funds tied up. When judging the amount of inventories to carry, the business must consider such things as the likely demand for the inventories, the possibility of supply shortages, the likelihood of price rises, the amount of storage space available and the perishability/susceptibility to obsolescence of the inventories. The management of inventories will be considered in more detail in Chapter 10.

This ratio is sometimes expressed in terms of months rather than days. Multiplying by 12 rather than 365 will achieve this.

Activity 3.7

Calculate the average inventories turnover period for Alexis plc for the year ended 31 March 2008.

The ratio for 2008 is:

$$\text{Average inventories turnover period} = \frac{(300 + 406)/2}{2{,}272} \times 365 = 56.7 \text{ days}$$

The inventories turnover period is virtually the same in both years.

Average settlement period for trade receivables

A business will usually be concerned with amount of funds tied up in trade receivables and try to keep this to a minimum. The speed of payment can have a significant effect on the business's cash flow. The **average settlement period for trade receivables ratio** calculates how long, on average, credit customers take to pay the amounts that they owe to the business. The ratio is as follows:

$$\text{Average settlement period for trade receivables} = \frac{\text{Trade receivables}}{\text{Credit sales revenue}} \times 365$$

A business will normally prefer a shorter average settlement period to a longer one as, once again, funds are being tied up that may be used for more profitable purposes. Although this ratio can be useful, it is important to remember that it produces an *average* figure for the number of days for which debts are outstanding. This average may be badly distorted by, for example, a few large customers who are very slow or very fast payers.

Since all sales made by Alexis plc are on credit, the average settlement period for trade receivables for the year ended 31 March 2007 is:

$$\text{Average settlement period for trade receivables} = \frac{240}{2,240} \times 365 = 39.1 \text{ days}$$

As no figure for opening trade receivables is available, only the year-end figure is used. This is common practice for calculating any ratio where averaging would be desirable but is impossible because of lack of the opening value.

Activity 3.8

Calculate the average settlement period for Alexis plc's trade receivables for the year ended 31 March 2008. (To be consistent with the 2007 calculation, use the year-end trade receivables figure rather than an average figure.)

The ratio for 2008 is:

$$\text{Average settlement period for trade receivables} = \frac{273}{2,681} \times 365 = 37.2 \text{ days}$$

On the face of it, this reduction in the settlement period is welcome. It means that less cash was tied up in trade receivables for each £1 of sales revenue in 2008 than in 2007. Only if the reduction were achieved at the expense of customer goodwill or a high direct financial cost might the desirability of the reduction be questioned. For example, the reduction may have been due to chasing customers too vigorously or as a result of incurring higher expenses, such as discounts allowed to customers who pay quickly.

Average settlement period for trade payables

The **average settlement period for trade payables ratio** measures how long, on average, the business takes to pay those who have supplied goods and services on credit. The ratio is calculated as follows:

$$\textbf{Average settlement period for trade payables} = \frac{\textbf{Trade payables}}{\textbf{Credit purchases}} \times \textbf{365}$$

This ratio provides an average figure, which, like the average settlement period for trade receivables ratio, can be distorted by the payment period for one or two large suppliers.

As trade payables provide a free source of finance for the business, it is perhaps not surprising that some businesses attempt to increase their average settlement period for trade payables. However, such a policy can be taken too far and result in a loss of good-will of suppliers. We shall return to the issues concerning the management of trade receivables and trade payables in Chapter 10.

For the year ended 31 March 2007, Alexis plc's average settlement period for trade payables is:

$$\text{Average settlement period for trade payables} = \frac{261}{1,804} \times 365 = 52.8 \text{ days}$$

Once again, the year-end figure rather than an average figure for trade payables has been used in the calculations.

Activity 3.9

Calculate the average settlement period for trade payables for Alexis plc for the year ended 31 March 2008. (For the sake of consistency, use a year-end figure for trade payables.)

.....

The ratio for 2008 is:

$$\text{Average settlement period for trade payables} = \frac{354}{2,378} \times 365 = 54.3 \text{ days}$$

There was an increase, between 2007 and 2008, in the average length of time that elapsed between buying inventories and services and paying for them. On the face of it, this is beneficial because the business is using free finance provided by suppliers. If, however, this is leading to a loss of supplier goodwill that could have adverse consequences for Alexis plc, it is not necessarily advantageous.

Sales revenue to capital employed

The **sales revenue to capital employed ratio** (or asset turnover ratio) examines how effectively the assets of the business are being used to generate sales revenue. It is calculated as follows:

$$\frac{\text{Sales revenue to}}{\text{capital employed ratio}} = \frac{\text{Sales revenue}}{\text{Share capital + Reserves + Non-current liabilities}}$$

Generally speaking, a higher asset turnover ratio is preferred to a lower one. A higher ratio will normally suggest that assets are being used more productively in the generation of revenue. However, a very high ratio may suggest that the business is 'overtrading on its assets', that is, it has insufficient assets to sustain the level of sales revenue achieved. (Overtrading will be discussed in more detail later in the chapter.) When comparing this ratio for different businesses, factors such as the age and condition of assets held, the valuation bases for assets and whether assets are leased or owned outright can complicate interpretation.

A variation of this formula is to use the total assets less current liabilities (which is equivalent to long-term capital employed) in the denominator (the lower part of the fraction). The identical result is obtained.

For the year ended 31 March 2007 this ratio for Alexis plc is:

$$\text{Sales revenue to capital employed} = \frac{2,240}{(638 + 763)/2} = 3.20 \text{ times}$$

Calculate the sales revenue to capital employed ratio for Alexis plc for the year ended 31 March 2008.

The sales revenue to capital employed ratio for the 2008 is:

$$\text{Sales revenue to capital employed} = \frac{2,681}{(763 + 834)/2} = 3.36 \text{ times}$$

This seems to be an improvement, since in 2008 more sales revenue was being generated for each £1 of capital employed (£3.36) than was the case in 2007 (£3.20). Provided that overtrading is not an issue and that the additional sales are generating an acceptable profit, this is to be welcomed.

Sales revenue per employee

The **sales revenue per employee ratio** relates sales revenue generated to a particular business resource, that is, labour. It provides a measure of the productivity of the workforce. The ratio is:

$$\textbf{Sales revenue per employee} = \frac{\textbf{Sales revenue}}{\textbf{Number of employees}}$$

Generally, businesses would prefer to have a high value for this ratio, implying that they are using their staff efficiently.

For the year ended 31 March 2007, the ratio for Alexis plc is:

$$\text{Sales revenue per employee} = \frac{£2,240m}{13,995} = £160,057$$

Calculate the sales revenue per employee for Alexis plc for the year ended 31 March 2008.

The ratio for 2008 is:

$$\text{Sales revenue per employee} = \frac{£2,681m}{18,623} = £143,962$$

This represents a fairly significant decline and probably one that merits further investigation. As we discussed previously, the number of employees had increased quite notably (by about 33 per cent) during 2008 and the analyst will probably try to discover why this had not generated sufficient additional sales revenue to maintain the ratio at its 2007 level. It could be that the additional employees were not appointed until late in the year ended 31 March 2008.

The efficiency, or activity, ratios may be summarised as follows:

	2007	2008
Average inventories turnover period	56.6 days	56.7 days
Average settlement period for trade receivables	39.1 days	37.2 days
Average settlement period for trade payables	52.8 days	54.3 days
Sales revenue to capital employed (asset turnover)	3.20 times	3.36 times
Sales revenue per employee	£160,057	£143,962

Activity 3.12

What do you deduce from a comparison of the efficiency ratios over the two years?

Maintaining the inventories turnover period at the 2007 level might be reasonable, though whether this represents a satisfactory period can probably only be assessed by looking at the business's planned inventories period. The inventories holding period for other businesses operating in carpet retailing, particularly those regarded as the market leaders, may have been helpful in formulating the plans. On the face of things, a shorter receivables collection period and a longer payables payment period are both desirable. On the other hand, these may have been achieved at the cost of a loss of the goodwill of customers and suppliers, respectively. The increased asset turnover ratio seems beneficial, provided that the business can manage this increase. The decline in the sales revenue per employee ratio is undesirable but, as we have already seen, is probably related to the dramatic increase in the level of staffing. As with the inventories turnover period, these other ratios need to be compared with the planned standard of efficiency.

Relationship between profitability and efficiency

In our earlier discussions concerning profitability ratios, we saw that return on capital employed (ROCE) is regarded as a key ratio by many businesses. The ratio is:

$$\text{ROCE} = \frac{\text{Operating profit}}{\text{Long-term capital employed}} \times 100$$

where long-term capital comprises share capital plus reserves plus long-term borrowings. This ratio can be broken down into two elements, as shown in Figure 3.1. The first ratio is the operating profit margin ratio, and the second is the sales revenue to capital employed (asset turnover) ratio, both of which we discussed earlier.

By breaking down the ROCE ratio in this manner, we highlight the fact that the overall return on funds employed within the business will be determined both by the profitability of sales and by efficiency in the use of capital.

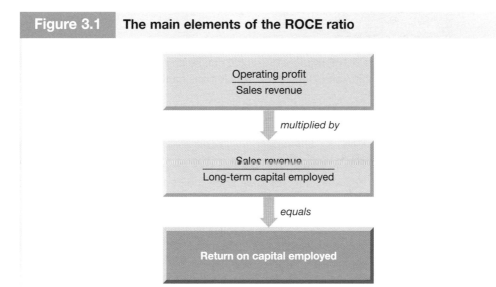

Figure 3.1 **The main elements of the ROCE ratio**

The ROCE ratio can be divided into two elements: operating profit to sales revenue and sales revenue to capital employed. By analysing ROCE in this way, we can see the influence of both profitability and efficiency on this important ratio.

Example 3.2

Consider the following information, for last year, concerning two different businesses operating in the same industry:

	Antler plc	Baker plc
Operating profit	£20m	£15m
Average long-term capital employed	£100m	£75m
Sales revenue	£200m	£300m

The ROCE for each business is identical (20 per cent). However, the manner in which that return was achieved by each business was quite different. In the case of Antler plc, the operating profit margin is 10 per cent and the sales revenue to capital employed ratio is 2 times (so ROCE = 10% × 2 = 20%). In the case of Baker plc, the operating profit margin is 5 per cent and the sales revenue to capital employed ratio is 4 times (and so ROCE = 5% × 4 = 20%).

Example 3.2 demonstrates that a relatively high sales revenue to capital employed ratio can compensate for a relatively low operating profit margin. Similarly, a relatively low sales revenue to capital employed ratio can be overcome by a relatively high operating profit margin. In many areas of retail and distribution (for example, supermarkets and delivery services), the operating profit margins are quite low but the ROCE can be high, provided that the assets are used productively (that is, low margin, high sales revenue).

Activity 3.13

Show how the ROCE ratio for Alexis plc can be analysed into the two elements for each of the years 2007 and 2008. What conclusions can you draw from your figures?

	ROCE	=	Operating profit margin	×	Sales revenue to capital employed
2007	34.7%		10.8%		3.19
2008	5.9%		1.8%		3.36

As we can see, the relationship between the three ratios holds for Alexis plc for both years. The small apparent differences arise because the three ratios are stated here only to one or two decimal places.

Although the business was more effective at generating sales revenue (sales revenue to capital employed ratio increased) in 2008 than in 2007, in 2008 it fell well below the level necessary to compensate for the sharp decline in the effectiveness of each sale (operating profit margin). As a result, the 2008 ROCE was well below the 2007 value.

Liquidity

Liquidity ratios are concerned with the ability of the business to meet its short-term financial obligations. The following ratios are widely used:

- current ratio
- acid test ratio.

These will now be considered.

Current ratio

The **current ratio** compares the 'liquid' assets (that is, cash and those assets held that will soon be turned into cash) of the business with the current liabilities. The ratio is calculated as follows:

$$\text{Current ratio} = \frac{\text{Current assets}}{\text{Current liabilities}}$$

Some people seem to believe that there is an 'ideal' current ratio (usually 2 times or 2 : 1) for all businesses. However, this fails to take into account the fact that different types of business require different current ratios. For example, a manufacturing business will often have a relatively high current ratio because it is necessary to hold inventories of finished goods, raw materials and work in progress. It will also normally sell goods on credit, thereby giving rise to trade receivables. A supermarket chain, on the other hand, will have a relatively low ratio, as it will hold only fast-moving inventories of finished goods and all of its sales will be made for cash (no credit sales). (See Real World 10.1 on p. 396.)

The higher the ratio, the more liquid the business is considered to be. As liquidity is vital to the survival of a business, a higher current ratio might be thought to be preferable to a lower one. If a business has a very high ratio, however, it may be that funds are tied up in cash or other liquid assets and are not, therefore, being used as productively as they might otherwise be.

As at 31 March 2007, the current ratio of Alexis plc is:

$$\text{Current ratio} = \frac{544}{291} = 1.9 \text{ times (or } 1.9 : 1)$$

Activity 3.14

Calculate the current ratio for Alexis plc as at 31 March 2008.

The ratio as at 31 March 2008 is:

$$\text{Current ratio} = \frac{679}{432} = 1.6 \text{ times (or } 1.6 : 1)$$

Although this is a decline from 2007 to 2008, it is not necessarily a matter of concern. The next ratio may provide a clue as to whether there seems to be a problem.

Acid test ratio

The **acid test ratio** is very similar to the current ratio, but it represents a more stringent test of liquidity. It can be argued that, for many businesses, inventories cannot be converted into cash quickly. (Note that, in the case of Alexis plc, the inventories turnover period was about 57 days in both years (see p. 80).) As a result, it may be better to exclude this particular asset from any measure of liquidity. The acid test ratio is a variation of the current ratio, but excluding inventories.

The minimum level for this ratio is often stated as 1.0 times (or 1 : 1; that is, current assets (excluding inventories) equals current liabilities). In many highly successful businesses that are regarded as having adequate liquidity, however, it is not unusual for the acid test ratio to be below 1.0 without causing particular liquidity problems. (See Real World 10.1 on p. 396.)

The acid test ratio is calculated as follows:

$$\textbf{Acid test ratio} = \frac{\textbf{Current assets (excluding inventories)}}{\textbf{Current liabilities}}$$

The acid test ratio for Alexis plc as at 31 March 2007 is:

$$\text{Acid test ratio} = \frac{544 - 300}{291} = 0.8 \text{ times (or } 0.8 : 1)$$

We can see that the 'liquid' current assets do not quite cover the current liabilities, so the business may be experiencing some liquidity problems.

Activity 3.15

Calculate the acid test ratio for Alexis plc as at 31 March 2008.

....

The ratio as at 31 March 2008 is:

$$\text{Acid test ratio} = \frac{679 - 406}{432} = 0.6 \text{ times}$$

The 2008 ratio is significantly below that for 2007. The 2008 level may well be a cause for concern. The rapid decline in this ratio should lead to steps being taken, at least, to stop further decline.

The liquidity ratios for the two-year period may be summarised as follows:

	2007	2008
Current ratio	1.9	1.6
Acid test ratio	0.8	0.6

Activity 3.16

What do you deduce from the liquidity ratios set out above?

....

Although it is not possible to make a totally valid judgement without knowing the planned ratios, there appears to have been a worrying decline in liquidity. This is indicated by both of these ratios. The apparent liquidity problem may, however, be planned, short term and linked to the expansion in non-current assets and staffing. It may be that when the benefits of the expansion come on stream, liquidity will improve. On the other hand, short-term claimants may become anxious when they see signs of weak liquidity. This anxiety could lead to steps being taken to press for payment, and this could cause problems for Alexis plc.

Financial gearing

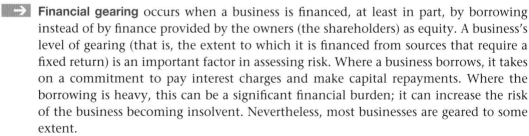

Financial gearing occurs when a business is financed, at least in part, by borrowing instead of by finance provided by the owners (the shareholders) as equity. A business's level of gearing (that is, the extent to which it is financed from sources that require a fixed return) is an important factor in assessing risk. Where a business borrows, it takes on a commitment to pay interest charges and make capital repayments. Where the borrowing is heavy, this can be a significant financial burden; it can increase the risk of the business becoming insolvent. Nevertheless, most businesses are geared to some extent.

Given the risks involved, we may wonder why a business would want to take on gearing (that is, to borrow). One reason may be that the owners have insufficient funds, so the only way to finance the business adequately is to borrow from others. Another reason is that gearing can be used to increase the returns to owners. This is possible provided the returns generated from borrowed funds exceed the cost of paying interest. The issue of gearing is important and we shall leave a detailed discussion of this topic until Chapter 8.

Two ratios are widely used to assess gearing:

* gearing ratio
* interest cover ratio.

Gearing ratio

The **gearing ratio** measures the contribution of long-term lenders to the long-term capital structure of a business:

$$\text{Gearing ratio} = \frac{\text{Long-term (non-current) liabilities}}{\text{Share capital + Reserves +}} \times 100$$
$$\text{Long-term (non-current) liabilities}$$

The gearing ratio for Alexis plc, as at 31 March 2007, is:

$$\text{Gearing ratio} = \frac{200}{(563 + 200)} \times 100 = 26.2\%$$

This ratio reveals a level of gearing that would not normally be considered to be very high.

Activity 3.17

Calculate the gearing ratio of Alexis plc as at 31 March 2008.

The ratio as at 31 March 2008 is:

$$\text{Gearing ratio} = \frac{300}{(534 + 300)} \times 100 = 36.0\%$$

This ratio reveals a substantial increase in the level of gearing over the year.

Interest cover ratio

The **interest cover ratio** measures the amount of operating profit available to cover interest payable. The ratio may be calculated as follows:

$$\text{Interest cover ratio} = \frac{\text{Operating profit}}{\text{Interest payable}}$$

The ratio for Alexis plc for the year ended 31 March 2007 is:

$$\text{Interest cover ratio} = \frac{243}{18} = 13.5 \text{ times}$$

This ratio shows that the level of operating profit is considerably higher than the level of interest payable. This means that a significant fall in operating profit could occur before operating profit levels failed to cover interest payable. The lower the level of operating profit coverage, the greater the risk to lenders that interest payments will not be met, and the greater the risk to the shareholders that the lenders will take action against the business to recover the interest due.

Activity 3.18

Calculate the interest cover ratio of Alexis plc for the year ended 31 March 2008.

The ratio for the year ended 31 March 2008 is:

$$\text{Interest cover ratio} = \frac{47}{32} = 1.5 \text{ times}$$

Alexis plc's gearing ratios are:

	2007	2008
Gearing ratio	26.2%	36.0%
Interest cover ratio	13.5 times	1.5 times

Activity 3.19

What do you deduce from a comparison of Alexis plc's gearing ratios over the two years?

The gearing ratio altered significantly. This is mainly due to the substantial increase in long-term lenders to the financing of the business.

The interest cover ratio has declined dramatically from a position where operating profit covered interest 13.5 times in 2007, to one where operating profit covered interest only 1.5 times in 2008. This was partly caused by the increase in borrowings in 2008, but mainly caused by the dramatic decline in profitability in that year. The later situation looks hazardous; only a small decline in future profitability in 2008 would leave the business with insufficient operating profit to cover the interest payments. The gearing ratio at 31 March 2008 would not necessarily be considered to be very high for a business that was trading successfully. It is the low profitability that is the problem.

Without knowing what the business planned these ratios to be, it is not possible to reach a valid conclusion on Alexis plc's gearing.

Real World 3.5 provides some evidence concerning the gearing of listed businesses.

REAL WORLD 3.5

The gearing of listed businesses

Larger listed businesses tend to have higher levels of gearing than smaller ones. A Bank of England report on the financing of small businesses found that the average level of gearing among smaller listed businesses was 27 per cent compared with 37 per cent for the top 350 listed businesses. Over recent years the level of borrowing by larger listed businesses has risen whereas the level of borrowing for smaller listed businesses has remained fairly stable. This difference in gearing levels between larger and smaller businesses flies in the face of conventional wisdom.

Recent government investigations have found that smaller listed businesses often find it hard to attract investors. Many large institutional investors, who dominate the stock market, are not interested in the shares of smaller listed businesses because the amount of investment required is too small. As a result, shares in smaller businesses are less marketable. In such circumstances, it may be imagined that smaller businesses would become more reliant on borrowing and so would have higher levels of gearing than larger businesses. However, this is clearly not the case.

Although smaller businesses increase the level of shareholder funds by paying relatively low dividends and retaining more profits, they tend to be less profitable than larger businesses. So, higher retained profits do not seem to explain this phenomenon satisfactorily.

The only obvious factors that could explain this difference between smaller and larger businesses are the level of tax relief on interest on borrowings, and borrowing capacity. Broadly, larger businesses pay tax at a higher rate than their smaller counterparts. This means that the tax benefits of borrowing tend to be greater per £ of interest paid for larger businesses than for smaller ones. It may well be that larger businesses can borrow at lower interest rates than smaller ones, if only because they tend to borrow larger sums and so economies of scale may apply. Also, larger businesses tend to be less likely to get into financial difficulties than smaller ones, so they may be able to borrow at lower interest rates.

Source: Adapted from 'Small companies surprise on lending', *Financial Times*, 25 April 2003.

Investment ratios

There are various ratios available that are designed to help investors assess the returns on their investment. The following are widely used:

- dividend payout ratio
- dividend yield ratio
- earnings per share
- price/earnings ratio.

Dividend payout ratio

The **dividend payout ratio** measures the proportion of earnings that a business pays out to shareholders in the form of dividends. The ratio is calculated as follows:

$$\text{Dividend payout ratio} = \frac{\text{Dividends announced for the year}}{\text{Earnings for the year available for dividends}} \times 100$$

In the case of ordinary shares, the earnings available for dividend will normally be the profit for the year (that is, the profit after taxation) less any preference dividends relating to the year. This ratio is normally expressed as a percentage.

The dividend payout ratio for Alexis plc for the year ended 31 March 2007 is:

$$\text{Dividend payout ratio} = \frac{40}{165} \times 100 = 24.2\%$$

The information provided by this ratio is often expressed slightly differently as the
➜ **dividend cover ratio**. Here the calculation is:

$$\text{Dividend cover ratio} = \frac{\text{Earnings for the year available for dividend}}{\text{Dividend announced for the year}}$$

In the case of Alexis plc (for 2007) it would be $165/40 = 4.1$ times. That is to say, the
earnings available for dividend cover the actual dividend by just over four times.

Activity 3.20

Calculate the dividend payout ratio of Alexis plc for the year ended 31 March 2008.

The ratio for 2008 is:

$$\text{Dividend payout ratio} = \frac{40}{11} \times 100 = 363.6\%$$

This would normally be considered to be a very alarming increase in the ratio over
the two years. Paying a dividend of £40m in 2008 would probably be regarded as very
imprudent.

Dividend yield ratio

➜ The **dividend yield ratio** relates the cash return from a share to its current market value.
This can help investors to assess the cash return on their investment in the business.
The ratio, expressed as a percentage, is:

$$\text{Dividend yield} = \frac{\text{Dividend per share}/(1 - t)}{\text{Market value per share}} \times 100$$

where t is the 'dividend tax credit' rate of income tax. This requires some explanation.
In the UK, investors who receive a dividend from a business also receive a tax credit.
As this tax credit can be offset against any tax liability arising from the dividends
received, the dividends are effectively issued net of income tax, at the dividend tax
credit rate.

Investors may wish to compare the returns from shares with the returns from other
forms of investment. As these other forms of investment are often quoted on a 'gross'
(that is, pre-tax) basis it is useful to 'gross up' the dividend to make comparison easier.
➜ We can achieve this by dividing the **dividend per share** by $(1 - t)$, where t is the
'dividend tax credit' rate of income tax.

Using the 2008/09 dividend tax credit rate of 10 per cent, the dividend yield for
Alexis plc for the year ended 31 March 2007 is:

$$\text{Dividend yield} = \frac{0.067^*/(1 - 0.10)}{2.50} \times 100 = 3.0\%$$

* Dividend proposed/number of shares = $40/(300 \times 2) = £0.067$ dividend per share (the 300 is multiplied by 2 because they are £0.50 shares).

Calculate the dividend yield for Alexis plc for the year ended 31 March 2008.

The ratio for 2008 is:

$$\text{Dividend yield} = \frac{0.067^*/(1 - 0.10)}{1.50} \times 100 = 4.9\%$$

* $40/(300 \times 2) = £0.067$.

Earnings per share

The **earnings per share (EPS)** ratio relates the earnings generated by the business, and available to shareholders, during a period to the number of shares in issue. For equity (ordinary) shareholders, the amount available will be represented by the profit for the year (profit after taxation) less any preference dividend, where applicable. The ratio for equity shareholders is calculated as follows:

$$\text{Earnings per share} = \frac{\text{Earnings available to ordinary shareholders}}{\text{Number of ordinary shares in issue}}$$

In the case of Alexis plc, the earnings per share for the year ended 31 March 2007 is as follows:

$$\text{EPS} = \frac{£165m}{600m} = 27.5p$$

Many investment analysts regard the EPS ratio as a fundamental measure of share performance. The trend in earnings per share over time is used to help assess the investment potential of a business's shares. Although it is possible to make total profit rise through ordinary shareholders investing more in the business, this will not necessarily mean that the profitability *per share* will rise as a result.

It is not usually very helpful to compare the EPS of one business with that of another. Differences in capital structure (for example, in the nominal value of shares issued) can render any such comparison meaningless. However, it can be very useful to monitor the changes that occur in this ratio for a particular business over time.

Calculate the earnings per share of Alexis plc for the year ended 31 March 2008.

The ratio for 2008 is:

$$\text{EPS} = \frac{£11m}{600m} = 1.8p$$

Price/earnings (P/E) ratio

The **price/earnings ratio** relates the market value of a share to the earnings per share. This ratio can be calculated as follows:

$$\text{P/E ratio} = \frac{\textbf{Market value per share}}{\textbf{Earnings per share}}$$

The P/E ratio for Alexis plc as at 31 March 2007 is:

$$\text{P/E ratio} = \frac{£2.50}{27.5\text{p}^*} = 9.1 \text{ times}$$

* The EPS figure (27.5p) was calculated on p. 93.

This ratio reveals that the capital value of the share is 9.1 times higher than its current level of earnings. The ratio is a measure of market confidence in the future of a business. The higher the P/E ratio, the greater the confidence in the future earning power of the business and, consequently, the more investors are prepared to pay in relation to the earnings stream of the business.

P/E ratios provide a useful guide to market confidence concerning the future and they can, therefore, be helpful when comparing different businesses. However, differences in accounting policies between businesses can lead to different profit and earnings per share figures, and this can distort comparisons.

Activity 3.23

Calculate the P/E ratio of Alexis plc as at 31 March 2008.

The ratio for 2008 is:

$$\text{P/E ratio} = \frac{£1.50}{1.8\text{p}} = 83.3 \text{ times}$$

The investment ratios for Alexis plc over the two-year period are as follows:

	2007	2008
Dividend payout ratio	24.2%	363.6%
Dividend yield ratio	3.0%	4.9%
Earnings per share	27.5p	1.8p
P/E ratio	9.1 times	83.3 times

Activity 3.24

What do you deduce from the investment ratios set out above?

Can you offer an explanation why the share price has not fallen as much as it might have done, bearing in mind the very poor (relative to 2007) trading performance in 2008?

Although the EPS has fallen dramatically and the dividend payment for 2008 seems very imprudent, the share price seems to have held up remarkably well (fallen from £2.50 to £1.50, see p. 72). This means that dividend yield and P/E value for 2008 look better than those for 2007. This is an anomaly of these two ratios, which stems from using a forward-looking value (the share price) in conjunction with historic data (dividends and earnings). Share prices are based on investors' assessments of the business's future. It seems with Alexis plc that, at the end of 2008, the 'market' was not happy with the business, relative to 2007. This is evidenced by the fact that the share price had fallen by £1 a share. On the other hand, the share price has not fallen as much as profit for the year. It appears that investors believe that the business will perform better in the future than it did in 2008. This may well be because they believe that the large expansion in assets and employee numbers that occurred in 2008 will yield benefits in the future: benefits that the business was not able to generate during 2008.

Real World 3.6 gives some information about the shares of several large, well-known UK businesses. This type of information is provided on a daily basis by several newspapers, notably the *Financial Times*.

REAL WORLD 3.6

Market statistics for some well-known businesses

The following data was extracted from the *Financial Times* on 25 January 2008, relating to the previous day's trading of the shares of some well-known businesses on the London Stock Exchange:

Share	Price	Chng	2008		Y'ld	P/E	Volume
			High	Low			000s
BP	531	+27.5	648	498	4.0	11.4	99,574
CadburySchweppes	552.50	−11.50	728	514	2.7	23.7	20,123
British Airways	326.50	+18	579.75	259	–	8.1	24,216
Marks and Spencer	445	+26.50	759	372.75	3.7	9.4	26,918
Carphone Warehouse	287.75	−4.25	384.25	265	1.2	34.4	24,803
Vodafone	171.50	+6.40	197.50	133.70	4.0	13.9	278,507

The column headings are as follows:

Price   Mid-market price in pence (that is, the price midway between buying and selling price) of the shares at the end of 24 January 2008.

Chng   Gain or loss in the mid-market price during 24 January 2008.

High/Low   Highest and lowest prices reached by the share during the last year.

Y'ld   Gross dividend yield, based on the most recent year's dividend and the current share price.

P/E   Price/earnings ratio, based on the most recent year's (after-tax) profit for the year and the current share price.

Volume   The number of shares (in thousands) that were bought/sold on 24 January 2008.

So, if we use BP, the oil business, as an example:

● the shares had a mid-market price of £5.31 each at the close of Stock Exchange trading on 24 January 2008;
● the shares had increased in price by 27.5 pence during trading on 24 January;
● the shares had highest and lowest prices during the last year of £6.48 and £4.98, respectively;

Real World 3.6 continued

- the shares had a dividend yield, based on the 24 January price (and the dividend for the most recent year), of 4.0 per cent;
- the shares had a P/E ratio, based on the 24 January price (and the after-tax earnings per share for the most recent year), of 11.4;
- during trading in the shares on 24 January, 99,574 of the business's shares had changed hands from one investor to another.

Real World 3.7 shows how investment ratios can vary between different industry sectors.

REAL WORLD 3.7

How investment ratios vary between industries

Investment ratios can vary significantly between businesses and between industries. To give some indication of the range of variations that occur, the average dividend yield ratios and average P/E ratios for listed businesses in twelve different industries are shown in Figures 3.2 and 3.3, respectively.

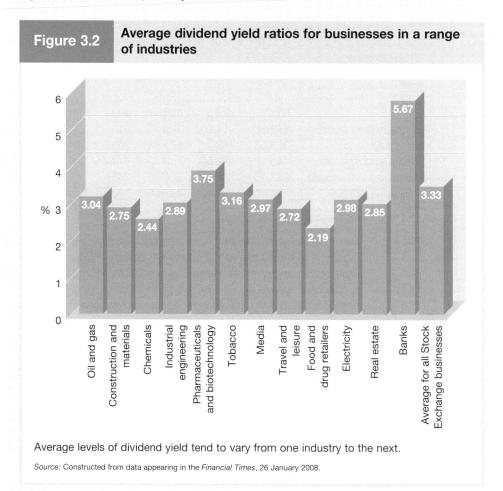

| Figure 3.2 | Average dividend yield ratios for businesses in a range of industries |

Average levels of dividend yield tend to vary from one industry to the next.

Source: Constructed from data appearing in the *Financial Times*, 26 January 2008.

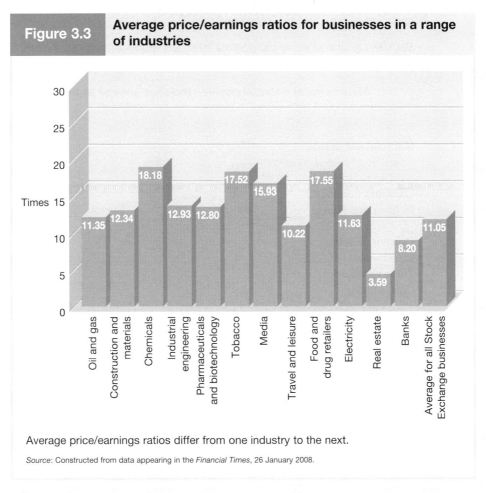

| Figure 3.3 | Average price/earnings ratios for businesses in a range of industries |

Average price/earnings ratios differ from one industry to the next.

Source: Constructed from data appearing in the *Financial Times*, 26 January 2008.

These dividend yield ratios are calculated from the current market value of the shares and the most recent year's dividend paid.

Some industries tend to pay out lower dividends than others, leading to lower dividend yield ratios. The average for all Stock Exchange listed businesses was 3.33% (as is shown in Figure 3.2), but there is a wide variation, with food and drug retailers at 2.19% and banks at 5.67%.

Some of the inter-industry differences in the dividend yield ratio can be explained by the nature of the calculation of the ratio. The prices of shares at any given moment are based on expectations of their economic futures; dividends are based on actual past events. A business that had a good trading year recently may have paid a dividend that, in the light of investors' assessment of the business's economic future, may be high (a high dividend yield).

P/E ratios are calculated from the current market value of the shares and the most recent year's earnings per share (EPS). Businesses that have a high share price relative to their recent historic earnings have high P/E ratios. This may be because their future is regarded as economically bright, which may be the result of investing heavily in the future at the expense of recent profits (earnings). On the other hand, high P/Es also arise where businesses have recent low earnings but investors believe that their future is brighter. The average for all Stock Exchange listed businesses was 11.05 (as is shown in Figure 3.3), but banks were as low as 8.20 times and food and drug retailers as high as 17.55 times.

Source: Figures constructed from FTSE Actuaries share Indices data in the *Financial Times*, 26 January 2008, p. 28.

Self-assessment question 3.1

Both Ali plc and Bhaskar plc operate electrical stores throughout the UK. The financial statements of each business for the year ended 30 June 2008 are as follows:

Statements of financial position (balance sheets) as at 30 June 2008

	Ali plc £000	Bhaskar plc £000
Non-current assets		
Property, plant and equipment		
(cost less depreciation)		
Land and buildings	360.0	510.0
Fixtures and fittings	87.0	91.2
	447.0	601.2
Current assets		
Inventories	592.0	403.0
Trade receivables	176.4	321.9
Cash at bank	84.6	91.6
	853.0	816.5
Total assets	1,300.0	1,417.7
Equity		
£1 ordinary shares	320.0	250.0
Retained earnings	367.6	624.6
	687.6	874.6
Non-current liabilities		
Borrowings – Loan notes	190.0	250.0
Current liabilities		
Trade payables	406.4	275.7
Tax due	16.0	17.4
	422.4	293.1
Total equity and liabilities	1,300.0	1,417.7

Income statements for the year ended 30 June 2008

	Ali plc £000	Bhaskar plc £000
Revenue	1,478.1	1,790.4
Cost of sales	(1,018.3)	(1,214.9)
Gross profit	459.8	575.5
Operating expenses	(308.5)	(408.6)
Operating profit	151.3	166.9
Interest payable	(19.4)	(27.5)
Profit before taxation	131.9	139.4
Tax	(32.0)	(34.8)
Profit for the year	99.9	104.6

All purchases and sales were on credit. Ali plc had announced its intention to pay a dividend of £135,000 and Bhaskar plc £95,000 in respect of the year. The market values of a share in Ali plc and Bhaskar plc at the end of the year were £6.50 and £8.20 respectively.

Required:
For each business, calculate two ratios that are concerned with liquidity, gearing and investment (six ratios in total). What can you conclude from the ratios that you have calculated?
The answer to this question may be found at the back of the book on p. 530.

Financial ratios and the problem of overtrading

→ **Overtrading** occurs where a business is operating at a level of activity that cannot be supported by the amount of finance that has been committed. For example, the business has inadequate finance to fund the level of trade receivables and inventories necessary for the level of sales revenue that it is achieving. This situation usually reflects a poor level of financial control over the business. The reasons for overtrading are varied. It may occur:

- in young, expanding businesses that fail to prepare adequately for the rapid increase in demand for their goods or services;
- in businesses where the managers may have miscalculated the level of expected sales demand or have failed to control escalating project costs;
- as a result of a fall in the value of money (inflation), causing more finance to be committed to inventories and trade receivables, even where there is no expansion in the real volume of trade;
- where the owners are unable both to inject further funds into the business and cannot persuade others to invest in the business.

Whatever the reason, the problems that it brings must be dealt with if the business is to survive over the longer term.

Overtrading results in liquidity problems such as exceeding borrowing limits, or slow repayment of lenders and trade payables. It can also result in suppliers withholding supplies, thereby making it difficult to meet customer needs. The managers of the business might be forced to direct all their efforts to dealing with immediate and pressing problems, such as finding cash to meet interest charges due or paying wages. Longer-term planning becomes difficult and managers may spend their time going from crisis to crisis. At the extreme, a business may fail because it cannot meet its maturing obligations.

Activity 3.25

If a business is overtrading, do you think the following ratios would be higher or lower than normally expected?

1 Current ratio.
2 Average inventories turnover period.
3 Average settlement period for trade receivables.
4 Average settlement period for trade payables.

Your answer should be as follows:

1 The current ratio would be lower than normally expected. This is a measure of liquidity, and lack of liquidity is an important symptom of overtrading.
2 The average inventories turnover period would be lower than normally expected. Where a business is overtrading, the level of inventories held will be low because of the problems of financing them. In the short term, sales revenue may not be badly affected by the low inventories levels and therefore inventories will be turned over more quickly.
3 The average settlement period for trade receivables may be lower than normally expected. Where a business is suffering from liquidity problems it may chase credit customers more vigorously in order to improve cash flows.
4 The average settlement period for trade payables may be higher than normally expected. The business may try to delay payments to its suppliers because of the liquidity problems arising.

To deal with the overtrading problem, a business must ensure that the finance available is consistent with the level of operations. Thus, if a business that is overtrading is unable to raise new finance, it should cut back its level of operations in line with the finance available. Although this may mean lost sales and lost profits in the short term, it may be necessary to ensure survival over the longer term.

Trend analysis

It is often helpful to see whether ratios are indicating trends. Key ratios can be plotted on a graph to provide a simple visual display of changes occurring over time. The trends occurring within a business may, for example, be plotted against trends for rival businesses or for the industry as a whole for comparison purposes. An example of trend analysis is shown in **Real World 3.8**.

REAL WORLD 3.8

Trend setting

In Figure 3.4 the current ratio of Tesco plc is plotted against the same ratio for two other businesses within the same industry – J. Sainsbury plc and Wm Morrison plc – over a seven-year period. We can see that the current ratio of Tesco plc has risen slightly over the period but it is, nevertheless, consistently lower than that of its main rivals, until 2005, when it overtook Morrison.

Figure 3.4	Graph plotting current ratio against time

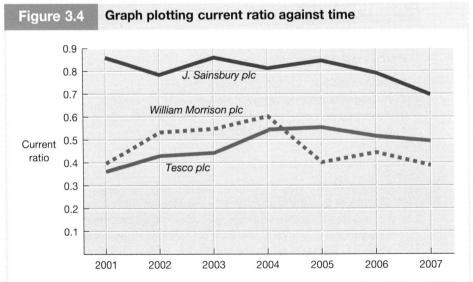

The current ratio for Tesco plc is plotted for the financial years ending 2001 to 2007. On the same graph, the current ratio for J. Sainsbury plc and Wm Morrison plc is plotted for the same financial years, enabling comparison to be made between the ratio for Tesco plc and those of its rivals.

Many larger businesses publish certain key financial ratios as part of their annual reports to help users identify significant trends. These ratios typically cover several years' activities. **Real World 3.9** shows part of the table of 'key performance measures' of Marks and Spencer plc (M&S), the well-known UK high street store.

REAL WORLD 3.9

Key performance measures of Marks and Spencer Group plc

	2007 52 weeks	2006 52 weeks	2005 52 weeks	2004 53 weeks	2003 52 weeks
Gross margin $\dfrac{\text{Gross profit}}{\text{Turnover (sales)}}$	38.9%	38.3%	34.7%	35.4%	34.8%
Net margin $\dfrac{\text{Operating profit}}{\text{Turnover (sales)}}$	12.2%	10.9%	8.0%	9.9%	8.6%
Net margin excluding property disposals and exceptional items	12.2%	11.0%	8.7%	10.2%	9.2%
Profitability $\dfrac{\text{Profit before tax}}{\text{Turnover (sales)}}$	10.9%	9.6%	6.7%	9.4%	8.4%
Profitability excluding property disposals and exceptional items	11.2%	9.6%	7.4%	9.7%	9.0%
Basic earnings per share $\dfrac{\text{Basic earnings}}{\text{Weighted average ordinary shares in issue}}$	39.1p	31.3p	17.6p	24.2p	21.8p
Earnings per share adjusted for property disposals and exceptional items	40.4p	31.4p	19.2p	24.7p	23.3p
Dividend per share declared in respect of the year	18.3p	14.0p	12.1p	11.5p	10.5p
Dividend cover $\dfrac{\text{Profit attributable to shareholders}}{\text{Dividends payable}}$	2.1×	2.2×	2.9×	2.1×	2.1×
Return on equity $\dfrac{\text{Profit attributable to shareholders}}{\text{Average equity shareholders' funds}}$	46.3%	50.0%	35.1%	25.2%	22.4%

Source: Marks and Spencer Group plc Annual Report 2007, p. 96. Reproduced by kind permission of Marks and Spencer Group plc. The results for 2003 and 2004 have not been restated following the adoption of International Financial Reporting Standards in 2005. This means that the results over the five years are not strictly comparable.

After many years of profitable growth, M&S suffered a decline in its fortunes during the late 1990s. This was seen by the directors, and by many independent commentators, as arising from the business allowing itself to be drawn away from its traditional areas of strength. Steps were taken to deal with the problem and the improvements since 2002 are very clear. Although the return on equity (return on ordinary shareholders' funds) is slightly lower than in 2006, it is significantly better than in the earlier three years. In 2005, both the gross profit and net (operating profit) margins are lower than in 2004, but both recovered strongly in 2006, with further improvements in 2007.

Using ratios to predict financial failure

Financial ratios, based on current or past performance, are often used to help predict the future. But both the choice of ratios and the interpretation of results are normally dependent on the judgement and opinion of the analyst. In recent years, however, attempts have been made to develop a more rigorous and systematic approach to the use of ratios for prediction purposes. In particular, researchers have shown an interest in the ability of ratios to predict the financial failure of a business.

By financial failure, we mean a business either being forced out of business or being severely adversely affected by its inability to meet its financial obligations. It is often referred to as 'going bust' or 'going bankrupt'. This, of course, is an area with which all those connected with the business are likely to be concerned.

Using single ratios

Many approaches that attempt to use ratios to predict future financial failure have been developed. Early research focused on the examination of ratios on an individual basis to see whether they were good or bad predictors of financial failure. Here, a particular ratio (for example the current ratio) for a business that had failed was tracked over several years leading up to the date of the failure. This was to see whether it was possible to say that the ratio had shown a trend that could have been taken as a warning sign.

Beaver (see reference 1 at the end of the chapter) carried out the first research in this area. He identified 79 businesses that had failed. He then calculated the average (mean) of various ratios for these 79 businesses, going back over the financial statements of each business for each of the ten years leading up to each one's failure. Beaver then compared these average ratios with similarly derived ratios for a sample of 79 businesses that did not fail over this period. (The research used a matched-pair design, where each failed business was matched with a non-failed business of similar size and industry type.) Beaver found that some ratios exhibited a marked difference between the failed and non-failed businesses for up to five years prior to failure. This is shown in Figure 3.5.

To explain Figure 3.5, let us take a closer look at graph (a). This plots the ratio, cash flow (presumably the operating cash flow figure, taken from the cash flow statement) divided by total debt (borrowings). For the non-failed businesses this stayed fairly steady at just below +0.45 over the period. For the failed businesses, however, this was already well below that of the non-failed businesses, at about +0.15, even five years before those businesses eventually failed. It then declined steadily until, by one year before the failure, it was less than −0.15. Note that the scale of the horizontal axis shows the most recent year before actual failure (Year 1) on the left and the earliest one (Year 5) on the right. The other graphs in Figure 3.5 show a similar picture for five other ratios. In each case there is a deteriorating average ratio for the failed businesses as the time of failure approaches.

What is shown in Figure 3.5 implies that failure could be predicted by careful assessment of the trend shown by particular key ratios.

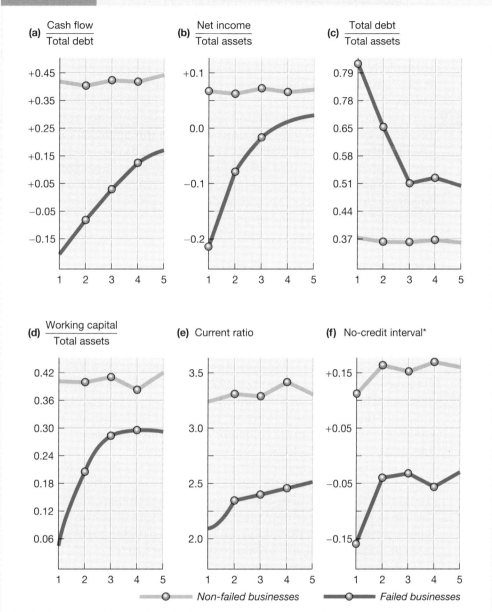

| Figure 3.5 | Average (mean) ratios of failed and non-failed businesses plotted against the number of years before failure |

Each of the ratios (a) to (f) above indicates a marked difference in the average ratio between the sample of failed businesses and a matched sample of non-failed businesses. The vertical scale of each graph is the average value of the particular ratio for each group of businesses (failed and non-failed). The horizontal axis is the number of years before failure. Thus Year 1 is the most recent year and Year 5 the earliest of the years. For each of the six ratios, the difference between the average for the failed and the non-failed businesses can be detected five years prior to the failure of the former group.

* The no-credit interval is the same as the cash generated from operations to maturing obligations ratio discussed earlier in the chapter.

Source: Beaver (see reference 1 at the end of the chapter).

Research by Zmijewski (see reference 2 at the end of the chapter), using a sample of 72 failed and 3,573 non-failed businesses over a six-year period, found that failed businesses were characterised by lower rates of return, higher levels of gearing, lower levels of coverage for their fixed interest payments and more variable returns on shares. While we may not find these results very surprising, it is interesting to note that Zmijewski, like a number of other researchers in this area, did not find liquidity ratios particularly useful in predicting financial failure. Intuition might have led us (wrongly it seems) to believe that the liquidity ratios would have been particularly helpful in this context.

The approach adopted by Beaver and Zmijewski is referred to as **univariate analysis** because it looks at one ratio at a time. Although this approach can produce interesting results, there are practical problems associated with its use. Let us say, for example, that past research has identified two ratios as being good predictors of financial failure. When applied to a particular business, however, it may be found that one ratio predicts financial failure whereas the other does not. Given these conflicting signals, how should the decision maker interpret the results?

Using combinations of ratios

The weaknesses of univariate analysis have led researchers to develop models that combine ratios in such a way as to produce a single index that can be interpreted more clearly. One approach to model development, much favoured by researchers, applies **multiple discriminate analysis** (MDA). This is, in essence, a statistical technique that is similar to regression analysis and which can be used to draw a boundary between those businesses that fail and those businesses that do not. This boundary is referred to as the **discriminate function**. In this context, MDA attempts to identify those factors likely to influence financial failure. However, unlike regression analysis, MDA assumes that the observations come from two different populations (for example, failed and non-failed businesses) rather than from a single population.

To illustrate this approach, let us assume that we wish to test whether two ratios (say, the current ratio and the return on capital employed) can help to predict failure. To do this, we can calculate these ratios, first for a sample of failed businesses and then for a matched sample of non-failed businesses. From these two sets of data we can produce a scatter diagram that plots each business according to these two ratios to produce a single coordinate. Figure 3.6 illustrates this approach.

Using the observations plotted on the diagram, we try to identify the boundary between the failed and the non-failed businesses. This is the diagonal line in Figure 3.6.

We can see that those businesses that fall below and to the left of the line are predominantly failed and those that fall to the right are predominantly non-failed ones. Note that there is some overlap between the two populations. The boundary produced is unlikely, in practice, to eliminate all errors. Some businesses that fail may fall on the side of the boundary with non-failed businesses, and the other way round as well. However, the analysis will *minimise* the misclassification errors.

The boundary shown in Figure 3.6 can be expressed in the form:

$$Z = a + (b \times \text{Current ratio}) + (c \times \text{ROCE})$$

where a is a constant and b and c are weights to be attached to each ratio. A weighted average or total score (Z) is then derived. The weights given to the two ratios will depend on the slope of the line and its absolute position.

Figure 3.6	**Scatter diagram showing the distribution of failed and non-failed businesses**

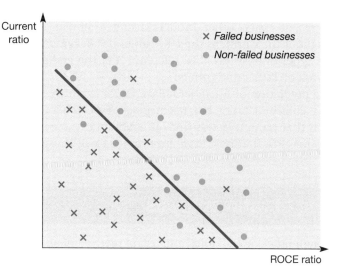

The distribution of failed and non-failed businesses is based on two ratios. The line represents a boundary between the samples of failed and non-failed businesses. Although there is some crossing of the boundary, the boundary represents the line that minimises the problem of mis-classifying particular businesses.

Z-score models

Altman (see reference 3 at the end of the chapter) was the first to develop a model (in 1968), using financial ratios, that was able to predict financial failure. In 2000 he revised that model. In fact, the revisions necessary to make the model effective in present times were quite minor. Altman's revised model, the Z-score model, is based on five financial ratios and is as follows:

$$Z = 0.717a + 0.847b + 3.107c + 0.420d + 0.998e$$

where a = Working capital/Total assets
b = Accumulated retained profits/Total assets
c = Operating profit/Total assets
d = Book (balance sheet) value of ordinary and preference shares/Total liabilities at book (balance sheet) value
e = Sales revenue/Total assets

In developing and revising this model, Altman carried out experiments using a paired sample of failed businesses and non-failed businesses and collected relevant data for each business for five years prior to failure. He found that the model represented by the formula above was able to predict failure for up to two years before it occurred. However, the predictive accuracy of the model became weaker the longer the time before the date of the actual failure.

The ratios used in this model were identified by Altman through a process of trial and error, as there is no underlying theory of financial failure to help guide researchers in their selection of appropriate ratios. According to Altman, those businesses with a Z-score of less than 1.23 tend to fail, and the lower the score the greater the probability of failure. Those with a Z-score greater than 4.14 tend not to fail. Those businesses with a Z-score between 1.23 and 4.14 occupied a 'zone of ignorance' and were difficult to classify. However, the model was able overall to classify 91 per cent of the businesses correctly. Altman based his model on US businesses.

In recent years, other models, using a similar approach, have been developed throughout the world. In the UK, Taffler has developed separate Z score models for different types of business. (See reference 4 at the end of the chapter for a discussion of the work of Taffler and others.)

The prediction of financial failure is not the only area where research into the predictive ability of ratios has taken place. Researchers have also developed ratio-based models that claim to assess the vulnerability of a business to takeover by another. This is another area that is of vital importance to all those connected with the business.

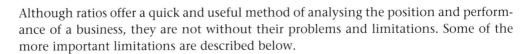

Limitations of ratio analysis

Although ratios offer a quick and useful method of analysing the position and performance of a business, they are not without their problems and limitations. Some of the more important limitations are described below.

Quality of financial statements

It must always be remembered that ratios are based on financial statements, and the results of ratio analysis are dependent on the quality of these underlying statements. Ratios will inherit the limitations of the financial statements on which they are based. A significant example of this arises from the application of the prudence convention to internally generated intangible non-current assets (as compared with purchased ones). This convention tends to lead to assets of considerable value, such as goodwill and brand names, being excluded from the balance sheet. This can mean that ratios such as ROSF, ROCE and the gearing ratio fail to take account of these assets.

- Creative accounting. Despite the proliferation of accounting rules and the independent checks that are imposed, there is evidence that the directors of some companies have employed particular accounting policies or structured particular transactions in such a way that portrays a picture of financial health that is in line with what they would like users to see rather than what is a true and fair view of financial position and performance. This practice is referred to as **creative accounting** and it can pose a major problem for those seeking to gain an impression of the financial health of a business.

Activity 3.26

Why might the directors of a business engage in creative accounting?

There are many reasons and these include:

- to get around restrictions (for example, to report sufficient profit to pay a dividend);
- to avoid government action (for example, the taxation of excessive profits);

- to hide poor management decisions;
- to achieve sales or profit targets, thereby ensuring that performance bonuses are paid to the directors;
- to attract new share capital or loan capital by showing a healthy financial position; and
- to satisfy the demands of major investors concerning levels of return.

The particular methods that unscrupulous directors use to manipulate the financial statements are many and varied. They can involve overstatement of revenues, manipulation of expenses, concealing losses and liabilities and overstating asset values.

Overstating revenues has been a particularly popular target for creative accounting. The methods used often involve the early recognition of sales income or the reporting of sales transactions that have no real substance. **Real World 3.10** is an extract from an article in *The Times*, which provides examples of both types of revenue manipulation.

REAL WORLD 3.10

Overstating revenue

Hollow swaps: telecoms companies sell useless fibre optic capacity to each other in order to generate revenues on their income statements. Example: Global Crossing.

Channel stuffing: a company floods the market with more products than its distributors can sell, artificially boosting its sales. SSL, the condom maker, shifted £60 million in excess stock on to trade customers. Also known as 'trade loading'.

Round tripping: also known as 'in-and-out trading'. Used to notorious effect by Enron. Two or more traders buy and sell energy among themselves for the same price and at the same time. Inflates trading volumes and makes participants appear to be doing more business than they really are.

Pre-dispatching: goods such as carpets are marked as 'sold' as soon as an order is placed . . . This inflates sales and profits.

Note that some of the techniques used, such as round tripping, may inflate the sales for a period but do not inflate reported profits. Nevertheless, this may still benefit the company. Sales growth has become an important yardstick of performance for some investors and can affect the value they place on the company.

Source: 'Dirty laundry: how companies fudge the numbers', *The Times*, Business Section, 22 September 2002. © NI Syndication Limited, 22 September 2002.

When examining the financial statements of a business, a number of checks may be carried out to help gain a 'feel' for their reliability. These can include checks to see whether:

- the reported profits are significantly higher than the operating cash flows for the period, which may suggest that profits have been overstated;
- the tax charge is low in relation to reported profits, which may suggest, again, that profits are overstated, although there may be other, more innocent, explanations;
- the valuation methods used for assets held are based on historic cost or current values, and if the latter approach has been used why and how the current values were determined;

- there have been any changes in accounting policies over the period, particularly in key areas such as revenue recognition, inventory valuation and depreciation;
- the accounting policies adopted are in line with those adopted by the rest of the industry;
- the auditors' report gives a 'clean bill of health' to the financial statements; and
- the 'small print', that is, the notes to the financial statements, is not being used to hide significant events or changes.

Although such checks are useful, they are not guaranteed to identify creative accounting practices, some of which may be very deeply seated.

Inflation

A persistent, though recently less severe, problem in most western countries is that the financial results of businesses can be distorted as a result of inflation. One effect of inflation is that the balance sheet values of assets held for any length of time may bear little relation to current values. Generally speaking, the balance sheet value of assets will be understated in current terms during a period of inflation as they are usually recorded at their original cost (less any amounts written off for depreciation). This means that comparisons, either between businesses or between periods, will be hindered. A difference in, say, ROCE may simply be owing to the fact that assets in one of the balance sheets being compared were acquired more recently (ignoring the effect of depreciation on the asset values). Another effect of inflation is to distort the measurement of profit. Sales revenue for a period is often matched against costs from an earlier period because there is often a time lag between acquiring a particular resource and using it to help generate sales revenue. For example, inventories may be acquired in one period and sold in a later period. During a period of inflation, this will mean that the expense does not reflect current prices. The cost of sales figure is usually based on the historic cost of the inventories concerned. As a result, expenses will be understated in the income statement and this, in turn, means that profit will be overstated. One effect of this will be to distort the profitability ratios discussed earlier.

The restricted vision of ratios

It is important not to rely exclusively on ratios, thereby losing sight of information contained in the underlying financial statements. As we saw earlier in the chapter, some items reported in these statements can be vital in assessing position and performance. For example, the total sales revenue, capital employed and profit figures may be useful in assessing changes in absolute size that occur over time, or differences in scale between businesses. Ratios do not provide such information. When comparing one figure with another, ratios measure *relative* performance and position, and thus provide only part of the picture. When comparing two businesses, therefore, it will often be useful to assess the absolute size of profits, as well as the relative profitability of each business. For example, Business A may generate £1m operating profit and have a ROCE of 15 per cent, and Business B may generate £100,000 operating profit and have a ROCE of 20 per cent. Although Business B has a higher level of *profitability*, as measured by ROCE, it generates lower total operating profits.

The basis for comparison

We saw earlier that if ratios are to be useful they require a basis for comparison. Moreover, it is important that the analyst compares like with like. However, no two businesses are identical, and the greater the differences between the businesses being compared, the greater the limitations of ratio analysis. Also, when comparing businesses, differences in such matters as accounting policies, financing methods (gearing levels) and financial year ends will add to the problems of evaluation.

Statement of financial position (balance sheet) ratios

Because the statement of financial position (balance sheet) is only a 'snapshot' of the business at a particular moment in time, any ratios based on balance sheet figures, such as the liquidity ratios, may not be representative of the financial position of the business for the year as a whole. For example, it is common for a seasonal business to have a financial year end that coincides with a low point in business activity. As a result, inventories and trade receivables may be low at the statement of financial position date, and so the liquidity ratios may also be low. A more representative picture of liquidity can only really be gained by taking additional measurements at other points in the year.

Real World 3.11 points out another way in which ratios are limited.

 REAL WORLD 3.11

Remember, it's people that really count . . .

Lord Weinstock (1924–2002) was an influential industrialist whose management style and philosophy helped to shape management practice in many UK businesses. During his long and successful reign at GEC plc, a major engineering business, Lord Weinstock relied heavily on financial ratios to assess performance and to exercise control. In particular, he relied on ratios relating to sales revenue, expenses, trade receivables, profit margins and inventories turnover. However, he was keenly aware of the limitations of ratios and recognised that, ultimately, people produce profits.

In a memo written to GEC managers he pointed out that ratios are an aid to good management rather than a substitute for it. He wrote:

> The operating ratios are of great value as measures of efficiency but they are only the measures and not efficiency itself. Statistics will not design a product better, make it for a lower cost or increase sales. If ill-used, they may so guide action as to diminish resources for the sake of apparent but false signs of improvement.
>
> Management remains a matter of judgement, of knowledge of products and processes and of understanding and skill in dealing with people. The ratios will indicate how well all these things are being done and will show comparison with how they are done elsewhere. But they will tell us nothing about how to do them. That is what you are meant to do.

Source: Extract from S. Aris, *Arnold Weinstock and the Making of GEC* (Aurum Press, 1998), published in *The Sunday Times*, 22 February 1998, p. 3.

SUMMARY

The main points of this chapter may be summarised as follows.

Ratio analysis

- Compares two related figures, usually both from the same set of financial statements.
- Is an aid to understanding what the financial statements really mean.
- Is an inexact science so results must be interpreted cautiously.
- Past periods, the performance of similar businesses and planned performance are often used to provide benchmark ratios.
- A brief overview of the financial statements can often provide insights that may not be revealed by ratios and/or may help in the interpretation of them.

Profitability ratios – concerned with effectiveness at generating profit

- Return on ordinary shareholders' funds (ROSF)
- Return on capital employed (ROCE)
- Operating profit margin
- Gross profit margin.

Efficiency ratios – concerned with efficiency of using assets/resources

- Average inventories turnover period
- Average settlement period for trade receivables
- Average settlement period for trade payables
- Sales revenue to capital employed
- Sales revenue per employee.

Liquidity ratios – concerned with the ability to meet short-term obligations

- Current ratio
- Acid test ratio.

Gearing ratios – concerned with the relationship between equity and debt financing

- Gearing ratio
- Interest cover ratio.

Investment ratios – concerned with returns to shareholders

- Dividend payout ratio
- Dividend yield ratio
- Earnings per share
- Price/earnings ratio.

Trend analysis

- Individual ratios can be tracked (for example, plotted on a graph) to detect trends.

Ratios as predictors of financial failure

- Univariate analysis – looking at just one ratio over time in an attempt to predict financial failure.
- Multiple discriminate analysis – looking at several ratios, put together in a model, over time, in an attempt to predict financial failure – Z-scores.

Limitations of ratio analysis

- Ratios are only as reliable as the financial statements from which they derive.
- Creative accounting can distort the portrayal of financial health.
- Inflation can also distort the information.
- Ratios have restricted vision.
- It can be difficult to find a suitable benchmark (for example, another business) as comparator.
- Some ratios could mislead due to the 'snapshot' nature of the statement of financial position (balance sheet).

→ Key terms

Return on ordinary shareholders' funds ratio (ROSF)   p. 73
Return on capital employed ratio (ROCE)   p. 74
Operating profit margin ratio   p. 76
Gross profit margin ratio   p. 77
Average inventories turnover period ratio   p. 80
Average settlement period for trade receivables ratio   p. 80
Average settlement period for trade payables ratio   p. 81
Sales revenue to capital employed ratio   p. 82
Sales revenue per employee ratio   p. 83

Current ratio   p. 86
Acid test ratio   p. 87
Financial gearing   p. 88
Gearing ratio   p. 89
Interest cover ratio   p. 89
Dividend payout ratio   p. 91
Dividend cover ratio   p. 92
Dividend yield ratio   p. 92
Dividend per share   p. 92
Earnings per share (EPS)   p. 93
Price/earnings ratio   p. 94
Overtrading   p. 99
Univariate analysis   p. 104
Multiple discriminate analysis   p. 104
Discriminate function   p. 104
Creative accounting   p. 106

For definitions of these terms see the Glossary, pp. 574–583.

References

1 'Financial ratios as predictors of failure', *Beaver, W. H.*, Empirical Research in Accounting: Selected studies, a supplement to the **Journal of Accounting Research**, 1966, pp. 71–111.

2 **Predicting corporate bankruptcy: an empirical comparison of the extent of financial distress models**, *Zmijewski, M. E.*, Research Paper, State University of New York, 1983.

3 'Predicting financial distress of companies: revisiting the Z-score and Zeta models', *Altman, E. I.*, Working paper, New York University, June 2000.

4 'Predicting corporate failure: empirical evidence for the UK', *Neophytou, E., Charitou, A. and Charalamnous, C.*, Working Paper 01-173, Department of Accounting and Management Science, University of Southampton, 2001.

Further reading

If you would like to explore the topics covered in this chapter in more depth, try the following books:

Financial analysis, *Gowthorpe, C.*, CIMA Publishing, 2007, chapters 16, 17 and 19.

Financial Accounting and Reporting, *Elliott, B. and Elliott, J.*, 12th edn, Financial Times Prentice Hall, 2007, chapters 28 and 29.

Financial Reporting and Analysis, *Revsine, L., Collins, D. and Bruce Johnson, W.*, 3rd edn, Prentice Hall, 2008, chapter 5.

Financial Statement Analysis, *Wild, J., Subramanyam, K. and Halsey, R.*, 9th edn, McGraw-Hill, 2006, chapters 8, 9 and 11.

REVIEW QUESTIONS

Answers to these questions can be found at the back of the book on p. 540.

3.1 Some businesses operate on a low operating profit margin (for example, a supermarket chain). Does this mean that the return on capital employed from the business will also be low?

3.2 What potential problems arise for the external analyst from the use of statement of financial position (balance sheet) figures in the calculation of financial ratios?

3.3 Is it responsible to publish *Z*-scores of businesses that are in financial difficulties? What are the potential problems of doing this?

3.4 Identify and discuss three reasons why the P/E ratio of two businesses operating within the same industry may differ.

EXERCISES

Exercises 3.5 to 3.7 are more advanced than 3.1 to 3.4. Those with coloured numbers have answers at the back of the book, starting on p. 551.

>
> If you wish to try more exercises, visit the students' side of this book's Companion Website.

3.1 Set out below are ratios relating to three different businesses. Each business operates within a different industrial sector.

Ratio	A plc	B plc	C plc
Operating profit margin	3.6%	9.7%	6.8%
Sales to capital employed	2.4 times	3.1 times	1.7 times
Inventory turnover period	18 days	n/a	44 days
Average settlement period for receivables	2 days	12 days	26 days
Current ratio	0.8 times	0.6 times	1.5 times

Required:
State, with reasons, which of the above is:

(a) A holiday tour operator
(b) A supermarket chain
(c) A food manufacturer.

3.2 Amsterdam Ltd and Berlin Ltd are both engaged in retailing, but they seem to take a different approach to it according to the following information:

Ratio	Amsterdam Ltd	Berlin Ltd
Return on capital employed (ROCE)	20%	17%
Return on ordinary shareholders' funds (ROSF)	30%	18%
Average settlement period for trade receivables	63 days	21 days
Average settlement period for trade payables	50 days	45 days
Gross profit margin	40%	15%
Operating profit margin	10%	10%
Average inventories turnover period	52 days	25 days

Required:

Describe what this information indicates about the differences in approach between the two businesses. If one of them prides itself on personal service and one of them on competitive prices, which do you think is which and why?

3.3 Conday and Co. Ltd has been in operation for three years and produces antique reproduction furniture for the export market. The most recent set of financial statements for the business is set out as follows:

Statement of financial position (balance sheet) as at 30 November

	£000
Non-current assets	
Property, plant and equipment (Cost less depreciation)	
Land and buildings	228
Plant and machinery	762
	990
Current assets	
Inventories	600
Trade receivables	820
	1,420
Total assets	2,410
Equity	
Ordinary shares of £1 each	700
Retained earnings	365
	1,065
Non-current liabilities	
Borrowings – 9% loan notes (Note 1)	200
Current liabilities	
Trade payables	665
Tax due	48
Short-term borrowings (all bank overdraft)	432
	1,145
Total equity and liabilities	2,410

Income statement for the year ended 30 November

	£000
Revenue	2,600
Cost of sales	(1,620)
Gross profit	980
Selling and distribution expenses (Note 2)	(408)
Administration expenses	(194)
Operating profit	378
Finance expenses	(58)
Profit before taxation	320
Tax	(95)
Profit for the year	225

Notes:

1 The loan notes are secured on the land and buildings.
2 Selling and distribution expenses include £170,000 in respect of bad debts.
3 A dividend of £160,000 was paid on the ordinary shares during the year.
4 The directors have invited an investor to take up a new issue of ordinary shares in the business at £6.40 each making a total investment of £200,000. The directors wish to use the funds to finance a programme of further expansion.

Required:

(a) Analyse the financial position and performance of the business and comment on any features that you consider to be significant.

(b) State, with reasons, whether or not the investor should invest in the business on the terms outlined.

3.4 The directors of Helena Beauty Products Ltd have been presented with the following abridged financial statements:

Helena Beauty Products Ltd
Income statement for the year ended 30 September

	2007		2008	
	£000	£000	£000	£000
Sales revenue		3,600		3,840
Cost of sales				
Opening inventories	320		400	
Purchases	2,240		2,350	
	2,560		2,750	
Closing inventories	(400)	(2,160)	(500)	(2,250)
Gross profit		1,440		1,590
Expenses		(1,360)		(1,500)
Profit for the year		80		90

Statement of financial position (balance sheet) as at 30 September

	2007	2008
	£000	£000
Non-current assets		
Property, plant and equipment	1,900	1,860
Current assets		
Inventories	400	500
Trade receivables	750	960
Cash at bank	8	4
	1,158	1,464
Total assets	3,058	3,324
Equity		
£1 ordinary shares	1,650	1,766
Retained earnings	1,018	1,108
	2,668	2,874
Current liabilities	390	450
Total equity and liabilities	3,058	3,324

Required:
Using six ratios, comment on the profitability (three ratios) and efficiency (three ratios) of the business as revealed by the statements shown above.

3.5 Threads Limited manufactures nuts and bolts, which are sold to industrial users. The abbreviated financial statements for 2007 and 2008 are as follows:

Income statements for the year ended 30 June

	2007 £000	2008 £000
Revenue	1,180	1,200
Cost of sales	(680)	(750)
Gross profit	500	450
Operating expenses	(200)	(208)
Depreciation	(66)	(75)
Operating profit	234	167
Interest	(–)	(8)
Profit before taxation	234	159
Tax	(80)	(48)
Profit for the year	154	111

Statements of financial position (balance sheets) as at 30 June

	2007 £000	2008 £000
Non-current assets		
Property, plant and equipment	702	687
Current assets		
Inventories	148	236
Trade receivables	102	156
Cash	3	4
	253	396
Total assets	955	1,083
Equity		
Ordinary share capital of £1 (fully paid)	500	500
Retained earnings	256	295
	756	795
Non-current liabilities		
Borrowings – Bank loan	–	50
Current liabilities		
Trade payables	60	76
Other payables and accruals	18	16
Tax due	40	24
Short-term borrowings (all bank overdraft)	81	122
	199	238
Total equity and liabilities	955	1,083

Dividends were paid on ordinary shares of £70,000 and £72,000 in respect of 2007 and 2008, respectively.

Required:

(a) Calculate the following financial ratios for *both* 2007 and 2008 (using year-end figures for balance sheet items):
  (i) return on capital employed
  (ii) operating profit margin
  (iii) gross profit margin
  (iv) current ratio
  (v) acid test ratio
  (vi) settlement period for trade receivables
  (vii) settlement period for trade payables
  (viii) inventories turnover period.

(b) Comment on the performance of Threads Limited from the viewpoint of a business considering supplying a substantial amount of goods to Threads Limited on usual trade credit terms.

3.6 The financial statements for Harridges Ltd are given below for the two years ended 30 June 2007 and 2008. Harridges Limited operates a department store in the centre of a small town.

Income statement for the years ended 30 June

	2007 £000	2008 £000
Sales revenue	2,600	3,500
Cost of sales	(1,560)	(2,350)
Gross profit	1,040	1,150
Wages and salaries	(320)	(350)
Overheads	(260)	(200)
Depreciation	(150)	(250)
Operating profit	310	350
Interest payable	(50)	(50)
Profit before taxation	260	300
Tax	(105)	(125)
Profit for the year	155	175

Statement of financial position (balance sheet) as at 30 June

	2007 £000	2008 £000
Non-current assets		
Property, plant and equipment	1,265	1,525
Current assets		
Inventories	250	400
Trade receivables	105	145
Cash at bank	380	115
	735	660
Total assets	2,000	2,185
Equity		
Share capital: £1 shares fully paid	490	490
Share premium	260	260
Retained earnings	350	450
	1,100	1,200
Non-current liabilities		
Borrowings – 10% loan notes	500	500
Current liabilities		
Trade payables	300	375
Other payables	100	110
	400	485
Total equity and liabilities	2,000	2,185

Dividends were paid on ordinary shares of £65,000 and £75,000 in respect of 2007 and 2008, respectively.

Required:

(a) Choose and calculate eight ratios that would be helpful in assessing the performance of Harridges Ltd. Use end-of-year values and calculate ratios for both 2007 and 2008.

(b) Using the ratios calculated in (a) and any others you consider helpful, comment on the business's performance from the viewpoint of a prospective purchaser of a majority of shares.

3.7 Genesis Ltd was incorporated in 2005 and has grown rapidly over the past three years. The rapid rate of growth has created problems for the business, which the directors have found difficult to deal with. Recently, a firm of management consultants has been asked to help the directors to overcome these problems.

In a preliminary report to the board of directors, the management consultants state: 'Most of the difficulties faced by the business are symptoms of an underlying problem of overtrading.'

The most recent financial statements of the business are set out below:

Statement of financial position (balance sheet) as at 31 October 2008

	£000	£000
Non-current assets		
Property, plant and equipment		
Land and buildings at cost	530	
Accumulated depreciation	(88)	442
Fixtures and fittings at cost	168	
Accumulated depreciation	(52)	116
Motor vans at cost	118	
Accumulated depreciation	(54)	64
		622
Current assets		
Inventories		128
Trade receivables		104
		232
Total assets		854
Equity		
Ordinary £0.50 shares		60
General reserve		50
Retained earnings		74
		184
Non-current liabilities		
Borrowings – 10% loan notes (secured)		120
Current liabilities		
Trade payables		184
Tax due		8
Short-term borrowings (all bank overdraft)		358
		550
Total equity and liabilities		854

Income statement for the year ended 31 October 2008

	£000	£000
Revenue		1,640
Cost of sales		
Opening inventories	116	
Purchases	1,260	
	1,376	
Closing inventories	(128)	(1,248)
Gross profit		392
Selling and distribution expenses		(204)
Administration expenses		(92)
Operating profit		96
Interest payable		(44)
Profit before taxation		52
Tax		(16)
Profit for the year		36

All purchases and sales were on credit.
A dividend was paid during the year on ordinary shares of £4,000.

Required:
(a) Explain the term 'overtrading' and state how overtrading might arise for a business.
(b) Discuss the kinds of problem that overtrading can create for a business.
(c) Calculate and discuss *five* financial ratios that might be used to establish whether the business is overtrading.
(d) State the ways in which a business may overcome the problem of overtrading.

4

Making capital investment decisions

INTRODUCTION

In this chapter we shall look at how businesses can make decisions involving investments in new plant, machinery, buildings and similar long-term assets. In making these decisions, businesses should be trying to pursue their key financial objective, which is to maximise the wealth of the owners (shareholders).

Investment appraisal is a very important area for businesses; expensive and far-reaching consequences can flow from bad investment decisions.

LEARNING OUTCOMES

When you have completed this chapter, you should be able to:

● Explain the nature and importance of investment decision making.

● Identify the four main investment appraisal methods found in practice.

● Use each method to reach a decision on a particular investment opportunity.

● Explain the methods used to monitor and control investment projects.

The nature of investment decisions

The essential feature of investment decisions is *time*. Investment involves making an outlay of something of economic value, usually cash, at one point in time, which is expected to yield economic benefits to the investor at some other point in time. Usually, the outlay precedes the benefits. Also, the outlay is typically one large amount and the benefits arrive as a series of smaller amounts over a fairly protracted period.

Investment decisions tend to be of profound importance to the business because:

● *Large amounts of resources are often involved.* Many investments made by businesses involve laying out a significant proportion of their total resources (see Real World 4.2). If mistakes are made with the decision, the effects on the businesses could be significant, if not catastrophic.
● *It is often difficult and/or expensive to bail out of an investment once it has been undertaken.* It is often the case that investments made by a business are specific to its needs. For example, a hotel business may invest in a new, custom-designed hotel complex. The specialist nature of this complex will probably lead to its having a rather limited second-hand value to another potential user with different needs. If the business found, after having made the investment, that room occupancy rates were not as buoyant as was planned, the only possible course of action might be to close down and sell the complex. This would probably mean that much less could be recouped from the investment than it had originally cost, particularly if the costs of design are included as part of the cost, as they logically should be.

Real World 4.1 gives an illustration of a major investment by a well-known business operating in the UK.

REAL WORLD 4.1

Brittany Ferries launches an investment

Brittany Ferries, the cross-Channel ferry operator, recently ordered a new ship to be named *Amorique*. The ship will cost the business about €81m and will be used on the Plymouth to Roscoff route as from autumn 2008. Although Brittany Ferries is a substantial business, this level of expenditure is significant. Clearly, the business believes that acquisition of the new ship will be profitable for it, but how would it have reached this conclusion? Presumably the anticipated future cash flows from passengers and freight operators will have been major inputs to the decision. The ship was specifically designed for Brittany Ferries, so it would be difficult for the business to recoup a large proportion of its €81m should these projected cash flows not materialise.

Source: 'New €81m passenger cruise-ferry to be named Amorique', www.brittany-ferries.co.uk.

The issues raised by Brittany Ferries' investment will be the main subject of this chapter.

Real World 4.2 indicates the level of annual net investment for a number of randomly selected, well-known UK businesses. It can be seen that the scale of investment varies from one business to another. (It also tends to vary from one year to the next for a particular business.) In nearly all of these businesses the scale of investment is very significant.

REAL WORLD 4.2

The scale of investment by UK businesses

	Expenditure on additional non-current assets as a percentage of:	
	Annual sales revenue	End-of-year non-current assets
BT plc (telecommunications)	15.9	17.5
Babcock International Group plc (support services)	6.8	20.6
Tesco plc (supermarkets)	5.5	11.6
J D Wetherspoon plc (pub operator)	12.5	9.0
Marks and Spencer plc (stores)	7.6	14.4
National Grid plc (utilities)	48.0	19.8
J. Sainsbury plc (supermarkets)	4.0	8.9
First Group plc (passenger transport)	5.7	13.1

Source: Annual reports of the businesses concerned for the financial year ending in 2007.

Real World 4.2 is limited to considering the non-current asset investment, but most non-current asset investment also requires a level of current asset investment to support it (additional inventories, for example), meaning that the real scale of investment is even greater, typically considerably so, than indicated above.

Activity 4.1

When managers are making decisions involving capital investments, what should the decision seek to achieve?

Investment decisions must be consistent with the objectives of the particular business. For a private-sector business, maximising the wealth of the owners (shareholders) is usually assumed to be the key financial objective.

Investment appraisal methods

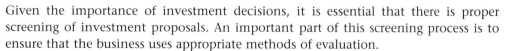

Given the importance of investment decisions, it is essential that there is proper screening of investment proposals. An important part of this screening process is to ensure that the business uses appropriate methods of evaluation.

Research shows that there are basically four methods used in practice by businesses throughout the world to evaluate investment opportunities. They are:

- accounting rate of return (ARR)
- payback period (PP)
- net present value (NPV)
- internal rate of return (IRR).

It is possible to find businesses that use variants of these four methods. It is also possible to find businesses, particularly smaller ones, which do not use any formal appraisal method but rely instead on the 'gut feeling' of their managers. Most businesses, however, seem to use one (or more) of these four methods.

We are going to assess the effectiveness of each of these methods and we shall see that only one of them (NPV) is a wholly logical approach. The other three all have flaws. We shall also see how popular these four methods seem to be in practice.

To help us to examine each of the methods, it might be useful to consider how each of them would cope with a particular investment opportunity. Let us consider the following example.

Example 4.1

Billingsgate Battery Company has carried out some research that shows that the business could provide a standard service that it has recently developed.

Provision of the service would require investment in a machine that would cost £100,000, payable immediately. Sales of the service would take place throughout the next five years. At the end of that time, it is estimated that the machine could be sold for £20,000.

Inflows and outflows from sales of the service would be expected to be as follows:

Time		£000
Immediately	Cost of machine	(100)
1 year's time	Operating profit before depreciation (£4 × 5,000)	20
2 years' time	Operating profit before depreciation (£4 × 10,000)	40
3 years' time	Operating profit before depreciation (£4 × 15,000)	60
4 years' time	Operating profit before depreciation (£4 × 15,000)	60
5 years' time	Operating profit before depreciation (£4 × 5,000)	20
5 years' time	Disposal proceeds from the machine	20

Note that, broadly speaking, the operating profit before deducting depreciation (that is, before non-cash items) equals the net amount of cash flowing into the business. Apart from depreciation, all of this business's expenses cause cash to flow out of the business. Sales revenues lead to cash flowing in. If, for the time being, we assume that inventories, trade receivables and trade payables remain constant, operating profit before depreciation will equal the cash inflow.

To simplify matters, we shall assume that the cash from sales and for the expenses of providing the service are received and paid, respectively, at the end of each year. This is clearly unlikely to be true in real life. Money will have to be paid to employees (for salaries and wages) on a weekly or a monthly basis. Customers will pay within a month or two of buying the service. On the other hand, making the assumption probably does not lead to a serious distortion. It is a simplifying assumption that is often made in real life, and it will make things more straightforward for us now. We should be clear, however, that there is nothing about any of the four methods that *demands* that this assumption is made.

Having set up the example, we shall now go on to consider how each of the appraisal methods works.

Accounting rate of return (ARR)

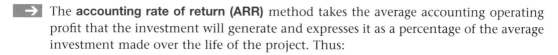

→ The **accounting rate of return (ARR)** method takes the average accounting operating profit that the investment will generate and expresses it as a percentage of the average investment made over the life of the project. Thus:

$$\text{ARR} = \frac{\text{Average annual operating profit}}{\text{Average investment to earn that profit}} \times 100\%$$

We can see from the equation that, to calculate the ARR, we need to deduce two pieces of information about the particular project:

- the annual average operating profit; and
- the average investment.

In our example, the average annual operating profit *before depreciation* over the five years is £40,000 (that is, £(20 + 40 + 60 + 60 + 20)/5). Assuming 'straight-line' depreciation (that is, equal annual amounts), the annual depreciation charge will be £16,000 (that is, £(100,000 – 20,000)/5). Thus the average annual operating profit *after depreciation* is £24,000 (that is, £40,000 – £16,000).

The average investment over the five years can be calculated as follows:

$$\text{Average investment} = \frac{\text{Cost of machine} + \text{Disposal value}}{2}$$

$$= \frac{£100,000 + £20,000}{2}$$

$$= £60,000$$

Thus, the ARR of the investment is:

$$\text{ARR} = \frac{£24,000}{£60,000} \times 100\% = 40\%$$

Users of ARR should apply the following decision rules:

- For any project to be acceptable it must achieve a target ARR as a minimum.
- Where there are competing projects that all seem capable of exceeding this minimum rate (that is, where the business must choose between more than one project), the one with the higher, or highest, ARR would normally be selected.

To decide whether the 40 per cent return is acceptable, we need to compare this percentage return with the minimum rate required by the business.

Activity 4.2

Chaotic Industries is considering an investment in a fleet of ten delivery vans to take its products to customers. The vans will cost £15,000 each to buy, payable immediately. The annual running costs are expected to total £20,000 for each van (including the driver's salary). The vans are expected to operate successfully for six years, at the end of which period they will all have to be sold, with disposal proceeds expected to be about £3,000 a van. At present, the business uses a commercial carrier for all of its

→

Activity 4.2 continued

deliveries. It is expected that this carrier will charge a total of £230,000 each year for the next six years to undertake the deliveries.

What is the ARR of buying the vans? (Note that cost savings are as relevant a benefit from an investment as are net cash inflows.)

The vans will save the business £30,000 a year (that is, £230,000 − (£20,000 × 10)), before depreciation, in total. Thus, the inflows and outflows will be:

Time		£000
Immediately	Cost of vans (10 × £15,000)	(150)
1 year's time	Net saving before depreciation	30
2 years' time	Net saving before depreciation	30
3 years' time	Net saving before depreciation	30
4 years' time	Net saving before depreciation	30
5 years' time	Net saving before depreciation	30
6 years' time	Net saving before depreciation	30
6 years' time	Disposal proceeds from the vans (10 × £3,000)	30

The total annual depreciation expense (assuming a straight-line method) will be £20,000 (that is, (£150,000 − £30,000)/6). Thus, the average annual saving, after depreciation, is £10,000 (that is, £30,000 − £20,000).

The average investment will be

$$\text{Average investment} = \frac{£150,000 + £30,000}{2}$$

$$= £90,000$$

and the ARR of the investment is

$$\text{ARR} = \frac{£10,000}{£90,000} \times 100\%$$

$$= 11.1\%$$

ARR and ROCE

We should note that ARR and the return on capital employed (ROCE) ratio, that we met in Chapter 3, take the same approach to performance measurement, in that they both relate accounting profit to the cost of the assets invested to generate that profit. ROCE is a popular means of assessing the performance of a business, as a whole, *after* it has performed. ARR is an approach that assesses the potential performance of a particular investment, taking the same approach as ROCE, but *before* it has performed.

As we have just seen, managers using ARR will require that any investment undertaken should achieve a target ARR as a minimum. Perhaps the minimum target ROCE would be based on the rate that previous investments had actually achieved (as measured by ROCE). Perhaps it would be the industry-average ROCE.

Since private sector businesses are normally seeking to increase the wealth of their owners, ARR may seem to be a sound method of appraising investment opportunities. Operating profit can be seen as a net increase in wealth over a period, and relating it to the size of investment made to achieve it seems a logical approach.

ARR is said to have a number of advantages as a method of investment appraisal. It was mentioned earlier that ROCE seems to be a widely used measure of business performance. Shareholders seem to use this ratio to evaluate management performance, and sometimes the financial objective of a business will be expressed in terms of a target ROCE. It therefore seems sensible to use a method of investment appraisal that is consistent with this overall approach to measuring business performance. It also gives the result expressed as a percentage. It seems that some managers feel comfortable using measures expressed in percentage terms.

Problems with ARR

Activity 4.3

ARR suffers from a very major defect as a means of assessing investment opportunities. Can you reason out what this is? Consider the three competing projects whose profits are shown below. All three involve investment in a machine that is expected to have no residual value at the end of the five years. Note that all of the projects have the same total operating profits over the five years.

Time		Project A	Project B	Project C
		£000	£000	£000
Immediately	Cost of machine	(160)	(160)	(160)
1 year's time	Operating profit after depreciation	20	10	160
2 years' time	Operating profit after depreciation	40	10	10
3 years' time	Operating profit after depreciation	60	10	10
4 years' time	Operating profit after depreciation	60	10	10
5 years' time	Operating profit after depreciation	20	160	10

(*Hint*: The defect is not concerned with the ability of the decision maker to forecast future events, although this too can be a problem. Try to remember the essential feature of investment decisions, which we identified at the beginning of this chapter.)

The problem with ARR is that it almost completely ignores the time factor. In this example, exactly the same ARR would have been computed for each of the three projects.

Since the same total operating profit over the five years (£200,000) arises in all three of these projects, and the average investment in each project is £80,000 (that is, £160,000/2), this means that each case will give rise to the same ARR of 50 per cent (that is, £40,000/£80,000).

Given a financial objective of maximising the wealth of the owners of the business, any rational decision maker faced with a choice between the three projects set out in Activity 4.3 would strongly prefer Project C. This is because most of the benefits from the investment arise within twelve months of investing the £160,000 to establish the project. Project A would rank second and Project B would come a poor third. Any appraisal technique that is not capable of distinguishing between these three situations is seriously flawed. We shall look at why timing is so important later in the chapter.

There are further problems associated with the use of ARR. One of these problems concerns the approach taken to derive the average investment in a project.

Example 4.2 illustrates the daft result that ARR can produce.

Example 4.2

George put forward an investment proposal to his boss. The business uses ARR to assess investment proposals using a minimum 'hurdle' rate of 27 per cent. Details of the proposal were as follows:

Cost of equipment	£200,000
Estimated residual value of equipment	£40,000
Average annual operating profit before depreciation	£48,000
Estimated life of project	10 years
Annual straight-line depreciation charge	£16,000 (that is, £(200,000 – £40,000)/10)

The ARR of the project will be:

$$\text{ARR} = \frac{48,000 - 16,000}{(200,000 + 40,000)/2} \times 100\% = 26.7\%$$

The boss rejected George's proposal because it failed to achieve an ARR of at least 27 per cent. Although George was disappointed, he realised that there was still hope. In fact, all that the business had to do was to give away the piece of equipment at the end of its useful life rather than to sell it. The residual value of the equipment then became zero and the annual depreciation charge became ([£200,000 – £0]/10) = £20,000 a year. The revised ARR calculation was then as follows:

$$\text{ARR} = \frac{48,000 - 20,000}{(200,000 + 0)/2} \times 100\% = 28\%$$

ARR is based on the use of accounting profit. When measuring performance over the whole life of a project, however, it is cash flows rather than accounting profits that are important. Cash is the ultimate measure of the economic wealth generated by an investment. This is because it is cash that is used to acquire resources and for distribution to owners. Accounting profit, on the other hand is more appropriate for reporting achievement on a periodic basis. It is a useful measure of productive effort for a relatively short period, such as a year or half year. It is really a question of 'horses for courses'. Accounting profit is fine for measuring performance over short period but cash is the appropriate measure when considering the performance over the life of a project.

The ARR method can also create problems when considering competing investments of different size.

Activity 4.4

Sinclair Wholesalers plc is currently considering opening a new sales outlet in Coventry. Two possible sites have been identified for the new outlet. Site A has an area of 30,000 sq m. It will require an average investment of £6m, and will produce an average operating profit of £600,000 a year. Site B has an area of 20,000 sq m. It will require an average investment of £4m, and will produce an average operating profit of £500,000 a year.

What is the ARR of each investment opportunity? Which site would you select, and why?

. . . .

The ARR of Site A is £600,000/£6m = 10 per cent. The ARR of Site B is £500,000/£4m = 12.5 per cent. Thus, Site B has the higher ARR. However, in terms of the absolute operating profit generated, Site A is the more attractive. If the ultimate objective is to increase the wealth of the shareholders of Sinclair Wholesalers plc, it might be better to choose Site A even though the percentage return is lower. It is the absolute size of the return rather than the relative (percentage) size that is important. This is a general problem of using comparative measures, such as percentages, when the objective is measured in absolute ones, like an amount of money. If businesses were seeking through their investments to generate a percentage rate of return on investment, ARR would be more helpful. The problem is that most businesses seek to achieve increases in their absolute wealth (measured in pounds, euros, dollars and so on), through their investment decisions.

Real World 4.3 illustrates how using percentage measures can lead to confusion.

 REAL WORLD 4.3

Increasing road capacity by sleight of hand

During the 1970s, the Mexican government wanted to increase the capacity of a major four-lane road. It came up with the idea of repainting the lane markings so that there were six narrower lanes occupying the same space as four wider ones had previously done. This increased the capacity of the road by 50 per cent (that is, $^2/_4 \times 100$). A tragic outcome of the narrower lanes was an increase in deaths from road accidents. A year later the Mexican government had the six narrower lanes changed back to the original four wider ones. This reduced the capacity of the road by 33 per cent (that is, $^2/_6 \times 100$). The Mexican government reported that, overall, it had increased the capacity of the road by 17 per cent (that is, 50% − 33%), despite the fact that its real capacity was identical to that which it had been originally. The confusion arose because each of the two percentages (50 per cent and 33 per cent) is based on different bases (four and six).

Source: Gigerenzer (see reference 1 at the end of the chapter).

Payback period (PP)

The **payback period (PP)** is the length of time it takes for an initial investment to be repaid out of the net cash inflows from a project. Since it takes time into account, the PP method seems to go some way to overcoming the timing problem of ARR – or at first glance it does.

It might be useful to consider PP in the context of the Billingsgate Battery Company example (see Activity 4.1). We should recall that essentially the project's cash flows are:

Time		£000
Immediately	Cost of machine	(100)
1 year's time	Operating profit before depreciation	20
2 years' time	Operating profit before depreciation	40
3 years' time	Operating profit before depreciation	60
4 years' time	Operating profit before depreciation	60
5 years' time	Operating profit before depreciation	20
5 years' time	Disposal proceeds	20

Note that all of these figures are amounts of cash to be paid or received (we saw earlier that operating profit before depreciation is a rough measure of the cash flows from the project).

As the payback period is the length of time it takes for the initial investment to be repaid out of the net cash inflows, it will be three years before the £100,000 outlay is covered by the inflows. This is still assuming that the cash flows occur at year ends. The payback period can be derived by calculating the cumulative cash flows as follows:

Time		Net cash flows £000	Cumulative cash flows £000	
Immediately	Cost of machine	(100)	(100)	
1 year's time	Operating profit before depreciation	20	(80)	(−100 + 20)
2 years' time	Operating profit before depreciation	40	(40)	(−80 + 40)
3 years' time	Operating profit before depreciation	60	20	(−40 + 60)
4 years' time	Operating profit before depreciation	60	80	(20 + 60)
5 years' time	Operating profit before depreciation	20	100	(80 + 20)
5 years' time	Disposal proceeds	20	120	(100 + 20)

We can see that the cumulative cash flows become positive at the end of the third year. Had we assumed that the cash flows arise evenly over the year, the precise payback period would be:

$$2 \text{ years} + (^{40}/_{60}) \text{ years} = 2^{2}/_{3} \text{ years}$$

where 40 represents the cash flow still required at the beginning of the third year to repay the initial outlay, and 60 is the projected cash flow during the third year.

We must now ask how to decide whether three years is an acceptable payback period. The decision rule for using PP is:

- For a project to be acceptable it would need to have a payback period shorter than a maximum payback period set by the business.
- If there were two (or more) competing projects whose payback periods were all shorter than the maximum payback period requirement, the project with the shorter (shortest) payback period should be selected.

If, for example, Billingsgate Battery had a maximum acceptable payback period of four years, the project would be undertaken. A project with a longer payback period than four years would not be acceptable.

Activity 4.5

What is the payback period of the Chaotic Industries project from Activity 4.2?

The inflows and outflows are expected to be:

Time		Net cash flows £000	Cumulative net cash flows £000	
Immediately	Cost of vans	(150)	(150)	
1 year's time	Net saving before depreciation	30	(120)	(−150 + 30)
2 years' time	Net saving before depreciation	30	(90)	(−120 + 30)
3 years' time	Net saving before depreciation	30	(60)	(−90 + 30)
4 years' time	Net saving before depreciation	30	(30)	(−60 + 30)
5 years' time	Net saving before depreciation	30	0	(−30 + 30)
6 years' time	Net saving before depreciation	30	30	(0 + 30)
6 years' time	Disposal proceeds from the machine	30	60	(30 + 30)

The payback period here is five years; that is, it is not until the end of the fifth year that the vans will pay for themselves out of the savings that they are expected to generate.

The PP method has certain advantages. It is quick and easy to calculate, and can be easily understood by managers. The logic of using PP is that projects that can recoup their cost quickly are economically more attractive than those with longer payback periods, that is, it emphasises liquidity. PP is probably an improvement on ARR in respect of the timing of the cash flows. PP is not, however, the whole answer to the problem.

Problems with PP

Activity 4.6

In what respect is PP not the whole answer as a means of assessing investment opportunities? Consider the cash flows arising from three competing projects:

Time		Project 1 £000	Project 2 £000	Project 3 £000
Immediately	Cost of machine	(200)	(200)	(200)
1 year's time	Operating profit before depreciation	40	10	80
2 years' time	Operating profit before depreciation	80	20	100
3 years' time	Operating profit before depreciation	80	170	20
4 years' time	Operating profit before depreciation	60	20	200
5 years' time	Operating profit before depreciation	40	10	500
5 years' time	Disposal proceeds	40	10	20

(*Hint*: Again, the defect is not concerned with the ability of the manager to forecast future events. This is a problem, but it is a problem whatever approach we take.)

The PP for each project is three years and so the PP method would regard the projects as being equally acceptable. It cannot distinguish between those projects that pay back a significant amount early in the three-year payback period and those that do not.

In addition, this method ignores cash flows after the payback period. A decision maker concerned with increasing owners' wealth would prefer Project 3 because the cash flows come in earlier (most of the initial cost of making the investment has been repaid by the end of the second year) and they are greater in total.

The cumulative cash flows of each project in Activity 4.6 are set out in Figure 4.1.

We can see that the PP method is not concerned with the profitability of projects; it is concerned simply with their payback period. Thus cash flows arising beyond the payback period are ignored. While this neatly avoids the practical problems of forecasting cash flows over a long period, it means that relevant information may be ignored.

We may feel that, by favouring projects with a short payback period, the PP method does at least provide a means of dealing with the problems of risk and uncertainty. However, this is a fairly crude approach to the problem. It looks only at the risk that the project will end earlier than expected. However, this is only one of many risk areas. What, for example, about the risk that the demand for the product may be less than expected? There are more systematic approaches to dealing with risk that can be used and we shall look at these in the following chapter.

PP takes some note of the timing of the costs and benefits from the project. Its key deficiency, however, is that it is not linked to promoting increases in the wealth of the business and its owners. PP will tend to recommend undertaking projects that pay for themselves quickly.

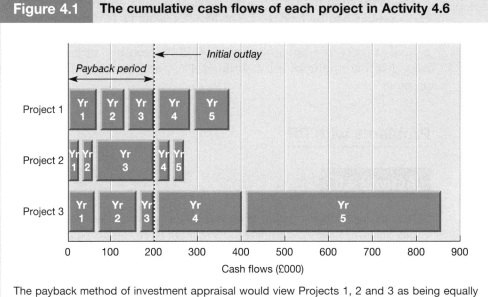

Figure 4.1   **The cumulative cash flows of each project in Activity 4.6**

The payback method of investment appraisal would view Projects 1, 2 and 3 as being equally attractive. In doing so, the method completely ignores the fact that Project 3 provides the payback cash earlier in the three-year period and goes on to generate large benefits in later years.

The PP method requires the managers of a business to select a maximum acceptable payback period. This maximum period, in practice, will vary from one business to the next. **Real World 4.4** provides some evidence of the length of payback period required by small to medium-size businesses when investing in new forms of energy generation.

REAL WORLD 4.4

Payback time

When it comes to self-generation of renewable energy, UK SMEs (small and medium-size enterprises) want an unrealistically quick return on investment according to research carried out by energy consultancy energyTEAM. Nearly three-quarters would need payback within three years in order to justify introducing such measures. Only four per cent are prepared for this process to take over five years despite growing concern over commercial energy usage. EnergyTEAM's study revealed that 40 per cent of enterprises with 50 to 500 employees would have to be convinced of a return on investment in just one year before they would proceed down the route of self-generation.

When asked which method of self-generation they would be most inclined to choose, over half of respondents highlighted solar power as the preferred method. This is despite the fact that solar has one of the largest payback times, at around ten years.

Brian Rickerby, joint Managing Director of energyTEAM, said, 'I can understand that seeking a quick, return is a pragmatic, business-like approach, but unfortunately this is not realistic when it comes to energy issues. Self-generation technologies must be viewed as a long-term strategy that will have a significant positive impact for many years to come.'

Source: 'SMEs' unrealistic demands on renewables', *Sustain*, Vol. 8, Issue 5, 2007, p. 74.

Net present value (NPV)

From what we have seen so far, it seems that to make sensible investment decisions, we need a method of appraisal that both:

● considers *all* of the costs and benefits of each investment opportunity; and
● makes a logical allowance for the *timing* of those costs and benefits.

The **net present value (NPV)** method provides us with this.

Consider the Billingsgate Battery Company's cash flows, which we should recall (from Activity 4.1) can be summarised as follows:

Time		£000
Immediately	Cost of machine	(100)
1 year's time	Operating profit before depreciation	20
2 years' time	Operating profit before depreciation	40
3 years' time	Operating profit before depreciation	60
4 years' time	Operating profit before depreciation	60
5 years' time	Operating profit before depreciation	20
5 years' time	Disposal proceeds	20

Given that the principal financial objective of the business is to increase owners' wealth, it would be very easy to assess this investment if all of the cash inflows and outflows were to occur now (all at the same time). All that we should need to do would be to add up the cash inflows (total £220,000) and compare them with the cash outflows (£100,000). This would lead us to the conclusion that the project should go ahead because the business, and its owners, would be better off by £120,000. Of course, it is not as easy as this because time is involved. The cash outflow (payment) will occur immediately if the project is undertaken. The inflows (receipts) will arise at a range of later times.

The time factor is an important issue because people do not normally see £100 paid out now as equivalent in value to £100 receivable in a year's time. If we were to be offered £100 in 12 months' time in exchange for paying out £100 now, we should not be prepared to do so unless we wished to do someone a favour.

Activity 4.7

Why would you see £100 to be received in a year's time as not equal in value to £100 to be paid immediately? (There are basically three reasons.)

The reasons are:

● interest lost
● risk
● effects of inflation.

We shall now take a closer look at these three reasons in turn.

Interest lost

If we are to be deprived of the opportunity to spend our money for a year, we could equally well be deprived of its use by placing it on deposit in a bank or building society. In this case, at the end of the year we could have our money back and have interest as well. Thus, by investing the funds in some other way, we shall be incurring an *opportunity cost*. An opportunity cost occurs where one course of action, for example making an investment, deprives us of the opportunity to derive some benefit from an alternative action, for example putting the money in the bank and earning interest.

From this we can see that any investment opportunity must, if it is to make us wealthier, do better than the returns that are available from the next best opportunity. Thus, if Billingsgate Battery Company sees putting the money in the bank on deposit as the alternative to investment in the machine, the return from investing in the machine must be better than that from investing in the bank. If the bank offered a better return, the business, and its owners, would become wealthier by putting the money on deposit.

Risk

Buying a machine to manufacture a product, or to provide a service, to be sold in the market, on the strength of various estimates made in advance of buying the machine, exposes the business to **risk**. Things may not turn out as expected.

Activity 4.8

Can you suggest some areas where things could go other than according to plan in the Billingsgate Battery Company example?

We have come up with the following:

- The machine might not work as well as expected; it might break down, leading to loss of the business's ability to provide the service.
- Sales of the service may not be as buoyant as expected.
- Labour costs may prove to be higher than expected.
- The sale proceeds of the machine could prove to be less than were estimated.

It is important to remember that the decision whether to invest in the machine must be taken *before* any of these things are known. It is only after the machine has been purchased that we could discover that the level of sales, which had been estimated before the event, is not going to be achieved. It is not possible to wait until we know for certain whether the market will behave as we expected before we buy the machine. We can study reports and analyses of the market. We can commission sophisticated market surveys, and these may give us more confidence in the likely outcome. We can advertise widely and try to promote sales. Ultimately, however, we have to decide whether to jump off into the dark and accept the risk if we want the opportunity to make profitable investments.

Real World 4.5 gives some some impression of the extent to which businesses believe that investment outcomes turn out as expected.

REAL WORLD 4.5

Size matters

A sample of 99 Cambridgeshire manufacturing businesses were surveyed and asked the extent to which past investments performed in line with earlier expectations. The results, broken down according to business size, are set out below.

	Size of business			
	Large	Medium	Small	All
Under-performed	8%	14%	32%	14%
Performed as expected	82%	72%	68%	77%
Over-performed	10%	14%	0%	9%

It seems that smaller businesses are much more likely to get it wrong than medium-size or larger businesses. This may be because small businesses are often younger and, therefore, less experienced in the techniques of both forecasting and managing investment projects. They are also likely to have less financial expertise. It also seems that small businesses have a distinct bias towards over-optimism and do not take full account of the possibility that things will turn out worse than expected.

Source: Baddeley, M., Unpacking the black box: An econometric analysis of investment strategies in real world firms, CEPP Working Paper No. 08/05, University of Cambridge, p. 14.

Normally, people expect to receive greater returns where they perceive risk to be a factor. Examples of this in real life are not difficult to find. One such example is that banks tend to charge higher rates of interest to borrowers whom the bank perceives as more risky. Those who can offer good security for a loan, and who can point to a regular source of income, tend to be charged lower rates of interest.

Going back to Billingsgate Battery Company's investment opportunity, it is not enough to say that we should not advise making the investment unless the returns from it are as high as those from investing in a bank deposit. Clearly we should want returns above the level of bank deposit interest rates, because the logical equivalent of investing in the machine is not putting the money on deposit but making an alternative investment that is risky.

In practice, we tend to expect a higher rate of return from investment projects where the risk is perceived as being higher. How risky a particular project is, and therefore how large this **risk premium** should be, are matters that are difficult to handle. It is usually necessary to make some judgement on these questions.

Inflation

If we are to be deprived of £100 for a year, when we come to spend that money it will not buy as many goods and services as it would have done a year earlier. Generally, we shall not be able to buy as many tins of baked beans or loaves of bread or bus tickets as we could have done a year earlier. This is because of the loss in the purchasing power of money, or **inflation**, which occurs over time. Clearly, the investor needs compensating for this loss of purchasing power if the investment is to be made. This compensation is on top of a return that takes account of what could have been gained from an alternative investment of similar risk.

In practice, interest rates observable in the market tend to take inflation into account. Rates that are offered to potential building society and bank depositors include an allowance for the rate of inflation that is expected in the future.

What will a logical investor do?

A logical investor who is seeking to increase his or her wealth will only be prepared to make investments that will compensate for the loss of interest and purchasing power of the money invested and for the fact that the returns expected may not materialise (risk). This is usually assessed by seeing whether the proposed investment will yield a return that is greater than the basic rate of interest (which would include an allowance for inflation) plus a risk premium.

These three factors (interest lost, risk and inflation) are set out in Figure 4.2.

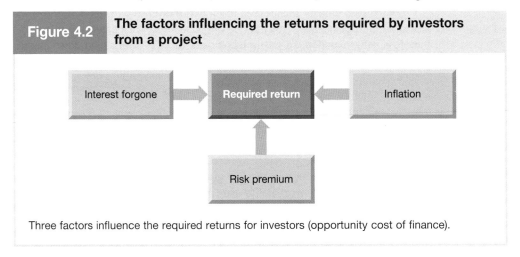

| Figure 4.2 | **The factors influencing the returns required by investors from a project** |

Three factors influence the required returns for investors (opportunity cost of finance).

Naturally, investors need at least the minimum returns before they are prepared to invest. However, it is in terms of the effect on their wealth that they should logically assess an investment project. Usually it is the investment with the highest percentage return that will make the investor most wealthy, but we shall see later in this chapter that this is not always the case. For the time being, therefore, we shall concentrate on wealth.

Let us now return to the Billingsgate Battery Company example. We should recall that the cash flows expected from this investment are:

Time		£000
Immediately	Cost of machine	(100)
1 year's time	Operating profit before depreciation	20
2 years' time	Operating profit before depreciation	40
3 years' time	Operating profit before depreciation	60
4 years' time	Operating profit before depreciation	60
5 years' time	Operating profit before depreciation	20
5 years' time	Disposal proceeds	20

We have already seen that it is not sufficient just to compare the basic cash inflows and outflows for the investment. It would be useful if we could express each of these cash flows in similar terms, so that we could make a direct comparison between the sum of the inflows over time and the immediate £100,000 investment. Fortunately, we can do this.

Let us assume that, instead of making this investment, the business could make an alternative investment with similar risk and obtain a return of 20 per cent a year.

Activity 4.9

We know that Billingsgate Battery Company could alternatively invest its money at a rate of 20 per cent a year. How much do you judge the present (immediate) value of the expected first year receipt of £20,000 to be? In other words, if instead of having to wait a year for the £20,000, and being deprived of the opportunity to invest it at 20 per cent, you could have some money now, what sum to be received now would you regard as exactly equivalent to getting £20,000 but having to wait a year for it?

We should obviously be happy to accept a lower amount if we could get it immediately than if we had to wait a year. This is because we could invest it at 20 per cent (in the alternative project). Logically, we should be prepared to accept the amount that, with a year's income, will grow to £20,000. If we call this amount PV (for present value) we can say:

$$PV + (PV \times 20\%) = £20,000$$

That is, the amount plus income from investing the amount for the year, equals the £20,000.

If we rearrange this equation we find:

$$PV \times (1 + 0.2) = £20,000$$

(Note that 0.2 is the same as 20 per cent, but expressed as a decimal.) Further rearranging gives:

$$PV = £20,000/(1 + 0.2) = £16,667$$

Thus, rational investors who have the opportunity to invest at 20 per cent a year would not mind whether they have £16,667 now or £20,000 in a year's time. In this sense we can say that, given a 20 per cent alternative investment opportunity, the present value of £20,000 to be received in one year's time is £16,667.

If we could derive the present value (PV) of each of the cash flows associated with Billingsgate's machine investment, we could easily make the direct comparison between the cost of making the investment (£100,000) and the various benefits that will derive from it in years 1 to 5. In fact, we can do this.

We can make a more general statement about the PV of a particular cash flow. It is:

PV of the cash flow of year n = actual cash flow of year n divided by $(1 + r)^n$

where n is the year of the cash flow (that is, how many years into the future) and r is the opportunity investing rate expressed as a decimal (instead of as a percentage).

We have already seen how this works for the £20,000 inflow for year 1 for the Billingsgate project. For year 2 the calculation would be:

$$\text{PV of year 2 cash flow (that is, £40,000)} = \frac{£40,000}{(1 + 0.2)^2} = \frac{£40,000}{(1.2)^2}$$

$$= \frac{£40,000}{1.44} = £27,778$$

Thus the present value of the £40,000 to be received in two years' time is £27,778.

Activity 4.10

See if you can show that an investor would find £27,778, receivable now, as equally acceptable to receiving £40,000 in two years' time, assuming that there is a 20 per cent investment opportunity.

The reasoning goes like this:

	£
Amount available for immediate investment	27,778
Add Interest for year 1 (20% × 27,778)	5,556
	33,334
Add Interest for year 2 (20% × 33,334)	6,667
	40,001

(The extra £1 is only a rounding error.)

This is to say that since the investor can turn £27,778 into £40,000 in two years, these amounts are equivalent. We can say that £27,778 is the present value of £40,000 receivable after two years (given a 20 per cent rate of return).

Now let us calculate the present values of all of the cash flows associated with the Billingsgate machine project and from them the *net present value (NPV)* of the project as a whole.

The relevant cash flows and calculations are as follows:

Time	Cash flow £000	Calculation of PV	PV £000
Immediately (time 0)	(100)	$(100)/(1 + 0.2)^0$	(100.00)
1 year's time	20	$20/(1 + 0.2)^1$	16.67
2 years' time	40	$40/(1 + 0.2)^2$	27.78
3 years' time	60	$60/(1 + 0.2)^3$	34.72
4 years' time	60	$60/(1 + 0.2)^4$	28.94
5 years' time	20	$20/(1 + 0.2)^5$	8.04
5 years' time	20	$20/(1 + 0.2)^5$	8.04
Net present value (NPV)			24.19

Note that $(1 + 0.2)^0 = 1$.

Once again, we must ask how we can decide whether the machine project is acceptable to the business. In fact, the decision rule for NPV is simple:

- If the NPV is positive the project should be accepted; if it is negative the project should be rejected.
- If there are two (or more) competing projects that have positive NPVs, the project with the higher (or highest) NPV should be selected.

In this case, the NPV is positive, so we should accept the project and buy the machine. The reasoning behind this decision rule is quite straightforward. Investing in the machine will make the business, and its owners, £24,190 better off than they would be by taking up the next best opportunity available to it. The gross benefits from investing in this machine are worth a total of £124,190 today, and since the business can 'buy' these benefits for just £100,000 today, the investment should be made. If, however, the present value of the gross benefits were below £100,000, it would be less than the cost of 'buying' those benefits.

Activity 4.11

What is the *maximum* the Billingsgate Battery Company would be prepared to pay for the machine, given the potential benefits of owning it?

The business would logically be prepared to pay up to £124,190 since the wealth of the owners of the business would be increased up to this price – although the business would prefer to pay as little as possible.

Using discount tables

Deducing the present values of the various cash flows is a little laborious using the approach that we have just taken. To deduce each PV we took the relevant cash flow and multiplied it by $1/(1 + r)^n$. There is a slightly different way to do this. Tables exist that show values of this **discount factor** for a range of values of r and n. Such a table appears at the end of this book, on p. 527. Take a look at it.

Look at the column for 20 per cent and the row for one year. We find that the factor is 0.833. This means that the PV of a cash flow of £1 receivable in one year is £0.833. So the present value of a cash flow of £20,000 receivable in one year's time is £16,660 (that is, 0.833 × £20,000), the same result as we found doing it in longhand.

Activity 4.12

What is the NPV of the Chaotic Industries project from Activity 4.2, assuming a 15 per cent opportunity cost of finance (discount rate)? You should use the discount table on p. 527.

Remember that the inflows and outflow are expected to be:

Time		£000
Immediately	Cost of vans	(150)
1 year's time	Net saving before depreciation	30
2 years' time	Net saving before depreciation	30
3 years' time	Net saving before depreciation	30
4 years' time	Net saving before depreciation	30
5 years' time	Net saving before depreciation	30
6 years' time	Net saving before depreciation	30
6 years' time	Disposal proceeds from the machine	30

The calculation of the NPV of the project is as follows:

Time	Cash flows	Discount factor (15% – from the table)	Present value
	£000		£000
Immediately	(150)	1.000	(150.00)
1 year's time	30	0.870	26.10
2 years' time	30	0.756	22.68
3 years' time	30	0.658	19.74
4 years' time	30	0.572	17.16
5 years' time	30	0.497	14.91
6 years' time	30	0.432	12.96
6 years' time	30	0.432	12.96
		NPV	(23.49)

Activity 4.13

How would you interpret this result?

....

The fact that the project has a negative NPV means that the present values of the benefits from the investment are worth less than the cost of entering into it. Any cost up to £126,510 (the present value of the benefits) would be worth paying, but not £150,000.

The discount table shows how the value of £1 diminishes as its receipt goes further into the future. Assuming an opportunity cost of finance of 20 per cent a year, £1 to be received immediately, obviously, has a present value of £1. However, as the time before it is to be received increases, the present value diminishes significantly, as is shown in Figure 4.3.

Figure 4.3	**Present value of £1 receivable at various times in the future, assuming an annual financing cost of 20 per cent**

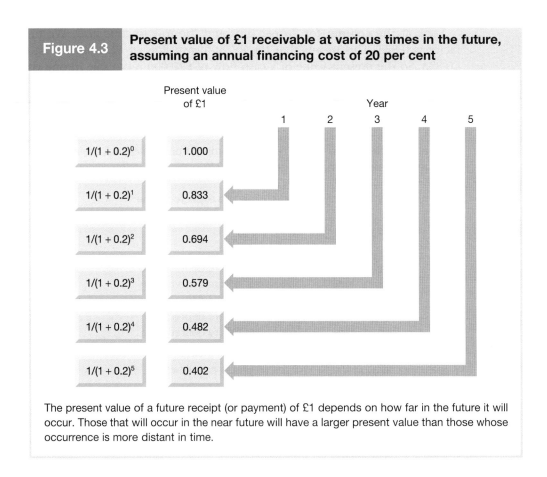

The present value of a future receipt (or payment) of £1 depends on how far in the future it will occur. Those that will occur in the near future will have a larger present value than those whose occurrence is more distant in time.

The discount rate and the cost of capital

We have seen that the appropriate discount rate to use in NPV assessments is the opportunity cost of finance. This is often referred to as the **cost of capital**. The way in which we determine the cost of capital for a particular business will be considered in some detail in Chapter 8.

Why NPV is better

From what we have seen, NPV seems to be a better method of appraising investment opportunities than either ARR or PP. This is because it fully takes account of each of the following:

- *The timing of the cash flows.* By discounting the various cash flows associated with each project according to when each one is expected to arise, NPV takes account of the time value of money. Associated with this is the fact that by discounting, using the opportunity cost of finance (that is, the return that the next best alternative opportunity would generate), the net benefit *after* financing costs have been met is identified (as the NPV of the project).
- *The whole of the relevant cash flows.* NPV includes *all* of the relevant cash flows irrespective of when they are expected to occur. It treats them differently according to their date of occurrence, but they are all taken into account in the NPV, and they all have an influence on the decision.
- *The objectives of the business.* NPV is the only method of appraisal in which the output of the analysis has a direct bearing on the wealth of the owners of the business (with a limited company, the shareholders). Positive NPVs enhance wealth; negative ones reduce it. Since we assume that private-sector businesses seek to increase owners' wealth, NPV is superior to the other two methods (ARR and PP) that we have already discussed.

We saw earlier that a business should take on all projects with positive NPVs, when their cash flows are discounted at the opportunity cost of finance. Where a choice has to be made between projects, the business should normally select the one with the higher or highest NPV.

NPV's wider application

NPV is considered the most logical approach to making business decisions about investments in productive assets. The same logic makes NPV equally valid as the best approach to take when trying to place a value on any economic asset, that is, an asset that seems capable of yielding financial benefits. This would include a share in a limited company and a loan. In fact, when we talk of *economic value*, we mean a value that has been derived by adding together the discounted (present) values of all future cash flows from the asset concerned.

Real World 4.6 provides an estimate of the NPV that is expected from one interesting project.

 REAL WORLD 4.6

A real diamond geezer   **FT**

Alan Bond, the disgraced Australian businessman and America's Cup winner, is looking at ways to raise money in London for an African diamond mining project. Lesotho Diamond Corporation (LDC), is a private company in which Mr Bond has a large interest. LDC's main asset is a 93 per cent stake in the Kao diamond project in the southern African kingdom of Lesotho.

Real World 4.6 continued

Mr Bond says, on his personal website, that the Kao project is forecast to yield 5m carats of diamonds over the next 10 years and could become Lesotho's biggest foreign currency earner.

SRK, the mining consultants, has estimated the net present value of the project at £129m.

It is understood that Mr Bond and his family own about 40 per cent of LDC. Mr Bond has described himself as 'spearheading' the Kao project.

Source: Adapted from Rebecca Bream, 'Bond seeks funds in London to mine African diamonds', www.ft.com, 23 April 2007.

Internal rate of return (IRR)

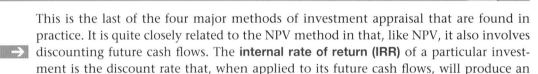

This is the last of the four major methods of investment appraisal that are found in practice. It is quite closely related to the NPV method in that, like NPV, it also involves discounting future cash flows. The **internal rate of return (IRR)** of a particular investment is the discount rate that, when applied to its future cash flows, will produce an NPV of precisely zero. In essence, it represents the yield from an investment opportunity.

Activity 4.14

We should recall that, when we discounted the cash flows of the Billingsgate Battery Company machine investment opportunity at 20 per cent, we found that the NPV was a positive figure of £24,190 (see p. 138). What does the NPV of the machine project tell us about the rate of return that the investment will yield for the business?

The fact that the NPV is positive when discounting at 20 per cent implies that the rate of return that the project generates is more than 20 per cent. The fact that the NPV is a pretty large figure implies that the actual rate of return is quite a lot above 20 per cent. We should expect increasing the size of the discount rate to reduce NPV, because a higher discount rate gives a lower discounted figure.

It is somewhat laborious to deduce the IRR by hand, since it cannot usually be calculated directly. Iteration (trial and error) is the approach that must usually be adopted. Fortunately, computer spreadsheet packages can deduce the IRR with ease. The package will also use a trial and error approach, but at high speed.

Despite it being laborious, we shall now go on and derive the IRR for the Billingsgate project by hand.

Let us try a higher rate, say 30 per cent, and see what happens.

Time	Cash flow	Discount factor	PV
	£000	(30%)	£000
Immediately (time 0)	(100)	1.000	(100.00)
1 year's time	20	0.769	15.38
2 years' time	40	0.592	23.68
3 years' time	60	0.455	27.30
4 years' time	60	0.350	21.00
5 years' time	20	0.269	5.38
5 years' time	20	0.269	5.38
		NPV	(1.88)

In increasing the discount rate from 20 per cent to 30 per cent, we have reduced the NPV from £24,190 (positive) to £1,880 (negative). Since the IRR is the discount rate that will give us an NPV of exactly zero, we can conclude that the IRR of Billingsgate Battery Company's machine project is very slightly below 30 per cent. Further trials could lead us to the exact rate, but there is probably not much point, given the likely inaccuracy of the cash flow estimates. It is probably good enough, for practical purposes, to say that the IRR is about 30 per cent.

The relationship between the NPV method discussed earlier and the IRR is shown graphically in Figure 4.4 using the information relating to the Billingsgate Battery Company.

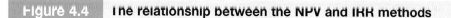

Figure 4.4   The relationship between the NPV and IRR methods

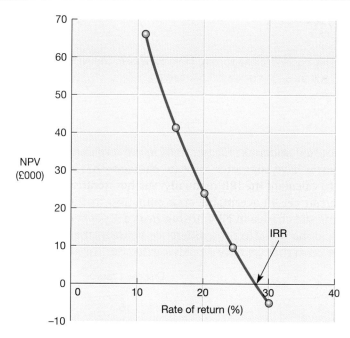

If the discount rate were zero, the NPV would be the sum of the net cash flows. In other words, no account would be taken of the time value of money. However, if we assume increasing discount rates, there is a corresponding decrease in the NPV of the project. When the NPV line crosses the horizontal axis there will be a zero NPV, and the point where it crosses is the IRR.

We can see that, where the discount rate is zero, the NPV will be the sum of the net cash flows. In other words, no account is taken of the time value of money. However, as the discount rate increases there is a corresponding decrease in the NPV of the project. When the NPV line crosses the horizontal axis there will be a zero NPV, and that represents the IRR.

Activity 4.15

What is the internal rate of return of the Chaotic Industries project from Activity 4.2?
   You should use the discount table on p. 527. (*Hint*: Remember that you already know the NPV of this project at 15 per cent (from Activity 4.12).)

Since we know that, at a 15 per cent discount rate, the NPV is a relatively large negative figure, our next trial is using a lower discount rate, say 10 per cent:

Time	Cash flows £000	Discount factor (10% – from the table)	Present value £000
Immediately	(150)	1.000	(150.00)
1 year's time	30	0.909	27.27
2 years' time	30	0.826	24.78
3 years' time	30	0.751	22.53
4 years' time	30	0.683	20.49
5 years' time	30	0.621	18.63
6 years' time	30	0.565	16.95
6 years' time	30	0.565	16.95
		NPV	(2.40)

This figure is close to zero NPV. However, the NPV is still negative and so the precise IRR will be a little below 10 per cent.

We could undertake further trials in order to derive the precise IRR. In practice, most businesses have computer software packages that will do this quickly. If, however, we have to calculate the IRR manually, further iterations can be time consuming.

We can get an acceptable approximation to the answer fairly quickly by first calculating the change in NPV arising from a 1 per cent change in the discount rate. This can be done by taking the difference between the two trials (that is, 15 per cent and 10 per cent) that we have already carried out (in Activities 4.12 and 4.15):

Trial	Discount factor %	Net present value £000
1	15	(23.49)
2	10	(2.40)
Difference	5	21.09

The change in NPV for every 1 per cent change in the discount rate will be:

$$(21.09/5) = 4.22$$

The reduction in the 10% discount rate required to achieve a zero NPV would therefore be:

$$[(2.40)/4.22] \times 1\% = 0.57\%$$

The IRR is therefore:

$$(10.00 - 0.57)\% = 9.43\%$$

However to say that the IRR is about 9 per cent is near enough for most purposes.

Note that this approach assumes a straight-line relationship between the discount rate and NPV. We can see from Figure 4.4 that this assumption is not strictly correct. Over a relatively short range, however, this simplifying assumption is not usually a problem and so we can still arrive at a reasonable approximation using the approach that we took in deriving the 9.43 per cent IRR.

Users of the IRR method should apply the following decision rules:

- For any project to be acceptable, it must meet a minimum IRR requirement. This is often referred to as the *hurdle rate* and, logically, this should be the opportunity cost of finance.
- Where there are competing projects (that is, the business can choose only one of two or more viable projects), the one with the higher (or highest) IRR should be selected.

IRR has certain attributes in common with NPV. All cash flows are taken into account, and their timing is logically handled.

Real World 4.7 provides some idea of the IRR for one form of renewable energy.

REAL WORLD 4.7

The answer is blowin' in the wind   **FT**

'Wind farms are practically guaranteed to make returns once you have a licence to operate,' says Bernard Lambilliotte, chief investment officer at Ecofin, a financial group that runs Ecofin Water and Power Opportunities, an investment trust.

'The risk is when you have bought the land and are seeking a licence,' says Lambilliotte. 'But once it is built and you are plugged into the grid it is risk-free. It will give an internal rate of return in the low to mid-teens.' Ecofin's largest investment is in Sechilienne, a French company that operates wind farms in northern France and generates capacity in the French overseas territories powered by sugar cane waste.

Source: Charles Batchelor, 'A hot topic, but poor returns', www.ft.com, 27 August 2005.

Real World 4.8 gives some examples of IRRs sought in practice.

REAL WORLD 4.8

Rates of return

IRR rates for investment projects can vary considerably. Here are a few examples of the expected or target returns from investment projects of large businesses.

- Forth Ports plc, a port operator, concentrates on projects that generate an IRR of at least 15 per cent.
- Rok plc, the builder, aims for a minimum IRR of 15 per cent from new investments.
- Hutchison Whampoa, a large telecommunications business, requires an IRR of at least 25 per cent from its telecom projects.
- Airbus, the plane maker, expects an IRR of 13 per cent from the sale of its A380 super-jumbo aircraft.
- Signet Group plc, the jewellery retailer, requires an IRR of 20 per cent over five years when appraising new stores.

Sources: 'FAQs, Forth Ports plc' (www.forthports.co.uk); Numis Broker Research Report, p. 31 (www.rokgroup.com) 17 August 2006; 'Hutchison Whampoa', Lex column, www.ft.com, 31 March 2004; and 'Airbus hikes A380 break-even target', www.ft.com, 20 October 2006; 'Risk and other factors', Signet Group plc (www.signetgroupplc.com) 2006.

Problems with IRR

The main disadvantage of IRR, relative to NPV, is the fact that it does not correctly address the question of wealth generation. It could therefore lead to the wrong decision being made. This is because IRR will always rank a project with an IRR of 25 per cent above that of a project with an IRR of 20 per cent, assuming an opportunity cost of finance of, say, 15 per cent. Although accepting the project with the higher percentage return will often generate more wealth, this may not always be the case. This is because IRR completely ignores the *scale of investment.*

With a 15 per cent cost of finance, £15 million invested at 20 per cent for one year will make us wealthier by £0.75 million (that is, $15 \times (20 - 15)\% = 0.75$). With the same cost of finance, £5 million invested at 25 per cent for one year will make us only £0.5 million (that is, $5 \times (25 - 15)\% = 0.50$). IRR does not recognise this. It should be acknowledged that it is not usual for projects to be competing where there is such a large difference in scale. Even though the problem may be rare and so, typically, IRR will give the same signal as NPV, a method that is always reliable (NPV) must be better to use than IRR. This problem with percentages is another example illustrated by the Mexican road discussed in Real World 4.3.

A further problem with the IRR method is that it has difficulty handling projects with unconventional cash flows. In the examples studied so far, each project has a negative cash flow arising at the start of its life and then positive cash flows thereafter. However, in some cases, a project may have both positive and negative cash flows at future points in its life. Such a pattern of cash flows can result in there being more than one IRR, or even no IRR at all. This would make the IRR method difficult to use, although it should be said that this is quite rare in practice.

Example 4.3

Let us assume that a project had the following pattern of cash flows:

Time	Cash flows
	£000
Immediately	(4,000)
One year's time	9,400
Two years' time	(5,500)

These cash flows will give a zero NPV at both 10 per cent and 25 per cent. Thus, we will have two IRRs, which can be confusing for decision makers. Assume, for example, the minimum acceptable IRR is 15 per cent. Should the project be accepted or rejected?

Figure 4.5 shows the NPV of the above project for different discount rates. Once again, where the NPV line touches the horizontal axis, there will be a zero NPV and that will also represent the IRR.

| Figure 4.5 | **The IRR method providing more than one solution** |

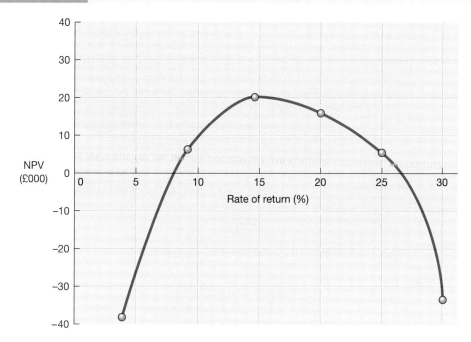

The point at which the NPV line touches the horizontal axis will be the IRR. The figure shows that the NPV of the project is zero at a 10 per cent discount rate and a 25 per cent discount rate. Hence there are two possible IRRs for this project.

Some practical points

When undertaking an investment appraisal, there are several practical points that we should bear in mind:

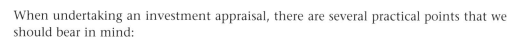

- *Past costs.* As with all decisions, we should take account only of **relevant costs** in our analysis. This means that only costs that vary with the decision should be considered. Thus, all past costs should be ignored as they cannot vary with the decision. In some cases, a business may incur costs (such as development costs and market research costs) *before* the evaluation of an opportunity to launch a new product. As those costs have already been incurred, they should be disregarded, even though the amounts may be substantial. Costs that have already been committed but not yet paid should also be disregarded. Where a business has entered into a binding contract to incur a particular cost, it becomes in effect a past cost even though payment may not be due until some point in the future.
- *Common future costs.* It is not only past costs that do not vary with the decision; some future costs may also be the same. For example, the cost of raw materials may not vary with the decision whether to invest in a new piece of manufacturing plant or to continue to use existing plant.
- *Opportunity costs.* Opportunity costs arising from benefits forgone must be taken into account. Thus, for example, when considering a decision concerning whether or not to continue to use a machine already owned by the business, the realisable value of the machine might be an important **opportunity cost**.

These points concerning costs are brought together in Activity 4.16.

Activity 4.16

A garage has sold an old car that it bought several months ago for £3,000. The car needs a replacement engine before it can be sold. It is possible to buy a reconditioned engine for £300. This would take seven hours to fit by a mechanic who is paid £12 an hour. At present, the garage is short of work, but the owners are reluctant to lay off any mechanics or even cut down their basic working week because skilled labour is difficult to find and an upturn in repair work is expected soon.

Without the engine, the car could be sold for an estimated £3,500. What is the minimum price at which the garage should sell the car, with a reconditioned engine fitted, to avoid making a loss? (Ignore any timing differences in receipts and payments.)

The minimum price is the amount required to cover the relevant costs of the job. At this price, the business will make neither a profit nor a loss. Any price below this amount will result in a reduction in the wealth of the business. Thus, the minimum price is:

	£
Opportunity cost of the car	3,500
Cost of the reconditioned engine	300
Total	3,800

The original cost of the car is a past cost and is, therefore, irrelevant. However, we are told that, without the engine, the car could be sold for £3,500. This is the opportunity cost of the car, which represents the real benefits forgone, and should be taken into account.

The cost of the new engine is relevant because, if the work is done, the garage will have to pay £300 for the engine; but will pay nothing if the job is not done. The £300 is a future cost that varies with the decision and should be taken into account.

The labour cost is irrelevant because the same cost will be incurred whether the mechanic undertakes the work or not. This is because the mechanic is being paid to do nothing if this job is not undertaken; thus the additional labour cost arising from this job is zero.

● *Taxation.* Owners will be interested in the after-tax returns generated from the business, and so taxation will usually be an important consideration when making an investment decision. The profits from the project will be taxed, the capital investment may attract tax relief, and so on. Tax is levied on these at significant rates. This means that, in real life, unless tax is formally taken into account, the wrong decision could easily be made. The timing of the tax outflow should also be taken into account when preparing the cash flows for the project.

● *Cash flows not profit flows.* We have seen that for the NPV, IRR and PP methods, it is cash flows rather than profit flows that are relevant to the assessment of investment projects. In an investment appraisal requiring the application of any of these methods we may be given details of the profits for the investment period. These need to be adjusted in order to derive the cash flows. We should remember that the operating profit *before* non-cash items (such as depreciation) is an approximation to the cash flows for the period, and so we should work back to this figure.

When the data are expressed in profit rather than cash flow terms, an adjustment in respect of working capital may also be necessary. Some adjustment should be made to take account of changes in working capital. For example, launching a new product may give rise to an increase in the net investment made in trade receivables, inventories and trade payables, requiring an immediate outlay of cash. This outlay for additional working capital should be shown in the NPV calculations as part of the initial cost. However, at the end of the life of the project, the additional working capital will be released. This divestment, resulting in an inflow of cash at the end of the project, should also be taken into account at the point at which it is received.

- *Year-end assumption*. In the examples and activities that we have considered so far in this chapter, we have assumed that cash flows arise at the end of the relevant year. This is a simplifying assumption that is used to make the calculations easier. (However, it is perfectly possible to deal more precisely with the cash flows.) The assumption is clearly unrealistic, as money will have to be paid to employees on a weekly or monthly basis and credit customers will pay within a month or two of buying the product or service. Nevertheless, it is probably not a serious distortion. We should be clear, however, that there is nothing about any of the four appraisal methods that demands that this assumption be made.
- *Interest payments*. When using discounted cash flow techniques (NPV and IRR), interest payments should not be taken into account in deriving the cash flows for the period. The discount factor already takes account of the costs of financing, and so to take account of interest charges in deriving cash flows for the period would be double counting.
- *Other factors*. Investment decision making must not be viewed as simply a mechanical exercise. The results derived from a particular investment appraisal method will be only one input to the decision-making process. There may be broader issues connected to the decision that have to be taken into account but which may be difficult or impossible to quantify.

The reliability of the forecasts and the validity of the assumptions used in the evaluation will also have a bearing on the final decision.

Activity 4.17

The directors of Manuff (Steel) Ltd are considering closing one of the business's factories. There has been a reduction in the demand for the products made at the factory in recent years, and the directors are not optimistic about the long-term prospects for these products. The factory is situated in the north of England, in an area where unemployment is high.

The factory is leased, and there are still four years of the lease remaining. The directors are uncertain whether the factory should be closed immediately or at the end of the period of the lease. Another business has offered to sublease the premises from Manuff at a rental of £40,000 a year for the remainder of the lease period.

The machinery and equipment at the factory cost £1,500,000, and have a balance sheet value of £400,000. In the event of immediate closure, the machinery and equipment could be sold for £220,000. The working capital at the factory is £420,000, and could be liquidated for that amount immediately, if required. Alternatively, the working capital can be liquidated in full at the end of the lease period. Immediate closure would result in redundancy payments to employees of £180,000.

If the factory continues in operation until the end of the lease period, the following operating profits (losses) are expected:

	Year 1 £000	Year 2 £000	Year 3 £000	Year 4 £000
Operating profit (loss)	160	(40)	30	20

→

Activity 4.17 continued

The above figures include a charge of £90,000 a year for depreciation of machinery and equipment. The residual value of the machinery and equipment at the end of the lease period is estimated at £40,000.

Redundancy payments are expected to be £150,000 at the end of the lease period if the factory continues in operation. The business has an annual cost of capital of 12 per cent. Ignore taxation.

Required:

(a) Determine the relevant cash flows arising from a decision to continue operations until the end of the lease period rather than to close immediately.

(b) Calculate the net present value of continuing operations until the end of the lease period, rather than closing immediately.

(c) What other factors might the directors take into account before making a final decision on the timing of the factory closure?

(d) State, with reasons, whether or not the business should continue to operate the factory until the end of the lease period.

Your answer should be as follows:

(a) *Relevant cash flows*

	Years				
	0	1	2	3	4
	£000	£000	£000	£000	£000
Operating cash flows (Note 1)		250	50	120	110
Sale of machinery (Note 2)	(220)				40
Redundancy costs (Note 3)	180				(150)
Sublease rentals (Note 4)		(40)	(40)	(40)	(40)
Working capital invested (Note 5)	(420)				420
	(460)	210	10	80	380

Notes:

1 Each year's operating cash flows are calculated by adding back the depreciation charge for the year to the operating profit for the year. In the case of the operating loss, the depreciation charge is deducted.

2 In the event of closure, machinery could be sold immediately. Thus an opportunity cost of £220,000 is incurred if operations continue.

3 By continuing operations, there will be a saving in immediate redundancy costs of £180,000. However, redundancy costs of £150,000 will be paid in four years' time.

4 By continuing operations, the opportunity to sublease the factory will be forgone.

5 Immediate closure would mean that working capital could be liquidated. By continuing operations this opportunity is forgone. However, working capital can be liquidated in four years' time.

(b) Discount rate 12 per cent	1.000	0.893	0.797	0.712	0.636
Present value	(460)	187.5	8.0	57.0	241.7
Net present value	34.2				

(c) Other factors that may influence the decision include:

● *The overall strategy of the business*. The business may need to set the decision within a broader context. It may be necessary to manufacture the products at the factory because they are an integral part of the business's product range. The business may wish to avoid redundancies in an area of high unemployment for as long as possible.

● *Flexibility*. A decision to close the factory is probably irreversible. If the factory continues, however, there may be a chance that the prospects for the factory will brighten in the future.

- *Creditworthiness of sub-lessee.* The business should investigate the creditworthiness of the sub-lessee. Failure to receive the expected sublease payments would make the closure option far less attractive.
- *Accuracy of forecasts.* The forecasts made by the business should be examined carefully. Inaccuracies in the forecasts or any underlying assumptions may change the expected outcomes.

(d) The NPV of the decision to continue operations rather than close immediately is positive. Hence, shareholders would be better off if the directors took this course of action. The factory should therefore continue in operation rather than close down. This decision is likely to be welcomed by employees and would allow the business to maintain its flexibility.

Investment appraisal in practice

Many surveys have been conducted in the UK into the methods of investment appraisal used by businesses. They have shown the following features:

- Businesses tend to use more than one method to assess each investment decision.
- The discounting methods (NPV and IRR) have become increasingly popular over time, with these two becoming the most popular in recent years.
- The continued popularity of PP, and to a lesser extent ARR, despite their theoretical shortcomings.
- A tendency for larger businesses to rely more heavily than smaller businesses on discounting methods.

Real World 4.9 shows the results of a fairly recent survey conducted of UK manufacturing businesses regarding their use of investment appraisal methods.

 REAL WORLD 4.9

A survey of UK business practice

A survey of 83 of the UK's largest manufacturing businesses examined the investment appraisal methods used to evaluate both strategic and non-strategic projects. Strategic projects usually aim to increase or change the competitive capabilities of a business, such as introducing a new manufacturing process. Although a definition was provided, survey respondents were able to decide for themselves what constituted a strategic project. The results of the survey are set out below:

Method	Non-strategic projects Mean score	Strategic projects Mean score
Net present value	3.6829	3.9759
Payback	3.4268	3.6098
Internal rate of return	3.3293	3.7073
Accounting rate of return	1.9867	2.2667

Response scale 1 = never, 2 = rarely, 3 = often, 4 = mostly, 5 = always.

Real World 4.9 continued

We can see that, for both non-strategic and strategic investments, the NPV method is the most popular. As the sample consists of large businesses (nearly all with total sales in excess of £100 million), a fairly sophisticated approach to evaluation might be expected. Nevertheless, for non-strategic investments, the payback method comes second in popularity. It drops to third place for strategic projects.

The survey also found that 98 per cent of respondents used more than one method and 88 per cent used more than three methods of investment appraisal.

Source: Based on information in F. Alkaraan and D. Northcott (see reference 2 at the end of the chapter).

A survey of US businesses also shows considerable support for the NPV and IRR methods. There is less support, however, for the payback method and ARR. **Real World 4.10** sets out some of the main findings.

A survey of US practice

A survey of the chief financial officers (CFOs) of 392 US businesses examined the popularity of various methods of investment appraisal. Figure 4.6 shows the percentage of businesses surveyed that always, or almost always, used the four methods discussed in this chapter.

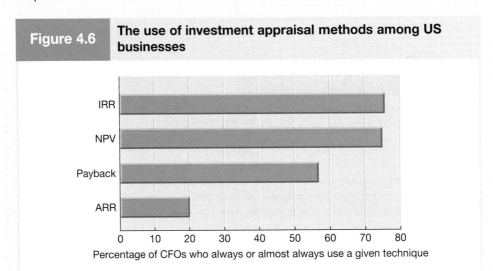

| Figure 4.6 | The use of investment appraisal methods among US businesses |

The figure shows that the IRR and NPV methods are both widely used and are much more popular than the payback and accounting rate of return methods. Nevertheless, the payback method is still used always, or almost always, by a majority of US businesses.

Source: Based on information in R. Graham and C. Harvey (see reference 3 at the end of the chapter).

Activity 4.18

Earlier in the chapter we discussed the theoretical limitations of the PP method. How do you explain the fact that it still seems to be a popular method of investment appraisal among businesses?

A number of possible reasons may explain this finding:

- PP is easy to understand and use.
- It can avoid the problems of forecasting far into the future.
- It gives emphasis to the early cash flows when there is greater certainty concerning the accuracy of their predicted value.
- It emphasises the importance of liquidity. Where a business has liquidity problems, a short payback period for a project is likely to appear attractive.

PP can provide a convenient, though rough and ready, assessment of the profitability of a project, in the way that it is used in Real World 4.11.

REAL WORLD 4.11

An investment lifts off   FT

SES Global is the world's largest commercial satellite operator. This means that it rents satellite capacity to broadcasters, governments, telecommunications groups and Internet service providers. It is a risky venture that few are prepared to undertake. As a result, a handful of businesses dominates the market.

Launching a satellite requires a huge initial outlay of capital, but relatively small cash outflows following the launch. Revenues only start to flow once the satellite is in orbit. A satellite launch costs around €250m. The main elements of this cost are the satellite (€120m), the launch vehicle (€80m), insurance (€40m) and ground equipment (€10m).

According to Romain Bausch, president and chief executive of SES Global, it takes three years to build and launch a satellite. However, the average lifetime of a satellite is fifteen years during which time it is generating revenues. The revenues generated are such that the payback period is around four to five years.

Source: Tim Burt, 'Satellites need space to earn', www.ft.com, 14 July 2003.

The popularity of PP may suggest a lack of sophistication by managers, concerning investment appraisal. This criticism is most often made against managers of smaller businesses. This point is borne out by both of the surveys discussed above which have found that smaller businesses are much less likely to use discounted cash flow methods (NPV and IRR) than are larger ones. Other surveys have tended to reach a similar conclusion.

IRR may be popular, because it expresses outcomes in percentage terms rather than in absolute terms. This form of expression appears to be more acceptable to managers, despite the problems of percentage measures that we discussed earler. This may be because managers are accustomed to using percentage figures as targets (for example, return on capital employed).

Real World 4.12 shows extracts from the 2006 annual report of a well-known business, Rolls-Royce plc, the builder of engines for aircraft and other purposes.

REAL WORLD 4.12

The use of NPV at Rolls-Royce

In its 2006 annual report and accounts, Rolls-Royce plc stated that:

> The Group continues to subject all investments to rigorous examination of risks and future cash flows to ensure that they create shareholder value. All major investments require Board approval. The Group has a portfolio of projects at different stages of their life cycles. Discounted cash flow analysis of the remaining life of projects is performed on a regular basis.

Source: Rolls-Royce plc Annual Report and Accounts 2006.

Rolls-Royce makes clear that it uses NPV (the report refers to creating shareholder value and to discounted cash flow, which strongly imply NPV). It is interesting to note that Rolls-Royce not only assesses new projects but also reassesses existing ones. This must be a sensible commercial approach. Businesses should not continue with existing projects unless those projects have a positive NPV based on future cash flows. Just because a project seemed to have a positive NPV before it started does not mean that this will persist, in the light of changing circumstances. Activity 4.17 considered a decision to close down a project.

Self-assessment question 4.1

Beacon Chemicals plc is considering buying some equipment to produce a chemical named X14. The new equipment's capital cost is estimated at £100,000. If its purchase is approved now, the equipment can be bought and production can commence by the end of this year. £50,000 has already been spent on research and development work. Estimates of revenues and costs arising from the operation of the new equipment appear in the table:

	Year 1	Year 2	Year 3	Year 4	Year 5
Sales price (£/litre)	100	120	120	100	80
Sales volume (litres)	800	1,000	1,200	1,000	800
Variable costs (£/litre)	50	50	40	30	40
Fixed costs (£000)	30	30	30	30	30

If the equipment is bought, sales of some existing products will be lost, and this will result in a loss of contribution of £15,000 a year over its life.

The accountant has informed you that the fixed costs include depreciation of £20,000 a year on the new equipment. They also include an allocation of £10,000 for fixed overheads. A separate study has indicated that if the new equipment were bought, additional overheads, excluding depreciation, arising from producing the chemical would be £8,000 a year. Production would require additional working capital of £30,000.

For the purposes of your initial calculations ignore taxation.

Required:
(a) Deduce the relevant annual cash flows associated with buying the equipment.
(b) Deduce the payback period.
(c) Calculate the net present value using a discount rate of 8 per cent.

(*Hint*: You should deal with the investment in working capital by treating it as a cash outflow at the start of the project and an inflow at the end.)
   The answer to this question may be found at the back of the book on p. 531.

The process of investment decision making

So far, we have been concerned with the methods available for evaluating investment opportunities that have already been identified. This topic is given a great deal of emphasis in the literature and whilst it is undoubtedly important, it is only *part* of the process of investment decision making. Other important aspects must also be considered.

The investment process can be seen as a sequence of six stages, with each requiring careful consideration. These six stages are set out in Figure 4.7 and described below.

Figure 4.7	**Managing the investment decision**

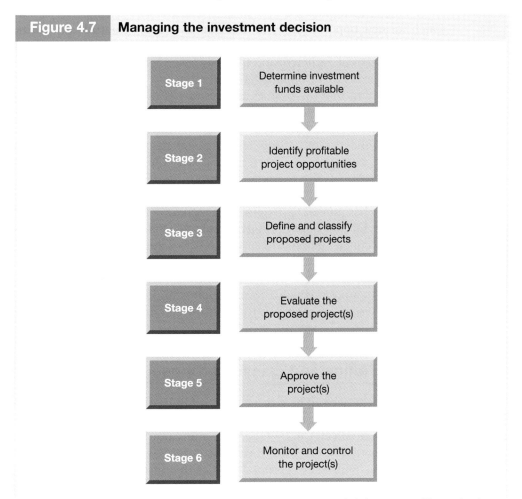

The management of an investment project involves a sequence of six key stages. The evaluation of projects using the appraisal techniques discussed earlier represents only one of these stages.

Stage 1: Determine investment funds available

The amount available for investment may be determined by the external market for funds or by internal management. Usually, it is the latter that is the more important. In either case, however, it may be that the funds allocated will be insufficient to undertake all the profitable opportunities available. When this occurs, some form of **capital rationing** has to be undertaken. This means that managers must allocate the available funds in a way that ensures their most profitable use. Competing investment opportunities must be prioritised and, to do this correctly, some modification to the NPV decision rule is necessary. This point is discussed further in the next chapter.

Stage 2: Identify profitable project opportunities

A vitally important part of the investment process is the search for profitable investment opportunities. A business should be proactive and should adopt a systematic approach towards identifying investment opportunities. To maintain a competitive edge, the search for new investment opportunities should be considered a normal part of the planning process. The range of investment opportunities available to a business may include the development of new products or services, improving existing products or services, entering new markets, and investing to increase capacity or efficiency. The search for new opportunities will often involve looking outside the business to identify changes in technology, customer demand, market conditions and so on. Information will need to be gathered, and this may take some time, particularly for unusual or non-routine investment opportunities.

It is important that the business's investments should fit in with its strategic plans. The business should seek out investment projects that use its strengths (such as management expertise in a particular activity) to exploit opportunities (for example, an expansion of the market). At the same time, investment projects selected should avoid exposing the business's weaknesses (such as a shortage of suitably skilled labour) or exposing it to threats (for example, other businesses poaching skilled staff). One business may be able to generate greater benefits from a particular project than another business that has different strengths and weaknesses.

The search for new opportunities is likely to be more successful where there is a culture that encourages employees at all levels to submit proposals. Various policies can be adopted to help develop such a culture. For example, some businesses encourage unrefined ideas to be submitted and will then invest resources to refine the potentially useful ideas to a point where a formal submission can be made. Some businesses will encourage investment proposals through the reward and appraisal systems operating for employees.

Stage 3: Refine and classify proposed project(s)

Promising ideas need to be converted into full-blown proposals. This means that further information will usually be required, much of it of a detailed nature. Collecting information, however, can be time consuming and costly, and so a two-stage process is often adopted. The first stage involves collecting enough information to allow a preliminary screening. Many proposals fall at this first hurdle because it soon becomes clear that they are unprofitable or unacceptable for other reasons. Proposals that are considered worthy of further investigation continue to the second stage. This stage involves developing the ideas further so that more detailed screening can be carried out.

It is often helpful to classify the investment opportunities identified. The following broad classifications have been suggested:

- *New product development.* Where businesses operate in fast-changing markets (for example, computer manufacturers), there must be a regular stream of new, innovative products under development.
- *Improving existing product sales.* To maintain or enhance competitive position, a business may continually seek to improve the quality or design of existing products.
- *Reducing costs.* New investments may result in considerable savings over the longer term. For example, purchasing a new machine may reduce the costs incurred from scrap, reworking, product labour costs and quality inspection.
- *Replacement of equipment.* Where equipment has reached the end of its economic life it may be necessary to replace the items simply to maintain the existing level of output.
- *Welfare and safety.* A business may seek to achieve certain standards or be required to adhere to new regulations relating to such issues as employee safety, environmental pollution, recycling and so on.

Activity 4.19

What do you think are the benefits of classifying investment proposals in this way? Could it be helpful when gathering information and making decisions?

Classification can be useful in deciding on the level of information required for a particular proposal. For example, equipment replacement may be a routine occurrence and so a replacement proposal may only require evidence that the particular piece of equipment has reached the end of its economic life. New product development, on the other hand, may require market research evidence, a marketing plan and detailed costings to support the proposal.

Classification can also help in deciding on the acceptance criteria to be applied. For example, equipment replacement may be considered low risk and this may be reflected in a low required rate of return. New product development, on the other hand, may be considered to be high risk and this may be reflected in a high rate of return. (Risk and return in relation to investment proposals are considered in detail in the next chapter.)

Stage 4: Evaluate proposed project(s)

Once a project has passed the preliminary screening stage and has been fully developed, a detailed evaluation is usually carried out. For projects of any size, this may involve providing answers to a number of key questions, including:

- What is the nature and purpose of the project?
- Does the project align with the overall objectives of the business?
- How much finance is required? Does this fit with the funds available?
- What other resources (such as expertise, IT, factory space and so on) are required for successful completion of the project?
- How long will the project last and what are its key stages?
- What is the expected pattern of cash flows?
- What are the major problems associated with the project and how can they be overcome?

- What is the NPV/IRR of the project? How does this compare with other opportunities available?
- Have risk and inflation been taken into account in the appraisal process and, if so, what are the results?

The ability and commitment of those responsible for proposing and managing the project will be vital to its success and so, when evaluating a new project, its proposers may also be evaluated. In some cases, senior managers may decide not to support a project that appears profitable on paper if they lack confidence in the ability of key individuals to see it through to completion.

Stage 5: Approve project(s)

Once those responsible for investment decision making are satisfied that the project should be undertaken, formal approval can be given. However, a decision on a project may be postponed if senior managers need more information from those proposing the project, or if revisions are required to the proposal. In some cases, the proposal may be rejected if it is considered unprofitable or likely to fail. Before rejecting a proposal, however, the implications of not pursuing the project for such areas as market share, staff morale and existing business operations must be carefully considered.

Approval may be authorised at different levels of the management hierarchy according to the type of investment and amount of finance required. For example, a plant manager may have authority to accept investment projects up to a maximum of, say, £100,000, and beyond this amount, authority from a capital expenditure committee, made up of senior managers and directors, may be required.

Stage 6: Monitor and control the project(s)

Making a decision to invest in, say, the plant needed to provide a new service does not automatically cause the investment to be made and provision of the service to go smoothly ahead. Managers will need to manage the project actively through to completion. This, in turn, will require further information gathering.

Management should receive progress reports at regular intervals concerning the project. These reports should provide information relating to the actual cash flows for each stage of the project, which can then be compared against the forecast figures provided when the proposal was submitted for approval. The reasons for significant variations should be ascertained, and corrective action taken where possible. Any changes in the expected completion date of the project or any expected variations in future cash flows from budget should be reported immediately; in extreme cases, managers may even abandon the project if circumstances appear to have changed dramatically for the worse. We saw in Real World 4.12 that Rolls-Royce undertakes this kind of reassessment of existing projects. No doubt most other well-managed businesses do this too.

In addition to financial measures, key non-financial measures, such as physical output, wastage rate, customer satisfaction scores and so on, may be used to monitor performance. Certain types of project, such as civil engineering and construction projects, may have 'milestones' (that is, particular levels of completion) to be reached by certain dates. The progress towards each milestone should be monitored carefully and early warnings should be given of any problems that are likely to prevent their achievement. Project management techniques (for example, critical path analysis) should be employed wherever possible and their effectiveness reported to senior management.

An important part of the control process is a **post-completion audit** of the project. This is, in essence, a review of the project performance in order to see whether it lived up to expectations and whether any lessons can be learned from the way that the investment process was carried out. In addition to an evaluation of financial costs and benefits, non-financial measures of performance, such as the ability to meet deadlines and levels of quality achieved, should also be reported.

The fact that a post-completion audit is an integral part of the management of the project should encourage those who submit projects to use realistic estimates. Where over-optimistic estimates are used in an attempt to secure project approval, the managers responsible will find themselves accountable at the post-completion audit stage.

Activity 4.20

Can you think of any drawbacks with the use of post-completion audits? Could they have an adverse effect on manager behaviour?

One problem that has been suggested is that a post-completion audit may inhibit managers from proposing and supporting projects that carry a high level of risk. If things go wrong, they could be blamed. This may result in only low-risk projects being submitted for consideration.

Another problem is that managers may feel threatened by the post-completion audit investigations and so will not cooperate fully with the audit team.

The behaviour of managers is likely to be influenced by the way in which the post-completion audit is conducted. If it is seen by managers as simply a device to apportion blame, then the problems mentioned in Activity 4.20 are more likely to occur. However, if it is used as a constructive tool where the main objective is to learn from experience, and the high-risk nature of particular projects is taken into account, the problems mentioned need not arise.

Post-completion audits can be difficult and time consuming to carry out, and so the likely benefits must be weighed against the costs involved. Senior management may feel, therefore, that only projects above a certain size should be subject to a post-completion audit.

Real World 4.13 identifies two large businesses that use post-completion audits when evaluating past investment projects.

REAL WORLD 4.13

Looking back

In its 2007 corporate governance report, Tesco plc, the supermarket chain, stated:

> All major initiatives require business cases to be prepared, normally covering a minimum period of five years. Post investment appraisals are also carried out.

In its 2007 corporate governance report, Artisan (UK) plc, the house builder and business park developer, stated:

> There is a group-wide policy governing appraisal and approval of investment expenditure and asset disposals. Post investment performance reviews are undertaken.

Sources: The websites of Tesco plc (www.tescocorporate.com) and Artisan (UK) plc (www.artisan-plc.co.uk).

Investment decisions and human behaviour

The sequence of stages described above may give the impression that investment decision making is an entirely rational process. However, studies have shown that, in practice, this may not always be the case. It has been argued that an investment project will often gather support among managers as it is being developed and that the greater the level of support, the greater the potential for bias in the information used to evaluate the project. This may mean that future cash flows are overestimated or the risks associated with the project are underestimated. It has also been suggested that the project sponsors will often seek political support among senior managers so that final approval of the project is simply a formality (see reference 1 at the end of the chapter). These behavioural aspects are beyond the scope of this book. Nevertheless, it is important to recognise that investment decisions are made by individuals who may have their own interests to satisfy.

As a footnote to our discussion of business investment decision making, **Real World 4.14** looks at one of the world's biggest investment projects which has proved to be a commercial disaster, despite being a technological success.

REAL WORLD 4.14

Wealth lost in the chunnel

The Channel Tunnel, which runs for 31 miles between Folkestone in the UK and Sangatte in northern France, was started in 1986 and opened for public use in 1994. From a technological and social perspective it has been a success, but from a financial point of view it has been a disaster. The tunnel was purely a private-sector venture for which a new business, Eurotunnel plc, was created. Relatively little public money was involved. To be a commercial success the tunnel needed to cover all of its costs, including interest charges, and leave sufficient to enhance the shareholders' wealth. In fact, the providers of long-term finance (lenders and shareholders) have lost virtually all of their investment. Although the main losers were banks and institutional investors, many individuals, particularly in France, bought shares in Eurotunnel.

Key inputs to the pre-1986 assessment of the project were the cost of construction and creating the infrastructure, the length of time required to complete construction and the level of revenue that the tunnel would generate when it became operational.

In the event:

- construction cost was £10bn – it was originally planned to cost £5.6bn;
- construction time was seven years – it was planned to be six years;
- revenues from passengers and freight have been well below projected – for example, 21 million annual passenger journeys on Eurostar trains were projected; the numbers have consistently remained at around 7 million.

The failure to generate revenues at the projected levels has probably been the biggest contributor to the problem. When preparing the projection before 1986, planners failed to take adequate account of two crucial factors:

- fierce competition from the ferry operators – at the time, many thought that the ferries would roll over and die; and
- the rise of no-frills, cheap air travel between the UK and the continent.

The commercial failure of the tunnel means that it will be very difficult in future for projects of this nature to be funded by private funds.

Sources: Annual reports of Eurotunnel plc; and J. Randall, 'How Eurotunnel went wrong', BBC news, http://newsvote.bbc.co.uk.

SUMMARY

The main points of this chapter may be summarised as follows.

The accounting rate of return (ARR) is the average accounting profit from the project expressed as a percentage of the average investment.

- Decision rule: projects with an ARR above a defined minimum are acceptable; the greater the ARR, the more attractive the project becomes.
- Conclusions on ARR:
  - it does not relate directly to shareholders' wealth – it can lead to illogical conclusions;
  - it takes almost no account of the timing of cash flows;
  - it ignores some relevant information and may take account of some that is irrelevant;
  - it is relatively simple to use;
  - it is much inferior to NPV.

The payback period (PP) is the length of time that it takes for the cash outflow for the initial investment to be repaid out of resulting cash inflows.

- Decision rule: projects with a PP up to defined maximum period are acceptable, the shorter the PP, the more desirable.
- Conclusions on PP:
  - it does not relate to shareholders' wealth, it ignores inflows after the payback date;
  - it takes little account of the timing of cash flows;
  - it ignores much relevant information;
  - it does not always provide clear signals and can be impractical to use;
  - it is much inferior to NPV, but it is easy to understand and can offer a liquidity insight, which might be the reason for its widespread use.

The net present value (NPV) is the sum of the discounted values of the net cash flows from the investment.

- Money has a time value.
- Decision rule: all positive NPV investments enhance shareholders' wealth; the greater the NPV, the greater the enhancement and the more desirable.
- PV of a cashflow = cashflow $\times 1/(1 + r)^n$, assuming a constant discount rate.
- The act of discounting brings cash flows at different points in time to a common valuation basis (their present value), which enables them to be directly compared.
- Conclusions on NPV:
  - it relates directly to shareholders' wealth objective;
  - it takes account of the timing of cash flows;
  - it takes all relevant information into account;
  - it provides clear signals and is practical to use.

Internal rate of return (IRR) is the discount rate that, when applied to the cash flows of a project, causes it to have a zero NPV.

- It represents the average percentage return on the investment, taking account of the fact that cash may be flowing in and out of the project at various points in its life.
- Decision rule: projects that have an IRR greater than the cost of capital are acceptable; the greater the IRR, the more attractive the project.

● Cannot normally be calculated directly; a trial and error approach is often necessary.
● Conclusions on IRR:
  - it does not relate directly to shareholders' wealth. It usually gives the same signals as NPV but can mislead where there are competing projects of different size;
  - it takes account of the timing of cash flows;
  - it takes all relevant information into account;
  - there are problems of multiple IRRs when there are unconventional cash flows;
  - it is inferior to NPV.

Use of appraisal methods in practice

● All four methods identified are widely used.
● The discounting methods (NPV and IRR) show a steady increase in usage over time.
● Many businesses use more than one method.
● Larger businesses seem to be more sophisticated in their choice and use of appraisal methods than smaller ones.

Management of the investment project has six stages

1 Determine investment funds available – dealing, if necessary with capital rationing problems.
2 Identify profitable project opportunities.
3 Refine and classify the project.
4 Evaluate the proposed project.
5 Approve the project.
6 Monitor and control the project – using a post-completion audit approach.

→ Key terms

Accounting rate of return (ARR) p. 125	**Discount factor** p. 139
Payback period (PP) p. 129	**Cost of capital** p. 140
Net present value (NPV) p. 133	**Internal rate of return (IRR)** p. 142
Risk p. 134	**Relevant costs** p. 147
Risk premium p. 135	**Opportunity cost** p. 147
Inflation p. 135	**Capital rationing** p. 156
	Post-completion audit p. 159

For definitions of these terms see the Glossary, pp. 574–583.

References

1 **Reckoning with Risk**, *Gigerenzer G.*, Penguin, 2002.

2 'Strategic capital investment decision-making: A role for emergent analysis tools? A study of practice in large UK manufacturing companies', *Alkaraan, F. and Northcott, D.* **The British Accounting Review** 38, 2006, p. 159.

3 'How do CFOs make capital budgeting and capital structure decisions?', *Graham, R. and Harvey, C.*, **Journal of Applied Corporate Finance**, vol. 15, no. 1, 2002.

Further reading

If you would like to explore the topics covered in this chapter in more depth, try the following books:

Business Finance: Theory and practice, *McLaney, E.*, 8th edn, Financial Times Prentice Hall, 2009, chapters 4, 5 and 6.

Corporate Finance and Investment, *Pike, R. and Neale, B.*, 5th edn, Prentice Hall, 2006, chapters 5, 6 and 7.

Corporate Financial Management, *Arnold, G.*, 3rd edn, Financial Times Prentice Hall, 2005, chapters 2, 3 and 4.

Management and Cost Accounting, *Drury, C.*, 8th edn, Thomson Learning, 2009, chapters 13 and 14.

REVIEW QUESTIONS

Answers to these questions can be found at the back of the book on p. 541.

4.1 Why is the net present value method of investment appraisal considered to be theoretically superior to other methods that are found in practice?

4.2 The payback method has been criticised for not taking the time value of money into account. Could this limitation be overcome? If so, would this method then be preferable to the NPV method?

4.3 Research indicates that the IRR method is extremely popular even though it has shortcomings when compared to the NPV method. Why might managers prefer to use IRR rather than NPV when carrying out discounted cash flow evaluations?

4.4 Why are cash flows rather than profit flows used in the IRR, NPV and PP methods of investment appraisal?

EXERCISES

Exercises 4.3 to 4.7 are more advanced than 4.1 to 4.3. Those with coloured numbers have answers at the back of the book, starting on p. 554.

>
> If you wish to try more exercises, visit the students' side of this book's Companion Website.

4.1 The directors of Mylo Ltd are currently considering two mutually exclusive investment projects. Both projects are concerned with the purchase of new plant. The following data are available for each project:

	Project	
	1	2
	£000	£000
Cost (immediate outlay)	(100)	(60)
Expected annual operating profit (loss):		
Year 1	29	18
2	(1)	(2)
3	2	4
Estimated residual value of the plant	7	6

The business has an estimated cost of capital of 10 per cent, and uses the straight-line method of depreciation for all non-current (fixed) assets when calculating operating profit. Neither project would increase the working capital of the business. The business has sufficient funds to meet all capital expenditure requirements.

Required:
(a) Calculate for each project:
   (i)   The net present value.
   (ii) The approximate internal rate of return.
   (iii) The payback period.

(b) State which, if any, of the two investment projects the directors of Mylo Ltd should accept, and why.

(c) State, in general terms, which method of investment appraisal you consider to be most appropriate for evaluating investment projects, and why.

4.2 Arkwright Mills plc is considering expanding its production of a new yarn, code name X15. The plant is expected to cost £1 million and have a life of five years and a nil residual value. It will be bought, paid for and ready for operation on 31 December Year 0. £500,000 has already been spent on development costs of the product, and this has been charged in the income statement in the year it was incurred.

The following results are projected for the new yarn:

	Year 1	Year 2	Year 3	Year 4	Year 5
	£m	£m	£m	£m	£m
Sales revenue	1.2	1.4	1.4	1.4	1.4
Costs, including depreciation	(1.0)	(1.1)	(1.1)	(1.1)	(1.1)
Profit before taxation	0.2	0.3	0.3	0.3	0.3

Tax is charged at 50 per cent on annual profits (before tax and after depreciation) and paid one year in arrears. Depreciation of the plant has been calculated on a straight-line basis. Additional working capital of £0.6 million will be required at the beginning of the project and released at the end of Year 5. You should assume that all cash flows occur at the end of the year in which they arise.

Required:

(a) Prepare a statement showing the incremental cash flows of the project relevant to a decision concerning whether or not to proceed with the construction of the new plant.

(b) Compute the net present value of the project using a 10 per cent discount rate.

(c) Compute the payback period to the nearest year. Explain the meaning of this term.

4.3 The accountant of your business has recently been taken ill through overwork. In his absence his assistant has prepared some calculations of the profitability of a project, which are to be discussed soon at the board meeting of your business. His workings, which are set out below, include some errors of principle. You can assume that the statement below includes no arithmetical errors.

	Year 1	Year 2	Year 3	Year 4	Year 5	Year 6
	£000	£000	£000	£000	£000	£000
Sales revenue		450	470	470	470	470
Less Costs:						
Materials		126	132	132	132	132
Labour		90	94	94	94	94
Overheads		45	47	47	47	47
Depreciation		120	120	120	120	120
Working capital	180					
Interest on working capital		27	27	27	27	27
Write-off of development costs		30	30	30		
Total costs	180	438	450	450	420	420
Operating profit/(loss)	(180)	12	20	20	50	50

$$\frac{\text{Total profit (loss)}}{\text{Cost of equipment}} = \frac{(\text{£}28,000)}{\text{£}600,000} = \text{Return on investment (4.7\%)}$$

You ascertain the following additional information:

● The cost of equipment includes £100,000, being the carrying (balance sheet) value of an old machine. If it were not used for this project it would be scrapped with a zero net realisable value. New equipment costing £500,000 will be purchased on 31 December Year 0. You should assume that all other cash flows occur at the end of the year to which they relate.

● The development costs of £90,000 have already been spent.
● Overheads have been costed at 50 per cent of direct labour, which is the business's normal practice. An independent assessment has suggested that incremental overheads are likely to amount to £30,000 a year.
● The business's cost of capital is 12 per cent.

Ignore taxation in your answer.

Required:
(a) Prepare a corrected statement of the incremental cash flows arising from the project. Where you have altered the assistant's figures you should attach a brief note explaining your alterations.
(b) Calculate:
  (i) The project's payback period.
  (ii) The project's net present value as at 31 December Year 0.
(c) Write a memo to the board advising on the acceptance or rejection of the project.

4.4 C. George (Controls) Ltd manufactures a thermostat that can be used in a range of kitchen appliances. The manufacturing process is, at present, semi-automated. The equipment used costs £540,000, and has a written-down (balance sheet) value of £300,000. Demand for the product has been fairly stable, and output has been maintained at 50,000 units a year in recent years.

The following data, based on the current level of output, have been prepared in respect of the product:

	Per unit	
	£	£
Selling price		12.40
Less		
Labour	3.30	
Materials	3.65	
Overheads: Variable	1.58	
Fixed	1.60	
		10.13
Operating profit		2.27

Although the existing equipment is expected to last for a further four years before it is sold for an estimated £40,000, the business has recently been considering purchasing new equipment that would completely automate much of the production process. The new equipment would cost £670,000 and would have an expected life of four years, at the end of which it would be sold for an estimated £70,000. If the new equipment is purchased, the old equipment could be sold for £150,000 immediately.

The assistant to the business's accountant has prepared a report to help assess the viability of the proposed change, which includes the following data:

	Per unit	
	£	£
Selling price		12.40
Less		
Labour	1.20	
Materials	3.20	
Overheads: Variable	1.40	
Fixed	3.30	
		9.10
Operating profit		3.30

Depreciation charges will increase by £85,000 a year as a result of purchasing the new machinery; however, other fixed costs are not expected to change.

In the report the assistant wrote:

> The figures shown above that relate to the proposed change are based on the current level of output and take account of a depreciation charge of £150,000 a year in respect of the new equipment. The effect of purchasing the new equipment will be to increase the operating profit to sales revenue ratio from 18.3% to 26.6%. In addition, the purchase of the new equipment will enable us to reduce our inventories level immediately by £130,000. In view of these facts, I recommend purchase of the new equipment.

The business has a cost of capital of 12 per cent. Ignore taxation.

Required:

(a) Prepare a statement of the incremental cash flows arising from the purchase of the new equipment.

(b) Calculate the net present value of the proposed purchase of new equipment.

(c) State, with reasons, whether the business should purchase the new equipment.

(d) Explain why cash flow forecasts are used rather than profit forecasts to assess the viability of proposed capital expenditure projects.

4.5   Newton Electronics Ltd has incurred expenditure of £5m over the past three years researching and developing a miniature hearing aid. The hearing aid is now fully developed, and the directors are considering which of three mutually exclusive options should be taken to exploit the potential of the new product. The options are as follows:

1   The business could manufacture the hearing aid itself. This would be a new departure, since the business has so far concentrated on research and development projects. However, the business has manufacturing space available that it currently rents to another business for £100,000 a year. The business would have to purchase plant and equipment costing £9m and invest £3m in working capital immediately for production to begin.

   A market research report, for which the business paid £50,000, indicates that the new product has an expected life of five years. Sales of the product during this period are predicted as follows:

	Predicted sales for the year ended 30 November				
	Year 1	Year 2	Year 3	Year 4	Year 5
Number of units ('000)	800	1,400	1,800	1,200	500

   The selling price per unit will be £30 in the first year but will fall to £22 in the following three years. In the final year of the product's life, the selling price will fall to £20. Variable production costs are predicted to be £14 a unit, and fixed production costs (including depreciation) will be £2.4m a year. Marketing costs will be £2m a year.

   The business intends to depreciate the plant and equipment using the straight-line method and based on an estimated residual value at the end of the five years of £1m. The business has a cost of capital of 10 per cent a year.

2   Newton Electronics Ltd could agree to another business manufacturing and marketing the product under licence. A multinational business, Faraday Electricals plc, has offered to undertake the manufacture and marketing of the product, and in return will make a royalty payment to Newton Electronics Ltd of £5 per unit. It has been estimated that the annual number of sales of the hearing aid will be 10 per cent higher if the multinational business, rather than Newton Electronics Ltd, manufactures and markets the product.

3   Newton Electronics Ltd could sell the patent rights to Faraday Electricals plc for £24m, payable in two equal instalments. The first instalment would be payable immediately and the second at the end of two years. This option would give Faraday Electricals the exclusive right to manufacture and market the new product.

Ignore taxation.

Required:

(a) Calculate the net present value of each of the options available to Newton Electronics Ltd.

(b) Identify and discuss any other factors that Newton Electronics Ltd should consider before arriving at a decision.

(c) State what you consider to be the most suitable option, and why.

4.6 Chesterfield Wanderers is a professional football club that has enjoyed considerable success in both national and European competitions in recent years. As a result, the club has accumulated £10m to spend on its further development. The board of directors is currently considering two mutually exclusive options for spending the funds available.

The first option is to acquire another player. The team manager has expressed a keen interest in acquiring Basil ('Bazza') Ramsey, a central defender, who currently plays for a rival club. The rival club has agreed to release the player immediately for £10m if required. A decision to acquire 'Bazza' Ramsey would mean that the existing central defender, Vinnie Smith, could be sold to another club. Chesterfield Wanderers has recently received an offer of £2.2m for this player. This offer is still open but will only be accepted if 'Bazza' Ramsey joins Chesterfield Wanderers. If this does not happen, Vinnie Smith will be expected to stay on with the club until the end of his playing career in five years' time. During this period, Vinnie will receive an annual salary of £400,000 and a loyalty bonus of £200,000 at the end of his five-year period with the club.

Assuming 'Bazza' Ramsey is acquired, the team manager estimates that gate receipts will increase by £2.5m in the first year and £1.3m in each of the four following years. There will also be an increase in advertising and sponsorship revenues of £1.2m for each of the next five years if the player is acquired. At the end of five years, the player can be sold to a club in a lower division and Chesterfield Wanderers will expect to receive £1m as a transfer fee. During his period at the club, 'Bazza' will receive an annual salary of £800,000 and a loyalty bonus of £400,000 after five years.

The second option is for the club to improve its ground facilities. The west stand could be extended and executive boxes could be built for businesses wishing to offer corporate hospitality to clients. These improvements would also cost £10m and would take one year to complete. During this period, the west stand would be closed, resulting in a reduction of gate receipts of £1.8m. However, gate receipts for each of the following four years would be £4.4m higher than current receipts. In five years' time, the club has plans to sell the existing grounds and to move to a new stadium nearby. Improving the ground facilities is not expected to affect the ground's value when it comes to be sold. Payment for the improvements will be made when the work has been completed at the end of the first year.

Whichever option is chosen, the board of directors has decided to take on additional ground staff. The additional wages bill is expected to be £350,000 a year over the next five years.

The club has a cost of capital of 10 per cent. Ignore taxation.

Required:

(a) Calculate the incremental cash flows arising from each of the options available to the club.

(b) Calculate the net present value of each of the options.

(c) On the basis of the calculations made in (b) above, which of the two options would you choose and why?

(d) Discuss the validity of using the net present value method in making investment decisions for a professional football club.

4.7 Haverhill Engineers Ltd manufactures components for the car industry. It is considering automating its line for producing crankshaft bearings. The automated equipment will cost £700,000. It will replace equipment with a scrap value of £50,000 and a book written-down value of £180,000.

At present, the line has a capacity of 1.25 million units per year but typically it has only been run at 80 per cent of capacity because of the lack of demand for its output. The new line has a capacity of 1.4 million units per year. Its life is expected to be five years and its scrap value at that time £100,000.

The accountant has prepared the following cost estimates based on the expected output of 1,000,000 units per year:

	New line (per unit) pence	Old line (per unit) pence
Materials	40	36
Labour	22	10
Variable overheads	14	14
Fixed overheads	44	20
	120	80
Selling price	150	150
Profit per unit	30	70

Fixed overheads include depreciation on the old machine of £40,000 per year and £120,000 for the new machine. It is considered that, for the business overall, fixed overheads are unlikely to change.

The introduction of the new machine will enable inventories to be reduced by £160,000. The business uses 10 per cent as its cost of capital. You should ignore taxation.

Required:
(a) Prepare a statement of the incremental cash flows arising from the project.
(b) Calculate the project's net present value.
(c) Calculate the project's approximate internal rate of return.
(d) Explain the terms net present value and internal rate of return. State which method you consider to be preferable, giving reasons for your choice.

5

Making capital investment decisions: further issues

INTRODUCTION

This chapter is concerned with issues relating to the application of the investment appraisal methods discussed in the previous chapter. The simple NPV decision rules mentioned in that chapter were: (1) that we should accept all projects with a positive NPV and (2) that, where there are competing projects, the one with the higher (or highest) NPV should be selected. There are circumstances, however, that call for a modification to these simple decision rules and, in this chapter, we consider three of these.

Inflation has been a persistent problem for most industrialised economies. We shall examine the problems that inflation creates, and the ways in which we can adjust for the effects of inflation when undertaking discounted cash flow analysis.

Investment appraisal involves making estimates about the future. However, producing reliable estimates can be difficult, particularly where the environment is fast-changing or where new products are being developed. Risk, which is the likelihood that what is estimated to occur will not actually occur, is an important part of investment appraisal. We conclude this chapter by considering the problem of risk and by discussing some of the methods available for dealing with risk.

LEARNING OUTCOMES

When you have completed this chapter, you should be able to:

● Explain the modifications needed to the simple NPV decision rules where there is capital rationing or where there are competing projects with unequal lives.

● Discuss the effect of inflation on investment appraisal and explain how inflation may be taken into account.

● Discuss the nature of risk and explain why it is important in the context of investment decisions.

● Describe the main approaches to the measurement of risk and discuss their limitations.

Investment decisions when funds are limited

We saw in the previous chapter that projects with a positive NPV should be undertaken if the business wishes to maximise shareholder wealth. What if, however, there aren't enough funds to undertake all projects with a positive NPV? Investors may not be prepared to provide the necessary funds or management may restrict the funds available for investment projects. Where funds are limited and, as a result, not all projects with a positive NPV can be undertaken, the basic NPV rules require modification. To illustrate the modification required, let us consider Example 5.1.

Example 5.1

Unicorn Engineering Ltd is considering three possible investment projects: X, Y and Z. The expected pattern of cash flows for each project is as follows:

	Project cash flows		
	X	Y	Z
	£m	£m	£m
Initial outlay	(8)	(9)	(11)
1 year's time	5	5	4
2 years' time	2	3	4
3 years' time	3	3	5
4 years' time	4	5	6.5

The business has a cost of capital of 12 per cent and the investment budget for the year that has just begun is restricted to £12 million. Each project is divisible (that is, it is possible to undertake part of a project if required).

Which investment project(s) should the business undertake?

Solution

If the cash flows for each project are discounted using the cost of capital as the appropriate discount rate, the NPVs are:

Project X			Project Y			Project Z		
Cash	Discount Rate	PV	Cash	Discount Rate	PV	Cash	Discount Rate	PV
£m	12%	£m	£m	12%	£m	£m	12%	£m
(8)	1.00	(8.0)	(9)	1.00	(9.0)	(11)	1.00	(11.0)
5	0.89	4.5	5	0.89	4.5	4	0.89	3.6
2	0.80	1.6	3	0.80	2.4	4	0.80	3.2
3	0.71	2.1	3	0.71	2.1	5	0.71	3.6
4	0.64	2.6	5	0.64	3.2	6.5	0.64	4.2
		NPV 2.8			NPV 3.2			NPV 3.6

It is tempting to think that the best approach to dealing with the limited availability of funds would be to rank the projects according to their NPV. Hence, Project Z would be ranked first, Project Y would be ranked second and Project X would be ranked last. Given that £12 million is available, this would lead to the acceptance of Project Z (£11 million) and part of Project Y (£1 million). The total NPV from the £12 million invested would, therefore, be:

$$£3.6m + \frac{£3.2m}{9} = £4m$$

However, this solution would not represent the most efficient use of the limited funds available.

The best approach, *when projects are divisible*, is to maximise the *present value per £ of scarce finance*. By dividing the present values of the future cash inflows by the outlay for each project, a figure that represents the present value per £ of scarce finance is obtained. This figure provides a measure that is known as the **profitability index**.

Using the information in the example, the following figures would be obtained for the profitability index for each project. (In each case, the top part of the fraction represents the future cash flows before deducting the investment outlays.)

	Project X	Project Y	Project Z
Profitability index:	$\dfrac{10.8}{8.0}$	$\dfrac{12.2}{9.0}$	$\dfrac{14.6}{11.0}$
	= 1.35	= 1.36	= 1.33

Note that all the projects provide a profitability index of greater than 1. This will always be so where the NPV from a project is positive.

Activity 5.1

What does the profitability index calculated in Example 5.1 suggest about the relative profitability of the projects? What would be the NPV of the £12 million invested, assuming the profitability index approach is used?

The above calculations indicate that Project Y provides the highest present value per £ of scarce finance and so should be ranked first. Project X should be ranked second and Project Z should be ranked third. To maximise the use of the limited funds available (£12 million), the business should, therefore, undertake all of Project Y (£9 million) and part of Project X (£3 million).

The total NPV of the £12 million invested would be £3.2 million + (3/8 × £2.8 million) = £4.3 million. Note that this figure is higher than the total NPV obtained where projects were ranked according to their absolute NPVs.

There may be a need for projects to be funded over more than one year and limits may be placed on the availability of funds in each year. In such circumstances, there will be more than one constraint to consider. A mathematical technique known as **linear programming** can be used to maximise the NPV, given that not all projects with a positive NPV can be undertaken. This technique adopts the same approach (that is, it maximises the NPV per £ of scarce finance) as that illustrated above. Computer software is available to undertake the analysis required for this kind of multi-period, rationing problem. A detailed consideration of linear programming is beyond the scope of this book; however, if you are interested in this technique, take a look at the suggested further reading at the end of the chapter.

Non-divisible investment projects

The profitability index approach is only suitable where projects are divisible. Where this is not the case, the problem must be looked at in a different way. The investment project, or combination of whole projects, that will produce the highest NPV for the limited finance available should be selected.

Activity 5.2

Recommend a solution for Unicorn Engineering Ltd if the investment projects were not divisible (that is, it was not possible to undertake part of a project) and the finance available was:

(a) £12 million
(b) £18 million
(c) £20 million.

If the capital available was £12 million, only Project Z should be recommended as this would provide the highest NPV (£3.6 million) for the funds available for investment. If the capital available was £18 million, Projects X and Y should be recommended as this would provide the highest NPV (£6 million). If the capital available was £20 million, Projects Y and Z should be recommended as this would provide the highest NPV (£6.8 million)

Mutually exclusive projects

A business may be faced with a situation where investment projects are mutually exclusive. For example, a business may be able to invest in either one project or another, similar, project but not both. In this kind of situation, the possible combinations available within the funding limit should be compared to see which provides the highest NPV.

Activity 5.3

What investment solution should be recommended if all three projects were divisible but the business could select *either* Project X or Project Z (that is, they were mutually exclusive)? Assume the capital available is £12 million.

In this case, the combinations that are possible within the £12 million finance limit should be compared. There are really only two combinations:

1 Project Y plus part of Project X, or
2 Project Y plus part of Project Z.

The outcomes from each combination are as follows:

	Combination 1		Combination 2	
	Outlay £m	*NPV* £m	*Outlay* £m	*NPV* £m
Project Y	9	3.2	9	3.2
Project X (3/8 of total)	3	1.1	–	–
Project Z (3/11 of total)	–	–	3	1.0
	12	4.3	12	4.2

We can see that the first combination is better as it has a slightly higher NPV.

Activity 5.4

Assume the budget limit was £18 million rather than £12 million. What would now be the recommended combination?

The calculations are as follows:

	Combination 1		Combination 2	
	Outlay	NPV	Outlay	NPV
	£m	£m	£m	£m
Project Y	9	3.2	9	3.2
Project X (whole)	8	2.8	–	–
Project Z (9/11)	–	–	9	2.9
	17	6.0	18	6.1

Now, the second combination is better as it would give a slightly higher NPV.

In the following section, we look at another situation where modification to the simple NPV decision rules is needed to make optimal investment decisions.

Comparing projects with unequal lives

On occasions, a business may find itself in a position where it has to decide between two (or more) competing investment projects, aimed a meeting a continuous need, which have different life spans. When this situation arises, accepting the machine with the shorter life may offer the business the opportunity to reinvest sooner in another project with a positive NPV. The opportunity for earlier reinvestment should be taken into account so that proper comparisons between competing projects can be made. This is not taken into account, however, in the simple form of NPV analysis.

To illustrate how direct comparisons between two (or more) competing projects with unequal lives can be made, let us consider Example 5.2.

Example 5.2

Khan Engineering Ltd has the opportunity to invest in two competing machines. Details of each machine are as follows:

	Machine A	Machine B
	£000	£000
Initial outlay	(100)	(140)
Cash flows		
1 year's time	50	60
2 years' time	70	80
3 years' time	–	32

The business has a cost of capital of 10 per cent.

State which of the two machines, if either, should be acquired.

Solution

One way to tackle this problem is to assume that the machines form part of a repeat chain of replacement and to compare the machines using the **shortest-common-period-of-time approach**. If we assume that investment in Machine A

Example 5.2 continued

can be repeated every two years and that investment in Machine B can be repeated every three years, the *shortest common period of time* over which the machines can be compared is six years (that is, 2 × 3).

The first step in this process of comparison is to calculate the NPV for each project over their expected lives. Thus, the NPV for each project will be as follows:

	Cash flows £000	Discount rate 10%	Present value £000
Machine A			
Initial outlay	(100)	1.00	(100.0)
1 year's time	50	0.91	45.5
2 years' time	70	0.83	58.1
			NPV 3.6
Machine B			
Initial outlay	(140)	1.00	(140.0)
1 year's time	60	0.91	54.6
2 years' time	80	0.83	66.4
3 years' time	32	0.75	24.0
			NPV 5.0

The next step is to calculate the NPV arising for each machine, over a six-year period, using the reinvestment assumption discussed above. That is, investment in Machine A will be repeated three times and investment in Machine B will be repeated twice during the six-year period.

This means that, for Machine A, the NPV over the six-year period will be equal to the NPV above (that is, £3,600) plus equivalent amounts two years and four years later. The calculation (in £000s) will be:

$$\text{NPV} = £3.6 + \frac{£3.6}{(1 + 0.1)^2} + \frac{£3.6}{(1 + 0.1)^4} = £9.1$$

These calculations can be shown in the form of a diagram as in Figure 5.1.

Figure 5.1   NPV for Machine A using a common period of time

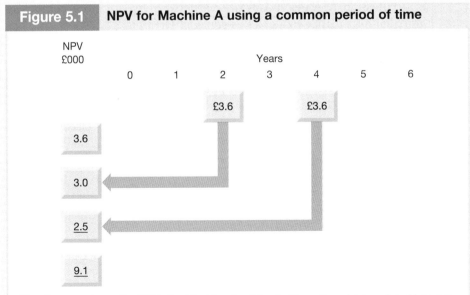

The diagram shows the NPVs for Machine A arising in Years 2 and 4 translated into present value terms.

Activity 5.5

What is the NPV for Machine B over the six-year period? Which machine is the better buy?

In the case of Machine B, the NPV over the six-year period will be equal to the NPV above plus the equivalent amount three years later. The calculation (in £000s) will be:

$$\text{NPV} = £5.0 + \frac{£5.0}{(1 + 0.1)^3} = £8.8$$

The calculations set out above suggest that Machine A is the better buy as it will have the higher NPV over the six-year period.

An alternative approach

When investment projects have a longer life span than those in Example 5.2, the calculations required using this method can be time consuming. Fortunately, there is another method that can be used which avoids the need for laborious calculations. This approach uses the annuity concept to solve the problem. An **annuity** is simply an investment that pays a constant sum each year over a period of time. Thus, fixed payments made in respect of a loan or mortgage or a fixed amount of income received from an investment bond would be examples of annuities.

To illustrate the annuity principle, let us assume that we are given a choice of purchasing a new car by paying either £6,000 immediately or three annual instalments of £2,410 commencing at the end of Year 1. Assuming interest rates of 10 per cent, the present value of the annuity payments would be:

	Cash outflows £	Discount rate 10%	Present value £
1 year's time	2,410	0.91	2,193
2 years' time	2,410	0.83	2,000
3 years' time	2,410	0.75	1,807
		NPV	6,000

As the present value of the immediate payment is £6,000, these calculations mean that we should be indifferent as to the form of payment as they are equal in present value terms.

In the example provided, a cash sum paid today is the equivalent of making three annuity payments over a three-year period. The second approach to solving the problem of competing projects that have unequal lives is based on the annuity principle. Put simply, the **equivalent-annual-annuity approach**, as it is referred to, converts the NPV of a project into an annual annuity stream over its expected life. This conversion is carried out for each competing project and the one that provides the highest annual annuity is the most profitable project.

To establish the equivalent annual annuity of the NPV of a project, we apply the formula:

$$\textbf{Annual annuity} = \frac{i}{1 - (1 + i)^{-n}}$$

where i is the interest rate and n is the number of years.

Thus, using the information from the car loan example above, the annual value of an annuity that lasts for three years, which has a present value of £6,000 and where the discount rate is 10 per cent, is:

$$\text{Annual annuity} = £6,000 \times \frac{0.1}{1 - (1 + 0.1)^{-3}}$$

$$= £6,000 \times 0.402 = £2,412$$

(*Note*: The small difference between this final figure and the one used in the example earlier is due to rounding.)

There are tables that make life easier by providing the annual equivalent factors for a range of possible discount rates. An example of such an annuity table is given on p. 528 at the end of this book.

Activity 5.6

Use the table provided in on p. 528 to calculate the equivalent annual annuity for each machine referred to in Example 5.2 above. Which machine is the better buy?

The equivalent annual annuity for Machine A is:

£3.6 × 0.5762 = £2.07

The equivalent annual annuity for Machine B is:

£5.0 × 0.4021 = £2.01

Machine A is, therefore, the better buy as it provides the higher annuity value. This is consistent with the finding of the shortest-common-period-of-time approach described earlier.

Self-assessment question 5.1

Choi Ltd is considering buying a new photocopier that could lead to considerable cost savings. There are two machines on the market that are suitable for the business. These machines have the following outlays and expected cost savings:

	Lo-tek	Hi-tek
	£	£
Initial outlay	(10,000)	(15,000)
Cost savings		
1 year's time	4,000	5,000
2 years' time	5,000	6,000
3 years' time	5,000	6,000
4 years' time	–	5,000

The business has a cost of finance of 12 per cent and will have a continuing need for the chosen machine.

Required:

(a) Evaluate each machine using both the shortest-common-period-of-time approach and the equivalent-annual-annuity approach.

(b) Which machine would you recommend and why?

The answer to this question may be found at the back of the book on p. 532.

The ability to delay

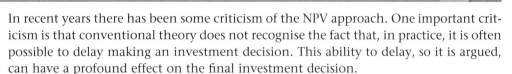

In recent years there has been some criticism of the NPV approach. One important criticism is that conventional theory does not recognise the fact that, in practice, it is often possible to delay making an investment decision. This ability to delay, so it is argued, can have a profound effect on the final investment decision.

Activity 5.7

What are the possible benefits of delaying an investment decision?

By delaying, it may be possible to acquire more information concerning the likely outcome of the investment proposal. If a business decides not to delay, the investment decision, once made, may be irreversible. This may lead to losses if conditions prove unfavourable.

It is argued, therefore, that if managers do not exercise their option to delay, there may be an opportunity cost in the form of the benefits lost from later information. This opportunity cost can be large, and so failure to take it into account could be a serious error. One way of dealing with this problem is to modify the NPV decision rule so that the present value of the future cash flows must exceed the initial outlay *plus* any expected benefits from delaying the decision in order to obtain additional information. In theory this may be fine, but the benefits will often be difficult to quantify.

The problem of inflation

Inflation is a problem that affects most modern economies. Although the rate of inflation may change over time, there has been a persistent tendency for the general price level to rise. It is important to recognise this phenomenon when evaluating investment projects, as inflation will affect both the cash flows and the discount rate over the life of the project.

During a period of inflation, the physical monetary amount required to acquire resources will rise over time and the business may seek to pass on any increase to customers in the form of higher prices. Inflation will also have an effect on the cost of financing the business, as investors seek to protect their investment from a decline in purchasing power by demanding higher returns. As a result of these changes, the cash flows and discount rates relating to the investment project will be affected.

To deal with the problem of inflation in the appraisal of investment projects, two possible approaches can be used:

● *Either* include inflation in the calculations by adjusting annual cash flows by the expected rate of inflation, and by using a discount rate that is also adjusted for inflation. This will mean estimating the actual monetary cash flows expected from the project and using a market rate of interest that will take inflation into account.
● *Or* exclude inflation from the calculations by adjusting cash flows accordingly and by using a 'real' discount rate that does not include any element to account for inflation.

Both methods, properly applied, will give the same result.

If all cash flows are expected to increase in line with the general rate of inflation, it would be possible to use net cash flows as the basis for any adjustments. However, it is unlikely that the relationship between the various items that go to make up the net cash flows of the business will remain constant over time. In practice, inflation is likely to affect each item differently. This means that separate adjustments for each of the monetary cash flows will be necessary.

Activity 5.8

Why is inflation likely to have a differing effect on the various items making up the net cash flow of a business?

Different costs may increase at different rates due to relative changes in demand. For example, labour costs may rise more quickly than materials costs, assuming that labour is in greater demand. Certain costs may be fixed over time (for example, lease payments) and may therefore be unaffected by inflation over the period of the project.

In a highly competitive environment, a business may be unable to pass on all of the increase in costs to customers and so will have to absorb some of the increase by reducing profits. Thus, cash inflows from sales may not fully reflect the rise in the costs of the various inputs, such as labour and materials.

To compute the real cash flows from a project, it will be necessary to calculate the monetary cash flows relating to each item and then deflate these amounts by the *general* rate of inflation. This adjustment will provide us with the *current general purchasing power* of the cash flows. This measure of general purchasing power is of more relevance to investors than if the cash flows were deflated by a specific rate of inflation relevant to each type of cash flow. Similarly, the real discount rate will be deduced by deflating the market rate of interest by the *general* rate of inflation.

Real World 5.1 sets out the findings of a survey of UK businesses which reveals how inflation is dealt with in practice.

REAL WORLD 5.1

Adjusting for inflation

The following table summarises the ways in which UK businesses adjust for inflation for investment appraisal purposes:

Approach used	Business size			
	Small %	Medium %	Large %	Total %
Specify cash flow in constant prices and apply a real rate of return	47	29	45	42
All cash flows expressed in inflated price terms and discounted at the market rate of return	18	42	55	39
Considered at risk analysis or sensitivity stage*	21	13	16	17
No adjustment	18	21	3	13
Other	0	0	3	1

* This approach is discussed later in the chapter.

Two points worth noting from the summary table are:

- Large and medium-sized businesses are more likely to inflate cash flows and to use a market rate of return than to use real cash flows and a real discount rate. For small businesses, however, it is the other way around.
- Small and medium-sized businesses are more likely to make no adjustment for inflation than large businesses.

Source: Arnold and Hatzopoulos (2000), quoted in *Corporate Financial Management*, G. Arnold, 3rd edn, Financial Times Prentice Hall, 2005, p. 201.

The problem of risk

Risk arises where the future is unclear and where a range of possible future outcomes exists. As the future is uncertain, there is a chance (or risk) that estimates made concerning the future will not occur. Risk is particularly important in the context of investment decisions. This is because of:

- the relatively long timescales involved – there is more time for things to go wrong between the decision being made and the end of the project; and
- the size of the investment – if things do go wrong, the impact can be both significant and lasting.

Sometimes, a distinction is made in the literature between risk and uncertainty. However, this distinction is not particularly useful for our purposes and in this chapter the two words are used interchangeably.

In the sections that follow, we examine various methods that can be used to help managers deal with the problem of risk. This examination will focus on the more useful and systematic approaches to dealing with risk that have been proposed. In practice, crude methods of dealing with risk are sometimes used, such as shortening the required payback period and employing conservative cash flows. However, these methods rely on arbitrary assumptions and have little to commend them. They have, therefore, been excluded from our examination.

The first three methods of dealing with risk that we consider were discussed briefly in Chapter 2 during our examination of projected financial statements. We now consider them in more detail as they are also relevant to investment decisions.

Sensitivity analysis

A popular way of assessing the level of risk is to carry out **sensitivity analysis**. We may recall from Chapter 2 that it involves an examination of key input values in order to see how changes in each input might influence the likely outcomes. One form of sensitivity analysis involves posing a series of 'what if?' questions. For example:

- What if sales volume is 5 per cent higher than expected?
- What if sales volume is 10 per cent lower than expected?

By answering these 'what if?' questions, the managers will have a range of possible outcomes to consider, which can be useful for investment appraisal purposes as well as for profit planning.

There is, however, another form of sensitivity analysis that is particularly useful in the context of investment appraisal. Where the result from an appraisal, using the best estimates, is positive, the value for each key factor can be examined to see by how much it could be changed before the project became unprofitable for that reason alone.

Let us suppose that the NPV for an investment in a machine to provide a particular service is estimated to be a positive value of £50,000. To carry out sensitivity analysis on this investment proposal, we should consider in turn each of the key input factors:

● initial cost of the machine
● sales volume and price
● relevant operating costs
● life of the machine
● financing cost.

We should try to find the value that each of them could have before the NPV figure becomes negative (that is, the value for the factor at which NPV is zero). The difference between the value for that factor at which the NPV is zero and the estimated value represents the 'margin of safety' for that particular factor. The process is set out in Figure 5.2.

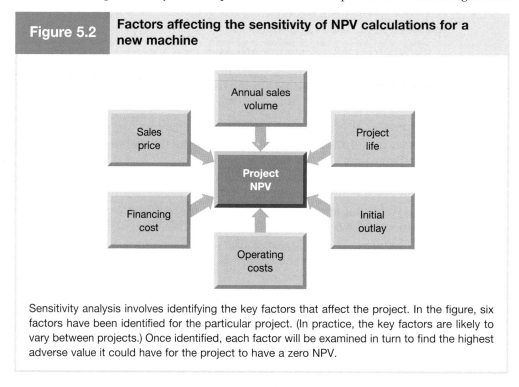

| Figure 5.2 | **Factors affecting the sensitivity of NPV calculations for a new machine** |

Sensitivity analysis involves identifying the key factors that affect the project. In the figure, six factors have been identified for the particular project. (In practice, the key factors are likely to vary between projects.) Once identified, each factor will be examined in turn to find the highest adverse value it could have for the project to have a zero NPV.

In your previous studies of accounting, you may have studied break-even analysis. This form of sensitivity analysis is, in essence, a form of break-even analysis. The point at which the NPV is zero is the point at which the project breaks even (that is, makes neither profit nor loss). The 'margin of safety' for a particular factor associated with the project can be interpreted in the same way as the margin of safety is interpreted in break-even analysis.

A computer spreadsheet model of the project can be extremely valuable when undertaking sensitivity analysis because it then becomes a simple matter to try various values for the key factors and to calculate the effect of changes in each. Example 5.3, which illustrates sensitivity analysis, is, however, straightforward and can be undertaken without recourse to a spreadsheet.

Example 5.3

S. Saluja (Property Developers) Ltd intends to bid at an auction, to be held today, for a manor house that has fallen into disrepair. The auctioneer believes that the manor house will be sold for about £450,000. The business wishes to renovate the property and to divide it into flats to be sold for £150,000 each. The renovation will be in two stages and will cover a two-year period. Stage 1 will cover the first year of the project. It will cost £500,000 and the six flats completed during this stage are expected to be sold for a total of £900,000 at the end of the first year. Stage 2 will cover the second year of the project. It will cost £300,000 and the three remaining flats are expected to be sold at the end of the second year for a total of £150,000.

The cost of renovation is subject to an agreed figure with local builders; however, there is some uncertainty over the remaining input values. The business estimates its cost of capital at 12 per cent a year.

Required:
(a) What is the NPV of the proposed project?
(b) Assuming none of the other inputs deviate from the best estimates provided:
   (i)   What auction price would have to be paid for the manor house to cause the project to have a zero NPV?
   (ii) What cost of capital would cause the project to have a zero NPV?
   (iii) What is the sale price of each of the flats that would cause the project to have a zero NPV? (Each flat will be sold for the same price: £150,000.)
(c) Is the level of risk associated with the project high or low?

Solution

(a) (i)   The NPV of the proposed project is as follows:

	Cash flows £	Discount factor 12%	Present value £
Year 1 (£900,000 – £500,000)	400,000	0.893	357,200
Year 2 (£450,000 – £300,000)	150,000	0.797	119,550
Less Initial outlay			(450,000)
		NPV	26,750

(b) (i)   To obtain a zero NPV, the auction price for the manor house would have to be £26,750 higher than the current estimate (that is, the amount of the estimated NPV). This would make a total price of £476,750, which is about 6 per cent above the current estimated price.

   (ii) As there is a positive NPV, the cost of capital that would cause the project to have a zero NPV must be higher than 12 per cent. Let us try 20 per cent.

	Cash flows £	Discount factor 20%	Present value £
Year 1 (£900,000 – £500,000)	400,000	0.833	333,200
Year 2 (£450,000 – £300,000)	150,000	0.694	104,100
Less Initial outlay			(450,000)
		NPV	(12,700)

Example 5.3 continued

As the NPV, using a 20 per cent discount rate, is negative, the 'break-even' cost of capital must lie somewhere between 12 per cent and 20 per cent. A reasonable approximation is obtained as follows:

	Discount rate	NPV
	%	£
	12	26,750
	20	(12,700)
Difference	8	Range 39,450

The change in NPV for every 1 per cent change in the discount rate will be:

$$\frac{39,450}{8} = 4,931$$

The reduction in the 20 per cent discount rate required to achieve a zero NPV would therefore be:

$$\frac{12,700}{4,931} = 2.6\%$$

The cost of capital (that is, the discount rate) would, therefore, have to be 17.4 per cent (20.0 – 2.6) for the project to have a zero NPV.

This calculation is, of course, the same as that used in the previous chapter when calculating the IRR of the project. In other words, 17.4 per cent is the IRR of the project.

(iii) To obtain a zero NPV, the sale price of each flat must be reduced so that the NPV is reduced by £26,750. In Year 1, six flats are sold, and in Year 2, three flats are sold. The discount factor for Year 1 is 0.893 and for Year 2 it is 0.797. We can derive the fall in value per flat (Y), to give a zero NPV, by using the equation:

$$(6Y \times 0.893) + (3Y \times 0.797) = £26,750$$
$$Y = £3,452$$

The sale price of each flat necessary to obtain a zero NPV is therefore:

$$£150,000 – £3,452 = £146,548$$

This represents a fall in the estimated price of 2.3 per cent.

(c) These calculations indicate that the auction price would have to be about 6 per cent above the estimated price before a zero NPV is obtained. The margin of safety is, therefore, not very high for this factor. The calculations also reveal that the price of the luxury flats would only have to fall by 2.3 per cent from the estimated price before the NPV is reduced to zero. Hence, the margin of safety for this factor is even smaller. However, the cost of capital is less sensitive to changes and there would have to be an increase from 12 per cent to 17.4 per cent before the project produced a zero NPV.

It seems from the calculations that the sale price of the flats is the most sensitive of the three inputs examined. A careful re-examination of the market value of the flats seems appropriate before a final decision is made.

Real World 5.2 describes the evaluation of a mining project that incorporated sensitivity analysis to test the robustness of the findings.

REAL WORLD 5.2

Golden opportunity

In 2006, Eureka Mining plc undertook an evaluation of the opportunity to mine copper and gold deposits at Miheevskoye, which is located in the Southern Urals region of the Russian Federation. Using three investment appraisal methods, the business came up with the following results:

	IRR %	Pre-tax NPV $USm	Payback period Years
	20.4%	178.8	3.8

Sensitivity analysis was carried out on four key variables – the price of copper, the price of gold, operating costs and capital outlay costs to help assess the riskiness of the project. The following table sets out the findings.

		IRR %	Pre-tax NPV $USm	Payback period Years
Copper price				
	Average spot copper price ($US/lb)*			
	1.10	8.8	(18.4)	8.1
	1.20	14.8	80.2	5.0
	1.40	25.7	277.3	3.0
	1.50	30.8	375.9	2.7
Gold price				
	Average spot gold price ($US/oz)*			
	450	18.9	152.0	4.0
	500	19.6	165.4	3.9
	600	21.2	192.2	3.6
	650	21.9	205.6	3.5
Operating costs				
Percentage change	*Average total costs (lb copper equivalent)*			
–20	$0.66	26.68	298.5	3.0
–10	$0.72	23.7	238.6	3.3
+10	$0.83	17.1	118.9	4.4
+20	$0.88	13.6	59.0	5.3
Capital costs				
	Initial capital ($USm)			
–20	360	28.6	261.8	2.8
–10	405	24.1	220.3	3.2
+10	495	17.3	137.2	4.4
+20	540	14.7	95.7	5.1

* The spot price is the price for immediate delivery of the mineral.

Real World 5.2 continued

In its report, the business stated:

> This project is most sensitive to percentage changes in the copper price which have the largest impact, whereas movements in the gold price have the least. The impact of changes in operating costs is more significant than capital costs.

Source: Adapted from 'Eureka Mining PLC – Drilling Report', 26 July 2006 (www.citywire.co.uk).

The following activity can also be attempted without recourse to a spreadsheet.

Activity 5.9

A business has the opportunity to invest £12 million immediately in new plant and equipment in order to produce a new product. The product will sell at £80 each and it is estimated that 200,000 units of the product can be sold in each of the next four years. Variable costs are £56 a unit and additional fixed costs (excluding depreciation) are £1.0 million in total. The residual value of the plant and machinery at the end of the life of the product is estimated to be £1.6 million.

The business has a cost of capital of 12 per cent.

Required:

(a) Calculate the NPV of the investment proposal.
(b) Carry out separate sensitivity analysis to indicate by how much the following factors would have to change in order to produce an NPV of zero.
   (i) Initial outlay on plant and machinery.
   (ii) Residual value of the plant and machinery.
   (iii) Discount rate.

(a) Annual operating cash flows are as follows:

	£m	£m
Sales (200,000 × £80)		16.0
Less		
Variable costs (200,000 × £56)	11.2	
Fixed costs	1.0	12.2
		3.8

Estimated cash flows are as follows:

	Year 0 £m	Year 1 £m	Year 2 £m	Year 3 £m	Year 4 £m
Plant and equipment	(12.0)				1.6
Operating cash flows		3.8	3.8	3.8	3.8
	(12.0)	3.8	3.8	3.8	5.4

The NPV of the project is:

	Year 0 £m	Year 1 £m	Year 2 £m	Year 3 £m	Year 4 £m
Cash flows	(12.0)	3.8	3.8	3.8	5.4
Discount rate (12%)	1.0	0.89	0.80	0.71	0.64
Present value	(12.0)	3.38	3.04	2.70	3.46
	NPV 0.58				

(b) (i) The increase required in the initial outlay on plant and equipment to achieve an NPV of zero will be £0.58 million (as the plant and equipment are already expressed in present value terms). This represents a 4.8 per cent increase on the current estimated figure of £12 million.

(ii) Using a discount rate of 14 per cent, the NPV of the project is:

	Year 0 £m	Year 1 £m	Year 2 £m	Year 3 £m	Year 4 £m
Cash flows	(12.0)	3.8	3.8	3.8	5.4
Discount rate (14%)	1.0	0.88	0.77	0.68	0.59
Present value	(12.0)	3.34	2.92	2.58	3.18
NPV	0.02				

This is very close to an NPV of zero and so 14 per cent is the approximate figure. This is 16.7 per cent higher than the cost of capital.

(iii) The fall in the residual value of the plant and equipment (R) that will lead to a zero NPV is:

$$(R \times \text{discount factor at the end of four years}) - \text{NPV of the project} = 0$$

By rearranging this equation, we have:

$$(R \times \text{Discount factor at the end of four years}) = \text{NPV of the project} = 0$$
$$R \times 0.64 = £0.58 \text{ million}$$
$$R = £0.58 \text{ million}/0.64$$
$$= £0.90 \text{ million}$$

This represents a 43.8 per cent decrease in the current estimated residual value.

Sensitivity chart

It is possible to portray the effect of changes to key variables on the NPV of a project by preparing a **sensitivity chart**. To illustrate how this chart is prepared, we can use the following information from the answer to Activity 5.9 above:

● The NPV of the project is estimated as £0.58m.
● An NPV of zero will occur where there is a:
  – 4.8% increase in initial outlay
  – 16.7% increase in the cost of capital
  – 43.8% decrease in the residual value of the plant and equipment.

In Figure 5.3, the NPV of the project is shown on the vertical axis and the percentage change in estimates on the horizontal axis. By using two co-ordinates – the estimated NPV without any change and the percentage change required to a produce a zero NPV – a line can be drawn for each variable to show its sensitivity to change. The steeper the slope of the line, the more sensitive the particular variable is to change. The visual representation in Figure 5.3 can help managers to see more clearly the sensitivity of each variable.

Strengths and weaknesses of sensitivity analysis

Sensitivity analysis should help managers to gain a feel for the investment project as they will be able to see the margin of safety for each factor. They should also be able

| Figure 5.3 | Sensitivity chart |

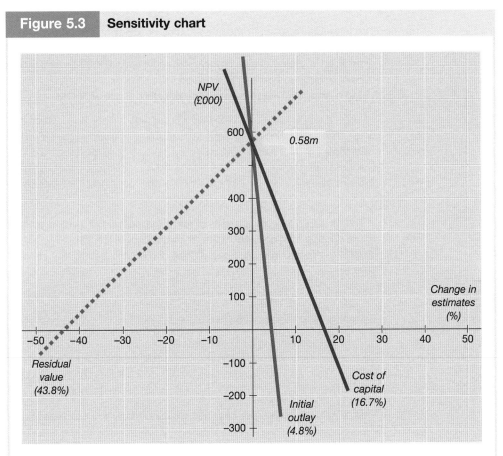

We can see that a 4.8% increase in initial outlay, a 16.7% increase in the cost of capital and 43.8% decrease in the residual value of plant and equipment will each result in a zero NPV. The slope of the line of each variable indicates sensitivity to change: the steeper the slope, the more sensitive the variable is to change.

to identify highly sensitive factors, which require careful study and which are also likely to require more detailed information. We should always bear in mind that the collection, reporting and evaluation of information can be costly and time consuming, and the more that managers can focus their efforts on the critical aspects of a decision the better. Sensitivity analysis can also be useful in directing the actions of managers. Where a project outcome has been identified as being highly sensitive to changes in a key factor, managers may decide to formulate plans to deal with possible variations from the estimated outcome.

Although sensitivity analysis is undoubtedly a useful tool for managers, it has two major drawbacks:

● It does not give managers clear decision rules concerning acceptance or rejection of the project. There is no single-figure outcome that will indicate whether the project is worth undertaking. This means that managers must rely on their own judgement.
● It is a static form of analysis. Only one factor is considered at a time while the rest are held constant. In practice, however, it is likely that more than one factor value will differ from the best estimates provided.

Scenario analysis

A slightly different approach, which overcomes the problem of dealing with a single variable at a time, is **scenario analysis**. This method was also briefly discussed in Chapter 2. We may recall that this approach changes a number of variables simultaneously so as to provide a particular 'state of the world', or scenario, for managers to consider. A popular form of scenario analysis is to provide three different 'states of the world', or scenarios, which set out:

- an optimistic view of likely future events
- a pessimistic view of likely future events
- a 'most likely' view of future events.

The approach is open to criticism because it does not indicate the likelihood of each scenario occurring nor does it identify the other possible scenarios that might occur. Nevertheless, the portrayal of optimistic and pessimistic scenarios may be useful in providing managers with some feel for the 'downside' risk and 'upside' potential associated with a project.

Simulations

We saw in Chapter 2 that an approach using **simulations** is really a development of sensitivity analysis discussed earlier. The starting point for carrying out a simulation exercise is to model the investment project. This involves identifying the key factors affecting the project and their interrelationships. Thus, the cash flows will have to be modelled to reveal the key factors influencing both the cash receipts and the cash payments and their interrelationships. Let us illustrate this point using a simple example. The cash received from sales may be modelled by the following equation:

Sales revenue = Selling price per unit × (Market share × Market size)

The modelling process will also require equations showing the factors determining the cash expenses and the interrelationships between these factors. The relationship between the cash inflows and outflows must also be modelled. As investment projects usually extend over more than one year, there may also be a need to model the relationship between the cash flows occurring in different periods. Thus, a fairly large number of equations may be required to model even a fairly simple investment project proposal.

Once the key factors have been identified and their relationships have been modelled, the next step is to specify the possible values for each of the factors within the model. A computer is then used to select one of the possible values from each distribution on a random basis. It then generates projected cash flows using the selected values for each factor. This process represents a single trial. The process is then repeated using other values for each factor until many possible combinations of values for the key factors have been considered. The results of the repeated sampling allow us to obtain a probability distribution of the values of the cash flows for the project (see Figure 5.4).

The use of simulations is meant to help managers in two ways. First, the process of building a model helps managers to understand more fully the nature of the project and the issues that must be resolved. Secondly, it provides managers with a distribution of project outcomes that can be used to assess the riskiness of the project. However,

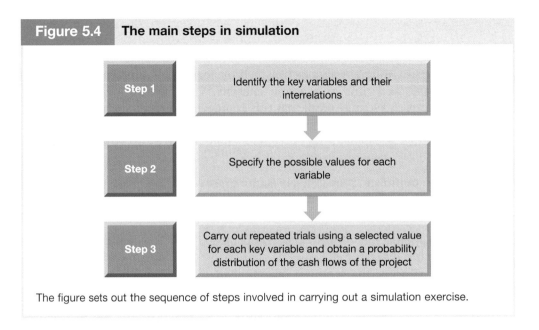

Figure 5.4 **The main steps in simulation**

Step 1 — Identify the key variables and their interrelations

Step 2 — Specify the possible values for each variable

Step 3 — Carry out repeated trials using a selected value for each key variable and obtain a probability distribution of the cash flows of the project

The figure sets out the sequence of steps involved in carrying out a simulation exercise.

these potential benefits must be weighed against the potential problems of producing simulations.

Simulation can be costly and time consuming. In practice, the task of producing a simulation model may be given to support staff, and managers may not be closely involved with its construction. When this task is delegated, the first potential benefit referred to above may easily be lost. Furthermore, there are usually problems in modelling the relationship between factors and in establishing the distribution of outcomes for each factor. The more complex the project, the more complex these problems are likely to be.

Risk preferences of investors

So far, the methods discussed have sought to identify the level of risk associated with a project. However, this is not, of itself, enough. The attitude of investors towards risk should also be determined. Unless we know how investors are likely to react to the presence of risk in investment opportunities, we cannot really make an informed decision.

In theory, investors may display three possible attitudes towards risk. They may be:

- **Risk-seeking investors**. Some investors enjoy a gamble. Given two projects with the same expected return but with different levels of risk, the risk-seeking investor would choose the project with the higher level of risk.
- **Risk-neutral investors**. Some investors are indifferent to risk. Thus, given two projects with the same expected return but with different levels of risk, the risk-neutral investor would have no preference. Both projects provide the same expected return and the fact that one project has a higher level of risk would not be an issue.
- **Risk-averse investors**. Some investors are averse to risk. Given two projects with the same expected return but with different levels of risk, a risk-averse investor would choose the project that has a lower level of risk.

While some investors may be risk seekers and some investors may be indifferent to risk, the evidence suggests that the vast majority of investors are risk averse. This does not mean, however, that they will not be prepared to take on risky investments. Rather, it means that they will require compensation in the form of higher returns from projects that have higher levels of risk. An explanation as to why this is the case can be found in utility theory.

Risk and utility theory

To describe utility theory, let us assume you can measure the satisfaction, or utility, you receive from money in the form of 'utils of satisfaction' and let us also assume that you are penniless. If a rich benefactor gives you £1,000, this may bring you a great deal of satisfaction as it would allow you to buy many things that you have yearned for. Let us say it provides you with 20 utils of satisfaction. If the benefactor gives you a further £1,000, this may also bring you a great deal of satisfaction, but not as much as the first £1,000 as your essential needs have now been met. Let us say, therefore, it provides you with 10 utils of satisfaction. If the benefactor then gives you a further £1,000, the additional satisfaction received from this additional sum may reduce to, say, 6 utils and so on. (The expression *diminishing marginal utility of wealth* is often used to describe the situation where the additional satisfaction received from wealth declines with each additional amount of wealth received.)

The relationship between the level of satisfaction received and the amount of wealth received can be expressed in the form of a **utility function**. For a risk-averse individual, the utility function, when shown graphically, would take the shape of a downward-sloping curve as shown in Figure 5.5. We can see clearly from this graph that each increment in wealth provides a diminishing level of satisfaction for the individual. We can also see that the increase in satisfaction from gaining additional wealth is not the same as the decrease in satisfaction from losing the same amount of wealth.

| Figure 5.5 | **Utility function for a risk-averse individual** |

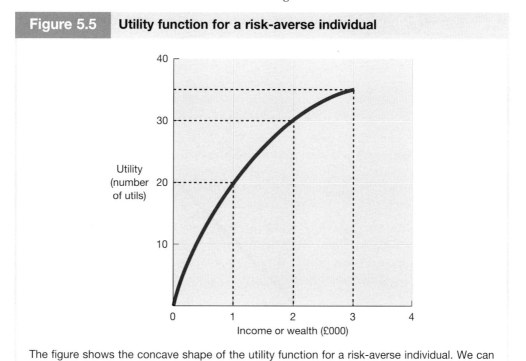

The figure shows the concave shape of the utility function for a risk-averse individual. We can see that each additional amount of wealth received provides a diminishing amount of satisfaction for the individual. The greater the aversion to risk, the more concave the utility function will become.

An individual with wealth of, say, £2,000 would receive satisfaction from this amount of 30 utils. If, however, the wealth of the individual fell by £1,000 for some reason, the loss of satisfaction would be greater than the satisfaction gained from receiving an additional £1,000. We can see the loss of satisfaction from a fall in wealth of £1,000 would be 10 utils, whereas the gain in satisfaction from receiving an additional £1,000 would only be 6 utils. As the satisfaction, or happiness, lost from a fall in wealth is greater than the satisfaction, or happiness, gained from acquiring an equivalent amount of wealth, the individual will be averse to risk and will only be prepared to undertake risk in exchange for the prospect of higher returns.

The particular shape of the utility curve will vary between individuals. Some individuals are likely to be more risk averse than others. The more risk averse an individual is, the more concave the shape of the curve will become. However, this general concave curve shape will apply to all risk-averse individuals.

For an individual who is indifferent to risk, the marginal satisfaction, or utility, of wealth will not diminish as described above. Instead, the marginal utility of wealth will remain constant. This means the individual's utility function will look quite different from that of a risk-averse individual.

Activity 5.10

Try to draw a graph that plots the utility of wealth against wealth for an individual who is indifferent to risk. Explain the shape of the graph line.

An individual who is indifferent to risk would have a utility function that can be plotted in the form of a straight line as shown in Figure 5.6.

This indicates that the satisfaction, or happiness, lost from a fall in wealth will be equal to the satisfaction, or happiness, gained from acquiring an equivalent amount of wealth.

Figure 5.6	Utility function for a risk-neutral individual

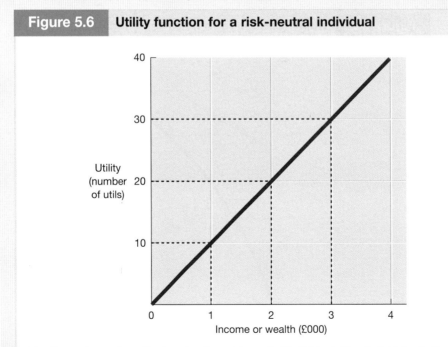

The figure shows the utility function for a risk-neutral individual. The straight line indicates that each additional util of wealth received will produce the same amount of satisfaction.

For a risk-seeking individual, the marginal satisfaction, or utility, of wealth will increase rather than decrease or remain constant. This means that the shape of a risk-seeking individual's utility function, when displayed in the form of a graph, will be quite different from the two described above.

Activity 5.11

Draw a graph plotting the utility of wealth against wealth for an individual who is risk seeking and explain the shape of the graph line.

The graph for a risk-seeking individual will be as shown in Figure 5.7. We can see from the graph that the curve is upward sloping. The satisfaction, or happiness, gained from an increase in wealth would be greater than the satisfaction, or happiness, lost from a decrease in wealth of an equivalent amount. This means the individual will be prepared to take on risks in order to obtain additional wealth.

Figure 5.7 | **Utility function for a risk-seeking individual**

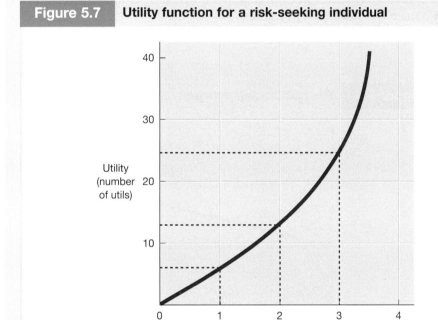

The figure shows the convex shape of the utility function for a risk-seeking individual. We can see that each additional amount of wealth received provides an increasing amount of satisfaction for the individual. The greater the attraction to risk, the more convex the utility function will become.

Although utility theory helps us to understand why investors are risk averse, it would not be possible to identify the utility functions of individual investors and then combine these in some way so as to provide a guide for management decisions. The practical value of this theory is, therefore, limited. In the real world, managers may make decisions based on their own attitudes towards risk rather than those of investors, or may make assumptions about the risk preferences of investors.

Risk-adjusted discount rate

We have seen from the section above that there is a relationship between risk and the rate of return required by investors. The reaction of a risk-averse individual will be to require a higher rate of return for risky projects. The higher the level of risk associated with a project, the higher the required rate of return. The **risk-adjusted discount rate** is based on this simple relationship between risk and return. Thus, when evaluating investment projects, managers will increase the NPV discount rate in the face of increased risk. In other words, a *risk premium* will be required for risky projects: the higher the level of risk, the higher the risk premium.

The risk premium is usually added to a 'risk-free' rate of return in order to derive the total return required. The risk-free rate is normally taken to be equivalent to the rate of return from long-term government loan stock. In practice, a business may divide projects up into risk categories (for example, low, medium and high risk) and then assign a risk premium to each risk category. The cash flows from a particular project will then be discounted using a rate based on the risk-free rate plus the appropriate risk premium. This relationship between risk and return, which we first discussed in Chapter 1, is illustrated in Figure 5.8.

| Figure 5.8 | The relationship between risk and return |

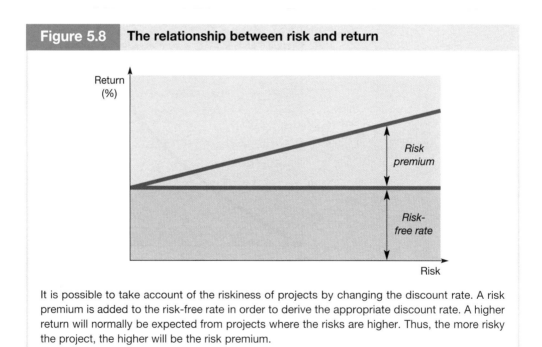

It is possible to take account of the riskiness of projects by changing the discount rate. A risk premium is added to the risk-free rate in order to derive the appropriate discount rate. A higher return will normally be expected from projects where the risks are higher. Thus, the more risky the project, the higher will be the risk premium.

The use of a risk-adjusted discount rate in investment appraisal provides a single-figure outcome that can be used to decide whether to accept or to reject a project. Often, managers have an intuitive grasp of the relationship between risk and return and so may well feel comfortable with this technique. However, there are practical difficulties with implementing this approach.

Activity 5.12

Can you think of what the practical problems with this approach might be?

Subjective judgement is required when assigning an investment project to a particular risk category and then in assigning a risk premium to each category. The choices made will reflect the personal views of the managers responsible and these may differ from the views of the shareholders they represent. The choices made can, nevertheless, make the difference between accepting and rejecting a particular project. (We shall see in Chapter 8, however, that there is a more sophisticated approach to deriving a risk premium that does not rely on subjective judgement.)

Expected net present value

Another means of assessing risk is through the use of statistical probabilities. It may be possible to identify a range of feasible values for a particular input, such as net cash flows, and to assign a probability of occurrence to each of these values. Using this information, we can derive an **expected value** which is a weighted average of the possible outcomes where the probabilities are used as weights. An **expected net present value (ENPV)** can then be derived using these expected values.

To illustrate this method in relation to an investment decision, let us consider Example 5.4.

Example 5.4

Patel Properties Ltd has the opportunity to acquire a lease on a block of flats that has only two years remaining before it expires. The cost of the lease would be £1,000,000. The occupancy rate of the block of flats is currently around 70 per cent and the flats are let almost exclusively to naval personnel. There is a large naval base located nearby and there is little other demand for the flats. The occupancy rate of the flats will change in the remaining two years of the lease depending on the outcome of a defence review. The navy is currently considering three options for the naval base. These are:

● *Option 1.* Increase the size of the base by closing down a naval base in another region and transferring the naval personnel to the base located near to the flats.
● *Option 2.* Close down the naval base near to the flats and leave only a skeleton staff there for maintenance purposes. The personnel would be moved to a base in another region.
● *Option 3.* Leave the naval base open but reduce staffing levels by 20 per cent.

The directors of Patel Properties Ltd have estimated the following net cash flows for each of the two years under each option and the probability of their occurrence:

	£	Probability
Option 1	800,000	0.6
Option 2	120,000	0.1
Option 3	400,000	0.3
		1.0

Note: The sum of the probabilities is 1.0 (that is, it is certain that one of the possible options will arise).

> **Example 5.4 continued**
>
> The business has a cost of capital of 10 per cent.
>
> Should the business purchase the lease on the block of flats?
>
> **Solution**
>
> To answer the question, the expected net present value (ENPV) of the proposed investment can be calculated. To do this, the weighted average of the possible outcomes for each year must first be calculated. This involves multiplying each cash flow by its probability of occurrence (as the probabilities are used as weights). The expected annual net cash flows will be:
>
> | | Cash flows | Probability | Expected cash flows |
> |---|---|---|---|
> | | £ | | £ |
> | Option 1 | 800,000 | 0.6 | 480,000 |
> | Option 2 | 120,000 | 0.1 | 12,000 |
> | Option 3 | 400,000 | 0.3 | 120,000 |
> | Expected net cash flows in each year | | | 612,000 |
>
> Having derived the expected net cash flows in each year, they can be discounted using a rate of 10 per cent to reflect the cost of capital.
>
> | | Expected cash flows | Discount rate 10% | Expected present value |
> |---|---|---|---|
> | | £ | | £ |
> | Year 1 | 612,000 | 0.909 | 556,308 |
> | Year 2 | 612,000 | 0.826 | 505,512 |
> | | | | 1,061,820 |
> | Less Initial investment | | | 1,000,000 |
> | Expected net present value (ENPV) | | | 61,820 |
>
> We can see that the ENPV is positive. Hence, the wealth of shareholders is expected to increase by purchasing the lease. (However, the size of the ENPV is small in relation to the initial investment and so the business may wish to check carefully the key assumptions used in the analysis before a final decision is made.)

The ENPV approach has the advantage of producing a single-figure outcome and of having a clear decision rule to apply (that is, if the ENPV is positive the business should invest, if it is negative it should not). However, this approach produces an average figure that may not be capable of actually occurring. This point was illustrated in Example 5.4 where the expected value of the net cash flows does not correspond to any of the stated options.

Using an average figure can also obscure the underlying risk associated with the project. Simply deriving the ENPV, as in Example 5.4, can be misleading. Without some idea of the individual possible outcomes and their probability of occurring, managers are in the dark. If either of Options 2 and 3 were to occur, the NPV of the investment would be negative (wealth destroying). It is 40 per cent probable that one of these options will occur, so this is a significant risk. Only if Option 1 were to occur (60 per cent probable), would investing in the flats represent a good decision. Of course, in advance of making the investment, which option will actually occur is not known.

None of the above should be taken to mean that the investment in the flats should not be made, simply that the managers are better placed to make a judgement where information on the possible outcomes is available. Thus, where the ENPV approach is being used, it is probably a good idea to reveal to managers the different possible outcomes and the probability attached to each outcome. By so doing, the managers will be able to gain an insight to the 'downside risk' attached to the project. This point is further illustrated by Activity 5.13.

Activity 5.13

Ukon Ltd is considering two competing projects. Details of each project are as follows:

● Project A has a 0.8 probability of producing a negative NPV of £500,000, a 0.1 probability of producing a positive NPV of £1.0 million, and a 0.1 probability of producing a positive NPV of £5.5 million.
● Project B has a 0.2 probability of producing a positive NPV of £125,000, a 0.3 probability of producing a positive NPV of £250,000, and a 0.5 probability of producing a positive NPV of £300,000.

What is the expected net present value (ENPV) of each project?

The ENPV of Project A is:

Probability	NPV	Expected value
	£	£
0.8	(500,000)	(400,000)
0.1	1,000,000	100,000
0.1	5,500,000	550,000
	ENPV	250,000

The ENPV of Project B is:

Probability	NPV	Expected value
	£	£
0.2	125,000	25,000
0.3	250,000	75,000
0.5	300,000	150,000
	ENPV	250,000

Although the ENPV of each project in Activity 5.13 is identical, this does not mean that the business will be indifferent about which project to undertake. Project A has a high probability of making a loss, whereas Project B is not expected to make a loss under either possible outcome. If we assume that investors are risk averse, they will prefer the business to take on Project B as this will provide the same level of expected return as Project A but has a lower level of risk.

It can be argued that the problem identified above may not be significant where the business is engaged in several similar projects, as it will be lost in the averaging process. However, in practice, investment projects may be unique events and this argument will not then apply. Also, where the project is large in relation to other projects undertaken the argument loses its force. There is also the problem that a factor that might cause one project to have an adverse outcome could also have adverse effects on other projects. For example, a large unexpected increase in the price of oil may have a simultaneous adverse effect on all of the investment projects of a particular business.

Event tree diagrams

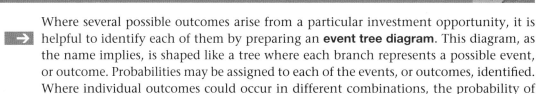

Where several possible outcomes arise from a particular investment opportunity, it is helpful to identify each of them by preparing an **event tree diagram**. This diagram, as the name implies, is shaped like a tree where each branch represents a possible event, or outcome. Probabilities may be assigned to each of the events, or outcomes, identified. Where individual outcomes could occur in different combinations, the probability of each combination can be derived by multiplying together the probabilities of each outcome.

Example 5.5 illustrates how a simple event tree may be prepared for an investment project with different possible outcomes that can combine in different ways.

Example 5.5

Zeta Computing Services Ltd has recently produced some software for a client organisation. The software has a life of two years and will then become obsolete. The cost of developing the software was £60,000. The client organisation has agreed to pay a licence fee of £80,000 a year for the software if it is used in only one of its two divisions and £120,000 a year if it is used in both of its divisions. The client may use the software for either one or two years in either division but will definitely use it in at least one division in each of the two years.

Zeta Computing Services Ltd believes there is a 0.6 chance that the licence fee received in any one year will be £80,000 and a 0.4 chance that it will be £120,000.

Produce an event tree diagram for the project.

Solution

The four possible outcomes attached to this project and their probability of occurrence (p) are as follows:

Outcome	Probability
1 Year 1 cash flow £80,000 ($p = 0.6$) and Year 2 cash flow £80,000 ($p = 0.6$). The probability of both years having cash flows of £80,000 will be (0.6×0.6)	= 0.36
2 Year 1 cash flow £120,000 ($p = 0.4$) and Year 2 cash flow £120,000 ($p = 0.4$). The probability of both years having cash flows of £120,000 will be (0.4×0.4)	= 0.16
3 Year 1 cash flow £120,000 ($p = 0.4$) and Year 2 cash flow £80,000 ($p = 0.6$). The probability of this sequence of cash flows occurring will be (0.4×0.6)	= 0.24
4 Year 1 cash flow £80,000 ($p = 0.6$) and Year 2 cash flow £120,000 ($p = 0.4$). The probability of this sequence of cash flows occurring will be (0.6×0.4)	= 0.24
	1.00

This information can be displayed in the form of an event tree diagram as shown in Figure 5.9.

Figure 5.9   Event tree diagram showing different possible project outcomes

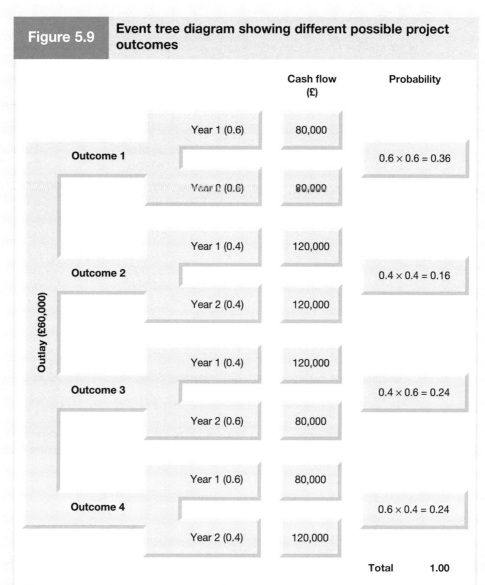

The event tree diagram sets out the different possible outcomes associated with a particular project and the probability of each outcome. We can see that each outcome is represented by a branch and that each branch has subsidiary branches. The sum of the probabilities attached to the outcomes must equal 1.00. In other words, it is certain that one of the possible outcomes will occur.

Activity 5.14

Kernow Cleaning Services Ltd provides street-cleaning services for local councils in the far south-west of England. The work is currently labour intensive and few machines are employed. However, the business has recently been considering the purchase of a fleet of street-cleaning vehicles at a total cost of £540,000. The vehicles have a life of four

Activity 5.14 continued

years and are likely to result in a considerable saving of labour costs. Estimates of the likely labour savings and their probability of occurrence are set out below:

	Estimated savings £	Probability of occurrence
Year 1	80,000	0.3
	160,000	0.5
	200,000	0.2
Year 2	140,000	0.4
	220,000	0.4
	250,000	0.2
Year 3	140,000	0.4
	200,000	0.3
	230,000	0.3
Year 4	100,000	0.3
	170,000	0.6
	200,000	0.1

Estimates for each year are independent of other years. The business has a cost of capital of 10 per cent.

Required:
(a) Calculate the expected net present value (ENPV) of the street-cleaning machines.
(b) Calculate the net present value (NPV) of the worst possible outcome and the probability of its occurrence.

(a) The first step is to calculate the expected annual cash flows:

Year 1	£	Year 2	£
£ 80,000 × 0.3	24,000	£140,000 × 0.4	56,000
£160,000 × 0.5	80,000	£220,000 × 0.4	88,000
£200,000 × 0.2	40,000	£250,000 × 0.2	50,000
	144,000		194,000

Year 3		Year 4	
£140,000 × 0.4	56,000	£100,000 × 0.3	30,000
£200,000 × 0.3	60,000	£170,000 × 0.6	102,000
£230,000 × 0.3	69,000	£200,000 × 0.1	20,000
	185,000		152,000

The expected net present value (ENPV) can now be calculated as follows:

Period	Expected cash flow £	Discount rate 10%	Expected PV £
0	(540,000)	1.000	(540,000)
1	144,000	0.909	130,896
2	194,000	0.826	160,244
3	185,000	0.751	138,935
4	152,000	0.683	103,816
		ENPV	(6,109)

(b) The worst possible outcome can be calculated by taking the lowest values of savings each year, as follows:

Period	Cash flow £	Discount rate 10%	PV £
0	(540,000)	1.000	(540,000)
1	80,000	0.909	72,720
2	140,000	0.826	115,640
3	140,000	0.751	105,140
4	100,000	0.683	68,300
			NPV (178,200)

The probability of occurrence can be obtained by multiplying together the probability of each of the worst outcomes above, that is, $0.3 \times 0.4 \times 0.4 \times 0.3 = 0.014$ (or 1.4 per cent).

Thus, the probability of occurrence is 1.4 per cent, which is very low.

Risk and the standard deviation

In the problems discussed so far, the number of possible outcomes relating to a particular project has been fairly small. Perhaps only two or three possible outcomes have been employed to illustrate particular principles. In reality, however, there may be a large number of outcomes that could occur. Indeed, a project may have thousands of possible outcomes, each with its own probability of occurrence. Although it would not be very realistic, let us suppose a particular project has a large number of possible outcomes and that we are able to identify each possible outcome and to assign a probability to it. This would mean that we could plot a probability distribution of the outcomes that could take the form of a continuous curve, such as the one shown in Figure 5.10.

Figure 5.10	**Probability distribution of outcomes for a single investment project**

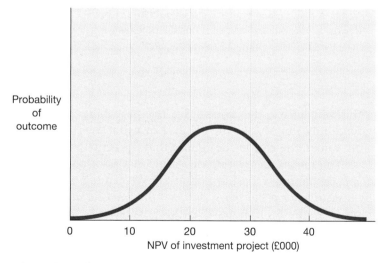

The figure shows the probability distribution of outcomes for a single investment project. We can see that the range of possible outcomes forms a continuous curve. The particular shape of the curve will vary according to the nature of the project.

The particular shape of the curve is likely to vary between investment projects. Variations in the shape of the curve can occur even where projects have identical expected values. To illustrate this point, the probability distribution for two separate projects that have the same expected value is shown in Figure 5.11. We can see, however, that Project A has a range of possible values that is much more tightly distributed around the expected value than Project B.

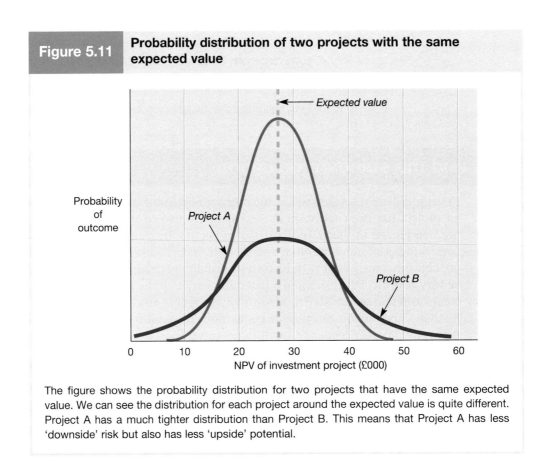

| Figure 5.11 | Probability distribution of two projects with the same expected value |

The figure shows the probability distribution for two projects that have the same expected value. We can see the distribution for each project around the expected value is quite different. Project A has a much tighter distribution than Project B. This means that Project A has less 'downside' risk but also has less 'upside' potential.

This difference in the shape of the two probability distributions can provide us with a useful indicator of risk. The graph shows that the tighter the distribution of possible future values, the greater the chance that the actual value will be close to the expected value. This means there is less 'downside' risk associated with the particular investment project (but also less 'upside' potential). We can say, therefore, that *the tighter the probability distribution of outcomes, the lower the risk associated with the investment project*. The graph in Figure 5.11 shows that the possible outcomes for Project A are much less spread out than those of Project B. Hence, Project A will be considered a less risky venture than Project B.

The variability of possible future values associated with a project can be measured using a statistical measure called the **standard deviation**. This is a measure of spread that is based on deviations from the mean, or expected value. To demonstrate how the standard deviation is calculated, let us consider Example 5.6.

Example 5.6

Telematix plc is considering two mutually exclusive projects: Cable and Satellite. The possible NPVs for each project and their associated probabilities are as follows:

Cable		Satellite	
NPV £m	Probability of occurrence	NPV £m	Probability of occurrence
10	0.1	15	0.6
20	0.5	20	0.2
25	0.4	40	0.2

To calculate the standard deviation, the ENPV for each project must be calculated. In the case of the Cable project, the ENPV is as follows:

(a) NPV £m	(b) Probability of occurrence	(c) = (a) × (b) ENPV £m
10	0.1	1.0
20	0.5	10.0
25	0.4	10.0
		21.0

The next step is to calculate the deviations around the ENPV by deducting the expected NPV from each possible outcome. For the Cable project, the following set of deviations will be obtained:

(a) Possible NPV £m	(b) ENPV £m	(c) = (a) – (b) Deviation £m
10	21	–11
20	21	–1
25	21	4

The calculations reveal two of the deviations are negative and one is positive. To prevent the positive and negative deviations from cancelling each other out, we can eliminate the negative signs by squaring the deviations. The sum of the squared deviations is referred to as the variance. The variance for the Cable project will be:

Deviations £m	Squared deviations £m
–11	121
–1	1
4	16
	Variance 138

The problem with the variance is that it provides a unit of measurement that is the square of the NPV deviations. In this case, the variance is 138 $(£m)^2$ which is difficult to interpret. To make things easier, it is a good idea to take the square root of the variance. The final step in calculating the standard deviation is to do just that. The standard deviation is:

$$\text{Standard deviation} = \sqrt{\text{Variance}}$$

→

Example 5.6 continued

For the Cable project, the standard deviation is:

$$\text{Standard deviation} = \sqrt{£138m}$$
$$= £11.74m$$

It was mentioned earlier that the standard deviation is a measure of spread. Thus, we can say that the higher the standard deviation for a particular investment project, the greater the spread, or variability, of possible outcomes.

Activity 5.15

Calculate the standard deviation for the Satellite project. Which project has the higher level of risk?

To answer this activity, the steps outlined above must be followed. Thus:

Step 1. Calculate the ENPV:

(a)	(b)	(c) = (a) × (b)
NPV	Probability of occurrence	ENPV
£m		£m
15	0.6	9.0
20	0.2	4.0
40	0.2	8.0
		21.0

Step 2. Calculate the deviations around the ENPV:

(a)	(b)	(c) = (a) – (b)
Possible NPV	ENPV	Deviation
£m	£m	£m
15	21	–6
20	21	–1
40	21	19

Step 3. Calculate the variance (that is, sum the squared deviations):

Deviations	Squared deviations
£m	£m
–6	36
–1	1
19	361
Variance	398

Step 4. Find the square root of the variance (that is, the standard deviation):*

$$\text{Standard deviation} = \sqrt{£398m}$$
$$= £19.95m$$

The Satellite project has the higher standard deviation and, therefore, the greater variability of possible outcomes. Hence, it has the higher level of risk.

* Computer software or calculators with statistical functions can be used to calculate the standard deviation and so this manual approach need not be used in practice. It is shown here for illustrative purposes.

The standard deviation and the normal distribution

If the distribution of possible outcomes has a symmetrical bell shape when plotted on a graph, it is referred to as a **normal distribution**. In Figure 5.12 we can see an example of a normal distribution. Note that this kind of distribution has a single peak and that there is an equal tapering off from the peak to each tail. In practice, distributions of data often display this pattern. Where a normal distribution occurs, it is possible to identify the extent to which possible outcomes will deviate from the mean or expected value. The following rules will apply:

● Approximately 68 per cent of possible outcomes will fall within one standard deviation from the mean or expected value.
● Approximately 95 per cent of possible outcomes will fall within two standard deviations from the mean or expected value.
● Approximately 100 per cent of possible outcomes will fall within three standard deviations from the mean or expected value.

Even when the possible outcomes do not form a precise symmetrical bell shape, or normal distribution, these rules can still be reasonably accurate. We shall see below how these rules may be useful in interpreting the level of risk associated with a project.

| Figure 5.12 | **The normal distribution and standard deviations** |

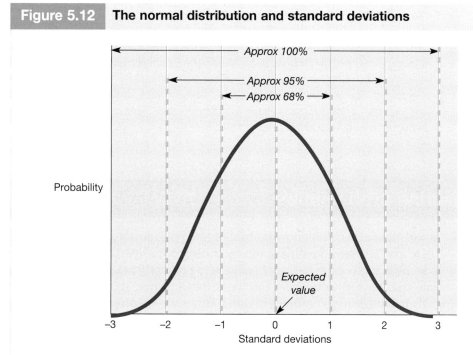

The figure shows the probability of an outcome being one, two and three standard deviations from the mean or expected value. Note that approximately 100 per cent of possible outcomes will fall within three standard deviations of the mean (assuming a normal distribution). There is only a very small probability of an outcome being more than three standard deviations from the mean.

The expected value–standard deviation rules

Where the expected value of the returns of investment opportunities and their standard deviation are known, we have both a measure of return and a measure of risk that can be used for making decisions. If investors are risk averse, they will be seeking the highest level of return for a given level of risk (or the lowest level of risk for a given level of return). The following decision rules can, therefore, be applied where the possible outcomes for investment projects are normally distributed.

Where there are two competing projects, X and Y, Project X should be chosen when either:

- the expected return of Project X is equal to, or greater than, that of Project Y and the standard deviation of Project X is lower than that of Project Y, or
- the expected return of Project X is greater than that of Project Y and the standard deviation of Project X is equal to, or lower than, that of Project Y.

The **expected value-standard deviation rules**, as they are known, do not cover all possibilities. For example, the rules cannot help us discriminate between two projects where one has both a higher expected return and a higher standard deviation. Nevertheless, they provide some help for managers.

Activity 5.16

Refer back to Example 5.6 above. Which project should be chosen and why? (Assume the possible outcomes are normally distributed.)

We can see from our earlier calculations that the Cable and Satellite projects have an identical expected net present value. However, the Cable project has a much lower standard deviation, indicating less variability of possible outcomes. Applying the decision rules mentioned above, this means that the Cable project should be selected; or to put it another way, a risk-averse investor would prefer the Cable project as it provides the same expected return for a lower level of risk.

Measuring probabilities

As we might expect, assigning probabilities to possible outcomes can often be a problem. There may be many possible outcomes arising from a particular investment project and to identify each outcome and then assign a probability to it may prove to be an impossible task. Nevertheless, there are circumstances where it is feasible to use probabilities.

Probabilities may be derived using either an objective or a subjective approach. **Objective probabilities** are based on information gathered from experience. For example, the transport manager of a business operating a fleet of motor vans may be able to provide information concerning the possible life of a newly purchased van based on the record of similar vans acquired in the past. From the information available, probabilities may be developed for different possible life spans. However, past experience may not always be a reliable guide to the future, particularly during a period of rapid change. In the case of the motor vans, for example, changes in design and technology or changes in the purpose for which the vans are being used may undermine the validity

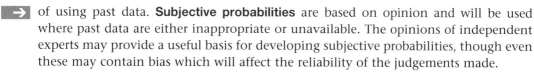

of using past data. **Subjective probabilities** are based on opinion and will be used where past data are either inappropriate or unavailable. The opinions of independent experts may provide a useful basis for developing subjective probabilities, though even these may contain bias which will affect the reliability of the judgements made.

Despite these problems, we should not dismiss the use of probabilities. They help to make explicit some of the risks associated with a project and can help managers to appreciate the uncertainties that must be faced. **Real World 5.3** provides an example of the use of probabilities to assess the risks associated with an investment project.

REAL WORLD 5.3

Assigning probabilities

In 2005, the transport strategy for South Hampshire included a light rail transit route linking Fareham, Gosport and Portsmouth. The proposed route was 14.3 km long and contained 16 stops. A thorough appraisal of the proposed investment was undertaken, which estimated an NPV of £272 million for the scheme. An integral part of the investment appraisal involved assigning probabilities to various risks identified with the scheme, including risks relating to design, construction and development, performance, operating costs, revenue streams and technology.

During the period of construction and development, a number of risks were identified. One such risk relates to cost overruns on the construction of a tunnel along part of the route. The total cost of the tunnel was estimated at £42.2 million but the following probabilities were assigned to various possible cost overruns.

Probability of occurrence %	Cost £000	Cost of risk £000	Expected cost £000
34	100	34	
46	1,000	460	
10	2,000	200	
5	4,000	200	
4	6,000	240	
1	10,000	100	1,234
100			

We can see from the table that it was estimated that there would be an 80 per cent chance of a cost overrun of £1.0 million or less and a 90 per cent chance that it would be £2.0 million or less.

Source: South Hampshire Rapid Transit Fareham–Gosport–Portsmouth Investment Appraisal, 2005, www.hants.gov.uk.

Portfolio effects and risk reduction

So far, our consideration of risk has looked at the problem from the viewpoint of an investment project being undertaken in isolation. However, in practice, a business will normally invest in a range, or *portfolio*, of investment projects rather than a single project. This approach to investment provides a potentially useful way of reducing risk. The problem with investing all available funds in a single project is, of course, that an unfavourable outcome could have disastrous consequences for the business. By investing in a spread of projects, an adverse outcome from a single project is less likely to have severe repercussions. The saying, 'don't put all your eggs in one basket', neatly sums up the best advice concerning investment policy.

→ Investing in a range of different projects is referred to as **diversification**, and holding a diversified portfolio of investment projects can reduce the total risk associated with the business. Indeed, in theory, it is possible to combine two risky investment projects so as to create a portfolio of projects that is riskless. To illustrate this point let us consider Example 5.7.

Example 5.7

Frank N. Stein plc has the opportunity to invest in two investment projects in Transylvania. The possible outcomes from each project will depend on whether the ruling party of the country wins or loses the next election. (For the sake of simplicity, we shall assume the ruling party will either win or lose outright and there is no possibility of another outcome, such as a hung parliament.) The NPV from each project under each outcome is estimated as follows:

	Project 1 NPV £m	Project 2 NPV £m
Ruling party wins	(20)	30
Ruling party loses	40	(30)

What should the business do to manage the risks involved in each project?

Solution

If the business invests in *both* projects, the total NPV under each outcome will be as follows:

	Project 1 NPV £m	Project 2 NPV £m	Total returns £m
Ruling party wins	(20)	30	10
Ruling party loses	40	(30)	10

We can see that, whatever the outcome of the election, the total NPV for the business will be the same (that is, £10 million). Although the possible returns from each project vary according to the results of the election, they are inversely related and so the total returns will be stabilised. As risk can be diversified away in this manner, the relationship between the returns from individual investment projects is an important issue for managers.

The coefficient of correlation

A business may eliminate the variability in total returns by investing in projects whose returns are inversely related, such as in the example above. Ideally, a business should invest in a spread of investment projects so that when certain projects generate low (or negative) returns, other projects are generating high returns, and vice versa. It is possible to measure the degree to which the returns from individual projects are related by using the **coefficient of correlation**. This coefficient is an abstract measure that ranges along a continuum between +1 and –1.

When the coefficient for two projects, X and Y, is positive, it means that increases in the returns from Project X will be accompanied by increases in returns from Project Y: the higher the positive measure, the stronger the relationship between the returns of the two projects. A coefficient of +1 indicates a perfect positive correlation and this means that the returns are moving together in perfect step. In Figure 5.13, we see a graph showing the returns for two investment projects that have a perfect positive correlation.

Figure 5.13	**Two projects whose returns have a perfect positive correlation**

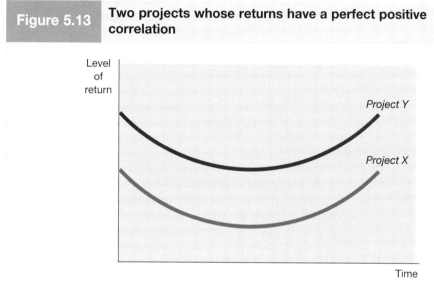

The diagram shows the returns from two projects moving in perfect step with each other. The rises and falls in returns in one project are precisely matched by rises and falls in returns in the other project.

If the coefficient of correlation is negative, increases in the returns from Project X will be accompanied by decreases in the returns from Project Y. A coefficient of –1 indicates a perfect negative correlation between two projects. In other words, the projects' returns will move together in perfect step, but in *opposite directions*.

Activity 5.17

Suppose the returns from Project Y had a perfect negative correlation with those of Project X. Draw a graph depicting the relationship between the two projects.

·····

The graph for two investment projects whose returns are perfectly negatively correlated is shown in Figure 5.14.

Activity 5.17 continued

Figure 5.14	**Two projects whose returns have a perfect negative correlation**

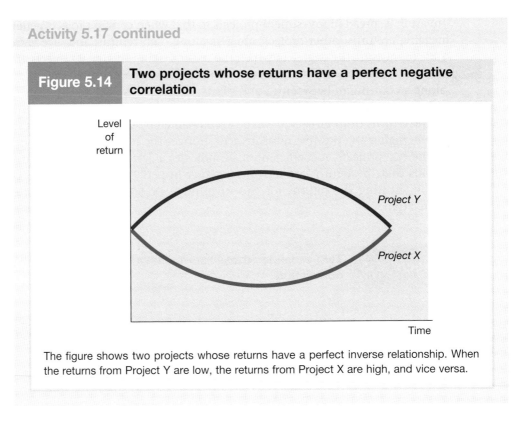

The figure shows two projects whose returns have a perfect inverse relationship. When the returns from Project Y are low, the returns from Project X are high, and vice versa.

If the coefficient of correlation between the returns of two projects is 0, this means that the returns from Project X and Project Y move independently of one another and so there is no relationship between them.

To eliminate risk completely, a business should invest in projects whose returns are perfectly negatively correlated. This will mean that the variability in returns between projects will cancel each other out and so risk will be completely diversified away. So far, so good – unfortunately, however, it is rarely possible to do this. In the real world, projects whose returns are perfectly negatively correlated are extremely difficult to find. Nevertheless, risk can still be diversified away to some extent by investing in projects whose returns do not have a perfect positive correlation. Provided the correlation between projects is less than +1, some offsetting will occur. The further the coefficient of correlation moves away from +1 and towards −1 on the scale, the greater this offsetting effect will be.

Activity 5.18

Should the managers of a business seek project diversification as their main objective?

The answer is no. Even if two projects could be found whose returns had a perfect negative correlation, this does not necessarily mean that they should be pursued. The expected returns from the projects must also be considered when making any investment decision.

One potential problem of diversification is that a range of different projects can create greater project management problems. Managers will have to deal with a variety of different projects with different technical and resource issues to resolve. The greater the number of projects, the greater the management problems are likely to be.

Real World 5.4 discusses the likely impact of a reduction in the level of diversification of one well-known business.

REAL WORLD 5.4

Rock and risk

In December 2006, the board of directors of Rank Group plc announced that it had agreed to sell Hard Rock, the rock-music-based entertainment business, to Seminole Hard Rock Entertainment Inc. for US$965 million. The directors of Rank acknowledged the effect of this sale on the remainder of the business as follows:

> The majority of the current Rank Group's profits are generated by three businesses: Hard Rock, Mecca Bingo and Grosvenor Casinos. The three businesses operate in different market segments and, notwithstanding global economic factors, the financial performance and prospects of the three businesses may be impacted by different and unrelated factors, which provide a benefit of diversification. Following the sale of Hard Rock, there could be a greater risk of share price volatility as this diversification will be more limited.

Source: Adapted from 'Proposed Disposal of Hard Rock and related Special Dividend and Share Consolidation. Notice of Extraordinary General Meeting', The Rank Group plc, December 2006 (www.rank.com).

Diversifiable and non-diversifiable risk

The benefits of risk diversification can be obtained by increasing the number of projects within the investment portfolio. As each investment project is added to the portfolio, the variability of total returns will diminish, provided that the projects are not perfectly correlated. However, there are limits to the benefits of diversification due to the nature of the risks faced. The total risk relating to a particular project can be divided into two types: **diversifiable risk** and **non-diversifiable risk**. As the names suggest, it is only the former type of risk that can be eliminated through diversification.

The two types of risk can be described as follows:

● *Diversifiable risk* is that part of the total risk that is specific to the project, such as changes in key personnel, legal regulations, the degree of competition and so on. By spreading available funds between investment projects, it is possible to offset adverse outcomes occurring in one project against beneficial outcomes in another. (Diversifiable risk is also referred to as avoidable risk, or unsystematic risk.)

● *Non-diversifiable risk* is that part of the total risk that is common to all projects and which, therefore, cannot be diversified away. This element of risk arises from general market conditions and will be affected by such factors as the rate of inflation, the general level of interest rates, exchange rate movements and the rate of growth within the economy. (Non-diversifiable risk is also referred to as unavoidable risk, or systematic risk.)

In Figure 5.15, the relationship between the level of portfolio risk and the size of the portfolio is shown. We can see that, as the number of projects increases, the diversifiable element of total risk is reduced. This does not mean, necessarily, that a business should invest in a large number of projects. Many of the benefits from diversification can often be reaped from investing in a relatively small number of projects. In Figure 5.15, we can see the additional benefits from each investment project diminish quite sharply.

Figure 5.15 **Reducing risk through diversification**

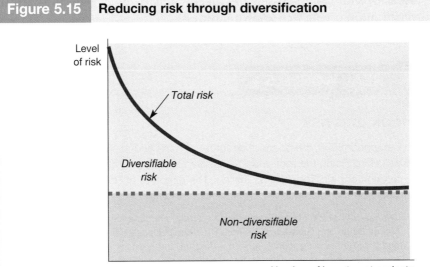

The figure shows that, as the size of the portfolio of projects is increased, the level of total risk is reduced. However, the rate of reduction in the level of total risk decreases quite sharply and soon reaches a point where investing in further projects to reduce risk is of little or no value.

This suggests that a business with a large portfolio of projects may gain very little from further diversification.

Non-diversifiable risk is based on general economic conditions and therefore all businesses will be affected. However, certain businesses are more sensitive to changes in economic conditions than others. For example, during a recession, some types of businesses will be badly affected, whereas others will be only slightly affected.

Activity 5.19

Provide two examples of businesses that are likely to be:

(a) badly affected by an economic recession
(b) only slightly affected by an economic recession.

The types of business that are likely to be badly hit by recession will include those selling expensive or luxury goods and services such as:

- hotels and restaurants
- travel companies
- house builders and construction companies
- airlines
- jewellers.

The types of business that are likely to be only slightly affected by recession will include those selling essential goods and services such as:

- gas and electricity suppliers
- water suppliers
- basic food retailers and producers
- undertakers.

The businesses that are likely to be badly affected by an economic recession will usually have a cyclical pattern of profits. Thus, during a period of economic growth, these businesses may make large profits, and during periods of recession they may make large losses. The businesses that are likely to be only slightly affected will tend to have a fairly stable pattern of profits over the economic cycle.

The distinction between diversifiable and non-diversifiable risk is an important issue to which we shall return when considering the cost of capital in the next chapter.

Risk assessment in practice

Surveys of UK businesses indicate that risk assessment methods have become more widely used over time. These surveys also indicate that sensitivity analysis and scenario analysis are the most popular methods. **Real World 5.5** sets out evidence from a fairly recent survey by Alkaraan and Northcott of large UK manufacturing businesses, which are consistent with these findings.

REAL WORLD 5.5

Assessing risk

The survey of 83 large UK manufacturing businesses by Alkaraan and Northcott (see Chapter 4), asked respondents to reveal their usage of risk analysis techniques when assessing investment projects. The following table sets out the results.

Method	Non-strategic investment projects Mean score	Strategic investment projects Mean score
1. Adjust required payback period to allow for risk	2.2892	2.6867
2. Adjust required return on investment to allow for risk	2.5181	3.1084
3. Adjust discount rate to allow for risk	2.6747	3.0723
4. Adjust forecast cash flows to allow for risk	2.8193	3.2169
5. Probability analysis	2.4337	2.6867
6. Computer simulation	1.8434	2.0000
7. Beta analysis (capital asset pricing model)*	1.7108	1.7590
8. Sensitivity/scenario analysis	3.1928	3.4699

Response scale: 1 = never, 2 = rarely, 3 = often, 4 = mostly, 5 = always.
* This method will be discussed in the following chapter.

The table shows that sensitivity/scenario analysis is the most popular way of dealing with risk. It also shows that some unsophisticated methods of dealing with risk, such as shortening the payback period and adjusting the cash flows, are more popular than sophisticated methods such as computer simulation. Statistical analysis showed that methods 1, 2 and 4 above were used significantly more for strategic investments than for non-strategic investments.

The survey also found that 89 per cent of businesses used sensitivity/scenario analysis, whilst 82 per cent raised the required rate of return, 77 per cent used probability analysis and 75 per cent shortened the payback period. Clearly, many businesses use more than one method of dealing with risk.

Source: Alkaraan and Northcott (see reference 1 at the end of the chapter).

SUMMARY

The main points in this chapter may be summarised as follows:

Investment decisions when funds are limited

- When projects are divisible, managers should maximise the present value per £ of scarce finance.
- The profitability index provides a measure of the present value per £ of scarce finance.
- Where funding requirements extend beyond a single period, linear programming can be used to maximise NPV.

Comparing projects with unequal lives

- These can be dealt with by assuming the projects form part of a repeat chain of replacement and then make comparisons using the shortest-common-period-of-time approach.
- Alternatively, the equivalent-annual-annuity approach converts the NPV of a project into an annual annuity stream over its expected life.

The problem of inflation

- Either include inflation by adjusting the annual cash flows and the discount rate to take account of price increases.
- Or exclude inflation by adjusting the cash flow to real terms and by using a 'real' discount rate.

Risk

- This is important because of the long time scales and amounts involved in investment decisions.
- Various methods of dealing with risk are available.

Sensitivity analysis

- This provides an assessment, taking each input factor in turn, of how much each one can vary from estimate before a project is not viable:
  - it provides useful insights to projects
  - it does not give a clear decision rule, but provides an impression
  - it can be rather static.

Scenario analysis

- This changes a number of variables simultaneously to provide a particular 'state of the world'.
- Usually three different states – optimistic, pessimistic and most likely – are portrayed.
- It does not indicate the likelihood of each state occurring or the other possible states that may occur.

Simulations

- This involves identifying the key variables of the project and their key relationships.
- Possible values are attached to each factor and a computer is used to select one of the possible values on a random basis to produce a projected cash flow.

- The process is repeated many times to obtain a probability distribution of the values of the cash flows.
- It can be costly and time consuming.

Risk preferences of shareholders

- Given a choice between two projects with the same expected return but with different levels of risk:
  - risk-seeking investors will choose the project with the higher level of risk
  - risk-neutral investors will have no preference
  - risk-averse investors will choose the project with the lower level of risk.
- Most investors appear to be risk averse.

Risk adjusted discount rate

- Risk-averse investors will require a risk premium for risky projects.
- Using a risk-adjusted discount rate, where a risk premium is added to the risk-free rate, is a logical response to risk.

Expected net present value (ENPV) approach

- This assigns probabilities to possible outcomes.
- The expected value is the weighted average of the possible outcomes where the probabilities are used as weights.
- The ENPV approach:
  - it provides a single value and a clear decision rule
  - the single ENPV figure can hide the real risk
  - it is useful for the ENPV figure to be supported by information on the range of possible outcomes
  - probabilities may be subjective (based on opinion) or objective (based on evidence).

The standard deviation

- Is a measure of spread based on deviations from the mean.
- Provides a measure of risk.

Portfolio effect

- By holding a diversified portfolio of investment projects, a business can reduce the total risk associated with its projects.
- Ideally, a business should hold a spread of projects, such that when certain projects generate low returns, others generate high returns.
- Only diversifiable risk can be eliminated through diversification.

→ **Key terms**

Profitability index   p. 173
Linear programming   p. 173
Shortest-common-period-of-time
   approach   p. 175
Annuity   p. 177
Equivalent-annual-annuity approach
   p. 177
Risk   p. 181
Sensitivity analysis   p. 181
Sensitivity chart   p. 187
Scenario analysis   p. 189
Simulation   p. 189
Risk-seeking investors   p. 190
Risk-neutral investors   p. 190
Risk-averse investors   p. 190
Utility function   p. 191

Risk-adjusted discount rate   p. 194
Expected value   p. 195
Expected net present value (ENPV)
   p. 195
Event tree diagram   p. 198
Standard deviation   p. 202
Normal distribution   p. 205
Expected value–standard deviation
   rules   p. 206
Objective probabilities   p. 206
Subjective probabilities   p. 207
Diversification   p. 208
Coefficient of correlation   p. 209
Diversifiable risk   p. 211
Non-diversifiable risk   p. 211

For definitions of these terms see the Glossary, pp. 574–583.

Reference

1. 'Strategic capital investment decision-making: A role for emergent analysis tools? A study of practice in large UK manufacturing companies', *Alkaraan, F. and Northcott, D.* **The British Accounting Review**, Vol. 38, 2006, pp. 149–73.

Further reading

If you wish to explore the topics discussed in this chapter in more depth, try the following books:

Business Finance: Theory and practice, *McLaney, E.*, 8th edn, Financial Times Prentice Hall, 2009, chapters 5 and 6.

Corporate Finance and Investment, *Pike, R. and Neale, B.*, 5th edn, Prentice Hall International, 2006, chapters 6–9.

Corporate Financial Management, *Arnold, G.*, 3rd edn, Financial Times Prentice Hall, 2005, chapters 3, 5, 6 and 7.

Fundamentals of Corporate Finance, *Ross, S., Westerfield, R. and Jordan, B.*, 8th edn, Irwin Professional Publishing, 2007, chapter 11.

REVIEW QUESTIONS

Answers to these questions can be found at the back of the book on p. 542.

5.1 There is evidence to suggest that some businesses fail to take account of inflation in investment decisions. Does it really matter given that, in recent years, the level of inflation has been low? What would be the effect on NPV calculations (that is, would NPV be overstated or understated) of dealing with inflation incorrectly by (a) discounting nominal cash flows at real discount rates and (b) discounting real cash flows at nominal discount rates?

5.2 What is risk and why is it an important issue for investment decision making?

5.3 What practical problems arise when using the risk-adjusted discount rate to deal with the problem of risk?

5.4 Explain why the standard deviation may be useful in measuring risk.

EXERCISES

Exercises 5.5 to 5.7 are more advanced than 5.1 to 5.4. Those with coloured numbers have answers at the back of the book, starting on p. 557.

 If you wish to try more exercises, visit the students' side of this book's Companion Website.

5.1 Lee Caterers Ltd is about to make an investment in new kitchen equipment. It is considering whether to replace the existing kitchen equipment with cook/freeze or cook/chill technology. The following cash flows are expected from each form of technology:

	Cook/chill	Cook/freeze
	£000	£000
Initial outlay	(200)	(390)
1 year's time	85	88
2 years' time	94	102
3 years' time	86	110
4 years' time	62	110
5 years' time	–	110
6 years' time	–	90
7 years' time	–	85
8 years' time	–	60

The business would expect to replace the new equipment purchased with similar equipment at the end of its life. The cost of finance for the business is 10 per cent.

Required:

Which type of equipment should the business invest in? Use both approaches considered in the chapter to support your conclusions.

5.2   D'Arcy (Builders) Ltd is considering three possible investment projects: A, B and C. The expected pattern of cash flows for each project is:

Project cash flows

	A	B	C
	£000	£000	£000
Initial outlay	(17)	(20)	(24)
1 year's time	11	12	9
2 years' time	5	7	9
3 years' time	7	7	11
4 years' time	6	6	13

The business has a cost of finance of 10 per cent and the capital expenditure budget for next year is £25 million.

Required:

Which investment project(s) should the business undertake assuming:

(a) each project is divisible; and

(b) each project is indivisible?

5.3   Simonson Engineers plc is considering the building of a new plant in Indonesia to produce products for the South-east Asian market. To date, £450,000 has been invested in market research and site surveys. The cost of building the plant will be £9 million and it will be in operation and paid for in one year's time. Estimates of the likely cash flows from the plant and their probability of occurrence are set out as follows:

	Estimated cash flows £m	Probability of occurrence
Year 2	2.0	0.2
	3.5	0.6
	4.0	0.2
Year 3	2.5	0.2
	3.0	0.4
	5.0	0.4
Year 4	3.0	0.2
	4.0	0.7
	5.0	0.1
Year 5	2.5	0.2
	3.0	0.5
	6.0	0.3

Estimates for each year are independent of each other. The cost of capital for the business is 10 per cent.

Required:

(a) Calculate the expected net present value of the proposed plant.

(b) Calculate the net present value of the worst possible outcome and the probability of its occurrence.

(c) Should the business invest in the new plant? Why?

5.4 Helena Chocolate Products Ltd is considering the introduction of a new chocolate bar into their range of chocolate products. The new chocolate bar will require the purchase of a new piece of equipment costing £30,000 which will have no other use and no residual value on completion of the project. Financial data relating to the new product are as follows:

	Per bar (£)
Selling price	0.60
Variable costs	0.22

Fixed costs of £20,000 a year will be apportioned to the new product. These costs represent a 'fair share' of the total fixed costs of the business. The costs are unlikely to change as a result of any decision to introduce new products into the existing range. Other developments currently being finalised will mean that the new product will have a life of only three years and the level of expected demand for the new product is uncertain. The marketing department has produced the following levels of demand and the probability of each for all three years of the product's life.

Year 1		Year 2		Year 3	
Sales (units)	Probability	Sales (units)	Probability	Sales (units)	Probability
100,000	0.2	140,000	0.3	180,000	0.5
120,000	0.4	150,000	0.3	160,000	0.3
125,000	0.3	160,000	0.2	120,000	0.1
130,000	0.1	200,000	0.2	100,000	0.1

A rival business has offered to buy the right to produce and sell the new chocolate bar for £100,000. The cost of finance is 10 per cent and interest charges on the money borrowed to finance the project are expected to be £3,000 per year.

Required:
(a) Compute the expected net present value of the product.
(b) Advise the directors on the appropriate course of action. Give reasons.

5.5 Devonia (Laboratories) Ltd has recently carried out successful clinical trials on a new type of skin cream which has been developed to reduce the effects of ageing. Research and development costs incurred by the business in relation to the new product amount to £160,000. In order to gauge the market potential of the new product, an independent firm of market research consultants was hired at a cost of £15,000. The market research report submitted by the consultants indicates that the skin cream is likely to have a product life of four years and could be sold to retail chemists and large department stores at a price of £20 per 100 ml container. For each of the four years of the new product's life, sales demand has been estimated as follows:

Number of 100 ml containers sold	Probability of occurrence
0.3	11,000
0.6	14,000
0.1	16,000

If the business decides to launch the new product it is possible for production to begin at once. The necessary equipment to produce the product is already owned by the business and originally cost £150,000. At the end of the new product's life it is estimated that the equipment could be sold for £35,000. If the business decides against launching the new product the equipment will be sold immediately for £85,000 as it will be of no further use to the business.

The new skin cream will require one hour's labour for each 100 ml container produced. The cost of labour for the new product is £8.00 an hour. Additional workers will have to be recruited to produce the new product. At the end of the product's life the workers are unlikely to be offered further work with the business and redundancy costs of £10,000 are expected. The cost of the ingredients for each 100 ml container is £6.00. Additional overheads arising from production of the product is expected to be £15,000 a year.

The new skin cream has attracted the interest of the business's competitors. If the business decides not to produce and sell the skin cream it can sell the patent rights to a major competitor immediately for £125,000.

Devonia (Laboratories) Ltd has a cost of capital of 12 per cent. Ignore taxation.

Required:
(a) Calculate the expected net present value (ENPV) of the new product.
(b) State, with reasons, whether or not Devonia (Laboratories) Ltd should launch the new product.
(c) Discuss the strengths and weaknesses of the expected net present value approach for making investment decisions.

5.6   Nimby plc is considering two mutually exclusive projects: Delphi and Oracle. The possible NPVs for each project and their associated probabilities are as follows:

Delphi		Oracle	
NPV	*Probability of occurrence*	*NPV*	*Probability of occurrence*
£m		*£m*	
20	0.2	30	0.5
40	0.6	40	0.3
60	0.2	65	0.2

Required:
(a) Calculate the expected net present value and the standard deviation associated with each project.
(b) Which project would you select and why? State any assumptions you have made in coming to your conclusions.
(c) Discuss the limitations of the standard deviation as a measure of project risk.

5.7   Plato Pharmaceuticals Ltd has invested £300,000 to date in developing a new type of insect repellent. The repellent is now ready for production and sale, and the marketing director estimates that the product will sell 150,000 bottles a year over the next five years. The selling price of the insect repellent will be £5 a bottle and variable costs are estimated to be £3 a bottle. Fixed costs (excluding depreciation) are expected to be £200,000 a year. This figure is made up of £160,000 additional fixed costs and £40,000 fixed costs relating to the existing business which will be apportioned to the new product.

In order to produce the repellent, machinery and equipment costing £520,000 will have to be purchased immediately. The estimated residual value of this machinery and equipment in five years' time is £100,000. The business calculates depreciation on a straight-line basis.

The business has a cost of capital of 12 per cent. Ignore taxation.

Required:
(a) Calculate the net present value of the product.
(b) Undertake sensitivity analysis to show by how much the following factors would have to change before the product ceased to be worthwhile:
   (i)   The discount rate.
   (ii) The initial outlay on machinery and equipment.
   (iii) The net operating cash flows.
   (iv) The residual value of the machinery and equipment.

6

Financing a business 1: sources of finance

INTRODUCTION

This is the first of two chapters that examine the financing of businesses. In this chapter, we identify the main sources of finance available to businesses and discuss the main features of each source. We also consider the factors to be taken into account when choosing among the various sources of finance available.

In the following chapter, we go on to examine capital markets, including the role and efficiency of the London Stock Exchange and the ways in which share capital can be issued. We also consider the ways in which smaller businesses, which do not have access to the London Stock Exchange, may raise finance.

LEARNING OUTCOMES

When you have completed this chapter, you should be able to:

- Identify the main sources of external finance available to a business and explain the advantages and disadvantages of each source.

- Identify the main sources of internal finance available to a business and explain the advantages and disadvantages of each source.

- Discuss the factors to be taken into account when choosing an appropriate source of finance.

Sources of finance

When considering the various sources of finance available, it is useful to distinguish between *external* and *internal* sources of finance. By external sources we mean those that require the agreement of someone beyond the directors and managers of the business. Thus, finance from an issue of new shares is an external source because it requires the agreement of potential shareholders. Internal sources of finance, on the other hand, do not require agreement from other parties and arise from management decisions. Thus, retained profits are a source of internal finance because the directors have the power to retain profits without the agreement of shareholders, whose profits they are.

Within each of the categories just described, we can further distinguish between *long-term* and *short-term* finance. There is no agreed definition concerning each of these terms but, for the purpose of this chapter, a source of long-term finance will be defined as one that is expected to provide finance for at least one year. Sources of short-term finance typically provide finance for a shorter period. As we shall see, sources that are seen as short term when first used by the business often end up being used for quite long periods.

We shall begin by considering the various external sources of finance available and then go on to consider the various internal sources.

External sources of finance

Figure 6.1 summarises the main external sources of long-term and short-term finance.

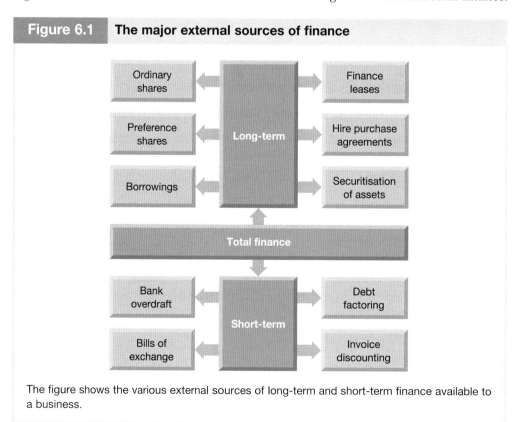

Figure 6.1 **The major external sources of finance**

The figure shows the various external sources of long-term and short-term finance available to a business.

External sources of long-term finance

As Figure 6.1 reveals, the major external sources of long-term finance are:

- ordinary shares
- preference shares
- borrowings
- finance leases, including sale- and leaseback arrangements
- hire purchase
- securitisation of assets.

We shall look at each of these sources in turn.

Ordinary shares

Ordinary shares represent the risk capital of a business and form the backbone of a business's financial structure. There is no fixed rate of dividend and ordinary share-holders will receive a dividend only if profits available for distribution still remain after other investors (preference shareholders and lenders) have received their dividend or interest payments. If the business is wound up, the ordinary shareholders will receive any proceeds from asset disposals only after lenders and creditors, and, in some cases, preference shareholders, have received their entitlements. Because of the high risks associated with this form of investment, ordinary shareholders will normally expect a relatively high rate of return.

Although ordinary shareholders have a potential loss liability, which is limited to the amount they have invested or agreed to invest, the potential returns from their invest-ment are unlimited. After preference shareholders and lenders have received their returns, all the remaining profits will accrue to the ordinary shareholders. Thus, while their 'downside' risk is limited, their 'upside' potential is not. Ordinary shareholders control the business through their voting rights, which give them the power to elect the directors and to remove them from office.

From the business's (the directors') perspective, ordinary shares can be a valuable form of financing compared to borrowing. It may be possible to avoid paying a dividend, whereas it is not usually possible to avoid interest payments.

Activity 6.1

Under what circumstances might a business wish to avoid paying a dividend?

Two circumstances spring to mind:

- An expanding business may prefer to retain funds in order to fuel future growth.
- A business in difficulties may need the funds to meet its operating costs and so may find making a dividend a real burden.

Real World 6.1 looks at the attitude of one well-known businessman to paying dividends.

REAL WORLD 6.1

No frills, no dividends and no brains

Michael O'Leary, the colourfully spoken chief executive of Ryanair Holdings plc, the 'no-frills' airline, was very clear on his attitude to dividends. He said, 'We are never paying a dividend as long as I live and breathe and as long as I'm the largest shareholder. If you are stupid enough to invest in an airline for its dividend flow you should be put back in the loony bin where you came from.'

Presumably, Ryanair is expanding at a rate that eats up all available finances.

Source: A. Osborne, 'Ryanair blunted by Buzz takeover', *Daily Telegraph*, 6 August 2004.

Although a business financed by ordinary shares can avoid making cash payments to shareholders when it is not prudent to do so, the market value of the shares may go down. The cost to the business of financing through ordinary shares may become higher if shareholders feel uncertain about future dividends. On the other hand, for a business like Ryanair, which is expanding its operations in a profitable way, share prices are likely to reflect this despite the lack of dividends.

It is also worth pointing out that the business does not obtain any tax relief on dividends paid to shareholders, whereas interest on borrowings is tax deductible. This makes it more expensive for the business to pay £1 of dividend than £1 of interest on borrowings.

Preference shares

Preference shares offer investors a lower level of risk than ordinary shares. Provided there are sufficient profits available, preference shares will normally be given a fixed rate of dividend each year and preference dividends will be paid the first slice of any dividend paid. Should the business be wound up, preference shareholders may be given priority over the claims of ordinary shareholders. (The business's particular documents of incorporation will state the precise rights of preference shareholders in this respect.)

Activity 6.2

Would you expect the returns to preference shares to be higher or lower than those to ordinary shares?

Preference shareholders will be offered a lower level of return than ordinary shareholders. This is because of the lower level of risk associated with this form of investment (preference shareholders have priority over ordinary shareholders regarding dividends, and perhaps capital repayment).

Preference shareholders are not usually given voting rights, although these may be granted where the preference dividend is in arrears. Both preference shares and ordinary shares are, in effect, redeemable. The business is allowed to buy back the shares from shareholders at any time.

Activity 6.3

Would you expect the market price of ordinary shares or of preference shares to be the more volatile? Why?

The share price, which reflects the expected future returns from the share, will normally be less volatile for preference shares than for ordinary shares. The dividends of preference shares tend to be fairly stable over time, and there is usually an upper limit on the returns that can be received.

Preference shares are no longer an important source of new finance. A major reason for this is that dividends paid to preference shareholders, like those paid to ordinary shareholders, are not allowable against taxable profits, whereas loan interest is an allowable expense. From the business's point of view, preference shares and loans are quite similar, so the tax benefits of loan interest is an important issue.

Loans (borrowings)

Most businesses rely on loans, or borrowings, as well as share capital to finance operations. Lenders enter into a contract with the business in which the rate of interest, dates of interest payments, capital repayments and security for the loan are clearly stated. If a business is successful, the lenders will not benefit beyond the fact that their claim will become more secure. If, on the other hand, the business experiences financial difficulties, the lenders may receive less than the terms of their contract with the business.

The major risk facing those who invest in loan capital is that the business will default on interest payments and capital repayments. To protect themselves against this risk, lenders often seek some form of **security** from the business. This may take the form of assets pledged either by a **fixed charge** on particular assets held by the business, or by a **floating charge**, which 'hovers' over the whole of the business's assets. A floating charge will cease to 'hover' and become fixed on particular assets in the event that the business defaults on its obligations.

Activity 6.4

What do you think is the advantage for the business of having a floating charge rather than a fixed charge on its assets?

A floating charge on assets will allow the managers of the business greater flexibility in their day-to-day operations than a fixed charge. Individual assets can be sold without reference to the lenders.

Not all assets will be acceptable to investors as a form of security. Assets to be pledged must normally be non-perishable, be capable of being sold easily and be fairly high in value relative to their size. (Property normally meet these criteria and so is often favoured by lenders.) The availability of asset-based security means that lenders, in the event of default, have the right to seize the assets pledged and sell these in order to obtain the amount owing. Any amounts remaining from the proceeds of the sale, after the investors' claims have been satisfied, will be returned to the business. In some cases, security offered by the borrower may take the form of a personal guarantee by the owners of the business or, perhaps, some third party.

Lenders may seek further protection through the use of **loan covenants**. These are obligations, or restrictions, on the business that form part of the loan contract. Such covenants may impose:

- the right of lenders to receive regular financial reports concerning the business;
- an obligation to insure the assets that are offered as security;
- a restriction on the right to issue further loan capital without prior permission of the existing lenders;
- a restriction on the ability of the managers of the business to sell certain assets held;
- a restriction on the level of dividend payments, or level of payments made to directors;
- minimum acceptable levels of liquidity or maximum acceptable levels of gearing.

Any breach of these restrictive covenants can have serious consequences for the business. The lender may demand immediate repayment of the loan in the event of a material breach.

Real World 6.2 describes how one well-known UK business was accused of breaching the covenants imposed by its lenders.

REAL WORLD 6.2

Capital problems

The stockbrokers Merrill Lynch (ML) claimed that GCap Media plc (Capital), the business that owns the London-based Capital Radio commercial station, breached its loan covenants. Capital's bankers required the business to maintain a net debt to annual earnings ratio of at most 3.0 and an interest cover ratio of at least 4.0. ML claims that both ratios were actually 3.3, meaning that Capital had broken the covenant on both counts. ML claimed that this had arisen as a result of falling advertising revenues for the radio station, particularly for its breakfast programme.

Capital denied breaching the covenants and referred to forecasts that it would do so as 'speculation'.

Source: Information taken from 'GCap attacks note on breaching covenants', *Financial Times*, 9 September 2006, www.ft.com.

The use of security and loan covenants can significantly lower the risk to which lenders are exposed and may make the difference between a successful and an unsuccessful issue of loan capital. They can also lower the cost of loan capital to the business as the required rate of return for lenders will vary according to the perceived level of risk of a business defaulting on its obligations.

It is possible for a business to issue loan capital that is subordinated to (that is, ranked below) other loan capital already in issue. This means that holders of this form of loan capital will not receive interest payments or capital repayments until the claims of senior loan holders (that is, lenders ranked above the subordinated lenders) have been satisfied. Any restrictive covenants imposed by senior loan holders relating to the issue of further loan capital will often ignore the issue of **subordinated loans** as this should not pose a threat to their claims. Holders of subordinated loans will normally expect to be compensated for the higher risks involved by a higher level of interest payment than that given to senior loan holders.

Term loans

→ One common form of long-term loan is the **term loan**. This type of loan is offered by banks and other financial institutions, and is usually tailored to the needs of the particular business. The amount of the loan, the time period, the repayment terms and the interest payable are all open to negotiation and agreement, which can be very useful. For example, where all of the funds to be borrowed are not required immediately, a business may agree with the lender that funds are drawn only as and when required. This means that interest will be paid only on amounts drawn and the business will not have to pay interest on amounts borrowed that are temporarily surplus to requirements. Term loans tend to be cheap to set up (from the borrower business's perspective) and can be quite flexible as to conditions.

Loan notes (or loan stock)

→ Another form of long-term loan finance is the **loan note** (or **loan stock**). Loan notes are frequently divided into units (rather like share capital), and investors are invited to purchase the number of units they require. The loan notes may be redeemable or irredeemable. Loan notes of public limited companies are often traded on the Stock Exchange, and their listed value will fluctuate according to the fortunes of the business, movements in interest rates and so on.

→ Loan notes are usually referred to as **bonds** in the USA and, increasingly, in the UK.

Eurobonds

→ **Eurobonds** are unsecured loan notes denominated in a currency other than the home currency of the business that issued them. They are issued by listed businesses (and other large organisations) in various countries, and the finance is raised on an international basis. They are often denominated in US dollars, but many are issued in other major currencies. They are bearer bonds (that is, the owner of the bond is not registered and the holder of the bond certificate is regarded as the owner) and interest is normally paid (without deduction of tax) on an annual basis.

Eurobonds are part of an international capital market, which is not subject to regulations imposed by authorities in particular countries. This partly explains why the cost of servicing eurobonds is usually lower than the cost of similar domestic bonds. Numerous financial institutions throughout the world have created a market for eurobonds, where holders of eurobonds are able to sell them to would-be holders. The business issuing the eurobonds usually makes them available to large banks and other financial institutions, which may either retain them as an investment or sell them to their clients.

The extent of borrowing, by UK businesses, in currencies other than sterling has expanded greatly in recent years. Businesses are often attracted to eurobonds because of the size of the international capital market. Access to a wider pool of potential investors can increase the chances of a successful issue. The lack of regulation in the eurobond market also means that national restrictions regarding loan issues may be overcome.

Real World 6.3 provides an example of one eurobond issue by a well-known UK business.

REAL WORLD 6.3

Healthy issue   **FT**

AstraZeneca plc, an international healthcare business, announced in September 2007 the successful issue of €750 million eurobonds. The bonds have a fixed rate of interest of 5.125 percent and will mature in January 2015. The money raised from the issue is intended for general business purposes and to repay loans taken out to acquire a US biotech business. David Brennan, chief executive officer of the AstraZeneca plc said:

> this transaction represents an enhancement of our financial flexibility by diversifying further our sources of funding.

Source: Information taken from 'Press release', AstraZeneca plc, 13 September 2007 (www.astrazeneca.com).

Activity 6.5

Would you expect the returns to loan capital to be higher or lower than those to preference shares?

Investors are usually prepared to accept a lower rate of return from loan capital. This is because they normally view loans as being less risky than preference shares. Lenders have priority over any claims from preference shareholders, and will usually have security for their loans.

The risk/return characteristics of loan, preference share and ordinary share finance are shown graphically in Figure 6.2.

Deep discount bonds

A business may issue redeemable loan notes that offer a rate of interest below the market rate. In some cases, the loan notes may have a zero rate of interest. Such loans are issued at a discount to their redeemable value and are referred to as **deep discount bonds**. Thus, loan notes may be issued at, say, £80 for every £100 of nominal value. Although lenders will receive little or no interest during the period of the loan, they will receive a £20 gain when it is finally redeemed at the full £100. The redemption yield, as it is referred to, is often quite high and, when calculated on an annual basis, may compare favourably with returns from other forms of loan capital with the same level of risk.

Deep discount bonds may have particular appeal to businesses with short-term cash flow problems. They receive an immediate injection of cash and there are no significant cash outflows associated with the loan notes until the maturity date. From an investment perspective, the situation is reversed. Deep discount bonds are likely to appeal to investors who do not have short-term cash flow needs since a large part of the return is received on maturity of the loan. However, deep discount bonds can often be traded on the London Stock Exchange if required, which will not affect the borrower but will enable the lender to obtain cash.

| **Figure 6.2** | **The risk/return characteristics of sources of long-term finance** |

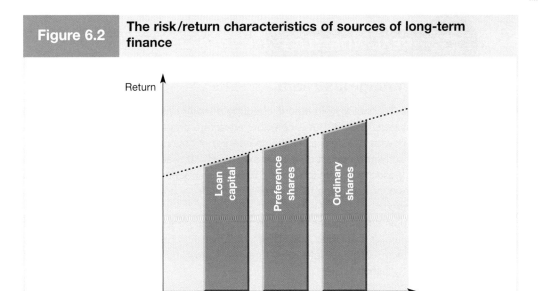

The higher the level of risk associated with a particular form of long-term finance, the higher will be the expected returns from investors. Ordinary shares are the most risky and have the highest expected return and, as a general rule, loan capital is the least risky and has the lowest expected return.

Convertible loan notes

Convertible loan notes (or convertible bonds) give investors the right to convert the loan notes into ordinary shares at a specified price and a given future date (or range of dates). The share price specified, which is known as the exercise price, will normally be higher than the market price of the ordinary shares at the time of the loan notes issue. There is no obligation to convert to ordinary shares. This will be done only if the market price of the shares at the conversion date exceeds the agreed conversion price. Until conversion takes place, the investor will remain a lender to the business, and will receive interest on the amount of the loan notes.

An investor may find this form of investment a useful 'hedge' against risk (that is, it can reduce the level of risk). This may be particularly useful when investment in a new business is being considered. Initially, the investment would be in the form of loan notes and regular interest payments will be made. If the business is successful, the investor can then decide to convert the investment into ordinary shares.

A business may also find this form of financing useful. If the business is successful the loan notes become self-liquidating (no cash payment is required) as investors will exercise their option to convert. The business may also be able to offer a lower rate of interest to investors because they expect future benefits to arise from the conversion. There will be, however, some dilution of control and possibly a dilution of earnings for existing shareholders if holders of convertible loan exercise their option to convert. (Dilution of earnings available to shareholders will not automatically occur as a result of the conversion of loan capital to share capital. There will be a saving in interest charges that will have an offsetting effect.)

Real World 6.4 describes plans for one convertible loan issue.

REAL WORLD 6.4

Swimming upstream

Tadpole Technology plc said it currently does not have sufficient working capital for its present requirements but it has now attracted 'considerable interest from both sophisticated private investors as well as a number of financial institutions'.

The software product developer said it has today sent out to its shareholders the details of a proposed loan note to raise up to 5 million pounds and has so far received indications of interest for approximately 4.5 million pounds, although binding subscriptions are yet to be secured.

Tadpole said in order to ensure that adequate working capital, sufficient for at least 12 months, is available, a minimum of 2.5 million pounds of loan notes will need to be subscribed for by no later than the day preceding a June 20 general meeting of the company's shareholders.

Tadpole chairman David Lee said: 'The level of funding that we are targeting will give us the time, working capital and resources to execute our expansion plans in the Software as a Service (SaaS) market.'

Source: www.lse.co.uk, 28 May 2008.

Measuring the riskiness of loan capital

A number of credit-rating agencies, including Moody's Investor Services and Standard and Poor Corporation (S&P), categorise loan capital issued by businesses according to their perceived default risk. The lower the risk of default, the higher will be the rating category assigned to the loan. The ratings used by the two leading agencies are very similar and are set out below (see **Real World 6.5**). To arrive at an appropriate loan rating, an agency may rely on various sources of information including published and unpublished reports, interviews with directors and visits to the business's premises.

REAL WORLD 6.5

The main debt-rating categories of two leading credit-rating agencies

Standard and Poor's	Moody's Investor Services	
AAA	Aaa	The lowest risk category. Lenders are well protected as the business has a strong capacity to pay the principal and interest.
AA	Aa	High-quality debt. Slightly smaller capacity to pay than the earlier category.
A	A	Good capacity to pay the principal and interest but the business may be more susceptible to adverse effects of changing circumstances and economic conditions.
BBB	Baa	Medium-quality debt. There is adequate capacity to pay the amounts due.

Standard and Poor's	Moody's Investor Services	
BB	Ba	Speculative aspects of the debt. Future capacity is not assured.
B	B	More speculative elements than the category above.
CCC	Caa	Poor-quality debt. Interest or capital may be at risk.
CC	Ca	Poorer-quality debt than the category above. The business is often in default.
C	C	Lowest-quality debt. No interest is being paid and the prospects for the future are poor.

These are the main categories of debt rating used; there are also sub-categories. For example S&P uses BB–, BB+ and so on.

Source: Adapted from Benninga, S. Z. and Sarig, O. H., *Corporate Finance: A valuation approach*, McGraw-Hill, 1997, p. 341. Copyright © 1997 The McGraw-Hill Companies, Inc.

Loan capital falling within any of the first four categories identified in Real World 6.5 is considered to be of high quality and is referred to as investment grade. Some institutional investors are restricted by their rules to investing only in investment-grade loans. For this reason, many businesses are concerned with maintaining investment-grade status.

Once loan capital has been assigned to a particular category, it will tend to remain in that category unless there is a significant change in circumstances. One example of a re-categorisation is given in **Real World 6.6** below.

REAL WORLD 6.6

Soaring higher   **FT**

British Airways was Wednesday propelled back into the investment-grade category for the first time in four years.

Standard & Poor's upgraded BA's long-term corporate credit rating one notch from BB+ to BBB–, the lowest investment-grade category. S&P also raised the long-term credit rating of BA's senior unsecured debt two notches from BB– to BB+.

Leigh Bailey, S&P credit analyst, said: 'The upgrade reflects the positive implications for BA's capital structure, future cash flows, and business operations of the proposed pension deficit solution and the debt reduction achieved in recent years'.

BA was downgraded to sub-investment grade or 'junk' status in July 2003 following the events of September 11, 2001 and the war in Iraq.

During that period the company has reduced its net debt from £6.6bn to £990m and steadily increased its operating margin.

Keith Williams, British Airways' chief financial officer, said on Wednesday: 'We have worked hard over the last four years strengthening the foundations of our business. Regaining investment grade status will enable us to invest in our future growth with confidence.'

The markets reacted positively to the upgrade. Shares in BA rose 7¼p to 431¾p Wednesday. Meanwhile, the cost of protecting its debt against default fell sharply.

Source: Joanna Chung, 'BA regains investment-grade status', www.ft.com, 20 June 2007.

Junk (high-yield) bonds

Loan notes rated below the first four categories identified in Real World 6.5 are often given the rather disparaging name of **junk bonds**. In some cases, loan notes with a junk bond rating began life with an investment grade rating but, because of a decline in the business's fortunes, have been downgraded. (Such a bond is known as a 'fallen angel'.)

Activity 6.6

Does it really matter if the loan notes of a business are downgraded to a lower category?

A downgrade is usually regarded as serious as it may well increase the cost of capital. Investors are likely to seek higher returns to compensate for the perceived increase in default risk.

In addition to increasing the cost of capital, a downgrade to junk bond status can adversely affect business relationships. **Real World 6.7** describes the possible risks for a major IT business of a downgrade and the efforts made by its managers to avoid this fate.

REAL WORLD 6.7

EDS warns of dividend cut   **FT**

Electronic Data Systems yesterday warned it might cut its dividends as part of efforts to improve its financial position by about $1bn and avoid a downgrade to junk bond status.

The move comes as the world's second-largest IT outsourcing company is trying to execute a large turnround plan and position itself for growth. If it were to lose its investment grade rating it would hamper its efforts to win new business.

In documents filed with the SEC, the group said dividends could be cut by about two-thirds this year. It is also considering selling equity or equity-linked securities to raise capital.

Earlier this year, EDS had been placed under review for downgrade by leading credit ratings agencies.

Although EDS said a downgrade to junk status would not materially affect its current business relationships, it could raise its cost of capital.

A downgrade would also make it more challenging to win outsourcing contracts, which usually run between five and ten years. It has to prove to customers that it has capital resources for such long-term projects. EDS is competing against aggressive and well-capitalised competitors such as IBM and Hewlett-Packard.

Source: 'EDS warns of a dividend cut', *Financial Times*, 11 May 2004.

Not all junk bonds start life with an investment-grade rating. Since the 1980s, loan notes with an initial low rating have been issued by US businesses. This type of borrowing provides investors with high interest rates to compensate for the high level of default risk (hence, their alternative name, *high-yield bonds*). Businesses that issue junk bonds, or high-yield bonds, are usually less financially stable than those offering investment-grade bonds. The junk bonds offered may also provide lower levels of security and weaker loan covenants than those normally associated with standard loan agreements.

Junk bonds became popular in the USA as they allowed some businesses to raise finance that was simply not available from other sources. Within a fairly short space of time, a market for this form of borrowing developed. Junk bonds are mainly used by businesses to finance everyday needs such as investment in inventories, receivables and non-current assets; however, they came to public attention through their use in financing hostile takeovers. There have been instances where a small business has taken on high levels of gearing, through the use of junk bonds, in order to finance a takeover of a much larger business. Following the takeover, non-core assets of the larger business have then been sold off to repay the junk bond holders.

The junk bond market in the USA has enjoyed a brief but turbulent history. There have been allegations of market manipulation, the collapse of a leading market maker and periods when default levels on junk bonds have been very high. Whilst these events have shaken investor confidence, the market has proved more resilient than many had expected. Nevertheless, there is always the risk that, in a difficult economic climate, investors will make a 'flight to quality' and the junk bond market will become illiquid.

Real World 6.8 describes a recent dramatic downturn in the market for junk bonds.

REAL WORLD 6.8

Temperature falls to freezing for junk bonds

Companies in Britain and Europe have failed to place a single high-yield bond since the credit crunch kicked off in August, and may now have to wait until next year before the credit market reopens for business. Société Générale said the monthly volume of junk bond issues peaked at €6.5bn (£4.69bn) in June, falling to zero in August, September, October, and November as investor flight from the market forced up yield spreads to stringent levels.

Far from returning to normal, the credit markets appear to tightening even further into the Christmas season.

The European Central Bank's October survey of 90 eurozone banks found that lenders had tightened conditions dramatically, both raising interest rates and slashing the maturity of loans.

Just two companies have even tried to venture into the treacherous high-yield bond market since the credit spigot was turned off in August, only to receive an icy reception.

The Scottish oil and gas exploration firm Melrose Resources shelved a €250m bond issue to help fund drilling in the Nile Delta and East Texas, saying that market conditions were not 'optimal'. The other was Singapore's semiconductor group United Test and Assembly.

The US junk bond market has also ground to a halt after holding up better than Europe in September and early October. The US wireless service group Alltel has cancelled a $6bn issue to finance its buy-out by Goldman Sachs and TPG Capital, after repeatedly failing to place chunks of the issue.

The Dutch plastics group Basell shelved a $21bn issue planned for this week needed to fund a merger with Lyondell.

Nadia Yoshiyama, high-yield strategist at Société Générale, said the main effect of the credit drought so far was to curb takeover and expansion plans.

'They don't have an immediate need for liquidity. Most of them refinanced and paid off bank debt earlier, so they can last into next year,' she said.

Source: Ambrose Evans-Pritchard, 'Temperature falls to freezing for junk bonds', www.telegraph.co.uk, 7 December 2007.

European investors show less interest in junk bonds than their US counterparts do. Perhaps this is because European investors tend to view ordinary shares as a high-risk/high-return investment and view loan capital as a form of low-risk/low-return investment. Junk bonds are a hybrid form of investment lying somewhere between ordinary shares and conventional loan notes. However, it can be argued that the same results as from junk bonds can be achieved through holding a balanced portfolio of ordinary shares and conventional loan notes.

Activity 6.7

Both preference shares and loan notes provide investors with a pre-determined rate of return. What factors might a business take into account when deciding on which of these two sources of finance should be issued?

The main factors are as follows:

- Preference shares have a higher rate of return than loan notes. From the investors' point of view, preference shares are more risky. The amount invested cannot be secured and the return is paid after the returns paid to lenders.
- A business has a legal obligation to pay interest and make capital repayments on loan notes at the agreed dates. It will usually make every effort to meet its obligations, as failure to do so can have serious consequences, as mentioned earlier. Failure to pay a preference dividend, on the other hand, is less important. There is no legal obligation to pay if profits are not available for distribution. Failure to pay a preference dividend may prove an embarrassment for the business, however, and may make it difficult to persuade investors to take up future preference share issues.
- Interest on loan notes can be deducted from profits for taxation purposes, whereas preference dividends cannot. As a result, the cost of servicing loan notes is, £ for £, usually much less for a business than the cost of servicing preference shares.
- The issue of loan notes may result in managers having to accept some restrictions on their freedom of action. Loan note agreements often contain covenants that can be onerous. However, no such restrictions can be imposed by preference shareholders.

A further point is that any preference shares issued form part of the permanent capital base of the business. If they are redeemed, the law requires that they be replaced, either by a new issue of shares or by a transfer from revenue reserves, so that the business's capital base stays intact. Loan notes, however, are not viewed, in law, as part of the business's permanent capital base and, therefore, there is no legal requirement to replace any loan notes that have been redeemed.

Mortgages

A **mortgage** is a form of loan that is secured on an asset, typically land and property. Financial institutions such as banks, insurance businesses and pension funds are often prepared to lend to businesses on this basis. The mortgage may be over a long period (20 years or more).

Warrants

Holders of **warrants** have the right, but not the obligation, to buy ordinary shares in a business at a given price (the 'exercise' price). As with convertible loan notes, the price at which shares may be bought is usually higher than the market price of those ordinary shares at the time of issue. The warrant will usually state the number of shares that the holder may buy and the time limit within which the option to buy shares can be exercised. Occasionally, perpetual warrants are issued that have no set time limits. Warrants do not confer voting rights or entitle the holders to make any claims on the assets of the business.

Share warrants are often sold to investors by the business concerned. In some cases, however, they are given away 'free' as a 'sweetener' to accompany the issue of loan notes. That is, they are used as an incentive to potential lenders. The issue of warrants in this way may enable the business to offer lower rates of interest on the loan notes or to negotiate less restrictive loan conditions. Warrants enable investors to benefit from any future increases in the business's ordinary share price, without having to buy the shares themselves. On the other hand, if the share price remains below the exercise price, the warrant will not be used and the investor will lose out.

Activity 6.8

Under what circumstances will the holders of share warrants exercise their option to purchase?

Holders will exercise this option only if the market price of the shares exceeds the exercise price within the specified time period. If the exercise price is higher than the market price, it will be cheaper for the investor to buy the shares in the market.

Share warrants may be detachable, which means that they can be sold separately from the loan notes. The warrants of businesses whose shares are listed on the Stock Exchange are often themselves listed, providing a ready market for buying and selling the warrants.

Issuing warrants to lenders may be particularly useful for businesses that are considered to be relatively risky. Lenders to such businesses may feel that a new project offers them opportunities for loss but no real opportunity to participate in any 'upside' potential from the risks undertaken. By issuing share warrants, a business gives lenders the opportunity to participate in future gains, which may make them more prepared to support risky projects.

Warrants have a gearing element, which means that changes in the value of the underlying shares can lead to a disproportionate change in value of the warrants. This makes them a speculative form of investment. To illustrate this gearing element, we will suppose that a share had a current market price of £2.50 and that an investor was able to exercise an immediate option to purchase a single share in the business at £2.00. The value of the warrant, in theory, would be £0.50 (that is, £2.50 – £2.00). Let us further suppose that the price of the share rose by 10 per cent to £2.75 before the warrant option was exercised. The value of the warrant would now rise to £0.75 (that is, £2.75 – £2.00), which represents a 50 per cent increase in value. This gearing effect can, of course, operate in the opposite direction as well.

It is probably worth mentioning the difference in status within a business between holders of convertible loan notes and holders of loans notes with share warrants attached if both groups decide to exercise their right to convert. Convertible loan note holders become ordinary shareholders and are no longer lenders to the business. They will have used the value of the loan notes to 'buy' the shares. Warrant holders become ordinary shareholders by paying cash for the shares. If the warrant holders hold loan notes as well, then their status as lenders is unaffected by exercising their right to buy the shares bestowed by the warrant. Thus, they become both ordinary shareholders and lenders to the business.

Both convertible loans and warrants are examples of **financial derivatives**. These are any form of financial instrument, based on share or loan capital, which can be used by investors to increase their returns or reduce risk.

Interest rates and interest rate risk

Interest rates on loan notes may be either floating or fixed. A **floating interest rate** means that the rate of return will rise and fall with market rates of interest. (But it is possible for a floating rate loan note to be issued that sets a maximum rate of interest and/or a minimum rate of interest payable.) The market value of the loan investment, however, is likely to remain fairly stable over time.

The converse will normally be true for loan notes with **fixed interest rates**. Interest payments will remain unchanged with rises and falls in market rates of interest, but the value of the loan investment will fall when interest rates rise, and will rise when interest rates fall.

Activity 6.9

Why do you think the value of fixed-interest loan notes will rise and fall with rises and falls in interest rates?

This is because investors will be prepared to pay less for loan notes that pay a rate of interest below the market rate of interest and will be prepared to pay more for loan notes that pay a rate of interest above the market rate of interest.

Movements in interest rates can be a significant issue for businesses that have high levels of borrowing. A business with a floating rate of interest may find that rate rises will place real strains on cash flows and profitability. Conversely, a business that has a fixed rate of interest will find that, when rates are falling, it will not enjoy the benefits of lower interest charges. To reduce or eliminate these risks, a business may enter into a **hedging arrangement**.

To hedge against the risk of interest rate movements, various devices may be employed: One popular device is the **interest rate swap**. This is an arrangement between two businesses whereby each business assumes responsibility for the other's interest payments. Typically, it involves a business with a floating-interest-rate loan swapping interest payment obligations with a business with a fixed-interest-rate loan. A swap agreement can be undertaken through direct negotiations with another business, but it is usually easier to negotiate through a bank or other financial intermediary. Although there is an agreement to swap interest payments, the legal responsibility for these payments will still rest with the business that entered into the original loan note agreement. Thus, the borrowing business may continue to make interest payments to the lender in line with the loan note agreement. However, at the end of an agreed period, a compensating cash adjustment between the two parties to the swap agreement will be made.

A swap agreement can be a useful hedging device where there are different views concerning future movements in interest rates. For example, a business with a floating rate agreement may believe that interest rates are going to rise, whereas a business with a fixed rate agreement may believe that interest rates are going to fall. However, swap agreements may also be used to exploit imperfections in the capital markets. It is sometimes the case that one business has an advantage over another when negotiating interest rates for a fixed loan agreement, but would prefer a floating loan agreement, whereas the other business is in the opposite position. When this occurs, both businesses can benefit from a swap agreement.

Real World 6.9 sets out the policies of two large businesses towards dealing with interest rate risk.

REAL WORLD 6.9

Managing interest rate risk

Wolseley plc, a major distributor of plumbing and heating products, states:

> The Group finances its operations through a mixture of retained profits and bank and other borrowings. The Group borrows in the desired currencies principally at floating rates of interest and then uses interest rate swaps to generate the desired interest rate profile, thereby managing the Group's exposure to interest rate fluctuations.

Source: Wolseley plc Annual Report 2007 (www.wolseleyplc.com).

Barratt Developments plc is a major UK builder and, in its annual report for 2007, loans and borrowings at the financial year end of almost £1.5 billion were revealed. The business states:

> The majority of the Group's facilities are floating rate, which exposes the Group to increased interest rate risk. The Group has therefore taken out £860.0m of floating to fixed interest rate swaps.

Source: Barratt Developments plc Annual Report and Accounts 2007, p. 58.

Finance leases

When a business needs a particular asset, such as a piece of equipment, instead of buying it direct from a supplier, the business may arrange for a bank (or other business) to buy it and then lease it to the business. The bank that owns the asset, and then leases it the business, is known as a 'lessor'. The business that leases the asset from the bank and then uses it is known as the 'lessee'.

A **finance lease**, as such an arrangement is known, is in essence a form of lending. This is because, had the lessee borrowed the funds and then used them to buy the asset itself, the effect would be much the same. The lessee would have use of the asset but would also have a financial obligation to the lender – just as with a leasing arrangement.

With finance leasing, legal ownership of the asset remains with the lessor; however, the lease agreement transfers to the lessee virtually all the rewards and risks associated with the item being leased. The finance lease agreement will cover a substantial part of the life of the leased item and, often, cannot be cancelled. **Real World 6.10** gives an example of the use of finance leasing by British Airways plc.

REAL WORLD 6.10

BA's leased assets are taking off

Many airline businesses use finance leasing as a means of acquiring new aeroplanes. The financial statements for British Airways plc (BA) for the year ended 31 March 2007 show that almost 29 per cent (totalling £1,698m) of the carrying value of its fleet of aircraft had been acquired through this method.

Source: British Airways plc Annual Report and Accounts 2007, p. 72.

A finance lease can be contrasted with an **operating lease** where the rewards and risks of ownership stay with the owner and where the lease is short term. An example of an operating lease is where a builder hires some earth-moving equipment for a week to carry out a particular job.

Over the years, some important benefits associated with finance leasing have disappeared. Changes in the tax laws no longer make it such a tax-efficient form of financing, and changes in accounting disclosure requirements no longer make it possible to conceal this form of 'borrowing' from investors. Nevertheless, the popularity of finance leases has continued. Other reasons must, therefore, exist for businesses to adopt this form of financing. These reasons are said to include the following:

- *Ease of borrowing*. Leasing may be obtained more easily than other forms of long-term finance. Lenders normally require some form of security and a profitable track record before making advances to a business. However, a lessor may be prepared to lease assets to a new business without a track record and to use the leased assets as security for the amounts owing.
- *Cost*. Leasing agreements may be offered at reasonable cost. As the asset leased is used as security, standard lease arrangements can be applied and detailed credit checking of lessees may be unnecessary. This can reduce administration costs for the lessor and, thereby, help in providing competitive lease rentals.
- *Flexibility*. Leasing can help provide flexibility where there are rapid changes in technology. If an option to cancel can be incorporated into the lease, the business may be able to exercise this option and invest in new technology as it becomes available. This will help the business to avoid the risk of obsolescence.
- *Cash flows*. Leasing, rather than buying an asset outright, means that large cash outflows can be avoided. The leasing option allows cash outflows to be smoothed out over the asset's life. In some cases, it is possible to arrange for low lease payments to be made in the early years of the asset's life, when cash inflows may be low, and for these to increase over time as the asset generates positive cash flows.

Real World 6.11 provides some impression of the importance of finance leasing over recent years.

REAL WORLD 6.11

Finance leasing in the UK

Figure 6.3 charts the changes in the value of finance leasing in the UK over the years 2002–6.

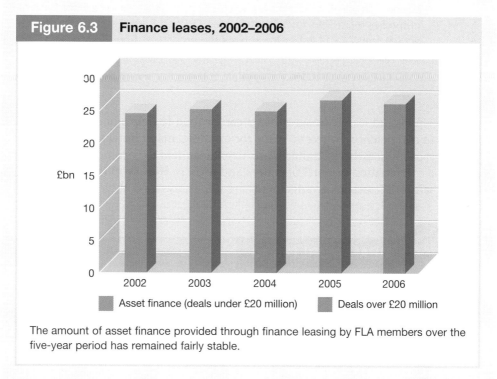

Figure 6.3   Finance leases, 2002–2006

The amount of asset finance provided through finance leasing by FLA members over the five-year period has remained fairly stable.

Source: Chart constructed from data published by the Finance and Leasing Association (www.fla.org.uk). Copyright © 2006 Finance and Leasing Association.

Sale-and-leaseback arrangements

A **sale-and-leaseback** arrangement involves a business raising finance by selling an asset to a financial institution. The sale is accompanied by an agreement to lease the asset back to the business to allow it to continue to use the asset. The lease rental payment is a business expense that is allowable against profits for taxation purposes.

There are usually rental reviews at regular intervals throughout the period of the lease, and the amounts payable in future years may be difficult to predict. At the end of the lease agreement, the business must either try to renew the lease or find an alternative asset. Although the sale of the asset will result in an immediate injection of cash for the business, it will lose benefits from any future capital appreciation on the asset. Where a capital gain arises on the sale of the asset to the financial institution, a liability for taxation may also arise. Property is often the asset that is the subject of such an arrangement. Many of the well-known UK high-street retailers (for example, Boots, Debenhams, Marks and Spencer and Sainsbury) have sold off their store sites under sale-and-leaseback arrangements.

Real World 6.12 provides one example of a sale-and-leaseback agreement.

Bingo

The Rank Group plc, the UK-based international gaming and leisure business, entered into an agreement for the sale and leaseback of 40 Mecca bingo clubs and four Grosvenor casinos. The deal, which was agreed on 14 July 2006, raised cash for Rank of £211m. The properties were sold to Solarus Estates Ltd and Earth Estates Ltd. Rank will now pay annual rents of £11.2m to lease back the properties, from Solarus and Earth, under 15-year leases.

Source: Information taken from 'Rank Group agrees sale and leaseback', 14 July 2006, www.ft.com.

Sale-and-leaseback agreements can be used to help a business focus on its core areas of competence. In recent years, for example, many hotel businesses have entered into sale-and-leaseback arrangements to enable them to become hotel operators rather than a combination of hotel operators and owners. **Real World 6.13**, however, suggests that sale-and-leaseback arrangements are not always a good idea.

REAL WORLD 6.13

Sell, sell, sell!

In the world of finance, companies' property portfolios still provoke oddly irrational reactions. 'Sell them! Release hidden value!' This is strange. The supposed remedy – sale and leaseback – rarely accomplishes this aim.

Typically, a company sells freehold properties that it occupies to a third party. In return it signs a lease of around 25 years. This is normally earnings neutral, releases no value, and is almost identical to long-term borrowing. Indeed debt rating agencies treat sale and leasebacks as debt. International accounting rules are likely to do so soon.

Despite this, a flurry of companies, including many UK retailers, have recently done such deals. Some argue they are reducing exposure to an overvalued asset class. But in reality, the rental terms received are usually fixed and reflect current market conditions. Were a crash to happen, the company would only capture lower rents at the end of lease period – which is too far off to matter.

Perhaps some companies cynically hope that, since property leases are off balance sheet, less vigilant investors may be duped. And those in financial distress – as BT Group and France Telecom were – can find sale and leasebacks a vital alternative to borrowing.

Yet the only convincing rationale is if deals transfer risk. In the hotel sector, operators such as Marriott have linked rental payments to their operating performance. Retailers will have to design similar structures if they want property deals to add value.

Source: 'Sale and leasebacks', Lex column www.ft.com, 1 March 2005.

Hire purchase

 Hire purchase is a form of credit used to acquire an asset. Under the terms of a hire purchase (HP) agreement a customer pays for an asset by instalments over an agreed period. Normally, the customer will pay an initial deposit (down payment) and then make instalment payments at regular intervals (perhaps monthly) until the balance outstanding has been paid. The customer will usually take possession of the asset after payment of the initial deposit, although legal ownership of the asset will not be transferred until the final instalment has been paid.

HP agreements will often involve three parties:

- the supplier
- the customer
- a financial institution.

Although the supplier will deliver the asset to the customer, the financial institution will buy the asset from the supplier and then enter into an HP agreement with the customer. This intermediary role played by the financial institution enables the supplier to receive immediate payment for the asset but allows the customer a period of extended credit.

Real World 6.14 describes how one well-known holiday operator uses hire purchase to help finance its assets.

REAL WORLD 6.14

Paying by instalments

Holidaybreak plc has a camping division that includes well-known brands such as Eurocamp and Keycamp. The division provides mobile homes for holidaymakers, and the company's 2007 annual report revealed that the cost of mobile homes purchased during the year was £10.9 m. The company states:

> we have hire purchase agreements with various UK financial institutions to finance the purchase of mobile homes. Just over half of expenditure on mobile homes is financed from this source.

Source: Holidaybreak plc Annual Report and Financial Statements 2007, p. 12.

HP agreements are similar to finance leases in so far as they allow a customer to obtain immediate possession of the asset without paying its full cost. Under the terms of an HP agreement, however, the customer will eventually become the legal owner of the asset, whereas under the terms of a finance lease, ownership will stay with the lessor.

Securitisation

→ **Securitisation** involves bundling together illiquid financial or physical assets of the same type in order to provide backing for issuing interest-bearing securities, such as bonds. This financing method was first used by US banks, which bundled together residential mortgage loans in order to provide asset backing for the issue of bonds to investors. (Mortgage loans held by a bank are financial assets that provide future benefits to the bank in the form of interest receivable.) The bonds issued were considered to be low risk as they were also backed by a guarantee from the bank. It was therefore possible for a bank to offer lower rates of interest on the bonds issued than on the interest accruing to the mortgage loans, which provided the asset backing.

Securitisation has now spread beyond the banking industry and has become an important source of finance for businesses in a wide range of industries. Future benefits from a variety of illiquid assets are now used as backing for bond issues, including:

- credit card receipts
- water industry charges
- rental income from university accommodation
- ticket sales for football matches
- royalties from music copyright
- consumer instalment contracts
- beer sales to pub tenants.

The effect of securitisation is to capitalise the claims to these future benefits. This capitalised amount is then sold to investors, through the financial markets, to raise finance for the business holding the claims.

Securitisation usually involves setting up a special-purpose vehicle (SPV) to acquire the assets from the business wishing to raise finance. This SPV will then arrange the issue of loan notes, such as a 10-year fixed rate bond, to investors. The interest to be paid on the loan notes to be issued will be met by the income generated from the securitised assets. When the securities mature, the amount to be repaid may come from receipts from the securitised assets, so long as the maturity dates are co-terminus. In other cases, repayment may come from the issue of new loan notes or from income generated by the securitised assets in excess of that needed to pay interest charges.

Securitised assets tend to be of good quality with regular and predictable income streams. To reassure investors, however, the assets offered may be higher in value than the securities issued (known as *overcollateralisation*) or some form of credit insurance may be available from a third party, such as a bank.

In addition to being a useful source of finance, a securitisation issue may be used to help manage risk. Where, for example, a bank has lent large amounts to a particular industry sector, it can reduce its exposure to the sector by bundling together some of the outstanding loan contracts and making a securitisation issue.

Real World 6.15 gives an insight to the reliance of some UK banks on the securitisation of customers' mortgages to raise finance.

REAL WORLD 6.15

Banking on bonds   FT

Securitisation of mortgage loans has become an important means of raising finance by UK banks. However, there is a wide variation in the use of this form of finance between the leading banks.

At one end of the scale, HSBC, RBS and Barclays have issued relatively few mortgage-backed bonds. But HBOS, the biggest mortgage lender, funds 17 per cent of all lending with securitisation. Abbey National uses securitisation for 22 per cent of its mortgage lending. Northern Rock used securitisation to fund 57 per cent of its loan book, according to Deutsche Bank data.

Following a crisis in the money markets in August 2007, banks found it almost impossible to sell any mortgage-backed bonds. It is clear, however, that some banks will have suffered more than others as a result.

Source: Adapted from Delphine Strauss, 'King fails to soothe lenders', 23 January 2008, www.ft.com.

External sources of short-term finance

Short term, in this context, is usually taken to mean up to one year. Figure 6.1 reveals that the major external sources of short-term finance are:

● bank overdrafts
● bills of exchange
● debt factoring
● invoice discounting.

Each of these sources is discussed below.

Bank overdrafts

A **bank overdraft** enables a business to maintain a negative balance on its bank account. It represents a very flexible form of borrowing as the size of an overdraft can (subject to bank approval) be increased or decreased more or less instantaneously. It is relatively inexpensive to arrange and interest rates are often very competitive. As with all loans, the rate of interest charged will vary according to how creditworthy the customer is perceived to be by the bank. An overdraft is fairly easy to arrange – sometimes it can be agreed by a telephone call to the bank. In view of these advantages, it is not surprising that an overdraft is an extremely popular form of short-term finance.

Banks prefer to grant overdrafts that are self-liquidating, that is, the funds applied will result in cash inflows that will extinguish the overdraft balance. The banks may ask for projected cash flow statements from the business to see when the overdraft will be repaid and how much finance is required. The bank may also require some form of security on amounts advanced.

One potential drawback with this form of finance is that it is repayable on demand. This may pose problems for a business that is illiquid. However, many businesses operate for many years using an overdraft, simply because the bank remains confident of their ability to repay and the arrangement suits the business. Thus, this form of borrowing, though in theory regarded as short term, can often become a source of long-term finance.

Bills of exchange

A **bill of exchange** is similar, in some respects, to an IOU. It is a written agreement that is addressed by one person to another, requiring the person to whom it is addressed to pay a particular amount at some future date. Bills of exchange are used in trading transactions and are offered by a buyer to a supplier in exchange for goods. The supplier who accepts the bill of exchange either may keep the bill until the date the payment is due (this is usually between 60 and 180 days after the bill is first drawn up) or may present it to a bank for payment. The bank will usually be prepared to pay the supplier the face value of the bill, less a discount, and will then collect the full amount of the bill from the buyer at the specified payment date. The advantage of using a bill of exchange is that it allows the buyer to delay payment for the goods purchased but provides the supplier with an opportunity to receive immediate payment from a bank if required. Nowadays, bills of exchange are not widely used for trading transactions within the UK, but are still used for overseas trading.

Debt factoring

Debt factoring is a service offered by a financial institution (known as a factor). Many of the large factors are subsidiaries of commercial banks. Debt factoring involves the factor taking over the trade receivables collection for a business. In addition to operating normal credit control procedures, a factor may offer to undertake credit investigations and advise on the creditworthiness of customers. It may also offer protection for approved credit sales. Two main forms of factoring agreement exist:

- *Recourse factoring*, where the factor assumes no responsibility for bad debts arising from credit sales.
- *Non-recourse factoring*, where, for an additional fee, the factor assumes responsibility for bad debts up to an agreed amount.

The factor is usually prepared to make an advance to the business of up to around 80 per cent of approved trade receivables (although it can sometimes be as high as 90 per cent). This advance is usually paid immediately after the goods have been supplied to the customer. The balance of the debt, less any deductions for fees and interest, will be paid after an agreed period or when the debt is collected. The charge made for the factoring service is based on total sales revenue and is often around 2–3 per cent of sales revenue. Any advances made to the business by the factor will attract a rate of interest similar to the rate charged on bank overdrafts.

Debt factoring is, in effect, outsourcing trade receivables collection to a specialist subcontractor. Many businesses find a factoring arrangement very convenient. It can result in savings in credit management and can create more certain cash flows. It can also release the time of key personnel for more profitable ends. This may be extremely important for smaller businesses that rely on the talent and skills of a few key individuals. In addition, the level of finance available will rise 'spontaneously' with the level of sales. The business can decide how much of the finance available is required and can use only that which it needs. However, there is a possibility that some will see a factoring arrangement as an indication that the business is experiencing financial difficulties. This may have an adverse effect on the confidence of customers, suppliers and staff. For this reason, some businesses try to conceal the factoring arrangement by collecting outstanding debts on behalf of the factor.

Not all businesses will find factoring arrangements the answer to their financing problems. Factoring agreements may not be possible to arrange for very small businesses (those with total sales revenue of, say, less than £100,000) because of the high set-up costs. In addition, businesses engaged in certain sectors such as retailers or building contractors, where trade disputes are part of the business culture, may find that factoring arrangements are simply not available.

Figure 6.4 shows the factoring process diagrammatically.

| Figure 6.4 | **The factoring process** |

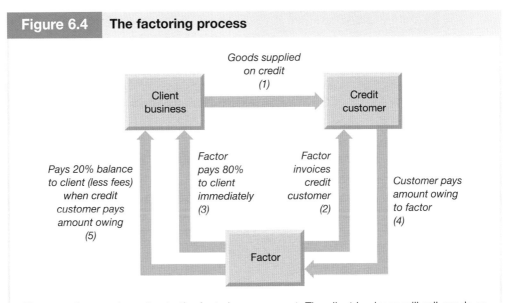

There are three main parties to the factoring agreement. The client business will sell goods on credit and the factor will take responsibility for invoicing the customer and collecting the amount owing. The factor will then pay the client business the invoice amount, less fees and interest, in two stages. The first stage typically represents 80 per cent of the invoice value and will be paid immediately after the goods have been delivered to the customer. The second stage will represent the balance outstanding and will usually be paid when the customer has paid the factor the amount owing.

When considering a factoring agreement, it is necessary to identify and carefully weigh the costs and likely benefits arising. Example 6.1 illustrates how this may be done.

EXAMPLE 6.1

Mayo Computers Ltd has annual sales revenue of £20 million before taking into account bad debts of £0.1 million. All sales made by the business are on credit and, at present, credit terms are negotiable by the customer. On average, the settlement period for trade receivables is 60 days. The business is currently reviewing its credit policies to see whether more efficient and profitable methods could be used.

The business is considering whether it should factor its trade receivables. The accounts department has recently approached a factoring business, which has agreed to provide an advance equivalent to 80 per cent of trade receivables (where the trade receivables figure is based on an average settlement period of 40 days) at an interest rate of 12 per cent. The factoring business will undertake collection of the trade receivables and will charge a fee of 2 per cent of total sales revenue for this service. The factoring service is also expected to eliminate bad debts and will lead to credit administration savings of £90,000. The settlement period for trade receivables will be reduced to an average of 40 days, which is equivalent to that of its major competitors.

The business currently has an overdraft of £4.8 million at an interest rate of 14 per cent a year. The bank has written recently to the business stating that it would like to see a reduction in this overdraft.

Example 6.1 continued

In evaluating the factoring arrangement, it is useful to begin by considering the cost of the existing arrangements:

Existing arrangements

	£000
Bad debts written off each year	100
Interest cost of average receivables outstanding [(£20m × 60/365) × 14%]	460
Total cost	560

The cost of the factoring arrangement can now be compared with the above:

Factoring arrangement

	£000
Factoring fee (£20m × 2%)	400
Interest on factor loan (assuming 80% advance and reduction in average credit period) [(£16m × 40/365) × 12%]	210
Interest on overdraft (remaining 20% of receivables financed in this way) [(£4m × 40/365) × 14%]	61
	671
Less Savings in credit administration	90
Cost of factoring	581

The net additional cost of factoring for the business would be £21,000 (£581,000 – £560,000).

Invoice discounting

Invoice discounting involves a factor or other financial institution providing a loan based on a proportion of the face value of a business's credit sales outstanding. The amount advanced is usually 75–80 per cent of the value of the approved sales invoices outstanding. The business must agree to repay the advance within a relatively short period – perhaps 60 or 90 days. Responsibility for collecting the trade receivables outstanding remains with the business and repayment of the advance is not dependent on the trade receivables being collected. Invoice discounting will not result in such a close relationship developing between the business and the financial institution as occurs with factoring. It may be a short-term arrangement whereas debt factoring usually involves a longer-term arrangement.

Nowadays, invoice discounting is a much more important source of funds to businesses than factoring. There are three main reasons for this.

● It is a confidential form of financing which the business's customers will know nothing about.
● The service charge for invoice discounting is only about 0.2–0.3 per cent of sales revenue compared to 2.0–3.0 per cent for factoring.
● A debt factor may upset customers when collecting the amount due, which may damage the relationship between the business and its customers.

Real World 6.16 shows the relative importance of invoice discounting and factoring.

REAL WORLD 6.16

The popularity of invoice discounting and factoring

Figure 6.5 charts the relative importance of invoice discounting and factoring in terms of the value of client sales revenue.

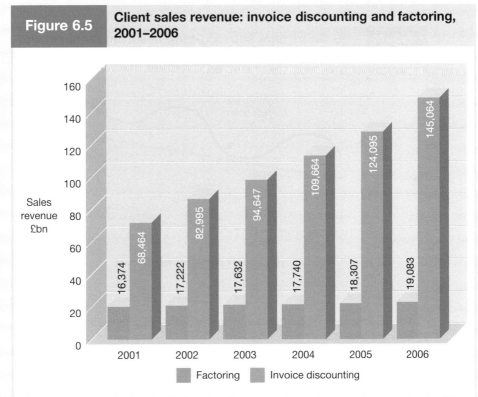

| Figure 6.5 | Client sales revenue: invoice discounting and factoring, 2001–2006 |

In recent years, client sales for invoice discounting have risen much more sharply than client sales for factoring. During 2006, for example, client sales for factoring grew by 4 per cent whereas invoice discounting grew by 17 per cent. Client sales for invoice discounting in 2006 were more than seven times the client sales for factoring.

Source: Chart constructed from data published by the Factors and Discounters Association (www.factors.org.uk). (The FDA has been renamed the Asset Based Finance Association.) Copyright © 2006. Factors and Discounters Association.

→   Factoring and invoice discounting are forms of **asset-based finance** as the assets of receivables are, in effect, used as security for the cash advances received by the business.

Long-term versus short-term borrowing

Having decided that some form of borrowing is required to finance the business, managers must then decide whether long-term or short-term borrowing is more appropriate. There are many issues to be taken into account, which include the following:

● *Matching*. The business may attempt to match the type of borrowing with the nature of the assets held. Thus, long-term borrowing might finance assets that form part of the permanent operating base of the business, including non-current assets and a certain level of current assets. This leaves assets held for a short period, such as current assets held to meet seasonal increases in demand (for example inventories), to be financed by short-term borrowing, because short-term borrowing tends to be more flexible in that funds can be raised and repaid at short notice. Figure 6.6 shows this funding division graphically.

Figure 6.6	**Short-term and long-term financing requirements**

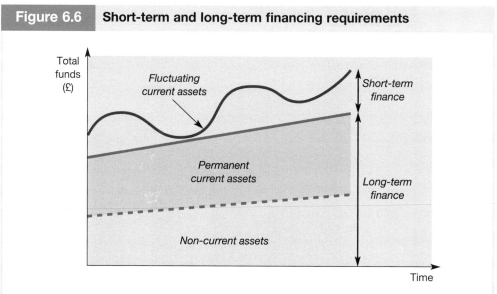

The broad consensus on financing seems to be that all of the permanent financial needs of the business should come from long-term sources. Only that part of current assets that fluctuates in the short term, probably on a seasonal basis, should be financed from short-term sources.

Activity 6.10

Some businesses may take up a less cautious financing position than that shown in Figure 6.6 and others may take up a more cautious one. How would the diagram differ under each of these options?

A less cautious position would mean relying on short-term finance to help fund part of the permanent capital base, so the arrow labelled 'short-term finance' would expand downwards. A more cautious position would mean relying on long-term finance to help finance the fluctuating assets of the business, so the arrow labelled 'long-term finance' would expand upwards.

● *Flexibility*. Short-term borrowing may be used as a means of postponing a commitment to long-term borrowing. This may be desirable if interest rates are high but are forecast to fall in the future. Short-term borrowing does not usually incur a financial penalty for early repayment, whereas a penalty may arise if long-term borrowing is repaid early.

- *Refunding risk*. Short-term borrowing has to be renewed more frequently than long-term borrowing. This may create problems for the business if it is in financial difficulties or if there is a shortage of funds available for lending.
- *Interest rates*. Interest payable on long-term borrowing is often higher than that for short-term borrowing, as lenders require a higher return where their funds are locked up for a long period. This fact may make short-term borrowing a more attractive source of finance for a business. However, there may be other costs associated with borrowing (arrangement fees, for example) to be taken into account. The more frequently borrowings are renewed, the higher these costs will be.

Internal sources of finance

In addition to external sources of finance there are certain internal sources of finance that a business may use to generate funds for particular activities. These sources usually have the advantage that they are flexible. They may also be obtained quickly – particularly working capital sources – and do not require the compliance of other parties. The main internal sources of funds are described below and summarised in Figure 6.7.

Figure 6.7	**Major internal sources of finance**

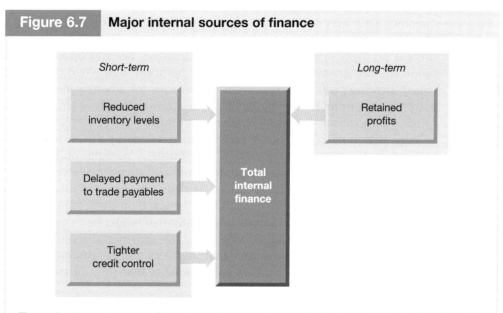

The major internal source of long-term finance is the profits that are retained rather than distributed to shareholders. The major internal sources of short-term finance involve reducing the level of trade receivables and inventories and increasing the level of trade payables.

Internal sources of long-term finance

Retained profits

Retained profits are the major source of finance (internal or external) for most businesses. By retaining profits within the business rather than distributing them to shareholders in the form of dividends, the business can increase its funds.

Activity 6.11

Are retained profits a free source of finance for the business?

It is tempting to think that retained profits are a cost-free source of funds for a business. However, this is not the case. If profits are reinvested rather than distributed in cash to shareholders, those shareholders cannot reinvest this cash in other forms of investment. They will therefore expect a rate of return from the profits reinvested which is equivalent to what they would receive if the funds had been invested in another opportunity with the same level of risk.

The reinvestment of profit, rather than the issue of new shares, can be a useful way of raising finance from ordinary share investors. No issue costs are incurred and the amount raised is certain once the profit has been made. When new shares are issued, on the other hand, issue costs may be substantial and there may be uncertainty over the success of the issue. Where new shares are issued to outside investors, some dilution of control may also be suffered by existing shareholders.

The decision to retain profits, rather than pay them out as dividends, is made by the directors. They may find it easier simply to retain profits rather than to ask investors to subscribe to a new share issue. Retained profits are already held by the business and so there is no delay in receiving the funds. Moreover, there is often less scrutiny when profits are being retained for reinvestment purposes than when new shares are being issued. Investors will examine closely the reasons for any new share issue. A problem with the use of profits as a source of finance, however, is that the timing and level of future profits cannot always be reliably determined.

Some shareholders may prefer profits to be retained by the business rather than distributed in the form of dividends. If the business ploughs profits back, it may be expected that it will expand and share values will increase as a result. In the UK, not all capital gains are liable for taxation. (For the tax year 2007/08, an individual with capital gains of less than £9,200 would not be taxed on those gains.) A further advantage of capital gains over dividends is that the shareholder has a choice as to when the gain is realised. In the UK, it is only when the gain is realised that capital gains tax comes into play. Research indicates that investors may be attracted to particular businesses because of the dividend/retention policies that they adopt. This point is considered in more detail in Chapter 8.

Retained profits and 'pecking order' theory

It has been suggested that businesses have a 'pecking order' when taking on long-term finance. This pecking order can be summarised as follows:

- Retained profits will be used to finance the business if possible.
- Where retained profits are insufficient, or unavailable, loan capital will be used.
- Where loan capital is insufficient, or unavailable, share capital will be used.

One explanation for such a pecking order is that the managers of the business have access to information that investors do not. Let us suppose that the managers have reliable information indicating that the prospects for the business are better than that predicted by the market. This means that shares will be undervalued and, so, to raise finance by an issue of shares under such circumstances would involve selling them at an undervalued price. This would, in effect, result in a transfer of wealth from existing shareholders to those investors who take up the new share issue. Hence, the managers, who are employed to act in the best interests of existing shareholders, will prefer to rely on retained profit, followed by loan capital, instead.

Activity 6.12

Why shouldn't the managers simply release any inside information to the market to allow the share price to rise and so make it possible to issue shares at a fair price?

There are at least two reasons why this may not be a good idea:

- It may be time consuming and costly to persuade the market that the prospects of the business are better than current estimates. Investors may find it hard to believe what the managers tell them.
- It may provide useful information to competitors about future developments.

Let us now suppose the managers of a business have access to bad news about the future. If the market knows that the business will rely on retained profit and loan capital when in possession of good news, it will assume that the issue of share capital can be taken as an indication that the business is in possession of bad news. Investors are, therefore, likely to believe that the shares of the business are currently overvalued and will not be interested in subscribing to a new issue. (There is some evidence to show that the value of shares will fall when a share issue is announced.) Hence, this situation will again lead managers to favour retained profits followed by loan capital, with share capital as a last resort.

The pecking order theory may partly explain the heavy reliance of businesses on retained profits, but it will not be the only influence on the financing decision. There are other factors to be taken into account when deciding on an appropriate source of finance, as we shall see in Chapter 8.

Internal sources of short-term finance

Figure 6.7 reveals that the major internal forms of short-term finance are:

- tighter credit control
- reducing inventory levels
- delaying payments to trade payables.

Each of these is discussed below.

Tighter credit control

By exerting tighter control over amounts owed by credit customers a business may be able to reduce the proportion of assets held in this form and so release funds for other purposes. Having funds tied up in trade receivables represents an opportunity cost in that those funds could be used for profit-generating activities. It is important, however, to weigh the benefits of tighter credit control against the likely costs in the form of lost customer goodwill and lost sales. To remain competitive, a business must take account of the needs of its customers and the credit policies adopted by rival businesses within the industry. We consider this further in Chapter 10.

Activity 6.13 below involves weighing the costs of tighter credit control against the likely future benefits.

Activity 6.13

Rusli Ltd provides a car valet service for car hire businesses when their cars are returned from hire. Details of the service costs are as follows:

	Per car	
	£	£
Car valet charge		20
Less Variable costs	14	
Fixed costs	4	18
Profit		2

Sales revenue is £10 million a year and is all on credit. The average credit period taken by Rusli Ltd's customers is 45 days, although the terms of credit require payment within 30 days. Bad debts are currently £100,000 a year. Trade receivables are financed by a bank overdraft with an interest cost of 10 per cent a year.

The credit control department of Rusli Ltd believes it can eliminate bad debts and can reduce the average credit period to 30 days if new credit control procedures are implemented. These procedures will cost £50,000 a year and are likely to result in a reduction in sales of 5 per cent a year.

Should the business implement the new credit control procedures?

(*Hint*: To answer this activity it is useful to compare the current cost of trade credit with the costs under the proposed approach.)

The current cost of trade credit is:

	£
Bad debts	100,000
Overdraft interest [(£10m × 45/365) × 10%]	123,288
	223,288

The annual cost of trade credit under the new policy will be:

	£
Overdraft interest [(95% × £10m) × (30/365) × 10%]	78,082
Cost of control procedures	50,000
Net cost of lost sales [(£10m/£20 × 5%)(20 − 14*)]	150,000
	278,082

* The loss will be the contribution from valeting the car, that is, the difference between the valet charge and the variable costs. The fixed costs are ignored as they do not vary with the decision.

The above figures reveal that the business will be worse off if the new policies are adopted.

Reducing inventory levels

This internal source of funds may prove attractive to a business. As with trade receivables, holding inventories imposes an opportunity cost on a business as the funds tied up cannot be used for other opportunities. If inventories are reduced, funds become available for those opportunities. However, a business must ensure there are sufficient inventories available to meet likely future sales demand. Failure to do so will result in lost customer goodwill and lost sales revenue.

The nature and condition of the inventories held will determine whether it is possible to exploit this form of finance. A business may have excessive inventories as a result of poor buying decisions. This may mean that a significant proportion of inventories held is slow moving or obsolete and cannot, therefore, be reduced easily. These issues are picked up again in Chapter 10.

Delaying payment to trade payables

By providing a period of credit, suppliers are in effect offering a business an interest-free loan. If the business delays payment, the period of the 'loan' is extended and funds are retained within the business. This can be a cheap form of finance for a business, although this is not always the case. If a business fails to pay within the agreed credit period, there may be significant costs: for example, the business may find it difficult to buy on credit when it has a reputation as a slow payer.

Some final points

The so-called short-term sources just described are short term to the extent that they can be reversed at short notice. For example, a reduction in the level of trade receivables can be reversed within a couple of weeks. Typically, however, once a business has established a reduced receivable collection period, a reduced inventory holding period and/or an expanded payables payment period, it will tend to maintain these new levels.

We shall see in Chapter 10 that, for many businesses, the funds invested in working capital items are vast. Through exercising tighter control of trade receivables and inventories and by exploiting opportunities to delay payment to trade payables, it may be possible to release substantial amounts for other purposes.

Self-assessment question 6.1

Helsim Ltd is a wholesaler and distributor of electrical components. The most recent draft financial statements of the business revealed the following:

Income statement for the year

	£m	£m
Sales revenue		14.2
Opening inventories	3.2	
Purchases	8.4	
	11.6	
Closing inventories	(3.8)	(7.8)
Gross profit		6.4
Administration expenses		(3.0)
Distribution expenses		(2.1)
Operating profit		1.3
Finance costs		(0.8)
Profit before taxation		0.5
Tax		(0.2)
Profit for the period		0.3

Self-assessment question 6.1 continued

Statement of financial position (balance sheet)
as at the end of the year

	£m
Non-current assets	
Property, plant and equipment	
Land and buildings	3.8
Equipment	0.9
Motor vehicles	0.5
	5.2
Current assets	
Inventories	3.8
Trade receivables	3.6
Cash at bank	0.1
	7.5
Total assets	12.7
Equity	
Share capital	2.0
Retained earnings	1.8
	3.8
Non-current liabilities	
Loan notes (secured on property)	3.5
Current liabilities	
Trade payables	1.8
Short-term borrowings	3.6
	5.4
Total equity and liabilities	12.7

Notes

1 Land and buildings are shown at their current market value. Equipment and motor vehicles are shown at their written-down values (that is, cost less accumulated depreciation).
2 No dividends have been paid to ordinary shareholders for the past three years.

In recent months, trade payables have been pressing for payment. The managing director has therefore decided to reduce the level of trade payables to an average of 40 days outstanding. To achieve this, he has decided to approach the bank with a view to increasing the overdraft (the short-term borrowings comprise only a bank overdraft). The business is currently paying 10 per cent a year interest on the overdraft.

Required:
(a) Comment on the liquidity position of the business.
(b) Calculate the amount of finance required to reduce trade payables, from the level shown on the balance sheet, to an average of 40 days outstanding.
(c) State, with reasons, how you consider the bank would react to the proposal to grant an additional overdraft facility.
(d) Identify four sources of finance (internal or external, but excluding a bank overdraft) that may be suitable to finance the reduction in trade payables, and state, with reasons, which of these you consider the most appropriate.

The answer to this question may be found at the back of the book on p. 533.

SUMMARY

The main points in this chapter may be summarised as follows:

Sources of finance

● Sources of long-term finance are expected to provide finance for at least one year whereas sources of short-term finance would provide it for a shorter period.

● External sources of finance require the agreement of outside parties, whereas internal sources of finance do not.

● The higher the level of risk associated with a particular form of finance, the higher the level of return expected from investors.

External sources of finance

● The main external sources of *long-term* finance are ordinary shares, preference shares, loans, leases, hire purchase agreements and securitisation of assets.

● Ordinary shares are normally considered to be the most risky form of investment and, therefore, provide the highest expected returns to investors. Loan notes are normally the least risky and provide the lowest expected returns to investors.

● Loan capital is relatively low risk because lenders are offered security for their loan; furthermore, covenants in the loan contract often impose obligations on managers, or restrictions on the actions of managers, that help protect the lenders.

● There are different types of loan capital including convertible loan notes, term loans, mortgages, Eurobonds, deep discount bonds and junk bonds.

● A number of credit-rating agencies attempt to categorise loan capital issued by businesses according to the level of default risk.

● Convertible loan notes offer the right of conversion to ordinary shares at a given future date and at a specified price. This will be done if the market price at the conversion date exceeds the specified price.

● Junk bonds are those that do not fall within the investment grade categories established by the credit-rating agencies.

● Warrants give holders the right, but not the obligation, to buy ordinary shares at a given price and are often used as a 'sweetener' to accompany a loan issue.

● Interest rates may be floating or fixed.

● Interest rate risk may be reduced, or eliminated, through the use of hedging arrangements such as interest rate swaps.

● A finance lease is, in essence, a form of lending that gives the lessee the use of an asset over most of its useful life in return for payment of a lease rental.

● A sale-and-leaseback arrangement involves the sale of an asset to a financial institution accompanied by an agreement to lease the asset back to the business.

● Securitisation involves bundling together homogeneous, illiquid assets to provide backing for the issue of bonds.

● The main external sources of *short-term* finance are bank overdrafts, debt factoring and invoice discounting.

● Bank overdrafts are flexible and cheap but are repayable on demand.

● Debt factoring and invoice discounting both use the trade receivables of a business as a basis for borrowing, with the latter being more popular because of relative cost and flexibility.

● When considering the choice between sources of long-term and short-term borrowing, a business should take into account factors such as matching the type of borrowing with the nature of the assets held, the need for flexibility, refunding risk, and interest rates.

Internal sources of finance

● An internal source of long-term finance is retained profits. It is by far the most important source of new long-term finance (internal or external) for UK businesses.

● Retained profits are not a free source of finance, as investors will require levels of return from retained profits similar to those from ordinary shares.

● The main internal sources of short-term finance are tighter credit control of receivables, reducing inventory levels and delaying payments to trade payables.

→ Key terms

Security p. 225	Floating interest rate p. 236
Fixed charge p. 225	Fixed interest rate p. 236
Floating charge p. 225	Hedging arrangement p. 236
Loan covenants p. 226	Interest rate swap p. 236
Subordinated loans p. 226	Finance lease p. 237
Term loan p. 227	Operating lease p. 238
Loan notes p. 227	Sale and leaseback p. 239
Eurobonds p. 227	Hire purchase p. 240
Bonds p. 227	Securitisation p. 241
Deep discount bonds p. 228	Bank overdraft p. 243
Convertible loan notes p. 229	Bill of exchange p. 243
Junk (high-yield) bonds p. 232	Debt factoring p. 244
Mortgage p. 234	Invoice discounting p. 246
Warrants p. 234	Asset-based finance p. 247
Financial derivative p. 236	

For definitions of these terms see the Glossary, pp. 574–583.

Further reading

If you wish to explore the topics discussed in this chapter in more depth, try the following books:

Corporate Finance and Investment, *Pike, R. and Neale, B.*, 5th edn, Financial Times Prentice Hall, 2006, chapters 15 and 16.

Corporate Financial Management, *Arnold, G.*, 3rd edn, Financial Times Prentice Hall, 2005, chapters 11 and 12.

Corporate Finance, *Brealey, R., Myers, S. and Allen, F.*, 9th edn, McGraw-Hill International, 2007, chapters 14, 25 and 26.

REVIEW QUESTIONS

Answers to these questions can be found at the back of the book on p. 543.

6.1 What are share warrants and what are the benefits to a business of issuing share warrants?

6.2 'Convertible loan capital is really a form of delayed equity.' Do you agree? Discuss.

6.3 What are the benefits of an interest swap agreement and how does it work?

0.4 Distinguish between invoice discounting and debt factoring.

EXERCISES

Exercises 6.4 to 6.7 are more advanced than 6.1 to 6.3. Those with coloured numbers have answers at the back of the book, starting on p. 560.

If you wish to try more exercises, visit the students' side of this book's Companion Website.

6.1 Answer *all* parts below.

Required:
Provide reasons why a business may decide to:
(a) Lease rather than buy an asset which is to be held for long-term use.
(b) Use retained profit to finance growth rather than issue new shares.
(c) Repay long-term loan capital earlier than the specified repayment date.

6.2 H. Brown (Portsmouth) Ltd produces a range of central heating systems for sale to builders' merchants. As a result of increasing demand for the business's products, the directors have decided to expand production. The cost of acquiring new plant and machinery and the increase in working capital requirements are planned to be financed by a mixture of long-term and short-term borrowing.

Required:
(a) Discuss the major factors that should be taken into account when deciding on the appropriate mix of long-term and short-term borrowing necessary to finance the expansion programme.
(b) Discuss the major factors that a lender should take into account when deciding whether to grant a long-term loan to the business.
(c) Identify three conditions that might be included in a long-term loan agreement, and state the purpose of each.

6.3 Securitisation is now used in a variety of different industries. In the music industry, for example, rock stars such as David Bowie, Michael Jackson and Iron Maiden have used this form of financing to their benefit.

Required:
(a) Explain the term 'securitisation'.
(b) Discuss the main features of this form of financing and the benefits of using securitisation.

6.4   Raphael Ltd is a small engineering business that has annual credit sales revenue of £2.4 million. In recent years, the business has experienced credit control problems. The average collection period for sales has risen to 50 days even though the stated policy of the business is for payment to be made within 30 days. In addition, 1.5 per cent of sales are written off as bad debts each year.

The business has recently been in talks with a factor that is prepared to make an advance to the business equivalent to 80 per cent of trade receivables, based on the assumption that customers will, in future, adhere to a 30-day payment period. The interest rate for the advance will be 11 per cent a year. The trade receivables are currently financed through a bank overdraft, which has an interest rate of 12 per cent a year. The factor will take over the credit control procedures of the business and this will result in a saving to the business of £18,000 a year; however, the factor will make a charge of 2 per cent of sales revenue for this service. The use of the factoring service is expected to eliminate the bad debts incurred by the business.

Required:

Calculate the net cost of the factor agreement to the business and state whether or not the business should take advantage of the opportunity to factor its trade receivables.

6.5   Cybele Technology Ltd is a software business that is owned and managed by two computer software specialists. Although sales have remained stable at £4 million per year in recent years, the level of trade receivables has increased significantly. A recent financial report submitted to the owners indicates an average settlement period for trade receivables of 60 days compared with an industry average of 40 days. The level of bad debts has also increased in recent years and the business now writes off approximately £20,000 of bad debts each year.

The recent problems experienced in controlling credit have led to a liquidity crisis for the business. At present, the business finances its trade receivables by a bank overdraft bearing an interest rate of 14 per cent a year. However, the overdraft limit has been exceeded on several occasions in recent months and the bank is now demanding a significant decrease in the size of the overdraft. To comply with this demand, the owners of the business have approached a factor who has offered to make an advance equivalent to 85 per cent of trade receivables, based on the assumption that the level of receivables will be in line with the industry average. The factor will charge a rate of interest of 12 per cent a year for this advance. The factor will take over the sales records of the business and, for this service, will charge a fee based on 2 per cent of sales. The business believes that the services offered by the factor should eliminate bad debts and should lead to administrative cost savings of £26,000 per year.

Required:

(a)   Calculate the effect on the profit of Cybele Technology Ltd of employing a debt factor. Discuss your findings.

(b)   Discuss the potential advantages and disadvantages for a business that employs the services of a debt factor.

6.6   Telford Engineers plc, a medium-sized Midlands manufacturer of automobile components, has decided to modernise its factory by introducing a number of robots. These will cost £20 million and will reduce operating costs by £6 million a year for their estimated useful life of 10 years starting next year (Year 10). To finance this scheme, the business can raise £20 million either by issuing:

1   20 million ordinary shares at 100p; or
2   loan notes at 7 per cent interest a year with capital repayments of £3 million a year commencing at the end of Year 11.

Telford Engineers' summarised financial statements appear below:

Summary of statements of financial position (balance sheets) at 31 December

	Year 6	Year 7	Year 8	Year 9
	£m	£m	£m	£m
Non-current assets	48	51	65	64
Current assets	55	67	57	55
Total assets	103	118	122	119
Equity	48	61	61	63
Non-current liabilities	30	30	30	30
Current liabilities				
Trade payables	20	27	25	18
Short-term borrowings	5	–	6	8
	25	27	31	26
Total equity and liabilities	103	118	122	119
Number of issued 25p shares	80m	80m	80m	80m
Share price	150p	200p	100p	145p

Note that the short-term borrowings consisted entirely of bank overdrafts.

Summary of income statements for years ended 31 December

	Year 6	Year 7	Year 8	Year 9
	£m	£m	£m	£m
Sales revenue	152	170	110	145
Operating profit	28	40	7	15
Interest payable	(4)	(3)	(4)	(5)
Profit before taxation	24	37	3	10
Tax	(12)	(16)	(0)	(4)
Profit for the year	12	21	3	6
Dividends paid during each year	6	8	3	4

For your answer you should assume that the tax rate for Year 10 is 30 per cent, that sales revenue and operating profit will be unchanged except for the £6 million cost saving arising from the introduction of the robots, and that Telford Engineers will pay the same dividend per share in Year 10 as in Year 9.

Required:
(a) Prepare, for each financing arrangement, Telford Engineers' projected income statement for the year ending 31 December Year 10 and a statement of its share capital, reserves and loans on that date.
(b) Calculate Telford's projected earnings per share for Year 10 for both schemes.
(c) Which scheme would you advise the business to adopt? You should give your reasons and state what additional information you would require.

6.7 Gainsborough Fashions Ltd operates a small chain of fashion shops in North Wales. In recent months the business has been under pressure from its suppliers to reduce the average credit period taken from three months to one month. As a result, the directors have approached the bank to ask for an increase in the existing overdraft for one year to be able to comply with the suppliers' demands. The most recent financial statements of the business are as follows:

Statement of financial position (balance sheet) as at 31 May

	£	£
Non-current assets		
Property, plant and equipment		
Fixtures and fittings at cost	90,000	
Accumulated depreciation	(23,000)	67,000
Motor vehicles at cost	34,000	
Accumulated depreciation	(27,000)	7,000
		74,000
Current assets		
Inventories at cost		198,000
Trade receivables		3,000
		201,000
Total assets		275,000
Equity		
£1 ordinary shares		20,000
General reserve		4,000
Retained earnings		17,000
		41,000
Non-current liabilities		
Borrowings – Loan notes repayable in just over one year's time		40,000
Current liabilities		
Trade payables		162,000
Accrued expenses		10,000
Borrowings – Bank overdraft		17,000
Tax due		5,000
		194,000
Total equity and liabilities		275,000

Abbreviated income statement for the year ended 31 May

	£
Sales revenue	740,000
Operating profit	38,000
Interest charges	(5,000)
Profit before taxation	33,000
Tax	(10,000)
Profit for the year	23,000

A dividend of £23,000 was paid for the year.

Notes
1   The loan notes are secured by personal guarantees from the directors.
2   The current overdraft bears an interest rate of 12 per cent a year.

Required:
(a)   Identify and discuss the major factors that a bank would take into account before deciding whether or not to grant an increase in the overdraft of a business.
(b)   State whether, in your opinion, the bank should grant the required increase in the overdraft for Gainsborough Fashions Ltd. You should provide reasoned arguments and supporting calculations where necessary.

7

Financing a business 2: raising long-term finance

INTRODUCTION

We begin this chapter by looking at the role of the London Stock Exchange (which we shall refer to as simply the Stock Exchange) in raising finance for large businesses. We shall then go on to consider whether shares listed on the Stock Exchange are efficiently priced. We shall see that efficient share pricing has important implications for businesses seeking to raise finance through the Stock Exchange. Following our examination of share pricing, we consider the different methods by which share capital may be issued.

Smaller businesses do not have access to the Stock Exchange and so must look elsewhere to raise long-term finance. In this chapter, we identify some of the main providers of long-term finance for smaller businesses.

LEARNING OUTCOMES

When you have completed this chapter, you should be able to:

- Discuss the role and nature of the Stock Exchange.

- Discuss the nature and implications of stock market efficiency.

- Outline the methods by which share capital may be issued.

- Identify the problems that smaller businesses experience in raising finance and describe the ways in which they may gain access to long-term finance.

The Stock Exchange

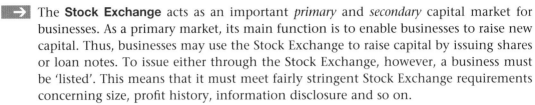

→ The **Stock Exchange** acts as an important *primary* and *secondary* capital market for businesses. As a primary market, its main function is to enable businesses to raise new capital. Thus, businesses may use the Stock Exchange to raise capital by issuing shares or loan notes. To issue either through the Stock Exchange, however, a business must be 'listed'. This means that it must meet fairly stringent Stock Exchange requirements concerning size, profit history, information disclosure and so on.

As a secondary market, the function of the Stock Exchange is to enable investors to transfer their securities (that is, shares and loan notes) with ease. It provides a 'second-hand' market where shares and loan notes already in issue may be bought and sold. This benefits listed businesses as investors are more likely to invest if they know their investment can be turned into cash whenever required. Listed businesses are, therefore, likely to find it easier to raise long-term finance and to do so at lower cost.

Although investors are not obliged to use the Stock Exchange as the means of transferring shares in a listed business, it is usually the most convenient way of buying or selling shares.

Listed businesses

Businesses listed on the Stock Exchange vary considerably in size, with market capitalisations ranging from below £2 million to more than £2,000 million. **Real World 7.1** provides some idea of the distribution of businesses across this wide range.

REAL WORLD 7.1

UK listed businesses by equity market value

The distribution of UK listed businesses by equity market value at the end of December 2007 is shown in Figure 7.1 below.

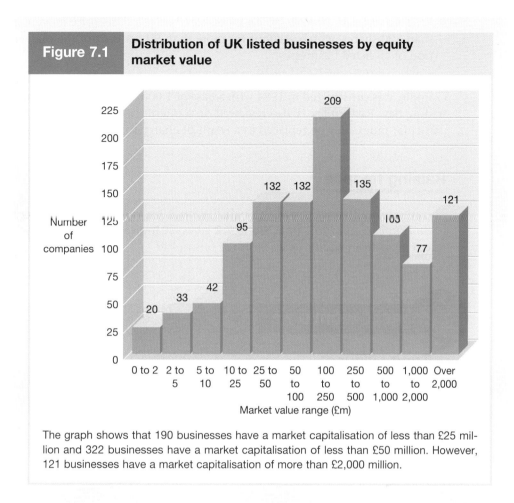

| Figure 7.1 | Distribution of UK listed businesses by equity market value |

The graph shows that 190 businesses have a market capitalisation of less than £25 million and 322 businesses have a market capitalisation of less than £50 million. However, 121 businesses have a market capitalisation of more than £2,000 million.

Source: Adapted from www.londonstockexchange.com, Primary Market Fact Sheet, December 2007.

Share price indices

There are various indices available to help monitor trends in overall share price movements of Stock Exchange listed businesses. **FTSE (Footsie) indices**, as they are called, derive their name from the organisations behind them: the Financial Times (FT) and the Stock Exchange (SE). The most common indices are:

- *FTSE 100.* This is probably the most well known share price index. It is based on the share price movements of the 100 largest businesses, by **market capitalisation**, listed on the Stock Exchange. (Market capitalisation is the total market value of the shares of the business.) Businesses within this index are often referred to as 'large cap' businesses.
- *FTSE Mid 250.* An index based on the share price movements of the next 250 largest businesses, by market capitalisation, listed on the Stock Exchange.
- *FTSE A 350.* This index combines businesses in the FTSE 100 and FTSE Mid 250 indices.

● *FTSE Actuaries All Share Index*. An index based on the share price movements of more than 800 shares, which account for more than 90 per cent of the market capitalisation of all listed businesses.

Each index is constructed using a base date and a base value (the FTSE 100 index, for example, was constructed in 1984 with a base of 1,000) and is updated throughout each trading day. Each index is also reviewed on a quarterly basis, and businesses within a particular index may be replaced as a result of changes in their relative size.

Raising finance

The amount of finance raised through the Stock Exchange each year varies according to economic conditions. **Real World 7.2** gives an indication of the amounts raised in recent years from equity issues by listed businesses.

REAL WORLD 7.2

Equity issues

The following amounts were raised from new equity capital issues by listed businesses through the main market of the London Stock Exchange over the three years 2005–2007.

	New equity capital raised	
	Number of businesses	Amount raised (£m)
2007	73	7,613.2
2006	77	8,415.4
2005	84	5,965.6

We can see that there have been significant fluctuations over the three-year period.

Source: Compiled from Main Market Fact sheets, December 2005, 2006 and 2007, London Stock Exchange (www.londonstockexchange.com).

Proceeds from a share issue may be uncertain, particularly when markets are volatile. **Real World 7.3** describes a recent equity issue by a well-known business that was affected by market volatility.

REAL WORLD 7.3

Timing is everything   **FT**

Timing is everything in life and for Moneysupermarket.com, everything amounts to about £216m.

The internet price comparison site floated on the stock exchange yesterday on the day of the biggest one-day percentage fall in four years.

Management at the company were ruing the delay in flotation caused by wrangling between Simon Nixon and Duncan Cameron, the two founders.

However, analysts say the recent volatility in world stock markets almost derailed the entire initial public offering and said Moneysupermarket.com was relieved to be able to achieve its planned float of 43.4 per cent of its equity at 170p a share.

It is believed that a week ago, bankers were confidently expecting a price closer to 202p, valuing the company at £1bn. Instead, its opening price meant Moneysupermarket.com had a capitalisation of £843m, reduced to £783m by close of trading.

'It's a blip,' Mr Nixon said. 'I suppose we have been a little bit unlucky, but the really positive thing for us is that we have been able to get our flotation going at all. It shows a lot of interest from investors.'

Mr Nixon has said he wanted to float several months ago, but could not reach agreement with Mr Cameron, with whom he divided all voting shares when they set up the company. The two had fallen out in 2001. They reached agreement last month, with Mr Cameron selling 90 per cent of his stake for £162m.

A person familiar with the deal said: 'The difference that market conditions made between the actual float price and what it might have been a week ago was a matter of days, not months, so it's unfair to blame Duncan Cameron. But it was a tough haggle and, if it hadn't take so long to finish, the company would have floated . . . for a lot more.'

Source: Ben Fenton, 'What a difference a delay makes for Moneysupermarket.com', www.ft.com, 27 July 2007.

The Stock Exchange can be a useful vehicle for owners to realise value from their business. By floating the business on the Stock Exchange, and thereby making shares available to other investors, the owners will be able to convert the value of their stake in the business into cash by selling shares. A share issue arising from the initial listing of the business is known as an *initial public offering (IPO)*. **Real World 7.4** describes how two of the owners of moneysupermarket.com (mentioned above) benefited from its IPO.

REAL WORLD 7.4

Cashing in

Paul Doughty, the CFO (chief financial officer) of moneysupermarket.com, is nearly £3m richer after his company's IPO despite a below-par fundraising.

The internet broker, which helps consumers to find the cheapest financial products, completed its float last week but ended up with an offer price of £1.70 a share, at the foot of the £1.70 to £2.10 range.

A company spokesperson confirmed that Doughty had cashed in 1.6m shares, but even with the disappointing showing, the CFO of the UK's leading price-comparison website made himself close to £3m.

If the IPO offer price had been set at the top end of the range, Doughty would have earned close to £3.5m. But his windfall was dwarfed by chief executive, Simon Nixon, who cashed in £60.3m shares, netting £100m. He still holds more than 57% of the company, which is worth more than £800m.

Source: David Jetuah, 'Internet FD is in the money after floatation', *Accountancy Age*, 2 August 2007, p. 3.

Advantages and disadvantages of a listing

In addition to the advantages already mentioned, it is claimed that a Stock Exchange listing can help a business by:

● raising its profile, which may be useful in dealings with customers and suppliers;
● ensuring that its shares are valued in an efficient manner (a point to which we return later);
● broadening its investor base;
● acquiring other businesses by using its own shares as payment rather than cash;
● attracting and retaining employees by offering incentives based on share ownership schemes.

Before a decision is made to float (that is, to list), however, these advantages must be weighed against the possible disadvantages of a listing.

Raising finance through the Stock Exchange can be a costly business. To make an initial public offering, a business will rely on the help of various specialists such as lawyers, accountants and bankers. However, their services do not come cheap. Typically, between 4 and 8 per cent of the total proceeds from a sale will be absorbed in professional fees. (See reference 1 at the end of the chapter.) In addition to these out-of-pocket expenses, a huge amount of management time is usually required to undertake an IPO through the Stock Exchange, which can result in missed business opportunities.

Another important disadvantage is the regulatory burden placed on listed businesses. Once a business is listed, there are continuing requirements that must be met, covering issues such as:

● disclosure of financial information
● informing shareholders of significant developments
● the rights of shareholders and lenders
● the obligations of directors.

These requirements can be onerous and can also involve substantial costs for the business.

Another potential disadvantage is that the activities of listed businesses are closely monitored by financial analysts, financial journalists and other businesses. Such scrutiny may be unwelcome, particularly if the business is dealing with sensitive issues or is experiencing operational problems.

If investors become disenchanted with the business, and the price of its shares falls, this may make it vulnerable to a takeover bid from another business. This risk has led some businesses to withdraw from the Stock Exchange. Sir Richard Branson, the principal shareholder of Virgin, floated this business on the Stock Exchange in 1986. However, 18 months later he decided to de-list the business. The value of the shares in Virgin fell substantially during a crash in stock market prices in 1987 and Sir Richard believed that this made the business vulnerable to a takeover. He wanted to retain control of the business and decided, therefore, to de-list the business (after buying back shares he had sold at the time of the listing).

A potential disadvantage for smaller listed businesses is that they may be overlooked by investors. Large institutional investors, which dominate the ownership of listed shares, usually buy shares in large tranches and so may focus on larger businesses because of the size of investment to be made. Smaller businesses may, therefore, find it difficult to raise fresh capital unless investors can be persuaded of their growth potential.

A final disadvantage claimed is that Stock Exchange investors suffer from a short-term investment perspective. It is argued that the investment myopia of investors puts pressure on listed businesses to produce good results in the short term, even though this may have adverse long-term effects. This claim is worthy of further investigation and so is considered in more detail below.

The problem of short termism

The conventional wisdom appears to be that listed businesses are under pressure to perform well over the short term by Stock Exchange investors. Furthermore, as a result of this pressure, businesses are inhibited from undertaking projects that will only yield benefits in the longer term. Instead, they will opt for investments that perform well over the short term, even though the long-term prospects may be poor. Although this view of Stock Exchange investors seems to be widely held, it is not well supported by the evidence. Indeed, there is some compelling evidence to the contrary.

Evidence of share price behaviour can be cited that suggests that investors take a long-term view when making investment decisions. Two such examples are:

● *Share price reaction to investment plans*. If a short-term view is taken by investors, any announcement by a business that it plans to undertake long-term investment or research would be treated as bad news. It should lead investors to sell their shares and this, in turn, would result in a fall in the business's share price. Conversely, any announcement by a business that long-term investment plans are to be scrapped would be treated as good news and should result in a rise in share price. In fact, the opposite share price reaction to that stated will usually occur.

● *Dividend payments*. Investors demanding short-term returns would be expected to value businesses with a high dividend yield more highly than businesses with a low dividend yield. This kind of behaviour would allow an astute investor to buy shares in low-yielding businesses at a lower price than their 'true' value and so, over time, make higher returns. However, the evidence suggests that businesses with low dividend yields are more highly regarded by investors than businesses with high dividend yields (see reference 2 at the end of the chapter).

If Stock Exchange investors are not to blame for the short-term perspective of managers, then who is to blame? Some believe that it is the managers themselves. It has been argued, for example, that managers have incorrect views about what Stock Exchange investors are really looking for. (There is certainly survey evidence to support the view that managers believe that investors have a short-term investment perspective.) It has also been suggested that managers adopt a short-term view because their rewards are linked to short-term results or because frequent job changes encourage the quest for short-term results. Finally, it has been suggested that the particular appraisal methods adopted by managers to evaluate investment opportunities encourage a short-term view (see reference 2 at the end of the chapter).

Activity 7.1

Can you think of an investment appraisal method, dealt with in Chapter 4, which may encourage a short-term view?

The payback method places emphasis on how quickly an investment repays its initial out-lay. This method is widely used and may encourage a short-term approach by managers. (An alternative explanation, however, is that the payback method is selected by managers because they adopt a short-term perspective.)

Some believe, however, that managers are not the real culprits and that it is high inflation and economic instability during the post-war years that have given managers a short-term perspective. Thus, to encourage long-term thinking we need a sustained period of stable monetary conditions.

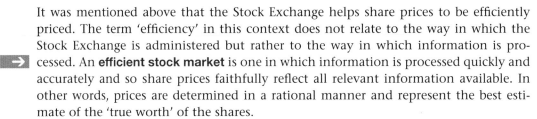

Stock market efficiency

It was mentioned above that the Stock Exchange helps share prices to be efficiently priced. The term 'efficiency' in this context does not relate to the way in which the Stock Exchange is administered but rather to the way in which information is pro-cessed. An **efficient stock market** is one in which information is processed quickly and accurately and so share prices faithfully reflect all relevant information available. In other words, prices are determined in a rational manner and represent the best esti-mate of the 'true worth' of the shares.

The term 'efficiency' does not imply that investors have perfect knowledge con-cerning a business and its future prospects and that this knowledge is reflected in the share price. Information may come to light concerning the business that investors did not previously know about and which may indicate that the current share price is higher or lower than its 'true worth'. However, in an efficient market, the new informa-tion will be quickly absorbed by investors and this will lead to an appropriate share price adjustment.

We can see that the term 'efficiency' in relation to the Stock Exchange is not the same as the economists' concept of perfect markets, which you may have come across in your previous studies. The definition of an efficient capital market does not rest on a set of restrictive assumptions regarding the operation of the market (for example, that relevant information is freely available, that all investors have access to all relevant information, and so on). In reality, such assumptions will not hold. The term 'efficient market' is a narrower concept that has been developed by studying the behaviour of stock markets in the real world. It simply describes the situation where relevant informa-tion is *quickly* and *accurately* reflected in share prices. The speed at which new informa-tion is absorbed in share prices will mean that not even nimble-footed investors will have time to make superior gains by buying or selling shares when new information becomes available.

To understand why the Stock Exchange may be efficient, it is important to bear in mind that shares listed on the Stock Exchange are scrutinised by many individuals, including skilled analysts, who are constantly seeking to make gains from identifying shares that are inefficiently priced. They are alert to new information and will react quickly when new opportunities arise. If, for example, a share can be identified as being below its 'true worth' investors would immediately exploit this information by buying shares in that business. When this is done on a large scale, the effect will be to drive up the price of the share, thereby eliminating any inefficiency within the market. Thus, as a result of the efforts to make gains from inefficiently priced shares, investors will, paradoxically, promote the efficiency of the market.

Three levels of efficiency have been identified concerning the operation of stock markets. These are as follows.

Weak form of efficiency

The weak form reflects the situation where past market information, such as the sequence of share prices, rates of return and trading volumes and so on, is fully reflected in current share prices and so should have no bearing on future share prices. Thus, future share price movements will be independent of past share price movements. Movements in share prices will follow a random path and, as a result, any attempt to study past prices in order to detect a pattern of price movements will fail. It is not, therefore, possible to make gains from simply studying past price movements. Investors and analysts who draw up charts of share price changes (which is known as technical analysis) in order to predict future price movements will, therefore, be wasting their time.

Semi-strong form of efficiency

The semi-strong form takes the notion of efficiency a little further and describes the situation where all publicly available information, including past share prices, is fully reflected in the current share price. Other publicly available forms of information will include published accounts, business announcements, newspaper reports, economic forecasts, and so on. These forms of information, which become available at random intervals, are quickly absorbed by the market and so investors who study relevant reports and announcements (known as fundamental analysis), in an attempt to make above-average returns on a consistent basis, will be disappointed. The information will already be incorporated into share prices.

Strong form of efficiency

The strong form is the ultimate form of efficiency and describes the situation where share prices fully reflect all available information, whether public or private. This means that the share price will be a good approximation to the 'true' value of the share. As all relevant information is absorbed in share prices, even those who have 'inside' information concerning a business, such as unpublished reports or confidential management decisions, will not be able to make superior returns, on a consistent basis, from using this information.

The various forms of efficiency described above can be viewed as a progression where each higher form of efficiency incorporates the previous form(s). Thus, if a stock market is efficient in the semi-strong form it will also be efficient in the weak form. Similarly, if a stock market is efficient in the strong form, it will also be efficient in the semi-strong and weak forms (see Figure 7.2).

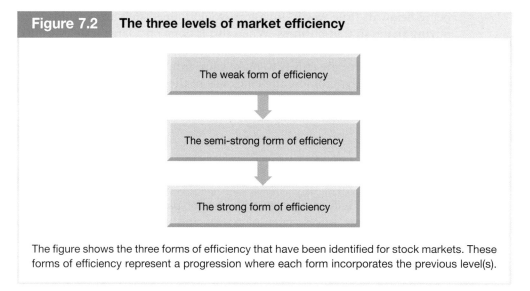

Figure 7.2 **The three levels of market efficiency**

The figure shows the three forms of efficiency that have been identified for stock markets. These forms of efficiency represent a progression where each form incorporates the previous level(s).

Activity 7.2

Can you explain why the relationship between the various forms of market efficiency explained above should be the case?

If a stock market is efficient in the semi-strong form it will reflect all publicly available information. This will include past share prices. Thus, the semi-strong form will incorporate the weak form. If the stock market is efficient in the strong form, it will reflect all available information; which includes publicly available information. Thus, it will incorporate the semi-strong and weak forms.

Activity 7.3 below tests your understanding of how share prices might react to a public announcement under two different levels of market efficiency.

Activity 7.3

Dornier plc is a large civil engineering business that is listed on the Stock Exchange. On 1 May it received a confidential letter stating that it had won a large building contract from an overseas government. The new contract is expected to increase the profits of the business by a substantial amount over the next five years. The news of the contract was announced publicly on 4 May.

How would the shares of the business react to the formal announcement on 4 May assuming (a) a semi-strong and (b) a strong form of market efficiency?

Under the semi-strong form, the formal announcement would lead to an increase in the value of the shares. Under the strong form of efficiency, however, there would be no share reaction as the information would already be incorporated in the share price.

Evidence on stock market efficiency

You may wonder what evidence exists to support each of the above forms of efficiency. For the weak form there is now a large body of evidence that spans many countries and many time periods. Much of this evidence has involved checking to see whether share price movements follow a random pattern: that is, finding out whether successive price changes were independent of each other. The research evidence generally confirms the existence of a random pattern of share prices. Research has also been carried out to assess the value of trading rules used by some investors. These rules seek to achieve superior returns by identifying trend-like patterns to determine the point at which to buy or sell shares. The research has produced mixed results but tends to demonstrate that trading rules are not worthwhile. However, the value of these rules is difficult to assess, partly because of their sheer number and partly because of the subjective judgement involved in interpreting trends.

Activity 7.4

If share prices follow a random pattern, does this not mean that the market is acting in an irrational (and inefficient) manner?

No. New information concerning a business is likely to arise at random intervals and so share price adjustments to the new information will arise at those random intervals. The randomness of share price movements is, therefore, to be expected if markets are efficient.

Although the weight of research evidence offers little support for the belief that share prices, or prices in other financial markets, exhibit repetitive patterns of behaviour, some analysts (known as technical analysts) continue to search for such patterns. **Real World 7.5** illustrates some of the techniques used by these analysts to help predict future price movements.

 **REAL WORLD 7.5**

Reading the signs

The charts in Figure 7.3 are taken from *The Independent* and show the techniques used by technical analysts being applied to different markets: the Dow Jones Index (a share price index of 30 industrial companies listed on the New York Stock Exchange), the share price of Vodafone plc (a major mobile phone operator) and to currency markets.

Real World 7.5 continued

| Figure 7.3 | Reading the signs |

USD/GBP

The most basic tool of technical analysis is the trend line, which must go through at least three points on a chart. Markets frequently trade within a channel of two parallel lines: the top one is called the resistance line, the lower one the support line. A break-out of the channel can indicate the end of a market trend.

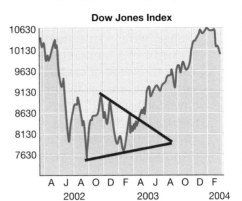

Dow Jones Index

The triangle is another popular trend indicator. Triangles show price convergence, and are formed during periods of consolidation in the markets, when the support and resistance lines converge, as shown here in the chart of the Dow Jones Index. A break-out from a triangle is seen as a strong indicator of market direction.

USD/EUR

The triangular formation in this recent chart of the US dollar/euro price also represents a period of consolidation in the market. However, the fact that this consolidation came after a price fall and the market then broke out of the triangle in the same downward direction makes this a particularly strong indicator.

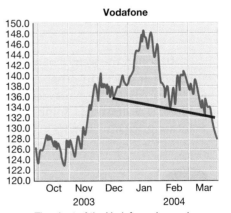

Vodafone

The chart of the Vodafone share price demonstrates a classic 'head and shoulders'. In this formation, the price reaches a peak and declines; rises above its former peak and declines; and rises a third time but not to the second peak, and then again declines. Chartists consider this formation a very negative market indicator.

The diagrams illustrate four techniques used by technical analysts to predict future market movements.

Source: 'Reading the signs', *The Independent*, 27 March 2004.

Research to test the semi-strong form of efficiency has usually involved monitoring the reaction of the share price to new information, such as profit announcements. This is done to see whether the market reacts to new information in an appropriate manner. The results usually show that share prices readjust quickly and accurately to any new information that affects the value of the business. This implies that investors cannot make superior returns by reacting quickly to new information. The results also show that investors are able to distinguish between new information that affects the value of the underlying business and new information that does not.

Other semi-strong tests have checked to whether it is possible to predict future returns by using available public information. These tests have produced more mixed results. One test involves the use of P/E ratios. We saw in Chapter 3 that the P/E ratio reflects the market's view of the growth prospects of a particular share: the higher the P/E ratio, the greater the growth prospects. Tests have shown, however, that shares with low P/E ratios outperform those with high P/E ratios. The market overestimates the growth prospects of businesses with high P/E ratios and underestimates the growth prospects of those with low P/E ratios. In other words, the market gets it wrong. We shall return to this point a little later.

Research to test the strong form of efficiency has often involved an examination of the performance of investment fund managers. These managers are highly skilled and have access to a wide range of information, not all of which may be in the public domain. If, despite their advantage over private investors, fund managers were unable to generate consistently superior performance over time, it would provide support for the view that markets are strong-form efficient. The results, alas, are mixed. Although earlier studies often supported the view that fund managers cannot outperform the market, more recent studies have suggested that some can.

Implications for managers

If stock markets are efficient, what should managers do? It seems that they must learn six important lessons.

Lesson 1: Timing doesn't matter

When managers are considering a new share issue, they may feel that the timing of the issue is important. If the stock market is inefficient, there is a risk that the price of a share will fall below its 'true worth' and making a new issue of the same shares at such a point could be very costly. The timing of new issues therefore becomes a critical management decision. However, if the market is efficient then, by definition, the price quoted for shares will faithfully reflect the available information. This implies that the timing of issues will not be critical as there is no optimal point in time for making a new issue. Even if the market is very depressed and share prices are very low, it cannot be assumed that things will improve. The share prices prevailing at the low point will still reflect the market's estimate of the future returns from the shares.

Activity 7.5

Why might a financial manager who accepts that the market is efficient in the semi-strong form nevertheless be justified in delaying the issue of new shares until what he or she believes will be a more appropriate time?

Activity 7.5 continued

The justification for delaying a new issue under the circumstance described would be that the manager believes the market has got it wrong. This situation could arise if the market has inadequate information with which to price the shares correctly. The manager may have access to inside information which, when made available to the market, will lead to an upward adjustment in share prices.

Lesson 2: Don't search for undervalued businesses

If the stock market accurately absorbs publicly available information concerning businesses, the prices quoted for shares will represent the best estimates available of their 'true worth'. This means that investors should not spend time trying to find undervalued shares in order to make gains. Unless they have access to information which the market does not have, they will not be able to 'beat the market' on a consistent basis. To look for undervalued shares will only result in time being spent and transaction costs being incurred to no avail. Similarly, managers should not try to identify undervalued shares in other businesses with the intention of identifying possible takeover targets. While there may be a number of valid and compelling reasons for taking over another business, the argument that shares of the target business are undervalued by the stock market is not one of them.

Lesson 3: Take note of market reaction

The investment plans and decisions of managers will be quickly and accurately reflected in the share price. Where these plans and decisions result in a fall in share price, managers may find it useful to review them. In effect, the market provides managers with a 'second opinion', which is both objective and informed. This opinion should not go unheeded.

Lesson 4: You can't fool the market

Some managers appear to believe that form is as important as substance when communicating new information to investors. This may induce them to 'window dress' the financial statements in order to provide a better picture of financial health than is warranted by the facts. However, the evidence suggests that the market is able to see through any cosmetic attempts to improve the financial picture. The market quickly and accurately assesses the economic substance of the business and will price the shares accordingly. Thus, accounting policy changes (such as switching depreciation methods, or switching inventory valuation methods, to boost profits in the current year) will be a waste of time.

Lesson 5: The market, not the business, decides the level of risk

Investors will correctly assess the level of risk associated with an investment and will impose an appropriate rate of return. Moreover, this rate of return will apply to whichever business undertakes that investment. Managers will not be able to influence the required rate of return by adopting particular financing strategies. This means, for example, that the issue of certain types of security, or combinations of securities, will not reduce the rate of return required by the market.

Lesson 6: Champion the interests of shareholders

It was mentioned in Chapter 1 that the primary objective of a business is the maximisation of shareholder wealth. If managers take decisions and actions that are consistent with this objective, it will be reflected in the share price. This is likely to benefit the managers of the business as well as the shareholders.

Are the stock markets really efficient?

The view that stock markets, at least in the major industrialised countries, are efficient has become widely accepted. However, there is a growing body of evidence that casts doubt on the efficiency of stock markets and which has reopened the debate on this topic. Below we consider some of the evidence.

Stock exchange regularities

Researchers have unearthed regular share price patterns in some of the major stock markets. These suggest an element of inefficiency as it would be possible to exploit these patterns in order to achieve superior returns over time. Some of the more important 'regularities' that have been identified are as follows:

- *Business size.* There is now a substantial body of evidence indicating that, other things being equal, small businesses yield higher returns than large businesses. The evidence concerning this phenomenon also shows that the superior returns from small businesses will change over time. The size effect, as it is called, is more pronounced at the turn of the year, for example, than at any other point.
- *Price/earnings (P/E) ratio.* It was mentioned earlier that research has shown that a portfolio of shares held in businesses with a low P/E ratio will outperform a portfolio of shares held in businesses with a high P/E ratio. This suggests that investors can make superior returns from investing in businesses with low P/E ratios.
- *Investment timing.* There are various studies indicating that superior returns may be gained by timing investment decisions appropriately. For example, it has been found that higher returns can be achieved by buying shares at the beginning of April, in the UK, and then selling them at the end of this month, than similar share trading in any other month. Some studies have shown that on Mondays there is an above-average fall in share prices. This may be because investors review their portfolio of shares at the weekend and then decide to sell unwanted shares when the market opens on Monday morning, thereby depressing prices. This suggests, of course, that it is better to buy rather than sell shares on a Monday. Other studies have revealed that the particular time of the day in which shares are traded can lead to superior returns.

Activity 7.6

Can you suggest why April may provide better returns than other months of the year?

One reason may be that a new tax year begins in this month. Investors may sell loss-making shares in March to offset any capital gains tax on shares sold at a profit during the tax year. As a result of these sales, share prices will become depressed. At the start of the new tax year, however, investors will start to buy shares again and so share prices will rise.

The key question is whether these regularities seriously undermine the idea of market efficiency. Many believe that they are of only minor importance and that, on the whole, the markets are efficient for most of the time. The view taken is that, in the real world, there are always likely to be inefficiencies. It can also be argued that if investors discover share price patterns, they will try to exploit these patterns in order to make higher profits. By so doing, they will eliminate the patterns and so make the markets even more efficient. However, others believe that these regularities confirm that stock market behaviour cannot simply be viewed through the lens of efficient markets.

Bubbles, bull markets and behavioural finance

In recent years, a new discipline called **behavioural finance** has emerged, which tries to provide a more complete understanding of the way in which markets behave. This new discipline takes account of the psychological traits of individuals when seeking to explain market behaviour. It does not accept that individuals always behave in a rational manner, and there is a plethora of research evidence in psychology to support this view. Many studies, for example, have shown that individuals make systematic errors when processing information. In the context of investment decisions, these biases can result in the mispricing of shares. Where this occurs, profitable opportunities can be exploited. A detailed study of these behavioural biases is beyond the scope of this book. However, it is worth providing an example to illustrate the challenge they pose to the notion of efficient markets.

One well-documented bias is the overconfidence that individuals place in their own information processing skills and judgement. Overconfidence may lead to various errors when making investment decisions, including:

- an underreaction to new share price information, which arises from a tendency to place more emphasis on new information confirming an original share valuation than new information challenging this valuation;
- a reluctance to sell shares that have incurred losses because it involves admitting to past mistakes;
- incorrectly assessing the riskiness of future returns;
- a tendency to buy and sell shares more frequently than is prudent.

Such errors may help to explain share price 'bubbles' and overextended 'bull' markets, where investor demand keeps share prices buoyant despite evidence suggesting that share prices are too high.

Share price bubbles, which inflate and then burst, appear in stock markets from time to time. When they inflate there is a period of high prices and high trading volumes, which is sustained by the enthusiasm of investors rather than by the fundamentals affecting the shares. During a bubble, investors appear to place too much faith in their optimistic views of future share price movements, and, for a while at least, ignore warning signals concerning future growth prospects. However, as the warning signals become stronger, the disparity between investors' views and reality eventually becomes too great and a correction occurs, bringing investors' views more into line with fundamental values. This realignment of investors' views leads to a large correction in share prices – in other words, the bubble bursts.

For similar reasons, overconfidence can result in overextended bull markets, where share prices become detached from fundamental values. **Real World 7.6** provides a warning of an incipient bubble in one emerging stock market.

REAL WORLD 7.6

Bubble trouble   **FT**

Jim Rogers, the investor and author, has warned of an 'incipient bubble' in the mainland Chinese stock market in an interview with the *Financial Times*.

Thanks to a stock market that has increased nearly sixfold in 28 months, China is now home to five of the world's 10 largest companies by market capitalisation compared with three for the US.

Analysts say this is clear evidence that the market is overvalued, especially considering the relatively poor quality of many listed Chinese companies when compared with their international counterparts.

Mr Rogers says he is heavily invested in China and has never sold a single Chinese share in his life but, if the market continues to climb, he will have to consider selling out.

'It may sound strange for someone who owns Chinese shares to say it would be good for stocks to go down 30 or 40 per cent but, if they don't, there'll be a bubble – and bubbles always end very badly,' he said.

Source: Jamil Anderlini, 'Pundit warns of "incipient bubble" in mainland equities', *Financial Times*, 30 October 2007.

How should managers act?

At present, the debate concerning the efficiency of markets rumbles on and further research is needed before a clear picture emerges. Although this situation may be fine for researchers, we are left with the problem of how managers should respond to an increasingly mixed set of messages concerning the behaviour of the stock markets. Probably the best advice is for managers to assume that, as a general rule, the markets are efficient, at least in the semi-strong form. The weight of evidence still supports this view, and failure to act in this way could be very costly indeed. Where it is clear, however, that some market inefficiency exists, managers should be prepared to take advantage of the opportunities that it provides.

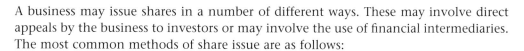

Share issues

A business may issue shares in a number of different ways. These may involve direct appeals by the business to investors or may involve the use of financial intermediaries. The most common methods of share issue are as follows:

- rights issues
- bonus issues
- offers for sale
- public issues
- placings.

Each of these is considered in turn.

Rights issues

Rights issues are made when businesses that have been established for some time seek to raise finance by issuing additional shares for cash. Company law gives existing shareholders the right of first refusal on these new shares, which are offered to them in proportion to their existing shareholding. Only where the existing shareholders waive their right would the share be offered to the investing public generally.

Rights issues, which are now the most common form of share issue, are a relatively cheap and straightforward way of issuing shares: issue expenses are quite low and issue procedures are simpler than for other forms of share issue. The fact that those offered new shares already have an investment in the business, which presumably suits their risk/return requirements, is likely to increase the chances of a successful issue.

Activity 7.7

What is the advantage to existing shareholders of having the right of first refusal on new shares issued for cash?

....

The main advantage is that control of the business by existing shareholders will not be diluted, provided they take up the offer of new shares.

A rights offer usually allows existing shareholders to acquire shares in the business at a price below the current market price. This means that entitlement to participate in a rights offer has a cash value. Existing shareholders who do not wish to take up the rights offer can sell their rights to other investors. Calculating the cash value of the rights entitlement is quite straightforward. An example can be used to illustrate how this is done.

Example 7.1

Shaw Holdings plc has 20 million ordinary shares of 50p in issue. These shares are currently valued on the Stock Exchange at £1.60 per share. The directors of Shaw Holdings plc believe the business requires additional long-term capital and have decided to make a one-for-four issue (that is, one new share for every four shares held) at £1.30 per share. What is the value of the rights per new share?

Solution

The first step in the valuation process is to calculate the price of a share following the rights issue. This is known as the *ex-rights price* and is simply a weighted average of the price of shares before the issue of rights and the price of the rights shares. In the above example we have a one-for-four rights issue. The theoretical ex-rights price is, therefore, calculated as follows:

	£
Price of four shares before the rights issue (4 × £1.60):	6.40
Price of taking up one rights share:	1.30
	7.70
Theoretical ex-rights price:	$\dfrac{7.70}{5}$
	£1.54

As the price of each share, in theory, should be £1.54 following the rights issue and the price of a rights share is £1.30, the value of the rights offer will be the difference between the two:

$$£1.54 - £1.30 = £0.24 \text{ per new share}$$

Market forces will usually ensure the actual price of rights and the theoretical price will be fairly close.

Activity 7.8

An investor with 2,000 shares in Shaw Holdings plc (see Example 7.1) has contacted you for investment advice. She is undecided whether to take up the rights issue, sell the rights or allow the rights offer to lapse.

Calculate the effect on the net wealth of the investor of each of the options being considered.

If the investor takes up the rights issue, she will be in the following position:

	£
Value of holding after rights issue [(2,000 + 500) × £1.54]	3,850
Less Cost of buying the rights shares (500 × £1.30)	(650)
	3,200

If the investor sells the rights, she will be in the following position:

	£
Value of holding after rights issue (2,000 × £1.54)	3,080
Sale of rights (500 × £0.24)	120
	3,200

If the investor lets the rights offer lapse, she will be in the following position:

	£
Value of holding after rights issue (2,000 × £1.54)	3,080

As we can see, the first two options should leave her in the same position concerning net wealth as she was before the rights issue. Before the rights issue she had 2,000 shares worth £1.60 each, or £3,200. However, she will be worse off if she allows the rights offer to lapse than under the other two options. In practice, the business may sell the rights offer on behalf of the investor and pass on the proceeds in order to ensure that she is not worse off as a result of the issue.

When considering a rights issue, the directors of a business must first consider the amount of funds that it needs to raise. This will depend on the future plans and commitments of the business. The directors must then decide on the issue price of the rights shares. Generally speaking, this decision is not of critical importance. In the example above, the business made a one-for-four issue with the price of the rights shares set at £1.30. However, it could have raised the same amount by making a one-for-two issue and setting the rights price at £0.65, or a one-for-one issue and setting the price at £0.325 and so on. The issue price that is finally decided upon will not affect the value of the underlying assets of the business or the proportion of the underlying assets and earnings of the business to which the shareholder is entitled. The directors must, however, ensure that the issue price is not *above* the current market price of the shares in order for the issue to be successful.

Activity 7.9

Why will a rights issue fail if the issue price of the shares is above the current market price of the shares?

If the issue price is above the current market price, it would be cheaper for the investor to purchase shares in the business in the open market (assuming transaction costs are not significant) than to acquire the shares by taking up the rights offer.

In practice, a rights issue will usually be priced at a significant discount to the market price of shares at the date of the rights announcement. Time will elapse between the announcement date of the rights issue and the date at which the rights shares must be subscribed, and during this period there is always a risk that the market price of the shares will fall and the rights issue price will be higher than the market price at the subscription date. If this occurs, the rights issue will fail for the reasons mentioned in Activity 7.9. The higher the discount offered, therefore, the lower the risk of such failure.

Despite the attractions of rights issues, it can be argued that the rights given to existing shareholders will prevent greater competition for new shares in the business. This may, in turn, increase the costs of raising finance for the business because other forms of share issue may be able to raise the required finance more cheaply.

Rights issues are frequently made to raise cash for expansion; however, **Real World 7.7** gives an example of where a rights issue was made to reduce the weight of debt.

REAL WORLD 7.7

TV and radio rights   **FT**

SMG, the embattled media company, sought the sanctuary of its investors yesterday, announcing a two-for-one rights issue to reduce debt from £131m to £40m.

The issue, fully underwritten, was also aimed at giving Rob Woodward, the chief executive, a period of calm in which to sell SMG's Virgin Radio at a better price than offered so far during a protracted process.

It is understood that after market volatility sank the option of a flotation, a sale of Virgin stalled because no bidder would offer more than £57m for the stations. SMG wrote down the value of Virgin to £85m in its financial results.

Mr Woodward said he had the support of his main shareholders for the rights issue, which will see investors offered two new shares at 15p for each one they hold and aims to raise £95m. After expenses, £91m will go towards reducing the debt, which will then be renegotiated with bankers.

Mr Woodward said this would save £20m yearly and free him to concentrate on the core business, SMG's two Scottish ITV franchises, while also avoiding a fire-sale of Virgin Radio.

Source: Ben Fenton, 'Rights issue to cut SMG debt by £91m', www.ft.com, 7 November 2007.

Bonus issues

A **bonus issue** should not be confused with a rights issue of shares. A bonus, or *scrip*, issue also involves the issue of new shares to existing shareholders in proportion to their existing shareholdings. However, shareholders do not have to pay for the new shares issued. The bonus issue is achieved by transferring a sum from the reserves to the paid-up share capital of the business and then issuing shares, equivalent in value to the amount transferred, to existing shareholders. As the reserves are already owned by the shareholders, they do not have to pay for the shares issued. In effect, a bonus issue will simply convert reserves into paid-up capital. To understand this conversion process, and its effect on the financial position of the business, let us consider Example 7.2.

Example 7.2

Wickham plc has the following abbreviated balance sheet as at 31 March:

	£m
Net assets	20
Financed by	
Share capital (£1 ordinary shares)	10
Reserves	10
	20

The directors decide to convert £5 million of the reserves to paid-up capital. As a result, it was decided that a one-for-two bonus issue should be made. Following the bonus issue, the balance sheet of Wickham plc will be as follows:

	£m
Net assets	20
Financed by	
Share capital (£1 ordinary shares)	15
Reserves	5
	20

We can see in Example 7.2 that the share capital of the business has increased and there has been a corresponding decrease in the reserves of the business. The net assets of the business remain unchanged by the bonus issue. Although each shareholder will own more shares following the bonus issue, the proportion held of the total number of shares in issue will remain unchanged and so the stake in the business and the net assets of the business will remain unchanged. Thus, bonus issues do not, of themselves, result in an increase in shareholder wealth. They will simply switch part of the owners' claim from reserves to share capital.

Activity 7.10

Assume that the market price per share in Wickham plc (see Example 7.2) before the bonus issue was £2.10. What will be the market price per share following the share issue?

The business has made a one-for-two issue. A holder of two shares would therefore be in the following position before the bonus issue:

2 shares held at £2.10 market price = £4.20

Activity 7.10 continued

As the wealth of the shareholder has not increased as a result of the issue, the total value of the shareholding will remain the same. This means that, as the shareholder holds one more share following the issue, the market value per share will now be:

$$\frac{£4.20}{3} = £\underline{1.40}$$

You may wonder from the calculations above why bonus issues are made by businesses, particularly as the effect of a bonus issue may be to reduce the reserves available for dividend payments. A number of reasons have been put forward to explain this type of share issue, which include the following:

- *Share price.* The share price of a business may be very high and, as a result, its shares may become more difficult to trade on the Stock Exchange. It seems that shares that trade within a certain price range generate more interest and activity within the market. If the number of shares in issue is increased, the market price of each share will be reduced, which may make the shares more marketable.
- *Lender confidence.* The effect of making a transfer from distributable reserves to paid-up share capital will be to increase the permanent capital base of the business. This move may increase confidence among lenders. In effect, a bonus issue will lower the risk of the business reducing its ordinary shareholders' investment through dividend distributions, thereby leaving lenders in an exposed position.
- *Market signals.* The directors may use a bonus issue as an opportunity to signal to investors their confidence in the future prospects of the business. The issue may be accompanied by the announcement of good news concerning the business (for example, securing a large contract or achieving an increase in profits). Under these circumstances, the share price may rise in the expectation that earnings/dividends per share will be maintained. Shareholders would, therefore, be better off following the issue. However, it is the *information content* of the bonus issue, rather than the issue itself, that will create this increase in wealth.

Real World 7.8 provides a recent example of a bonus issue.

REAL WORLD 7.8

Increasing marketability   FT

Shares in Henry Boot have enjoyed a good run over the past year from below 700p to £11.10 by this week's end. The property and construction group, where about half of the shares are family-controlled, wants to increase liquidity by a bonus issue that will increase fivefold the shares in circulation. Investors will gain four new shares for each one held, bringing a big price adjustment after the annual meeting in May. The bonus issue follows a successful year for the Sheffield-based group, which this week reported a 41 per cent rise in annual sales to £142.3m, helped by a rise in the value of land sales.

Source: James Wilson, 'Rise possible following bonus issue adjustment', www.ft.com, 24 March 2007.

Offer for sale

An **offer for sale** involves a business, which trades as a public limited company, selling a new issue of shares to a financial institution known as an issuing house. However, shares that are already in issue may also be sold to an issuing house. In this case, existing shareholders agree to sell their shares to the issuing house. The issuing house will, in turn, sell the shares purchased from either the business or its shareholders to the public. The issuing house will publish a prospectus that sets out details of the business and the type of shares to be sold, and investors will be invited to apply for shares.

The advantage of this type of issue, from the business's viewpoint, is that the sale proceeds of the shares are certain. It is the issuing house that will take on the risk of selling the shares to investors. This type of issue is often used when a business seeks a listing on the Stock Exchange and wishes to raise a large amount of funds.

Public issue

A **public issue** involves a business making a direct invitation to the public to purchase shares in the business. Typically, this is done through a newspaper advertisement, and the invitation to the public will be accompanied by the publication of a prospectus. The shares may, once again, be either a new issue or shares already in issue. An issuing house may be asked by the business to help administer the issue of the shares to the public and to offer advice concerning an appropriate selling price. However, the business rather than the issuing house will take on the risk of selling the shares. An offer for sale and a public issue will both result in a widening of share ownership in the business.

Setting a share price

When making an issue of shares, the business or the issuing house will usually set a price for the shares. However, establishing a share price may not be an easy task, particularly where the market is volatile or where the business has unique characteristics. If the share price is set too high, the issue will be undersubscribed and the business (or issuing house) will not receive the amount expected. If the share price is set too low, the issue will be oversubscribed and the business (or issuing house) will receive less than could have been achieved.

One way of dealing with the pricing problem is to make a **tender issue** of shares. This involves the investors determining the price at which the shares are issued. Although the business (or issuing house) may publish a reserve price to help guide investors, it will be up to the individual investor to determine the number of shares to be purchased and the price the investor wishes to pay. Once the offers from investors have been received, a price at which all the shares can be sold will be established (known as the striking price). Investors that have made offers at, or above, the striking price will be issued shares at the striking price and offers received below the striking price will be rejected. Note that all of the shares will be issued at the same price, irrespective of the prices actually offered by individual investors.

Example 7.3 illustrates the way in which a striking price is achieved.

Example 7.3

Celibes plc made a tender offer of shares and the following offers were received by investors:

Share price £	No. of shares tendered at this particular price 000s	Cumulative no. of shares tendered 000s
£2.80	300	300
£2.40	590	890
£1.90	780	1,670
£1.20	830	2,500

The directors of Celibes plc wish to issue 2,000,000 shares, at a minimum price of £1.20.

The striking price would have to be £1.20 as, above this price, there would be insufficient interest to issue 2,000,000 shares. At the price of £1.20, the total number of shares tendered exceeds the number of shares available and so a partial allottment would be made. Normally, each investor would receive 4 shares for every 5 shares tendered (that is 2,000/2,500).

Activity 7.11

Assume that, rather than issue a fixed number of shares, the directors of Celibes plc (see Example 7.3) wish to maximise the amount raised from the share issue. What would be the appropriate striking price?

The price at which the amount raised from the issue can be maximised is calculated as follows:

Share price £	Cumulative no. of shares 000s	Share sale proceeds £000
£2.80	300	840
£2.40	890	2,136
£1.90	1,670	3,173
£1.20	2,500	3,000

The table shows that the striking price should be £1.90 to maximise the share sale proceeds.

Although tender issues are used occasionally, they are not popular with investors and are, therefore, not in widespread use.

Placing

 A **placing** does not involve an invitation to the public to subscribe to shares. Instead, the shares are 'placed' with selected investors, such as large financial institutions. This can be a quick and relatively cheap method of raising funds because savings can be made in advertising and legal costs. However, it can result in the ownership of the business being concentrated in a few hands and may prevent small investors from participating in the new issue of shares. Usually, businesses seeking relatively small amounts of cash will employ this form of issue.

Real World 7.9 describes how one business used a placing to raise finance.

REAL WORLD 7.9

Placing for growth   **FT**

Ultimate Leisure, the Newcastle bar and nightclub operator, is raising £25m through a share placement with existing backers to pursue 'substantive acquisitive growth'.

The company intends to place 14.8m shares with its two largest investors, Reuben Brothers and the Dawnay, Day Group.

The placing price of 169p per share is at a 5 per cent discount compared with the company's closing share price on January 19. The share placement scheme will raise both backers' combined control in Ultimate to more than 30 per cent.

The group, which operates the 'Chase', 'Blubambu' and 'Coyote Wild' nightclub brands, said it is reviewing a number of acquisitions.

Both Reuben Brothers and Dawnay, Day have indicated that they would support a new equity issue.

Source: Lucy Warwick-Ching, 'Ultimate outlines £25m share placing plan', www.ft.com, 23 January 2007.

Long-term finance for the smaller business

Although the Stock Exchange provides an important source of long-term finance for large businesses, it is not really suitable for smaller businesses. The aggregate market value of shares that are to be listed on the Stock Exchange must be at least £700,000 and, in practice, the amounts are much higher because of the listing costs identified earlier. Thus, smaller businesses must look elsewhere for help in raising long-term finance. However, various reports and studies over more than seventy years have highlighted the problems that they encounter in doing so. These problems can be a major obstacle to growth and include:

- a lack of financial management skills (leading to difficulties in developing credible business plans that will satisfy lenders);
- a lack of knowledge concerning the availability of sources of long-term finance;
- insufficient security for loan capital;
- failure to meet rigorous assessment criteria (for example, a good financial track record over five years);
- an excessively bureaucratic screening process for loan applications (see reference 3 at the end of the chapter).

In addition to the problems mentioned, the cost of finance is often higher for smaller businesses than for larger businesses because of the higher risks involved.

Not all financing constraints are externally imposed; some arise from the attitude of owners. Owners of small businesses are often unwilling to raise new finance through the issue of ordinary shares if it involves a dilution of control. It is also claimed that some refuse to consider loan finance because they do not believe in borrowing (see reference 4 at the end of the chapter).

Although obtaining long-term finance is not always easy for smaller businesses (and one consequence may be excessive reliance on short-term sources of finance, such as bank overdrafts), things have improved over recent years. Some of the more important sources of long-term finance that are now available are considered below.

Private equity

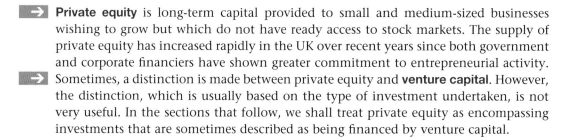

Private equity is long-term capital provided to small and medium-sized businesses wishing to grow but which do not have ready access to stock markets. The supply of private equity has increased rapidly in the UK over recent years since both government and corporate financiers have shown greater commitment to entrepreneurial activity. Sometimes, a distinction is made between private equity and **venture capital**. However, the distinction, which is usually based on the type of investment undertaken, is not very useful. In the sections that follow, we shall treat private equity as encompassing investments that are sometimes described as being financed by venture capital.

Types of investment

Private equity providers are interested in investing in small and medium-sized businesses with good growth potential. These businesses must also have owners with the ambition and determination to realise this potential. Although private equity-backed businesses usually have higher levels of risk than would be acceptable to other providers of finance, they also have the potential for higher returns. An investment is often made for a period of five years or more, with the amount varying according to need.

Private equity is used to fund different types of business needs, including:

- *Start-up capital.* This is available for businesses that are still at the concept stage of development through to those that are ready to commence trading. Finance is usually provided to help design, develop or market new products and services.
- *Other early stage capital.* This is available to businesses that have undertaken their development work and are ready to begin operations.
- *Expansion (development) capital.* This provides funding for growing businesses needing additional working capital, new equipment, and so on. It may also include rescue finance, which is used to turn around a business after a period of poor performance.
- *Refinancing bank borrowings.* This is aimed at reducing the level of gearing.
- *Secondary purchases.* This refers to finance used to purchase shares in order to buy out part of the ownership of a business or to buy out another private equity firm.
- *Buy-out capital.* This is finance to acquire an existing business. A management buy-out (MBO) is where the funds are used to help the existing management team to acquire the business, and an institutional buy-out (IBO) is where the private equity firm acquires the business and installs a management team of its choice.
- *Buy-in capital.* This is finance to acquire an existing business by an external management team. This kind of acquisition is known as a management buy-in (MBI). Buy-outs/buy-ins often occur when a large business wishes to divest itself of one of its operating units or when a family business wishes to sell out because of succession problems.

In practice, private equity providers make much higher levels of investment in growth businesses and management acquisitions than in business start-ups. Although business start-ups may be important to the health of the economy, they are very high risk: investing in existing businesses is a much safer bet. Furthermore, start-up businesses often require relatively small amounts of finance and so the high cost of investigating and monitoring the investment can make this type of investment unprofitable.

Real World 7.10 provides an impression of private equity investment in UK businesses.

REAL WORLD 7.10

Nothing ventured, nothing gained

Figures 7.4 and 7.5 show the private equity investments made in UK businesses during 2006, according to financing stage. Figure 7.4 reveals the total amounts invested and Figure 7.5 reveals the total number of businesses in which investments were made.

Figure 7.4	Amount invested, by financing stage, 2006

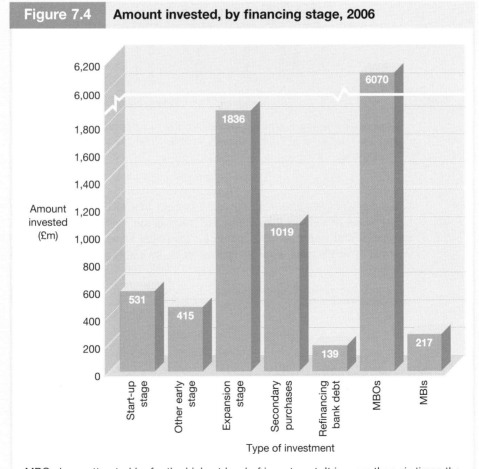

MBOs have attracted by far the highest level of investment. It is more than six times the total invested in start-up and other early-stage businesses. This imbalance has been even higher in previous years.

→

Real World 7.10 continued

| Figure 7.5 | Number of businesses backed, by financing stage, 2006 |

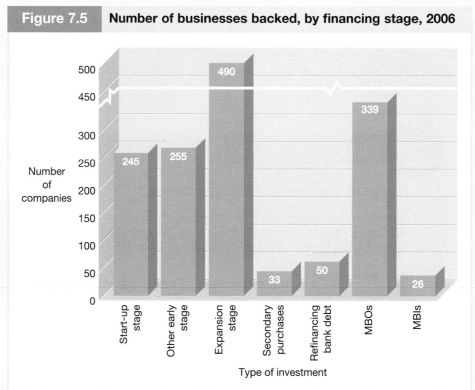

Businesses seeking expansion capital are the most popular type of investment. Note that the number of MBO investments is lower than the total start-up and early-stage investments.

When comparing Figures 7.4 and 7.5, it is clear that MBOs receive, on average, much higher levels of funding than start-ups. The average funding for MBOs is £17.9 million compared with less than £2.2 million for start-ups. More than half of the total amount invested in MBOs was used to finance deals involving more than £100 million equity invested.

Source: Charts compiled from information in *BVCA Report on Investment Activity 2006*, British Private Equity and Venture Capital Association (www.bvca.co.uk).

The investment process

Private equity investment involves a five-step process that is similar to the investment process undertaken within a business. The five steps are set out in Figure 7.6, and below we consider each of these five steps.

Step 1: Obtaining the funds

Private equity firms obtain their funds from various sources including large financial institutions (for example, pension funds, mutual funds and banks), government

Figure 7.6	The investment process

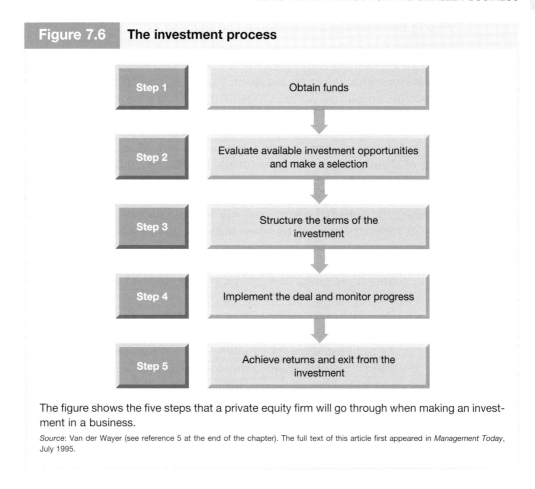

The figure shows the five steps that a private equity firm will go through when making an investment in a business.

Source: Van der Wayer (see reference 5 at the end of the chapter). The full text of this article first appeared in *Management Today*, July 1995.

agencies, wealthy individuals and direct appeals to the public. Once obtained, there can be a two- or three-year time lag before the funds are invested in suitable businesses. This is partly because the businesses take time to identify and partly because, once found, they require careful investigation.

Step 2: Evaluating investment opportunities and making a selection

When a suitable business is identified, the management plans will be reviewed and an assessment made of the investment potential, including the potential for growth. This will involve an examination of:

- the market for the products
- the business processes and the ways in which they can be managed
- the ambition and quality of the management team
- the opportunities for improving performance
- the types of risks involved and the ways in which they can be managed
- the track record and future prospects of the business.

Private equity firms will also be interested to see whether the likely financial returns are commensurate with the risks that have to be taken. The internal rate of return (IRR) method is often used in helping to make this assessment, and an IRR in excess of 20 per cent is normally required (see reference 6 at the end of the chapter).

Step 3: Structuring the terms of the investment

When structuring the financing agreement, private equity firms try to ensure that their own exposure to risk is properly managed. This will involve establishing control mechanisms within the financing agreements to protect their investment. One important control mechanism is the requirement to receive information on the progress of the business at regular intervals. The information provided, as well as information collected from other sources, will then be used as a basis for providing a staged injection of funds. In this way, progress is regularly reviewed and, where serious problems arise, the option of abandoning further investments in order to contain any losses is retained.

In some cases, the private equity firm may reduce the amount of finance at risk by establishing a financing syndicate with other private equity firms. However, this will also reduce the potential returns and will increase the possibility of disputes between syndicate members, particularly when things do not go according to plan.

Private equity firms will usually expect the owner/managers to demonstrate their commitment by investing in the business. Although the amounts they invest may be small in relation to the total investment, they should be large in relation to their personal wealth.

Step 4: Implementing the deal and monitoring progress

Private equity firms usually work closely with client businesses throughout the period of the investment and it is quite common for them to have a representative on the board of directors to keep an eye on their investment. They may also provide a form of consultancy service by offering expert advice on technical and marketing matters.

Business plans, which were prepared at the time of the initial investment, will be monitored to see whether they are achieved. Those businesses that meet their key targets are likely to find the presence of the private equity firms less intrusive than those that do not. Monitoring is likely to be much closer at the early stages of the investment until certain problems, such as the quality of management and cost overruns, become less of a risk (see reference 7 at the end of the chapter).

Step 5: Achieving returns and exiting from the investment

A major part of the total returns from the investment is usually achieved through the final sale of the investment. The particular method of divestment is, therefore, of great concern to the private equity firm. The most common forms of divestment are through:

- a trade sale (that is, where the investment is sold to another business)
- flotation of the business on the Stock Exchange, or sale of the quoted equity
- sale of the investment to the management team (buy-back)
- sale of the investment to another private equity firm or financial institution.

In some cases, there will be an 'involuntary exit' when the business fails, in which case the investment must be written off. Private equity firms may also supply loan capital and preference shares to help finance a business, which will be repaid by the business.

Real World 7.11 shows the amounts divested by various methods during 2006 by private equity firms.

Looking for an exit route

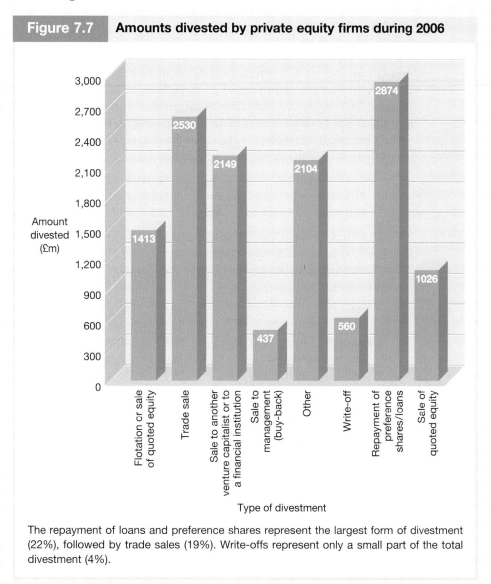

Figure 7.7 **Amounts divested by private equity firms during 2006**

The repayment of loans and preference shares represent the largest form of divestment (22%), followed by trade sales (19%). Write-offs represent only a small part of the total divestment (4%).

Source: Compiled from information in *BVCA Report on Investment Activity 2006*, British Private Equity and Venture Capital Association (www.bvca.co.uk).

Private equity and borrowing

A private equity firm will often require a business to borrow a significant proportion of its needs from a bank or other financial institution, thereby reducing its own financing commitment. Cash flows generated by the business during the investment period are then used to reduce or eliminate the outstanding loan.

Example 7.4 provides a simple illustration of this process.

Example 7.4

Ippo Ltd is a private equity firm that has recently purchased Andante Ltd for £80 million. The business requires an immediate injection of £60 million to meet its needs and Ippo Ltd has insisted that this be raised by a 10 per cent bank loan. Ippo Ltd intends to float Andante Ltd in four years' time to exit from the investment and then expects to receive £160 million on the sale of its shares. During the next four years, the cash flows generated by Andante Ltd (after interest has been paid) will be used to eliminate the outstanding loan.

The net cash flows (before interest) of the business, over the four years leading up to the flotation, are predicted to be as follows:

Year	1	2	3	4
	£m	£m	£m	£m
	20.0	20.0	20.1	15.0

Ippo Ltd has a cost of capital of 18 per cent and uses the internal rate of return (IRR) method to evaluate investment projects.

The following calculations reveal that the loan can be entirely repaid over the next four years.

	Yr 1	Yr 2	Yr 3	Yr 4
	£m	£m	£m	£m
Net cash flows	20.0	20.0	20.1	15.0
Loan interest (10%)	(6.0)	(4.6)	(3.1)	(1.4)
Cash available to repay loan	14.0	15.4	17.0	13.6
Loan at start of year	60.0	46.0	30.6	13.6
Cash available to repay loan	14.0	15.4	17.0	13.6
Loan at end of year	46.0	30.6	13.6	–

There are no cash flows remaining after the loan is repaid and so Ippo Ltd will receive nothing until the end of the fourth year, when the shares are sold.

The IRR of the investment will be the discount rate which, when applied to the net cash inflows, will provide an NPV of zero. Thus,

$$(\text{£160m} \times \text{Discount factor}) - \text{£80m} = 0$$
$$\text{Discount factor} = 0.50$$

A discount rate of approximately 19 per cent will give a discount factor of 0.5 in four years' time.

Thus, the IRR of the investment is approximately 19 per cent. This is higher than the costs of capital of Ippo Ltd and so the investment will increase the wealth of its shareholders.

Taking on a large loan imposes a tight financial discipline on the managers of a business as there must always be enough cash to make interest payments and capital repayments. This should encourage them to be aggressive in chasing sales and to bear down on costs. Taking on a loan can also boost the returns to the private equity firm.

Activity 7.12

Assume that:

(a) Ippo Ltd (see Example 7.4) provides additional ordinary share capital at the beginning of the investment period of £60 million, thereby eliminating the need for Andante Ltd to take on a bank loan;

(b) any cash flows generated by Andante Ltd would be received by Ippo Ltd in the form of annual dividends.

What would be the IRR of the total investment in Andante Ltd for Ippo Ltd?

The IRR can be calculated using the trial and error method as follows. At discount rates of 10 per cent and 16 per cent, the NPV of the investment proposal is:

		Trial 1		Trial 2	
Year	Cash flows	Discount rate	Present value	Discount rate	Present value
	£m	10%	£m	16%	£m
0	(140.0)	1.00	(140.0)	1.00	(140.0)
1	20.0	0.91	18.2	0.86	17.2
2	20.0	0.83	16.6	0.74	14.8
3	20.1	0.75	15.1	0.64	12.9
4	175.0	0.68	119.0	0.55	96.3
			NPV 28.9		NPV 1.2

The calculations reveal that, at a discount rate of 16 per cent, the NPV is close to zero. Thus, the IRR of the investment is approximately 16 per cent, which is lower than the cost of capital. This means that the investment will reduce the wealth of the shareholders of Ippo Ltd.

The calculations in Example 7.4 and Activity 7.12 show that, by Andante Ltd taking on a bank loan, returns to the private equity firm are increased. This 'gearing effect', as it is called, is discussed in more detail in the next chapter.

Self-assessment question 7.1

Ceres plc is a large conglomerate which, following a recent strategic review, has decided to sell its agricultural foodstuffs division. The managers of this operating division believe that it could be run as a separate business and are considering a management buy-out. The division has made an operating profit of £10 million for the year to 31 May Year 6 and the board of Ceres plc has indicated that it would be prepared to sell the division to the managers for a price based on a multiple of 12 times the operating profit for the most recent year.

The managers of the operating division have £5 million of the finance necessary to acquire the division and have approached Vesta Ltd, a private equity firm, to see whether it would be prepared to assist in financing the proposed management buy-out. The divisional managers have produced the following forecast of operating profits for the next four years:

Year to 31 May	Year 7	Year 8	Year 9	Year 10
	£m	£m	£m	£m
Operating profit	10.0	11.0	10.5	13.5

Self-assessment question 7.1 continued

To achieve the profit forecasts shown above, the division will have to invest a further £1 million in working capital during the year to 31 May Year 8. The division has premises costing £40 million and plant and machinery costing £20 million. In calculating operating profit for the division, these assets are depreciated, using the straight-line method, at the rate of 2 per cent on cost and 15 per cent on cost, respectively.

Vesta Ltd has been asked to invest £45 million in return for 90 per cent of the ordinary shares in a new business specifically created to run the operating division. The divisional managers would receive the remaining 10 per cent of the ordinary shares in return for their £5 million investment. The managers believe that a bank would be prepared to provide a 10 per cent loan for any additional finance necessary to acquire the division. (The premises of the division are currently valued at £80 million and so there would be adequate security for a loan up to this amount.) All net cash flows generated by the new business during each financial year will be applied to reducing the balance of the loan and no dividends will be paid to shareholders until the loan is repaid. (There are no other cash flows apart from those mentioned above.) The loan agreement will be for a period of eight years. However, if the business is sold during this period, the loan must be repaid in full by the shareholders.

Vesta Ltd intends to realise its investment after four years when the fixed assets and working capital (excluding the bank loan) of the business are expected to be sold to a rival at a price based on a multiple of 12 times the most recent annual operating profit. Out of these proceeds, the bank loan will have to be repaid by existing shareholders before they receive their returns. Vesta Ltd has a cost of capital of 25 per cent and employs the internal rate of return method to evaluate investment proposals.

Ignore taxation.

Workings should be in £millions and should be made to one decimal place.

Required:

(a) Calculate:
   (i) The amount of the loan outstanding at 31 May Year 10 immediately prior to the sale of the business.
   (ii) The approximate internal rate of return for Vesta Ltd of the investment proposal described above.
(b) State, with reasons, whether or not Vesta Ltd should invest in this proposal.

The answer to this question may be found at the back of the book on p. 534.

Cause for concern?

Private equity firms have recently extended their reach by acquiring listed businesses. Following acquisition, a listed business is usually de-listed and then restructured, perhaps with the intention of re-flotation at some future date. The acquisition of well-known, listed businesses, such as Alliance Boots, has placed private equity firms under greater scrutiny and concerns have been expressed over their business methods. The main concerns are the:

● job losses and asset sales that accompany restructuring;
● very high levels of gearing employed, which place a business at risk;
● lack of transparency in business dealings;
● lack of accountability to employees and the communities in which they operate;

- adverse effect on the Stock Exchange's role, resulting from the acquisition and de-listing of large businesses;
- problems of identifying those who bear the financial risk because of the complexity of many financing deals;
- tax benefits received by private equity firms.

Although some changes to levels of transparency and tax relief have been made, critics of private equity firms remain largely unappeased. **Real World 7.12**, however, suggests that some of the concerns mentioned are unfounded.

REAL WORLD 7.12

Heroes not villains

Companies bought by private equity firms do not destroy jobs on a large scale, a study suggests. The private equity industry has been accused of 'quick flips' – stripping company assets and axing jobs before selling firms or closing them down.

The research conducted by Josh Lerner of Harvard Business School does away with some of the myths surrounding private equity.

For starters, the time that private equity firms hold on to their investments is growing, and currently stands at a bit more than five years.

Their management seems to be making an impact. In the United States every year just 1.2 per cent of private equity-owned firms are being forced into bankruptcy. In contrast, about 1.6 per cent of firms issuing bonds go bankrupt. It is worse for troubled firms that have to issue so-called junk bonds; 4.7 per cent of them tend to fail.

The picture gets a bit murkier when it comes to jobs, the research suggests. In the two years before being taken private, companies tend to lose 4 per cent more jobs than their peers – an indication that these firms are in serious trouble to start with.

In the two years after takeover, these companies cut 7 per cent more jobs than rivals. After that employment levels are comparable. However, the sharper job cuts are partially offset by the fact that private equity-owned firms are growing faster and create 6 per cent more jobs at new factories than their rivals. More importantly though, these figures do not take account of the jobs saved because private equity-controlled firms are less likely to go bankrupt.

Source: Tim Weber, 'Private equity defends job record', BBC News (http://bbc.co.uk/news), 26 January 2008.

As a footnote to this section, it is worth mentioning that the methods employed by private equity firms are producing echoes elsewhere. Other businesses, particularly those feeling vulnerable to a takeover from a private equity firm, have adopted similar methods, such as high gearing and downsizing, in order to remain viable and independent.

Private equity returns

Private equity is generally assumed to generate high returns for investors and there is plenty of anecdotal evidence to support this assumption. Nevertheless, studies in the USA suggest that, *on average*, returns from private equity over recent decades are not impressive when compared with stock market returns (see reference 8 at the end of this chapter). This is a somewhat surprising conclusion given the rigorous investment appraisal procedures employed and the large amounts invested by private equity firms. It might be expected that their returns would significantly outperform stock market returns. In fact, studies in both the UK and USA suggest that, once an adjustment is made for the risk premium arising from high levels of gearing, average returns from private equity at best are mediocre and at worst significantly underperform the market (see references 8 and 9 at the end of this chapter). This average performance, however, masks a much wider range of returns than with listed equity shares. For the investor in private equity funds, therefore, the choice of investment fund is critical.

Business angels

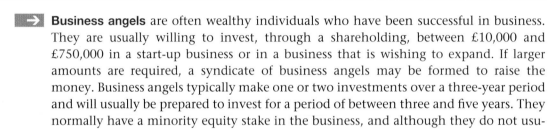

→ **Business angels** are often wealthy individuals who have been successful in business. They are usually willing to invest, through a shareholding, between £10,000 and £750,000 in a start-up business or in a business that is wishing to expand. If larger amounts are required, a syndicate of business angels may be formed to raise the money. Business angels typically make one or two investments over a three-year period and will usually be prepared to invest for a period of between three and five years. They normally have a minority equity stake in the business, and although they do not usually become involved in its day-to-day management, they tend to take an interest, more generally, in the way that the business is managed.

Business angels fill an important gap in the market as the size and nature of investments they find appealing are often not so appealing to private equity firms. They can be attractive to small businesses because they may:

● make investment decisions quickly, particularly if they are familiar with the industry in which the new business operates;
● offer useful skills, experience and business contacts;
● accept lower financial returns than those required from private equity firms in order to have the opportunity to become involved in a new and interesting project.

Business angels offer an informal source of share finance and it is not always easy for owners of small businesses to identify a suitable angel. However, numerous business angel networks have now developed to help owners of small businesses find their 'perfect partner'.

Government assistance

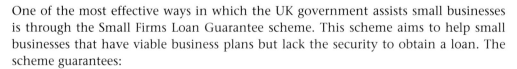

One of the most effective ways in which the UK government assists small businesses is through the Small Firms Loan Guarantee scheme. This scheme aims to help small businesses that have viable business plans but lack the security to obtain a loan. The scheme guarantees:

● 75 per cent of the amount borrowed, for which the borrower pays a premium of 2 per cent on the outstanding loan;
● loans of up to £250,000 for a maximum period of 10 years.

The scheme is available for businesses that are no more than five years old and have annual sales revenue of up to £5.6m.

In addition to other forms of financial assistance, such as government grants and tax incentives for investors to buy shares in small businesses, the government also helps by providing information concerning the sources of finance available.

Alternative Investment Market (AIM)

Several European stock markets have been established recently that specialise in the shares of smaller businesses. These include the **Alternative Investment Market (AIM)**, which is the largest and most successful. AIM is a second-tier market of the London Stock Exchange. It was established in 1995 and has enjoyed an astonishing rate of growth. During the first year of operations, AIM-listed business raised £94.8m through this market but by 2007 this had risen to £16,183.9m. (See reference 10 at the end of the chapter.)

AIM offers businesses many of the benefits of a listing without the burdensome regulatory environment that accompanies a listing on the main market. The main regulatory differences between the two markets' tiers can be summarised as follows:

Main market	AIM
● Minimum 25 per cent shares in public hands	● No minimum shares to be in public hands
● Normally, 3-year trading record required	● No trading record requirement
● Prior shareholder approval required for substantial acquisitions and disposals	● No prior shareholder approval for transactions
● Pre-vetting of admission documents by the UK Listing Authority	● Admission documents not pre-vetted by the Stock Exchange or UK Listing Authority
● Minimum market capitalisation	● No minimum market capitalisation

Source: Adapted from information on London Stock Exchange website (www.londonstockexchange.com).

AIM offers growing businesses a stepping stone to the main market – though not all AIM-listed businesses wish to make this step – and offers private equity firms a useful exit route from their investments. AIM has proved to be successful in attracting investors as it offers them a range of benefits, which include:

- a broad range of businesses in which to invest
- low failure rates among AIM-listed businesses
- good market liquidity, at least for larger businesses, and
- a good track record of share performance when compared to the main market.

Research shows that shares of smaller businesses are more actively traded on AIM than similar-size businesses on the main market (see reference 11 at the end of the chapter).

Real World 7.13 shows the distribution of businesses, by market capitalisation, within this market.

REAL WORLD 7.13

Distribution of AIM-listed businesses by equity market value

The distribution of businesses by equity market value at the end of December 2007 is shown in Figure 7.8 below.

| Figure 7.8 | Distribution of AIM businesses by equity market value |

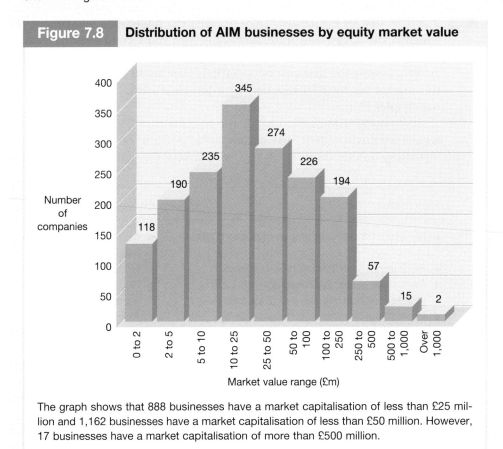

The graph shows that 888 businesses have a market capitalisation of less than £25 million and 1,162 businesses have a market capitalisation of less than £50 million. However, 17 businesses have a market capitalisation of more than £500 million.

Source: After AIM market statistics, www.londonstockexchange.com, December 2007.

Amazon.com: a case history

The internet retailer Amazon.com has grown considerably during its short life. In **Real World 7.14** we can see how that growth was financed in the early years. To begin with, the business relied heavily on the founder and his family for finance. However, as the business grew, other ways of raising finance, as described in the chapter, have become more important. The table in Real World 7.14 charts the progress of the business in its early years.

REAL WORLD 7.14

Financing Amazon.com – the early years

Financing of Amazon.com (1994–99)

Dates	Share price	Source of funds
1994: July to November	$0.0010	**Founder:** Jeff Bezos starts Amazon.com with $10,000; borrows $44,000
1995: February to July	$0.1717	**Family:** founder's father and mother invest $245,000
1995: August to December	$0.1287–0.3333	**Business angels:** 2 angels invest $54,408
1995/96: December to May	$0.3333	**Business angels:** 20 angels invest $937,000
1996: May	$0.3333	**Family:** founder's siblings invest $20,000
1996: June	$2.3417	**Private equity firms:** 2 private equity funds invest $8m
1997: May	$18.00	**IPO*:** 3m shares issued raising $49.1m
1997/98: December to May	$52.11	**Bond issue:** $326m bond issue

* Initial public offering of shares.

Source: Reproduced from Van Osnabrugge, M. and Robinson, R. J., *Angel Investing: Matching Start-up Funds with Start-up Companies – A Guide for Entrepreneurs and Individual Investors.* Copyright © 2000 Jossey-Bass Inc. Reprinted with permission of John Wiley & Sons, Inc.

SUMMARY

The main points in the chapter may be summarised as follows:

The Stock Exchange

- The Stock Exchange is an important primary and secondary market in capital for large businesses.
- Obtaining a Stock Exchange listing can help a business to raise finance and help to raise its profile but obtaining a listing can be costly and the regulatory and other burdens can be onerous.
- Stock Exchange investors are often accused of adopting a short-term perspective although there is no real evidence to support this.
- A stock market is efficient if information is processed by investors quickly and accurately so that prices faithfully reflect all relevant information.
- Three forms of efficiency have been suggested: the weak form, the semi-strong form and the strong form.
- If a stock market is efficient, managers of a listed business should learn six important lessons:
  - timing doesn't matter
  - don't search for undervalued businesses

  – take note of market reaction
  – you can't fool the market
  – the market decides the level of risk
  – champion the interests of shareholders.

● Stock market 'regularities' and research into investor behaviour have cast doubt on the notion of market efficiency.

Share issues

● Share issues that involve the payment of cash by investors can take the form of a rights issue, public issue, offer for sale or a placing.

● A rights issue is made to existing shareholders. Most share issues are of this type as the law requires that shares that are to be issued for cash must first be offered to existing shareholders.

● A public issue involves a direct issue to the public and an offer for sale involves an indirect issue to the public.

● A placing is an issue of shares to selected investors.

● A bonus (scrip) issue involves issuing shares to existing shareholders but the shareholders do not have to pay for them. The issue is achieved by transferring a sum from reserves to the share capital of the business.

● A tender issue allows the investors to determine the price at which the shares are issued.

Smaller businesses

● Smaller businesses do not have access to the Stock Exchange main market and so must look elsewhere for funds.

● Private equity (venture capital) is long-term capital for small or medium-sized businesses that are not listed on the Stock Exchange. These businesses often have higher levels of risk but provide the private equity firm with the prospect of higher levels of return.

● Private equity firms are interested in businesses with good growth prospects and offer finance for start-ups, business expansions and buy-outs.

● The investment period is usually five years or more and the private equity firms may exit by a trade sale, flotation, buy-back or sale to another financial institution.

● Business angels are wealthy individuals who are willing to invest in businesses at an early stage of development.

● The government assists small businesses through guaranteeing loans and by providing grants and tax incentives.

● The Alternative Investment Market (AIM) specialises in the shares of smaller businesses.

● AIM is a second-tier market of the Stock Exchange, which offers businesses the benefits of listing without the burdensome regulatory environment.

→ Key terms

Stock Exchange p. 262	**Public issue** p. 283
FTSE (Footsie) indices p. 263	**Tender issue** p. 283
Market capitalisation p. 263	**Placing** p. 285
Efficient stock market p. 268	**Private equity (Venture capital)** p. 286
Behavioural finance p. 276	
Rights issue p. 278	**Business angels** p. 296
Bonus issue p. 280	**Alternative Investment Market (AIM)** p. 297
Offer for sale p. 283	

For definitions of these terms see the Glossary, pp. 574–583.

References

1 **Practical Guide to Listing**, London Stock Exchange, p. 24 (www.londonstockexchange.com).

2 **Myths Surrounding Short-termism**, *Marsh, P.*, Mastering Finance, Financial Times Pitman Publishing, 1998, pp. 168–74.

3 **SME Finance and Regulation**, *Institute of Chartered Accountants in England and Wales*, 2000.

4 **Report of the Committee of Inquiry on Small Firms** (Bolton Committee), 1971, Cmnd 4811, HMSO.

5 'The venture capital vacuum', *Van der Wayer, M.*, **Management Today**, July 1995, pp. 60–4.

6 **A Guide to Private Equity**, British Private Equity and Venture Capital Association, www.bvca.co.uk.

7 'Venture capital as an alternative means to allocate capital: an agency-theoretic view', *Norton, E.*, **Entrepreneurship**, Winter 1995, pp. 19–30.

8 'The enigma of private equity', *J. Lerner*, www.ft.com, 24 April 2007.

9 'Taming private equity', **Sunday Times Business News**, 10 June 2007, p. 5.

10 'AIM market statistics, January 2008', London Stock Exchange (www.londonstockexchange.com).

11 'Aim makes its mark on the investment map', **Financial Times**, 9 February 2004.

Further reading

If you wish to explore the topics discussed in this chapter in more depth, try the following books:

Corporate Finance and Investment, *Pike, R. and Neale, B.*, 5th edn, Financial Times Prentice Hall, 2006, chapters 2 and 23.

Corporate Financial Management, *Arnold, G.*, 3rd edn, Financial Times Prentice Hall, 2005, chapters 9 and 10.

Principles of Corporate Finance, *Brealey, R. and Myers, C.*, 9th edn, McGraw-Hill International, 2007, chapter 13.

Investment Analysis and Portfolio Management, *Reilly, F. and Brown, K.*, 8th edn, Thomson South-Western, 2006, chapters 6 and 15.

REVIEW QUESTIONS

Answers to these questions can be found at the back of the book on p. 544.

7.1 UK private equity firms have been criticised for the low level of funding invested in business start-ups by comparison with the levels invested by their US counterparts. Can you think of possible reasons why such a difference may exist?

7.2 Why might a listed business revert to being an unlisted business?

7.3 Distinguish between an offer for sale and a public issue of shares.

7.4 What kind of attributes should the owners and managers of a business possess to attract private equity finance?

EXERCISES

Exercises 7.5 to 7.7 are more advanced than 7.1 to 7.4. Those with coloured numbers have answers at the back of the book, starting on p. 562.

 If you wish to try more exercises, visit the students' side of this book's Companion Website.

7.1 'Private equity' is an important source of risk capital for smaller businesses.'

Required:
(a) Explain the term 'private equity' and discuss the main types of business that are likely to prove attractive to private equity firms.
(b) Identify the main issues that the board of directors of a business should take into account when deciding whether to use private equity finance.
(c) Identify and discuss the factors that a private equity firm will take into account when assessing an investment proposal.

7.2 (a) Explain what is meant by the term 'efficient market hypothesis' and discuss the three main forms of market efficiency.
(b) Explain the implications of an efficient market for the managers of a business that is listed on the London Stock Exchange.

7.3 'Smaller businesses experience greater problems in raising finance than larger businesses.'

Required:
(a) Discuss the problems that smaller businesses may confront when trying to obtain long-term finance.
(b) Describe how smaller businesses may gain access to long-term finance.

7.4 Pizza Shack plc operates a chain of pizza restaurants in the south of England. The business started operations five years ago and has enjoyed uninterrupted and rapid growth. The directors of the business, however, believe that future growth can only be achieved if the business seeks a listing on the London Stock Exchange. If the directors go ahead with a listing, the financial advisers to the business have suggested that an issue of ordinary shares by tender at a minimum price of £2.20 would be an appropriate method of floating the business. The advisers have suggested that three million ordinary shares should be issued in the first instance although the directors of the business are keen to raise the maximum amount of funds possible.

Initial research carried out by the financial advisers suggests that the following demand for shares at different market prices is likely:

Share price	Number of shares tendered at each share price
£	000s
3.60	850
3.20	1,190
2.80	1,380
2.40	1,490
2.00	1,540
1.60	1,560
	8,010

Required:

(a) Discuss the advantages and disadvantages of making a tender issue of shares.

(b) Calculate the expected proceeds from the tender issue, assuming the business:
   (i) issues 3 million shares
   (ii) wishes to raise the maximum amount of funds possible.

7.5 The board of directors of Wicklow plc is considering an expansion of production capacity following an increase in sales over the past two years. The most recent financial statements for the business are set out below.

Statement of financial position (balance sheet) as at 30 November Year 5

	£m
Non-current assets	
Property, plant and equipment	
Premises	22.0
Machinery and equipment	11.0
Fixtures and fittings	8.0
	41.0
Current assets	
Inventory	14.0
Trade receivables	22.0
Cash at bank	2.0
	38.0
Total assets	79.0
Equity	
£0.50 ordinary shares	20.0
Retained earnings	19.0
	39.0
Non-current liabilities	
Borrowings – 12% loan	20.0
Current liabilities	
Trade payables	20.0
Total equity and liabilities	79.0

Income statement for the year ended 30 November Year 5

	£m
Sales revenue	95.0
Operating profit	8.0
Interest charges	(2.4)
Profit before taxation	5.6
Tax (30%)	(1.7)
Profit for the year	3.9

A dividend of £1.2 million was proposed and paid during the year.

The business plans to invest a further £15 million in machinery and equipment and is considering two possible financing options. The first option is to make a one-for-four rights issue. The current market price per share is £2.00 and the rights shares would be issued at a discount of 25 per cent on this market price. The second option is to take a further loan that will have an initial annual rate of interest of 10 per cent. This is a variable rate and, while interest rates have been stable for a number of years, there has been recent speculation that interest rates will begin to rise in the near future.

The outcome of the expansion is not certain. The management team involved in developing and implementing the expansion plans has provided three possible outcomes concerning profit before interest and tax for the following year:

	Change in profits before interest and tax from previous year
Optimistic	+30%
Most likely	+10%
Pessimistic	−20%

The dividend per share for the forthcoming year is expected to remain the same as for the year ended 30 November Year 5.

Wicklow plc has a lower level of gearing than most of its competitors. This has been in accordance with the wishes of the Wicklow family, which has a large shareholding in the business. The share price of the business has shown rapid growth in recent years and the P/E ratio for the business is 20.4 times, which is much higher than the industry average of 14.3 times.

Costs of raising finance should be ignored.

Required:
(a) Prepare calculations that show the effect of each of the possible outcomes of the expansion programme on:
  (i) earnings per share
  (ii) the gearing ratio (based on year-end figures), and
  (iii) the interest cover ratio of Wicklow plc, under both of the financing options.
(b) Assess each of the financing options available to Wicklow plc from the point of view of an existing shareholder and compare the possible future outcomes with the existing situation.

7.6 Devonian plc has the following long-term capital structure as at 30 November Year 4:

	£m
Ordinary shares 25p fully paid	50.0
General reserve	22.5
Retained earnings	25.5
	98.0

The business has no long-term loans.

In the year to 30 November Year 4, the operating profit (profit before interest and taxation) was £40 million and it is expected that this will increase by 25 per cent during the forthcoming year. The business is listed on the London Stock Exchange and the share price as at 30 November Year 4 was £2.10.

The business wishes to raise £72 million in order to re-equip one of its factories and is considering two possible financing options. The first option is to make a one-for-five rights issue at a discount price of £1.80 per share. The second option is to take out a long-term loan at an interest rate of 10 per cent a year. If the first option is taken, it is expected that the price/earnings (P/E) ratio will remain the same for the forthcoming year. If the second option is taken, it is estimated that the P/E ratio will fall by 10 per cent by the end of the forthcoming year.

Assume a tax rate of 30 per cent.

Required:
(a) Assuming a rights issue of shares is made, calculate:
  (i) the theoretical ex-rights price of an ordinary share in Devonian plc
  (ii) the value of the rights for each original ordinary share.
(b) Calculate the price of an ordinary share in Devonian plc in one year's time assuming:
  (i) a rights issue is made
  (ii) a loan issue is made.
  Comment on your findings.
(c) Explain why rights issues are usually made at a discount.
(d) From the business's viewpoint, how critical is the pricing of a rights issue likely to be?

7.7 Carpets Direct plc wishes to increase the number of its retail outlets in the south of England. The board of directors has decided to finance this expansion programme by raising the funds from existing shareholders through a one-for-four rights issue. The most recent income statement of the business is as follows:

Income statement for the year ended 30 April

	£m
Sales revenue	164.5
Operating profit	12.6
Interest	(6.2)
Profit before taxation	6.4
Tax	(1.9)
Profit for the year	4.5

An ordinary dividend of £2.0 million was proposed and paid during the year.

The share capital of the business consists of 120 million ordinary shares with a par value of £0.50 per share. The shares of the business are currently being traded on the Stock Exchange at a price/earnings ratio of 22 times and the board of directors has decided to issue the new shares at a discount of 20 per cent on the current market value.

Required:
(a) Calculate the theoretical ex-rights price of an ordinary share in Carpets Direct plc.
(b) Calculate the price at which the rights in Carpets Direct plc are likely to be traded.
(c) Identify and evaluate, at the time of the rights issue, each of the options arising from the rights issue to an investor who holds 4,000 ordinary shares before the rights announcement.

8

The cost of capital and the capital structure decision

INTRODUCTION

We have seen that the cost of capital has an important role to play when appraising investment opportunities. In this chapter, we shall consider how the cost of capital can be calculated. Following this, we turn our attention to the factors that should be taken into account when making capital structure decisions and, in particular, the impact of gearing on the risks and returns to ordinary shareholders. We touched on this area in Chapter 3 and will now consider it in more detail. We conclude the chapter by examining the debate concerning whether there is an optimal capital structure for a business.

LEARNING OUTCOMES

When you have completed this chapter, you should be able to:

● Calculate the weighted average cost of capital for a business and assess its usefulness when making investment decisions

● Calculate the degree of financial gearing for a business and explain its significance.

● Evaluate different capital structure options available to a business.

● Explain the key points in the debate over whether a business has an optimal capital structure.

Cost of capital

We saw in Chapter 4 that the cost of capital is used as the appropriate discount rate in NPV calculations and as the appropriate 'hurdle rate' when assessing IRR calculations. As investment projects are normally financed from long-term capital, the discount rate, or hurdle rate, applied to new investment projects should reflect the expected returns required by investors in long-term capital. From the viewpoint of the business, these returns represent its **cost of capital**. This is an *opportunity* cost as it represents the return that investors expect from investments of similar risk.

The cost of capital must be calculated with care as failure to do so could be damaging to the business.

Activity 8.1

What adverse consequences might result from failing to calculate the cost of capital correctly?

Where a business, which uses the NPV approach to investment appraisal, calculates its cost of capital incorrectly, the wrong discount rate will be applied to investment projects. If the cost of capital is understated, it may lead to projects that will reduce shareholder wealth being accepted. This can happen when the understated cost of capital produces a positive NPV, whereas the correct cost of capital produces a negative NPV. If, on the other hand, the cost of capital figure is overstated, this may result in the rejection of profitable projects. This can happen when the overstated cost of capital produces a negative NPV, whereas the correct cost of capital produces a positive NPV.

Similar problems can occur where a business adopts the IRR method and uses the cost of capital as the hurdle rate.

In Chapter 6, we saw that the main forms of *external* long-term capital for businesses include:

● ordinary shares
● preference shares
● loan capital.

In addition, an important form of *internal* long-term capital is:

● retained profit.

In the sections that follow, we shall see how the cost of each element of long-term capital may be deduced. We shall also see that there is a strong link between the cost of each element and its value: both are determined by the level of return. As a result, our discussions concerning the cost of capital will also embrace the issue of value. For reasons that should soon become clear, we consider first how each element of capital is valued and then go on to deduce its cost to the business.

Ordinary (equity) shares

There are two major approaches to determining the cost of ordinary shares to a business: the dividend-based approach and the risk/return-based approach. Each approach is discussed below.

Dividend-based approach

Investors hold assets (including ordinary shares) in the expectation of receiving future benefits. In broad terms, the value of an asset can be defined in terms of the stream of future benefits that arise from holding that asset. When considering ordinary shares, we can say that the value of an ordinary share can be defined in terms of the future dividends that investors receive by holding the share. To be more precise, the value of an ordinary share will be the present value of the expected future dividends from the particular share.

In mathematical terms, the value of an ordinary share (P_0) can be expressed as follows:

$$P_0 = \frac{D_1}{(1 + K_0)^1} + \frac{D_2}{(1 + K_0)^2} + \frac{D_?}{(1 + K_0)^3} + \cdots + \frac{D_n}{(1 + K_0)^n}$$

where: P_0 = the current market value of the share

D = the expected future dividend in years 1 to n

n = the number of years over which the business expects to issue dividends

K_0 = the cost of ordinary shares to the business (that is, the required return for investors).

Activity 8.2

The valuation approach above takes into account the expected dividend stream over the whole life of the business. Is this really relevant for an investor who holds a share for a particular period of time (say five years) and then sells the share?

The valuation approach should still be relevant. The market value of the share at the time of sale should reflect the present value of the (remaining) future dividends. Thus, when determining an appropriate selling price, the expected dividend stream beyond the point at which the share is held should be highly relevant to the investor.

The valuation model above can be used to determine the *cost* of ordinary shares to the business (K_0). Assuming the value of an ordinary share and the expected future dividends is known, the cost of an ordinary share will be the discount rate that, when applied to the stream of expected future dividends, will produce a present value that is equal to the current market value of the share. Thus, the required rate of return for ordinary share investors (that is, the cost of ordinary shares to the business) is similar to the internal rate of return (IRR) used to evaluate investment projects.

To deduce the required rate of return for investors, we can use the same trial and error approach as that used to deduce the internal rate of return for investment projects. In practice, however, this trial and error approach is rarely used, as simplifying assumptions are normally employed concerning the pattern of dividends, which make the calculations easier. These simplifying assumptions help us to avoid some of the problems associated with predicting the future dividend stream from an ordinary share.

One of two simplifying assumptions concerning the pattern of future dividends will often be employed. The first assumption is that dividends will remain constant over time. Where dividends are expected to remain constant for an infinite period, the fairly complicated equation to deduce the current market value of a share stated above can be reduced to:

$$P_0 = \frac{D_0}{K_0}$$

This equation (which is the equation for capitalising a perpetual annuity) can be rearranged to provide an equation for deducing the *cost* of ordinary shares to the business. Hence:

$$K_0 = \frac{D_0}{P_0}$$

Activity 8.3

Kowloon Investments plc has ordinary shares in issue that have a current market value of £2.20. The annual dividend to be paid by the business in future years is expected to be 40p. What is the cost of the ordinary shares to the business?

The cost will be:

$$K_0 = \frac{D_0}{P_0} = \frac{0.40}{2.20} = 0.182 \text{ or } 18.2\%$$

The second simplifying assumption that may be employed is that dividends will grow at a constant rate over time. Where dividends are expected to have a constant growth rate, the equation to deduce the current market value of a share can be reduced to:

$$P_0 = \frac{D_1}{K_0 - g}$$

where g is the expected annual growth rate. (The model assumes K_0 is greater than g.)

This equation can also be rearranged to provide an equation for deducing the *cost* of ordinary share capital. Hence:

$$K_0 = \frac{D_1}{P_0} + g$$

Determining the future growth rate in dividends (g) can be a problem. One approach is to use the average past rate of growth in dividends (adjusted, perhaps, for any new information concerning future prospects). There are, however, several other approaches and a business must select whichever is likely to give the most accurate results.

Activity 8.4

Avalon plc has ordinary shares in issue that have a current market price of £1.50. The dividend expected for next year is 20p per share and future dividends are expected to grow at a constant rate of 3 per cent a year.
What is the cost of the ordinary shares to the business?

The cost is:

$$K_0 = \frac{D_1}{P_0} + g = \frac{0.20}{1.50} + 0.03 = 0.163 \text{ or } 16.3\%$$

It should now be clear why we began by looking at how a share is valued before going on to deduce its cost. We have now seen how the value of an ordinary share to an investor and the cost of capital for the business are linked and how valuation models can help in deriving the required returns from investors. This relationship between value and the cost of capital also applies to preference shares and to loan capital, as we shall see in later sections.

Risk/return approach

An alternative approach to deducing the returns required by ordinary shareholders is to use the **capital asset pricing model (CAPM)**. This approach builds on the ideas that we discussed in Chapter 5.

We may recall that, when discussing the attitude of investors towards risk and the risk-adjusted discount rate, the following points were made:

- Investors who are risk averse will seek additional returns to compensate for the risks associated with a particular investment. These additional returns are referred to as the *risk premium.*
- The higher the level of risk, the higher the risk premium that will be demanded.
- The risk premium is an amount required by investors that is over and above the returns from investing in risk-free investments.
- The total returns required from a particular investment will, therefore, be made up of a risk-free rate plus any risk premium.

The relationship between risk and return is depicted in Figure 8.1.

Figure 8.1 **The relationship between risk and return**

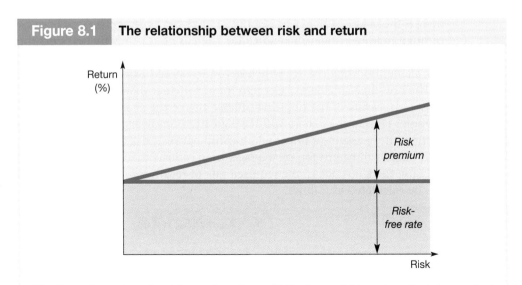

The figure shows how the risk premium rises with the level of risk and so the total required returns will rise as the level of risk increases.

Although the above ideas were made in respect of investment projects undertaken by a business, they are equally valid when considering investments in ordinary shares. CAPM (pronounced 'cap-M') is based on the above ideas and so the required rate of return to ordinary share investors (and, therefore, the cost of ordinary shares to the business) is viewed as being made up of a risk-free rate of return *plus* a risk premium. This means that, to calculate the required return, we have to derive the risk-free rate of return and the risk premium associated with a particular share.

Deriving the risk-free rate of return is fairly straightforward, provided we assume that the returns from government bonds can be used as an approximation. These offer the most secure return available as the government guarantees payment. A thornier problem, however, is deriving the risk premium for a particular share. CAPM does this by adopting a three-stage process, which is as follows:

1 Measure the risk premium for the ordinary share market as a whole. This figure will be the difference between the returns from the ordinary share market and the returns from an investment in risk-free investments.
2 Measure the returns from a particular share in relation to the returns from the ordinary share market as a whole.
3 Apply this relative measure of returns to the ordinary share market risk premium (calculated in stage 1) to derive the risk premium for the particular share.

The second and third stages of the process require further explanation.

We may recall from Chapter 6 that total risk is made up of two elements: *diversifiable* and *non-diversifiable* risk. Diversifiable risk is that part of the risk that is specific to the investment project and which can be eliminated by spreading available funds among investment projects. Non-diversifiable risk is that part of total risk that is common to all projects and which, therefore, cannot be diversified away. This element of risk arises from general market conditions.

This distinction between the two types of risk is also relevant to investors. The total risk associated with holding shares is also made up of diversifiable and non-diversifiable risk. By holding a portfolio of shares, an investor can eliminate diversifiable risk, which is specific to the share, leaving only non-diversifiable risk, which is common to all shares.

We know that risk-averse investors will only be prepared to take on increased risk if there is the prospect of increased returns. However, as diversifiable risk can be eliminated through holding a diversified portfolio, there is no reason why investors should receive additional returns for taking on this form of risk. It is, therefore, only the non-diversifiable risk element of total risk for which investors should expect additional returns.

The non-diversifiable risk element for a particular share can be measured using **beta**. This is a measure of the non-diversifiable risk of the share in relation to the market as a whole. Thus, a risky share will have greater non-diversifiable risk than the market as a whole. If we assume a linear relationship between risk and return, the returns from a risky share will be greater, on average, than returns than the market as a whole.

Using the above ideas, the required rate of return for investors for a particular share can be calculated as follows:

$$K_0 = K_{RF} + b(K_m - K_{RF})$$

where: K_0 = the required return for investors for a particular share
K_{RF} = the risk-free rate on government bonds
b = beta of the particular share
K_m = the expected returns to the market for the next period
$(K_m - K_{RF})$ = the expected market average risk premium for the next period.

This equation reflects the idea that the required return for a particular share is made up of two elements: the risk-free return plus a risk premium. We can see the risk premium is equal to the expected risk premium for the market as a whole multiplied by the beta of the particular share. This adjustment to the market risk is undertaken to derive the relative risk associated with the particular share. (As stated earlier, beta measures the non-diversifiable risk of a particular share in relation to the market as a whole.)

The expected market average risk premium can be derived by reference to past periods, on the assumption that past periods provide a good predictor of future periods. A market average is usually calculated for a relatively long period, as share returns can fluctuate wildly over the short term. The CAPM equation shows that the risk premium can be deduced by subtracting the returns from government bonds (the risk-free rate) from the average returns to the market. **Real World 8.1** shows the returns from gilts (government bonds), the average market returns and the equity market risk premium for a variety of time periods.

 REAL WORLD 8.1

Ordinary share risk premiums

The following table shows the returns from the equity market, the returns from gilts and the equity risk premium for 2006 and for different time periods ending in 2006.

	(a) Equity market returns %	(b) Gilt returns %	(a) – (b) Equity market risk premium %
2006	11.4	−4.4	15.8
Last 10 years	4.9	4.6	0.3
Last 20 years	6.9	5.6	1.3
Last 50 years	7.1	2.2	4.9
Last 107 years*	5.3	1.1	4.2

* Whole sample period.

We can see that the risk premium differs significantly over the different times periods.

Source: 2007 Equity Gilt study Barclays Capital (www.barcap.com).

Where a share has the same average return as the market as a whole, it will have a beta measure of 1.0. Where a share has an average return of half the average market return, it will have a beta of 0.5 and where a share has an average return that is twice the average market return, it will have a beta of 2.0. Many shares have a beta that is fairly close to the market beta of 1.0, with most falling within the range 0.5 to 2.0. The beta value of a share can change over time, particularly if the business changes its operating activities.

Betas are normally measured using regression analysis on past data, again, on the assumption that past periods provide a good predictor of future periods. The monthly returns from a particular share (that is, dividends plus any increase in share value) for a period are regressed against the returns from the market as a whole (as represented by some Stock Exchange index such as the FTSE 100).

To illustrate this approach, let us assume that the monthly returns from a particular share and the returns to the market are plotted on a graph, as shown in Figure 8.2. A line of best fit can then be drawn, using regression analysis. Note the slope of this line. We can see that, for this particular share, the returns do not change as much as the returns for the market as a whole. In other words, the beta is less than 1.

Figure 8.2	**Relationship between the returns from an individual share and returns from the market**

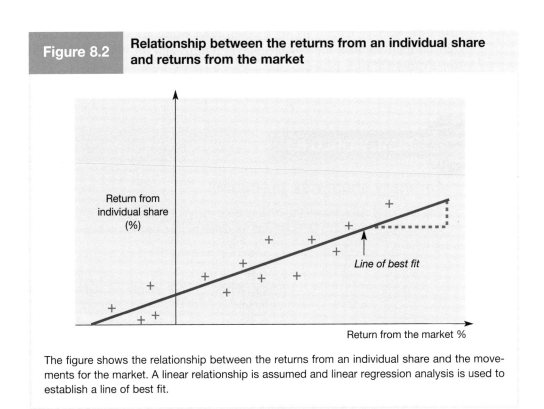

The figure shows the relationship between the returns from an individual share and the movements for the market. A linear relationship is assumed and linear regression analysis is used to establish a line of best fit.

Measures of beta for the shares of UK listed businesses are available from various information agencies such as the London Business School Risk Measurement Service and Bloomberg. Calculating beta, therefore, is not usually necessary. **Real World 8.2** provides examples of betas of some well-known UK listed businesses.

REAL WORLD 8.2

Betas in practice

Betas for some well-known UK listed businesses are set out in Figure 8.3.

| Figure 8.3 | Betas for a sample of well-known UK listed businesses |

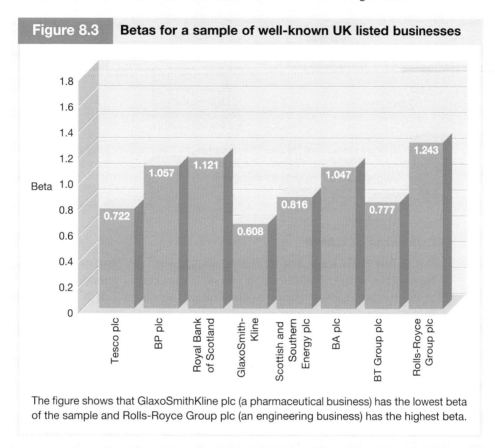

The figure shows that GlaxoSmithKline plc (a pharmaceutical business) has the lowest beta of the sample and Rolls-Royce Group plc (an engineering business) has the highest beta.

Source: Graph compiled from information taken from www.bloomberg.com, 9 February 2008.

Activity 8.5

Lansbury plc has recently obtained a measure of its beta from a business information agency. The beta obtained is 1.2. The expected returns to the market for the next period is 10 per cent and the risk-free rate on government securities is 3 per cent. What is the cost of ordinary shares to the business?

....

Using the CAPM formula we have:

$$K_0 = K_{RF} + b(K_m - K_{RF}) = 3\% + 1.2(10\% - 3\%) = 11.4\%$$

Figure 8.4 below illustrates the main elements in calculating the cost of ordinary shares using CAPM.

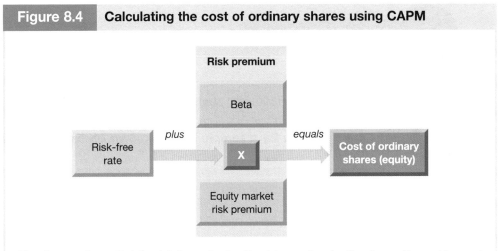

Figure 8.4   Calculating the cost of ordinary shares using CAPM

The diagram shows that the risk-free rate plus the risk premium for the share will equal the cost of ordinary shares. The risk premium is derived by multiplying the equity (ordinary share) market risk premium by the beta for the share.

Criticisms of CAPM

CAPM has been subject to criticism, which will not be considered in detail as it is beyond the scope of this book. If you are interested in pursuing this issue, take a look at the further reading section at the end of this chapter. It is probably enough to say that there are various technical problems concerning the measurement of beta values, returns to the market and the risk-free rate of return. Furthermore, some tests of the model have cast doubt on the relationship between beta values and expected returns, and some have found that beta is not the only factor influencing share returns.

Whilst we await the development of more complete model of the risk/return relationship, however, CAPM is still a useful way to estimate ordinary share returns.

CAPM and business practice

Having ploughed through the above sections on CAPM, you may like to know that it is actually used in practice. **Real World 8.3** briefly sets out the findings of two surveys, which shed some light on how UK listed businesses compute their cost of ordinary share capital.

REAL WORLD 8.3

A beta way to do it

Two surveys have revealed that CAPM is the most popular way of computing the cost of ordinary share capital among UK listed businesses:

- A postal survey of 193 UK listed business revealed that CAPM is used by 47.2 per cent of respondents. The dividend-based approach came a poor second with only 27.5 per cent of respondents using it (see reference 1 at the end of the chapter).
- An interview-based survey of 18 UK listed businesses revealed that CAPM is used by 13 (78 per cent) of respondents (see reference 2 at the end of the chapter).

Differences in usage of CAPM between these two surveys may be due to the fact that the first survey included businesses of all sizes whereas the second survey looked only at very large businesses. Larger businesses may adopt a more sophisticated approach to calculating the cost of ordinary shares than smaller businesses.

Retained profit

Retained profit is an important source of finance from ordinary shareholders and, as we saw in Chapter 6, it cannot be regarded as 'cost free'. If profits are reinvested by the business, the shareholders will expect to receive returns on these funds that are equivalent to the returns expected from investments in opportunities with similar levels of risk. The ordinary shareholders' interest in the business is made up of ordinary share capital plus any retained profits, and the expected returns from each will, in theory, be the same. Hence, when we calculate the cost of ordinary share capital, we are also calculating the cost of any retained profits. (In practice, however, we may require a slightly higher return from any new shares issued to compensate for the issue costs.)

Loan capital

We begin this section concerning loan capital as we began the sections relating to ordinary shares. That is, we shall consider the value of this element first and then go on to consider its cost. It cannot be emphasised enough that these two aspects are interrelated: they are really two sides of the same coin.

Loan capital may be irredeemable (that is, the business is not expected to repay the principal sum and so interest will be paid indefinitely). Where the rate of interest on the loan is fixed, the equation used to derive the value of irredeemable loan capital is similar to the equation used to derive the value of ordinary shares, where the dividends remain constant over time. The equation for the value of irredeemable loan capital is:

$$P_d = \frac{I}{K_d}$$

where: P_d = the current market value of the loan capital

K_d = the cost of loan capital to the business

I = the annual rate of interest on the loan capital.

This equation can be rearranged to provide an equation for deducing the *cost* of loan capital. Hence:

$$K_d = \frac{I}{P_d}$$

Interest payments on loan capital are an allowable expense for taxation purposes and so the net cash flows incurred in servicing the loan capital will be the rate of interest payable *less* the tax charge, which can be offset. For investment appraisal purposes, we take the post-tax net cash flows resulting from a project, and so, when calculating the appropriate discount rate, we should be consistent and use the post-tax rates for the cost of capital. The post-tax cost of loan capital will be:

$$K_d = \frac{I(1-t)}{P_d}$$

where *t* is the rate of tax payable.

Activity 8.6

Tan and Co plc has irredeemable loan capital outstanding on which it pays an annual rate of interest of 10 per cent. The current market value of the loan capital is £88 per £100 nominal value and the tax rate is 20 per cent. What is the cost of the loan capital to the business?

Using the above formula, the cost is:

$$K_d = \frac{I(1-t)}{P_d}$$

$$= \frac{10(1-0.20)}{88} = 9.1\%$$

Note that the rate of interest payable on the nominal value of the loan capital does not represent the relevant cost. Rather, we are concerned with the *opportunity* cost of the loan capital. This represents the return that can be earned by investing in an opportunity that has the same level of risk. The *current market rate of interest* of the loan capital, as calculated above, will provide us with a measure of the relevant opportunity cost.

Where the loan capital is redeemable, deriving the cost of capital figure is a little more complex. However, the principles and calculations required to derive the relevant figure have already been covered in Chapter 4. An investor who purchases redeemable loan capital will pay an initial outlay and then expect to receive annual interest payments plus a repayment of capital at the end of the loan period. The required rate of return for the investor will be the discount rate which, when applied to the future cash flows, will produce a present value that is equal to the current market value of the investment. Thus, the rate of return can be computed in the same way as the IRR is computed for other forms of investment opportunity. Let us consider Example 8.1.

Example 8.1

Lim Associates plc issues £20 million loan capital on which it pays an annual rate of interest of 10 per cent on the nominal value. The issue price of the loan capital is £88 per £100 nominal value and the tax rate is 20 per cent. The loan capital is due to be redeemed in four years' time at its nominal value.

What are the annual cash flows for this issue?

Solution

The cash flows for this issue of loan capital will be as follows:

		Cash flows £m
Year 0	Current market value [£20m × (88/100)]	17.6
Years 1–3	Interest payable (£20m × 10%)	(2.0)
Year 4	Redemption value (–£20m) + Interest (–£2m)	(22.0)

To derive the cost of loan capital to the business, the trial and error approach that is used in calculating the IRR can be used.

Activity 8.7

Calculate the cost of loan capital for Lim Associates plc. (*Hint*: Start with a discount rate of 10 per cent.)

Using a discount rate of 10 per cent, the NPV is calculated as follows:

	Cash flows	Discount rate	PV of cash flows
	£m	10%	£m
Year 0	17.6	1.00	17.6
Year 1	(2.0)	0.91	(1.0)
Year 2	(2.0)	0.83	(1.7)
Year 3	(2.0)	0.75	(1.5)
Year 4	(22.0)	0.68	(15.0)
		NPV	(2.4)

The discounted future cash outflows exceed the issue price of the loan capital and so the NPV is negative. This means that the discount rate is too low. Let us try 15 per cent.

	Cash flows	Discount rate	PV of cash flows
	£m	15%	£m
Year 0	17.6	1.00	17.6
Year 1	(2.0)	0.87	(1.7)
Year 2	(2.0)	0.76	(1.5)
Year 3	(2.0)	0.66	(1.3)
Year 4	(22.0)	0.57	(12.5)
		NPV	0.6

This discount rate is a little too high as the discounted cash outflows are less than the issue price of the loan capital. Thus, the appropriate rate lies somewhere between 10 and 15 per cent.

Trial	Discount factor	Net present value
		£m
1	10%	(2.4)
2	15%	0.6
Difference	5%	3.0

The change in NPV for every 1 per cent change in the discount rate will be:

$$£3.0m/5 = £0.6m$$

Thus, the reduction in the 15 per cent discount rate required to achieve a zero NPV will be 1 per cent as a 15 per cent discount rate produced an NPV of £0.6 million. In other words, the discount rate is 14 per cent. This, however, represents the pre-tax cost of loan capital. The tax rate is 20 per cent and so the post-tax cost of loan capital is 14 per cent $\times (1 - 0.2) = 11.2$ per cent.

Preference shares

Let us again begin by a consideration of the value of this element of capital before moving on to calculate its cost. Preference shares may be either redeemable or irredeemable. They are similar to loan capital in so far as the holders receive an agreed rate of return each year (which is expressed in terms of the nominal value of the shares). However, preference shares differ from loan capital in that the annual dividends paid to preference shareholders do not represent a tax-deductible expense. Thus, the full cost of the annual dividend payments must be borne by the business. As the rate of dividend on the preference shares is normally fixed, the equation used to derive the value of irredeemable preference shares is again similar to the equation used to derive the value of ordinary shares, where the dividends remain constant over time. The equation for irredeemable preference shares is:

$$P_p = \frac{D_p}{K_p}$$

where: P_p = the current market price of the preference shares
K_p = the cost of preference shares to the business
D_p = the annual dividend payments.

This equation can be rearranged to provide an equation for deducing the *cost* of irredeemable preference shares. Hence:

$$K_p = \frac{D_p}{P_p}$$

Activity 8.8

Iordanova plc has 12 per cent irredeemable preference shares in issue with a nominal (par) value of £1. The shares have a current market price of £0.90 (excluding dividends).
　What is the cost of these shares?

The cost is:

$$K_p = \frac{D_p}{P_p}$$

$$= \frac{12}{90}$$

$$= 13.3\%$$

The cost of redeemable preference shares can be deduced using the IRR approach, which was used earlier to determine the cost of redeemable loan capital.

Activity 8.9

L. C. Conday plc has £50 million 10 per cent £1 preference shares in issue. The current market price is £0.92 and the shares are due to be redeemed in three years' time at their nominal value.
　What is the cost of these shares? (*Hint:* Start with a discount rate of 11 per cent.)

The annual cash flows are as follows:

		Cash flows £m
Year 0	Current market value (£50m × 0.92)	46.0
Years 1–2	Dividends (£50m × 10%)	5.0
Year 3	Redemption value (£50m) + Dividend (£5m)	55.0

Using a discount rate of 11 per cent, the NPV is as follows:

	Cash flows £m	Discount rate 11%	PV of cash flows £m
Year 0	46.0	1.00	46.0
Year 1	(5.0)	0.90	(4.5)
Year 2	(5.0)	0.81	(4.0)
Year 3	(55.0)	0.73	(40.1)
		NPV	(2.6)

This discount rate is too low as the discounted future cash outflows exceed the issue price of the preference share capital. Let us try 13 per cent:

	Cash flows £m	Discount rate 13%	PV of cash flows £m
Year 0	46.0	1.00	46.0
Year 1	(5.0)	0.89	(4.4)
Year 2	(5.0)	0.78	(3.9)
Year 3	(55.0)	0.69	(38.0)
		NPV	(0.3)

The discounted cash outflows are almost equal to the issue price of the preference share capital. Thus, the cost of preference shares is approximately 13 per cent.

Weighted average cost of capital (WACC)

When making financing decisions, the managers of a business are assumed to have a target capital structure in mind. Although the relative proportions of equity, preference shares and loans may vary over the short term, these proportions are assumed to remain fairly stable when viewed over the medium to longer term. The existence of a fairly stable capital structure is consistent with the view that managers believe that a particular financing mix will minimise the cost of capital of the business, or, to put it another way, a particular financing mix provides an optimal capital structure for the business. (Whether or not there is such a thing as an optimal capital structure is discussed later in the chapter.) However, a target capital structure is unlikely to be set in stone. It may change from time to time in response to changes in the tax rates, interest rates, and so on, which affect the cost of particular elements of the capital structure.

The existence of a stable capital structure (presumably reflecting the target capital structure) has important implications for the evaluation of investment projects. It has already been argued that the required rates of return from investors (that is, the costs of capital to the business) should provide the basis for determining an appropriate discount rate for investment projects. If we accept that a business will maintain a fairly stable capital structure over the period of the project, then the average cost of capital can provide an appropriate discount rate.

The average cost of capital can be calculated by taking the cost of the individual elements and then weighting each element in proportion to the target capital structure (by market value) of the business. Example 8.2 illustrates how the **weighted average cost of capital (WACC)** is calculated.

Example 8.2

Danton plc has 10 million ordinary shares in issue with a current market value of £2.00 per share. The expected dividend for next year is 16p per share and this is expected to grow each year at a constant rate of 4 per cent. The business also has:

- 10.0 million 9 per cent £1 irredeemable preference shares in issue with a market price of £0.90 per share, and
- £20 million of irredeemable loan capital in issue with a nominal rate of interest of 6 per cent and which is quoted at £80 per £100 nominal value.

Assume a tax rate of 20 per cent and that the current capital structure reflects the target capital structure of the business.

What is the weighted average cost of capital of the business?

Solution

The first step is to calculate the cost of the individual elements of capital. The cost of ordinary shares in Danton plc is calculated as follows:

$$K_0 = \frac{D_1}{P_0} + g \text{ (see note)}$$

$$= \frac{16}{200} + 0.04$$

$$= 12\%$$

Note: The dividend valuation model has been used to calculate the cost of ordinary shares; however, the CAPM model could have been used instead if the relevant information had been available.

The cost of the preference share capital is as follows:

$$K_p = \frac{D_p}{P_p}$$

$$= \frac{9}{90}$$

$$= 10\%$$

The cost of loan capital is:

$$K_d = \frac{I(1-t)}{P_d}$$

$$= \frac{6(1-0.2)}{80}$$

$$= 6.0\%$$

Having derived the cost of the individual elements, we can now calculate the weighted average cost of these elements. The WACC will be:

	(a) Market value £m	(b) Proportion of total market value	(c) Cost %	(d) = (b × c) Contribution to WACC
Ordinary shares (10m × £2) (see note)	20	0.44	12	5.3
Preference shares (10m × £0.90)	9	0.20	10	2.0
Loan capital (£20m × 0.8)	16	0.36	6	2.2
	45	1.00		
WACC				**9.5%**

Note: The market value of the capital rather than the nominal value has been used in the calculations. This is because we are concerned with the opportunity cost of capital invested, as explained earlier.

Figure 8.5 sets out the approach used to calculate the WACC of a business.

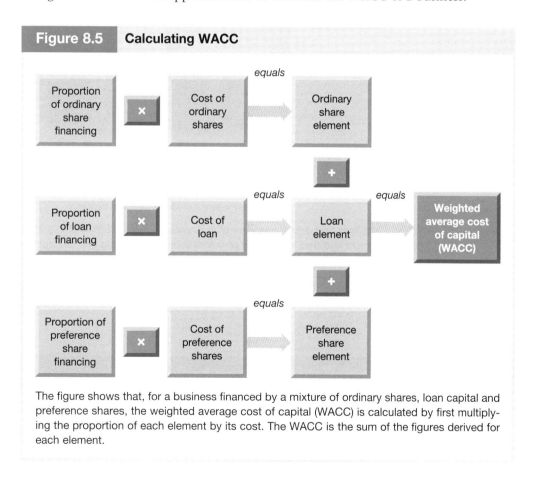

Figure 8.5   Calculating WACC

The figure shows that, for a business financed by a mixture of ordinary shares, loan capital and preference shares, the weighted average cost of capital (WACC) is calculated by first multiplying the proportion of each element by its cost. The WACC is the sum of the figures derived for each element.

Whether businesses maintain a target capital structure in practice has been the subject of some debate. **Real World 8.4** provides some evidence from the USA concerning this issue.

REAL WORLD 8.4

Targets in practice

A survey of 392 US businesses reveals mixed support for the idea of a target capital structure. Figure 8.6 below sets out the evidence.

| Figure 8.6 | **Use of target capital structures by US businesses** |

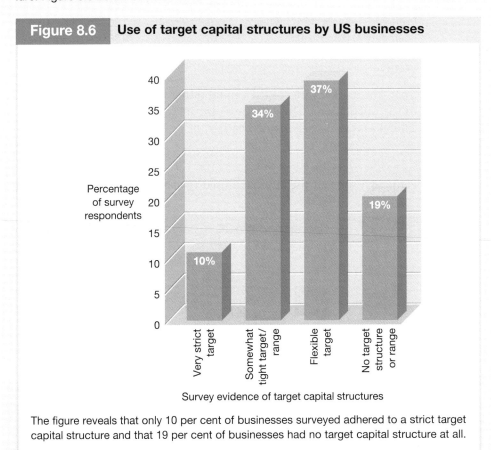

Percentage of survey respondents

Survey evidence of target capital structures

The figure reveals that only 10 per cent of businesses surveyed adhered to a strict target capital structure and that 19 per cent of businesses had no target capital structure at all.

Source: J. Graham and C. Harvey, 'How do CFOs make capital budgeting and capital structure decisions?' Paper prepared for *Journal of Applied Corporate Finance*, Vol. 15, No. 1, 2002.

Specific or average cost of capital?

In practice, an investment project may be financed by raising funds from a particular source. It is, therefore, tempting to think that the appropriate cost of capital for the project will be the cost of the particular source of finance used. However, this is not the case. When new funds are needed for an investment project, it is not normally feasible to raise the funds in exactly the same proportions as in the existing capital structure. To minimise the cost of raising funds, it will usually make sense for a business to raise funds from one source and, later, to raise funds from another, even though this may lead to deviations in the required capital structure over the short term. The fact that a particular source of new funds is used for a project will be determined by the requirements for the long-term capital structure of the business rather than the requirements of the project.

Using the specific cost of funds raised for the project could lead to illogical decisions being made. Assume that a business is considering an investment in two identical machines and that each machine has an estimated IRR of 12 per cent. Let us further assume that the first machine will be financed using loan capital with a post-tax cost of 10 per cent. However, as debt capacity of the business will then be used up, the second machine must be financed by ordinary (equity) share capital at a cost of 14 per cent. If the specific cost of capital is used to evaluate investment decisions, the business would be in the peculiar position of accepting the investment in the first machine, because the IRR exceeds the cost of capital, and rejecting the second (identical) machine because the IRR is lower than the cost of capital! By using the WACC, we avoid this kind of problem. Each machine will be evaluated according to the average cost of capital, which should then result in consistent decisions being made.

Real World 8.5 reveals the weighted average cost of capital for some large businesses.

REAL WORLD 8.5

WACC in practice

WACC figures for a sample of large businesses, operating in different industrial sectors, are shown below.

Name	Type of business	WACC (%)
Pennon Group plc	Water, sewerage and waste management	5.1
Kingfisher plc	Home improvement	7.4
Sage Group plc	Accounting and business software	7.4
United Business Media	Business media	8.0
Prudential plc	Insurance	9.6
Man Group plc	Investment products and brokers	12.1
Rolls-Royce plc	Engineering	12.75

We can see that the WACC figures cover a fairly wide range.

Sources: Relevant business websites and annual reports covering the period 2005–2007.

Limitations of the WACC approach

The WACC approach has been criticised for failing to take proper account of risk in investment decisions. In practice, different investment opportunities are likely to have different levels of risk and so the cost of capital for each project should be adjusted accordingly. We may recall from Chapter 5 that investors who are risk averse require higher returns to compensate for higher levels of risk. This means that the WACC is really only suitable where an investment project is expected to have the same level of risk as existing investments, or the proposed project is fairly small and is, therefore, not expected to have a significant effect on the overall risk level of the business.

It was mentioned earlier that the WACC approach assumes that the capital structure of the business remains stable over the period of the investment project. If there are changes in the proportions of each capital element over time, the WACC approach would be difficult to justify.

Cost of capital – some evidence

Real World 8.6 provides some evidence on the frequency with which the cost of capital is reviewed in practice and the use of WACC as the appropriate discount rate in capital investment decisions.

REAL WORLD 8.6

Counting the cost

The survey of 193 UK listed businesses mentioned in Real World 8.3 above revealed the frequency with which businesses reassess their cost of capital. As the financial environment continually changes, we should expect businesses to reassess their cost of capital fairly frequently. The frequency with which the businesses surveyed reassess their cost of capital is shown in Figure 8.7. These findings indicate that an annual reassessment is preferred by more than half of respondents.

A further finding concerns the extent to which the weighted average cost of capital was used in evaluating investment decisions. Figure 8.8 shows the discount rates that were used for investment projects. We saw above that WACC is normally the appropriate discount rate to use when evaluating investment projects. The reasons for using the cost of

Figure 8.7	**Frequency with which businesses reassess their cost of capital**

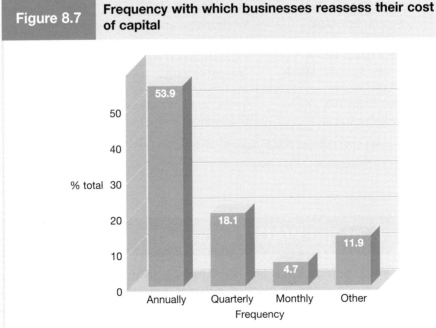

The figure shows that nearly all of the businesses surveyed reassess their cost of capital on at least an annual basis. Those falling into the 'other' category reassess every six months (2.6 per cent) when long-term interest rates change (3.1 per cent) and on a project-by-project basis (6.2 per cent).

Source: Adapted from E. McLaney, J. Pointon, M. Thomas and J. Tucker, 'Practioners' perspectives on the UK cost of capital', *European Journal of Finance*, 10, pp. 123–138, April 2004.

ordinary shares only or a long-term borrowing rate require further investigation. The use of the ordinary share cost of capital would be appropriate only where the business was entirely financed by ordinary shares and the riskiness of the project was in line with that of the business as a whole. The use of a long-term borrowing rate is even more difficult to understand as it fails to take into account the required rate of return to investors.

| Figure 8.8 | **The discount rate used for investment projects** |

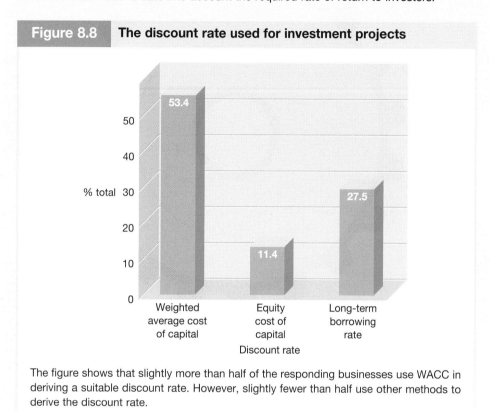

The figure shows that slightly more than half of the responding businesses use WACC in deriving a suitable discount rate. However, slightly fewer than half use other methods to derive the discount rate.

Source: Charts taken from E. McLaney, J. Pointon, M. Thomas and J. Tucker, 'Practitioners' perspectives on the UK cost of capital', *European Journal of Finance*, 10, pp. 123–38, April 2004.

Financial gearing

We have already seen that the presence of capital with a fixed rate of return, such as loans and preference shares, in the long-term capital structure of a business is referred to as 'gearing' (or to be more precise 'financial gearing'). The term 'gearing' is used because fixed-return capital can accentuate any changes in profit before interest and taxation (PBIT) on the returns to ordinary shareholders. The effect is similar to the effect of two intermeshing cog wheels of unequal size (see Figure 8.9). The movement in the larger cog wheel (profit before interest and taxation) causes a more than proportionate movement in the smaller cog wheel (returns to ordinary shareholders).

The effect of financial gearing on the returns to ordinary shareholders is demonstrated in the Example 8.3.

Figure 8.9 The effect of financial gearing

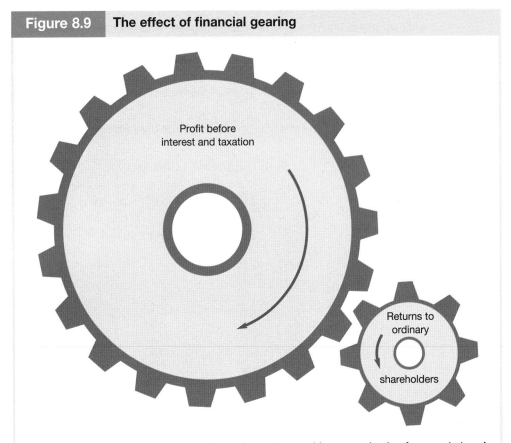

The gearing effect is similar to the effect of two intermeshing cog wheels of unequal size. A movement in the larger cog (profit before interest and taxation) brings about a disproportionately large movement in the smaller cog (returns to ordinary shareholders).

Example 8.3

Alpha plc and Gamma plc have both been recently created and have identical operations. The long-term capital structure of each business is as follows:

	Alpha plc	Gamma plc
	£m	£m
£1 ordinary shares	200	340
12% preference shares	100	50
10% loan notes	100	10
	400	400

Although both businesses have the same total long-term capital, we can see that the level of financial gearing differs significantly between the two businesses.

A widely used measure of gearing, which we came across in Chapter 3, is as follows:

$$\text{Financing gearing ratio} = \frac{\text{Loan capital} + \text{Preference shares (if any)}}{\text{Total long-term capital}} \times 100\%$$

For Alpha plc and Gamma plc, the ratios are 50 per cent [(200/400) × 100%] and 15 per cent [(60/400) × 100%], respectively. These ratios indicate that Alpha has a high level of financial gearing, that is, a high proportion of fixed-return capital (loan capital plus preference shares) in relation to its total long-term capital, and Gamma has a relatively low level of financial gearing.

To consider the effect of financial gearing on the returns to ordinary shareholders, let us assume that, in Year 1, the businesses generated identical profits before interest and taxation (PBIT) of £80 million. The earnings per share (EPS) for the ordinary share investors of each business for Year 1 can be calculated as follows:

	Alpha plc £m	Gamma plc £m
PBIT	80.0	80.0
Loan interest	(10.0)	(1.0)
Profit before taxation	70.0	79.0
Tax (say, 30%)	(21.0)	(23.7)
Profit for the year	49.0	55.3
Preference dividend paid	(12.0)	(6.0)
Profit available to ordinary shareholders	37.0	49.3

The EPS for ordinary share investors of Alpha plc are 18.5p (that is, £37m/200m) and for Gamma plc they are 14.5p (that is, £49.3m/340m).

We can see that ordinary share investors in Alpha plc earn higher returns in Year 1 than those in Gamma plc. This arises from the use of a higher level of fixed-return capital (loan capital and preference share capital) in the capital structure. When additional profits generated from the use of fixed-return capital exceed the additional fixed payments (interest charges and preference dividends) incurred, the surplus will accrue to the ordinary shareholders. Alpha plc has a higher proportion of fixed-return capital and a lower proportion of ordinary share (equity) capital than Gamma plc. This means that, where a large surplus is available, ordinary shareholders in Alpha plc will receive higher earnings per share.

However, the financial gearing effect can operate in both directions. To illustrate this point, let us assume that the profit before interest and taxation for Year 2 is much lower than for Year 1, say £40 million, for each business. The earnings per share for ordinary shareholders for Year 2 would then be as follows:

	Alpha plc £m	Gamma plc £m
PBIT	40.0	40.0
Loan interest	(10.0)	(1.0)
Profit before taxation	30.0	39.0
Tax (say, 30%)	(9.0)	(11.7)
Profit for the year	21.0	27.3
Preference dividend	(12.0)	(6.0)
Profit available to ordinary shareholders	9.0	21.3
EPS	4.5p	6.3p

The cost of servicing the fixed-return capital in Year 2 is unchanged for both businesses, but Alpha plc has the higher costs to bear. The surplus available to ordinary shareholders of Alpha plc in Year 2 is, therefore, much lower. We can see that they suffer a greater decrease in earnings per share, and receive lower earnings per share in total, than shareholders in Gamma plc.

Real World 8.7 describes how investment trusts, which invest in other businesses, change their level of gearing, according to the perceived level of risk.

REAL WORLD 8.7

Gearing levels fall amid fears over risks   **FT**

Investment trust managers, who control £62bn of assets, have almost halved their levels of borrowing, or gearing, over the past two years because of fears about the strength of the stock market recovery and regulatory concerns.

The average level of gearing of the conventional investment trust has fallen from 20 per cent at the end of March 2003 to 11 per cent at the end of March this year, according to the Association of Investment Trust Companies. Some specialist sectors, including UK high income, have maintained higher levels of gearing.

'Managers are taking a cautious view of markets and boards are becoming wary of taking any risk at all in terms of gearing,' says Iain Scouller, analyst at UBS.

JP Morgan Fleming's European Fledgling investment trust cut its gearing from 18 to 2 per cent at the beginning of this month. 'The managers felt there had been a period of strong performance and it was time to slightly reduce its risk profile,' says David Barron, head of investment trusts. 'We felt it was time to lock in some of those gains.'

Some managers are maintaining their gearing levels but switching from expensive long-term borrowing into short-term arrangements. 'Long-term arrangements worked well in the 1990s but managers were hit hard in the bear (sellers) market,' said Charles Cade, analyst at Close Wins, a market maker. 'Now they want flexible gearing that changes with market conditions.'

Investment trusts make a selling point of their ability to gear up in the good times. They contrast themselves with unit trusts which are only permitted to borrow up to 10 per cent of their net asset value.

There is no official upper limit on investment trust borrowing but trusts are limited by what investors would think was prudent and by the willingness of banks to lend. One manager said gearing of more than 25 per cent could make a trust hard to market.

Investment trusts gear up when they believe they can make a higher return on their investment than the interest they are paying on their borrowing. Additional borrowing also means they can take advantage of opportunities without having to sell existing investments.

The downside of gearing is that if markets fall and the performance of the assets in the portfolio is poor, then the losses will be magnified by high borrowings.

Source: Charles Batchelor, 'Gearing levels fall amid fears over risks', www.ft.com 29 April 2005.

Degree of financial gearing

The effect of financial gearing, as we have just seen, is that any increase in the profit before interest and taxation for a financially geared business will result in a disproportionate increase in earnings per share, and any decrease in profit before interest and taxation will result in a disproportionate decrease in earnings per share. The higher the level of financial gearing, the more sensitive earnings per share become to changes in

→ profit before interest and taxation for any given level. The **degree of financial gearing** provides a measure of the financial gearing effect and can be calculated as follows:

$$\text{Degree of financial gearing} = \frac{\% \text{ change in EPS}}{\% \text{ change in PBIT}}$$

For Alpha plc, the degree of financial gearing, based on the changes between Year 1 and Year 2, will be:

$$\text{Degree of financial gearing} = \frac{-75.7\%}{-50\%} = 1.5$$

Activity 8.10

What is the degree of financial gearing for Gamma plc?

It can be calculated as follows:

$$\text{Degree of financial gearing} = \frac{\% \text{ change in EPS}}{\% \text{ change in PBIT}} = \frac{-56.6\%}{-50\%} = 1.1$$

In both cases, the figure derived is greater than 1, which indicates the presence of financial gearing. The higher the figure derived, the greater the sensitivity of earnings per share to changes in profit before interest and taxation.

This measure of financial gearing indicates that, in the case of Alpha plc, a 1.0 per cent change in profit before interest and taxation from the base level of £80 million will result in a 1.5 per cent change in earnings per share, whereas for Gamma plc, a 1.0 per cent change in profit before interest and taxation from the base level of £80 million will only result in a 1.1 per cent change in earnings per share.

Another way of arriving at the degree of financial gearing for a particular level of profit before interest and taxation is as follows:

$$\text{Degree of financial gearing} = \frac{\text{PBIT}}{\text{PBIT} - I - [P \times 100/(100 - t)]}$$

where: I = interest charges
P = preference dividend
t = tax rate.

(Note that the preference dividend is 'grossed up' to a pre-tax amount by multiplying the dividend by $100/(100 - t)$. This is done to ensure consistency with the other variables in the equation.)

The above equation has the advantage that a single measure of PBIT is all that is required to derive the degree of financial gearing. For Alpha plc, the measure will be calculated as follows for Year 1:

$$\text{Degree of financial gearing} = \frac{80}{80 - 10 - [12 \times 100/(100 - 30)]} = \frac{80}{52.9} = 1.5$$

This equation will yield the same results as the earlier equation shown above.

Activity 8.11

Using the above equation, calculate the degree of financial gearing for Gamma plc for Year 1.

The calculation is:

$$\text{Degree of financial gearing} = \frac{\text{PBIT}}{\text{PBIT} - I - [P \times 100/(100 - t)]}$$

$$= \frac{80}{80 - 1 - [6 \times 100/(100 - 30)]}$$

$$= \frac{80}{70.4} = 1.1$$

The impact of financial gearing for a business will become less pronounced as the level of profit before interest and taxation increases in relation to fixed-return payments (interest charges and preference dividends). Where profit before interest and taxation barely covers the fixed-return payments, even small changes in the former figure can have a significant impact on earnings per share. This high degree of sensitivity will be reflected in the degree of financial gearing measure. However, as profit before interest and taxation increases in relation to fixed-return charges, earnings per share will become less sensitive to changes. As a result, the degree of financial gearing measure will be lower.

Activity 8.12

What is the degree of financial gearing for Alpha plc and Gamma plc for Year 2?

For Alpha plc, the degree of financial gearing in Year 2 (when profit before interest and taxation is much lower) will be:

$$\text{Degree of financial gearing} = \frac{\text{PBIT}}{\text{PBIT} - I - [P \times 100/(100 - t)]}$$

$$= \frac{40}{40 - 10 - [12 \times 100/(100 - 30)]}$$

$$= 3.1$$

For Gamma plc, the degree of financial gearing in Year 2 will be:

$$\text{Degree of financial gearing} = \frac{\text{PBIT}}{\text{PBIT} - I - [P \times 100/(100 - t)]}$$

$$= \frac{40}{40 - 1 - [6 \times 100/(100 - 30)]}$$

$$= 1.3$$

We can see that EPS for both businesses is now more sensitive to changes in the level of PBIT than in the previous year, when profits were higher. However, returns to ordinary shareholders in Alpha plc, which has a higher level of financial gearing, have become much more sensitive to change than returns to ordinary shareholders in Gamma plc.

Gearing and capital structure decisions

When evaluating capital structure decisions, the likely impact of gearing on the expected risks and returns for ordinary shareholders should be taken into account. To do this, projected financial statements and gearing ratios, which we considered in earlier chapters, can be helpful. Example 8.4 illustrates the way in which a capital structure decision may be evaluated.

Example 8.4

Semplice Ltd manufactures catering equipment for restaurants and hotels. The statement of financial position of the business as at 31 May Year 4 is as follows:

Statement of financial position (balance sheet) as at 31 May Year 4

	£m
Non-current assets	
Premises	40.2
Machinery and equipment	17.4
	57.6
Current assets	
Inventory	22.5
Trade receivables	27.6
Cash at bank	1.3
	51.4
Total assets	109.0
Equity	
£0.25 ordinary shares	15.0
Retained earnings	46.2
	61.2
Non-current liabilities	
12% loan notes	20.0
Current liabilities	
Trade payables	25.2
Tax due	2.6
	27.8
Total equity and liabilities	109.0

An abridged income statement for the year ended 31 May Year 4 is as follows:

Income statement for the year ended 31 May Year 4

	£m
Sales revenue	137.4
Operating profit (profit before interest and taxation)	23.2
Interest payable	(2.4)
Profit before taxation	20.8
Tax	(5.2)
Profit for the year	15.6

A dividend of £6.0m was paid and proposed during the year.

Example 8.4 continued

The board of directors of Semplice Ltd has decided to invest £20 million in new machinery and equipment to meet an expected increase in sales for the business's products. The expansion in production facilities is expected to result in an increase of £6 million in annual operating profit (profit before interest and taxation).

To finance the proposed investment, the board of directors is considering either:

1 a rights issue of eight million ordinary shares at a premium of £2.25 per share, or
2 the issue of £20 million 10 per cent loan notes at par (nominal) value.

The directors wish to increase the dividend per share by 10 per cent in the forthcoming year irrespective of the financing method chosen.

Assume a tax rate of 25 per cent.

Which financing option should be chosen?

Solution

A useful starting point in tackling this problem is to prepare a projected income statement for the year ended 31 May Year 5 under each financing option.

Projected income statement for the year ended 31 May Year 5

	Shares	Loan notes
	£m	£m
Profit before interest and taxation (23.2 + 6.0)	29.2	29.2
Interest payable	(2.4)	(4.4)
Profit before taxation	26.8	24.8
Tax (25%)	(6.7)	(6.2)
Profit for the year	20.1	18.6

Having prepared these statements, we should consider the impact of each financing option on the overall capital structure of the business. The projected capital structure under each option will be:

	Shares	Loan notes
	£m	£m
Equity		
Share capital – £0.25 ordinary shares (Note 1)	17.0	15.0
Share premium (Note 2)	18.0	
Retained earnings (Note 3)	58.8	58.2
	93.8	73.2
Loan capital	20.0	40.0

Notes

1 The share premium account represents the amount received from the issue of shares that is above the nominal value of the shares. The amount is calculated as follows: 8 million × £2.25 = £18 million.
2 The number of shares in issue (25p shares) for the share issue option is 68 million (£17m/£0.25) and for the loan note option is 60 million (£15m/£0.25).
3 The retained earnings will be £58.8 (46.2 + 20.1 − 7.5 (dividends)) for the shares option and £58.2 (46.2 + 18.6 − 6.6 (dividend)) for the loan notes option.

To help us further, gearing ratios and profitability ratios may be calculated under each option.

Activity 8.13

Using the projected figures above, compute the return on ordinary shareholders' funds ratio, earnings per share, interest cover ratio and gearing ratio, assuming the business issues:

(a) shares, and
(b) loan notes.

These ratios are as follows:

	Shares	Loan notes

Return on ordinary shareholders' funds (ROSF)

$$\text{ROSF} = \frac{\text{Earnings available to ordinary shareholders}}{\text{Ordinary shares plus reserves}}$$

	Shares	Loan notes
Share issue $= \dfrac{£12.6m}{£93.8m} \times 100\%$	13.4%	
Loan notes $= \dfrac{£12.0m}{£73.2m} \times 100\%$		16.4%

Earnings per share (EPS)

$$\text{EPS} = \frac{\text{Earnings available to ordinary shareholders}}{\text{No. of ordinary shares}}$$

	Shares	Loan notes
Share issue $= \dfrac{£20.1m}{£68m}$	29.6p	
Loan notes $= \dfrac{£18.6m}{£60m}$		31.0p

Interest cover ratio

$$\frac{\text{Profit before interest and taxation}}{\text{Interest payable}}$$

	Shares	Loan notes
Share issue $= \dfrac{£29.2m}{£2.4m}$	12.2 times	
Loan notes $= \dfrac{£29.2m}{£4.4m}$		6.6 times

Gearing ratio

Gearing ratio

$$= \frac{\text{Loan capital}}{\text{(Ordinary shares + Reserves + Loan capital)}} \times 100\%$$

	Shares	Loan notes
Share issue $= \dfrac{£20.0m}{(93.8 + 20)} \times 100\%$	17.6%	
Loan note issue $= \dfrac{£20.0m + £20.0m}{(73.2 + 40)} \times 100\%$		35.3%

The calculations we have undertaken in Activity 8.13 should help us assess the implications of each financing option.

Activity 8.14

Briefly evaluate each of the proposed financing options from the perspective of an existing shareholder.

....

The loan notes option provides the investor with better returns. We can see that EPS is slightly higher and the ROSF is 3 per cent higher than under the share option. However, the loan notes option also produces a higher level of gearing and, therefore, a higher level of risk. Although the gearing ratio for the loan notes option does not seem excessive, it does represent a significant increase to the existing level of 24.6 per cent (that is, £20m/£81.2m) and is twice as high as the share option. The interest cover for the loan notes option is almost half that for the share option. Nevertheless, the profit before interest and taxation comfortably exceeds the interest charges.

The investor must decide whether the fairly small increase in returns warrants the increase in gearing that must be undertaken to achieve those returns.

Real World 8.8 shows how Tesco plc, the UK and, increasingly, international supermarket chain, was able to use financial gearing to boost ROSF in the early 2000s.

REAL WORLD 8.8

Changing gear at Tesco

Figure 8.10 plots the ROSF, ROCE and interest cover ratios over the period 2001 to 2007.

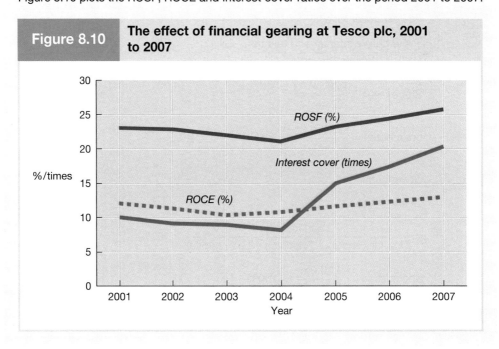

Figure 8.10 The effect of financial gearing at Tesco plc, 2001 to 2007

Tesco was able to boost returns to shareholders (ROSF), despite the business not producing a better ROCE (which reduced slightly between 2001 and 2003). This was achieved as a result of increasing financial gearing (as measured by interest cover) over that period. After 2004, Tesco started to reduce gearing again. Now ROSF continued to increase, but as a result of increasing ROCE.

Source: Based on information contained in Tesco plc Annual Reports from 2003 to 2007.

Gearing and signalling

When a decision to change the existing level of gearing is announced, investors may interpret this as a signal concerning future prospects. For example, an increase in the level of gearing may be taken by investors to indicate management's confidence in future profitability and, as a result, share prices may rise. Managers must therefore be sensitive to the possible signals that are being transmitted to the market by their actions and, where necessary, provide further explanation.

Constructing a PBIT–EPS indifference chart

Managers may wish to know the returns to ordinary shareholders at different levels of profit before interest and taxation for each of the financing options being considered. This can be presented in the form of a chart and, to show how this is done, we can use the information contained in the answer to Example 8.4 above. The chart, which is referred to as a **PBIT–EPS indifference chart**, is set out in Figure 8.11. We can see that its vertical axis plots the earnings per share and its horizontal axis plots the profit before interest and taxation.

Figure 8.11	**PBIT–EPS indifference chart for two financing options**

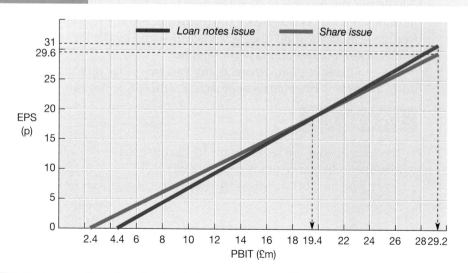

The chart reveals the returns to shareholders, as measured by earnings per share, for different levels of profit before interest and taxation of two financing options. The point at which the two lines intersect represents the level of profit before interest and tax at which both financing options provide the same rate of return to shareholders. This is referred to as the indifference point.

To show the returns to shareholders at different levels of profit, we need two co-ordinates for each financing scheme. The first of these will be the profit before interest and taxation necessary to cover the fixed-return charges (the interest payable). For the loan notes issue, it is £4.4 million and for the ordinary share issue, it is £2.4 million (see income statements above). At these points, there will be nothing available to the ordinary shareholders and so earnings per share will be zero. These points will be plotted on the vertical axis.

The second coordinate for each financing scheme will be the earnings per share at the expected profit before interest and taxation. (However, an arbitrarily determined level of profit before interest and taxation could also be used.) For the loan notes issue, the earnings per share at the expected profit before interest and taxation is 31.0p, and for the ordinary share issue it is 29.6p (see earlier calculations). By joining the two coordinates relevant to each financing scheme, we have a straight line that reveals the earnings per share at different levels of profit before interest and taxation.

We can see from the chart that, at lower levels of profit before interest and taxation, the ordinary share issue provides better returns to shareholders. However, the loan notes issue line has a steeper slope and returns to ordinary shareholders rise more quickly. We can see that beyond a profit before interest and taxation of £19.4 million, ordinary shareholders begin to reap the benefits of gearing and their returns become higher under this alternative. The profit before interest and taxation of £19.4 million is referred to as the **indifference point** (that is, the point at which the two financing schemes provide the same level of return to ordinary shareholders).

The distance between the indifference point and the expected level of profit before interest and taxation provides us with a 'margin of safety'. The chart reveals that there is a reasonable margin of safety for the loan notes option: there would have to be a fall in profit before interest and taxation of about 34 per cent before the ordinary share option became more attractive. Thus, provided the managers were confident that the expected levels of profit could be maintained, the loan notes option would be more attractive.

A business may consider issuing preference shares to finance a particular project. As preference dividends are paid out of profits *after taxation* this means that, when we are calculating the first coordinate for the chart, the profits *before* interest and taxation must be sufficient to cover both the dividends and the relevant tax payments. In other words, we must 'gross up' the preference dividend by the relevant tax rate to derive the profits before interest and taxation figure.

The indifference point between any two financing options can also be derived by using a simple mathematical approach. Example 8.5 illustrates the process.

Example 8.5

The information for Semplice plc in Example 8.4 above can be used to illustrate how the indifference point is calculated.

Let x be the PBIT at which the two financing options provide the same EPS.

	Shares £m	Loan notes £m
Profit before interest and taxation	x	x
Interest payable	(2.4)	(4.4)
Profit before taxation	$(x - 2.4)$	$(x - 4.4)$
Tax (25%)	$0.25(x - 2.4)$	$0.25(x - 4.4)$
Profit after taxation	$0.75(x - 2.4)$	$0.75(x - 4.4)$
EPS	$\dfrac{0.75(x - £2.4m)}{68m}$	$\dfrac{0.75(x - £4.4m)}{60m}$

Thus, the EPS of the two financing options will be equal when:

$$\frac{0.75(x - £2.4\text{m})}{68\text{m}} = \frac{0.75(x - £4.4\text{m})}{60\text{m}}$$

We can solve this equation as follows:

$$45x - £108\text{m} = 51x - £224.4\text{m}$$
$$6x = £116.4\text{m}$$
$$x = \underline{£19.4\text{m}}$$

Self-assessment question 8.1

Russell Ltd installs and services heating and ventilation systems for commercial premises. The most recent financial statements of the business are set out below:

Statement of financial position (balance sheet) as at 31 May Year 4

	£000
Non-current assets	
Machinery and equipment	555.2
Motor vehicles	186.6
	741.8
Current assets	
Inventory	293.2
Trade receivables	510.3
Cash at bank	18.4
	821.9
Total assets	1,563.7
Equity	
£1 ordinary shares	400.0
General reserve	52.2
Retained earnings	380.2
	832.4
Non-current liabilities	
12% loan notes (repayable Year 10/11)	250.0
Current liabilities	
Trade payables	417.3
Tax due	64.0
	481.3
Total equity and liabilities	1,563.7

Income statement for the year ended 31 May Year 4

	£000
Sales revenue	5,207.8
Operating profit (profit before interest and taxation)	542.0
Interest payable	(30.0)
Profit before taxation	512.0
Tax (25%)	(128.0)
Profit for the year	384.0

Self-assessment question 8.1 continued

A dividend of £153,600 was proposed and paid during the year.

The business wishes to invest in more machinery and equipment in order to cope with an upsurge in demand for its services. Additional operating profit (profit before interest and taxation) of £120,000 per year is expected if an investment of £600,000 is made in plant and machinery.

The directors of the business are considering an offer from a private equity firm to finance the expansion programme. The finance will be made available immediately through either:

(i)   an issue of £1 ordinary shares at a premium on par of £3 per share, or
(ii) an issue of £600,000 10% loan notes at par (nominal) value.

The directors of the business wish to maintain the same dividend payout ratio in future years as in past years, whichever method of finance is chosen.

Required:
(a) For each of the financing schemes:
   (i)   Prepare a projected income statement for the year ended 31 May Year 5
   (ii) Calculate the projected earnings per share for the year ended 31 May Year 5
   (iii) Calculate the projected level of gearing as at 31 May Year 5.
(b) Briefly assess both of the financing schemes under consideration from the viewpoint of the existing shareholders.
(c) Calculate the level of operating profit (profit before interest and taxation) at which the earnings per share under each of the financing options will be the same.

The answer to this question may be found at the back of the book on p. 535.

What determines the level of gearing?

In practice, the level of gearing adopted by a business is likely to be influenced by the attitude of owners, managers and lenders. The factors that each of these groups may bear in mind when making gearing decisions are considered below.

The attitude of the owners

The attitude of owners is likely to be influenced by the following:

● *Control.* Owners may be reluctant to issue more ordinary shares where it results in a dilution of control. If this is the case, loan capital may be viewed as a better option.
● *Flexibility.* Loan capital can often be raised much more quickly than share capital, which can be important when a business operates in a fast-changing environment.
● *Debt capacity.* Too high a level of gearing may eliminate the capacity for future borrowing.
● *Risk.* Risk-averse investors will only be prepared to take on more risk if there is the opportunity for higher rates of return. Thus, higher gearing must offer the prospect of higher returns.
● *Returns.* The potential benefits for owners of gearing have already been discussed. Where shareholders are receiving relatively poor returns, they may be reluctant to provide additional share capital. Instead, they may encourage managers to try to increase their returns through higher gearing.

The attitude of management

Although managers are employed to operate a business in the owners' best interests, they may not always do this. Managers may resist high levels of gearing if they feel that it places their income and jobs at risk. They make a big investment of 'human capital' in the business and become dependent on its continuing financial health. Managers cannot diversify this 'human capital' risk in the way that investors can diversify their financial capital risk. Managers may also object to the tight financial discipline that loan capital imposes on them. They may feel under constant pressure to ensure that sufficient cash is available to cover interest payments and capital repayments.

These objections may lead them to avoid making investments that require funding through loan capital.

The attitude of lenders

When deciding whether to provide loan finance, lenders will be concerned with the ability of the business to repay the amount borrowed and to pay interest at the due dates. There are various factors that will have a bearing on these issues.

Activity 8.15

What factors are likely to influence the ability of a business to repay the amount borrowed and to pay interest at due dates?

The following factors are likely to be important:

- *Profitability.* Where a business has a stable level of profits, lenders may feel that there is less risk to their investment than where profits are volatile. Profit stability will depend on such factors as the nature of the products sold, the competitive structure of the industry and so on.
- *Cash-generating ability.* Where a business is able to generate strong, predictable cash flows, lenders may feel there is less risk to their investment.
- *Security for the loan.* The nature and quality of assets held by a business will determine whether there is adequate security for a loan. Generally speaking, lenders prefer assets that have a ready market value, which can be easily transferred and which will not deteriorate quickly (for example, property).
- *Fixed cost.* A business that operates with a high level of fixed costs has a high level of risk as fixed costs have to be paid irrespective of the level of sales and profits. Lenders may feel that a business with high fixed costs will only add to these by borrowing and this may increase the overall level of risk to unacceptable levels.

This is not an exhaustive list: you may have thought of other factors.

Levels of gearing can vary significantly between industries. Generally speaking, levels of gearing will be higher in industries where profits are stable (which lenders are likely to prefer). Thus, higher levels of gearing are likely to occur in utilities such as electricity, gas and water businesses, which are less affected by economic recession, changes in consumer tastes and so forth, than most businesses.

The capital structure debate

It may come as a surprise to discover that there is some debate in the finance literature over whether the capital structure decision really is important. There is controversy over whether the 'mix' of long-term funds employed can have an effect on the overall cost of capital of a business. If a particular mix of funds can produce a lower cost of capital, then the way in which the business is financed is important as it can affect its value. (In broad terms, the value of a business can be defined as the net present value of its future cash flows. Lowering the cost of capital, which is used as the discount rate, will increase the value of the business.)

There are two schools of thought concerning the capital structure decision, which we shall refer to as the traditional school and modernist school. The position of each is described below.

The traditional view

According to the traditional school, the capital structure decision is very important. The traditionalists point out that the cost of loan capital is cheaper than the cost of ordinary (equity) share capital (see Chapter 6). This difference in the relative cost of finance suggests that, by increasing the level of borrowing (or gearing), the overall cost of capital of the business can be reduced. However, there are drawbacks to taking on additional borrowing. As the level of borrowing increases, ordinary shareholders will require higher levels of return on their investments to compensate for the higher levels of financial risk that they will have to bear. Existing lenders will also require higher levels of return.

The traditionalists argue, however, that at fairly low levels of borrowing, the benefits of raising finance through the use of loan capital will outweigh any costs that arise. This is because ordinary shareholders and lenders will not view low levels of borrowing as having a significant effect on the level of risk that they have to bear and so will not require a higher level of return in compensation. As the level of borrowing increases, however, things will start to change. Ordinary shareholders and existing lenders will become increasingly concerned with the higher interest charges that must be met and the risks this will pose to their own claims on the income and assets of the business. As a result, they will seek compensation for this higher level of risk in the form of higher expected returns.

The situation just described is set out in Figure 8.12. We can see that, where there are small increases in borrowing, ordinary shareholders and existing lenders do not require greatly increased returns. However, at significantly higher levels of borrowing, the risks involved take on greater importance for investors and this is reflected in the sharp rise in the returns required from each group. Note that the overall cost of capital (which is a weighted average of the cost of ordinary shares and loan capital) declines when small increases in the level of borrowing occur. However, at significantly increased levels of borrowing, the increase in required returns from ordinary (equity) shareholders and lenders will result in a sharp rise in the overall cost of capital.

An important implication of the above analysis is that managers of the business should try to establish that mix of loan/equity finance that will minimise the overall cost of capital. At this point, the business will be said to achieve an **optimal capital structure**. Minimising the overall cost of capital in this way will maximise the value of the business (that is, the net present value of future cash flows). This relationship

| Figure 8.12 | The traditional view of the relationship between levels of borrowing and expected returns |

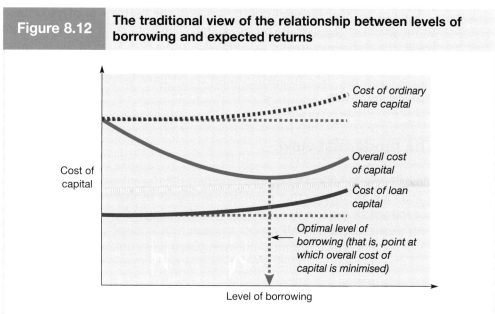

The figure assumes that at low levels of borrowing, ordinary (equity) shareholders will not require a higher level of return to compensate for the higher risk incurred. As loan finance is cheaper than ordinary share finance, this will lead to a fall in the overall cost of capital. However, this situation will change as the level of borrowing increases. At some point, the increased returns required by ordinary shareholders will begin to outweigh the benefits of cheap loan capital and so the overall cost of capital will start to rise. The implication is, therefore, that there is an optimum level of gearing for a business.

between the level of borrowing, the cost of capital and business value is illustrated in Figure 8.13.

| Figure 8.13 | The relationship between the level of borrowing, the cost of capital and business value: the traditional view |

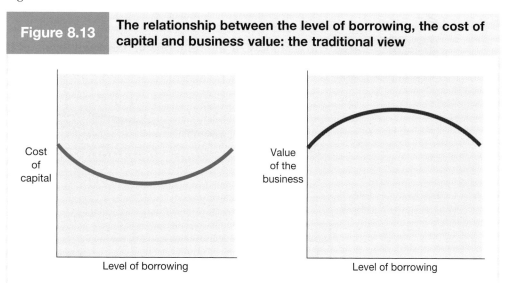

The first graph plots the cost of capital against the level of borrowing. We saw earlier that the traditionalist view suggests that, in the first instance, the cost of capital will fall as the level of borrowing increases. However, at higher levels of borrowing, the overall cost of capital will begin to increase. The second graph plots the level of borrowing against the value of the business. This is the inverse of the first graph. As the cost of capital decreases so the value increases, and vice versa.

We can see that the graph of the value of the business displays an inverse pattern to the graph of the overall cost of capital. (This is because a lower cost of capital will result in a higher net present value for the future cash flows of the business.) This relationship suggests that the financing decision is critically important. Failure to identify and achieve the right financing 'mix' could have serious adverse consequences for shareholder wealth.

The modernist view

Modigliani and Miller (MM), who represent the modernist school, challenged the traditional view by arguing that the required returns to shareholders and to lenders would not follow the pattern as set out above. They argued that shareholders in a business with financial gearing will expect a return that is equal to the returns expected from investing in a similar ungeared business plus a premium, which rises in *direct proportion* to the level of gearing. Thus, the increase in returns required for ordinary shareholders as compensation for increased financial risk will rise in constant proportion to the increase in the level of borrowing over the *whole range of borrowing*. This pattern contrasts with the traditional view, of course, which displays an uneven change in the required rate of return over the range of borrowing.

The MM analysis also assumes that the returns required from borrowers would remain constant as the level of borrowing increases. This latter point may appear strange at first sight. However, if lenders have good security for the loans made to the business, they are unlikely to feel at risk from additional borrowing and will not, therefore, seek additional returns. This is provided, of course, that the business does not exceed its borrowing capacity.

The MM position is set out in Figure 8.14. As you can see from this figure, the overall cost of capital remains constant at varying levels of borrowing. This is because the

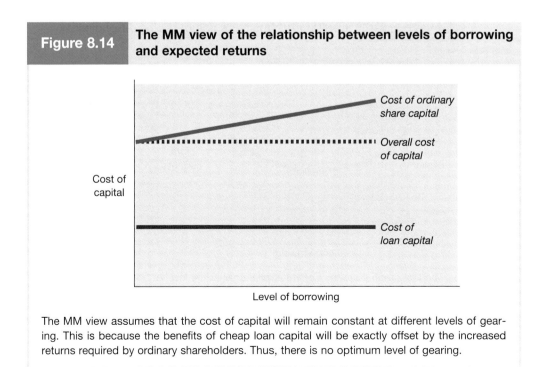

Figure 8.14	**The MM view of the relationship between levels of borrowing and expected returns**

The MM view assumes that the cost of capital will remain constant at different levels of gearing. This is because the benefits of cheap loan capital will be exactly offset by the increased returns required by ordinary shareholders. Thus, there is no optimum level of gearing.

benefits obtained from raising finance through borrowing, which is cheaper than share capital, is exactly offset by the increase in required returns from ordinary shareholders.

An important implication of the MM view is that the financing decision is not really important. Figure 8.14 shows that there is no optimal capital structure for a business, as suggested by the traditionalists, because the overall cost of capital remains constant. This means that one particular capital structure is no better or worse than any other and so managers should not spend time on evaluating different forms of financing 'mixes' for the business. Instead, they should concentrate their efforts on evaluating and managing the investments of the business.

Activity 8.16

In Figure 8.13 we saw the traditional view of the relationships between the cost of capital and the level of borrowing and the value of the business and the level of borrowing. How would the MM view of these two relationships be shown in graphical form?

The relationship between (i) the level of borrowing and the cost of capital and (ii) the level of borrowing and the value of the business, as viewed by MM, is set out in Figure 8.15.

| Figure 8.15 | **The relationship between the level of borrowing, the cost of capital and business value: the MM view** |

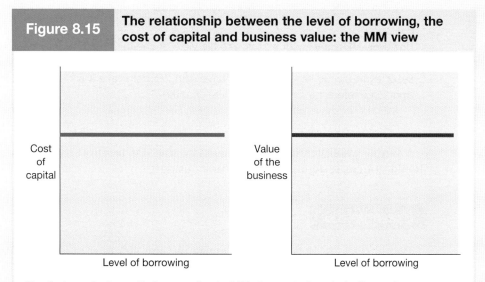

The first graph shows that, according to MM, the cost of capital will remain constant at different levels of borrowing. The second graph shows the implication of this for the value of the business. As the cost of capital is constant, the net present value of future cash flows from the business will not be affected by the level of borrowing. Hence, the value of the business will remain constant.

Although the views of Modigliani and Miller were first published in the late 1950s, they are described as modernists because they base their position on economic theory (unlike the traditional school). They argue that the value of a business is determined by the future income from its investments, and the risk associated with those investments, and not by the way in which this income is divided among the different providers of finance. In other words, it is not possible to increase the value of a business (that is, lower the overall cost of capital) simply by borrowing, as the traditionalists suggest.

MM point out that borrowing is not something that only businesses are able to undertake. Borrowing can also be undertaken by individual investors. As business borrowing can be replicated by individual investors, there is no reason why it should create additional value for the investor. **(Un)Real World 8.9** explains the theory from a lighter perspective.

(UN)REAL WORLD 8.9

To really understand MM . . . start with a pizza

We have just seen that it is the income-generating power and risks associated with the underlying investments of the business, rather than the different ways in which a business may be financed, that determine the value of a business. This point was once explained by Miller (of Modigliani and Miller fame) as follows:

> Think of the firm as a gigantic pizza, divided into quarters. If now, you cut each quarter in half into eighths, the M&M proposition says that you will have more pieces, but not more pizza.

In other words, different financing methods will have an effect on how the business investments and income stream will be divided up but will not affect the value of these.

Footnote:
However, Miller's view of pizzas, like his view of capital structure, may be controversial. When Yogi Berra, a US baseball player, was asked whether he would like his pizza cut into six or eight pieces he is reputed to have said, 'Better make it six, I don't think I can eat eight' (see reference 4 at the end of the chapter).

A simple example may help to illustrate the MM position that business borrowing should not create additional value for a business.

Example 8.6

Two businesses, Delta plc and Omega plc, are identical except for the fact that Delta plc is financed entirely by ordinary shares and Omega plc is 50 per cent financed by loans. The profit before interest for each business for the year is £2 million. The ordinary shareholders of Delta plc require a return of 12 per cent and the ordinary shareholders of Omega plc require a return of 14 per cent. Omega plc pays 10 per cent interest per year on the £10 million loans outstanding. (Tax is ignored for reasons that we shall discuss later.)

	Delta plc £m	Omega plc £m
Profits before interest	2.0	2.0
Interest payable	–	(1.0)
Available to ordinary shareholders	2.0	1.0

The market value of the total ordinary shares of each business will be equivalent to the profits capitalised at the required rate of return. Thus, the market value of each business is as follows:

	Delta plc £m	Omega plc £m
Market value of ordinary (equity) shares:		
(£2m/0.12)	16.7	
(£1m/0.14)		7.1
Market value of loan capital	–	10.0
Market value of each business	<u>16.7</u>	<u>17.1</u>

MM argue that differences in the way in which each business is financed cannot result in a higher value for Omega plc as shown above. This is because an investor who owns, say, 10 per cent of the shares in Omega plc would be able to obtain the same level of income from investing in Delta plc, for the same level of risk as the investment in Omega plc and for a lower net investment. The investor, by borrowing an amount equivalent to 10 per cent of the loans of Omega plc (that is, an amount proportional to the ownership interest in Omega plc), and selling the shares held in Omega plc in order to finance the purchase of a 10 per cent equity stake in Delta plc, would be in the following position:

	£000
Return from 10% equity investment in Delta plc	200
Interest on borrowing (£1,000 × 10%)	(100)
Net return	100
Purchase of shares (10% × £16.7m)	1,670
Amount borrowed	(1,000)
Net investment in Delta plc	670

The investor with a 10 per cent stake in the ordinary share capital of Omega plc is, currently, in the following position:

	£000
Return from 10% investment in Omega plc	100
Net investment in Omega plc: existing shareholding (10% × £7.1m)	710

As we can see, the investor would be better off by taking on personal borrowing in order to acquire a 10 per cent share of the ordinary share capital of the ungeared business, Delta plc, than by continuing to invest in the geared business, Omega plc. The effect of a number of investors switching investments in this way would be to reduce the value of the shares in Omega plc (thereby increasing the returns to ordinary shareholders in Omega plc), and to increase the value of shares in Delta plc (thereby reducing the returns to equity in Delta plc). This switching from Omega plc to Delta plc (which is referred to as an **arbitrage transaction**) would continue until the returns from each investment were the same, and so no further gains could be made from such transactions. At this point, the value of each business would be identical.

The MM analysis, while extremely rigorous and logical, is based on a number of restrictive assumptions. These include the following.

Perfect capital markets

The assumption of perfect capital markets means that there are no share transaction costs and investors and businesses can borrow unlimited amounts at the same rates of interest. Although these assumptions may be unrealistic, they may not have a significant effect on the arguments made. Where the prospect of 'arbitrage' gains (that is, selling shares in an overvalued business and buying shares in an undervalued business) are substantial, share transaction costs are unlikely to be an important issue as the potential benefits will outweigh the costs. It is only at the margin that share transaction costs will take on significance.

Similarly, the assumption that investors can borrow unlimited amounts at the same rate of interest may only take on significance at the margin. We have seen that the UK stock market is dominated by large investment institutions such as pension funds, unit trusts and insurance businesses that hold a very large proportion of all shares issued by listed businesses. These institutions may well be able to borrow very large amounts at similar rates to those offered to a business.

No bankruptcy costs

Assuming that there are no bankruptcy costs means that, if a business were liquidated, no legal and administrative fees would be incurred and the business assets could be sold at a price that would enable shareholders to receive cash equal to the market value of their shareholding prior to the liquidation. This assumption will not hold true in the real world where bankruptcy costs can be very high.

However, it is only at high levels of gearing that bankruptcy costs are likely to be a real issue. We saw in Chapter 6 that borrowing leads to a commitment to pay interest and to repay capital: the higher the level of borrowing, the higher the level of commitment and the higher the risk that this commitment will not be met. In the case of a low-geared, or moderately geared, business it may be possible to take on additional borrowing, if necessary, to meet commitments whereas a highly geared business may have no further debt capacity.

Risk

It is assumed that businesses exist that have identical operating risks but which have different levels of borrowing. Although this is unlikely to be true, it does not affect the validity of MM's arguments.

No taxation

A world without corporate or personal income taxes is clearly an unrealistic assumption. The real issue, however, is whether this undermines the validity of MM's arguments. We shall, therefore, consider next the effect on the MM position of introducing taxes.

MM and the introduction of taxation

MM were subject to much criticism for not dealing with the problem of taxation in their analysis. This led them to revise their position so as to include taxation. They acknowledged in their revised analysis that the tax relief from interest payments on loans provides a real benefit to ordinary shareholders. The more the level of borrowing increases, the more tax relief the business receives and so the smaller the tax liability of the business will become.

We should recall that the original MM position was that the benefits of cheap loan capital will be exactly offset by increases in the required rate of return by ordinary share investors. Tax relief on loan interest should, therefore, represent an additional benefit to shareholders. As the amount of tax relief increases with the amount of borrowing, the overall cost of capital (after tax) will be lowered as the level of borrowing increases.

The implication of this revised position is that there is an optimum level of gearing and it is at 100 per cent gearing. In Figure 8.16, we can see the MM position after taxation has been introduced.

Figure 8.16	The MM view of the relationship between levels of borrowing and expected returns (including tax effects)

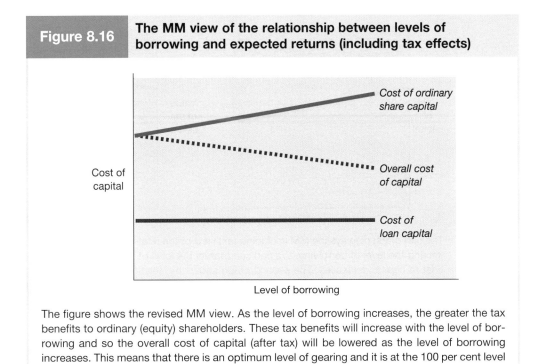

The figure shows the revised MM view. As the level of borrowing increases, the greater the tax benefits to ordinary (equity) shareholders. These tax benefits will increase with the level of borrowing and so the overall cost of capital (after tax) will be lowered as the level of borrowing increases. This means that there is an optimum level of gearing and it is at the 100 per cent level of gearing.

Thus, the MM position moves closer to the traditional position in so far as it recognises that there is a relationship between the value of the business and the way in which it is financed. It also recognises that there is an optimum level of gearing.

The relationship between (a) the level of borrowing and the cost of capital and (b) the level of borrowing and business value, after taking into account the tax effects, is set out in Figure 8.17.

Activity 8.17

What do you think is the main implication of the above analysis for managers who are trying to decide on an appropriate capital structure?

This revised MM analysis implies that a business should borrow to capacity as this will lower the post-tax cost of capital and thereby increase the value of the business.

In practice, however, few businesses follow the policy just described. When borrowing reaches very high levels, lenders are likely to feel that their security is threatened and ordinary share investors will feel that bankruptcy risks have increased. Thus, both groups are likely to seek higher returns, which will, in turn, increase the overall cost of capital. (A business would have to attract *risk-seeking* investors in order to prevent a rise in its cost of capital.)

Figure 8.17	The relationship between the level of borrowing, the cost of capital and business value: the MM view (including tax effects)

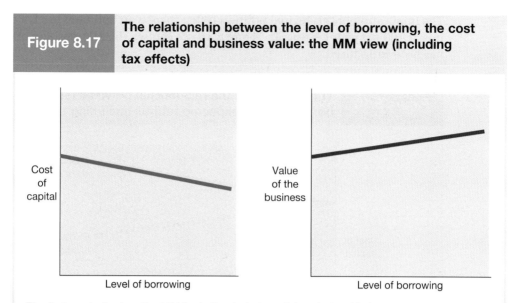

The first graph displays the MM (including tax) view of the relationship between the cost of capital and the level of borrowing. We can see that as the level of borrowing increases, the overall cost of capital decreases. The second graph shows the relationship between the value of the business and the level of borrowing. A decrease in the overall cost of capital results in a rise in the value of the business and so, as the level of borrowing increases, the value of the business increases.

The debate concerning capital structure still rumbles on. Although the arguments of the traditional school have been undermined by the inexorable logic of MM, it does seem that, in the real world, businesses tend to settle for moderate rather than high levels of gearing as recommended by the MM (including tax) arguments. We have just seen that the risk of bankruptcy and the effect of this on the attitudes of shareholders and lenders may prevent a business from taking on very high levels of gearing. Nevertheless, it could be argued that, from an ordinary share investor's viewpoint, the business should continue to borrow until the risks of incurring bankruptcy costs outweigh the benefits from higher gearing.

Real World 8.10 describes how the level of borrowing of BAA, the airport operator, has raised concerns.

 **REAL WORLD 8.10**

In the wrong gear? FT

When a consortium led by Spain's Ferrovial bought BAA last year, it was expected to refinance rapidly both the acquisition loans and the outstanding bonds it assumed. Several delays later, it has pushed back the refinancing until March.

There is no suggestion that BAA is breaching its borrowing terms. But the company made an underlying loss of €153m in the first nine months.

Of £11.7bn of gross borrowings, BAA wants to refinance £4.6bn of senior debt and £4.5bn of bonds, in a securitisation against Heathrow and Gatwick. Additionally, it plans to borrow even more against these assets to fund capital expenditure (capex).

The numbers, however, look worrying. Earnings before interest, tax, depreciation and amortisation in 2008 are estimated at £1.2bn, rising to £1.3bn by 2010. This is not enough to fund interest costs, which should be in the order of £800m annually, as well as capex, which Collins Stewart estimates at an annual £1.4bn for the next five years. So, either borrowing will rise significantly more or BAA's capital structure will have to change.

Source: 'BAA's finances' www.ft.com, 9 November 2007.

SUMMARY

The main points in this chapter may be summarised as follows:

Cost of capital

- The opportunity cost reflects the returns that investors would expect to earn from investments with the same level of risk.
- There are two major approaches to determining the cost of ordinary (equity) shares, the dividend-based approach and the risk/return (CAPM) approach.
- The dividend-based approach reflects the fact that a share can be valued according to the future dividends received.
- Dividend valuation models often assume constant dividends over time ($K_0 = D_0/P_0$) or that dividends will grow at a constant rate [$K_0 = (D_1/P_0) + g$].
- The risk/return approach is based on the idea that the cost of an ordinary share is made up of a risk-free rate of return plus a risk premium.
- The risk premium is calculated by measuring the risk premium for the market as a whole, then measuring the returns from a particular share in relation to the market and applying this measure to the market risk premium [$K_0 = K_{RF} + b(K_m - K_{RF})$].
- The cost of irredeemable loan capital can be derived in a similar way to that of ordinary shares where the dividend stays constant ($K_d = I(1 - t)/P_d$).
- The cost of redeemable loan capital can be computed using an IRR approach.
- The cost of preference share capital can be derived in a similar way to that of ordinary shares where the dividend stays constant ($K_p = D_p/P_p$).
- The weighted average cost of capital (WACC) is derived by taking the cost of each element of capital and weighting each element in proportion to the target capital structure.

Financial gearing

- The effect of financial gearing is that changes in profit before interest and taxation (PBIT) result in disproportionate changes in the returns to ordinary shareholders.
- The degree of financial gearing measures the sensitivity of changes in returns to ordinary shareholders to changes in PBIT.
- A PBIT–EPS indifference chart can be constructed to reveal the returns to shareholders at different levels of PBIT for different financing options.
- Gearing levels will be determined by the attitude of owners, managers and lenders.

The capital structure debate

- There are two schools of thought.
- The traditional view is that the capital structure decision is important whereas the modernist view is that it is not.

Traditional viewpoint

- Traditionalists argue that, at lower levels of gearing, shareholders and lenders are unconcerned about risk; however, at higher levels they become concerned and demand higher returns.
- This leads to an increase in WACC.
- WACC decreases at lower levels of gearing (because investors do not demand increased returns) but then increases.
- This means that there is an optimum level of gearing.

Modernist viewpoint

- Modernists (MM) argue that shareholders are always concerned about the level of gearing.
- Cheaper loan finance is offset by increasing cost of ordinary shares and so the cost of capital remains constant.
- This means that there is no optimum level of gearing.
- If tax is introduced, the modernist view is changed.
- The tax benefits arising from interest payments should be exploited by taking on loan capital up to the point where these benefits are outweighed by the potential costs of bankruptcy.

→ **Key terms**

Cost of capital p. 308
Capital asset pricing model (CAPM)
  p. 311
Beta p. 312
Weighted average cost of capital (WACC) p. 322

Degree of financial gearing p. 331
PBIT–EPS indifference chart p. 337
Indifference point p. 338
Optimal capital structure p. 342
Arbitrage transactions p. 347

For definitions of these terms see the Glossary, pp. 574–583.

References

1 'Practitioners' perspectives on the UK cost of capital', *McLaney, E., Pointon, J., Thomas, M. and Tucker J.*, **European Journal of Finance**, April 2004, pp. 123–38.

2 **The Cost of Capital in the UK**, *Gregory, A. and Rutterford, J. (with Zaman, M.)*, Chartered Institute of Management Accountants Research Monograph, 1999.

3 'How do CFOs make capital budgeting and capital structure decisions?', *Graham, J. and Harvey, C.*, **Journal of Applied Corporate Finance**, vol. 15, no. 1 (2002).

4 Quoted in **Finance for Executives**, *Hawawini, G. and Viallet, C.*, 2nd edn, South Western/ Thomson Learning, 2002, p. 353.

Further reading

If you wish to explore the topics discussed in this chapter in more depth, try the following books:

Business Finance: Theory and Practice, *McLaney, E.*, 9th edn., Financial Times Prentice Hall, 2009, chapters 10 and 11.

Corporate Finance and Investment, *Pike, R. and Neale, B.*, 5th edn., Financial Times Prentice Hall, 2006, chapters 20 and 21.

Corporate Financial Management, *Arnold, G.*, 3rd edn., Financial Times Prentice Hall, 2005, chapters 8 and 19.

Investment Analysis and Portfolio Management, *Reilly, F. and Brown, K.*, 8th edn., Thomson South Western, 2006, chapters 8 and 9.

REVIEW QUESTIONS

Answers to these questions can be found at the back of the book on p. 545.

8.1 How might a business find out whether a particular planned level of gearing would be acceptable to investors?

8.2 What factors might a prospective lender take into account when deciding whether to make a long-term loan to a particular business?

8.3 Should the specific cost of raising finance for a particular project be used as the appropriate discount rate for investment appraisal purposes?

8.4 What are the main implications for the financial manager who accepts the arguments of:

(a) the traditional approach
(b) the MM (excluding tax effects) approach
(c) the MM (including tax effects) approach

concerning capital structure?

EXERCISES

Exercises 8.5 to 8.7 are more advanced than 8.1 to 8.4. Those with coloured numbers have answers at the back of the book, starting on p. 563.

 If you wish to try more exercises, visit the students' side of this book's Companion Website.

8.1 Riphean plc and Silurian plc are two businesses operating in different industries from one another. They are both financed by a mixture of ordinary share and loan capital and both are seeking to derive the cost of capital for investment decision making purposes. The following information is available concerning the two businesses for the year to 30 November Year 8:

	Riphean plc	Silurian plc
Profit for the year	£3.0m	£4.0m
Gross dividends	£1.5m	£2.0m
Market value per ordinary share	£4.00	£1.60
Number of ordinary shares	5m	10m
Gross interest yield on loan capital	8%	12%
Market value of loan capital	£10m	£16m

The annual growth rate in dividends is 5 per cent for Riphean plc and 8 per cent for Silurian plc. Assume a 30 per cent tax rate.

Required:

(a) Explain what is meant by the term 'cost of capital' and state why it is important for a business to calculate its cost of capital correctly.

(b) Calculate the weighted average cost of capital of Riphean plc and Silurian plc using the information provided.

(c) Discuss two possible reasons why the cost of ordinary share capital differs between the two businesses.

(d) Discuss two limitations of using the weighted average cost of capital when making investment decisions.

8.2 Celtor plc is a property development business operating in the London area. The business has the following capital structure as at 30 November Year 9:

	£000
£1 ordinary shares	10,000
Retained earnings	20,000
9% loan notes	12,000
	42,000

The ordinary shares have a current market value of £3.90 and the current level of dividend is 20p per share. The dividend has been growing at a compound rate of 4 per cent a year in recent years. The loan notes of the business are irredeemable and have a current market value of £80 per £100 nominal. Interest due on the loan notes at the year end has recently been paid.

The business has obtained planning permission to build a new office block in a redevelopment area. The business wishes to raise the whole of the finance necessary for the project by the issue of more irredeemable 9 per cent loan notes at £80 per £100 nominal. This is in line with a target capital structure set by the business where the amount of loan capital will increase to 70 per cent of ordinary share capital within the next two years. The tax rate is 25 per cent.

Required:

(a) Explain what is meant by the term 'cost of capital'. Why is it important for a business to calculate its cost of capital with care?

(b) Calculate the weighted average cost of capital of Celtor plc that should be used for future investment decisions.

8.3 Grenache plc operates a chain of sports shops throughout the UK. In recent years competition has been fierce and profits and sales have declined. The most recent financial statements of the business are as follows:

Statement of financial position (balance sheet) as at 30 April Year 7

	£m
Non-current assets	
Premises	46.3
Fixtures, fittings and equipment	16.1
	62.4
Current assets	
Inventory	52.4
Trade receivables	2.3
Cash	1.2
	55.9
Total assets	118.3
Equity	
£1 ordinary shares	25.0
Retained earnings	18.6
	43.6
Non-current liabilities	
10% loan notes	25.0
Current liabilities	
Trade payables	48.1
Tax due	1.6
	49.7
Total equity and liabilities	118.3

Income statement for the year ended 30 April Year 7

	£m
Sales revenue	148.8
Operating profit	15.7
Interest payable	(2.5)
Profit before taxation	13.2
Tax (25%)	(3.3)
Profit for the year	9.9

A dividend of £5.2 million was proposed and paid during the year.

A new managing director was appointed during Year 7 to improve the performance of the business. She plans a 'sand and surf' image for the business in order to appeal to the younger market. This will require a large investment in new inventories and a complete redesign and refurbishment of the shops. The cost of implementing the plan is estimated to be £30 million.

The business is considering two possible financing options. The first option is to issue further 10 per cent loan notes at nominal value. The second option is to make a rights issue based on a 20 per cent discount on the current market value of the shares. The market capitalisation of the business is currently £187.5 million.

The future performance following the re-launch of the business is not certain. Three scenarios have been prepared concerning the possible effects on annual operating profits (profits before interest and taxation):

Scenario	Change in operating profits compared to most recent year
	%
Optimistic	+40
Most likely	+15
Pessimistic	−25

The dividend per share to be proposed and paid will increase by 10 per cent during the forthcoming year if there is an increase in profit but will decrease by 20 per cent if there is a reduction in profit.

The business has a current gearing ratio that is broadly in line with its competitors.

Required:

(a) Prepare, in so far as the information allows, a forecast income statement for the forthcoming year for each scenario assuming:
   (i) a loan notes issue is made
   (ii) a rights issue of shares is made.
   Workings should be in £m and to one decimal place.

(b) Calculate the earnings per share and gearing ratio for the forthcoming year for each scenario assuming:
   (i) a loan notes issue is made
   (ii) a rights issue of shares is made.

(c) Assess the future plans and financing options being considered from the perspective of a current shareholder and state what additional information, if any, you may require to make a more considered assessment.

8.4   Trexon plc is a major oil and gas exploration business that has most of its operations in the Middle East and South East Asia. Recently, the business acquired rights to explore for oil and gas in the Gulf of Mexico. Trexon plc proposes to finance the new operations from the issue of ordinary shares. At present, the business is financed by a combination of ordinary share capital and loan capital. The ordinary shares have a nominal value of £0.50 and a current market value of £2.60. The current level of dividend is £0.16 per share and this has been growing at a compound rate of 6 per cent a year in recent years. The loan capital is irredeemable and has a current market value of £94 per £100 nominal. Interest on the loan capital is at the rate of 12 per cent and interest due at the year end has recently been paid. At present, the business expects 60 per cent of its finance to come from ordinary share capital and the rest from loan capital. In the future, however, the business will aim to finance 70 per cent of its operations from ordinary share capital.

When the proposal to finance the new operations via the rights issue of shares was announced at the annual general meeting of the business, objections were raised by two shareholders present, as follows:

● *Shareholder A argued:* 'I fail to understand why the business has decided to issue shares to finance the new operation. Surely it would be better to reinvest profit, as this is, in effect, a free source of finance.'
● *Shareholder B argued:* 'I also fail to understand why the business has decided to issue shares to finance the new operation. However, I do not agree with the suggestion made by Shareholder A. I do not believe that shareholder funds should be used at all to finance the new operation. Instead, the business should issue more loan capital, as it is cheap relative to ordinary share capital and would, therefore, reduce the overall cost of capital of the business.'

Tax is at the rate of 35 per cent.

Required:
(a) Calculate the weighted average cost of capital of Trexon plc that should be used in future investment decisions.
(b) Comment on the remarks made by:
  (i) Shareholder A, and
  (ii) Shareholder B.

8.5 Ashcroft plc, a family-controlled business, is considering raising additional funds to modernise its factory. The scheme is expected to cost £2.34 million and will increase annual operating profits (profits before interest and tax) from 1 January Year 4 by £0.6 million. A summarised statement of financial position and an income statement are shown below. Currently the share price is 200p.

Two schemes have been suggested: (a) 1.3 million shares could be issued at 180p (net of issue costs); (b) a consortium of six City institutions has offered to buy loan notes from the business totalling £2.34 million. Interest would be at the rate of 13 per cent per year and capital repayments of equal annual instalments of £234,000 starting on 1 January Year 5 would be required.

Statement of financial position (balance sheet) as at 31 December Year 3

	£m
Non-current assets	1.4
Current assets	
Inventory	2.4
Trade receivables	2.2
	4.6
Total assets	6.0
Equity	
Share capital, 25p ordinary shares	1.0
Retained earnings	1.5
	2.5
Current liabilities	
Trade payables	3.2
Tax due	0.3
	3.5
Total equity and liabilities	6.0

Income statement for the year ended 31 December Year 3

	£m
Sales revenue	11.2
Operating profit	1.2
Tax	(0.6)
Profit for the year	0.6

Dividends of £0.3m were proposed and paid during the year. Assume tax is charged at the rate of 50 per cent.

Required:

(a) Compute the earnings per share for Year 4 under the loan notes and the ordinary share alternatives.

(b) Compute the level of operating profit (profit before interest and taxation) at which the earnings per share under the two schemes will be equal.

(c) Discuss the considerations the directors should take into account before deciding between loan notes or ordinary share finance.

8.6 Hatleigh plc is a medium-sized engineering business based in South Wales. The financial statements for the year ended 30 April 2008 are as follows:

Statement of financial position (balance sheet) as at 30 April 2008

	£000
Non-current assets	
Premises	3,885
Plant and machinery	2,520
Motor vehicles	1,470
	7,875
Current assets	
Inventory: Raw materials	824
Work in progress	2,120
Finished goods	5,436
Trade receivables	8,578
	16,958
Total assets	24,833
Equity	
Share capital (25p shares)	8,000
Retained earnings	5,034
	13,034
Non-current liabilities	
10% loan notes 2013–14 (secured on premises)	3,500
Current liabilities	
Trade payables	3,322
Bank overdraft	4,776
Tax due	201
	8,299
Total equity and liabilities	24,833

Income statement for the year ended 30 April 2008

	£000
Sales revenue	34,246
Cost of sales	(24,540)
Gross profit	9,706
Expenses	(7,564)
Operating profit	2,142
Interest	(994)
Profit before taxation	1,148
Tax (35%)	(402)
Profit for the year	746

A dividend of £600,000 was proposed and paid during the year.

The business made a one-for-four rights issue of ordinary shares during the year. Sales for the forthcoming year are forecast to be the same as for the year to 30 April Year 2008. The gross profit margin is likely to stay the same as in previous years but expenses (excluding interest payments) are likely to fall by 10 per cent as a result of economies.

The bank has been concerned that the business has persistently exceeded the agreed overdraft limits and, as a result, the business has now been asked to reduce its overdraft to £3 million over the next three months. The business has agreed to do this and has calculated that interest on the bank overdraft for the forthcoming year will be £440,000 (after taking account of the required reduction in the overdraft). In order to achieve the reduction in overdraft, the chairman of Hatleigh plc is considering either the issue of more ordinary shares for cash to existing shareholders at a discount of 20 per cent, or the issue of more 10% loan notes redeemable 2013–14 at the end of July 2008. It is believed that the share price will be £1.50 and the 10% loan notes will be quoted at £82 per £100 nominal value at the end of July 2008. The bank overdraft is expected to remain at the amount shown in the statement of financial position until that date. Any issue costs relating to new shares or loan notes should be ignored.

Required:

(a) Calculate:
   (i) the total number of shares, and
   (ii) the total par value of loan notes
   which will have to be issued in order to raise the funds necessary to reduce the overdraft to the level required by the bank.

(b) Calculate the projected earnings per share for the year to 30 April 2009 assuming:
   (i) the issue of shares, and
   (ii) the issue of loan notes
   are carried out to reduce the overdraft to the level required by the bank.

(c) Critically evaluate the proposal of the chairman to raise the necessary funds by the issue of:
   (i) shares, and
   (ii) loan notes.

8.7 Jubilee plc operates four wholesale food outlets in Scotland. After several years of sales and profits growth the business has recently experienced some financial problems. The financial statements for the year ended 31 May Year 6 are shown below:

Statement of financial position (balance sheet) as at 31 May Year 6

	£000
Non-current assets	
Premises	4,600
Fixtures and fittings	90
Motor vans	115
	4,805
Current assets	
Inventory	5,208
Trade receivables	5,240
Cash	6
Total assets	10,454
Equity	
£1 ordinary shares	1,400
Retained earnings	2,706
	4,106
Non-current liabilities	
11% loan notes Years 10–11 (secured on premises)	3,800
Current liabilities	
Trade payables	4,100
Tax due	53
Bank overdraft	3,200
Total equity and liabilities	7,353

Income statement for the year ended 31 May Year 6

	£000
Sales revenue	45,000
Cost of sales	(36,000)
Gross profit	9,000
Expenses	(7,600)
Operating profit	1,400
Interest payable	(1,050)
Profit before taxation	350
Tax (30%)	(105)
Profit for the year	245

Dividends of £140,000 were proposed and paid during the year.

Inventory levels remained constant throughout the year. All sales and purchases are on credit.

In recent months the business has failed to pay trade payables within the agreed credit periods. In order to restore its credit standing, the business wishes to reduce its trade payables to an average of 30 days' credit (all purchases are on credit). In addition, the business wishes to refurbish its outlets and to acquire a computerised accounting system at a total cost of £700,000. To finance these requirements, the business is considering making a rights issue of shares at a discount of 25 per cent on the market value. At present, shares are trading on the Stock Exchange at £1.60. Alternatively, the business may make an issue of 10% loan notes at a price of £96 per £100 nominal value to be secured on the premises.

In the forthcoming year, sales are expected to increase by 10 per cent and the gross profit margin is likely to remain the same as for the year ended 31 May Year 6. Expenses are likely to rise by 5 per cent during the forthcoming year. Interest charges on the overdraft are expected to be lower, due largely to falling interest rates, at £260,000. Dividends per share are planned to be the same as in the year to 31 May Year 6.

The raising of the necessary finance is expected to take place at the beginning of the year to 31 May Year 7. Issue costs relating to new shares and loan notes can be ignored.

Required:

(a) Treating separately each method of raising finance, calculate:
   (i)   the total number of shares, and
   (ii) the total par (nominal) value of loan notes
   that have to be issued in order to raise the finance required.

(b) Calculate the forecast earnings per share for the year to 31 May Year 7 assuming:
   (i)   a rights issue of shares is made, and
   (ii) an issue of loan notes is made
   to raise the necessary finance.

(c) Calculate the gearing ratio as at 31 May Year 7 assuming:
   (i)   a rights issue of shares is made, and
   (ii) an issue of loan notes is made.

(d) Discuss the major factors to be considered by Jubilee plc when deciding between a rights issue of shares and an issue of loan notes to raise the necessary finance.

Workings should be to the nearest £000.

9

Developing a dividend policy

INTRODUCTION

The issue of dividend policy has aroused much controversy over the years. At the centre of this controversy is whether the pattern of dividends adopted by a business has any effect on shareholders' wealth. In this chapter, we examine the arguments that have been raised. Although the importance of dividend policy to shareholders remains a moot point, there is evidence to suggest that managers perceive the dividend decision to be important. We consider the attitudes of managers towards dividends and examine the factors that are likely to influence dividend policy in practice. We also consider the alternatives to a cash dividend that might be used.

LEARNING OUTCOMES

When you have completed this chapter, you should be able to:

● Describe the nature of dividends and the way in which they are paid.

● Explain why dividends should have no effect on shareholder wealth in a world of perfect and efficient markets.

● Discuss the factors that influence dividend policy in practice.

● Discuss other ways in which cash may be distributed to shareholders.

The payment of dividends

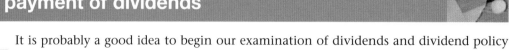

It is probably a good idea to begin our examination of dividends and dividend policy by describing briefly what dividends are and how they are paid. **Dividends** represent a return by a business to its shareholders. This return is normally paid in cash, although it would be possible for it to be paid with assets other than cash. In your previous studies, you may have discovered that there are legal limits on the amount that can be distributed in the form of dividend payments to shareholders.

Activity 9.1

Why does the law impose limits on the amount of cash that can be distributed as dividends?

If there were no legal limits, it would be possible for shareholders to withdraw their investment from the business and so leave the lenders and creditors in an exposed financial position. The law tries to protect lenders and creditors by preventing excessive withdrawals of shareholder capital. One way in which this can be done is through placing restrictions on dividend payments.

The law states that dividends can only be paid to shareholders of private limited companies out of *realised* profits. In essence, the maximum amount available for distribution will be the accumulated trading profits (less any losses) *plus* any profits on the disposal of non-current (fixed) assets. Any surpluses arising from the revaluation of non-current assets will represent an unrealised profit that cannot be distributed. However, shareholders of public companies can be paid out of the net accumulated profits whether the profits are realised or unrealised.

Activity 9.2

Bio-tech Ltd, a private limited company, started trading in Year 1 and made a trading profit of £200,000 in this year. In Year 2, the business made a trading loss of £150,000 but made a profit on the sale of its buildings of £30,000. Other non-current assets were revalued during the year leading to an increase in the revaluation reserve of £60,000. Assuming that no dividend was paid in Year 1, what is the maximum dividend that could be paid by Bio-tech Ltd in Year 2?

Bio-tech Ltd is a private limited company, hence the maximum dividend is calculated as follows:

	£
Trading profit Year 1	200,000
Profit on sale of non-current asset Year 6	30,000
	230,000
Trading loss Year 2	(150,000)
Maximum amount available for distribution	80,000

Businesses rarely make dividend payments based on the maximum amount available for distribution. The dividend paid is normally much lower than the trading profits for the particular year and so will 'cover' the dividend payment by a comfortable margin.

Dividends can also take the form of bonus shares. Instead of receiving cash, the shareholders may receive additional shares in the business. We consider this particular form of dividend (often referred to as a scrip dividend) later in the chapter.

Dividends are often paid twice yearly by large listed businesses. The first dividend is paid after the interim (half yearly) results have been announced and is a sort of 'payment on account'. The second and final dividend is paid after the year end. The final dividend will be paid after the annual financial reports have been published, and after the shareholders have agreed, at the annual general meeting, to the dividend payment proposed by the directors.

As shares are bought and sold continuously by investors, it is important to establish which investors have the right to receive the dividends declared. To do this, a **record date** is set by the business. Investors whose names appear in the share register on the record date will receive the dividends payable. When the share prices quoted on the Stock Exchange include accrued dividends payable, they are said to be quoted **cum dividend**. However, on a specified day before the record date, the quoted share prices will exclude the accrued dividend and so will become **ex dividend**. Assuming no other factors affect the share price, the ex-dividend price should be lower than the cum dividend price by the amount of the dividend payable. This is because a new shareholder would not qualify for the dividend and so the share price can be expected to fall by the amount of the dividend.

Most listed businesses produce a financial calendar for investors. The calendar, which is often included in the published financial reports and websites, sets out the key dates for investors for the forthcoming year. **Real World 9.1** provides an example of such a calendar for a large business.

REAL WORLD 9.1

Financial calendar

The 2008 financial calendar for The Admiral Group plc, an insurance business, is shown below.

Financial Calendar

Next Event

Tuesday 4 March 2008	2007 Full Year Results

Date	*Event*
Wednesday 09 April 2008	Final 2007 Ex Dividend
Friday 11 April 2008	Final 2007 Dividend Record Date
Tuesday 29 April 2008	Annual General Meeting
Wednesday 07 May 2008	Final 2007 Dividend Payment Date
Wednesday 30 July 2008	2008 Interim Results
Wednesday 27 August 2008	Interim 2008 Ex Dividend
Friday 29 August 2008	Interim 2008 Dividend Record Date
Thursday 25 September 2008	Interim 2008 Payment Date

Source: www.admiralgroup.co.uk.

Dividend policies in practice

It was mentioned above that businesses rarely distribute all of the profits available to shareholders in the form of dividend. Usually, the dividends paid are lower than the profits available for this purpose. The extent to which the profits generated during a particular period, and available for distribution, cover the dividend payment can be expressed in the **dividend cover ratio**. This ratio is calculated as follows:

$$\text{Dividend cover} = \frac{\text{Earnings for the year available for dividends}}{\text{Dividends announced for the year}}$$

The dividend cover ratio has already been discussed in Chapter 3. We may recall that the higher the ratio, the lower the risk that dividends to shareholders will be affected by adverse trading conditions. The inverse of this ratio is known as the **dividend payout ratio**, which was also discussed in Chapter 3. The lower this ratio, the lower the risk that dividends will be affected by adverse trading conditions.

In practice, businesses often express their dividend policy based on a target dividend cover ratio, or target dividend payout ratio. They may also express their policy in the form of a target for a particular rate of growth in dividends. **Real World 9.2** provides a recent example of each.

REAL WORLD 9.2

Dividend policies

J. Sainsbury plc, the supermarket chain, has stated that:

> Going forward we expect dividend cover to range between 1.5 times and 1.75 times.

Cadburyschweppes plc, the confectioner, has stated:

> The Board intends to target a dividend payout ratio of 40%–50% with a higher payout ratio in the near term reflecting confidence in the earnings potential of the new Group.

National Grid, the energy group, has outlined plans to:

> raise its dividend by 15 per cent this year and then by 8 per cent a year until 2012, reflecting the energy group's confidence in its growth prospects.

Sources: (1) J. Sainsbury plc, 'Preliminary Results for the 52 weeks ended 24 March 2007'; (2) Press release, 19 June 2007, www.cadburyschweppes.com; (3) Rebecca Bream, 'Dividends to rise at National Grid', www.ft.com, 1 February 2008.

Real World 9.3 provides an impression of the average dividend coverage ratios for listed businesses in selected industries. The factors that determine the particular level of dividend cover adopted are considered later in the chapter.

REAL WORLD 9.3

Dividend coverage ratios

Figure 9.1 shows the average dividend coverage ratios chosen by listed businesses in a range of industries.

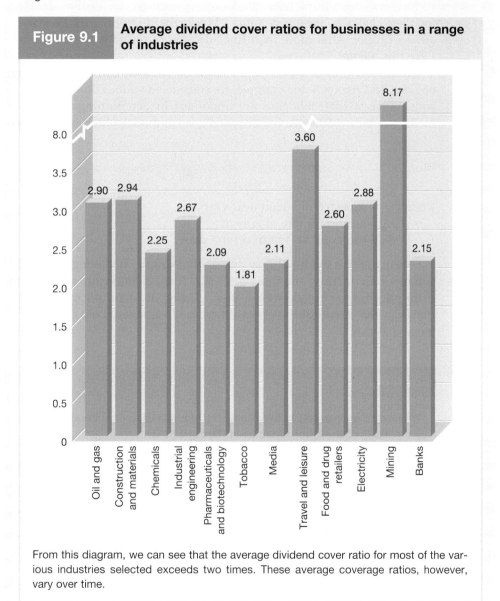

Figure 9.1	Average dividend cover ratios for businesses in a range of industries

From this diagram, we can see that the average dividend cover ratio for most of the various industries selected exceeds two times. These average coverage ratios, however, vary over time.

Source: Compiled from data in *Financial Times*, 25 January 2008, p. 36.

Dividend cover ratios vary between countries based on the particular conditions that exist. Where there is access to capital markets, profit retention becomes less important for businesses and so dividend distributions can be higher. Other factors, such as the treatment of dividends for taxation purposes can also have an influence.

Dividend policy and shareholder wealth

Much of the interest surrounding dividend policy has been concerned with the relationship between dividend policy and shareholder wealth. Put simply, the key question to be answered is: can the pattern of dividends adopted by a business influence shareholder wealth? (Note that it is the *pattern* of dividends rather than dividends themselves which is the issue. Shareholders must receive cash at some point in order for their shares to have any value.) While the question may be stated simply, the answer cannot. After more than three decades of research and debate we have yet to solve this puzzle.

The notion that dividend policy is important may seem, on the face of it, to be obvious. In Chapter 8, for example, we considered various dividend valuation models, which suggest that dividends are important in determining share price. One such model, we may recall, was the dividend growth model which is as follows:

$$P_0 = \frac{D_1}{K_0 - g}$$

where: D_1 = expected dividend next year
g = a constant rate of growth
K_0 = the expected return on the share.

Looking at this model, it may appear that simply increasing the dividend (D_1) will automatically increase the share price (P_0). If the relationship between dividends and share price was as just described, then, clearly, dividend policy would be important. However, the relationship between these two variables is not likely to be as straightforward as this.

Activity 9.3

Why might an increase in the dividend (D_1) not lead to an increase in share price (P_0)? (*Hint*: Think of the other variables in the equation.)

An increase in dividend payments will only result in an increase in share price if there is no consequential effect on the dividend growth rate. It is likely, however, that an increase in dividend will result in a fall in this growth rate, as there will be less cash to invest in the business. Thus, the beneficial effect on share price arising from an increase in next year's dividend may be cancelled out by a decrease in future years' dividends.

The traditional view of dividends

The dividend policy issue, like the capital structure issue discussed in the previous chapter, has two main schools of thought: the traditional view and the modernist view. The early finance literature accepted the view that dividend policy was important for shareholders. It was argued that a shareholder would prefer to receive £1 today rather than to have £1 reinvested in the business, even though this might yield future dividends. The reasoning for this was that future dividends (or capital gains) are less certain and so will be valued less highly. The saying 'a bird in the hand is worth two in the bush' is often used to describe this argument. Thus, if a business decides to replace an immediate and certain cash dividend with uncertain future dividends, shareholders will discount the future dividends at a higher rate in order to take account of this greater uncertainty. Referring back to the dividend growth model, the traditional view suggests that K_0 will rise if there is an increase in D_1, as dividends received later will not be valued so highly.

If this line of reasoning is correct, the effect of applying a higher discount rate to future dividends will mean that the share value of businesses that adopt a high retention policy will be adversely affected. The implication for managers is, therefore, quite clear. They should adopt as generous a dividend distribution policy as possible, given the investment and financing policies of the business, as this will represent the optimal dividend policy for the business. As the level of payout will affect shareholder wealth, the dividend payment decision will be an important policy decision for managers.

The modernist (MM) view of dividends

Miller and Modigliani (MM) have challenged this view of dividend policy. They argue that, given perfect and efficient markets, the pattern of dividend payments adopted by a business will have no effect on shareholder wealth. Where such markets exist, the wealth of shareholders will be affected solely by the investment projects that the business undertakes. To maximise shareholder wealth, therefore, the business should take on all investment projects that have a positive NPV. The way in which the returns from these investment projects are divided between dividends and retention is unimportant. Thus, a decision to pay a lower dividend will simply be compensated for by an increase in share price.

MM point out that it is possible for an individual investor to 'adjust' the dividend policy of a business to conform to his or her particular requirements. If a business does not pay a dividend, the shareholder can create 'home-made' dividends by selling a portion of the shares held. If, on the other hand, a business provides a dividend that the shareholder does not wish to receive, the amount can be reinvested in additional shares in the business. In view of this fact, there is no reason for an investor to value the shares of one business more highly than another simply because it adopts a particular dividend policy.

The implications of the MM position for managers are quite different from the implications of the traditional position described earlier. The MM view suggests that there is no such thing as an optimal dividend policy, and that one policy is as good as another (that is, the dividend decision is irrelevant to shareholder wealth). Thus managers should not spend time considering the most appropriate policy to adopt, but should, instead, devote their energies to finding and managing profitable investment opportunities.

The MM position explained

MM believe that dividends simply represent a movement of funds from inside the business to outside the business. This change in the location of funds should not have any effect on shareholder wealth. The MM position is set out in Example 9.1.

Example 9.1

Merton plc has the following statement of financial position as at 31 December Year 5:

Statement of financial position (balance sheet) as at 31 December Year 5

	£000
Assets at market value (exc. cash)	60
Cash	30
Total assets	90
Ordinary (equity) capital (30,000 shares) plus reserves	90

Suppose that the business decides to distribute all the cash available (that is, £30,000) to shareholders by making a 100p dividend per share. This will result in a fall in the value of assets to £60,000 (that is, £90,000 – £30,000) and a fall in the value of its shares from £3 (that is, £90,000/30,000) to £2 (that is, £60,000/30,000). The statement of financial position following the dividend payment will therefore be as follows:

Statement of financial position (balance sheet) following the dividend payment

	£000
Assets at market value (exc. cash)	60
Cash	–
Total assets	60
Ordinary (equity) capital (30,000 shares) plus reserves	60

Before the dividend distribution, an investor holding 10 per cent of the shares in Merton Ltd will have:

	£
3,000 shares at £3 per share	9,000

Following the distribution, the investor will have:

3,000 shares at £2 per share	6,000
plus a cash dividend of 3,000 × £1.00	3,000
	9,000

In other words, the total wealth of the investor remains the same.

If the investor did not want to receive the dividends, the cash received could be used to purchase more shares in the business. Although the number of shares held by the investor will change as a result of this decision, his or her *total wealth* will remain the same. If, on the other hand, Merton Ltd did not issue a dividend, and the investor wished to receive one, he or she could create the desired dividend by simply selling a portion of the shares held. Once again, this will change the number of shares held by the investor, but will not change the total amount of wealth held.

What about the effect of a dividend payment on the amounts available for investment? We may feel that a high dividend payment will mean that less can be retained by the business, and this may, in turn, mean that the business will be unable to invest in projects that have a positive NPV. If this occurs, then shareholder wealth will be adversely affected. However, if we assume perfect and efficient capital markets exist, the business will be able to raise the finance required for investment purposes and will not have to rely on profit retention. In other words, dividend policy and investment policy can be regarded as quite separate issues.

The wealth of existing shareholders should not be affected by raising finance from new issues rather than retention. Activity 9.4 reinforces this point.

Activity 9.4

Suppose that Merton plc (see Example 9.1) replaces the £30,000 paid out as dividends by an issue of shares to new shareholders. Show the statement of financial position after the new issue and calculate the value of shares held by existing shareholders after the issue.

The statement of financial position following the new issue will be almost the same as before the dividend payment was made. However, the number of shares in issue will increase. If we assume that the new shares can be issued at a fair value (that is, current market value), the number of shares in issue will increase by 15,000 shares (£30,000/£2.00 = 15,000).

Statement of financial position (balance sheet) following the issue of new shares

	£000
Assets at market value (exc. cash)	60
Cash	30
	90
Ordinary (equity) capital (45,000 shares) plus reserves	90

The existing shareholders will own 30,000 of the 45,000 shares in issue and will therefore own net assets worth £60,000 (30,000/45,000 × £90,000). In other words, their wealth will not be affected by the financing decision.

What about the traditional argument in support of dividend policy (that is, should investors prefer 'a bird in the hand')? The answer to this question is: probably not. The problem with the argument described earlier is that it is based on a misconception of the nature of risk. The risks borne by a shareholder will be determined by the level of business borrowing and the nature of the business operations. These risks do not necessarily increase over time and are not affected by the dividend policy of the business. Dividends will only reduce risk if the amount received by the shareholder is then placed in a less risky form of investment (with a lower level of return). This could equally be achieved, however, through the sale of the shares in the business.

Activity 9.5

There is one situation where even MM would accept that 'a bird in the hand is worth two in the bush' (that is, that immediate dividends are preferable). Can you think what it is? (*Hint*: Think of the way in which shareholder wealth is increased.)

Shareholder wealth is increased by the business accepting projects that have a positive NPV. If the business starts to accept projects with a negative NPV, this would decrease shareholder wealth. In such circumstances, a rational shareholder would prefer to receive a dividend rather than to allow the business to reinvest the profits of the business.

The MM assumptions

The logic of the MM arguments has proved to be unassailable and it is now widely accepted that, in a world of perfect and efficient capital markets, dividend policy should have no effect on shareholder wealth. The burning issue, however, is whether or not the MM analysis can be applied to the real world of imperfect markets. There are three key assumptions on which the MM analysis rests, and which have aroused much debate. These assumptions are, in essence, that we live in a 'frictionless' world where there are:

- no share issue costs
- no share transaction costs, and
- no taxation.

The first assumption means that money paid out in dividends can be replaced by the business through a new share issue without incurring additional costs. Thus, a business need not be deterred from paying a dividend simply because it needs cash to invest in a profitable project, as the amount can be costlessly replaced. In the real world, however, share issue costs can be significant.

The second assumption means that investors can make 'home-made' dividends or reinvest in the business at no extra cost. In other words, there are no barriers to investors pursuing their own dividend and investment strategies. Once again, in the real world, costs will be incurred when shares are purchased or sold by investors. The creation of 'home-made' dividends as a substitute for business dividend policy may pose other practical problems for the shareholder, such as the indivisibility of shares, resulting in shareholders being unable to sell the exact amount of shares required, and the difficulty of selling shares in unlisted companies. These problems, it is argued, can lead to investors becoming reliant on the dividend policy of the business as a means of receiving cash income. It can also lead them to have a preference for one business rather than another, because of the dividend policies adopted.

The third assumption concerning taxation is unrealistic and, in practice, tax may be an important issue for investors. It is often argued that, in the UK, the taxation rules can have a significant influence on investor preferences. It may be more tax efficient for an investor to receive benefits in the form of capital gains rather than dividends because, below a certain threshold (£9,200 or less for 2007/08), capital gains arising during a particular financial year are not taxable, whereas all dividends are taxable. In addition, it is possible for an investor to influence the timing of capital gains by choosing when to sell shares, whereas the timing of dividends is normally outside the investor's control.

Activity 9.6

In a world where taxation is an important issue for investors, how will the particular dividend policy adopted by a business affect its share price?

If, as a result of the tax system, investors prefer capital gains to dividends, a business with a high dividend payout ratio would be valued less than a similar business with a low payout ratio.

Although differences between the tax treatment of dividend income and capital gains still exist, changes in taxation policy have narrowed these differences in recent years. One important policy change has been the creation of tax shelters (for example, Individual Savings Accounts, or ISAs), which allow investors to receive dividend income and capital gains free of taxation.

The three assumptions discussed undoubtedly weaken the MM analysis when applied to the real world. However, this does not necessarily mean that their analysis is destroyed. Indeed, the research evidence tends to support their position. One direct way to assess the validity of MM's arguments, in the real world, is to see whether there is a positive relationship between the dividends paid by businesses and their share price. If such a relationship exists then MM's arguments would lose their force. The majority of studies, however, have failed to find any significant correlation between dividends and share prices.

The importance of dividends

Whether or not we accept the MM analysis, there is little doubt that, in practice, the pattern of dividends is seen by investors and corporate managers to be important. It seems that there are three possible reasons to explain this phenomenon. These are:

- the clientele effect
- the information signalling effect
- the need to reduce agency costs.

Each of these is considered below.

The clientele effect

It was mentioned earlier that share transaction costs may result in investors becoming reliant on the dividend policies of businesses. It was also argued that the tax position of investors can exert an influence on whether dividends or capital gains are preferred. These factors may, in practice, mean that dividend policy will exert an important influence on investor behaviour. Investors may seek out businesses whose dividend policies match closely their particular needs. Thus, businesses with particular dividend policies may attract particular types of investors. This phenomenon is referred to as the **clientele effect**.

The existence of a clientele effect has important implications for managers. First, dividend policy should be clearly set out and consistently applied. Investors attracted to a particular business because of its dividend policy will not welcome unexpected changes. Secondly, managers need not concern themselves with trying to accommodate all the different needs of shareholders. The particular distribution policy adopted by the business will tend to attract a certain type of investor depending on his or her cash needs and taxation position.

Investors should be wary, however, of making share investment decisions based primarily on dividend policy. Minimising costs may not be an easy process for investors. Those, for example, requiring a regular cash income, and who seek out businesses with high dividend payout ratios, may find that any savings in transaction costs are cancelled out by incurring other forms of cost.

Activity 9.7

What kind of costs may be borne by investors who invest in high-dividend payout businesses, do you think?

Being committed to a high-dividend payout may prevent a business from investing in profitable projects that would have increased shareholder wealth. Hence, there could be a loss of future benefits for the investor. If, however, a business decides to raise finance to replace the amount distributed in dividends, the cost of raising the required finance will be borne by existing shareholders.

Investors must, therefore, look beyond the dividend policy of a business in order to make a sensible investment decision.

The evidence concerning the clientele effect is fairly mixed. Although there are studies, based on both US and UK data, that support the existence of a clientele effect, other studies have cast doubt on these findings. More research, perhaps using different approaches to examining the issue, is required for a clearer picture to emerge.

Information signalling

In an imperfect world, managers of a business will have greater access to information regarding the profits and performance of the business than investors. This **information asymmetry**, as it is called, between managers and investors allows dividends to be used by managers as a means of passing on to investors information concerning the business. Thus, new information relating to future prospects may be signalled through changes in dividend policy. If, for example, managers are confident about the business's prospects, there may be **information signalling** to this effect through an increase in dividends.

Activity 9.8

Why would managers wish to use dividends as a means of conveying information about the business's prospects? Why not simply issue a statement to shareholders? Try to think of at least one reason why managers may prefer a less direct approach.

At least three reasons have been put forward to explain why dividend signalling may be preferred. First, it may be that the managers do not want to disclose the precise nature of the events that improve the business's prospects. Suppose, for example, that a business has signed a large government defence contract, which will be formally announced by the government at some time in the future. In the intervening period, however, the price of the shares in the business may be depressed and the managers may be concerned that the business is vulnerable to a takeover. The managers might, under the circumstances, wish to boost the share price without specifying the nature of the good news.

Secondly, issuing a statement about, say, improved future prospects may not be convincing, particularly if earlier statements by managers have proved incorrect. Statements are 'cheap' whereas an increase in dividends would be more substantial evidence of the managers' confidence in the future. Thirdly, managers may feel that an explicit statement concerning future prospects will attract criticism from shareholders if things do not work out as expected. They may, therefore, prefer more coded messages to avoid being held to account at a later date.

Sending a positive signal to the market by increasing dividends is an expensive way to send a message. It may also seem wasteful (particularly where investors do not wish to receive higher dividends for tax reasons). However, it may be the only feasible way of ensuring that investors take seriously the good news that managers wish to convey.

Various studies have been carried out to establish the 'information content' of dividends. Some of these studies have looked at the share price reaction to *unexpected* changes in dividends. If signalling exists, an unexpected dividend announcement should result in a significant share price reaction. The results from these studies suggest that signalling does exist, that is, a dividend increase (positive signal) results in an increase in share price, and a dividend decrease (negative signal) results in a decrease in share price. One interesting feature of the evidence is that the market reaction to dividend reductions is much greater than the market reaction to dividend increases. It appears that investors regard dividend reductions much more seriously.

Real World 9.4 provides a recent example of how the signalling effect can add to the problems of determining an appropriate dividend for the year.

REAL WORLD 9.4

Bankers' dilemma   FT

As senior bank executives prepare to update investors on their results, they are paying even closer attention than usual to their year-end dividend payments.

As the sell-off in UK bank shares has gathered pace in recent months, the dividend yield for the sector has risen to 7.5 per cent – a level that suggests investors believe dividends cannot be sustained.

However, Credit Suisse analysts say every big UK bank is expected to increase its final dividend, after boosting the pay-out at the half-year stage.

This leaves banks with a difficult decision: any increase in the final dividend will be interpreted as a signal the bank can sustain a higher pay-out in spite of the downturn.

However, if any bank decided just to maintain the final dividend at the same level as last year, this would be widely interpreted as a dividend cut.

Source: 'Focus on dividend payments', www.ft.com, 18 February 2008.

Reducing agency costs

In recent years, *agency theory* has become increasingly influential in the financial management literature. Agency theory views a business as a coalition of different interest groups (managers, shareholders, lenders, and so on) in which each group is seeking to maximise its own welfare. According to this theory, one group connected with the business may engage in behaviour that results in costs being borne by another group. However, the latter group may try to restrain the action of the former group, through contractual or other arrangements, so as to minimise these costs. Two examples of where a conflict of interest arises between groups, and the impact on dividend policy, are considered below.

The first example concerns a conflict of interest between shareholders and managers. If the managers (who are agents of the shareholders) decide to invest in lavish offices, expensive cars and other 'perks', they will be pursuing their own interests at a cost to the shareholders. (This potential conflict was briefly discussed in Chapter 1.) Shareholders may avoid incurring these agency costs, however, by reducing the cash available for managers to spend. They may insist that surplus cash be distributed to them in the form of a dividend. Managers may decide to support this policy to demonstrate their commitment to the shareholders' interests. Agency costs can prevent managers from receiving full recognition for their achievements, and helping to reduce these costs could be to their benefit.

The second example concerns a conflict between shareholders and lenders. Shareholders may seek to reduce their stake in the business by withdrawing cash in the form of dividends. This may be done to reduce their exposure to the risks associated with the business. However, this is likely to be to the detriment of lenders, who will become more exposed to these risks. The lenders may, therefore, try to prevent this kind of behaviour by restricting the level of dividends to be paid to shareholders.

Activity 9.9

How can lenders go about restricting shareholders' rights to dividends? (*Hint*: Think back to Chapter 6.)

Lenders can insist that loan covenants, which restrict the level of dividend payable, be included in the loan agreement.

Agency costs will be more of an issue where there is a clear separation between the shareholders and the managers of the business.

Figure 9.2 sets out the main reasons why dividends seem to be important in the real world.

Figure 9.2   Reasons for the importance of dividends

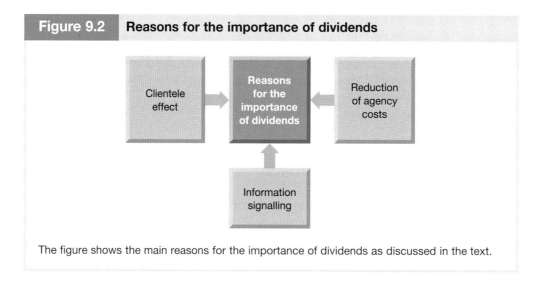

The figure shows the main reasons for the importance of dividends as discussed in the text.

Factors determining the level of dividends

We have now seen that there are three possible reasons why investors and managers regard dividends as being important. In addition, there are various issues that have a bearing on the level of dividends paid by a business. These include the following.

Investment opportunities

Businesses that have good investment opportunities may try to retain profits rather than distribute them. As we saw in Chapter 6, retained profits come first in the 'pecking order' when raising long-term finance, and are easily the most important source of long-term finance for businesses.

Investment opportunities may vary over the life cycle of a business and so its retention/dividend policies may also vary. In the early phase, when businesses are growing quickly, a policy of either low dividends or no dividends may be chosen in order to retain profits for reinvestment, but at a more mature stage of the business cycle, when investment opportunities are restricted, a policy of higher dividends may be chosen.

Real World 9.5 provides an example of how one business varied its dividend policy over time.

REAL WORLD 9.5

The joys of middle age   FT

With depressing regularity, we are told that it is essential to plan early for our later years. Surely this applies to companies as well as individuals? And perhaps even to one that is, rightly, lauded as one of Asia's great corporate growth stories at the moment: Samsung Electronics.

This year will be Samsung's best yet. Net profits at the high-tech conglomerate are expected to more than double to $10bn – more than Dell and Nokia put together, as South Korean analysts have gleefully pointed out. But 2004 could also turn out to be a high-water mark for Samsung.

The growth rate for semiconductors, which contributes half of operating profits, is likely to halve to single digits in the coming year – as most chip-makers, including Samsung and most recently Philips, have warned. Margins on mobile phones and prices of liquid crystal displays, the other two money spinners, are also under pressure. All in all, Samsung is unlikely to be firing on all cylinders again for quite a while and consensus estimates expect a 12 per cent drop in earnings in 2005.

Beyond the various industry cycles it is exposed to, Samsung faces the trickier problem of increasing size. With revenues above $50bn, it is now so large that it will take a spectacular new best-seller to have much impact on its top and bottom lines. It seems likely, therefore, that when profit growth resumes in 2006, as analysts expect, it will be more sedentary. LG Securities forecasts compound three-year earnings growth of less than 10 per cent for 2005, compared with 35 per cent over the past three years.

Encouragingly, Samsung has recently started to acknowledge its approaching maturity – at least implicitly. In July, the group doubled its interim dividend and earlier this month it announced a $1.75bn share buy-back, its fourth in two years. Taken together, this amounts to a payout ratio of nearly 50 per cent for the first half of 2004. Assuming a similarly sized final dividend, Samsung will hand back about 30 per cent of its annual profits to shareholders.

Source: 'Samsung and the joys of middle age: sharing out the cash', www.ft.com, 27 September 2004.

Financing opportunities

In some cases, raising external finance for new investment may be a problem and so profit retention may be the only option available. It can be argued that, where such a problem exists, and investors are indifferent about dividends, it would make sense for managers to regard dividends as simply a residual, that is, the managers should make dividend distributions only where the expected return from investment opportunities is below the required return for investors. The implication of this policy is that dividends could fluctuate each year according to the investment opportunities available: the greater the investment needs of the business, the less that is available for distribution, and vice versa. This line of argument is consistent with the **residual theory of dividends**. Where, however, a business is able to finance easily and cheaply from external sources, there is less need to rely on retained profits, which can then be distributed in the form of dividends.

Legal requirements

Company law restricts the amount that a business can distribute in the form of dividends. We saw earlier that the law states that, for private limited companies, dividends can only be paid to shareholders out of *realised* profits. In essence, the maximum amount available for distribution will be the accumulated trading profits (less any losses) plus any profits on the disposal of assets.

Loan commitments

There may be covenants included in a loan contract that restrict the level of dividends available for distribution to shareholders during the loan period. These covenants, as we saw in Chapter 6, are designed to protect the lenders' investment in the business. Even where a loan agreement does not impose any restriction on dividend payments, a business must retain its capacity to make interest and debt payments when they fall due. **Real World 9.6** provides an example of a business that is expected to cut its dividend for this reason.

REAL WORLD 9.6

When things go stale   **FT**

Shares of Premier Foods, owner of the Hovis bread brand, have tumbled 70 per cent in the past year and closed at a record low of 97p yesterday, down 9p on the day. The fall came amid concerns the group would cut its dividend next month to avoid defaulting on its debt payments.

Premier is believed to be trying to push through a 6p price rise on its Hovis bread with supermarkets over the next two months as its finances are squeezed by record wheat prices. This would be on top of two price rises last year.

Source: 'Premier Foods reaches its nadir', www.ft.com, 26 February 2008.

Profit stability

Businesses that have a stable pattern of profits over time are in a better position to make higher dividend payouts than businesses that have a volatile pattern of profits.

Activity 9.10

Why should this be the case?

Businesses that have a stable pattern of profits are able to plan with greater certainty and are less likely to feel a need to retain profits for unexpected events.

Control

A high profit retention/low dividend policy can help avoid the need to issue new shares, and so existing shareholders' control will not be diluted. (Even though existing shareholders have pre-emptive rights, they may not always be in a position to purchase new shares issued by the business.)

Threat of takeover

A further aspect of control concerns the relationship between dividend payments and the threat of takeover. It has been suggested, for example, that a high retention/low distribution policy can increase the vulnerability of a business to takeover.

Activity 9.11

Why might it be suggested that a low payout policy increases the threat of takeover? Is this a very convincing point?

If a predator is seeking to acquire the business, it may be able to convince shareholders that the dividends paid are too low and that the existing management is not maximising their wealth. Thus, a low dividend policy may make the task of acquisition much easier. Such arguments, however, are only likely to appeal to unsophisticated shareholders. More sophisticated shareholders will recognise that dividends represent only part of the total return from the shares held. (However, if profits are retained rather than distributed, they must be employed in a profitable manner. Failure to do this will make the threat of takeover greater.)

Dividend policy may, however, help avert the threat of takeover. Issuing a large dividend may signal to the market the managers' confidence in the prospects of the business. This should, in turn, increase the value of the shares and so make a takeover more costly for the predator business. However, the market may not necessarily interpret a large dividend in this way. Investors may regard a large dividend as a desperate attempt by the directors to gain their support and so will discount the dividend received.

Real World 9.7 cites an example of a dividend increase that some interpreted as a defensive move.

REAL WORLD 9.7

On the defensive?

FT

Scottish and Southern Energy has unveiled a new dividend policy, including an 18 per cent increase in this year's pay-out, triggering talk that it is defending itself against a possible takeover.

The energy group said yesterday it would propose a final dividend for the year to the end of March of 39.9p, bringing the total to 55p, 18.3 per cent higher than for last year. SSE added that the higher pay-out this year would provide 'a significantly higher base for future dividend growth'.

For the next three years, the company intends to deliver dividend growth of at least 4 per cent a year, with 'at least sustained real growth in dividend' in future years. The new policy replaces a previous aim of at least 4 per cent growth this year and next with sustained growth thereafter.

SSE's shares bucked the market trend and rose more than 20p early yesterday but slipped back to close just 1p higher at £14.66.

Some analysts said SSE's dividend increase could be interpreted as a defensive move. The battle to control Endesa, the Spanish energy company, has led to widespread speculation about which European utility will be next to be taken over, with SSE seen as an obvious target.

Source: Rebecca Bream and Toby Shelley, 'SSE to raise dividend 18 per cent in new pay-out policy', www.ft.com, 6 March 2007.

Market expectations

Investors may have developed certain expectations concerning the level of dividend to be paid. These expectations may be formed as a result of earlier statements made by the managers of the business. If these expectations are not met, there may be a loss of investor confidence in the business.

Inside information

The managers of a business may have inside information concerning the prospects of a business which cannot be published but which indicates that the shares are currently undervalued by investors. In such a situation, it may be sensible to rely on internal shareholder funds (that is, retained profit) rather than issuing more shares. Although this may lead to lower dividends, it could enhance the wealth of the existing shareholders.

Figure 9.3 sets out the main influences on the level of dividends declared by a business.

The dividend policy of other businesses

The dividend policy adopted by a business may be considered in relation to those of other comparable businesses. Indeed, it has been suggested that investors make comparisons between businesses and that a significant deviation in dividend policy from

Figure 9.3	**Factors influencing the level of dividends**

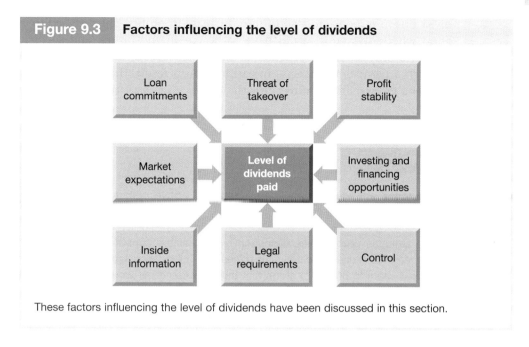

These factors influencing the level of dividends have been discussed in this section.

the sector norm will attract criticism. The implication seems to be that managers should shape the dividend policy of their business according to what comparable businesses are doing. This however, may be neither practical nor desirable.

To begin with, there is the problem of identifying comparable businesses. In practice, there may be real differences between businesses concerning risk characteristics, rate of growth and accounting policies adopted. There may also be real differences between businesses concerning the influences mentioned above such as investment opportunities, loan covenants, and so on. Even if comparable businesses could be found, the use of such businesses as a benchmark assumes that they adopt dividend polices that are optimal, which may not be the case.

These problems suggest that dividend policy is best determined according to the particular requirements of the business. If the policy adopted differs from the norm, the managers should be able to provide reasons to investors.

Dividend policy and management attitudes: some evidence

An interesting aspect of dividend policy concerns the attitudes and behaviour of managers. One of the earliest pieces of research on this topic was undertaken in the USA by Lintner (see reference 1 at the end of the chapter) who carried out interviews with managers in 28 businesses. Although this research is now quite old, it is still considered to be one of the most accurate descriptions of how managers set dividend policy in practice.

Lintner found that managers considered the dividend decision to be an important one and were committed to long-term target dividend payout ratios. He also found that managers were concerned more with variations in dividends than with the absolute amount of dividends paid. Managers held the view that investors preferred a smooth increase in dividends payments over time and were reluctant to increase the level of dividends in response to a short-term increase in profits. They wished to avoid a situation where dividends would have to be cut in the future, and so dividends were increased only when it was felt that the higher level of dividends could be sustained through a permanent increase in earnings. As a result, there was a time lag between dividend growth and earnings growth.

Activity 9.12

Are these attitudes of managers described above consistent with another view of dividends discussed earlier?

The attitudes of managers described by Lintner are consistent with more recent work concerning the use of dividends as a means of information signalling. The managers interviewed seem to be aware of the fact that a dividend cut would send negative signals to investors.

In a later study, Fama and Babiak (see reference 2 at the end of the chapter) found that businesses distributed about half of their profits in the form of dividends. However, significant increases in earnings would only be followed by a *partial adjustment* to dividends in the first year. On average, the increase in dividends in the first year was only about one-third of the increase that would have been consistent with maintaining the target payout ratio. The smooth and gradual adjustment of dividends to changes in profits revealed by this study is consistent with the earlier study by Lintner and confirms that managers wish to ensure a sustainable level of dividends.

Where a business experiences adverse trading conditions, DeAngelo and others (see reference 3 at the end of the chapter) found that managers are often reluctant to reduce dividend payments immediately. Instead, they will try to maintain the existing level of dividends until it is clear that the former profit levels cannot be achieved. At this point, the managers will usually make a single large reduction, rather than a series of small reductions to a new level of dividends.

An important study by Baker and others (see reference 4 at the end of the chapter) asked US managers to express their views concerning dividend policy. Some of the key findings regarding managers' attitudes are shown in **Real World 9.8**.

 **REAL WORLD 9.8**

Managers' attitudes towards dividends

Baker and others surveyed 188 managers of US, dividend-paying, listed businesses. The researchers wished to establish the views of managers concerning dividend policies adopted, why dividends are important and whether dividends affected the value of the business. Figure 9.4 sets out some of the key statements that managers were asked to consider and their responses.

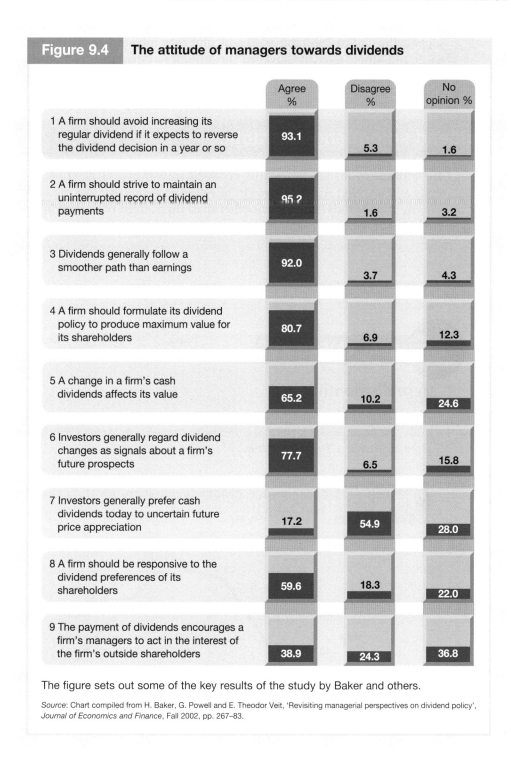

Figure 9.4   The attitude of managers towards dividends

	Agree %	Disagree %	No opinion %
1 A firm should avoid increasing its regular dividend if it expects to reverse the dividend decision in a year or so	93.1	5.3	1.6
2 A firm should strive to maintain an uninterrupted record of dividend payments	95.2	1.6	3.2
3 Dividends generally follow a smoother path than earnings	92.0	3.7	4.3
4 A firm should formulate its dividend policy to produce maximum value for its shareholders	80.7	6.9	12.3
5 A change in a firm's cash dividends affects its value	65.2	10.2	24.6
6 Investors generally regard dividend changes as signals about a firm's future prospects	77.7	6.5	15.8
7 Investors generally prefer cash dividends today to uncertain future price appreciation	17.2	54.9	28.0
8 A firm should be responsive to the dividend preferences of its shareholders	59.6	18.3	22.0
9 The payment of dividends encourages a firm's managers to act in the interest of the firm's outside shareholders	38.9	24.3	36.8

The figure sets out some of the key results of the study by Baker and others.

Source: Chart compiled from H. Baker, G. Powell and E. Theodor Veit, 'Revisiting managerial perspectives on dividend policy', *Journal of Economics and Finance*, Fall 2002, pp. 267–83.

The study reveals that the majority of managers acknowledge the importance of a smooth, uninterrupted pattern of dividends. This is in line with the earlier findings of Lintner. The study also reveals that the majority of managers acknowledge the signalling effect and clientele effect but not the role of dividends in reducing agency costs. These views, therefore, do not chime precisely with the theories concerning why dividends are important. Finally, the study reveals that the majority of managers do not support the bird-in-the-hand argument, and they therefore reject the traditional view. Baker and others recently surveyed the attitudes of managers of Canadian businesses and found similar results to those above. (See reference 5 at the end of the chapter.)

Dividend smoothing in practice

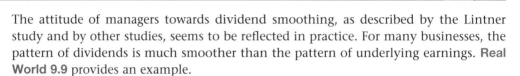

The attitude of managers towards dividend smoothing, as described by the Lintner study and by other studies, seems to be reflected in practice. For many businesses, the pattern of dividends is much smoother than the pattern of underlying earnings. **Real World 9.9** provides an example.

REAL WORLD 9.9

A real smoothie

HMV Group plc is a major music and games retailer. Over the five-year period to 28 April 2007, the basic earnings per share (EPS) and dividend per share (DPS) for the business were as set out in Figure 9.5 below.

Figure 9.5	**Earnings and dividends per share for HMV Group plc over time**

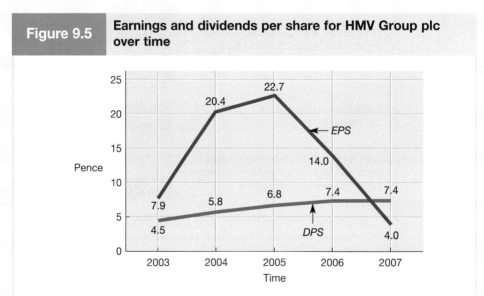

The figure shows that, whereas earnings per share have been fairly erratic, dividends per share have followed a smooth, broadly upward path over the five-year period.

Source: Chart compiled from information in HMV plc Annual Report and Accounts 2007, p. 84.

Self-assessment question 9.1

Sandarajan plc is a business that has recently obtained a listing on the Stock Exchange. The business operates a chain of supermarkets in Northern Ireland and was the subject of a management buy-out five years ago. In the period since the buy-out, the business has grown rapidly. The managers and a private equity firm owned 80 per cent of the shares prior to the Stock Exchange listing. However, this has now been reduced to 20 per cent. The record of the business over the past five years is as follows:

Year	Profit for the year £000	Dividend £000	No. of shares issued 000s
1	420	220	1,000
2	530	140	1,000
3	650	260	1,500
4	740	110	1,500
5 (most recent)	880	460	1,500

Required:

(a) Comment on the dividend policy of the business prior to the Stock Exchange listing.

(b) What advice would you give to the managers of the business concerning future dividend policy?

The answer to this question may be found at the back of the book on p. 536.

What should managers do?

Having read the above sections, you may be wondering what advice we should give to managers who are wrestling with the problem of dividend policy and who are looking for help. Probably the best advice we can give is to make the dividend policy that is adopted clear to investors and then make every effort to keep to that policy. Investors are unlikely to welcome 'surprises' in dividend policy and may react by selling their shares and investing in businesses that have more stable and predictable dividend policies. Uncertainty over dividend policy will lower the value of the business's shares and will increase the cost of capital. If, for any reason, managers have to reduce the dividends for a particular year, they should prepare investors for the change in dividend payout and state clearly the reasons for that change.

Alternatives to cash dividends

In some cases, a business may decide to make distributions to shareholders in a form different from a cash dividend. The two most important of these are scrip dividends and share repurchases. Below we consider each of these options.

Scrip dividends

A business may make a **scrip dividend** (or bonus share dividend) rather than making a cash distribution to shareholders. Thus, if a business announced a 20 per cent scrip dividend this would mean that each shareholder would receive a 20 per cent increase in the number of shares held. We saw in Chapter 6, however, that scrip issues (or bonus issues) do not result in an increase in shareholder wealth. Making a scrip issue is, in essence, a bookkeeping transaction that will not, of itself, create value. Nevertheless, the market may respond positively to a scrip dividend if it is seen as a sign of the directors' confidence concerning the future. The scrip issue may suggest that the directors will maintain the same dividend per share in the future, despite the increase in the number of shares in issue. Various research studies have shown a positive response to scrip dividend announcements by the market. However, if a business does not maintain or increase its dividend per share in subsequent periods, the positive effect on share prices will be lost.

In some cases, shareholders may be given the choice between a scrip dividend and a cash dividend. Those shareholders who choose the scrip dividend will increase their proportion of the total shares issued relative to that held by the shareholders who take the cash option. For tax purposes, shareholders who receive a scrip dividend will be treated, broadly speaking, as having received the cash dividend option from the business.

Share repurchase

In recent years, share repurchases have become a popular way of making distributions to shareholders. They are often undertaken either:

● to return cash to shareholders that is surplus to requirements; or
● to adjust the capital structure to a more suitable level of gearing;

Businesses with surplus cash may prefer to repurchase shares rather than to pay higher dividends. A repurchase has the advantage that it is a one-off event which does not oblige the business to make similar distributions in the future. Although the same effect may be achieved by a 'special' dividend to shareholders, a repurchase focuses on those shareholders wishing to receive cash. There is also the advantage that payments to shareholders can be spread over a longer period.

A repurchase of shares has the effect of reducing the amount of equity in relation to the amount of loan capital within a business. Shareholders may therefore benefit from a gearing effect, which may boost earnings per share and the share price. However, a rise in share price will not automatically occur: the additional benefits of higher gearing must outweigh the additional risks.

In recent years, doubts have emerged concerning the benefits of share repurchases (or 'buy-backs' as they are sometimes called) as a means of improving shareholder returns. **Real World 9.10** describes how one major business appears to have moved away from this form of distributing cash to investors.

REAL WORLD 9.10

To buy-back or not to buy-back?   FT

BP's decision to raise its dividends at the expense of share buy-backs marks a shift in the way the oil group rewards investors.

It also comes at a time of mounting scepticism about whether buy-backs are an effective way of boosting investment performance.

In a buy-back, a company purchases its own shares for cancellation, via a broker, reducing the shares in issue and so boosting earnings per share.

BP has been one of the UK's leading proponents, buying back almost $50bn (£25.5bn) of its own shares since 2000, equal to 16 per cent of its shares in issue.

However, it said yesterday it would 'shift the balance' between buy-backs and dividends as it hiked its quarterly dividend by 31 per cent amid growing confidence that higher oil prices are here to stay.

Although BP has pledged to continue buying back, some analysts argue the method is ineffective.

Keith Macquarie, an analyst at Collins Stewart, recently accused companies of 'destroying billions in shareholder value through ill-judged buy-back decisions' after concluding the excess returns associated with buy-backs were 'negligible'.

Figures from Morgan Stanley have shown the companies that pursued buy-backs in 2006 collectively underperformed the wider market. 'Just doing a buy-back is no guarantee of outperformance. In fact, on average, stocks (shares) that have conducted buy-backs have actually underperformed,' said Graham Secker, strategist at Morgan Stanley.

The popularity of buy-backs has surged in recent years as improved cash-flows have allowed companies to return billions of pounds to shareholders. Mr Secker estimates UK companies bought back about £32bn of their own shares last year, while others put the figures as high as £45bn.

However, the flexibility that makes buy-backs popular with company boards is also its weakness. Mr Secker said: 'Dividends are a much better indicator of corporate confidence. Companies only cut their dividends as a last resort, whereas buy-backs are more transitory.'

BP is a case in point: the company is acutely aware of the embarrassment caused by its humiliating decision in 1992 to cut its dividend in half.

Mr Macquarie applauded the BP move. He said the dividend hike 'sends a positive message, improves certainty of returns and equality of treatment for all shareholders'.

Source: Robert Orr, 'Dividend hike marks shift in investor rewards', www.ft.com, 5 February 2008.

Managers must take care to ensure equity between shareholders during a share repurchase. In some cases, the market may undervalue the shares of a business, perhaps because it does not have access to information known to the managers of the business. If this situation exists, the shareholders who hold on to their shares will benefit at the expense of those who sell. In other cases, the market for shares in the business may be slow and the effect of repurchasing a large number of shares may be to create an artificially high price. This will benefit those who sell at the expense of those who continue to hold shares.

SUMMARY

The main points in this chapter may be summarised as follows:

Dividends

- Dividends represent a return by a business to its shareholders.
- There are legal limits on dividend distributions to protect creditors and lenders.
- They are usually paid twice a year by large businesses.
- Cum dividend share prices include the accrued dividend; ex dividend prices exclude the dividend.
- Businesses often have a target dividend cover ratio or target dividend payout ratio.

Dividend policy and shareholder wealth

- There are two major schools of thought concerning the effect of dividends on share-holder wealth.
- The traditional school argues that investors prefer dividends now because the amounts are more certain.
- The implications for managers are that they should adopt as generous a dividend policy as possible.
- The modernists (MM) argue that, given perfect and efficient markets, the pattern of dividends has no effect on shareholder wealth.
- The implication for managers is that one policy is as good as another and so they should not spend time considering which policy should be adopted.
- The MM position assumes no share issue costs, no share transaction costs and no taxation; these assumptions weaken (but do not necessarily destroy) their arguments.

Dividends in practice

- Dividends appear to be important to investors.
- The clientele effect, signalling effect and the need to reduce agency costs may explain this.
- The level of dividends distributed is dependent on various factors, including: investment and financing opportunities, legal and loan requirements, profit stability, control issues (including takeover threats), market expectations and inside information.

Management attitudes

- Managers perceive dividends as being important for investors.
- They prefer a smooth increase in dividends and are reluctant to cut dividends.

Alternatives to cash dividends

- Scrip dividends are a bookkeeping transaction, but the market may see them as a sign of managers' confidence in the future, and respond positively.
- Share repurchases involve repurchasing and then cancelling shares.

→ Key terms

Dividend p. 364	**Clientele effect** p. 373
Record date p. 365	**Information asymmetry** p. 374
Cum dividend p. 365	**Information signalling** p. 374
Ex dividend p. 365	**Residual theory of dividends** p. 378
Dividend cover ratio p. 366	**Scrip dividend** p. 386
Dividend payout ratio p. 366	

For definitions of these terms see the Glossary, pp. 574–583.

References

1 'Distribution of incomes of corporations among dividends, retained earnings and taxes', *Lintner, J.*, **American Economic Review**, no. 46, May 1956, pp. 97–113.

2 'Dividend policy: an empirical analysis', *Fama, E. F. and Babiak, H.*, **Journal of the American Statistical Association**, December 1968.

3 'Dividends and losses', *DeAngelo, H., DeAngelo, L. and Skinner, D.*, **Journal of Finance**, December 1992, pp. 281–9.

4 'Revisiting managerial perspectives on dividend policy', *Baker, H., Powell, G. and Theodore Veit, E.*, **Journal of Economics and Finance**, Fall 2002, pp. 267–83.

5 'The perception of dividends by Canadian managers: New survey evidence', *Baker, H., Saadi, S. and Dutta, S.*, **International Journal of Managerial Finance**, Vol. 3, No. 1, 2007, pp. 70–91.

Further reading

If you wish to explore the topics discussed in this chapter in more depth, try the following books:

Business Finance: Theory and practice, *McLaney, E.*, 8th edn., Financial Times Prentice Hall, 2009, chapter 12.

Corporate Finance and Investment, *Pike, R. and Neale, B.*, 5th edn., Financial Times Prentice Hall, 2006, chapter 17.

Corporate Financial Management, *Arnold, G.*, 3rd edn., Financial Times Prentice Hall, 2005, chapter 22.

Principles of Corporate Finance, *Brealey, F., Myers, S. and Allen, F.*, 9th edn., McGraw-Hill, 2008, chapter 17.

REVIEW QUESTIONS

Answers to these questions can be found in at the back of the book on p. 545.

9.1   Why should a business wish to repurchase some of its shares?

9.2   'The business's dividend decision is really a by-product of its capital investment decision.' Discuss.

9.3   Is it really important for a business to try to meet the needs of different types of investors when formulating its dividend policy?

9.4   Describe how agency theory may help to explain the dividend policy of businesses.

EXERCISES

Exercises 9.3 to 9.6 are more advanced than 9.1 and 9.2. Those with coloured numbers have answers at the back of the book, starting on p. 566.

 If you wish to try more exercises, visit the students' side of this book's Companion Website.

9.1   The dividend policy of businesses has been the subject of much debate in the financial management literature.

Required:
Discuss the view that dividends can increase the wealth of shareholders.

9.2   Identify and discuss the factors that may influence the dividend policies of businesses.

9.3   The following listed businesses each have different policies concerning distributions to shareholders:

● *North plc* pays all profits available for distribution to shareholders in the form of a cash dividend each year.
● *South plc* has yet to pay any cash dividends to shareholders and has no plans to make dividend payments in the foreseeable future.
● *West plc* repurchases shares from shareholders as an alternative to a dividend payment.
● *East plc* offers shareholders the choice of either a small but stable cash dividend or a scrip dividend each year.

Required:
Discuss the advantages and disadvantages of each of the above policies.

9.4   Fellingham plc has 20 million ordinary £1 shares in issue. No shares have been issued during the past four years. The business's earnings and dividends record taken from the historic accounts showed:

	Year 1	Year 2	Year 3	Year 4 (most recent)
Earnings per share	11.00p	12.40p	10.90p	17.20p
Dividend per share	10.00p	10.90p	11.88p	12.95p

At the annual general meeting for Year 1, the chairman had indicated that it was the intention to consistently increase annual dividends by 9 per cent, anticipating that, on average, this would maintain the spending power of shareholders and provide a modest growth in real income.

In the event, subsequent average annual inflation rates, measured by the general index of prices, have been:

Year 2	11%
Year 3	10%
Year 4	8%

The ordinary shares are currently selling for £3.44, excluding the Year 4 dividend.

Required:

Comment on the declared dividend policy of the business and its possible effects on both Fellingham plc and its shareholders, illustrating your answer with the information provided.

9.5 Mondrian plc is a new business that aims to maximise the wealth of its shareholders. The board of directors is currently trying to decide upon the most appropriate dividend policy to adopt for the business's shareholders. However, there is strong disagreement among three of the directors concerning the benefits of declaring cash dividends:

- *Director A* argues that cash dividends would be welcome by investors and that as high a dividend payout ratio as possible would reflect positively on the market value of the business's shares.
- *Director B* argues that whether a cash dividend is paid or not is irrelevant in the context of shareholder wealth maximisation.
- *Director C* takes an opposite view to Director A and argues that dividend payments should be avoided as they would lead to a decrease in shareholder wealth.

Required:

(a) The arguments for and against the position taken by each of the three directors.
(b) Assuming the board of directors decides to pay a dividend to shareholders, what factors should be taken into account when determining the level of dividend payment?

9.6 Traminer plc provides software solutions for the airline industry. At present, shares in the business are held by the senior managers and by a venture capital business. However, Traminer plc intends to seek a Stock Exchange listing and to make 75 per cent of the ordinary shares available to the investing public. The board of directors recently met to decide upon a dividend policy for the business once it has become listed. However, the meeting ended without agreement. The chairman argued that the existing dividend policy need not be changed whereas the chief executive argued that it should be changed. The operations director expressed the view that, as the pattern of dividends had no effect on the shareholders' wealth, the debate was irrelevant.

Information relating to the business over the past five years is set out below:

Year ended 30 April	Ordinary shares in issue 000	Profit for the year £000	Ordinary share dividends £000
2004	500	840	420
2005	500	1,190	580
2006	800	1,420	340
2007	1,000	1,940	450
2008	1,000	2,560	970

Required:

(a) Explain the rationale for the view expressed by the operations director.

(b) Evaluate the rationale explained in (a) above and include in your evaluation two reasons why, in practice, managers consider the pattern of dividends to be important to shareholders.

(c) Evaluate the dividend policy pursued by Traminer plc over the past five years and comment on the points expressed by the chairman and the chief executive.

10

Managing working capital

INTRODUCTION

In this chapter we shall consider the factors that must be taken into account when managing the working capital of a business. Each element of working capital will be identified and the major issues surrounding them will be discussed. Working capital represents a significant investment for many businesses and so its proper management and control can be vital. We saw in Chapter 4 that an investment in working capital is typically an important aspect of new investment proposals. Some useful tools in the management of working capital are forecasts, which were considered in Chapter 2, and financial ratios, which we examined in Chapter 3.

LEARNING OUTCOMES

When you have completed this chapter, you should be able to:

● Identify the main elements of working capital.

● Discuss the purpose of working capital and the nature of the working capital cycle.

● Explain the importance of establishing policies for the control of working capital.

● Explain the factors that have to be taken into account when managing each element of working capital.

The nature and purpose of working capital

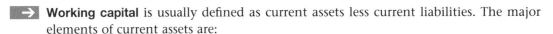

Working capital is usually defined as current assets less current liabilities. The major elements of current assets are:

- inventories
- trade receivables
- cash (in hand and at bank).

The major elements of current liabilities are:

- trade payables
- bank overdrafts.

The size and composition of working capital can vary between industries. For some types of business, the investment in working capital can be substantial. For example, a manufacturing business will typically invest heavily in raw material, work in progress and finished goods, and will normally sell its goods on credit, giving rise to trade receivables. A retailer, on the other hand, will hold only one form of inventories (finished goods), and will usually sell goods for cash. Many service businesses hold no inventories. Most businesses buy goods and/or services on credit, giving rise to trade payables. Few, if any, businesses operate without a cash balance, though in some cases it is a negative one (a bank overdraft).

Working capital represents a net investment in short-term assets. These assets are continually flowing into and out of the business, and are essential for day-to-day operations. The various elements of working capital are interrelated, and can be seen as part of a short-term cycle. For a manufacturing business, the working capital cycle can be depicted as shown in Figure 10.1.

Figure 10.1	**The working capital cycle**

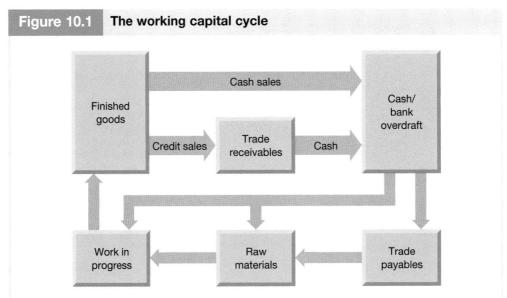

Cash is used to pay trade payables for raw materials, or raw materials are bought for immediate cash settlement. Cash is also spent on labour and other items that turn raw materials into work in progress and, finally, into finished goods. The finished goods are sold to customers either for cash or on credit. In the case of credit customers, there will be a delay before the cash is received from the sales. Receipt of cash completes the cycle.

For a retailer the situation would be as in Figure 10.1 except that there would be no work in progress and the raw materials and the finished inventories would be the same. For a purely service business, the working capital cycle would also be similar to that depicted in Figure 10.1 except that there would be no inventories of raw materials and finished goods. There may well be work in progress, however, since many services, for example a case handled by a firm of solicitors, will take some time to complete and costs will build up before the client is billed for them.

Managing working capital

The management of working capital is an essential part of the business's short-term planning process. It is necessary for management to decide how much of each element should be held. As we shall see later in this chapter, there are costs associated with holding either too much or too little of each element. Management must be aware of these costs, which include opportunity costs, in order to manage effectively. Hence, the potential benefits must be weighed against the likely costs in an attempt to achieve the optimum investment.

The working capital needs of a particular business are likely to change over time as a result of changes in the business environment. This means that working capital decisions are constantly being made. Managers must try to identify changes in an attempt to ensure that the level of investment in working capital is appropriate.

Activity 10.1

What kinds of changes in the commercial environment might lead to a decision to change the level of investment in working capital? Try to identify four possible changes that could affect the working capital needs of a business.

These may include the following:

- changes in interest rates
- changes in market demand
- changes in the seasons
- changes in the state of the economy.

You may have thought of others.

In addition to changes in the external environment, changes arising within the business could alter the required level of investment in working capital. Examples of such internal changes include using different production methods (resulting, perhaps, in a need to hold less inventories) and changes in the level of risk that managers are prepared to take.

The scale of working capital

We might imagine that, compared with the scale of investment in non-current assets by the typical business, the amounts involved with working capital are pretty trivial. This would be unrealistic – the scale of the working capital elements for most businesses is vast.

Real World 10.1 gives some impression of the working capital involvement for five UK businesses, either very well known by name, or whose products are everyday commodities for most of us. These businesses were randomly selected, except that each one is high profile and from a different industry. For each business the major statement of financial position (balance sheet) items are expressed as a percentage of the total investment by the providers of long-term finance (equity and non-current liabilities).

REAL WORLD 10.1

A summary of the statements of financial position (balance sheets) of five UK businesses

Business:	Next plc	British Airways plc	Rolls-Royce plc	Tesco plc	Severn Trent plc
Balance sheet date:	28.1.07	31.3.07	31.12.06	24.2.07	31.3.07
Non-current assets	71	103	57	122	112
Current assets					
Inventories	34	1	23	12	–
Trade receivables	69	8	39	6	8
Other receivables	–	4	10	–	–
Cash and near cash	15	30	35	9	3
	118	43	107	27	11
Total assets	189	146	164	149	123
Equity and non-current liabilities	100	100	100	100	100
Current liabilities					
Trade payables	75	35	52	36	8
Taxation	10	1	3	3	1
Other short-term liabilities	–	5	3	–	–
Overdrafts and short-term loans	4	5	6	10	14
	89	46	64	49	23
Total equity and liabilities	189	146	164	149	123

The non-current assets, current assets and current liabilities are expressed as a percentage of the total net long-term investment (equity plus non-current liabilities) of the business concerned. Next is a major retail and home shopping business. British Airways (BA) is a major airline. Rolls-Royce makes aero and other engines. Tesco is one of the major UK supermarkets. Severn Trent is a major supplier of water, sewerage services and waste management, mainly in the UK.

Source: Table constructed from information appearing in the annual reports of the five businesses concerned.

The totals for current assets are pretty large when compared with the total long-term investment. This is particularly true of Next and Rolls-Royce. The amounts vary considerably from one type of business to the next. When we look at the nature of working capital held we can see that Next, Rolls-Royce and Tesco, which produce and/or sell goods, are the only ones that hold significant amounts of inventories. The other two businesses are service providers and so inventories are not a significant item. We can see from the table that Tesco does not sell a lot on credit and very few of BA's and Severn Trent's sales are on credit as these businesses have little invested in trade receivables. It is interesting to note that Tesco's trade payables are much higher than its inventories. Since most of these payables will be suppliers of inventories, it means that the business is able, on average, to have the cash from a particular sale in the bank before it needs to pay for the goods concerned.

These types of variation in the amounts and types of working capital elements are typical of other businesses.

In the sections that follow, we shall consider each element of working capital separately and how they might be properly managed. It seems from the evidence presented in **Real World 10.2** that there is much scope for improvement in working capital management among European businesses.

REAL WORLD 10.2

Working capital not working hard enough!

According to a survey of 1,000 of Europe's largest businesses, working capital is not as well managed as it could be. The survey, conducted in 2007 by REL Consultancy Group and CFO Europe, suggests that larger European businesses have €611bn tied up in working capital that could be released through better management of inventories, trade receivables and trade payables. The potential for savings represents a total of 32 per cent of the total working capital invested (excluding automobile businesses). Although this represents an improvement on the results shown by similar surveys undertaken by REL and CFO Europe over each of the previous five years, it seems that reductions in the holding of inventories and receivables were partially offset by a reduction in trade payables, which increased working capital needs.

The total investment in each element of working capital, along with the estimated excess investment in each element, for the top 1,000 European countries is shown in Figure 10.2.

The figure shows that inventory is the working capital element that has potential for most improvement.

Figure 10.2	Total and excess working capital of large European businesses

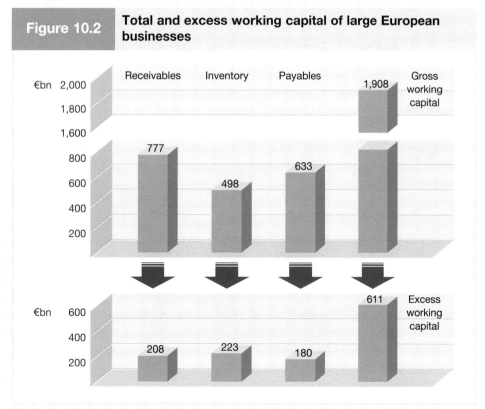

Source: 'US and European companies leave billions of dollars, euros untapped in working capital' in REL Consultancy Group and CFO Europe, *Annual Working Capital Survey* (2007), www.relconsult.com, 29 August 2007, p. 4.

Managing inventories

A business may hold inventories for various reasons, the most common of which is to meet the immediate day-to-day requirements of customers and production. However, a business may hold more than is necessary for this purpose if it is believed that future supplies may be interrupted or scarce. Similarly, if the business believes that the cost of inventories will rise in the future, it may decide to stockpile.

For some types of business the inventories held may represent a substantial proportion of the total assets held. For example, a car dealership that rents its premises may have nearly all of its total assets in the form of inventories. Inventories levels of manufacturers tend to be higher than in many other types of business as it is necessary to hold three kinds of inventories: raw materials, work in progress and finished goods. Each form of inventories represents a particular stage in the production cycle. For some types of business, the level of inventories held may vary substantially over the year owing to the seasonal nature of the industry. An example of such a business is a greetings card manufacturer. For other businesses, inventories levels may remain fairly stable throughout the year.

Where a business holds inventories simply to meet the day-to-day requirements of its customers and for production, it will normally seek to minimise the amount of inventories held. This is because there are significant costs associated with holding inventories. These include:

● storage and handling costs
● financing costs
● the costs of pilferage and obsolescence
● the cost of opportunities forgone in tying up funds in this form of asset.

To gain some impression of the level of cost involved in holding inventories **Real World 10.3** estimates the *financing* cost for four well-known businesses.

REAL WORLD 10.3

Inventories financing cost

The cost of holding inventories for each of four well-known businesses, based on their respective opportunity costs of capital, is calculated below.

Business	Type of operations	Cost of capital (a) %	Average inventories held* (b) £m	Cost of holding inventories (a) × (b) £m	Profit before tax £m	Cost as a % of profit before tax %
Rolls-Royce	Engineering	12.75	1,378	176	1,391	12.7
Pearson	Media	7.7	364	28	466	6.0
Carphone Warehouse	Mobile phone retailer	6.8	150	10.2	68	15.0
Scottish & Newcastle	Brewer	7.0	223	16.0	222	7.2

* Based on opening and closing inventories for the relevant year.

We can see that for Rolls-Royce and Carphone Warehouse, inventories financing costs are significant in relation to the profits generated. These figures do not take account of other costs of inventories holding mentioned above, like the cost of providing a secure store for the inventories. Clearly, the efficient management of inventories is an important issue for many businesses.

Source: Annual reports of the companies cited for 2005/6 or 2006/7.

As we have just seen, the cost of holding inventories can be very large. A business must also recognise, however, that, if the level of inventories held is too low, there will also be associated costs.

Activity 10.2

What costs might a business incur as a result of holding too low a level of inventories? Try to jot down at least three types of cost.

In answering this activity you may have thought of the following costs:

- loss of sales, from being unable to provide the goods required immediately;
- loss of customer goodwill, for being unable to satisfy customer demand;
- high transport costs incurred to ensure that inventories are replenished quickly;
- lost production due to shortage of raw materials;
- inefficient production scheduling due to shortages of raw materials;
- purchasing inventories at a higher price than might otherwise have been possible in order to replenish inventories quickly.

Before we go on to deal with the various approaches that can be taken to managing inventories, **Real World 10.4** provides an example of how badly things can go wrong if inventories are not adequately controlled.

REAL WORLD 10.4

Pallets lost at Brambles

Brambles Industries plc (BI) is an Anglo-Australian industrial services business, formed in 2001 when the industrial services subsidiary of GKN plc, the UK engineering business, was merged with the Australian business Brambles Ltd.

BI uses 'pallets' on which it delivers its products to customers. These are returnable by customers so BI holds a 'pool' of pallets. Each pallet costs the business about £10. Unfortunately, BI lost 14 million pallets during the year ended in June 2002 as a result of poor control and this led to a significant decline in the business's profits and share price.

At BI's annual general meeting in Sydney, Australia, one of the shareholders was quoted as saying: 'Running a pallet pool is not rocket science. I can teach one of my employees about pallets in 20 minutes.'

Source: Information taken from an article appearing in the *Financial Times*, 27 November 2002.

To try to ensure that the inventories are properly managed, a number of procedures and techniques may be used. These are reviewed below.

Forecasting future demand

One of the best ways to ensure that there will be inventories available to meet future production and sales requirements is to make appropriate forecasts. These forecasts should deal with each product that the business makes and/or sells. It is important that every attempt is made to ensure that forecasts are realistic, as they will determine future ordering and production levels. The forecasts may be derived in various ways. We saw in Chapter 2 that they may be developed using statistical techniques such as time series analysis, or they may be based on the judgement of the sales and marketing staff.

Financial ratios

One ratio that can be used to help monitor inventories levels is the average inventories turnover period, which we examined in Chapter 3. As we should recall, this ratio is calculated as follows:

$$\text{Average inventories turnover period} = \frac{\text{Average inventories held}}{\text{Cost of sales}} \times 365$$

This will provide a picture of the average period for which inventories are held, and can be useful as a basis for comparison. It is possible to calculate the average inventories turnover period for individual product lines as well as for inventories as a whole.

Recording and reordering systems

The management of inventories in a business of any size requires a sound system of recording inventories movements. There must be proper procedures for recording inventories purchases and usages. Periodic inventories checks may be required to ensure that the amount of physical inventories held is consistent with what is indicated by the inventories records.

There should also be clear procedures for the reordering of inventories. Authorisation for both the purchase and the issue of inventories should be confined to a few senior staff. This should avoid problems of duplication and lack of coordination. To determine the point at which inventories should be reordered, information will be required concerning the **lead time** (that is, the time between the placing of an order and the receipt of the goods) and the likely level of demand.

Activity 10.3

An electrical retailer stocks a particular type of light switch. The annual demand for the light switch is 10,400 units, and the lead time for orders is four weeks. Demand for the light switch is steady throughout the year. At what quantity of the light switch should the business reorder, assuming that it is confident of the information given above?

The average weekly demand for the switch is 10,400/52 = 200 units. During the time between ordering new switches and receiving them, the quantity sold will be 4 × 200 units = 800 units. So the business should reorder no later than when the level held reaches 800 units, in order to avoid running out of inventories.

In most businesses, there will be some uncertainty surrounding the above factors and so a buffer or safety inventories level may be maintained in case problems occur. The amount of the buffer to be held is really a matter of judgement. This judgement will depend on:

- the degree of uncertainty concerning the above factors;
- the likely costs of running out of the item concerned;
- the cost of holding the buffer inventories.

The effect of holding a buffer will be to raise the inventories level (the reorder point) at which an order for new inventories is placed.

Activity 10.4

Assume the same facts as in Activity 10.3. However, we are also told that the business maintains buffer inventories of 300 units. At what level should the business reorder?

Reorder point = expected level of demand during the lead time plus the level of buffer
inventories
= 800 + 300
= 1,100 units

Carrying buffer inventories will increase the cost of holding inventories; however, this must be weighed against the cost of running out of inventories, in terms of lost sales, production problems and so on.

Real World 10.5 provides an example of how small businesses can use technology in inventories reordering to help compete against their larger rivals.

 ## REAL WORLD 10.5

Taking on the big boys

The use of technology in inventories recording and reordering may be of vital importance to the survival of small businesses that are being threatened by larger rivals. One such example is that of small independent bookshops. Technology can come to their rescue in two ways. First, electronic point-of-sale (EPOS) systems can record books as they are sold and can constantly update records of inventories held. Thus, books that need to be reordered can be quickly and easily identified. Secondly, the reordering process can be improved by using web-based technology, which allows books to be ordered in real time. Many large book wholesalers provide free web-based software to their customers for this purpose and try to deliver books ordered during the next working day. This means that a small bookseller, with limited shelf space, may keep one copy only of a particular book but maintain a range of books that competes with that of a large bookseller.

Source: Information taken from 'Small stores keep up with the big boys', *Financial Times*, 5 February 2003, at www.ft.com.

Levels of control

Senior managers must make a commitment to the management of inventories. However, the cost of controlling inventories must be weighed against the potential benefits. It may be possible to have different levels of control according to the nature of the inventories held. The **ABC system of inventories control** is based on the idea of selective levels of control.

A business may find that it is possible to divide its inventories into three broad categories: A, B and C. Each category will be based on the value of inventories held, as is illustrated in Example 10.1.

Alascan Products plc makes door handles and door fittings. It makes them in brass, in steel and in plastic. The business finds that brass fittings account for 10 per cent of the physical volume of the finished inventories that it holds, but these represent 65 per cent of its total value. This is treated as Category A inventories. There are sophisticated recording procedures, tight control is exerted over inventories movements and there is a high level of security where the brass inventories is stored. This is economic because the inventories represents a relatively small proportion of the total volume.

The business finds that steel fittings account for 30 per cent of the total volume of finished inventories and represent 25 per cent of its total value. This is treated as Category B inventories, with a lower level of recording and management control being applied.

The remaining 60 per cent of the volume of inventories is plastic fittings, which represent the least valuable items that account for only 10 per cent of the total value of finished inventories held. This is treated as Category C inventories, so the level of recording and management control would be lower still. Applying to these inventories the level of control that is applied to Category A or even Category B inventories would be uneconomic.

Categorising inventories in this way seeks to direct management effort to the most important areas, and tries to ensure that the costs of controlling inventories are appropriate to its importance.

Figure 10.3 shows the nature of the ABC approach to inventories control.

Inventories management models

Economic order quantity

It is possible to use decision models to help manage inventories. The **economic order quantity (EOQ)** model is concerned with answering the question 'How much inventories should be ordered?' In its simplest form, the EOQ model assumes that demand is constant, so that inventories will be depleted evenly over time, and replenished just at the point that it runs out. These assumptions would lead to a 'saw-tooth' pattern to represent inventories' movements, as shown in Figure 10.4.

The EOQ model recognises that the key costs associated with inventories management are the cost of holding the inventories and the cost of ordering it. The model can

Figure 10.3   **ABC method of analysing and controlling inventories**

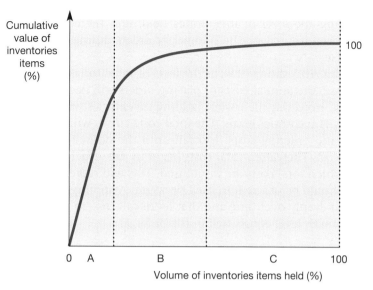

Category A contains inventories that, though relatively few in quantity, account for a large proportion of the total value. Category B inventories consists of those items that are less valuable but more numerous. Category C comprises those inventories items that are very numerous but relatively low in value. Different inventories' control rules would be applied to each category. For example, only Category A inventories would attract the more expensive and sophisticated controls.

Figure 10.4   **Patterns of inventories movements over time**

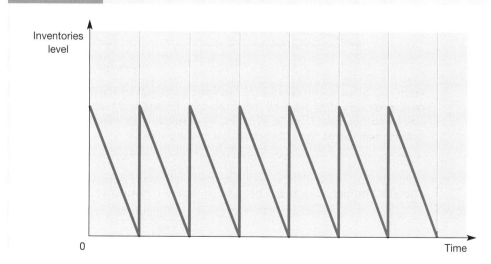

Here we assume that there is a constant rate of usage of the inventories item, and that inventories is reduced to zero just as new inventories arrives. At time 0 there is a full level of inventories. This is steadily used as time passes; and just as it falls to zero it is replaced. This pattern is then repeated.

be used to calculate the optimum size of a purchase order by taking account of both of these cost elements. The cost of holding inventories can be substantial, and so management may try to minimise the average amount of inventories held. However, by reducing the level of inventories held, and therefore the holding costs, there will be a need to increase the number of orders during the period, and so ordering costs will rise.

Figure 10.5 shows how, as the level of inventories and the size of inventories orders increase, the annual costs of placing orders will decrease because fewer orders will be placed. However, the cost of holding inventories will increase, as there will be higher average inventories levels. The total costs curve, which is based on the sum of holding costs and ordering costs, will fall until the point E, which represents the minimum total cost. Thereafter, total costs begin to rise. The EOQ model seeks to identify point E at which total costs are minimised. This will represent half of the optimum amount that should be ordered on each occasion. Assuming, as we are doing, that inventories is used evenly over time and that levels fall to zero before being replaced, the average inventories level equals half of the order size.

Figure 10.5	**Inventories holding and order costs**

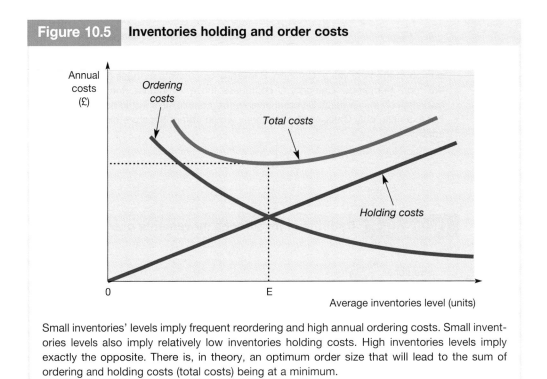

Small inventories' levels imply frequent reordering and high annual ordering costs. Small inventories levels also imply relatively low inventories holding costs. High inventories levels imply exactly the opposite. There is, in theory, an optimum order size that will lead to the sum of ordering and holding costs (total costs) being at a minimum.

The EOQ model, which can be used to derive the most economic order quantity, is:

$$EOQ = \sqrt{\frac{2DC}{H}}$$

where: D = the annual demand for the inventories item (expressed in units of the inventories item);

C = the cost of placing an order;

H = the cost of holding one unit of inventories for one year.

Activity 10.5

HLA Ltd sells 2,000 bags of cement each year. It has been estimated that the cost of holding one bag of cement for a year is £4. The cost of placing an order for new inventories is estimated at £250.

Calculate the EOQ for bags of cement.

Your answer to this activity should be as follows:

$$EOQ = \sqrt{\frac{2 \times 2,000 \times 250}{4}} = 500 \text{ bags}$$

This will mean that the business will have to order bags of cement four times each year (that is 2,000/500) in batches of 500 bags so that sales demand can be met.

Note that the cost of the inventories concerned, which is the price paid to the supplier, does not directly impact on the EOQ model. The EOQ model is concerned only with the administrative costs of placing each order and the costs of looking after the inventories. Where the business operates an ABC system of inventories control, however, more expensive inventories items will have greater holding costs. For example, Category A inventories would tend to have a lower EOQ than Category B ones. So the cost of the inventories may have an indirect effect on the economic order size that the model recommends.

The basic EOQ model has a number of limiting assumptions. In particular, it assumes that:

- demand for the particular inventories item can be predicted with accuracy;
- demand is constant over the period and does not fluctuate through seasonality or for other reasons;
- no 'buffer' inventories are required;
- there are no discounts for bulk purchasing.

However, the model can be developed to overcome each of these limiting assumptions. Many businesses use this model (or a development of it) to help in the management of inventories.

Materials requirement planning systems

A **materials requirement planning (MRP) system** takes planned sales demand as its starting point. It then uses a computer package to help schedule the timing of deliveries of bought-in parts and materials to coincide with production requirements. It is a coordinated approach that links materials and parts deliveries to the scheduled time of their input to the production process. Ordering only those items that are necessary to ensure the flow of production is likely to reduce inventories levels. MRP is really a 'top-down' approach to inventories management, which recognises that inventories ordering decisions cannot be viewed as being independent of production decisions. In recent years, this approach has been extended to provide a fully integrated approach to production planning. The approach also takes account of other manufacturing resources such as labour and machine capacity.

Just-in-time inventories management

In recent years, many businesses have tried to eliminate the need to hold inventories by adopting **just-in-time (JIT) inventories management**. This approach was first used in the US defence industry during the Second World War, but was first used on a wide scale by Japanese manufacturing businesses. The essence of JIT is, as the name suggests, to have supplies delivered to the business just in time for them to be used in the production process or in a sale. Adopting this approach means that the inventories holding costs rest with suppliers rather than with the business itself. On the other hand, a failure by a particular supplier to deliver on time could cause enormous problems and costs to the business. Thus JIT can save cost, but it tends to increase risk.

For JIT to be successful, it is important that the business informs suppliers of its inventories requirements in advance, and that suppliers, in their turn, deliver materials of the right quality at the agreed times. Failure to do so could lead to a dislocation of production or supply to customers and could be very costly. Thus a close relationship is required between the business and its suppliers.

This close relationship enables suppliers to schedule their own production to that of their customers. This should mean that between supplier and customer there will be a net saving in the amount of inventories that need to be held, relative to that which would apply were JIT not in operation.

Although a business that applies JIT will not have to hold inventories, there may be other costs associated with this approach. As the suppliers may need to hold inventories for the customer, they may try to recoup this additional cost through increased prices. On the other hand, the close relationship between customer and supplier should enable the supplier to predict its customers' inventories needs. This means that suppliers can tailor their own production to that of the customer. The close relationship necessary between the business and its suppliers may also prevent the business from taking advantage of cheaper sources of supply if they become available.

Many people view JIT as more than simply an inventories control system. The philosophy underpinning this approach is concerned with eliminating waste and striving for excellence. There is an expectation that suppliers will always deliver inventories on time and that there will be no defects in the items supplied. There is also an expectation that, for manufacturers, the production process will operate at maximum efficiency. This means there will be no production breakdowns and the queuing and storage times of products manufactured will be eliminated, as only that time spent directly on processing the products is seen as adding value. While these expectations may be impossible to achieve, they do help to create a culture that is dedicated to the pursuit of excellence and quality.

Real World 12.6 and **Real World 12.7** show how two very well-known businesses operating in the UK (one a retailer, the other a manufacturer) use JIT to advantage.

REAL WORLD 10.6

JIT at Boots

The Boots Company plc, the UK's largest healthcare retailer, has improved inventories management at its stores. The business is working towards a JIT system where delivery from its one central warehouse in Nottingham will be made every day to each retail branch, with nearly all of the inventories lines being placed directly on to the sales shelves, not into a branch inventories store room. The business says that this will bring significant savings of stores staff time and lead to significantly lower levels of inventories being held, without any lessening of the service offered to customers. The new system is expected to lead to major economic benefits for the business.

Source: Information taken from The Boots Company plc Annual Report and Accounts 2005.

REAL WORLD 10.7

JIT at Nissan

Nissan Motors UK Limited, the UK manufacturing arm of the world-famous Japanese car business, has a plant in Sunderland in the north-east of England. Here it operates a well-developed JIT system. Sommer supplies carpets and soft interior trim from a factory close to the Nissan plant. It makes deliveries to Nissan once every 20 minutes on average, so as to arrive exactly as they are needed in production. This is fairly typical of all of the 200 suppliers of components and materials to the Nissan plant.

Source: Information taken from Partnership Sourcing Best Practice Case Study (www.pslcbi.com/studies/docnissan.htm).

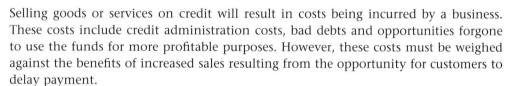

Managing receivables

Selling goods or services on credit will result in costs being incurred by a business. These costs include credit administration costs, bad debts and opportunities forgone to use the funds for more profitable purposes. However, these costs must be weighed against the benefits of increased sales resulting from the opportunity for customers to delay payment.

Selling on credit is very widespread and is the norm outside the retail industry. When a business offers to sell its goods or services on credit, it must have clear policies concerning:

- which customers should receive credit;
- how much credit should be offered;
- what length of credit it is prepared to offer;
- whether discounts will be offered for prompt payment;
- what collection policies should be adopted;
- how the risk of non-payment can be reduced.

In this section, we shall consider each of these issues.

Which customers should receive credit and how much should they be offered?

A business offering credit runs the risk of not receiving payment for goods or services supplied. Thus, care must be taken over the type of customer to whom credit facilities are offered and how much credit is allowed. When considering a proposal from a customer for the supply of goods or services on credit, the business must take a num- ber of factors into account. The following **five Cs of credit** provide a business with a useful checklist.

- *Capital.* The customer must appear to be financially sound before any credit is extended. Where the customer is a business, its financial statements should be examined. Particular regard should be given to the customer's likely future profitability and liquidity. In addition, any major financial commitments (for example, capital expenditure, contracts with suppliers) must be taken into account.

- *Capacity.* The customer must appear to have the capacity to pay amounts owing. Where possible, the payment record of the customer to date should be examined. If the customer is a business, the type of business operated and the physical resources of the business will be relevant. The value of goods that the customer wishes to buy on credit must be related to the customer's total financial resources.
- *Collateral.* On occasions, it may be necessary to ask for some kind of security for goods supplied on credit. When this occurs, the business must be convinced that the customer is able to offer a satisfactory form of security.
- *Conditions.* The state of the industry in which the customer operates, and the general economic conditions of the particular region or country, may have an important influence on the ability of a customer to pay the amounts outstanding on the due date.
- *Character.* It is important for a business to make some assessment of the customer's character. The willingness to pay will depend on the honesty and integrity of the individual with whom the business is dealing. Where the customer is a limited company this will mean assessing the characters of its directors. The business must feel satisfied that the customer will make every effort to pay any amounts owing.

It is clear from the above that the business will need to gather information concerning the ability and willingness of the customer to pay the amounts owing at the due dates.

Activity 10.6

Assume that you are the credit manager of a business and that a limited company approaches you with a view to buying goods on credit. What sources of information might you decide to use to help assess the financial health of the potential customer?

There are various possibilities. You may have thought of some of the following:

- *Trade references.* Some businesses ask potential customers to supply them with references from other suppliers who have made sales on credit to them. This may be extremely useful provided that the references supplied are truly representative of the opinions of a customer's suppliers. There is a danger that a potential customer will be selective when giving details of other suppliers, in an attempt to create a more favourable impression than is deserved.
- *Bank references.* It is possible to ask the potential customer for a bank reference. Although banks are usually prepared to supply references, the contents of such references are not always very informative. If customers are in financial difficulties, the bank may be unwilling to add to their problems by supplying poor references. It is worth remembering that the bank's loyalty is likely to be with the customer rather than the enquirer. The bank will usually charge a fee for providing a reference.
- *Published financial statements.* A limited company is obliged by law to file a copy of its annual financial statements with the Registrar of Companies. These financial statements are available for public inspection and provide a useful source of information. Apart from the information contained in the financial statements, company law requires public limited companies to state in the directors' report the average time taken to pay suppliers. The annual reports of many companies are available on their own websites or on computer-based information systems (for example, FAME).

- *The customer*. Interviews with the directors of the customer's business and visits to its premises may be carried out to gain an impression of the way that the customer conducts its business. Where a significant amount of credit is required, the business may ask the customer for access to internal budgets and other unpublished financial information to help assess the level of risk involved.
- *Credit agencies*. Specialist agencies exist to provide information that can be used to assess the creditworthiness of a potential customer. The information that a credit agency supplies may be gleaned from various sources, including the financial statements of the customer and news items relating to the customer from both published and unpublished sources. The credit agencies may also provide a credit rating for the business. Agencies will charge a fee for their services.
- *Register of County Court Judgments*. Any money judgments given against the business or an individual in a county court will be maintained on the register for six years. This register is available for inspection by any member of the public for a small fee.
- *Other suppliers*. Similar business will often be prepared to exchange information concerning slow payers or defaulting customers through an industry credit circle. This can be a reliable and relatively cheap way of obtaining information.

How much credit should be offered?

Once a customer is considered creditworthy, credit limits for the customer should be established and procedures should be laid down to ensure that these limits are adhered to. Unfortunately, there are no theories or models to help a business decide on the appropriate credit limit to adopt; it is really a matter of judgement. Some businesses adopt simple 'rule of thumb' methods based on either the amount of sales made to the customer (say, twice the monthly sales figure for that customer) or a maximum the business is prepared to be owed (say, a maximum of 20 per cent of the working capital).

Length of credit period

A business must determine what credit terms it is prepared to offer its customers. The length of credit offered to customers can vary significantly between businesses, and may be influenced by such factors as:

- the typical credit terms operating within the industry;
- the degree of competition within the industry;
- the bargaining power of particular customers;
- the risk of non-payment;
- the capacity of the business to offer credit;
- the marketing strategy of the business.

The last point identified may require some explanation. If, for example, a business wishes to increase its market share, it may decide to be more generous in its credit policy in an attempt to stimulate sales. Potential customers may be attracted by the offer of a longer credit period. However, any such change in policy must take account of the likely costs and benefits arising.

To illustrate this point, consider Example 10.2.

Example 10.2

Torrance Ltd produces a new type of golf putter. The business sells the putter to wholesalers and retailers and has an annual turnover of £600,000. The following data relate to each putter produced.

	£
Selling price	40
Variable costs	(20)
Fixed cost apportionment	(6)
Profit	14

The business's cost of capital is estimated at 10 per cent a year.

Torrance Ltd wishes to expand the sales volume of the new putter. It believes that offering a longer credit period can achieve this. The business's average receivables collection period is currently 30 days. It is considering three options in an attempt to increase sales revenue. These are as follows:

	Option		
	1	*2*	*3*
Increase in average collection period (days)	10	20	30
Increase in sales revenue (£)	30,000	45,000	50,000

To enable the business to decide on the best option to adopt, it must weigh the benefits of the options against their respective costs. The benefits arising will be represented by the increase in profit from the sale of additional putters. From the cost data supplied we can see that the contribution (that is, selling price (£40) less variable costs (£20)) is £20 a putter, that is, 50 per cent of the selling price. So, whatever increase there may be in sales revenue, the additional contributions will be half of that figure. The fixed costs can be ignored in our calculations, as they will remain the same whichever option is chosen.

The increase in contribution under each option will therefore be:

	Option		
	1	*2*	*3*
50% of the increase in sales revenue (£)	15,000	22,500	25,000

The increase in trade receivables under each option will be as follows:

	Option		
	1	*2*	*3*
	£	£	£
Projected level of trade receivables			
40 × £630,000/365 (Note 1)	69,041		
50 × £645,000/365		88,356	
60 × £650,000/365			106,849
Current level of trade receivables			
30 × £600,000/365	(49,315)	(49,315)	(49,315)
Increase in trade receivables	19,726	39,041	57,534

The increase in receivables that results from each option will mean an additional finance cost to the business.

The net increase in the business's profit arising from the projected change is:

	Option		
	1	*2*	*3*
	£	£	£
Increase in contribution (see above)	15,000	22,500	25,000
Increase in finance cost (Note 2)	(1,973)	(3,904)	(5,753)
Net increase in profits	13,027	18,596	19,247

The calculations show that Option 3 will be the most profitable one.

Notes:

1 If the annual sales revenue totals £630,000 and 40 days' credit are allowed (both of which will apply under Option 1), the average amount that will be owed to the business by its customers, at any point during the year, will be the daily sales revenue (that is, £630,000/365) multiplied by the number of days that the customers take to pay (that is, 40).

   Exactly the same logic applies to Options 2 and 3 and to the current level of trade receivables.

2 The increase in the finance cost for Option 1 will be the increase in trade receivables (£19,726) × 10 per cent. The equivalent figures for the other options are derived in a similar way.

Example 10.2 illustrates the way in which a business should assess changes in credit terms. However, if there is a risk that, by extending the length of credit, there will be an increase in bad debts, this should also be taken into account in the calculations, as should any additional trade receivable collection costs that will be incurred.

Real World 10.8 shows how the length of credit taken by some larger UK businesses leads to problems for smaller businesses.

REAL WORLD 10.8

Credit where it's due   FT

Late payment to small companies has got progressively worse over the past three years and they need to employ stricter credit management techniques, a survey released today claims.

Siemens Financial Services, a subsidiary of Siemens, the German engineering group, studied the accounts of thousands of UK companies. It found that smaller firms had to wait for 80 days to get paid by customers in 2006, compared with 69 days in 2004.

In contrast, medium-size and large companies have seen their 'days sales outstanding' hold steady over the period at 62 days and 47 days respectively.

Rod Tonna-Barthet, sales director at SFS, said the results showed that 'small firms are suffering' as a result of medium-size and large companies using competitive pressures to extend payment terms.

Source: J. Chisolm, 'Late payment hits small companies', www.ft.com, 29 January 2007.

An alternative approach to evaluating the credit decision

It is possible to view the credit decision as a capital investment decision. Granting trade credit involves an outlay of resources in the form of cash (which has been temporarily forgone) in the expectation that future cash flows will be increased (through higher sales) as a result. A business will usually have choices concerning the level of investment to be made in credit sales and the period over which credit is granted. These choices will result in different returns and different levels of risk. There is no reason in principle why the NPV investment appraisal method, which we considered in Chapter 4, should not be used to evaluate these choices. We have seen that the NPV method takes into account both the time value of money and the level of risk involved.

Approaching the problem as an NPV assessment is not different in principle from the way that we dealt with the decision in Example 10.2. In both approaches the time value of money is considered, but in Example 10.2 we did it by charging interest on the outstanding trade payables.

Cash discounts

→ A business may decide to offer a **cash discount** (or discount for prompt payment) in an attempt to encourage prompt payment from its credit customers. The size of any discount will be an important influence on whether a customer decides to pay promptly.

From the business's viewpoint, the cost of offering discounts must be weighed against the likely benefits in the form of a reduction both in the cost of financing receivables and in the amount of bad debts.

In practice, there is always the danger that a customer may be slow to pay and yet may still take the discount offered. Where the customer is important to the business it may be difficult to insist on full payment. An alternative to allowing the customer to take discounts by reducing payment is to agree in advance to provide discounts for prompt payment through quarterly credit notes. As credit notes will be given only for those debts paid on time, the customer will often make an effort to qualify for the discount.

Self-assessment question 10.1

Williams Wholesalers Ltd at present requires payment from its customers by the end of the month after the month of delivery. On average, customers take 70 days to pay. Sales revenue amounts to £4m a year and bad debts to £20,000 a year.

It is planned to offer customers a cash discount of 2 per cent for payment within 30 days. Williams estimates that 50 per cent of customers will accept this facility but that the remaining customers, who tend to be slow payers, will not pay until 80 days after the sale. At present the business has an overdraft facility at an interest rate of 13 per cent a year. If the plan goes ahead, bad debts will be reduced to £10,000 a year and there will be savings in credit administration expenses of £6,000 a year.

Required:
Should Williams Wholesalers Ltd offer the new credit terms to customers? You should support your answer with any calculations and explanations that you consider necessary.

The answer to this question may be found at the back of the book on p. 537.

Debt factoring and invoice discounting

We saw in Chapter 6 (p. 244) that trade receivables can, in effect, be turned into cash by either factoring them or having sales invoices discounted. These both seem to be fairly popular approaches to managing trade receivables.

Collection policies and reducing the risk of non-payment

A business offering credit must ensure that amounts owing are collected as quickly as possible so that the risk of non-payment is minimised. Various steps can be taken to achieve this, including the following.

Develop customer relationships

For major customers it is often useful to cultivate a relationship with the key staff responsible for paying sales invoices. So doing may increase the chances of prompt. For less important customers, the business should at least identify key staff responsible for paying invoices, who can be contacted in the event of a payment problem.

Publicise credit terms

The credit terms of the business should be made clear in all relevant correspondence, such as order acknowledgements, invoices and statements. In early negotiations with the prospective customer, credit terms should be openly discussed and an agreement reached.

Issue invoices promptly

An efficient collection policy requires an efficient accounting system. Invoices (bills) must be sent out promptly to customers, as must monthly statements. Reminders must also be despatched promptly to customers who are late in paying. If a customer fails to respond to a reminder, the accounting system should alert managers so that a stop can be placed on further deliveries.

Monitor outstanding debts

Management can monitor the effectiveness of collection policies in a number of ways. One method is to calculate the **average settlement period for trade receivables** ratio, which we met in Chapter 3. This ratio, we should recall, is calculated as follows:

$$\text{Average settlement period for trade receivables} = \frac{\text{Average trade receivables}}{\text{Credit sales}} \times 365$$

Although this ratio can be useful, it is important to remember that it produces an *average* figure for the number of days for which debts are outstanding. This average may be badly distorted by a few large customers who are very slow or very fast payers.

Produce an ageing schedule of trade receivables

A more detailed and informative approach to monitoring receivables may be to produce an **ageing schedule of trade receivables**. Receivables are divided into categories according to the length of time they have been outstanding. An ageing schedule can be produced, on a regular basis, to help managers see the pattern of outstanding receivables. An example of an ageing schedule is set out in Example 10.3.

Example 10.3

Ageing schedule of trade receivables at 31 December

Customer	Days outstanding				Total
	1 to 30 days £	31 to 60 days £	61 to 90 days £	More than 90 days £	£
A Ltd	20,000	10,000	–	–	30,000
B Ltd	–	24,000	–	–	24,000
C Ltd	12,000	13,000	14,000	18,000	57,000
Total	32,000	47,000	14,000	18,000	111,000

This shows a business's trade receivables figure at 31 December, which totals £111,000. Each customer's balance is analysed according to how long the amount has been outstanding. (This business has just three credit customers.)

Thus we can see from the schedule that A Ltd has £20,000 outstanding for 30 days or fewer (that is, arising from sales during December) and £10,000 outstanding for between 31 and 60 days (arising from November sales). This information can be very useful for credit control purposes.

Many accounting software packages now include this ageing schedule as one of the routine reports available to managers. Such packages often have the facility to put customers 'on hold' when they reach their credit limits. Putting a customer on hold means that no further credit sales will be made to that customer until amounts owing from past sales have been settled.

Identify the pattern of receipts

A slightly different approach to exercising control over receivables is to identify the pattern of receipts from credit sales on a monthly basis. This involves monitoring the percentage of trade receivables that pays (and the percentage of debts that remain unpaid) in the month of sale and the percentage that pays in subsequent months. To do this, credit sales for each month must be examined separately. To illustrate how a pattern of credit sales receipts is produced, consider a business that made credit sales of £250,000 in June and received 30 per cent of the amount owing in the same month, 40 per cent in July, 20 per cent in August and 10 per cent in September. The pattern of credit sales receipts and amounts owing is shown in Example 10.4.

Example 10.4

Pattern of credit sales receipts

	Receipts from June credit sales £	Received %	Amount outstanding from June sales at month end £	Outstanding %
June	75,000	30	175,000	70
July	100,000	40	75,000	30
August	50,000	20	25,000	10
September	25,000	10	–	–

Figure 10.6	Comparison of actual and budgeted receipts over time for Example 10.4

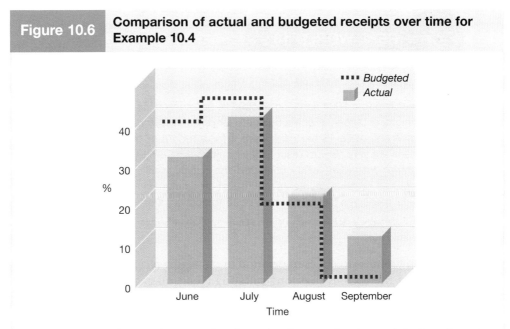

The graph shows the actual pattern of cash receipts from credit sales made in June. It can be seen that 30 per cent of the sales income for June is received in that month; the remainder is received in the following three months. The (assumed) budgeted pattern of cash receipts for June sales is also depicted. By comparing the actual and budgeted pattern of receipts, it is possible to see whether credit sales are being properly controlled and to decide whether corrective action is required.

Example 10.4 shows how sales made in June were received over time. This information can be used as a basis for control. The actual pattern of receipts can be compared with the expected (budgeted) pattern of receipts in order to see if there was any significant deviation (see Figure 10.6). If this comparison shows that debtors are paying more slowly than expected, management may decide to take corrective action.

Answer queries quickly

It is important for relevant staff to deal with customer queries on goods and services supplied quickly and efficiently. Customers are unlikely to make payment until their queries have been dealt with.

Deal with slow payers

It is almost inevitably the case that a business making significant sales on credit will be faced with customers who do not pay. When this occurs, there should be agreed procedures for dealing with the situation. However, the cost of any action to be taken against delinquent credit customers must be weighed against the likely returns. For example, there is little point in taking legal action against a customer, incurring large legal expenses, if there is evidence that the customer does not have the necessary resources to pay. Where possible, an estimate of the cost of bad debts should be taken into account when setting prices for products or services.

Real World 10.9 shows that businesses are not always as efficient as they might be with their management of trade receivables.

REAL WORLD 10.9

Would you credit it?

According to a 2004 survey of 6,500 UK businesses, 44 per cent of businesses leave it a fortnight, or longer, after the due date for payment before sending reminders to their credit customers, while 13 per cent leave it for a month or more. In other words, many businesses are very slow to react to their customers failing to pay on time.

Intrim Justia UK, who conducted the survey, said: 'A clear credit policy, consistent checks on overdue payments and robust credit management systems are just some of the critical measures that businesses need to adopt.'

Source: Information taken from Jonathon Moules, 'Late reminders lead to late payments', *Financial Times*, 12 July 2004.

As a footnote to our consideration of managing receivables, **Real World 10.10** outlines some of the excuses that long-suffering credit managers must listen to when chasing payment for outstanding debt.

REAL WORLD 10.10

It's in the post

Accountants' noses should be growing, if we're to believe a new survey listing the bizarre excuses given by businesses that fail to pay their debts.

'The director's been shot' and 'I'll pay you when God tells me to' are just two of the most outrageous excuses listed in a survey published by the Credit Services Association, the debt collection industry body.

The commercial sector tends to blame financial problems, and excuses such as 'you'll get paid when we do' and 'the finance director is off sick' are common. However, those in the consumer sector apparently feel no shame in citing personal relationship problems as the reason for not paying the bill.

Source: *Accountancy*, April 2000, p. 18. This extract is reproduced with the kind permission of Accountancy Magazine.

Reducing the risk of non-payment

Efficient collection policies are important in reducing the risk of non-payment. However, there are other ways in which a business can reduce this type of risk. Possibilities include:

● Requiring customers to pay part of their sales value in advance of the goods being sent.
● Agreeing to offset amounts owed for the purchase of goods against amounts due for goods supplied to the same business.
● Requiring a third-party guarantee from a financially sound business such as a bank or parent company.
● Making it a condition of sale that the legal title to the goods is not passed to the customer until the goods are paid for.
● Taking out insurance to cover the costs of any legal expenses incurred in recovering the debt. (Some customers may refuse to pay if they feel the business does not have the resources to pursue the debt through the courts.)

- Taking out insurance against risk of non-payment. Trade credit insurance can cover the whole of the credit sales of the business up to an agreed limit or can cover a number of specified customers.

The practical circumstances will determine which of the above methods is appropriate to use. For example, it would not be feasible to try to retain the legal title to raw materials or components which are intended to become part of a finished product. Remember also that, in a highly competitive environment, customers may be unwilling to accept stringent conditions. The risk of non-payment must always be weighed against the risk of lost sales.

Managing cash

Why hold cash?

Most businesses hold a certain amount of cash. The amount of cash held tends to vary considerably between businesses.

Activity 10.7

Why do you think a business may decide to hold at least some of its assets in the form of cash? (*Hint*: There are broadly three reasons.)

The three reasons are:

1 To meet day-to-day commitments, a business requires a certain amount of cash. Payments for wages, overhead expenses, goods purchased and so on must be made at the due dates. Cash has been described as the lifeblood of a business. Unless it circulates through the business and is available for the payment of claims as they become due, the survival of the business will be at risk. Profitability is not enough; a business must have sufficient cash to pay its debts when they fall due.

2 If future cash flows are uncertain for any reason, it would be prudent to hold a balance of cash. For example, a major customer that owes a large sum to the business may be in financial difficulties. Given this situation, the business can retain its capacity to meet its obligations by holding a cash balance. Similarly, if there is some uncertainty concerning future outlays, a cash balance will be required.

3 A business may decide to hold cash to put itself in a position to exploit profitable opportunities as and when they arise. For example, by holding cash, a business may be able to acquire a competitor's business that suddenly becomes available at an attractive price.

How much cash should be held?

Although cash can be held for each of the reasons identified, doing so may not always be necessary. If a business is able to borrow quickly, the amount of cash it needs to hold can be reduced. Similarly, if the business holds assets that can easily be converted to cash (for example, marketable securities such as shares in Stock Exchange listed businesses or government bonds), the amount of cash held can be reduced.

The decision as to how much cash a particular business should hold is a difficult one. Different businesses will have different views on the subject.

What do you think are the major factors that influence how much cash a business will hold? See if you can think of five possible factors.

You may have thought of the following:

- *The nature of the business*. Some businesses, such as utilities (for example, water, electricity and gas suppliers), may have cash flows that are both predictable and reasonably certain. This will enable them to hold lower cash balances. For some businesses, cash balances may vary greatly according to the time of year. A seasonal business may accumulate cash during the high season to enable it to meet commitments during the low season.
- *The opportunity cost of holding cash*. Where there are profitable opportunities it may not be wise to hold a large cash balance.
- *The level of inflation*. Holding cash during a period of rising prices will lead to a loss of purchasing power. The higher the level of inflation, the greater will be this loss.
- *The availability of near-liquid assets*. If a business has marketable securities or inventories that may easily be liquidated, high cash balances may not be necessary.
- *The availability of borrowing*. If a business can borrow easily (and quickly) there is less need to hold cash.
- *The cost of borrowing*. When interest rates are high, the option of borrowing becomes less attractive.
- *Economic conditions*. When the economy is in recession, businesses may prefer to hold cash so that they can be well placed to invest when the economy improves. In addition, during a recession, businesses may experience difficulties in collecting trade receivables. They may therefore hold higher cash balances than usual in order to meet commitments.
- *Relationships with suppliers*. Too little cash may hinder the ability of the business to pay suppliers promptly. This can lead to a loss of goodwill. It may also lead to discounts being forgone.

Controlling the cash balance

Several models have been developed to help control the cash balance of the business. One such model proposes the use of upper and lower control limits for cash balances and the use of a target cash balance. The model assumes that the business will invest in marketable investments that can easily be liquidated. These investments will be purchased or sold, as necessary, in order to keep the cash balance within the control limits.

The model proposes two upper and two lower control limits (see Figure 10.7). If the business exceeds an *outer* limit, the managers must decide whether the cash balance is likely to return to a point within the *inner* control limits set, over the next few days. If this seems likely, then no action is required. If, on the other hand, it does not seem likely, management must change the cash position of the business by either lending or borrowing (or possibly by buying or selling marketable securities).

In Figure 10.7 we can see that the lower outer control limit has been breached for four days. If a four-day period is unacceptable, managers must sell marketable securities to replenish the cash balance.

| Figure 10.7 | **Controlling the cash balance** |

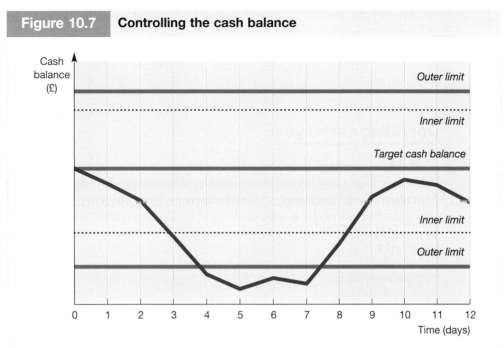

Management sets the upper and lower limits for the business's cash balance. When the balance goes beyond either of these limits, unless it is clear that the balance will return fairly quickly to within the limit, action will need to be taken. If the upper limit is breached, some cash will be placed on deposit or used to buy some marketable securities. If the lower limit is breached, the business will need to borrow some cash or sell some securities.

The model relies heavily on management judgement to determine where the control limits are set and the period within which breaches of the control limits are acceptable. Past experience may be useful in helping managers decide on these issues. There are other models, however, that do not rely on management judgement. Instead, these use quantitative techniques to determine an optimal cash policy. One model proposed, for example, is the cash equivalent of the inventories economic order quantity model, discussed earlier in the chapter.

Cash flow statements and managing cash

To manage cash effectively, it is useful for a business to prepare a projected cash flow statement. This is a very important tool for both planning and control purposes. Projected cash flow statements were considered in Chapter 2, and so we shall not consider them again in detail. However, it is worth repeating that these statements enable managers to see how planned events are expected to affect the cash balance. The projected cash flow statement will identify periods when cash surpluses and cash deficits are expected.

When a cash surplus is expected to arise, managers must decide on the best use of the surplus funds. When a cash deficit is expected, managers must make adequate provision by borrowing, liquidating assets or rescheduling cash payments or receipts to deal with this. Projected cash flow statements are useful in helping to control the cash held. The actual cash flows can be compared with the planned cash flows for the period. If there is a significant divergence between the projected, or forecast, cash flows and the actual cash flows, explanations must be sought and corrective action taken where necessary.

To refresh your memory on cash budgets, it would probably be worth looking back at Chapter 2, p. 39.

Although cash budgets are prepared primarily for internal management purposes, prospective lenders sometimes require them when a loan to a business is being considered.

Operating cash cycle

When managing cash, it is important to be aware of the **operating cash cycle (OCC)** of the business. For a retailer, for example, this may be defined as the period between the outlay of cash necessary for the purchase of inventories and the ultimate receipt of cash from the sale of the goods. In the case of a business that purchases goods on credit for subsequent resale on credit (for example, a wholesaler), the OCC is as shown in Figure 10.8.

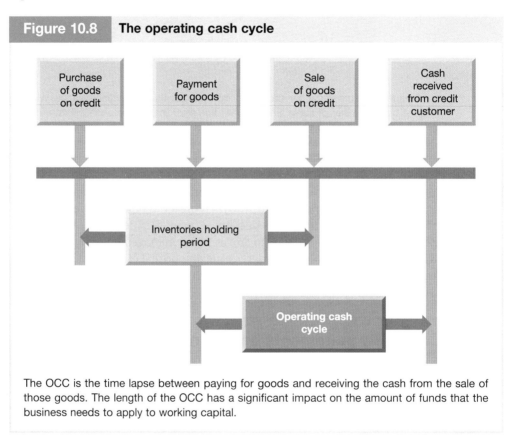

Figure 10.8 **The operating cash cycle**

The OCC is the time lapse between paying for goods and receiving the cash from the sale of those goods. The length of the OCC has a significant impact on the amount of funds that the business needs to apply to working capital.

Figure 10.8 shows that payment for inventories acquired on credit occurs some time after those inventories have been purchased and, therefore, no immediate cash outflow arises from the purchase. Similarly, cash receipts from credit customers will occur some time after the sale is made, and so there will be no immediate cash inflow as a result of the sale. The OCC is the period between the payment made to the supplier for goods concerned and the cash received from the credit customer. Although Figure 10.8 depicts the position for a wholesaling business, the precise definition of the OCC can easily be adapted for other types of business.

The OCC is important because it has a significant influence on the financing requirements of the business. Broadly, the longer the cycle, the greater the financing requirements of the business and the greater the financial risks. For this reason, the business is likely to want to reduce the OCC to the minimum possible period.

For the type of business mentioned above, which buys and sells on credit, the OCC can be calculated from the financial statements by the use of certain ratios. It is calculated as shown in Figure 10.9.

Figure 10.9 Calculating the operating cash cycle

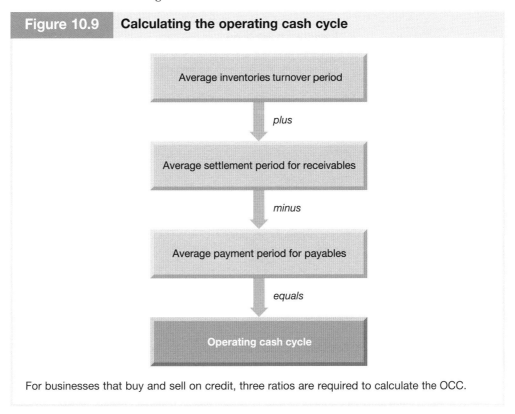

For businesses that buy and sell on credit, three ratios are required to calculate the OCC.

Activity 10.9

The financial statements of Freezeqwik Ltd, a distributor of frozen foods, are set out below for the year ended 31 December last year.

Income statement for the year ended 31 December last year

	£000	£000
Sales revenue		820
Cost of sales		
Opening inventories	142	
Purchases	568	
	710	
Closing inventories	166	(544)
Gross profit		276
Administration expenses		(120)
Distribution expenses		(95)
Operating profit		61
Financial expenses		(32)
Profit before taxation		29
Taxation		(7)
Profit for the year		22

→

Statements of financial position (balance sheet) as at 31 December last year

	£000
Non-current assets	
Property, plant and equipment	
Premises at valuation	180
Fixtures and fittings at cost less depreciation	82
Motor vans at cost less depreciation	102
	364
Current assets	
Inventories	166
Trade receivables	264
Cash	24
	454
Total assets	818
Equity	
Ordinary share capital	300
Share premium account	200
Retained earnings	152
	652
Current liabilities	
Trade payables	159
Taxation	7
	166
Total equity and liabilities	818

All purchases and sales are on credit. There has been no change in the level of trade receivables or payables over the period.

Calculate the length of the OCC for the business and go on to suggest how the business may seek to reduce this period.

The OCC may be calculated as follows:

Number of days

Average inventories turnover period:

$$\frac{(\text{Opening inventories} + \text{Closing inventories})/2}{\text{Cost of sales}} \times 365$$

$$= \frac{(142 + 166)/2}{544} \times 365 \qquad\qquad 103$$

Average settlement period for trade receivables:

$$\frac{\text{Trade receivables}}{\text{Credit sales}} \times 365 = \frac{264}{820} \times 365 \qquad\qquad 118$$

Average settlement period for trade payables:

$$\frac{\text{Trade payables}}{\text{Credit purchases}} \times 365 = \frac{159}{568} \times 365 \qquad\qquad (102)$$

OCC $\qquad\qquad\qquad\qquad\qquad\qquad\qquad\qquad\qquad\qquad$ 119

The business can reduce the length of the OCC in a number of ways. The average inventories holding period seems quite long. At present, average inventories held represent more than three months' sales requirements. Lowering the level of inventories held will reduce this. Similarly, the average settlement period for trade receivables seems long, at nearly four months' sales. Imposing tighter credit control, offering discounts, charging interest on overdue accounts and so on may reduce this. However, any policy decisions concerning inventories and trade receivables must take account of current trading conditions.

Extending the period of credit taken to pay suppliers could also reduce the OCC. However, for reasons that will be explained later, this option must be given careful consideration.

Real World 10.11 shows the average operating cash cycle for large European companies and large US companies.

REAL WORLD 10.11

Cycling along

The annual survey of working capital by REL Consulting and CFO Europe (see Real World 10.2 above) calculates the average operating cash cycle for the top 1,000 European and top 1,000 US businesses. Comparative figures for the five-year period ending in 2006 are shown in Figure 10.10.

We can see that European businesses have a higher average OCC than their US counterparts in each of the five years.

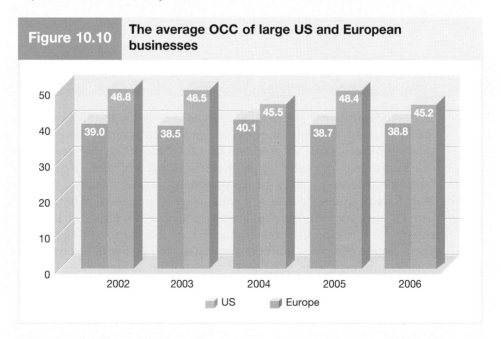

| Figure 10.10 | The average OCC of large US and European businesses |

Source: Diagram adapted from diagram in 'US and European companies leave billions of dollars, euros untapped in working capital', www.relconsult.com, 29 August 2007, p. 5.

Cash transmission

A business will normally wish to benefit from receipts from customers at the earliest opportunity. The benefit is immediate where payment is made in cash. However, when payment is made by cheque, there is normally a delay of three to four working days before the cheque can be cleared through the banking system. The business must therefore wait for this period before it can benefit from the amount paid in. In the case of a business that receives large amounts in the form of cheques, the opportunity cost of this delay can be significant.

To avoid this delay, a business could require payments to be made in cash. This is not usually very practical, mainly because of the risk of theft and/or the expense of conveying cash securely. Another option is to ask for payment to be made by standing order or by direct debit from the customer's bank account. This should ensure that the amount owing is always transferred from the bank account of the customer to the bank account of the business on the day that has been agreed.

It is also possible for funds to be transferred directly to a business's bank account. As a result of developments in computer technology, customers can pay for items by using debit cards, which results in the appropriate account being instantly debited and the seller's bank account being instantly credited with the required amount. This method of payment is widely used by large retail businesses, and may well extend to other types of business.

Bank overdrafts

Bank overdrafts are simply bank current accounts that have a negative balance. They are a type of bank loan. We looked at these in Chapter 6 in the context of short-term bank borrowing (p. 243). They can be a useful tool in managing the business's cash flow requirements.

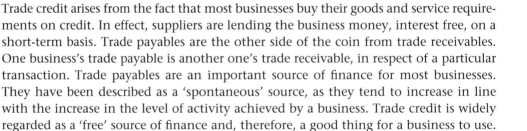

Managing trade payables

Trade credit arises from the fact that most businesses buy their goods and service requirements on credit. In effect, suppliers are lending the business money, interest free, on a short-term basis. Trade payables are the other side of the coin from trade receivables. One business's trade payable is another one's trade receivable, in respect of a particular transaction. Trade payables are an important source of finance for most businesses. They have been described as a 'spontaneous' source, as they tend to increase in line with the increase in the level of activity achieved by a business. Trade credit is widely regarded as a 'free' source of finance and, therefore, a good thing for a business to use. There may be real costs, however, associated with taking trade credit.

First, customers who take credit may not be as well treated as those who pay immediately. For example, when goods are in short supply, credit customers may receive lower priority when the goods available are allocated. In addition, credit customers may be less favoured in terms of delivery dates or the provision of technical support services. Sometimes, the goods or services provided may be more costly if credit is required. However, in most industries, trade credit is the norm. As a result, the above costs will not apply except, perhaps, to customers that abuse the credit facilities. A business that purchases supplies on credit will normally have to incur additional administration and accounting costs in dealing with the scrutiny and payment of invoices, maintaining and updating payables' accounts and so on.

These points are not meant to imply that taking credit is a burden to a business. There are, of course, real benefits that can accrue. Provided that trade credit is not abused, it can represent a form of interest-free loan. It can be a much more convenient method of paying for goods and services than paying by cash, and, during a period of inflation there will be an economic gain by paying later rather than sooner for goods and services purchased. For most businesses, these benefits will exceed the costs involved.

In some cases, delaying payment to payables can be a sign of financial problems. One such example is given in **Real World 10.12**.

REAL WORLD 10.12

NHS waiting times
FT

The National Health Service is delaying paying bills and cutting orders for supplies as it tries to balance its books, according to the trade associations whose members supply the service with everything from scanners to diagnostic tests.

Ray Hodgkinson, director-general of the British Healthcare Trades Association, said that while the picture was highly variable 'some of our members are having real trouble getting money out of NHS trusts'.

Most had standing orders that said bills should be paid within 30 days, Mr Hodgkinson said. 'But some are not paying for 60 or 90 days and even longer. They are in breach of their standing orders and for a lot of our members who are small businesses this is creating problems with cash flow. There is no doubt there is slow payment on a significant scale.'

Doris-Ann Williams, director-general of the British In-Vitro Diagnostics Association, whose members provide diagnostics supplies and tests, said: 'We are starting to see invoices not being paid and orders not being closed until the start of the new financial year [in April].

'All sorts of measures are being taken to try not to spend money in this financial year.'

Having seen orders dry up and bills not paid this time last year as the NHS headed for a £500m-plus financial deficit, she added that this was 'starting to seem like an annual event'.

Source: N. Timmins, 'NHS paying bills late in struggle to balance books, say suppliers', www.ft.com, 13 February 2007.

Taking advantage of cash discounts

Where a supplier offers a discount for prompt payment, the business should give careful consideration to the possibility of paying within the discount period. An example may be useful to illustrate the cost of forgoing possible discounts.

Example 10.5

Hassan Ltd takes 70 days to pay for goods from its supplier. To encourage prompt payment, the supplier has offered the business a 2 per cent discount if payment for goods is made within 30 days.

Hassan Ltd is not sure whether it is worth taking the discount offered.

If the discount is taken, payment could be made on the last day of the discount period (that is, the 30th day). However, if the discount is not taken, payment will be made after 70 days. This means that, by not taking the discount, the business will receive an extra 40 days' (that is, 70 − 30) credit. The cost of this extra credit to the business will be the 2 per cent discount forgone. If we annualise the cost of this discount forgone, we have:

$$365/40 \times 2\% = 18.3\%*$$

We can see that the annual cost of forgoing the discount is very high, and so it may be profitable for the business to pay the supplier within the discount period, even if it means that it will have to borrow to enable it to do so.

* This is an approximate annual rate. For the more mathematically minded, the precise rate is:

$$\{[(1 + 2/98)^{9.125}] - 1\} \times 100\% = 20.2\%$$

Controlling trade payables

→ To help monitor the level of trade credit taken, management can calculate the **average settlement period for trade payables**. As we saw in Chapter 3, this ratio is:

$$\textbf{Average settlement period for trade payables} = \frac{\textbf{Average trade payables}}{\textbf{Credit purchases}} \times 365$$

Once again, this provides an average figure, which could be misleading. A more informative approach would be to produce an ageing schedule for payables. This would look much the same as the ageing schedule for receivables described earlier.

SUMMARY

The main points of this chapter may be summarised as follows.

Working capital

- Working capital is the difference between current assets and current liabilities.
- That is, working capital = inventories + receivables + cash − payables − bank overdrafts.
- An investment in working capital cannot be avoided in practice – typically large amounts are involved.

Inventories

- There are costs of holding inventories, which include:
  - lost interest
  - storage cost

- insurance cost
- obsolescence.

● There are also costs of not holding sufficient inventories, which include:

- loss of sales and customer goodwill
- production dislocation
- loss of flexibility – cannot take advantage of opportunities
- reorder costs – low inventories imply more frequent ordering.

● Practical points on inventories management include:

- identify optimum order size – models can help with this
- set inventories reorder levels
- use forecasts
- keep reliable inventories records
- use accounting ratios (for example, inventories turnover period ratio)
- establish systems for security of inventories and authorisation
- consider just-in-time (JIT) inventories management.

Trade receivables

● When assessing which customers should receive credit, the five Cs of credit can be used:

- capital
- capacity
- collateral
- condition
- character.

● The costs of allowing credit include:

- lost interest
- lost purchasing power
- costs of assessing customer creditworthiness
- administration cost
- bad debts
- cash discounts (for prompt payment).

● The costs of denying credit include:

- loss of customer goodwill.

● Practical points on receivables management:

- establish a policy
- assess and monitor customer creditworthiness
- establish effective administration of receivables
- establish a policy on bad debts
- consider cash discounts
- use financial ratios (for example, average settlement period for trade receivables ratio)
- use ageing summaries.

Cash

● The costs of holding cash include:

- lost interest
- lost purchasing power.

- The costs of holding insufficient cash include:
  - loss of supplier goodwill if unable to meet commitments on time
  - loss of opportunities
  - inability to claim cash discounts
  - costs of borrowing (should an obligation need to be met at short notice).
- Practical points on cash management:
  - establish a policy
  - plan cash flows
  - make judicious use of bank overdraft finance – it can be cheap and flexible
  - use short-term cash surpluses profitably
  - bank frequently
  - operating cash cycle (for a wholesaler) = length of time from buying inventories to receiving cash from receivables less payables' payment period (in days)
  - transmit cash promptly.
- An objective of working capital management is to limit the length of the operating cash cycle (OCC), subject to any risks that this may cause.

Trade payables

- The costs of taking credit include:
  - higher price than purchases for immediate cash settlement
  - administrative costs
  - restrictions imposed by seller.
- The costs of not taking credit include:
  - lost interest-free borrowing
  - lost purchasing power
  - inconvenience – paying at the time of purchase can be inconvenient.
- Practical points on payables management:
  - establish a policy
  - exploit free credit as far as possible
  - use accounting ratios (for example, average settlement period for trade payables ratio).

→ **Key terms**

Working capital p. 394	**Five Cs of credit** p. 407
Lead time p. 400	**Cash discount** p. 412
ABC system of inventories control p. 402	**Average settlement period for trade receivables** p. 413
Economic order quantity (EOQ) p. 402	**Ageing schedule of trade receivables** p. 413
Materials requirement planning (MRP) system p. 405	**Operating cash cycle (OCC)** p. 420
Just-in-time (JIT) inventories management p. 405	**Average settlement period for trade payables** p. 426

For definitions of these terms see the Glossary, pp. 574–583.

Further reading

If you would like to explore the topics covered in this chapter in more depth, try the following books:

Business Finance: Theory and Practice, *McLaney, E.*, 8th edn., Financial Times Prentice Hall, 2009, chapter 13.

Corporate Finance, *Brealey, B., Myers, S. and Allen, F.*, 9th edn., McGraw-Hill, 2008, chapters 30 and 31.

Corporate Finance and Investment, *Pike, R. and Neale, B.*, 5th edn., Prentice Hall, 2006, chapters 13 and 14.

Corporate Financial Management, *Arnold, G.*, 3rd edn., Financial Times Prentice Hall, 2005, chapter 13.

REVIEW QUESTIONS

Answers to these questions may be found at the back of the book on p. 546.

10.1 Tariq is the credit manager of Heltex plc. He is concerned that the pattern of monthly cash receipts from credit sales shows that credit collection is poor compared with earlier forecasts. Heltex's sales director believes that Tariq is to blame for this situation, but Tariq insists that he is not. Why might Tariq not be to blame for the deterioration in the credit collection period?

10.2 How might each of the following affect the level of inventories held by a business?

(a) An increase in the number of production bottlenecks experienced by the business.
(b) A rise in the level of interest rates.
(c) A decision to offer customers a narrower range of products in the future.
(d) A switch of suppliers from an overseas business to a local business.
(e) A deterioration in the quality and reliability of bought-in components.

10.3 What are the reasons for holding inventories? Are these reasons different from the reasons for holding cash?

10.4 Identify the costs of holding:

(a) too little cash;
(b) too much cash.

EXERCISES

Exercises 10.4 to 10.7 are more advanced than 10.1 to 10.3. Those with coloured numbers have an answer at the back of the book, starting on p. 568.

  If you wish to try more exercises, visit the students' side of this book's Companion Website.

10.1 Hercules Wholesalers Ltd has been particularly concerned with its liquidity position in recent months. The most recent income statement and statement of financial position of the business are as follows:

Income statement for the year ended 31 December last year

	£000	£000
Sales revenue		452
Cost of sales		
Opening inventories	125	
Purchases	341	
	466	
Closing inventories	(143)	(323)
Gross profit		129
Expenses		(132)
Loss for the year		(3)

Statement of financial position (balance sheet) as at 31 December last year

	£000
Non-current assets	
Property, plant and equipment	
Premises at valuation	280
Fixtures and fittings at cost less depreciation	25
Motor vehicles at cost less depreciation	52
	357
Current assets	
Inventories	143
Trade receivables	163
	306
Total assets	663
Equity	
Ordinary share capital	100
Retained earnings	158
	258
Non-current liabilities	
Borrowings – Loans	120
Current liabilities	
Trade payables	145
Borrowings – Bank overdraft	140
	285
Total equity and liabilities	663

The trade receivables and payables were maintained at a constant level throughout the year.

Required:

(a) Explain why Hercules Wholesalers Ltd is concerned about its liquidity position.

(b) Calculate the operating cash cycle for Hercules Wholesalers Ltd based on the information above. (Assume a 360-day year.)

(c) State what steps may be taken to improve the operating cash cycle of the business.

10.2 International Electric plc at present offers its customers 30 days' credit. Half the customers, by value, pay on time. The other half take an average of 70 days to pay. The business is considering offering a cash discount of 2 per cent to its customers for payment within 30 days.

The credit controller anticipates that half of the customers who now take an average of 70 days to pay (that is, a quarter of all customers) will pay in 30 days. The other half (the final quarter) will still take an average of 70 days to pay. The scheme will also reduce bad debts by £300,000 a year.

Annual sales revenue of £365m is made evenly throughout the year. At present the business has a large overdraft (£60m) with its bank at an interest cost of 12 per cent a year.

Required:

(a) Calculate the approximate equivalent annual percentage cost of a discount of 2 per cent, which reduces the time taken by credit customers to pay from 70 days to 30 days. (*Hint*: This part can be answered without reference to the narrative above.)

(b) Calculate the value of trade receivables outstanding under both the old and new schemes.

(c) How much will the scheme cost the business in discounts?

(d) Should the business go ahead with the scheme? State what other factors, if any, should be taken into account.

(e) Outline the controls and procedures that a business should adopt to manage the level of its trade receivables.

10.3 The managing director of Sparkrite Ltd, a trading business, has just received summary sets of financial statements for last year and this year:

Sparkrite Ltd
Income statements for years ended 30 September last year and this year

	Last year		This year	
	£000	£000	£000	£000
Sales revenue		1,800		1,920
Cost of sales				
Opening inventories	160		200	
Purchases	1,120		1,175	
	1,280		1,375	
Closing inventories	(200)		(250)	
		(1,080)		(1,125)
Gross profit		720		795
Expenses		(680)		(750)
Profit for the year		40		45

Statements of financial position (balance sheets) as at 30 September last year and this year

	Last year	This year
	£000	£000
Non-current assets	950	930
Current assets		
Inventories	200	250
Trade receivables	375	480
Bank	4	2
	579	732
Total assets	1,529	1,662
Equity		
Fully paid £1 ordinary shares	825	883
Retained earnings	509	554
	1,334	1,437
Current liabilities	195	225
Total equity and liabilities	1,529	1,662

The finance director has expressed concern at the increase in inventories and trade receivables levels.

Required:
(a) Show, by using the data given, how you would calculate ratios that could be used to measure inventories and trade receivables levels during last year and this year.
(b) Discuss the ways in which the management of Sparkrite Ltd could exercise control over:
(i) inventories levels;
(ii) trade receivables levels.

10.4 Your superior, the general manager of Plastics Manufacturers Limited, has recently been talking to the chief buyer of Plastic Toys Limited, which manufactures a wide range of toys for young children. At present, Plastic Toys is considering changing its supplier of plastic granules and has offered to buy its entire requirement of 2,000 kg a month from you at the going market rate, provided that you will grant it three months' credit on its purchases. The following information is available:

1 Plastic granules sell for £10 a kg, variable costs are £7 a kg, and fixed costs £2 a kg.
2 Your own business is financially strong, and has sales revenue of £15 million a year. For the foreseeable future it will have surplus capacity, and it is actively looking for new outlets.

3 Extracts from Plastic Toys' financial statements:

	Year 1 £000	Year 2 £000	Year 3 £000
Sales revenue	800	980	640
Profit before interest and tax	100	110	(150)
Capital employed	600	650	575
Current assets			
Inventories	200	220	320
Receivables	140	160	160
	340	380	480
Current liabilities			
Payables	180	190	220
Overdraft	100	150	310
	280	340	530
Working capital	60	40	(50)

Required:

(a) Write some short notes suggesting sources of information that you would use to assess the creditworthiness of potential customers who are unknown to you. You should critically evaluate each source of information.

(b) Describe the accounting controls that you would use to monitor the level of your business's trade receivables.

(c) Advise your general manager on the acceptability of the proposal. You should give your reasons and do any calculations you consider necessary. (*Hint*: To answer this question you must weigh the costs of administration and cash discounts against the savings in bad debts and interest charges.)

10.5 Mayo Computers Ltd has annual sales of £20m. Bad debts amount to £0.1m a year. All sales made by the business are on credit, and, at present, credit terms are negotiable by the customer. On average, the settlement period for trade receivables is 60 days. Trade receivables are financed by an overdraft bearing a 14 per cent rate of interest per year. The business is currently reviewing its credit policies to see whether more efficient and profitable methods could be employed. Only one proposal has so far been put forward concerning the management of trade credit.

The credit control department has proposed that customers should be given a $2\frac{1}{2}$ per cent discount if they pay within 30 days. For those who do not pay within this period, a maximum of 50 days' credit should be given. The credit department believes that 60 per cent of customers will take advantage of the discount by paying at the end of the discount period, and the remainder will pay at the end of 50 days. The credit department believes that bad debts can be effectively eliminated by adopting the above policies and by employing stricter credit investigation procedures, which will cost an additional £20,000 a year. The credit department is confident that these new policies will not result in any reduction in sales revenue.

Required:

Calculate the net annual cost (savings) to the business of abandoning its existing credit policies and adopting the proposals of the credit control department. (*Hint*: To answer this question you must weigh the costs of administration and cash discounts against the savings in bad debts and interest charges.)

10.6 Boswell Enterprises Ltd is reviewing its trade credit policy. The business, which sells all of its goods on credit, has estimated that sales revenue for the forthcoming year will be £3m under the existing policy. Credit customers representing 30 per cent of trade receivables are expected to pay one month after being invoiced and 70 per cent are expected to pay two months after being invoiced. These estimates are in line with previous years' figures.

At present, no cash discounts are offered to customers. However, to encourage prompt payment, the business is considering giving a $2^1/_2$ per cent cash discount to credit customers who pay in one month or less. Given this incentive, the business expects credit customers accounting for 60 per cent of trade receivables to pay one month after being invoiced and those accounting for 40 per cent of trade receivables to pay two months after being invoiced. The business believes that the introduction of a cash discount policy will prove attractive to some customers and will lead to a 5 per cent increase in total sales revenue.

Irrespective of the trade credit policy adopted, the gross profit margin of the business will be 20 per cent for the forthcoming year and three months' inventories will be held. Fixed monthly expenses of £15,000 and variable expenses (excluding discounts), equivalent to 10 per cent of sales revenue, will be incurred and will be paid one month in arrears. Trade payables will be paid in arrears and will be equal to two months' cost of sales. The business will hold a fixed cash balance of £140,000 throughout the year, whichever trade credit policy is adopted. Ignore taxation.

Required:

(a) Calculate the investment in working capital at the end of the forthcoming year under:
   (i)   the existing policy;
   (ii) the proposed policy.

(b) Calculate the expected profit for the forthcoming year under:
   (i)   the existing policy;
   (ii) the proposed policy.

(c) Advise the business whether it should implement the proposed policy.

(*Hint*: The investment in working capital will be made up of inventories, trade receivables and cash, *less* trade payables and any unpaid expenses at the year end.)

10.7 Delphi plc has recently decided to enter the expanding market for minidisc players. The business will manufacture the players and sell them to small TV and hi-fi specialists, medium-sized music stores and large retail chain stores. The new product will be launched next February and predicted sales revenue for the product from each customer group for February and the expected rate of growth for subsequent months are as follows:

Customer type	February sales revenue £000	Monthly compound sales revenue growth %	Credit sales months
TV and hi-fi specialists	20	4	1
Music stores	30	6	2
Retail chain stores	40	8	3

The business is concerned about the financing implications of launching the new product, as it is already experiencing liquidity problems. In addition, it is concerned that the credit control department will find it difficult to cope. This is a new market for the business and there are likely to be many new customers who will have to be investigated for creditworthiness.

Workings should be in £000 and calculations made to one decimal place only.

Required:

(a) Prepare an ageing schedule of the monthly receivables balance relating to the new product for each of the first four months of the new product's life, and comment on the results. The schedule should analyse the receivables outstanding according to customer type. It should also indicate, for each customer type, the relevant percentage outstanding in relation to the total amount outstanding for each month.

(b) Identify and discuss the factors that should be taken into account when evaluating the creditworthiness of the new business customers.

11

Measuring and managing for shareholder value

INTRODUCTION

For some years, shareholder value has been a 'hot' issue among managers. Many leading businesses now claim that the quest for shareholder value is the driving force behind their strategic and operational decisions. In this chapter, we begin by considering what is meant by the term 'shareholder value', and in the sections that follow, we look at some of the main approaches to measuring shareholder value.

LEARNING OUTCOMES

When you have completed this chapter, you should be able to:

- Describe the shareholder value approach and explain its implications for the management of a business.

- Discuss the reasons why new ways of measuring shareholder value are necessary.

- Explain SVA and EVA® and describe their role in measuring and delivering shareholder value.

- Explain MVA and TSR and evaluate their usefulness for investors.

The quest for shareholder value

→ Let us start by considering what the term **shareholder value** means. In simple terms, it is about putting the needs of shareholders at the heart of management decisions. It is argued that shareholders invest in a business with a view to maximising their financial returns in relation to the risks that they are prepared to take. As managers are appointed by the shareholders to act on their behalf, management decisions and actions should reflect a concern for maximising shareholder returns. Although the business may have other 'stakeholder' groups, such as employees, customers and suppliers, it is the shareholders that should be seen as the most important group.

This, of course, is not a new idea. Take a look at most books on finance or economics, including this one, and you will see that maximising shareholder returns is assumed to be the key objective of a business. However, not everyone accepts this idea. Some believe that a balance must be struck between the competing claims of the various stakeholders. A debate about whether shareholders should be regarded as the most important group is beyond the scope of this chapter. What we can say, however, is that changes in the economic environment over recent years have often forced managers to focus their attention on the needs of shareholders.

In the past, shareholders have been accused of being too passive and of accepting too readily the profits and dividends that managers have delivered. However, this has changed. Nowadays, shareholders are much more assertive and, as owners of the business, are in a position to insist that their needs are given priority. Since the 1980s we have witnessed the deregulation and globalisation of business as well as enormous changes in technology. The effect has been to create a much more competitive world. This has meant not only competition for products and services but also competition for funds. Businesses must now compete more strongly for shareholder funds and so must offer competitive rates of return.

Thus, self-interest may be the most powerful reason for managers to commit themselves to maximising shareholder returns. If they do not do this, there is a real risk either that shareholders will replace them with managers who will, or that shareholders will allow the business to be taken over by another business, with managers who are dedicated to maximising shareholder returns.

Creating shareholder value

Creating shareholder value involves a four-stage process. The first stage is to set objectives for the business that recognise the central importance of maximising shareholder returns. This will set a clear direction for the business. The second stage is to establish an appropriate means of measuring the returns, or value, that have been generated for shareholders. For reasons that we shall discuss later, the traditional methods of measuring returns to shareholders are inadequate for this purpose. The third stage is to manage the business in order to ensure that shareholder returns are maximised. This means setting demanding targets and then achieving them through the best possible use of resources, the use of incentive systems and the embedding of a shareholder value culture throughout the business. The final stage is to measure the shareholder returns over a period of time to see whether the objectives have actually been achieved. These stages are set out in Figure 11.1.

Figure 11.1	Creating shareholder value

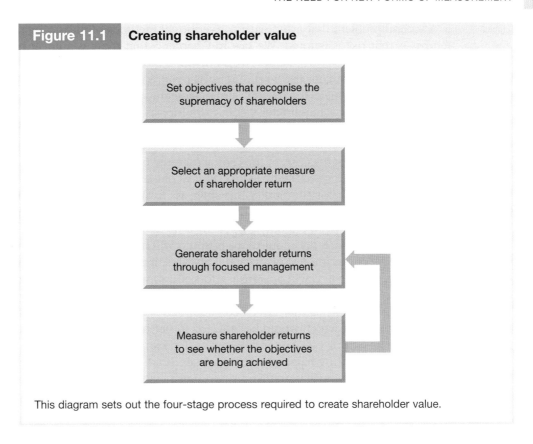

This diagram sets out the four-stage process required to create shareholder value.

The need for new forms of measurement

Once a commitment is made to maximising shareholder returns, an appropriate measure is then needed to help assess the returns to shareholders over time. Many argue that conventional methods for measuring shareholder returns are seriously flawed and so should not be used.

Activity 11.1

What are the conventional methods of measuring shareholder returns?

Managers normally use accounting profit or some ratio that is based on accounting profit, such as return on shareholders' funds or earnings per share.

One problem with using accounting profit, or a ratio based on profit, is that profit is measured over a relatively short period of time (usually one year). However, when we talk about maximising shareholder returns, we are concerned with maximising returns over the long term. It has been suggested that using profit as the key measure will run the risk that managers will take decisions that improve performance in the short term but which my have an adverse effect on long-term performance. For example, profits may be increased in the short term by cutting back on staff training and research expenditure. This type of expenditure, however, may be vital to long-term survival.

A second problem that arises with conventional methods of measuring shareholder returns is that risk is ignored. We saw in Chapter 5 that there is a linear relationship between the level of returns achieved and the level of risk that must be taken to achieve those returns. The higher the level of returns required, the higher the level of risk that must be taken to achieve the returns. A management strategy that produces an increase in profits can reduce shareholder value if the increase in profits achieved is not commensurate with the increase in the level of risk. Thus, profit alone is not enough.

A third problem with the use of profit, or a ratio based on profit, is that it does not take account of all of the costs of the capital invested by the business. The conventional approach to measuring profit will deduct the cost of loan capital (that is, interest charges) in arriving at profit for the period but there is no similar deduction for the cost of shareholder funds. (Remember that dividends are not deducted in arriving at the profit figure and, anyway, represent only part of the total return to shareholders.) Critics of the conventional approach point out that a business will not make a profit, in an economic sense, unless it covers the cost of all capital invested, including shareholder funds. Unless this is done, the business will operate at a loss and so shareholder value will be reduced.

A final problem is that the accounting profit reported by a business can vary according to the particular policies that have been adopted. Some businesses adopt a very conservative approach, which would be reflected in particular accounting policies such as the immediate writing off of intangible assets (for example, research and development), the use of the reducing balance method of depreciation (which favours high depreciation charges in the early years), and so on. Businesses that do not adopt conservative accounting policies would report profits more quickly. The writing off of intangible assets over a long period (or perhaps, not writing off intangible assets at all), the use of the straight-line method of depreciation, and so forth, will mean that profits are reported more quickly.

In addition, there are some businesses that may adopt particular accounting policies or structure transactions in a particular way in order to portray a picture of financial health that is in line with what those who prepared the financial statements would like to see rather than what is a true and fair view of financial performance and position. This practice, which we discussed in Chapter 3, is referred to as 'creative accounting' and has been a major problem for accounting rule makers.

Net present value (NPV) analysis

To summarise the points made above, we can say that in order to measure changes in shareholder value, what we really need is a measure that will consider the long term, take account of risk and the cost of shareholders' funds, and will not be affected by accounting policy choices. Fortunately, we have a measure that can, in theory, do just this.

Net present value analysis was discussed in Chapter 4. We saw that if we want to know the net present value (NPV) of an asset (whether this is a physical asset such as a machine or a financial asset such as a share), we must discount the future cash flows generated by the asset over its life. Thus:

$$\text{NPV} = C_1 \frac{1}{(1+r)^1} + C_2 \frac{1}{(1+r)^2} + C_3 \frac{1}{(1+r)^3} + \cdots$$

where: C = cash flows at time t (1, 2, 3, . . .)
r = the required rate of return.

Shareholders have a required rate of return and managers must strive to generate long-term cash flows for shares (in the form of dividends or proceeds that investors receive from the sale of the shares) that meet this rate of return. A negative present value will indicate that the cash flows generated do not meet the minimum required rate of return. If a business is to create value for its shareholders, it must generate cash flows that exceed the required returns of shareholders. In other words, the cash flows generated must produce a positive present value.

The NPV method fulfils the criteria that we mentioned earlier for the following reasons:

- It considers the long term. The returns from an investment, such as shares, are considered over the whole of the investment's life.
- It takes account of the cost of capital and risk. Future cash flows are discounted using the required rates of returns from investors (that is, both long-term lenders and shareholders). Moreover, this required rate of return will reflect the level of risk associated with the investment. The higher the level of risk, the higher the required level of return.
- It is not sensitive to the choice of accounting policies. Cash, rather than profit, is used in the calculations and is a more objective measure of return.

Extending NPV analysis: shareholder value analysis

We know from our earlier study of NPV that, when evaluating an investment project, shareholder wealth will be maximised when the net present value of cash flows generated by the project is maximised. In essence, the business is simply a portfolio of investment projects and so the same principles should apply when considering the business as a whole. **Shareholder value analysis (SVA)** is founded on this basic idea.

The SVA approach involves evaluating strategic decisions according to their ability to maximise value, or wealth, for shareholders. To undertake this evaluation, conventional measures are discarded and replaced by discounted cash flows. We have seen that the net present value of a project represents the value of that particular project. Given that the business can be viewed as a portfolio of projects, the value of the business as a whole can, therefore, be viewed as the net present value of the cash flows that it generates. SVA seeks to measure the discounted cash flows of the business as a whole and then seeks to identify that part which is available to the shareholders.

Activity 11.2

If the net present value of future cash flows generated by the business represents the value of the business as a whole, how can we derive that part of the value of the business that is available to shareholders?

A business will normally be financed by a combination of loan capital and ordinary shareholders' funds. Thus, holders of loan capital will also have a claim on the total value of the business. That part of the total business value that is available to ordinary shareholders can therefore be derived by deducting from the total value of the business (total NPV), the market value of any loans outstanding. Hence:

Shareholder value = Total business value − Market value of outstanding loans

Measuring free cash flows

The cash flows used to measure total business value are the **free cash flows**. These are the cash flows generated by the business that are available to ordinary shareholders and long-term lenders. In other words, they are equivalent to the net cash flows from operations after deducting tax paid and cash for additional investment. These free cash flows can be deduced from information contained within the income statement and statement of financial position (balance sheet) of a business.

It is probably worth going through a simple example to illustrate how the free cash flows can be calculated in practice.

Example 11.1

Sagittarius plc generated sales of £220 million during the year and has an operating profit margin of 25 per cent of sales. Depreciation charges for the year were £8.0 million and the cash tax rate for the year was 20 per cent of operating profit. During the year, £11.3 million was invested in additional working capital and £15.2 million was invested in additional non-current assets. A further £8.0 million was invested in the replacement of existing non-current assets.

The free cash flows are calculated as follows:

	£m	£m
Sales		220.0
Operating profit (25% × £220m)		55.0
Add Depreciation charge		8.0
Operating cash flows		63.0
Less Cash tax (20% × £55m)		(11.0)
Operating cash flows after tax		52.0
Less Additional working capital	(11.3)	
Additional non-current assets	(15.2)	
Replacement non-current assets	(8.0)	(34.5)
Free cash flows		17.5

We can see from Example 11.1 that, to derive the operating cash flows, we add the depreciation charge to the operating profit figure. We can also see that the cost of replacement of existing non-current assets is deducted from the operating cash flows in order to deduce the free cash flows. When we are trying to predict future free cash flows, one way of arriving at an approximate figure for the cost of replacing existing assets is to assume that the depreciation charge for the year is equivalent to the replacement charge for non-current assets. This would mean that the two adjustments mentioned cancel each other out and the calculation above could be shortened to:

	£m	£m
Sales		220.0
Operating profit (25% × £220m)		55.0
Less Cash tax (20% × £55m)		(11.0)
		44.0
Less: Additional working capital	(11.3)	
Additional non-current assets	(15.2)	(26.5)
Free cash flows		17.5

This shortened approach enables us to identify the key variables in determining free cash flows as being:

- sales
- operating profit margin
- cash tax rate
- additional investment in working capital
- additional investment in non-current assets (NCA).

Figure 11.2 sets out the process in the form of a flow chart.

Figure 11.2   Measuring free cash flows

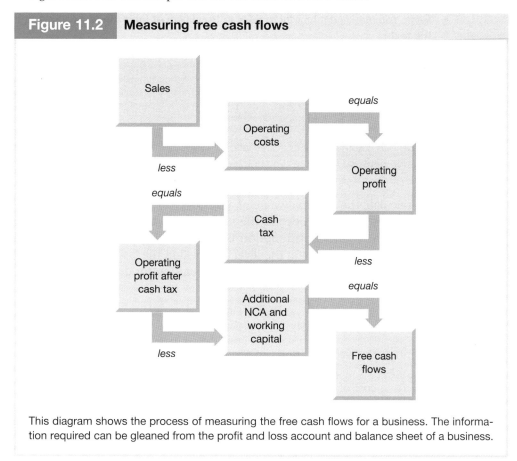

This diagram shows the process of measuring the free cash flows for a business. The information required can be gleaned from the profit and loss account and balance sheet of a business.

The five variables identified are **value drivers** of the business that reflect key business decisions. These decisions convert into free cash flows and finally into shareholder value.

The free cash flows should be measured over the life of the business. However, this is usually a difficult task. To overcome the problem, it is helpful to divide the future cash flows into two elements:

- cash flows over the planning horizon and which may be forecast with a reasonable level of reliability; and
- cash flows occurring beyond the planning horizon, which will be represented by a terminal value.

It is a good idea to try to make the planning horizon as long as possible. This is because the discounting process ensures that values beyond the planning horizon are given little weight. As can be imagined, cash flows in the distant future can be extremely difficult to forecast with accuracy and so the less weight given to them, the better.

Activity 11.3

Libra plc has an estimated terminal value (representing cash flows beyond the planning horizon) of £100 million. What is the present value of this figure assuming a discount rate of 12 per cent and a planning horizon of:

(a) 5 years
(b) 10 years
(c) 15 years?

(*Hint*: You may find it helpful to refer to the discount tables in Appendix A at the end of the text.)

The answers are:

(a) £100m × 0.567 = £56.7m
(b) £100m × 0.322 = £32.2m
(c) £100m × 0.183 = £18.3m

We can see that there is a dramatic difference in the present value of the terminal calculation between the three time horizons, given a 12 per cent discount rate.

To calculate the terminal value of a business, it is usually necessary to make simplifying assumptions. It is beyond the scope of this book to discuss this topic in detail. However, one common assumption is that returns beyond the planning horizon will remain constant (perhaps at the level achieved in the last year of the planning period). Using the formula for a perpetuity, the calculation for determining the terminal value (TV) will be:

$$TV = C_1/r$$

where: C_1 = the free cash flows in the following year
r = the required rate of return from investors (that is, the weighted average cost of capital).

This formula provides a capitalised value for future cash flows. Thus, if an investor receives a constant cash flow of £100 per year and has a required rate of return of 10 per cent, the capitalised value of these cash flows will be £100/0.1 = £1,000. In other words, the future cash flows are worth £1,000, when invested at the required rate of return, to the investor. This formula is similar to the dividend formula, where dividends are assumed to be constant, that we covered in Chapter 8.

Let us go through an example to illustrate the way in which shareholder value can be calculated.

Example 11.2

The directors of United Pharmaceuticals plc are considering the purchase of all the shares in Bortex plc, which produces vitamins and health foods. Bortex plc has a strong presence in the UK and it is expected that the directors of the business will reject any bids that value the shares of the business at less than £11.00 per share.

Bortex plc generated sales for the most recent year end of £3,000 million. Extracts from the statement of financial position (balance sheet) of the business at the end of the most recent year are as follows:

	£m
Equity	
Share capital (£1 ordinary shares)	400.0
Retained earnings	380.0
	780.0
Non-current liabilities	
Loan capital	120.0

Forecasts that have been prepared by the business planning department of Bortex plc are as follows:

- Sales will grow at 10 per cent a year for the next five years.
- The operating profit margin is currently 15 per cent and is likely to be maintained at this rate in the future.
- The cash tax rate is 25 per cent.
- Replacement non-current asset investment (RNCAI) will be in line with the annual depreciation charge each year.
- Additional non-current asset investment (ANCI) over the next five years will be 10 per cent of sales growth.
- Additional working capital investment (AWCI) over the next five years will be 5 per cent of sales growth.

After five years, the sales of the business will stabilise at their Year 5 level.

The business has a cost of capital of 10 per cent and the loan capital figure in the balance sheet reflects its current market value.

The free cash flow calculation will be as follows:

	Year 1 £m	Year 2 £m	Year 3 £m	Year 4 £m	Year 5 £m	After Year 5 £m
Sales	3,300.0	3,630.0	3,993.0	4,392.3	4,831.5	4,831.5
Operating profit (15%)	495.0	544.5	599.0	658.8	724.7	724.7
Less Cash tax (25%)	(123.8)	(136.1)	(149.8)	(164.7)	(181.2)	(181.2)
Operating profit after cash tax	371.2	408.4	449.2	494.1	543.5	543.5
Less						
ANCAI (Note 1)	(30.0)	(33.0)	(36.3)	(39.9)	(43.9)	–
AWCI (Note 2)	(15.0)	(16.5)	(18.2)	(20.0)	(22.0)	–
Free cash flows	326.2	358.9	394.7	434.2	477.6	543.5

Notes

1 The additional non-current asset investment is 10 per cent of sales growth. In the first year, sales growth is £300m (that is, £3,300m – £3,000m). Thus, the investment will be 10% × £300m = £30m. Similar calculations are carried out for the following years.

2 The additional working capital investment is 5 per cent of sales growth. In the first year the investment will be 5% × £300m = £15m. Similar calculations are carried out in following years.

Having derived the free cash flows (FCF), we can calculate the total business value as follows:

Year	FCF £m	Discount rate 10.0%	Present value £m
1	326.2	0.91	296.8
2	358.9	0.83	297.9
3	394.7	0.75	296.0
4	434.2	0.68	295.3
5	477.6	0.62	296.1
Terminal value (543.5/0.10)	5,435.0	0.62	3,369.7
Total business value			4,851.8

Activity 11.4

What is the shareholder value figure for the business in Example 11.2? Would the sale of the shares at £11 per share really add value for the shareholders of Bortex plc?

Shareholder value will be the total business value less the market value of the loan capital. Hence, shareholder value is:

	£m
£4,851.8m – £120m	= 4,731.8
The proceeds from the sale of the shares to	
United Pharmaceuticals would yield 400m × £11	= 4,400.0

Thus, from the point of view of the shareholders of Bortex plc, the sale of the business at the share price mentioned would not increase shareholder value.

Figure 11.3 sets out the key steps in calculating SVA.

Figure 11.3   Deriving shareholder value

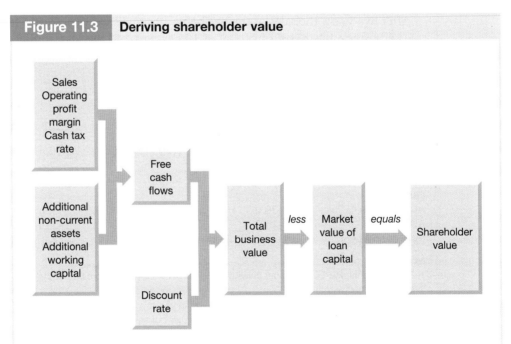

This diagram shows how shareholder value is derived. The five value drivers mentioned earlier – sales, operating profit, cash tax, additional non-current assets and additional working capital – will determine the free cash flows. These cash flows will be discounted using the required rate of return from investors to determine the total value of the business. If we deduct the market value of any loan capital from this figure, we are left with a measure of shareholder value.

Managing the business with shareholder value analysis

We saw earlier that the adoption of SVA indicates a commitment to managing the business in a way that maximises shareholder returns. Those who support this approach argue that SVA can be a powerful tool for strategic planning. For example, SVA can be extremely useful when considering major shifts of direction such as:

- acquiring new businesses
- selling existing businesses
- developing new products or markets
- reorganising or restructuring the business.

This is because SVA takes account of all the elements that determine shareholder value.

To illustrate this point let us suppose that a business develops a new product that is quite different from those within its existing range of products and appeals to a quite different market. Profit forecasts may indicate that the product is likely to be profitable, and so a decision to launch the product may be made. However, this decision may increase the level of risk for the business and, if so, investors will demand higher levels of return. In addition, there may have to be a significant investment in additional non-current assets and working capital in order to undertake the venture. When these factors are taken into account, using the type of analysis shown above, it may be found that the present value of the venture is negative. In other words, shareholder value will be destroyed.

SVA is also useful in focusing attention on the value drivers that create shareholder wealth. For example, we saw earlier that the key variables in determining free cash flows were:

- sales
- operating profit margin
- cash tax rate
- additional investment in working capital
- additional investment in non-current assets.

In order to improve free cash flows and, in turn, shareholder value, management targets can be set for improving performance in relation to each value driver and responsibility for achieving these targets can be assigned.

Activity 11.5

What do you think are the practical problems of adopting an SVA approach?

Two practical problems spring to mind:

- Forecasting future cash flows lies at the heart of this approach. In practice, forecasting can be difficult and simplifying assumptions will usually have to be made.
- SVA requires more comprehensive information (for example, information concerning the value drivers) than the traditional measures discussed earlier.

You may have thought of other problems.

Implications of SVA

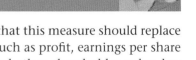

It is worth emphasising that supporters of SVA believe that this measure should replace the traditional accounting measures of value creation such as profit, earnings per share and return on ordinary shareholders' funds. To see whether shareholder value has increased or decreased, we must compare shareholder value at the beginning and the end of a period.

We can see that SVA is a radical departure from the conventional approach to managing a business. It will require different performance indicators, different financial reporting systems, and different management incentive methods. It may also require a change of culture within the business to accommodate the shareholder value philosophy as not all employees may be focused on the need to maximise shareholder wealth.

Economic value added (EVA®)

Economic value added (EVA®) has been developed and trademarked by a US management consultancy firm, Stern Stewart. However, EVA® is based on the idea of economic profit, which has been around for many years. The measure reflects the point made earlier that for a business to be profitable in an economic sense, it must generate returns that exceed the required returns from investors. It is not enough simply to make an accounting profit because this measure does not take full account of the returns required from investors.

EVA® indicates whether the returns generated exceed the required returns from investors. The formula is as follows:

$$\text{EVA}^{®} = \text{NOPAT} - (\text{R} \times \text{C})$$

where: NOPAT = net operating profit after tax

R = required returns from investors (that is, the weighted average cost of capital)

C = capital invested (that is, the net assets of the business).

Only when EVA® is positive can we say that the business is increasing shareholder wealth. To maximise shareholder wealth, managers must increase EVA® by as much as possible.

Activity 11.6

What can managers do in order to increase EVA®? (*Hint*: Use the formula shown above as your starting point.)

The formula suggests that in order to increase EVA®, managers may try the following tactics:

- Increase NOPAT. This may be done by either reducing expenses or increasing sales.
- Use capital invested more efficiently. This means selling off assets that are not generating returns which exceed their cost and investing in assets that do.
- Reduce the required rates of return for investors. This may be achieved by changing the capital structure in favour of loan capital (which is cheaper to service than share capital). This strategy, however, can create problems, as discussed in Chapter 8.

EVA® relies on conventional financial statements to measure the wealth created for shareholders. However, the NOPAT and capital figures shown on these statements are used only as a starting point. They have to be adjusted because of the problems and limitations of conventional measures. According to Stern Stewart, the major problem is that profit and capital are understated because of the conservative bias in accounting measurement. Profit is understated as a result of arbitrary write-offs such as research and development expenditure written off and also as a result of excessive provisions being created (such as allowances for trade receivables). Capital is also understated because assets are reported at their original cost (less amounts written off), which can produce figures considerably below current market values. In addition, certain assets such as internally generated goodwill and brand names are omitted from the financial statements because no external transactions have occurred.

Stern Stewart has identified more than 100 adjustments that could be made to the conventional financial statements to eliminate the conservative bias. However, the firm believes that, in practice, only a handful of adjustments are probably needed to the accounting figures of any particular business. Unless an adjustment is going to have a significant effect on the calculation of EVA®, it is really not worth making. The adjustments made should reflect the nature of the particular business. Each business is unique and so must customise the calculation of EVA® to its particular circumstances. (Depending on your viewpoint, this aspect of EVA® can be seen either as indicating flexibility or as being open to manipulation.)

Common adjustments that have to be made include:

- *Research and development (R&D) costs and marketing costs*. These costs should be written off over the period that they benefit. In practice, however, they are often written off in the period in which they are incurred. This means that any amounts written off immediately should be added back to the assets on the balance sheet, thereby increasing invested capital, and then written off over time.
- *Restructuring costs*. This item can be viewed as an investment in the future rather than an expense to be written off. Supporters of EVA® argue that by restructuring, the business is better placed to meet future challenges and so any amounts incurred should be added back to assets.
- *Marketable investments*. Investment in shares and loan capital are not included as part of the capital invested in the business. This is because the income from marketable investments is not included in the calculation of operating profit. (Income from this source will be added in the income statement *after* operating profit has been calculated.)

Let us now consider a simple example to show how EVA® may be calculated.

Example 11.3

Scorpio plc was established two years ago and has produced the following statement of financial position and income statement at the end of the second year of trading.

Statement of financial position (balance sheet) as at the end of the second year

	£m
Non-current assets	
Plant and equipment	80.0
Motor vehicles	12.4
Marketable investments	6.6
	99.0
Current assets	
Inventories	34.5
Receivables	29.3
Cash	2.1
	65.9
Total assets	164.9
Equity	
Share capital	60.0
Retained earnings	23.7
	83.7
Non-current liabilities	
Loan capital	50.0
Current liabilities	
Trade payables	30.3
Taxation	0.9
	31.2
Total equity and liabilities	164.9

Income statement for the second year

	£m
Sales revenue	148.6
Cost of sales	(76.2)
Gross profit	72.4
Wages	(24.5)
Depreciation of plant and equipment	(12.8)
Marketing costs	(22.5)
Allowances for trade receivables	(4.5)
Operating profit	8.1
Income from investments	0.4
	8.5
Interest payable	(0.5)
Ordinary profit before taxation	8.0
Restructuring costs	(2.0)
Profit before taxation	6.0
Tax	(1.8)
Profit for the year	4.2

Discussions with the finance director reveal the following:

1 Marketing costs relate to the launch of a new product. The benefits of the marketing campaign are expected to last for three years (including this most recent year).

2 The allowance for trade receivables was created this year and the amount is very high. A more realistic figure would be £2.0 million.

3 Restructuring costs were incurred as a result of a collapse in a particular product market. By restructuring the business, benefits are expected to flow for an infinite period.

4 The business has a 10 per cent required rate of return for investors.

The first step in calculating EVA® is to adjust the net operating profit after tax to take account of the various points revealed from the discussion with the finance director. The revised figure is calculated as follows:

NOPAT adjustment

	£m	£m
Operating profit		8.1
Less Tax		(1.8)
		6.3

EVA® adjustments
(to be added back to profit)

	£m	£m
Marketing costs (2/3 × 22.5)	15.0	
Excess allowance	2.5	17.5
Adjusted NOPAT		23.8

The next step is to adjust the net assets (as represented by equity and loan capital) to take account of the points revealed.

Adjusted net assets (or capital invested)

	£m	£m
Net assets per statement of financial position		133.7
Add Marketing costs (Note 1)	15.0	
Allowance for trade receivables	2.5	
Restructuring costs (Note 2)	2.0	19.5
		153.2
Less Marketable investments (Note 3)		(6.6)
Adjusted net assets		146.6

Notes:

1 The marketing costs represent two years' benefits added back (2/3 × £22.5m).

2 The restructuring costs are added back to the net assets as they provide benefits over an infinite period. (Note that they were not added back to the operating profit as these costs were deducted after arriving at operating profit in the income statement.)

3 The marketable investments do not form part of the operating assets of the business and the income from these investments is not part of the operating income.

Activity 11.7

What is the EVA® for the second year of the business in Example 11.3?

EVA® can be calculated as follows:

$$\text{EVA}^® = \text{NOPAT} - (R \times C) = £23.8m - (10\% \times £146.6m)$$
$$= \underline{£9.1m} \text{ (to one decimal place)}$$

We can see that EVA® is positive and so the business increased shareholder wealth during the year.

Although EVA® is used by many large businesses, both in the USA and Europe, it tends to be used for management purposes only: few businesses report this measure to shareholders. One business that does, however, is Whole Foods Market, a leading retailer of natural and organic foods, which operates more than 270 stores in the USA and the UK. **Real World 11.1** describes the way in which the business uses EVA® and its EVA® results.

REAL WORLD 11.1

The whole picture

Whole Foods Market aims to improve its business by achieving improvements to EVA®. To encourage managers along this path, an incentive plan, based on improvements to EVA® has been introduced. The plan embraces senior executives, regional managers and store managers and the bonuses awarded form a significant part of their total remuneration. To make the incentive plan work, measures of EVA® based on the whole business, the regional level and the store level, are calculated. More than five hundred managers are already included in the incentive plan and this number is expected to increase in the future.

EVA® is used to evaluate capital investment decisions such as the acquisition of new stores and the refurbishment of existing stores. Unless there is clear evidence that value will be added, investment proposals are rejected. EVA® is also used to improve operational efficiency. It was mentioned earlier that one way in which EVA® can be increased is through an improvement in NOPAT. The business is, therefore, continually seeking ways to improve sales and profit margins and to bear down on costs.

The business publishes its EVA® for the year as part of the annual financial reporting process. This is a welcome feature, particularly as it is being used to reward managers. Where EVA® is being used for this purpose, investors should be able to see clearly the basis for managerial rewards.

EVA® for 2005 and 2006 are shown below. The relevant tax rate for each year was 40% and the cost of capital was 9%.

	Years ended	
	24 September 2006	*25 September 2005*
	$000	$000
NOPAT	215,281	165,579
Less Capital cost	(150,871)	(139,793)
EVA®	64,410	25,786
Improvement in EVA®	38,624	

Source: Based on information in www.wholefoodsmarket.com.

The main advantage of this measure is the discipline to which managers are subjected as a result of the charge for capital that has been invested. Before any increase in shareholder wealth can be recognised, an appropriate deduction is made for the use of business resources. Thus, EVA® encourages managers to use these resources efficiently. Where managers are focused simply on increasing profits, there is a danger that the resources used to achieve any increase in profits will not be taken into proper account.

The benefits of EVA® may be undermined, however, if a short-term perspective is adopted. **Real World 11.2** describes the problems of a large engineering business that is using EVA® and, where it is claimed, the technique may be distorting management behaviour.

REAL WORLD 11.2

Hard times   **FT**

Klaus Kleinfeld, Siemens' chief executive, is stuck in an unfortunate position after a deeply testing period at the helm of Europe's largest engineering group.

On the one side he is receiving pressure from investors fed up with a stagnating share price and profitability that continues to lag behind most of the German group's main competitors. But from the other he is under attack from the powerful IG Metall union aimed at holding him back from doing any serious restructuring.

'He is having to walk a tightrope,' says a former senior Siemens director. 'His focus right now has to be on fixing the problem areas and very quickly.'

Ben Uglow, an analyst at Morgan Stanley, says 'I think the real question now in Siemens is one of management incentivisation. I think Kleinfeld has done a good job in the last year of refocusing the portfolio but some of his big chiefs have let him down.' Many investors are concerned that the margin targets that Mr Kleinfeld set last year for all his divisions to reach by April 2007 are distorting matters by making managers relax if they have already exceeded them.

Mr Kleinfeld and other directors disagree vehemently. Management pay is based on the 'economic value added' each division provides against each year's budget, not on specific margin targets. But a former senior director says this has led to a lack of investment in some parts of the business as managers look to earn as much as possible.

Source: Richard Milne, 'Siemens chief finds himself in a difficult balancing act', www.ft.com, 6 November 2006.

EVA® and SVA compared

Although at first glance it may appear that EVA® and SVA are worlds apart, this is not the case. In fact the opposite is true. EVA® and SVA are closely related and, in theory at least, should produce the same figure for shareholder value. The way in which shareholder value is calculated using SVA has already been described. The EVA® approach to calculating shareholder value adds the capital invested to the present value of future EVA® flows and then deducts the market value of any loan capital. Figure 11.4 illustrates the two approaches to determining shareholder value.

Figure 11.4   Two approaches to determining shareholder value

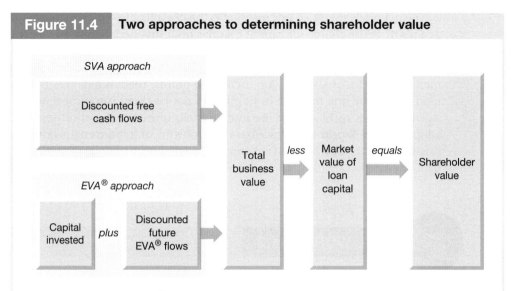

This figure shows how EVA® and SVA can both provide a measure of shareholder value. Total business value can be derived either by discounting the free cash flows over time or by discounting the EVA® flows over time and adding the capital invested. Whichever approach is used, the market value of loan capital must then be deducted to derive shareholder value.

Let us go through a simple example to illustrate this point.

Example 11.4

Leo Ltd has just been formed and has been financed by a £20 million issue of share capital and a £10 million issue of loan capital. The proceeds of the issue have been invested in non-current (fixed) assets with a life of three years and during this period these assets will depreciate by £10 million per year. The operating profit after tax is expected to be £15 million each year. There will be no replacement of non-current assets during the three-year period and no investment in working capital. At the end of the three years, the business will be wound up and the non-current assets will have no residual value.

The required rate of return by investors is 10 per cent.

The SVA approach to determining shareholder value will be as follows:

Year	FCF	Discount rate	Present value
	£m	10%	£m
1	25.0*	0.91	22.8
2	25.0	0.83	20.7
3	25.0	0.75	18.7
		Total business value	62.2
		Less Loan capital	(10.0)
		Shareholder value	52.2

* The free cash flows will be the operating profit after tax *plus* the depreciation charge (that is, £15m + £10m). In this case, there are no replacement non-current assets against which the depreciation charge can be netted off. It must therefore be added back.

The EVA® approach to determining shareholder value will be as follows:

Year	Opening capital invested (C) £m	Capital charge (10% × C) £m	Operating profit after tax £m	EVA® £m	Discount rate 10%	Present value of EVA® £m
1	30.0*	3.0	15.0	12.0	0.91	10.9
2	20.0	2.0	15.0	13.0	0.83	10.8
3	10.0	1.0	15.0	14.0	0.75	10.5
						32.2
					Opening capital	30.0
						62.2
					Less Loan capital	(10.0)
					Shareholder value	52.2

* The capital invested decreases each year by the depreciation charge (that is, £10 million).

EVA® or SVA?

Although both EVA® and SVA are consistent with the objective of maximising shareholder wealth and, in theory, should produce the same decisions and results, the supporters of EVA® claim that this measure has a number of practical advantages over SVA. One such advantage is that EVA® sits more comfortably with the conventional financial reporting systems and financial reports. There is no need to develop entirely new systems to implement EVA® as it can be calculated by making a few adjustments to the conventional income statement and statement of financial position.

It is also claimed that EVA® is more useful as a basis for rewarding managers. Both EVA® and SVA support the idea that management rewards be linked to increases in shareholder value. This should ensure that the interests of managers are closely aligned to the interests of shareholders. Under the SVA approach, management rewards will be determined on the basis of the contribution made to the generation of long-term cash flows. However, there are practical problems in using SVA for this purpose.

Activity 11.8

What are the practical problems that may arise when using SVA calculations to reward managers? (*Hint*: Think about how SVA is calculated.)

The SVA approach measures changes in shareholder value by reference to predicted changes in future cash flows and it is unwise to pay managers on the basis of predicted rather than actual achievements. If the predictions are optimistic, the effect will be that the business rewards optimism rather than real achievement. There is also a risk that unscrupulous managers will manipulate predicted future cash flows in order to increase their rewards.

Under EVA®, managers can receive bonuses based on actual achievement during a particular period. If management rewards are linked to a single period, however, there is a danger that managers will place undue attention on increasing EVA® during this period rather than over the long term. The objective should be to maximise EVA® over the longer term. Where a business has a stable level of sales, operating assets and borrowing, a current-period focus is likely to be less of a problem than where these elements are unstable over time. A stable pattern of operations minimises the risk that improvements in EVA® during the current period are achieved at the expense of future periods. Nevertheless, any reward system for managers must encourage a long-term perspective and so rewards should be based on the ability of managers to improve EVA® over a number of years rather than a single year.

Real World 11.3 describes the way in which one business uses EVA® to reward its managers.

REAL WORLD 11.3

Rewarding managers

Hanson PLC, a major supplier of heavy building materials, adopts a bonus system for its directors based on EVA®. EVA® generated is accumulated in a 'bonus bank' and the directors are paid a portion of the EVA® bonus bank during a particular year; the remainder is carried forward for payment in future years. The following is an extract from the 2006 Annual Report and Form 20-F of the business:

Annual bonus scheme

The annual bonus scheme for the Executive Directors and other senior executives is aligned with changes in shareholder value through the economic value added methodology. The main principle of economic value added is to recognise that over time a company should generate returns in excess of its cost of capital – the return that lenders and shareholders expect of the Company each year.

The annual bonus scheme is calibrated by reference to target levels of bonus and, for the Executive Directors and other senior executives, works on a bonus banking arrangement whereby each year the improvement in the group's overall economic value added for that year determines whether there is a bonus bank addition or deduction. Following the addition or deduction, the participant receives one-third of the accumulated bonus bank. There is neither a cap (maximum addition into the bonus bank each year) nor a floor (maximum deduction from the bonus bank each year).

The bonus bank has two main functions; firstly it ensures that individuals do not make short-term decisions such as deferring essential expenditure from one year to the next and receive a bonus for doing so; and secondly, the bonus bank can act as a retention tool.

For 2006, the target level of bonus for A J Murray was 62.5% of basic salary and for G Dransfield 37.5% of basic salary. No bonus entitlement arose for J C Nicholls who left the Company on October 31, 2006.

Improvement in the group's overall economic value added for the year to December 31, 2006 determined the bonus bank addition for the Executive Directors. The strong operating and profit performance in 2006 led to improvement in the group's economic value added and resulted in additions to the bonus bank of 69.4% of basic salary for A J Murray and 41.6% of basic salary for G Dransfield. The bonuses paid in respect of the year to December 31, 2006 to the Executive Directors were £509,262 for A J Murray and £161,986 for G Dransfield.

Source: Hanson PLC Annual Report and Form 20-F 2006, www.hanson.biz.

It is worth noting that Stern Stewart believes that bonuses, calculated as a percentage of EVA®, should form a very large part of the total remuneration package for managers. Thus, the higher the EVA® figure, the higher the rewards to managers – with no upper limits. The philosophy is that EVA® should make managers wealthy provided it makes shareholders extremely wealthy. A bonus system should encompass as many managers as possible in order to encourage a widespread commitment to implementing EVA®.

EVA® in practice

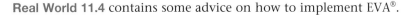

Real World 11.4 contains some advice on how to implement EVA®.

REAL WORLD 11.4

The thoughts of Robert Goizueto

Robert Goizueto was the chief executive of Coca-Cola Co. for many years and was an ardent supporter of EVA®. He offered two pieces of advice for those wishing to implement this technique:

- *Keep it simple.* By this he meant that EVA® should be the only method of value measurement used by managers. To do otherwise would lessen the impact of EVA® and would also make the management of the business unnecessarily complicated.
- *Make it accountable.* By this he meant that managers should be rewarded for increasing EVA®. In this way, the managers' own interests become indistinguishable from those of the owners of the business.

Source: See Ehrbar (reference 1 at the end of the chapter).

Market value added (MVA)

Stern Stewart developed EVA® to provide a means of motivating managers and other employees to achieving shareholder value. It is really designed for internal management purposes. However, a further measure has been developed by the same management consultants to complement EVA® and to provide shareholders with a way of tracking changes in shareholder value over time. **Market value added (MVA)** attempts to measure the gains or losses in shareholder value by measuring the difference between the market value of the business and the total investment that has been made in it over the years. The market value of the business is usually taken to be the market value of shares and loan capital. The total investment is the long-term capital invested, which is made up of loan capital plus share capital plus retained earnings. Figure 11.5 illustrates the derivation of market value added.

Figure 11.5 Market value added (MVA)

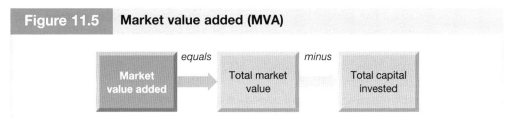

This figure shows how market value added represents the difference between the total market value (loan capital plus share capital) and the total amount invested in the business.

It is worth going through a simple example to show how market value can be calculated.

Example 11.5

Cosmo plc began trading ten years ago. It has two million £1 ordinary shares in issue that have a current market value of £5 per share. These shares were issued at their nominal value when the business was founded. The business also has £6 million 10 per cent loan capital. The book value of the loan capital is the same as its current market value. In addition, the business has retained earnings of £3 million.

The market value added can be calculated as follows:

	£m	£m
Market value of investments		
Ordinary shares (2m × £5)		10
Loan capital		6
		16
Total amount invested		
Ordinary shares (2m × £1)	2	
Retained earnings	3	
Loan capital	6	11
Market value added		5

We can see that market valued added is, in essence, a very simple idea. The cash value of the investment is compared with the cash invested. If the cash value of the investment is more than the cash invested, there has been an increase in shareholder value. If the cash value of the investment is less than the cash invested, there has been a decrease in shareholder value. There are, however, complications in measuring the figure for cash invested, which arise because of the conservative bias in accounting measurement. Thus, the adjustments to the balance sheet that are necessary for the proper calculation of EVA® are also required when measuring MVA.

The measurement of the cash value of capital invested is straightforward. The market value of each share is simply multiplied by the number of shares in issue in order to derive the total market value of the shares. If shares are not listed on the Stock Exchange it is not really possible to measure MVA, unless perhaps a bid for the business has been received from a possible buyer.

In Example 11.5, it was assumed that the market value and book value of loan capital are the same. This is a common assumption used in practice, and where this assumption is made, the calculation of MVA reduces to the difference between the market value of shares and the sum of the nominal value of those shares and retained earnings. Thus, in the example, MVA is simply the difference between £10m and £5m (£2m + £3m) = £5m.

In the example, we calculated MVA over the whole life of the business. The problem with doing this, in the case of an established business, is that it would not be clear when the value was actually created. The pattern of value creation over time may be useful in the assessment of past and likely future performance. It is perfectly feasible, however, to measure the change in MVA over any period by comparing the opening and closing positions for that period.

The link between MVA and EVA®

Stern Stewart argues that there is a strong relationship between MVA and EVA®. The theoretical underpinning of this relationship is clear. We saw earlier that the value of a business is equal to the present value of future expected EVA® plus the capital invested. Thus:

Business value = Capital invested + PV of future EVA®

This equation could be rearranged so that:

$$\text{PV of future EVA®} = \text{Business value} - \text{Capital invested} \quad (11.1)$$

We have also seen that market value added is the difference between the value of the business and the capital invested. Thus:

$$\text{MVA} = \text{Business value} - \text{Capital invested} \quad (11.2)$$

By comparing equations (11.1) and (11.2) we can see that:

PV of future EVA® = MVA

Stern Stewart states that the relationship described holds in practice as well as in theory. The firm has produced evidence to show that the correlation between MVA and EVA® is much stronger than the correlation between MVA and other measures of performance such as earnings per share, return on shareholders' funds, or cash flows.

Given that MVA reflects the expected future EVA® of a business, it follows that an investor using this measure will be able to see whether a business generates returns above the cost of capital invested. If a business only manages to provide returns in line with the cost of capital, the EVA® will be zero and so there will be no MVA. Thus, MVA can be used to impose a capital discipline on managers in the same way that EVA® does.

Limitations of MVA

MVA has a number of limitations as a tool for investors. To begin with, it has a fairly narrow scope. As mentioned earlier, MVA relies on market share prices and so it can only really be calculated for those businesses that are listed on a stock exchange. Similarly, MVA can only be used to assess the business as a whole as there are no separate market share prices available for strategic business units.

The interpretation of MVA can also be a problem. It is a measure of the absolute change occurring over time and so its significance is difficult to assess when deciding among competing investment opportunities involving businesses of different sizes or trading over different periods. Consider the following financial information relating to three separate businesses:

Business	Total market value (a) £m	Total capital invested (b) £m	Market value added (a) – (b) £m	No. of years trading
Alpha	250	120	130	18
Beta	480	350	130	16
Gamma	800	670	130	15

The table shows that each business has an identical MVA; but does this mean that each business has performed equally well? We can see that they operate with different amounts of capital invested and have operated over different periods.

The problems identified are not insurmountable but they reveal the difficulties of relying on an absolute measure when making investment decisions.

Activity 11.9

How could the problems of interpretation mentioned above be overcome?

The problem of the different time periods is probably best dealt with by comparing the businesses over the same time period. The problem of scale is probably best dealt with by comparing the MVA for each business with the capital invested in the business. (MVA/Capital provides a relative measure of wealth creation for investors.)

The most successful businesses at generating MVA are also the largest. Because MVA is an absolute measure of performance, large businesses have a greater potential to generate MVA. However, they also have a greater potential to destroy MVA.

Self-assessment question 11.1

Cupid plc produced the following balance sheet at the end of the third year of trading:

Statement of financial position (balance sheet) as at the end of the third year

	£m
Non-current assets	
Property	60.0
Computing equipment	90.0
Motor vehicles	22.0
	172.0
Current assets	
Inventories	39.0
Receivables	53.0
Cash	12.0
	104.0
Total assets	276.0

	£m
Equity	
£1 ordinary shares	60.0
Retained earnings	81.0
	141.0
Non-current liabilities	
Loan capital	90.0
Current liabilities	
Trade payables	45.0
Total equity and liabilities	276.0

An analysis of the underlying records reveals the following:

1 R&D costs relating to the development of a new product in the current year had been written off at a cost of £10 million. However, this is a prudent approach and the benefits are expected to last for ten years.
2 Property has a current value of £200 million.
3 The current market value of an ordinary share is £8.50.
4 The book value of the loan capital reflects its current market value.

Required:
Calculate the MVA for the business over its period of trading.
The answer to this question may be found at the end of the book, on p. 537.

Total shareholder return

Total shareholder return (TSR) has been used for many years by investors as a means of assessing value created and is often used as a basis for management reward systems. The total return from a share is made up of two elements: the increase (or decrease) in share value over a period plus (minus) any dividends paid during the period. To illustrate how total shareholder return is calculated, let us assume that a business commenced trading by issuing shares of £0.50 each at their nominal value (P_0) and by the end of the first year of trading the shares had increased in value to £0.55 (P_1). Furthermore, the business paid a dividend of £0.06 (D_1) per share during the period. We can calculate the total shareholder return as follows:

$$\text{Total shareholder return} = \frac{D_1 + (P_1 - P_0)}{P} \times 100\%$$

$$= \frac{0.06 + (0.55 - 0.50)}{0.50} \times 100\% = 22\%$$

The figure calculated has little information value when taken alone. It can only really be used to assess performance when compared with some benchmark.

Activity 11.10

What benchmark would be most suitable?

Perhaps the best benchmark to use would be the returns made by similar businesses operating in the same industry over the same period of time.

The reason that a benchmark using the returns of similar businesses is usually suitable is because it will compare the returns generated by the business with those generated from other investment opportunities that have the same level of risk. We have seen in earlier chapters that the level of return from an investment should always be related to the level of risk that has to be taken.

TSR in practice

Real World 11.5 provides an example of a business that sets a target TSR in relation to other, broadly similar, businesses.

REAL WORLD 11.5

Setting a target TSR

Unilever plc is a leading consumer goods business selling well-known brands of washing powder, toothpaste, creams, oils and so on. In its 2006 annual report, the business states:

> Unilever's TSR performance is compared with a peer group of competitors over a three-year rolling performance period. This period is sensitive enough to reflect changes but long enough to smooth out short-term volatility.

Unilever's position over a five-year period is shown in Figure 11.6.

Figure 11.6	**Unilever's position relative to the TSR reference group**

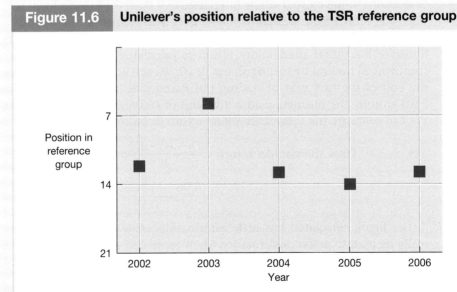

The reference group, including Unilever, consists of 21 businesses. Unilever's position is based on a three-year rolling period.

Source: Unilever plc, Annual Report and Accounts 2006, p. 27.

Many large businesses now publish total shareholder returns in their annual reports. **Real World 11.6** provides an example.

REAL WORLD 11.6

Tesco's TSR

Tesco plc, a major food retailer, publishes its TSR for a six-year period, along with movements in the FTSE 100 index for the same period. The TSR for the business, which is displayed graphically, is reproduced in Figure 11.7.

Figure 11.7	Tesco plc: total shareholder returns, February 2001– February 2007

We can see from this graph that shareholder returns vary over time and so a measure of total shareholder return is likely to be sensitive to the particular time period chosen.

Source: Tesco plc, Annual Report and Financial Statements 2007, p. 31.

TSR and managers' rewards

Where TSR is to be used as a basis for management reward, the issue of risk is very important. Higher returns can be achieved by taking on higher-risk projects. Managers should not be given rewards for increasing returns through this means.

Figure 11.8 sets out the main value measures that we have discussed in this chapter.

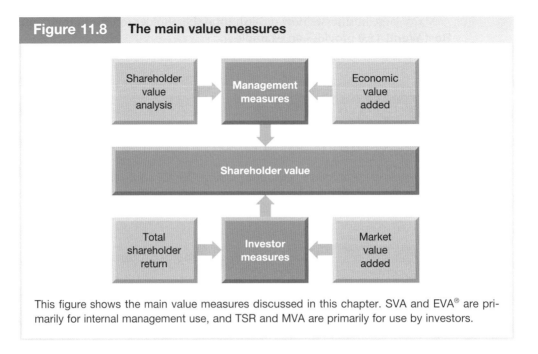

Figure 11.8 **The main value measures**

This figure shows the main value measures discussed in this chapter. SVA and EVA® are primarily for internal management use, and TSR and MVA are primarily for use by investors.

Criticisms of the shareholder value approach

In recent years, there has been growing criticism of the shareholder value approach. It is claimed that the pursuit of shareholder value has resulted in conflicts between shareholders and other stakeholders and has created a crisis for the world of business. There is no reason in theory, however, why such problems should occur. We have seen that shareholder value reflects a concern for long-term value creation, and to achieve this, the interests of other stakeholders cannot be trampled over. Nevertheless, it is easy to see how, in practice, the notion of shareholder value may be corrupted.

The quest for shareholder value implies a concern for improving the efficiency of current operations and for exploiting future growth opportunities. The latter of these is by far the more difficult task. The future is unpredictable and risks abound. Managers must therefore tread carefully. They must be painstaking in their analysis of future opportunities and in developing appropriate strategies. However, this is not always done. **Real World 11.7** describes the issues encountered by mobile phone operators in pursuit of growth and why things went horribly wrong.

REAL WORLD 11.7

Future imperfect

Telecommunication businesses became convinced that their future lay in G3 technology. They believed that there would be huge demand for the new technology from customers who were desperate to use their mobile phones for music downloads, picture and video exchange and for internet access. As a result they paid huge sums to acquire G3 operating licences. These costly investments, however, were an act of faith rather than a result of rigorous planning. There was no detailed analysis of who would use the new technology, how it would be paid for and when it would be required.

As the future unfolded, it became clear that the existing technology would not fade as quickly as predicted and that far too much has been paid for the G3 licences. The end result was a massive loss of shareholder value.

Source: Based on 'Companies must achieve the right balance for a successful strategy', *Financial News*, 22 February 2004.

Given the problems of exploiting future growth opportunities, managers may prefer to focus on improving efficiency. This is usually achieved by bearing down on costs through working assets harder, shedding staff and putting pressure on suppliers to lower prices. If, however, these cost reduction measures are taken too far, the result will be an emaciated business which is unable to take advantage of future growth opportunities and which has its major stakeholder groups locked in conflict.

To be successful, the shareholder value approach must strike the right balance between a concern for efficiency and a concern for future growth; a concern for efficiency alone is not enough. In order to achieve this balance, the way in which managers are assessed and rewarded must reflect the importance of both.

Measuring the value of future growth

If managers are to be assessed and rewarded, at least in part, on the basis of developing future growth potential, a suitable measure of this potential is required. According to Stern Stewart, the EVA® approach can provide such a measure.

We saw earlier that the value of a business can be described as:

Business value = Capital invested + PV of future EVA®

If a business has no growth potential and EVA® remains constant, we can use the formula for a perpetuity, so that the present value of future EVA® is:

$$\textbf{PV of future EVA}^\circledR = \frac{\textbf{EVA}^\circledR}{r}$$

where: r = required returns from investors (that is, the weighted average cost of capital). Thus, the value of a business with no growth potential is:

$$\textbf{Business value = Capital invested} + \frac{\textbf{EVA}^\circledR}{r}$$

Where the business has growth potential (as measured by growth in EVA®), business value (as measured by the market value of share and loan capital), will be greater than this. The value placed on future growth potential by investors is, therefore:

$$\textbf{Value of future growth potential} = \textbf{Business value} - \left(\textbf{Capital invested} + \frac{\textbf{EVA}^\circledR}{r}\right)$$

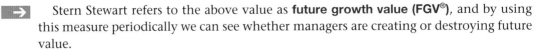

Stern Stewart refers to the above value as **future growth value (FGV®)**, and by using this measure periodically we can see whether managers are creating or destroying future value.

The percentage contribution to the value of the business arising from investor expectations concerning future growth in EVA® is:

$$\text{Percentage contribution to business value} = \left(\frac{\text{FGV}^{®}}{\text{Business value}} \right) \times 100\%$$

This measure can be used to see whether managers are striking the right balance between efficiency and future growth.

Activity 11.11

Centaur plc has five million shares in issue with a market value of £8.40 per share. The company has £14.2 million capital invested and for the most recent year, EVA® was £1.8 million. The required return from investors is 10 per cent a year.

What is the percentage contribution to the market value of the business arising from future growth?

$$\text{Assuming no growth, PV of future EVA}^{®} = \frac{\text{EVA}^{®}}{r}$$

$$= \frac{£1.8m}{0.10}$$

$$= £18.0m$$

$$\text{Value of future growth potential (FGV}^{®}) = \text{Business value} - \left(\text{Capital invested} + \frac{\text{EVA}^{®}}{r} \right)$$

$$= (5m \times £8.40) - (£14.2m + £18.0m)$$

$$= £9.8m$$

$$\text{Percentage contribution to business value} = \left(\frac{\text{FGV}^{®}}{\text{Business value}} \right) \times 100\%$$

$$= \frac{£9.8m}{(5m \times £8.40)} \times 100\%$$

$$= 23.3\%$$

Implementing the shareholder value approach

We have seen above that shareholder value may not always be implemented properly within a business. **Real World 11.8** sets out four different levels of implementation of shareholder value that may be found in practice.

REAL WORLD 11.8

Walking the talk

The extent to which a shareholder value philosophy is adopted within businesses varies. It has been suggested that four distinct levels can be identified.

Level 1

At this base level, the term 'shareholder value' is employed only as a business mantra and no real effort is made to implement shareholder value policies or techniques. Existing policies and techniques, however, may be re-labelled to give the impression that a shareholder value approach is being actively pursued. Whilst the term 'shareholder value' may be used in published financial statements, websites and other forms of communications, it is simply to impress investors and others.

Level 2

At this level, shareholder value is seen in fairly narrow terms as being concerned with greater efficiency. The business will, however, demonstrate serious intent by reorganising to reflect a concern for a shareholder value, by, for example, setting up shareholder value committees. It will also introduce shareholder value measures, such as EVA®, and use these measures as a means of incentivising and rewarding senior managers.

Level 3

This level of adoption recognises that shareholder value must be concerned with long-term growth as well as greater efficiency. These twin concerns will, furthermore be proclaimed in communications with managers and investors. A concern for long-term growth, however, is not deeply rooted within the culture of the business. An emphasis will remain on short-term growth and managers are aware that they will be judged and rewarded on this basis. The lack of commitment to long-term growth strategies means these will be abandoned without much struggle in the face of outside pressures.

Level 4

At this final level, long-term growth and efficiency are fully recognised within the business and will inform all major decisions. Policies, measures and managerial rewards will all be attuned to the successful pursuit of both. The business will communicate its growth vision to investors and will not be easily deflected from its long-term strategies. What is being said and what is being done will be in harmony.

Source: Based on 'Companies must achieve the right balance for a successful strategy', *Financial News*, 22 February 2004.

SUMMARY

The main points in this chapter may be summarised as follows:

Shareholder value

- This means putting shareholders' interests at the heart of management decisions.
- To create shareholder value, the objectives of the business must reflect a concern for shareholder value, there must be appropriate methods of measurement, the business

must be managed to create shareholder value and there must be periodic assessment of whether shareholder value has been achieved.

Measuring shareholder value – internal (management) measures

- Conventional forms of accounting measurement are inadequate – they focus on the short term, ignore risk, fail to take proper account of the cost of capital invested and are influenced by accounting methods employed.
- Two main approaches are used to measure shareholder value: shareholder value analysis (SVA) and economic value added (EVA®).
- SVA is based on the concept of net present value analysis.
- It identifies key value drivers for generating shareholder value.
- EVA® provides a means of measuring whether the returns generated by the business exceed the required returns from investors.
- EVA® = NOPAT – $(R \times C)$
- EVA® relies on conventional financial statements, which are adjusted because of their limitations.
- In theory, EVA® and SVA should produce the same decisions and results.

Measuring shareholder value – external (investor) measures

- There are two main approaches: market value added (MVA) and total shareholder return (TSR).
- MVA measures the difference between the market value of the business and the investment made in the business.
- MVA = Present value of EVA®.
- MVA is really only suitable for listed businesses.
- Interpreting MVA can be a problem.
- TSR measures the total return to shareholders over a period.
- TSR is made up of the increase (decrease) in share value and the dividends paid.
- TSR can be sensitive to the time period chosen.

Criticisms of the shareholder value approach

- There are two elements to shareholder value: efficiency of current operations and future growth.
- Undue emphasis on efficiency can undermine the prospects for future growth.

Measuring the value of future growth

- One approach is to use the EVA® methodology.
- Value of future growth potential = Market value of the business – (Capital invested + EVA®/r).
- To check whether managers strike the right balance between efficiency and future growth, the future growth potential can be compared with the market value of the business.

References

1 EVA: The real key to creating wealth, *Ehrbar, A.*, John Wiley, 1998.

Further reading

If you wish to explore the topic of shareholder value in more depth, try the following books:

Executive Corporate Finance: The business of enhancing shareholder value, *Asaf, S.,* Financial Times Prentice Hall, 2004.

Measuring Value for Shareholders, *Institute of Chartered Accountants in England and Wales Faculty of Finance and Management*, Good Practice Guideline No. 33, March 2001.

Corporate Financial Management, *Arnold G.*, 3rd edn, Financial Times Prentice Hall, 2005, chapters 17 and 18.

The EVA Challenge: Implementing valued added changes in an organization, *Stern, J. and Shielly, J.*, John Wiley, 2003.

REVIEW QUESTIONS

Answers to these questions may be found at the back of the book on p. 547.

11.1 The shareholder value approach to managing businesses takes a different approach from the stakeholder approach to managing businesses. In the latter case, the different stakeholders of the business (employees, customers, suppliers and, so on) are considered of equal importance and so the interests of shareholders will not dominate. Is it possible for these two approaches to managing businesses to coexist in harmony within a particular economy?

11.2 Why is MVA not really suitable as a tool for internal management purposes?

11.3 Should managers take changes in the total market value of the shares (that is, share price × number of shares issued) over time as an indicator of shareholder value created (or lost)?

11.4 It has been argued that many businesses are overcapitalised. If this is true, what may be the reasons for businesses having too much capital and how can EVA® help avoid this problem?

EXERCISES

Questions 11.4 and 11.5 are more advanced than 11.1 to 11.3. Those with coloured numbers have an answer at the back of the book, starting on p. 570.

> If you wish to try more exercises, visit the students' side of this book's Companion Website.

11.1 Aquarius plc has estimated the following free cash flows for its five-year planning period:

Year	Free cash flows
	£m
1	35.0
2	38.0
3	45.0
4	49.0
5	53.0

Required:
How might it be possible to check the accuracy of these figures? What internal and external sources of information might be used to see whether the figures are realistic?

11.2 Aries plc was recently formed and issued 80 million £0.50 shares at par and loan capital of £24m. The business used the proceeds from the capital issues to purchase the remaining lease on some commercial properties that are rented out to small businesses. The lease will expire in four years' time and during that period the annual operating profits are expected to be £12 million each year. At the end of the three years, the business will be wound up and the lease will have no residual value.

The required rate of return by investors is 12 per cent.

Required:
Calculate the expected shareholder value generated by the business over the four years, using:

(a) The SVA approach
(b) The EVA®approach.

11.3 Virgo plc is considering introducing a system of EVA® and wants its managers to focus on the longer term rather than simply focus on the year-to-year EVA® results. The business is seeking your advice as to how a management bonus system could be arranged so as to ensure the longer term is taken into account. The business is also unclear as to how much of the managers' pay should be paid in the form of a bonus and when such bonuses should be paid. Finally, the business is unclear as to where the balance between individual performance and corporate performance should be struck within any bonus system.

The finance director has recently produced figures that show that if Virgo plc had used EVA® over the past three years, the results would have been as follows:

	£m
2006	25
2007	(20)
2008	10

Required:
Set out your recommendations for a suitable bonus system for the divisional managers of the business.

11.4 Leo plc is considering entering a new market. A new product has been developed at a cost of £5 million and is now ready for production. The market is growing and estimates from the finance department concerning future sales of the new product are as follows:

Year	Sales
	£m
1	30.0
2	36.0
3	40.0
4	48.0
5	60.0

After Year 5, sales are expected to stabilise at the Year 5 level.
You are informed that:

- The operating profit margin from sales in the new market is likely to be a constant 20 per cent of sales revenue.
- The cash tax rate is 25 per cent of operating profit.
- Replacement non-current asset investment (RNC) will be in line with the annual depreciation charge each year.
- Additional non-current asset investment (ANC) over the next five years will be 15 per cent of sales growth.
- Additional working capital investment (AWCI) over the next five years will be 10 per cent of sales growth.

The business has a cost of capital of 12 per cent. The new market is considered to be no more risky than the markets in which the business already has a presence.

Required:
Using an SVA approach, indicate the effect of entering the new market on shareholder value.

11.5 Pisces plc produced the following statement of financial position and income statement at the end of the third year of trading:

Statement of financial position (balance sheet)
as at the end of the third year

	£m
Non-current assets	
Property	40.0
Machinery and equipment	80.0
Motor vans	18.6
Marketable investments	9.0
	147.6
Current assets	
Inventories	45.8
Receivables	64.6
Cash	1.0
	111.4
Total assets	259.0
Equity	
Share capital	80.0
Retained earnings	36.5
	116.5
Non-current liabilities	
Loan capital	80.0
Current liabilities	
Trade payables	62.5
Total equity and liabilities	259.0

Income statement for the third year

	£m
Sales revenue	231.5
Cost of sales	(143.2)
Gross profit	88.3
Wages	(43.5)
Depreciation of machinery and equipment	(14.8)
R&D costs	(40.0)
Allowance for trade receivables	(10.5)
Operating loss	(20.5)
Income from investments	0.6
	(19.9)
Interest payable	(0.8)
Ordinary loss before taxation	(20.7)
Restructuring costs	(6.0)
Loss before taxation	(26.7)
Tax	–
Loss for the year	(26.7)

An analysis of the underlying records reveals the following:

1 R&D costs relate to the development of a new product in the previous year. These costs are written off over a two-year period (starting last year). However, this is a prudent approach and the benefits are expected to last for 16 years.

2 The allowance for trade receivables was created this year and the amount is very high. A more realistic figure for the allowance would be £4 million.

3 Restructuring costs were incurred at the beginning of the year and are expected to provide benefits for an infinite period.

4 The business has a 7 per cent required rate of return for investors.

Required:

Calculate the EVA® for the business for the third year of trading.

12

Business mergers and share valuation

INTRODUCTION

In this chapter, we consider various aspects of mergers and takeovers. We begin by examining the reasons for mergers and takeovers and then go on to consider the ways in which they can be financed. We also identify the likely winners and losers in a takeover and the defences available to a business seeking to fend off a hostile bid. In the final part of this chapter, we consider how the shares of a business can be valued. This is relevant to a range of financial decisions, including mergers and takeovers.

LEARNING OUTCOMES

When you have completed this chapter, you should be able to:

- Identify and discuss the main reasons for mergers and takeovers.

- Discuss the advantages and disadvantages of each of the main forms of purchase consideration used in a takeover.

- Identify the likely winners and losers from takeover activity.

- Outline the tactics that may be used to defend against a hostile bid.

- Identify and discuss the main methods of valuing the shares of a business.

Mergers and takeovers

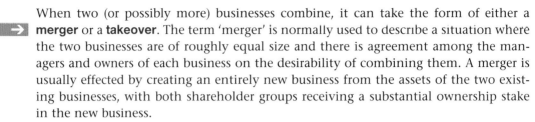

When two (or possibly more) businesses combine, it can take the form of either a **merger** or a **takeover**. The term 'merger' is normally used to describe a situation where the two businesses are of roughly equal size and there is agreement among the managers and owners of each business on the desirability of combining them. A merger is usually effected by creating an entirely new business from the assets of the two existing businesses, with both shareholder groups receiving a substantial ownership stake in the new business.

The term 'takeover' is normally used to describe a situation where a larger business acquires control of a smaller business, which is then absorbed by the larger business. When a takeover occurs, the shareholders of the target business may cease to have any financial interest in the business and the resources of the business may come under entirely new ownership. (The particular form of consideration used to acquire the shares in the target business will determine whether the shareholders continue to have a financial interest in the business.) Although the vast majority of takeovers are not contested, there are occasions when the management of the target business will fight to retain its separate identity.

In practice, however, many business combinations do not fit into these neat categories and it may be difficult to decide whether a merger or a takeover has occurred. The distinction between the two forms of combination used to be important in the context of financial reporting, as different accounting rules existed for each type of combination. However, changes to these rules have meant that the distinction is really no longer an issue. In this chapter, no distinction will be made between the terms 'merger' and 'takeover' and we shall use the terms interchangeably.

Mergers and takeovers can be classified according to the relationship between the businesses being merged.

- A **horizontal merger** occurs when two businesses in the same industry, and at the same point in the production/distribution process, decide to combine.
- A **vertical merger** occurs when two businesses in the same industry, but at different points in the same production/distribution process, decide to combine.
- A **conglomerate merger** occurs when two businesses in unrelated industries decide to combine.

Activity 12.1

Can you think of an example of each type of merger for a tyre retailer?

An example of a horizontal merger would be where a tyre retailer merges with another tyre retailer to form a larger retail business. An example of a vertical merger would be where a tyre retailer merges with a manufacturer of tyres. This would mean that the combined business operates at different points in the production/distribution chain. An example of a conglomerate merger would be where a tyre retailer merges with an ice cream manufacturer.

Merger and takeover activity

Although mergers and takeovers are a normal part of the business landscape, there are surges in merger and takeover activity from time to time. Each surge will have its own particular combination of economic, political and technological factors to create the required environment. Important economic factors usually include rising share prices and low interest rates, which make financing mergers and takeovers much easier.

Real World 12.1 provides some impression of the pattern of merger and takeover activity over recent times.

REAL WORLD 12.1

The urge to merge

Figure 12.1 below shows the pattern of takeover activity in the UK over the period 1977–2006.

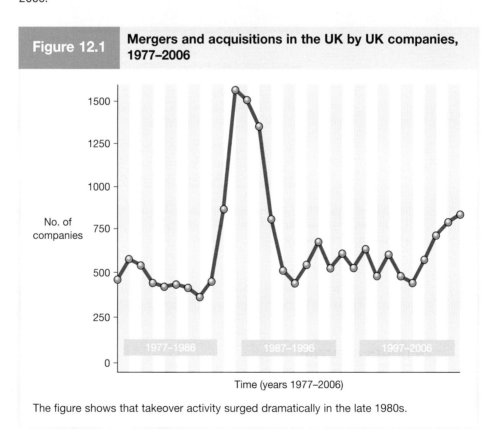

| Figure 12.1 | Mergers and acquisitions in the UK by UK companies, 1977–2006 |

The figure shows that takeover activity surged dramatically in the late 1980s.

Source: Based on information from www.statistics.gov.uk, the website of the Office for National Statistics.

The rationale for mergers

In economic terms, a merger will be worthwhile only if combining the two businesses will lead to gains that would not arise if the two businesses had stayed apart. We saw in the previous chapter that the value of a business can be defined in terms of the *present value of its future cash flows*. Thus, if a merger is to make economic sense, the present value of the combined business should be equal to the present value of future cash flows of the bidding and target businesses *plus* a gain from the merger. Figure 12.2 illustrates this point.

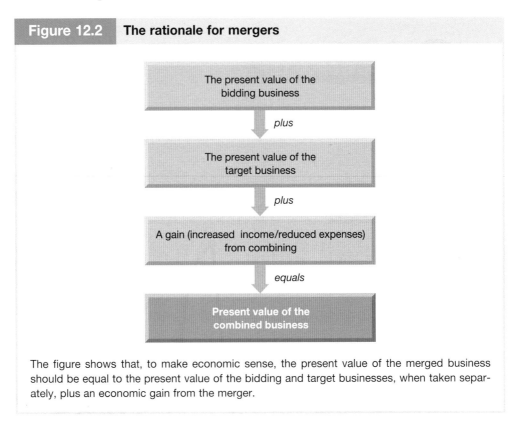

Figure 12.2 **The rationale for mergers**

The present value of the bidding business

plus

The present value of the target business

plus

A gain (increased income/reduced expenses) from combining

equals

Present value of the combined business

The figure shows that, to make economic sense, the present value of the merged business should be equal to the present value of the bidding and target businesses, when taken separately, plus an economic gain from the merger.

There are various ways in which an economic gain may be achieved through a merger or takeover; the more important of these are described below.

Benefits of scale

A merger or takeover will result in a larger business being created that may enable certain benefits of scale to be achieved. For example, a larger business may be able to negotiate lower prices with suppliers in exchange for larger orders. A merger or takeover may also provide the potential for savings, as some operating costs may be duplicated (for example, administrative costs, IT costs, marketing costs, research and development costs). These benefits are more likely to be gained from horizontal and vertical mergers than from conglomerate mergers; it is more difficult to achieve economies where the businesses are unrelated. The benefits outlined, however, must be weighed against the increased costs of organising and controlling a larger business.

Real World 12.2 describes the anticipated benefits of scale arising from a merger between Microsoft and Yahoo!. A letter sent from Steve Ballmer, CEO of Microsoft, to the Chairman and CEO of Yahoo!, proposed a merger of the two technology giants.

REAL WORLD 12.2

Searching for a partner

FT

In 2008, Microsoft, the software giant, made an abortive attempt to merge with Yahoo! the internet search engine. The management of Microsoft believed that, by combining the two businesses, a more efficient business could be created that would improve services to customers and add value for shareholders. The arguments put forward by Microsoft in support of a merger largely centred round the benefits of scale that could be reaped.

In a letter to the board of Yahoo!, Steven Ballmer, the chief executive of Microsoft, outlined four main advantages of combining as follows:

1. *Advertising growth*   It was argued that synergies were possible in advertising that related to both search and non-search related advertising. It was felt that the benefits of these synergies would be appealing to advertisers and to publishers. It was also argued that capital spending on developing new software, such as a search index, could be consolidated.
2. *R&D capacity*   Both businesses employ talented software engineers and it was argued that these could be brought together to focus on building a single advertising platform and a single search index. It was also argued that much new development and innovation relied on engineering scale, which the businesses did not have as separate entities but which would be available through combining.
3. *Operational efficiencies*   By removing operating activities that were currently being duplicated and unnecessary elements of business infrastructure, the combined entity would benefit from significant savings. This, in turn, would improve financial performance.
4. *Emerging technology*   It was argued that emerging opportunities such as on-line commerce, social media, mobile services and video services could be developed more successfully by using the combined engineering capability of the two businesses.

Although the letter stressed that the industry was moving towards greater consolidation and the time was therefore right for such a merger, the board of Yahoo! rejected the overtures. Microsoft had spent a considerable amount of time and resources in developing its merger proposals and so was left nursing its losses.

As a footnote to this failed merger attempt, it is worth mentioning that not all financial analysts and commentators were convinced that the benefits of a merger between the two internet giants were as potent as suggested by Steven Ballmer. Although many recognised

Real World 12.2 continued

the need for Microsoft to increase its scale in order to combat its loss of market share in internet search queries and to improve its relatively poor internet advertising revenues, some felt that the merger was unlikely to seriously threaten the dominance of Google in these markets.

Mark Mahaney at Citigroup posed two simple questions:

'Would Microsoft owning Yahoo! change consumers' clear strong preference for Google's search engine? We doubt it.

Would advertisers – who have been appreciative of a third search engine in the past, though disappointed with Microsoft traction – switch ad dollars from Google? We doubt it.'

Source: Adapted from 'Letter from Steve Ballmer to Yahoo!', FT.com, 1 February 2008, and Computing the future for Yahoo and Microsoft, C. Nuttall and R. Waters, 4 May 2007.

Activity 12.2

Is it necessary for a business to merge with, or take over, another business in order to reap the benefits of scale? Can these benefits be obtained by other means?

A business may be able to obtain lower prices from suppliers, reduced research and development costs, and so forth, by joining a consortium of businesses or by entering into joint ventures with other businesses. This form of cooperation can result in benefits of scale and yet avoid the costs of a merger. (However, there will be costs in negotiating a detailed joint venture agreement.)

Eliminating competition

A business may combine with, or take over another business in order to eliminate competition and to increase the market share of its goods. This, in turn, can lead to increased profits.

Activity 12.3

What type of merger will achieve this objective? What are the potential problems of this kind of merger from the consumer's point of view?

A horizontal merger will normally be required to increase market share. The potential problems of such mergers are that consumers will have less choice following the merger and that the market power of the merged business will lead to an increase in consumer prices. For these reasons, governments often try to ensure that the interests of the consumer are protected when mergers resulting in a significant market share are proposed. (This point is considered in more detail later in the chapter.)

Underutilised resources

The full potential of a business may not be achieved because of a weak management team. In such a situation, there is an opportunity to install a stronger management team that could do better. This argument is linked to what is sometimes referred to as the 'market for corporate control'. The term is used to describe the idea that mergers and takeovers are motivated by teams of managers that compete for the right to control business resources. The market for corporate control ensures that weak management teams will not survive and that, sooner or later, they will be succeeded by stronger management teams. The threat of takeover, however, may motivate managers to improve their performance. This suggests that mergers and takeovers are good for the economy as they help to ensure that resources are fully utilised and that shareholder wealth maximisation remains the top priority.

Complementary resources

Two businesses may have complementary resources which, when combined, will allow higher profits to be made than if the businesses remain separate. By combining the two businesses, the relative strengths of each business will be brought together and this may lead to additional profits being generated. It may be possible, of course, for each business to overcome its particular deficiency and continue as a separate entity. Even so, it may still make sense to combine.

Activity 12.4

Why might there still be an argument in favour of a merger, even though a business could overcome any deficiency on its own?

Combining the resources of two businesses may lead to a quicker exploitation of the strengths of each business than if the businesses remained separate.

Real World 12.3 sets out the overtures made by the chief executive of Comcast, a major cable networks business, to Michael Eisner, chief executive of the Walt Disney Company, for a merger of the two businesses. These overtures, which were made in an open letter, pointed to the complementary resources of each business.

REAL WORLD 12.3

Dear Mickey

FT

Dear Michael,

I am writing following our conversation earlier this week in which I proposed that we enter into discussions to merge Disney and Comcast to create a premier entertainment and communications company. It is unfortunate that you are not willing to do so. Given this, the only way for us to proceed is to make a public proposal directly to you and your Board.

We have a wonderful opportunity to create a company that combines distribution and content in a way that is far stronger and more valuable than either Disney or Comcast can be standing alone . . .

Under our proposal, your shareholders would own approximately 42% of the combined company. The combined company would be uniquely positioned to take advantage of an extraordinary collection of assets. Together, we would unite the country's premier cable provider with Disney's leading filmed entertainment, media networks and theme park properties.

In addition to serving over 21 million cable subscribers, Comcast is also the country's largest high speed internet service provider with over 5 million subscribers. As you have expressed on several occasions, one of Disney's top priorities involves the aggressive pursuit of technological innovation that enhances how Disney's content is created and delivered.

We believe this combination helps accelerate the realisation of that goal – whether through existing distribution channels and technologies such as video-on-demand and broadband video streaming or through emerging technologies still in development – to the benefit of all our shareholders, customers and employees.

We believe that improvements in operating performance, business creation opportunities and other combination benefits will generate enormous value for the shareholders of both companies.

Together, as an integrated distribution and content company, we will be best positioned to meet our respective competitive challenges. We have a stable and respected management team with a great track record for creating shareholder value . . .

Very truly yours
Brian L. Roberts

Source: 'Dear Mickey: open letter to Disney', www.ft.com, 11 February 2004.

Footnote: Alas, Mickey did not write back and so the merger proposal was withdrawn.

Surplus funds

A business may operate within an industry that offers few investment opportunities. In such a situation, the management may find that it has surplus cash which is not earning a reasonable return. The solution to this problem may be to invest in a new industry where there is no shortage of profitable investment opportunities. A business that acquires an existing business within the new industry will thereby quickly acquire the necessary specialist managerial and technical know-how.

Activity 12.5

Could management deal with the problem of surplus funds in some other way? Why might this other way not be acceptable to shareholders and managers?

The surplus funds could be distributed to shareholders through a special dividend or a share repurchase arrangement. However, shareholders may not like this idea because there may be a tax liability arising from the distribution. Managers may also not like this idea as it will result in reduced resources for them to manage. (It is also worth mentioning that lenders may not like the idea of funds being returned to shareholders, as it may increase their (the lenders') exposure to risk.)

The motives for mergers and takeovers considered above are consistent with the objective of enhancing the wealth of shareholders. However, other motives, which are more difficult to justify, may provide the driving force for business combinations. The following are examples.

Diversification

A business may invest in another business, operating in a different industry, in order to reduce risk. We may recall that in Chapter 5 the benefits of diversification in dealing with the problem of risk were discussed. At first sight, such a policy may seem appealing. However, we must ask ourselves whether diversification by *management* will provide any benefits to shareholders that the *shareholders themselves* cannot provide more cheaply. It is often easier and cheaper for a shareholder to deal with the problem of risk by holding a diversified portfolio of shares than for the business to acquire another. It is quite likely that the latter approach will be expensive, as a premium may have to be paid to acquire the shares and external investment advisers and consultants may have to be hired at substantial cost.

Activity 12.6

Who do you think might benefit from diversification?

Diversification may well benefit the managers of the bidding business. Managers cannot diversify their investment of time and effort in the business easily. Managing a more diversified business reduces the risks of unemployment and lost income for managers.

There may be circumstances, however, where shareholders are in a similar position to managers. For example, owner-managers may find it difficult to diversify their time and wealth because they are committed to the business. In these particular circumstances, there is a stronger case for diversifying the business.

Real World 12.4 describes the difficult problems that US conglomerates are facing.

Decline sets in at the conglomerate   FT

For nearly half a century the diversified business group was a cornerstone of American capitalism, but now many are either disappearing or struggling to justify their existence. Their predicament is made all the more serious by the rise of nimbler predators – private-equity groups betting that the old business-guru mantra got it backwards: the parts of a conglomerate are actually worth more than the whole.

Last week Altria put an end to a 20-year marriage of convenience between its tobacco and food businesses by spinning off Kraft from Philip Morris. A day later, American Standard split its $10bn-a-year toilets, brakes and air conditioning business. It will soon be followed by Tyco, which is poised to ask investors to forgive and forget its recent scandals by breaking itself in three.

Other once-mighty groups such as Cendant, the property-to-travel giant, and Viacom, Sumner Redstone's media powerhouse, have already unravelled decades of acquisitions to split into their component parts. Those that remain, like GE and its rival Honeywell, are reshaping their portfolio in an effort to convince sceptical investors of their worth. So far, their calls have gone unheeded, with share prices in both languishing below their historic highs.

'The conglomerates are dead,' says Chris Zook, head of the global strategy practice at Bain, the management consultancy. 'With some rare exceptions, the conglomerates' business model belongs to the past and is unlikely to reappear.'

The struggles of some of the oldest names in US business raise the prospect of a fundamental shift in corporate America's make-up. Supporters of conglomerates argue that their diversified structure has enabled them to safeguard industries, and their millions of employees, that would have struggled on their own.

Leaving such businesses to private-equity groups, whose focus is on asset trades and cost-cutting, or turning them into stand-alone operations exposed to the whims of the equity market might lead to further dramatic reductions in the US industrial base.

Lewis Campbell, chief executive of Textron, widely regarded as America's first conglomerate, recalls that when its Cessna aircraft unit was hit by a downturn in 2001–03, the investment needed to turn it around came from other parts of the helicopters-to-lawnmowers group. 'Where would Cessna's employment level and profitability be now if we were not a diversified, multi-industry company?' he asks.

To be sure, conglomerates are alive and kicking in Asian economies, from Japan to India, and even in the US not all diversified groups are gasping for air. Companies such as Warren Buffett's Berkshire Hathaway – with interests ranging from car insurance to Fruit of the Loom apparel – and, to a lesser extent, Rupert Murdoch's multi-media News Corporation have reaped rewards from operating across several industries.

But the rare successes highlight the problems of the rapidly shrinking US conglomerate sector. Indeed, the strategy of a renowned investor such as Mr Buffett is remarkably similar to the leaders of the conglomerates of old: buying companies whose diverse dynamics together cushion the whole group from the vagaries of business cycles.

'Conglomerates were the most exciting corporate form to appear in more than a generation,' wrote the late Robert Sobel in his 1984 *The Rise and Fall of the Conglomerate Kings*. 'They shook up the business scene as no other phenomenon had since the era of trust creation at the turn of the century.'

A bespectacled first world war veteran called Royal Little is credited with starting the trend in 1953 when his Textron, then a maker of rayon, bought a car upholstery supplier. The acquisition helped the company to weather a downturn in textile supplies and the recession of the late 1950s, emboldening Mr Little to go for an even more extravagant move: the purchase of Bell Aerospace, the helicopter manufacturer.

Companies such as Litton Industries, International Telephone & Telegraph and Gulf + Western followed suit, acquiring many unrelated businesses in a quest to expand earnings and revenues.

The success of the early conglomerates was predicated on the simple tenet that businesses find strength in numbers. This strategy of harvesting synergies between businesses, or simply cross-subsidising weaker operations with revenues generated by the more profitable ones, was warmly received by investors looking for safe, reliable earnings streams. That, in turn, gave conglomerates a powerful weapon: highly-rated stock that could be used to acquire even more companies, further expanding earnings power.

Over the past few decades, this virtuous circle has been progressively undone by profound changes in the US financial and business world.

On the financial front, Wall Street has grown to dislike the 'one-stop shop' nature of the conglomerate. As capital markets have become more global and liquid, fund managers believe that they can diversify risk, and gain better returns, by buying shares across several sectors rather than by delegating that choice to a conglomerate's chief executive.

At the same time, academic and empirical evidence began to show that, far from delivering the promised synergies, conglomerates' bias towards ploughing surplus resources back into their weaker businesses led to waste and inefficiency. 'Conglomerates that engage in "winner picking" find it optimal to allocate scarce capital internally to mediocre projects,' say Heitor Almeida and Daniel Wolfenzon, two New York University academics, in a recent study.

Indeed, academic studies dispelled the theory that acquisitions and cross-subsidies boost earnings and share prices, calculating that conglomerates are valued at average discounts of 10–12 per cent to the rest of the stock market.

Henry Silverman, who built Cendant through an acquisition spree in the 1990s and then disbanded it in 2005, summed up the conglomerates' plight when he said the company had been a 'financial success but a stock market failure'.

'This is a classic case of the sum of the parts is worth more than the whole,' he said in announcing the break-up.

Sluggish share prices have been mirrored by financial performance. Looking at data from the past decade, Bain found that conglomerates have 50 per cent less chance of achieving sustained earnings growth than more focused groups.

Klaus Kleinfeld, chief executive of Siemens, the German conglomerate, rejects this view, arguing that the ability of diversified groups to cross-fertilise ideas, products and talent gives them an inherent advantage over focused companies. 'Customers want a stable partner that can offer a variety of services. Customers do rely on us being around for a long time,' he says.

If he is right, conglomerates should come back in favour during an economic slowdown, when investors flee to the relative safety of broad-based companies whose earnings are less sensitive to a downturn.

But investment professionals argue that a cyclical return to favour of conglomerates is unlikely because today's financial markets offer investors more sophisticated risk management tools. 'Investing in a conglomerate is not the only way to diversify your risk, as it perhaps was 30 years ago,' says one. 'The financial instruments we have today mean anyone can diversify risk effectively by going on [the broking site] E*Trade.'

Real World 12.4 continued

The space in the business landscape left by the slow unwinding of the conglomerates is likely to be taken over by aggressive private-equity groups. Armed with cash raised from indulgent lenders, the buy-out groups are assembling large collections of varied businesses.

Even Jeffrey Immelt, Mr Welch's successor at the helm of GE, arguably the quintessential modern conglomerate, acknowledges private equity's coming of age. 'Private-equity funds are the conglomerates of this era,' he recently told the FT. '[Trade buyers] have not seized the moment in terms of doing deals they could have done to build their companies for the long term.'

It is perhaps ironic that private equity should fatten its portfolios with businesses hived off from old-style conglomerates, such as Cendant's Travelport and GE's speciality materials unit. The crucial difference between the new hoarders of businesses and their predecessors, however, is that the former have it in mind to sell them again within years.

But that comes after private equity applies, and extracts benefits from, another lesson learnt from the conglomerates of old: that diffuse businesses can be held together by a common set of managerial skills and processes.

Experts argue the conglomerates that will survive and prosper are the ones that succeed in linking their disparate operations through a common denominator of management and business principles. It is no coincidence that two surviving conglomerates, GE and Washington-based Danaher, have each created management 'playbooks' to remind their employees of their shared business goals and values.

'I am not prepared to bury the conglomerate just yet,' says Cynthia Montgomery, professor of management at Harvard Business School. 'There will always be a role for them because they bring managerial expertise and discipline.'

Perhaps the longer-lasting heirs to the conglomerates will be companies that spread themselves across more than one industry but do not overstretch into wildly different sectors. Bain's Mr Zook points to Apple as a company that branched out of its traditional computer business by harnessing a neighbouring technology with the iPod.

Google is following a similar path, building on its dominance of online search to expand into the global advertising market.

'It is not a matter of being diversified or not, it is the degree of diversification,' says Michael Patsalos-Fox, chairman of the Americas region for McKinsey, the management consultancy. 'A modest degree of diversification can lead to superior shareholder returns because companies that only do one thing eventually run out of rope.'

Source: Francesco Guerrera, 'Decline of the conglomerates', www.ft.com, 4 February 2007.

Management interests and goals

A merger or takeover may be undertaken to fulfil the personal goals or interests of managers. They may acquire another business simply to reduce the risks that they face or to increase the amount of resources that they control. **Real World 12.5** also points out that managers may enjoy the excitement of mergers and takeovers.

REAL WORLD 12.5

Mergers can be fun

Mergers and acquisitions can be very exciting and managers often enjoy 'the thrill of the chase'. Warren Buffett, one of the world's most successful investors and chief executive officer of Berkshire Hathaway, has stated:

> Leaders, business or otherwise, seldom are deficient in animal spirits and often relish increased activity and challenge. At Berkshire, the corporate pulse never beats faster than when an acquisition is in prospect.

Source: Warren Buffett's letter to Berkshire Hathaway Inc. shareholders, 1981, www.berkshirehathaway.com.

The personal goals and interests of managers may also explain why some proposed takeovers are fiercely contested by them.

Management interests and the agency problem

Although shareholders have the final say concerning whether a business should be acquired, they will rely heavily on information supplied to them by the managers. If the managers are determined to pursue their own goals, shareholders may not receive all the information required to make the correct decision. This is linked to the agency problem that was first discussed in Chapter 1. As we may recall, there is a risk that managers, who are employed to act on behalf of shareholders, will operate in a way that is designed to maximise their own benefits.

A merger, however, can sometimes be the solution to the agency problem. Where managers are not acting in the interests of the shareholders and are busy pursuing their own interests and goals, the effect is likely to be a decline in business performance and share price. The market for corporate control, mentioned earlier, should ensure that the business is taken over by another whose managers are committed to serving the interests of shareholders.

Forms of purchase consideration

When a business takes over another business, payment for the shares acquired may be made in different ways.

Activity 12.7

What different methods of payment may be used?

The main methods of payment are:

- cash
- shares in the bidding business
- loan capital in the bidding business.

Some combination of the methods listed in Activity 12.7 may, of course, also be used. Below we consider the advantages and disadvantages of each form of payment from the point of view of both the bidding business's shareholders and the target business's shareholders.

Cash

Payment by cash means the amount of the purchase consideration will be both certain and clearly understood by the target business's shareholders. This may improve the chances of a successful bid. It will also mean that shareholder control of the bidding business will not be diluted as no additional shares will be issued.

Raising the necessary cash, however, can create problems for the bidding business, particularly when the target business is large. It may only be possible to raise the amount required by a loan or share issue or by selling off assets, which the bidding business's shareholders may not like. On occasions, it may be possible to spread the cash payments over a period. However, deferred payments are likely to weaken the attraction of the bid to the target business's shareholders.

The receipt of cash will allow the target business's shareholders to adjust their share portfolios without incurring transaction costs on disposal. However, transaction costs will be incurred when new shares or loan capital are acquired to replace the shares sold. Moreover, the receipt of cash may result in a liability to capital gains tax (which arises on gains from the disposal of certain assets, including shares).

Shares

The issue of shares in the bidding business as purchase consideration will avoid any strain on its cash position. However, some dilution of existing shareholder control will occur and there may also be a risk of dilution in earnings per share. (Dilution will occur if the additional earnings from the merger divided by the number of new shares issued is lower than the existing earnings per share.) The directors must ensure that the authorised share capital of the business is sufficient to make a new issue and, more importantly, that the market value of the business's shares does not fall during the course of the takeover. A substantial fall in share price will reduce the value of the bid and could undermine the chances of acceptance. The cost of this form of financing must also be taken into account. We saw in Chapter 8 that the cost of servicing share capital is relatively expensive.

The target business's shareholders may find a share-for-share exchange attractive. As they currently hold shares, they may wish to continue with this form of investment rather than receive cash or other forms of security. A share-for-share exchange does not result in a liability for capital gains tax. (For capital gains tax purposes, no disposal is deemed to have occurred when this type of transaction takes place.) The target shareholders will also have a continuing ownership link with the original business, although it will now be part of a larger business. However, the precise value of the offer may be difficult to calculate owing to movements in the share prices of the two businesses.

Loan capital

Like the issue of shares, the issue of loan capital is simply an exchange of paper and so it avoids any strain on the cash resources of the bidding business. It has, however, certain advantages over shares in that the issue of loan capital involves no dilution of shareholder control and the service costs will be lower. A disadvantage of a loan-capital-for-share exchange is that it will increase the gearing of the bidding business and, therefore, the level of financial risk. The directors of the bidding business must ensure that the issue of loan capital is within its borrowing limits.

Loan capital may be acceptable to shareholders in the target business if they have doubts over the future performance of the combined business. Loan capital provides investors with both a fixed level of return and security for their investment. When a takeover bid is being made, convertible loan capital may be offered as purchase consideration.

Activity 12.8

What is the attraction of this form of loan capital from the point of view of the target business's shareholders?

The issue of convertible loan capital would give target business shareholders a useful hedge against uncertainty. This type of loan capital will provide relative security in the early years with an option to convert to ordinary shares at a later date. Investors will, of course, only exercise this option if things go well for the combined business.

There may be various factors influencing the form of consideration used by bidding businesses. Market conditions may be a critical factor. Research evidence suggests that ordinary shares are more likely to be used following a period of strong stock market performance. Recent high returns are seen as making shares more attractive to investors.

Businesses with good growth opportunities are more likely to use ordinary shares when financing acquisitions. It seems that growth businesses prefer to use ordinary shares as this form of finance is less constraining than the issue of loan capital or the payment of cash. Businesses with poor growth opportunities, however, may not be able to offer ordinary shares in payment.

Real World 12.6 reveals the ways in which mergers have been financed in recent years.

REAL WORLD 12.6

How mergers are financed

The popularity of each form of bid consideration varies over time. Figure 12.3 shows that, in recent years, cash has usually been the most popular.

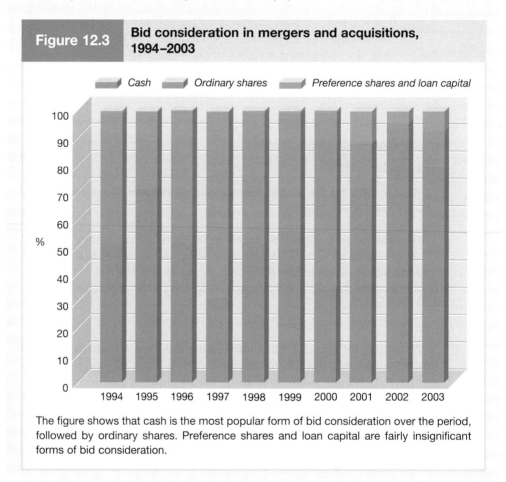

Figure 12.3	Bid consideration in mergers and acquisitions, 1994–2003

The figure shows that cash is the most popular form of bid consideration over the period, followed by ordinary shares. Preference shares and loan capital are fairly insignificant forms of bid consideration.

Source: Based on information from www.statistics.gov.uk, the website of the Office for National Statistics.

It is interesting to note that research in the UK and the USA suggests that businesses using ordinary shares as a means of acquisition achieve significantly poorer returns following the acquisition than those using cash (see reference 1 at the end of the chapter). The reasons for this are not entirely clear. Perhaps the relatively poor performance of share-for-share deals indicates that the bidding businesses' shares were too highly valued to begin with.

When another business is purchased, the debts of that business may be taken over. This can, of course, be regarded as part-payment for the assets acquired. **Real World 12.7** shows how the acquisition of HP Bulmer Holdings, the cider maker, was financed by Scottish and Newcastle plc.

REAL WORLD 12.7

Paying for Bulmer

In 2003, the Boards of Scottish and Newcastle plc and HP Bulmer Holdings agreed terms for the acquisition of Bulmer. The total consideration amounted to £200 million, which was made up of:

- £64 million in cash and loans
- £136 million by the issue of 38m ordinary shares.

In addition, Scottish and Newcastle took over £107 million of Bulmer's debt.

Source: Scottish and Newcastle plc Annual Report 2003.

Who benefits?

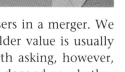

In this section, we shall try to identify the likely winners and losers in a merger. We begin by considering the shareholders, as the pursuit of shareholder value is usually claimed to be the driving force behind merger activity. It is worth asking, however, whether the reality matches the rhetoric. The answer, it seems, will depend on whether the bidding shareholders or the target shareholders are being discussed. Where mergers create value, it is often unevenly allocated. (See reference 2 at the end of the chapter.)

Shareholders in the target business

Studies, in both the UK and the USA, show that shareholders in the target business are usually the main beneficiaries. They are likely to receive substantial benefits from a takeover through a premium on the share price. Rose has summed up the position as follows:

> The bidder usually has to pay a premium over the pre-bid price of up to 100 per cent of the latter, with a mean of about 25 per cent in the UK and some 15 per cent in the US. In some cases the premium may appear to be small but this may merely reflect the fact that the 'pre-bid' price had already incorporated the possibility of a forthcoming bid. Bid premia tend to be higher in the case of contested bids, depending very much on whether another bidder is thought to be in the wings. (See reference 3 at the end of the chapter.)

Activity 12.9

Why might a bidding business be prepared to pay a premium above the market value for the shares of a business?

Various reasons have been put forward to explain this phenomenon. They include the following:

- The managers of the bidding business have access to information that is not available to the market and which is not, therefore, reflected in the share price. (This assumes that the market is not efficient in the strong form.)

Activity 12.9 continued

- The managers of the bidding business may simply misjudge the value of the target business.
- The managers may feel that there will be significant gains arising from combining the two businesses that are worth paying for. In theory, the maximum price a buyer will be prepared to pay will be equivalent to the present value of the business plus any gains from the merger.
- Management hubris. Where there is more than one bidder or where the takeover is being resisted, the managers of a bidding business may fail to act rationally and may raise the bid price above an economically justifiable level. This may be done in order to salvage management pride as they may feel humiliated by defeat.

Share prices in the target business will usually reflect the bid premium for as long as the bid is in progress. Where a takeover bid is unsuccessful and the bid withdrawn, the share price of the target business will usually return to its pre-offer level. However, shares may fall below their pre-bid prices if investors believe that the managers have failed to exploit a profitable opportunity. The same fate may be experienced by shares in the bidding business.

Real World 12.8 sets out details of recent merger and takeover bids.

REAL WORLD 12.8

Bids and bidders   **FT**

The following is an extract from a table concerning takeover bids and mergers that was published in the *Financial Times*.

Current takeover bids and mergers

Company bid for	Value of bid per share**	Market price	Pre-bid price	Value of bid** £m	Bidder
Biffa	350*	347.25	328	1.225bn	Wasteacquisitionco
CODA	205*	204.75	183.75	157.8	Agresso Ltd
Computerland UK	270*	262.5	206	27.58	Capita Group
Foseco (b)	295*	293	284	491.07	Cookson Grp
Global Marine Energy	16*	15.5	9.38	11.57	EMER Intl Grp
Imprint	115*	111.75	106.25	44.08	Premier UK
Inspicio♦	225*	225.5	198	228.6	Angus Newco
Resolution (12)	720*	693.5	707	4.942bn	Impala Hldg
Reuters Group	654.9§§	608.00	605.5	8.231bn	Thomson-Reuters
Rio Tinto (16)	5,712§	5,407	5,596	56.980bn	BHP Billiton

Prices in pence unless otherwise indicated. * All-cash offer. § All share offer. §§ Merger shares and cash. ♦ Unconditional in all respects. ** Based on closing prices 13 March 2008.

Source: Financial Times, Money section, 15–16 March 2008, p. M20.

Activity 12.10

Calculate the bid premium (in percentage terms) for each of the target businesses and comment on the findings.

The size of the bid premia can be calculated as follows:

Company bid for	Value of bid per share	Pre-bid price	Bid premium percentage
	(a)	(b)	$\dfrac{(a) - (b)}{(b)} \times 100$
Biffa	350	328	6.7
CODA	205	183.75	11.6
Computerland UK	270	206	31.1
Foseco (b)	295	284	3.9
Global Marine Energy	16	9.38	70.6
Imprint	115	106.25	8.2
Inspicio	225	198	13.6
Resolution	720	707	1.8
Reuters Group	654.9	605.5	8.2
Rio Tinto (16)	5,712	5,596	2.1

We can see that the bid premia cover a wide range from 1.8 per cent to 70.6 per cent. The current market value of the shares will normally increase following a bid and will move closer to the bid price. Occasionally, the market value of the shares may exceed the bid price, probably in anticipation of a higher offer being made.

Shareholders in the bidding business

Shareholders of the bidding business usually have little to celebrate. Although early studies offered some evidence that a merger provided them with either a small increase or no increase in the value of their investment, more recent studies suggest that, over the long run, takeovers produce a significant decrease in shareholder value (see reference 4 at the end of the chapter). Some studies also suggest that conglomerate takeovers provide the worst performance as indicated by both lower profitability and higher subsequent sell-offs of the acquired business (see reference 5 at the end of the chapter).

Activity 12.11

Why might shares in the bidding business lose value as a result of a takeover of a target business? Try to think of two reasons why this may be so.

Various reasons have been suggested. These include:

● *Overpayment*. The bidding business may pay too much to acquire the target business. We saw earlier that large premia are often paid to acquire another business and this may result in a transfer of wealth from the bidding business shareholders to the target business shareholders.

Activity 12.11 continued

- *Integration problems*. Following a successful bid, it may be difficult to integrate the target business's operations. There may be problems relating to organisational structure, key personnel, management style, management rivalries, and so on, which work against successful integration. These problems are most likely to arise in horizontal mergers where an attempt is made to fuse the systems and operations of the two separate businesses into a seamless whole. There are likely to be fewer problems where a conglomerate merger is undertaken and where there is no real attempt to adopt common systems or operations.
- *Management neglect*. There is a risk that, following the takeover, managers may relax and expect the combined business to operate smoothly. If the takeover has been bitterly contested, the temptation for management to ease back after the struggle may be very strong.
- *Hidden problems*. Problems relating to the target business may be unearthed following the takeover. This is most likely to arise where a thorough investigation was not carried out prior to the takeover.

Managers

Any discussion concerning winners and losers in a merger should include the senior managers of the bidding business and the target business. They are important stakeholders in their respective businesses and play an important role in takeover negotiations. This does not always mean, however, that they will benefit from a merger.

Activity 12.12

Following a successful bid, what is the likelihood of the senior managers in (a) the bidding business, and (b) the target business, benefiting from the merger?

(a) The managers of the bidding business are usually beneficiaries as they will manage an enlarged business, which will, in turn, result in greater status, income and security.

(b) The position of senior managers in the acquired business is less certain. In some cases, they may be retained and may even become directors of the enlarged business. In other cases, however, the managers may lose their jobs. A study by Franks and Mayer found that nearly 80 per cent of executive directors in a target business either resign or lose their job within two years of a successful takeover (see reference 6 at the end of the chapter).

Where managers in the target business lose their job, compensation may be payable. **Real World 12.9** outlines the compensation due to the directors of Safeway plc, a supermarket chain, in the event of a takeover. The business was subject to a number of takeover bids during 2003 and was eventually taken over by another supermarket chain, Wm Morrison plc.

REAL WORLD 12.9

Easing the pain

FT

Safeway's executive directors will be paid a total of more than £5.5m in compensation in the event that the supermarket group is taken over.

According to the group's annual report, published yesterday, David Webster, executive chairman, was paid £810,000 last year. He is entitled to one-and-a-half times his salary in the event of a takeover.

Carlos Criado-Perez, chief executive, was paid £802,000. He will be paid his basic annual salary of £654,000 plus a change-of-control payment that could be more than £1m.

Long-serving executives Simon Laffin, finance director, and Lawrence Christensen, operations director, are each entitled to two years' notice – and would double their basic salaries of £343,000 and £301,000 respectively.

Richard Williams and Jack Sinclair – information technology director and trading and marketing director – are each on one-year's notice periods and would be paid their basic annual salaries of £301,000 and £291,000 respectively.

Source: 'Safeway directors' £5.5m compensation', *Financial Times*, 10 June 2003.

Advisers

Mergers and takeovers can be very rewarding for investment advisers and lawyers employed by each business during the bid period. It seems that, whatever the outcome of the bid, they are winners. **Real World 12.10** describes a particularly rewarding merger for advisers.

REAL WORLD 12.10

Nice work (if you can get it)

FT

Five banks look set to share a double payday of more than $100m following Mittal's successful takeover of Arcelor.

Goldman Sachs, Citigroup, Credit Suisse, Société Générale and HSBC – which provided both merger advice and the financing package – will take the bulk of the fees, helping to boost year-end bonus coffers.

An additional nine banks will also be involved in the syndication of Mittal's €10.8bn loan to finance the cash element of the deal.

The deal will also generate substantial fees for the Arcelor advisory team, which comprised BNP Paribas, Deutsche Bank, Merrill Lynch, UBS, Banco Santander Central Hispano, Morgan Stanley and Calyon. Advisers acting for the target often receive higher fees because of the risk of losing a retained client.

Source: Lina Saigol, 'MITTA/ARCELOR: $100m payday for advisers', www.ft.com, 27 June 2006.

Why do mergers occur?

The substantial body of evidence that now exists, covering different time periods and across several different countries, indicating the dubious value of takeovers for bidding business shareholders, raises the question of why businesses persist in acquiring other businesses. The answer is still unclear. Perhaps it is because takeovers satisfy the interests of managers, or perhaps it reflects Samuel Johnson's view of remarriage – the triumph of hope over experience.

Real World 12.11 sets out the thoughts of Warren Buffet on why mergers occur.

REAL WORLD 12.11

A modern fairy tale

Many managements apparently were overexposed in impressionable childhood years to the story in which the imprisoned handsome prince is released from a toad's body by a kiss from a beautiful princess. Consequently, they are certain their managerial kiss will do wonders for the profitability of Company T[arget] . . . Investors can always buy toads at the going price for toads. If investors instead bankroll princesses who wish to pay double for the right to kiss the toad, those kisses had better pack some real dynamite. We've observed many kisses but very few miracles. Nevertheless, many managerial princesses remain serenely confident about the future potency of their kisses – even after their corporate backyards are knee-deep in unresponsive toads . . .

We have tried occasionally to buy toads at bargain prices with results that have been chronicled in past reports. Clearly our kisses fell flat. We have done well with a couple of princes – but they were princes when purchased. At least our kisses didn't turn them into toads. And, finally, we have occasionally been quite successful in purchasing fractional interests in easily identifiable princes at toadlike prices.

Source: Warren Buffett's letter to Berkshire Hathaway Inc. shareholders, 1981, www.berkshirehathaway.com.

Ingredients for successful mergers

Although many mergers and takeovers do not add value for the bidding business's shareholders, not all are unsuccessful. Why do some succeed? What are the magic ingredients of success? PA Consulting Group, a leading firm of management consultants, has tried to address these questions. Based on work with clients and research into mergers and acquisitions, the Group argues that consistent success in acquiring businesses can only be achieved if the following three factors are present:

- *Commitment.* This involves maintaining a clear focus on creating long-term value and committing the required resources to the merger process. It also involves reviewing performance in managing a merger in order to learn lessons for next time.
- *Competence.* To assess properly the risks and opportunities of a merger, a business must be able to assess its own strengths and weaknesses. It must be able to assess whether the areas of competence that it possesses will create value from the merger. Business platforms (such as IT and manufacturing processes) that support core competences should be designed in such a way that they can be easily and quickly expanded to accommodate newly acquired businesses.

● *Control*. There must be strategic analysis of acquisitions to help determine when, where and what to buy. There must also be a careful assessment of risks, including financial and operating risks. Systematic and rigorous planning must be applied throughout the whole transaction – starting with the bid and continuing throughout the subsequent integration process. (See reference 7 at the end of the chapter.)

These key elements are set out in Figure 12.4.

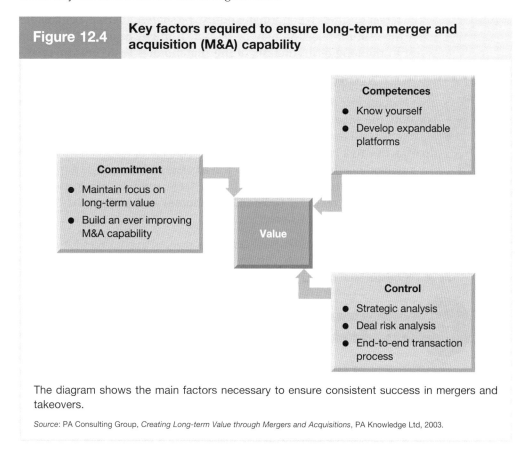

Figure 12.4 **Key factors required to ensure long-term merger and acquisition (M&A) capability**

The diagram shows the main factors necessary to ensure consistent success in mergers and takeovers.

Source: PA Consulting Group, *Creating Long-term Value through Mergers and Acquisitions*, PA Knowledge Ltd, 2003.

Rejecting a takeover bid

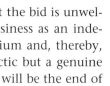

A takeover bid may, of course, be rejected. This need not imply that the bid is unwelcome and that shareholders are committed to maintaining the business as an independent entity. It may simply be a tactic to increase the bid premium and, thereby, increase shareholder wealth. If, however, it is not a negotiating tactic but a genuine attempt to remain independent, there is no certainty that rejection will be the end of the story. The spurned business may decide to press ahead with a hostile bid. Some of the defensive tactics that can be used against such a bid are considered below.

Defensive tactics

Various tactics may be used to fend off a hostile bid. Some of these must be put in place before a hostile bid is received, whereas others can be deployed when the bid has been made. Defensive tactics include the following:

- *Conversion to private company status.* By converting to private limited company status, the business makes its shares more difficult to acquire. This conversion must, however, be undertaken before a bid has been received.
- *Employee share option schemes.* Encouraging employees to acquire shares in the business increases the proportion of shareholders that are likely to resist a bid. This is a further example of a defence that must be in place before a bid is received.
- *Circularising shareholders.* When an offer has been received, the managers (directors) of the target business will normally notify the shareholders in a circular letter. In this letter the case for rejection may be set out. It might be argued, for example, that it is not in the long-term interests of the shareholders to accept the offer, or that the price offered is too low. In support of such arguments, the managers may disclose hitherto confidential information such as profit forecasts, future dividend payments, asset valuations, details of new contracts, and so on. This may have the effect of boosting the share price, thereby making the takeover more expensive.
- *Making the business unattractive.* The managers may take steps to make the business unattractive to a bidder. In the colourful language of mergers, this may involve taking a **poison pill** through the sale of prized assets of the business (the **crown jewels**). Other tactics include agreements to pay large sums to directors for loss of office resulting from a takeover (**golden parachutes**) and the purchase of certain assets that the bidding business does not want.

Real World 12.12 describes how generous severance packages for employees, in the event that they lose their job, can be used to thwart potential takeovers. Recently two large US businesses appear to have used this ploy.

REAL WORLD 12.12

Severance packages   **FT**

Electronic Arts will be recalculating the cost and benefits of its proposed $2bn acquisition of Take-Two today after the rival video game publisher announced a generous severance package for its employees.

In a regulatory filing late on Friday, Take-Two said its board had approved a package for employees in the event that they lose their jobs as a result of a take-over. They would receive as much as 1.5 times their salary and bonus for up to 18 months.

EA has already expressed its 'surprise', and analysts and corporate governance experts had raised eyebrows, at the compensation package Take-Two's management team won for itself last month while talks with EA were being held in private.

Salaries and possible bonuses were more than tripled and restricted shares were awarded worth millions of dollars. The executive team is not included in the new severance terms.

Take-Two's severance packages are similar to the change of control packages announced by Yahoo for its employees last month, a move described in one lawsuit brought against the internet company as being part of its effort to thwart Microsoft's takeover bid by increasing the cost by at least $1bn.

Source: Chris Nuttall, 'Take-Two's severance plan puts EA on notice', www.ft.com, 10 March 2008.

- **Pac-man defence**. This involves the target business launching a counterbid for the bidding business. However, this tactic is difficult to carry out where the target business is much smaller than the predator business. (The name given to this particular tactic derives from a well-known computer game.)

- **White knight**. A target business may avoid a takeover by an unwelcome bidder by seeking out another business (a 'white knight') with which to combine. This tactic will normally be used only as a last resort, however, as it will result in the loss of independence. There is also a risk that the white knight will be less gallant after the merger than was hoped.

- **White squire**. This is a variation of the white knight tactic. In this case, another business that is regarded as supportive will purchase a block of shares in the target business that is big enough to prevent any real prospect of a takeover but will not provide a controlling interest. The white squire will usually be given some incentive to 'ride to the rescue' of the target business. This might take the form of a seat on the board or a discount on the price of the shares purchased.

Real World 12.13 shows that modern tactics used to resist takeover attempts are pretty tame when compared with those used in the USA during the nineteenth century.

REAL WORLD 12.13

Defensive tactics – Western style

The following is a brief description of a 'Wild West' style takeover battle that involved an attempt to take control of the Eirie Railroad in 1868:

> The takeover attempt pitted Cornelius Vanderbilt against Daniel Drew, Jim Fisk and Jay Gould. As one of the major takeover defences, the defenders of the Eirie Railroad issued themselves large quantities of stock (that is, shares), even though they lacked the authorisation to do so. At that time, bribery of judges and elected officials was common, and so legal remedies for violating corporate laws were particularly weak. The battle for control of the railroad took a violent turn when the target corporation hired guards, equipped with firearms and cannons, to guard their headquarters. The takeover attempt ended when Vanderbilt abandoned his assault on the Eirie Railroad and turned his attention to weaker targets.

Source: Mergers and Acquisitions, P. Gaughan, HarperCollins, 1991, p. 13.

Overcoming resistance to a bid

Managers of the bidding business may try to overcome resistance to the bid by circularising shareholders of the target business with information that counters any claims made against the commercial logic of the bid or the offer price. They may also increase the offer price for the shares in the target business. In some cases, the original offer price may be pitched at a fairly low level as a negotiating ploy. The offer price will then be increased at a later date, thereby allowing the target business's managers and shareholders to feel that they have won some sort of victory.

Protecting the interests of shareholders and the public

To protect the interests of shareholders of both the bidding business and the target business, there is the City Code on Takeovers and Mergers. This Code seeks to ensure that shareholders are supplied with all the information necessary to make a proper decision and that the information supplied gives a fair and accurate representation of the facts. Any forecasts supplied by the bidding business or the target business must be carefully prepared and the key assumptions underpinning the forecast figures must be stated. The Code expects all shareholders to be treated equally when a merger or takeover is being negotiated.

Protecting the interests of the public also becomes a consideration when larger businesses combine. Where a business with UK turnover in excess of £70 million is being taken over, or where the combined business has a 25 per cent share of a particular market, the proposed merger can be referred to the **Competition Commission**. This is an independent public body that considers the effect of mergers and takeovers on the level of competition operating within particular markets. If the Commission believes a merger would result in a substantial lessening of competition in a particular market, it has the power to take action. This includes preventing the merger from taking place. When a merger is referred to the Commission (usually by the Office of Fair Trading), detailed enquiries are carried out, which may take some time. A large business that is the target of a hostile bid may, therefore, seek a referral in the hope that the delays and trouble caused by a Commission enquiry will make it less attractive to the bidding business.

In addition to national rules, the European Union has competition rules to eliminate restrictive practices that may affect trade between EU member states. These rules can restrict mergers that could distort competition or could lead to an abuse of a dominant market position. Recent reforms now mean that EU member states will normally enforce EU competition rules.

Restructuring a business: divestments and demergers

A business may wish to decrease, rather than increase, its scale of their operations. Restructuring a business in this way can be achieved through either a divestment or a demerger. Each of these is discussed below.

Divestment

A **divestment** or *sell-off* of business operations may be undertaken for various reasons including:

● *Financial problems.* A business that is short of cash or too highly geared may sell off certain operations to improve its financial position.
● *Defensive tactics.* A business that is vulnerable to a takeover may take pre-emptive action by selling its 'crown jewels'.
● *Strategic focus.* A business may wish to focus exclusively on core operations that are in line with its strategic objectives. As a result, non-core operations will be sold off.
● *Poor performance.* Where the performance of a particular business operation is disappointing, it may be sold off to enable more profitable use of resources.

Divestment and the agency problem

When a sell-off is undertaken, the managers of the particular business operations may bid to become the new owners. This, however, may give rise to an agency problem for the shareholders.

Activity 12.13

What kind of agency problem may arise for shareholders?

The managers have a duty to act in the interests of the shareholders. However, when a management buy-out is in prospect, the managers have a conflict of interest. On the one hand, they have a duty to ensure that the sale of the business will maximise the wealth of the owners and, on the other, they will be keen to acquire the business for as low a price as possible. There is a risk, therefore, that unscrupulous managers will suppress important information or will fail to exploit profitable opportunities in the period leading up to a buy-out in order to obtain the business operations at a cheap price. Shareholders must be aware of this risk and must seek independent advice concerning the value and potential of the business operations for which the managers are bidding.

If the bid by managers is successful, the purchase arrangement is referred to as a *management buy-out*. We saw in Chapter 7 that management buy-outs are often financed by private equity firms, who usually acquire a shareholding in the business.

Demerger

Rather than business operations being sold off to a third party, they may be transferred to a new business. This kind of restructuring is referred to as a **demerger** or **spin-off**. In this case, ownership of the business operations remains unchanged as the current owners will be given shares in the newly created business. The allocation of shares to the owners is usually made in proportion to their shareholdings in the existing business. A demerger can be undertaken for various reasons, including:

- *Market appeal*. Where part of the business operations is unattractive to investors (for example, very high risk), sentiment towards the business as a whole may be adversely affected. By spinning off the unattractive operations, the business may increase its market appeal.
- *Defensive tactics*. A business may have certain operations that are prized by another business. By spinning off particular operations, the business may successfully avoid the risk of takeover. (As mentioned above, a divestment can also be used for this purpose.)
- *Unlocking potential*. Where a business is a conglomerate, it is usually extremely difficult to manage effectively a diverse range of businesses. A decision to spin off part of its operations should make the business easier to manage and more focused. It will also give the managers of the operations that have been spun off greater autonomy, which may in turn lead to improved performance.
- *Investors' needs*. Investors in a conglomerate are unlikely to find the various operations in which the business is engaged equally attractive. The creation of separate businesses for different kinds of business operations should benefit investors as they will be able to adjust their portfolios to reflect more accurately the required level of investment for each business operation.

Real World 12.14 describes the trend of airline businesses towards selling off, or spinning off, ancillary businesses.

REAL WORLD 12.14

In a spin

FT

Investors' patience with US airlines may be wearing thin. While many of the biggest carriers have signalled they are weighing plans to sell or spin off ancillary businesses – from frequent-flyer programmes to aircraft maintenance divisions – news of the possible spin-offs has drawn the same foot taps that greet a long-overdue flight.

'They don't have all the time in the world,' said Hannes Smarason, chief executive of FL Group, the Iceland-based investment firm that has urged American Airlines parent AMR to shed its AAdvantage rewards plan. 'We hope to see them move aggressively.'

Investors such as Mr Smarason, whose $7.5bn firm owns a 9.1 per cent stake in American, say the divestitures would release value hidden within a cyclical industry challenged by fierce competition and unprecedented energy costs. Some of these businesses might generate steadier returns – after all, aircraft need repairs whether oil trades at $30 or $90 a barrel – if they're run separately.

Many investors point to Air Canada parent ACE Aviation, which spun out stakes in four of its businesses, as a blueprint for the transactions the largest US carriers should pursue.

Elsewhere, particularly in Europe, other airline groups have pursued similar strategies, most notably British Airways, which hived off non-core units such as catering and ground services in the late 1990s.

American told investors this month for the first time it was reviewing options for American Eagle, a regional air service; AAdvantage; its maintenance and repair arm; and American Beacon Advisors, an investment-management firm.

It also offered investors a glimpse of how some of those divisions perform – another first. American is working with advisers, including bankers at Rothschild, to evaluate plans for each of the divisions.

Delta Air Lines executives say they will decide whether to sell its regional carrier, Comair, within months.

Continental Airlines has said it will look at alternatives for its frequent-flyer arm, and USAirways is studying the merits of a spin-off for its rewards plan.

United Airlines parent UAL was in talks with private equity firms and strategic buyers to sell its maintenance business, chief financial officer Jake Brace said.

Northwest Airlines chief executive Douglas Steenland, who said on Monday that asset spin-offs had 'the potential for significant value creation', is also studying ways to break off the carrier's rewards division.

'For each of these businesses, there are arguments for some type of value-enhancing activity,' American finance chief Thomas Horton said during an analyst call. 'But there are also strategic and practical challenges.'

Not the least of which, industry executives, bankers and analysts say, is how the airline structures the contract defining its business relationship with the spin-off once they are separated, and how it values the division. Making the deal too lucrative for one side can imperil the other's future.

'We do not want to create a long-term issue for the business,' Larry Kellner, Continental Airlines chief executive, told the FT.

The carriers' relationships with organised labour could also influence how and when these businesses are separated. 'Nobody said it would be easy,' FL Group's Mr Smarason said of the challenges a frequent-flyer spin-off would pose.

While encouraged by American's willingness to at least raise the possibility of one or more spin-offs, Mr Smarason wants greater clarity on when the airline would reach a decision. 'They don't want to do it but, because stock prices are so lacklustre, they're facing pressure,' Calyon analyst Ray Neidl said.

'There's a sense of urgency because it's the right thing to do,' said Mr Brace, noting United might have a deal on its maintenance business to take to its employees' unions by the first quarter.

Source: 'Airline shareholders look for spin-off plans', www.ft.com, 30 October 2007.

As a footnote to the topics of divestment and demerger, it is worth pointing out that both forms of restructuring result in a smaller business. Thus some of the benefits of size, such as the benefits of scale, will be lost.

The valuation of shares

An important aspect of any merger or takeover negotiation is the value to be placed on the shares of the businesses to be merged or acquired. In this section, we explore the various methods that can be used to derive an appropriate share value for a business. Share valuation methods are not, of course, used only in the context of merger or takeover negotiations. They will also be required in other circumstances such as business flotations and liquidations. Nevertheless, mergers and takeovers are an important area for the application of share valuation methods.

In theory, the value of a share can be defined in terms of either the current value of the assets held or the future cash flows generated from those assets. In a world of perfect information and perfect certainty, share valuation would pose few problems. However, in the real world, measurement and forecasting problems conspire to make the valuation process difficult. Various valuation methods have been developed to deal with these problems, but they often produce quite different results.

The main methods employed to value a share can be divided into three broad categories:

- methods based on the value of the business's assets
- methods that use stock market information
- methods that are based on future cash flows.

Let us now examine some of the more important methods falling within each of these categories using the following example.

Example 12.1

CDC Ltd owns a chain of tyre and exhaust fitting garages in the west of England. The business has been approached by ATD plc, which owns a large chain of petrol stations, with a view to a takeover of CDC Ltd. ATD plc is prepared to make an offer in cash or a share-for-share exchange. The most recent financial statements of CDC Ltd are summarised below.

Example 12.1 continued

Income statement for the year ended 30 November Year 8

	£m
Sales revenue	18.7
Profit before interest and tax	6.4
Interest	(1.6)
Profit before taxation	4.8
Tax	(1.2)
Profit for the year	3.6

Statement of financial position (balance sheet) as at 30 November Year 8

	£m
Non-current assets (cost less depreciation)	
Property	4.0
Plant and machinery	5.9
	9.9
Current assets	
Inventories	2.8
Receivables	0.4
Bank	2.6
	5.8
Total assets	15.7
Equity	
£1 ordinary shares	2.0
Retained earnings	3.6
	5.6
Non-current liabilities	
Loan notes	3.6
Current liabilities	
Payables	5.9
Tax	0.6
	6.5
Total equity and liabilities	15.7

The accountant for CDC Ltd has estimated the future free cash flow of the business to be as follows:

Year 9	Year 10	Year 11	Year 12	Year 13
£4.4m	£4.6m	£4.9m	£5.0m	£5.4m

Note: After Year 13, the free cash flows remain constant at £5.4 million for the following 12 years.

The business has a cost of capital of 10 per cent.

CDC Ltd has recently had a professional valuer establish the current resale value of its assets. The current resale value of each asset was as follows:

	£m
Property	18.2
Plant and machinery	4.2
Inventories	3.4

The current resale values of the remaining assets are considered to be in line with their values as shown on the statement of financial position.

A company that is listed on the Stock Exchange and which is in the same business as CDC Ltd has a gross dividend yield of 5 per cent and a price/earnings ratio of 11 times.

The financial director believes that replacement costs are £1 million higher than the resale values for both land and premises, and plant and machinery, and £0.5 million higher than the resale value of the inventories. The replacement costs of the remaining assets are considered to be in line with their statement of financial position values. In addition, the financial director believes the goodwill of the business has a replacement value of £10 million. The values of the liabilities of the company, as shown on the statement of financial position, also reflect their current market values.

Asset-based methods

Asset-based methods attempt to value a share by reference to the value of the assets held by the business. Shareholders own the business and, therefore, own the underlying net assets (total assets less liabilities) of the business. This means that a single share can be valued by dividing the value of the net assets of the business by the number of shares in issue.

Statement of financial position (balance sheet) method

The simplest method is to use the statement of financial position (balance sheet) values of the assets held. The **statement of financial position (balance sheet) method** will determine the value of an ordinary share (P_0) as follows:

$$P_0 = \frac{\text{Total assets at statement of financial position values} - \text{Total liabilities}}{\text{Number of ordinary shares issued}}$$

Where the business has preference shares in issue, these must also be deducted (at their statement of financial position value) from the total assets in order to obtain the value of an ordinary share.

Activity 12.14

Calculate the statement of financial position value of an ordinary share in CDC Ltd.

The value of an ordinary share will be:

$$P_0 = \frac{[15.7 - (3.6 + 6.5)]}{2.0} = £2.80$$

The statement of financial position (balance sheet) method has the advantage that the valuation process is straightforward and the data are easy to obtain. However, the value of a share derived in this way is likely to represent a conservative value. This is because certain intangible assets, such as internally generated goodwill and brand names, may not be recorded on the statement of financial position and will, therefore, be ignored for the purposes of valuation. In addition, those assets that are shown on the statement of financial position are often recorded at their historic cost (less any depreciation to date, where relevant), and these figures may be below their current market values. During a period of inflation, the current market values of certain assets held, such as property, will normally exceed the historic cost figures recorded on the statement of financial position.

Often, a share value based on statement of financial position values is calculated to obtain a minimum value for a share. A bidder, for example, may compare the bid price with this value to measure the 'downside' risk associated with acquiring a business. Where the bid price is close to the statement of financial position value, the level of investment risk is likely to be small. It is fairly rare for the shares of a business to have a current market value that is below the statement of financial position value.

Current market value methods

Another approach to share valuation is to use the current market value, rather than the statement of financial position value, of assets held. In economic theory, the value of any asset (including a share in a business) should reflect the present value of the future benefits that it generates. The current market value of an asset should reflect the market's view of the present value of these future benefits as investors will be prepared to pay up to the present value of the future benefits to acquire the asset. Current market values can be expressed in terms of either **net realisable values** or **replacement costs**. In practice, both valuation approaches may be used.

● *Liquidation method.* The **liquidation method** values the assets held according to the net realisable values (that is, selling price less any costs of selling) that could be obtained in an orderly liquidation of the business. This method adopts the same basic equation as before, but uses net realisable values instead of statement of financial position values for assets and liabilities. Thus, the liquidation value for an ordinary share is calculated as follows:

$$P_0 = \frac{\text{Total assets at net realisable values} - \text{Total liabilities at current market values}}{\text{Number of ordinary shares issued}}$$

Activity 12.15

Calculate the value of an ordinary share in CDC Ltd using the liquidation method.

The liquidation value for an ordinary share will be:

$$P_0 = \frac{[(18.2 + 4.2 + 3.4 + 0.4 + 2.6) - (6.5 + 3.6)^*]}{2.0}$$

$$= £9.35$$

* We are told in Example 12.1 that the figures for liabilities on the statement of financial position reflect their current market values.

Although an improvement on the statement of financial position method, the liquidation method is also likely to reflect a conservative value. This is because it fails to take account of the value of the business as a going concern. Usually, the going concern value of a business will be higher than the sum of the individual values of the assets when sold piecemeal, because of the benefits of combining the assets. Net realisable values represent a lower limit for the current market value of assets held. The value of an asset in use is likely to be greater than the net realisable value of that asset. If this were not the case, a business would, presumably, sell the asset rather than keep it.

Using net realisable values can pose a number of practical problems. Where, for example, the asset is unique, such as a custom-built piece of equipment, it may be particularly hard to obtain a reliable value. Realisable values can vary according to the circumstances of the sale. The amount obtained in a hurried sale may be considerably below that which could be obtained in an orderly, managed sale.

- *Replacement cost method.* Replacement cost can also be used as an indicator of the market value of the assets held by a business. It will represent the cost of replacing a particular asset with an identical asset. The value of an ordinary share, based on replacement cost, will be calculated as follows:

$$P_0 = \frac{\text{Total assets at replacement cost} - \text{Total liabilities at current market values}}{\text{Number of ordinary shares issued}}$$

The replacement cost approach will take account of assets that can be sold on an individual basis as well as of goodwill, which will exist only where the business is a going concern. When this is done, the amount derived will represent an upper limit for the market value of assets held.

Activity 12.16

Calculate the value of an ordinary share in CDC Ltd using the replacement cost method.

The replacement cost approach will yield the following value for an ordinary share:

$$P_0 = \frac{(19.2 + 5.2 + 3.9 + 0.4 + 2.6 + 10.0) - (3.6 + 6.5)}{2.0}$$

$$= £15.6$$

Adopting the replacement cost method can lead to practical difficulties. Factors such as technological change may make it difficult to calculate an accurate replacement cost as the asset may no longer be in production.

Stock market methods

Where a business is listed on the Stock Exchange, the quoted share price provides an indication of value. We saw in Chapter 6 that there is evidence to suggest that share prices react quickly and in an unbiased manner to new information that becomes publicly available, and so, in that sense, the stock market can be described as efficient. As information is fully absorbed in share prices it can be argued that, until new information becomes available, shares are correctly valued. The efficiency of the stock market is largely due to the efforts of investors who closely monitor listed businesses in an attempt to identify undervalued shares. The activities of these investors ensure that undervalued shares do not stay undervalued for very long as they will buy the shares and so drive up the price.

It is possible to use stock market information and ratios to help value the shares of an unlisted business. The first step in this process is to find a listed business within the same industry that has similar risk and growth characteristics. Stock market ratios relating to the listed business can then be applied to the unlisted business in order to derive a share value. Two ratios that can be used in this way are the price/earnings (P/E) ratio and the dividend yield ratio.

Price/earnings (P/E) ratio method

The P/E ratio relates the current share price to the current earnings of the business. We may recall from Chapter 3 that the ratio is calculated as follows:

$$\text{P/E ratio} = \frac{\text{Market value per share}}{\text{Earnings per share}}$$

The P/E ratio reflects the market's view of the likely future growth in earnings. The higher the P/E ratio, the more highly regarded are the future growth prospects.

The equation above can be rearranged so that:

$$\text{Market value per share } (P_0) = \text{P/E ratio} \times \text{Earnings per share}$$

Thus, we can see that the market value is a multiple of the benefits (earnings) that the share will provide.

The P/E ratio of a listed business can be applied to the earnings of a similar unlisted business to derive a share value. Using the rearranged equation above, the value of an ordinary share of an unlisted business is calculated as follows:

$$P_0 = \begin{array}{c}\text{P/E ratio of similar} \\ \text{listed business}\end{array} \times \begin{array}{c}\text{Earnings per share} \\ \text{(of unlisted business)}\end{array}$$

Activity 12.17

Calculate the value of an ordinary share in CDC Ltd, using the P/E ratio method.

The value of an ordinary share using the P/E ratio method will be:

$$P_0 = 11 \times \frac{\text{£3.6 (earnings available to shareholders)}}{\text{2.0 (number of ordinary shares)}}$$

$$= \text{£19.80}$$

Although the calculations are fairly simple, this valuation approach should not be viewed as a mechanical exercise. Care must be taken to ensure that differences between the two businesses do not invalidate the valuation process. As can be imagined, a potential problem with this method is finding a listed business with similar risk and growth characteristics. Other differences, such as differences in accounting policies and accounting year ends between the two businesses, can lead to problems when applying the P/E ratio to the earnings of the unlisted business. An unlisted business may adopt different policies on such matters as directors' remuneration, which will require adjustment before applying the P/E ratio.

It should be borne in mind that shares in unlisted businesses are less marketable than those of similar listed businesses. To take account of this difference, a discount is usually applied to the share value derived by using the above equation. A discount of 30 per cent is not uncommon, although determining an appropriate discount figure is difficult.

Dividend yield ratio method

→ The **dividend yield ratio** offers another approach to valuing the shares of an unlisted business. This ratio relates the cash return from dividends to the current market value per share and we saw in Chapter 3 that it is calculated as follows:

$$\text{Dividend yield} = \frac{\text{Gross dividend per share}}{\text{Market value per share}} \times 100$$

The dividend yield can be calculated for shares listed on the Stock Exchange as both the market value per share and the gross dividend per share will normally be known. However, for unlisted businesses, the market value per share is not normally known and, therefore, this ratio cannot normally be applied.

The above equation can be expressed in terms of the market value per share by rearranging as follows:

$$\text{Market value per share } (P_0) = \frac{\text{Gross dividend per share}}{\text{Divided yield}} \times 100$$

This rearranged equation can be used to value the shares of an unlisted business. For this purpose, the gross dividend per share of the unlisted business, whose shares are to be valued, and the dividend yield of a similar listed business are used in the equation.

Activity 12.18

Calculate the value of an ordinary share in CDC Ltd using the dividend yield method. (Assume a lower rate of tax of 10 per cent.)

The value of an ordinary share using the dividend yield method will be:

$$P_0 = \frac{0.5 \times 100/90^*}{5} \times 100$$

$$= £11.11$$

* We may recall from Chapter 3 that the dividend as shown in the accounts must be 'grossed up' in order to obtain the gross dividend required for the equation.

This approach to share valuation has a number of weaknesses. Once again, we are faced with the problem of finding a similar listed business as a basis for the valuation. We must also recognise that dividend policies may vary considerably between businesses in the same industry, and may also vary between listed and unlisted businesses. Unlisted businesses, for example, are likely to be under less pressure to distribute profits in the form of dividends than listed businesses.

Dividends represent only part of the earnings stream of a business, and to value shares on this basis may be misleading. The valuation obtained will be largely a function of the dividend policy adopted (which is at the discretion of management) rather than the earnings generated. Where a business does not make dividend distributions, this method cannot be applied.

Cash flow methods

We have already seen that the value of an asset is equivalent to the present value of the future cash flows that it generates. The most direct, and theoretically appealing, approach is, therefore, to value a share on this basis. The dividend valuation method and free cash flow method adopt this approach and both are discussed below.

Dividend valuation method

The cash returns from holding a share take the form of dividends received. It is possible, therefore, to view the value of a share in terms of the stream of future dividends that are received. We have already seen in Chapter 8 that the value of a share will be the *discounted value of the future dividends received* and can be shown as:

$$P_0 = \frac{D_1}{(1 + K_0)} + \frac{D_2}{(1 + K_0)^2} + \ldots + \frac{D_n}{(1 + K_0)^n}$$

where: $D_{1,2\ldots,n}$ = the dividend received in periods 1, 2 . . . , n
K_0 = the required rate of return on the share.

Although this model is theoretically appealing, there are practical problems in forecasting future dividend payments and in calculating the required rate of return on the share. The first problem arises because dividends tend to fluctuate over time. If, however, dividends can be assumed to remain constant over time, we have already seen that the discounted dividend model can be reduced to:

$$P_0 = \frac{D_1}{K_0}$$

where D_1 = the dividend received at the end of period 1.

Activity 12.19

Assume that CDC Ltd has a constant dividend payout and the cost of ordinary share capital is estimated at 12 per cent. Calculate the value of an ordinary share in the business using the discounted dividend approach.

The value of an ordinary share using the discounted dividend approach will be:

$$P_0 = \frac{0.5 \text{ (that is, 1.0m/2.0m)}}{0.12}$$

$$= £4.17$$

The assumption of constant dividends, however, may not be very realistic, as many businesses attempt to increase their dividends to shareholders over time.

We saw in Chapter 8 that, where businesses increase their dividends at a constant rate of growth, the discounted dividend model can be revised to:

$$P_0 = \frac{D_1}{(K_0 - g)}$$

where g = the constant growth rate in dividends (the model assumes K_0 is greater than g).

In practice, an attempt may be made to forecast dividend payments for a manageable period (say, five years). After this period, accurate forecasting may become too difficult, and so a constant growth rate may be assumed for dividends received beyond the forecast horizon. Thus, the future dividend stream is divided into two separate elements: the first element based on dividend estimates over a particular forecast horizon, and the second representing dividends beyond the forecast horizon (and involving the use of a simplifying assumption). Although avoiding one problem, this approach creates another of deciding on an appropriate growth rate to use.

Figure 12.5 illustrates the process just described.

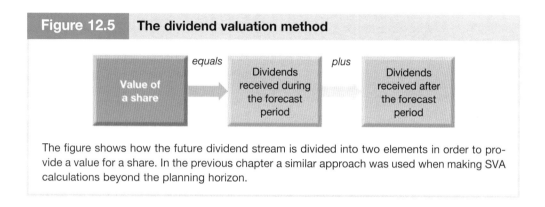

Figure 12.5 The dividend valuation method

The figure shows how the future dividend stream is divided into two elements in order to provide a value for a share. In the previous chapter a similar approach was used when making SVA calculations beyond the planning horizon.

The use of dividends as a basis for valuation can create difficulties because of their discretionary nature. Different businesses will adopt different dividend payout policies and this can affect the calculation of share values. In some cases, no dividends may be declared by a business for a considerable period. There are, for example, high-growth businesses that prefer to plough back profits into the business rather than make dividend payments.

Free cash flow method

Another approach to share valuation is to value the free cash flows that are generated by a business over time. Free cash flows were considered in Chapter 11. They represent the cash flows available to lenders and shareholders after any new investments in assets. In other words, they are equivalent to the net cash flows from operations after deducting tax paid and cash for investment.

The valuation process is the same as the process that we looked at in the preceding chapter. To value shares using free cash flows, we have to discount the future free cash flows over time, using the cost of capital. The present value of the free cash flows, after deducting amounts owing to long-term lenders at current market values, will represent that portion of the free cash flows that accrue to the ordinary shareholders. If this amount is divided by the number of ordinary shares in issue, we have a figure for the value of an ordinary share. Hence, the value of an ordinary share will be:

$$P_0 = \frac{\text{Present value of future free cash flows} - \text{Long-term loans at current market values}}{\text{Number of ordinary shares issued}}$$

Activity 12.20

Calculate the value of an ordinary share in CDC Ltd, using the free cash flow method.

The value of an ordinary share will be:

	Cash flow	Discount rate	Present value
	£m	10%	£m
Year 9	4.4	0.91	4.00
Year 10	4.6	0.83	3.82
Year 11	4.9	0.75	3.68
Year 12	5.0	0.68	3.40
Next 13 years	5.4	4.90*	26.46
			41.36

$$P_0 = \frac{PV - \text{Long-term loans at current market value}^\dagger}{\text{Number of ordinary shares}}$$

$$= \frac{41.36 - 3.6^\ddagger}{2.0} = \text{£18.88}$$

* This is the total of the individual discount rates for the 13-year period. This short cut can be adopted where cash flows are constant. For the sake of simplicity, it is assumed that there are no cash flows after the 13-year period.

† This method, unlike the statement of financial position methods discussed earlier, does not deduct short-term liabilities in arriving at a value per share. This is because they are dealt with in the calculation of free cash flows.

‡ We are told in the example that the statement of financial position values of liabilities reflect their current market values.

We have seen in Chapter 11 that a major problem with this method is that of accurate forecasting. However, this can be tackled in the same way as described above. Free cash flows may be forecast over a manageable time horizon (say, five years) and then a terminal value substituted for free cash flows arising beyond that period. Determining the terminal value is, of course, a problem – and an important one – as it may be a significant proportion of the total cash flows.

In the previous chapter we used an example to illustrate the valuation of a business where it was assumed that returns remained constant after the planning period and used the following formula for a perpetuity in order to determine the terminal value (TV):

$$\text{TV} = \frac{C_1}{r}$$

where: C_1 = the free cash flows in the following year

r = the required rate of return from investors.

However, another approach would be to assume a constant growth rate over time, just as we did with dividends earlier. The terminal value of the business as a whole (TV$_B$) would then be:

$$\text{TV}_B = \frac{C_1}{(r - g)}$$

where: C = free cash flows in the following year

r = the cost of capital

g = the constant rate of growth in free cash flows.

Although free cash flows may appear to be clearly defined, in practice there may be problems. The discretionary policies of management concerning new investments will have a significant influence on the free cash flow figure calculated. Free cash flows are likely to fluctuate considerably between periods. Unlike earnings, management has no incentive to smooth out cash flows over time. However, for valuation purposes, it may be useful to smooth out cash flow fluctuations between periods in order to establish trends over time.

Other methods of share valuation

We have now discussed the main methods of valuing shares; however, other methods can be found in practice. One such method is to use the ratio between a key financial measure, such as sales, and share value using information from a similar business. Example 12.2 illustrates how this method works in practice.

Example 12.2

Aztec Ltd has sales of £12 million and has 500,000 shares in issue. A similar business, Inca plc, has sales of £30 million and a market capitalisation (that is, total value of ordinary shares in issue) of £10 million.

What is the value of an ordinary share in Aztec Ltd?

Solution

Inca plc has £3 of sales for every £1 of market capitalisation. Using this ratio of 3 : 1, the total value of the ordinary shares in Aztec Ltd will be £4 million (that is, £12m/3).

Dividing £4 million (the total value of shares) by 500,000 (the number of shares in issue) will provide a value of £8 for each share.

Although the calculations required are straightforward, it is assumed that the relationship between sales and market capitalisation will hold from one business to another. This, however, may be a 'heroic' assumption. The fact that a business sells the same kind of products or services does not mean that it will have the same profitability, asset structure, risk and growth prospects. Ultimately, it is these factors that determine value.

The relationship between market capitalisation and other key financial measures, such as profit or the carrying value of assets, may also be used as a basis for valuation. The approach used in each case is basically the same – and so are the problems.

A further method of valuing shares is the EVA® method that we discussed in Chapter 11. We may recall that the value of a business could be derived as follows:

Business value = Capital invested + PV of future EVA®

To derive the total value of the ordinary shares, the value of any loan capital must be deducted. By dividing total value of shares by the number of shares in issue, we can derive a value for an ordinary share. (We saw in Chapter 11 that this method should arrive at the same business value as the free cash flow approach discussed earlier.)

Valuing a newly established business: an example

Although valuing well-established businesses poses problems, those problems can appear trivial when struggling with the difficulties of valuing newly established businesses. These businesses will have no track record and may be making little or no profit. **Real World 12.15** reveals how analysts might go about valuing a biotech business that is making losses but which has promising new drugs in the pipeline.

REAL WORLD 12.15

Putting a price on a promise   **FT**

So how do you put a realistic valuation on companies that offer little more than promise. Is it just made up?

No. While it may appear more art than a science, there is a generally accepted approach to how analysts value loss-making biotech companies. It is far from perfect and carries the ever-present risk of drugs failing, but it does allow for a form of comparison between companies.

Where do they start?

In a similar way to how analysts might work out a discounted cash flow for an entire company, in which they try to put a value on what predicted future income would be worth today. In a sense, the analysts treat each promising experimental drug within a portfolio as a mini-company. They then carry out a discounted cash flow of each drug to establish a net present value. They then add together the net present value of each drug, along with any cash in the bank, and come up with a present value for the company.

Do they include every drug in a company's development pipeline?

No. Generally, they only include drugs that are already being tested on humans. This is a contentious issue for smaller companies with drugs at the research stage, which are usually assigned no value. They would need to know the potential future sales of a drug to work out a net present value.

How do they do that?

The key thing is to determine what expected peak sales would be if – and it is a big if – a drug successfully makes it all the way through human trials. The year of peak sales is usually taken to be five years from the launch.

Will this depend on the number of potential patients?

Absolutely. The analyst will look at information provided by the company and the wealth of source material available on the internet to determine the size of the patient group that could be treated by a certain drug – that is, how many people actually suffer from a certain disease or condition.

And do they look at the worldwide potential?

They concentrate on North America, western Europe and Japan, the places where people will pay lots of money for drugs.

What if there is competition from existing drugs to treat a condition?

If there is a competitive market with limited advantage offered by the new drug in terms of reducing side-effects or increasing effectiveness, the assumption will be that it will win 10 per cent market share. If there is no other treatment that addresses the same needs as the new drug, a penetration rate of about 50 per cent is assumed.

We have worked out the potential size of the patient population and market share, how do they come up with a price?

This is obviously tricky for a drug that addresses an unmet need, which would involve a certain amount of guesswork. But for those that will compete, you look at the price of the existing drugs. For example, a cancer treatment could cost $15,000 (£8,900). So, if we multiply the potential number of patients by the price, this gives us estimated peak yearly sales,

Does the biotech company receive all of this?

Not likely. Most biotech businesses do not have a sales and marketing division capable of selling large numbers of drugs, and relatively little capital. They often need to license promising drugs to bigger pharmaceutical companies, which help pay for development and would be responsible for sales. Because of this, they will only usually expect a royalty on future sales.

How much of a percentage should they expect on a royalty deal?

This depends on how canny management is when negotiating, but the most important aspect is how far along in development a drug is when a licensing deal is signed. The later it is, the better the royalty level the small biotech can expect.

For Phase I drugs, the earliest stage of human trials, the royalty is usually in the single digits. For Phase II it would be double digits. But this is very changeable, depending on how promising a drug is and the analyst would expect some guidance from a company.

Are there any other costs that need to be taken into account?

Yes. The cost of overheads needs to be factored in. This would usually reduce by another 30 per cent the return expected by the biotech from each drug.

What about tax?

Most biotechs are lossmaking, but if you wanted to be conservative you could take off another 30 per cent. So, we have a figure that represents the potential return on a drug. But that assumes it makes it through human trials and is approved by regulators.

We know that rarely happens.

Very true. For this reason, the analyst applies a probability factor for each drug to account for risk, depending on what stage they are at in development.

If it is in Phase I, the chance of success is 10 per cent, Phase II 30 per cent and Phase III 50–70 per cent. This can vary according to the quality of the data and the inherent riskiness of some drugs, but consistency is important to allow for the comparison of one company's drug pipeline with another's. Add all these factors together and we have an expected peak return for a drug that takes account of risk.

How do we translate that into what it is worth now – its net present value?

The assumption is that a patent on a drug will usually last about 10 years. So, for the first five years the expected return increases until it hits the peak. The peak sales figure is then carried forward for another five years. The analyst discounts the expected returns for each of these 10 years to determine what each amount is worth now, and adds those numbers together to give the net present value.

Real World 12.15 continued

What is discounting?

A discounted cash flow puts a figure on what someone should be willing to pay today to receive the anticipated cash flow in future years. Biotech drugs are assigned a relatively high discount rate of 13 per cent because people would expect a return commensurate with the risk. This means that if someone were to invest £100 in their drugs now, they should expect a return of 13 per cent for each year the drug was available on the market. A safer bet, such as Tesco, has a discount rate of between 7 and 8 per cent, which reflects the much higher likelihood that you will actually see a return on your investment.

Source: 'Trying to put a price on a promise', *Financial Times,* 9 March 2004.

Self-assessment question 12.1

Permian Holdings plc is a large conglomerate company that is listed on the London Stock Exchange. The board of directors of Permian Holdings plc has decided to restructure the business and, as part of the restructuring plan, it has been agreed to spin off one of its largest subsidiaries, Miocene plc, as a separate business. Miocene plc will not seek an immediate Stock Exchange listing.

The most recent financial statements of Miocene plc are set out below.

Statement of financial position (balance sheet) as at 30 November 2008

	£m
Non-current assets (cost less depreciation)	
Property	33.2
Plant and equipment at cost	24.3
Fixtures and fittings at cost	10.4
	67.9
Current assets	
Inventories	34.8
Trade receivables	29.6
	64.4
Total assets	132.3
Equity	
Ordinary £0.25 shares	10.0
Share premium account	5.0
Retained earnings	45.1
	60.1
Non-current liabilities	
10% loan notes	21.0
Current liabilities	
Trade payables	35.9
Tax	3.9
Bank overdraft	11.4
	51.2
Total equity and liabilities	132.3

Income statement for the year ended 30 November 2008

	£m
Sales revenue	153.6
Cost of sales	(102.4)
Gross profit	51.2
Selling and distribution expenses	(12.3)
Administrative expenses	(10.2)
Operating profit	28.7
Finance expenses	(3.6)
Profit before taxation	25.1
Tax	(7.9)
Profit for the year	17.2

The following additional information has been gathered concerning Miocene plc:

1 A firm of independent valuers has recently established the current realisable value of the business's assets as:

	£m
Property	65.4
Plant and equipment	18.8
Fixtures and fittings	4.6
Inventories	38.9

The statement of financial position value of trade receivables reflects their current realisable values.

2 A similar business to Miocene plc is listed on the London Stock Exchange and has a price/earnings (P/E) ratio of 11.

3 The profit for the year for Miocene plc for the forthcoming year is expected to be the same as for the year to 30 November 2008. The dividend payout ratio is expected to be 40 per cent and dividends are expected to grow at 4 per cent per year for the foreseeable future.

4 The business has an estimated cost of ordinary shares of 10 per cent.

Required:

(a) Calculate the value of a share in Miocene plc using the following valuation methods:
  (i) Statement of financial position (balance sheet) basis
  (ii) Liquidation basis
  (iii) P/E basis
  (iv) Dividend growth basis.

(b) Explain what is meant by the term 'spin-off' in the context of restructuring and suggest reasons why Permian plc might undertake this form of restructuring.

The answer to this question may be found at the end of the book, on p. 538.

Choosing a valuation model

When deciding on the appropriate valuation model to employ, we need to consider the purpose for which the shares are being valued. Different valuation models may be appropriate for different circumstances. For example, an 'asset stripper' (that is, someone who wishes to acquire a business with a view to selling off its individual assets) would probably be most interested in the liquidation basis of valuation. A financial adviser to a new business being floated on the stock market, on the other hand, may rely more heavily on the P/E ratio method or the free cash flow method. We saw earlier that the former approach takes account of share values of similar businesses already listed on the Stock Exchange.

In cases such as mergers and takeovers, share valuations derived from the models can be used as a basis for negotiation. In such circumstances, they can be used to help set boundaries within which a final share value will be determined. The final figure will, however, be influenced by various factors including the negotiating skills and the relative bargaining position of the parties.

SUMMARY

The main points in this chapter may be summarised as follows:

Mergers and takeovers

- A merger is when two businesses of equal size combine; a takeover is when a larger business absorbs a smaller business.
- Mergers can be achieved through horizontal or vertical integration or by combining with unrelated businesses.
- There are surges in merger activity from time to time, usually as a result of a combination of political, economic and technological factors.
- To make economic sense, the merged business should generate greater cash flows than if the two businesses remained apart.

Rationale for mergers

- There are various reasons for a merger, which include:
  - benefits of scale
  - eliminating competition
  - exploiting underutilised resources
  - combining complementary resources
  - using surplus funds
  - diversification
  - pursuing managers' interests.
- The last two of these may not be consistent with the objective of maximising shareholder wealth.

Forms of purchase consideration

- Payment for the shares in an acquired business may take the form of:
  - cash
  - shares
  - loan capital.

Who benefits?

- Shareholders in the target business see an increase in the value of their investment.
- Shareholders in the bidding business often see a decrease in the value of their investment.
- Managers of the bidding business may gain through an increase in status, income and security.

- Managers of the target business often leave within a few years of the takeover.
- Financial advisers and lawyers usually benefit from a merger.

Resisting a takeover bid

- Various tactics may be employed to resist a bid, including:
  - conversion to private company status
  - employee share option schemes
  - circularising shareholders
  - making the business unattractive
  - pac-man defence
  - white knight defence
  - white squire defence.
- Managers of the bidding business may try to overcome resistance by circularising shareholders to explain the logic of the case or by increasing the bid price.

Protecting shareholders and the public

- The City Code on Mergers and Takeovers aims to ensure that shareholders are given every opportunity to evaluate a merger on its merits.
- To protect the public interest, the Competition Commission has the power to investigate mergers where a substantial lessening of competition may occur, and to take appropriate action.
- In the case of cross-border mergers, the EU has rules to protect competition.

Restructuring the business

- A divestment involves selling off part of the business operations.
- A demerger, or spin-off, involves transferring business operations to a new business that is owned by the current shareholders.

Valuing shares in a business

- Shares may be valued on the following bases:
  - methods based on the value of the assets (balance sheet method, liquidation method, replacement cost method)
  - methods based on stock market ratios (P/E ratio method and dividend yield method)
  - methods based on future cash flows (dividend valuation method and free cash flow method).
- The choice of valuation methods will depend on the reasons for the valuation.

→ **Key terms**

Merger p. 474	**White squire** p. 497
Takeover p. 474	**Competition Commission** p. 498
Horizontal merger p. 474	**Divestment** p. 498
Vertical merger p. 474	**Demerger (spin-off)** p. 499
Conglomerate merger p. 474	**Statement of financial position**
Poison pill p. 496	**(balance sheet) method** p. 503
Crown jewels p. 496	**Net realisable value** p. 504
Golden parachutes p. 496	**Replacement cost** p. 504
Pac-man defence p. 496	**Liquidation method** p. 504
White knight p. 497	**Dividend yield ratio** p. 507

For definitions of these terms see the Glossary, pp. 574–583.

References

1 'The long-run performance of UK acquirers: motives underlying the method of payment and their influence on subsequent performance', *Gregory, A.*, University of Exeter Discussion Paper, 1998.

2 **Takeovers, Restructuring and Corporate Governance**, *Weston, F., Siu, J. and Johnson, B.*, 3rd edn, Prentice Hall, 2001, chapter 8.

3 'The market for corporate control', *Rose, H.*, Financial Times Mastering Management Series, supplement issue no. 2, February 1996.

4 'An examination of the long run performance of UK acquiring firms', *Gregory, A.*, Working Papers in Accounting and Finance, The University of Wales, Aberystwyth, 1997.

5 'Gains and losses from mergers: the evidence', *Ravenscroft, D.*, **Managerial Finance**, vol. 17, (1991), no. 1.

6 'Corporate ownership and corporate control: a study of France, Germany and the UK', *Franks, J. and Mayer, C.*, **Economic Policy**, no. 10 (1994).

7 'Creating Long-term Value through Mergers and Acquisitions', *PA Consulting Group*, PA Knowledge Ltd, 2003.

Further reading

If you wish to explore the topics discussed in this chapter in more depth, try the following books:

Corporate Financial Management, *Arnold, G.*, 3rd edn, Financial Times Prentice Hall, 2005, chapters 20 and 23.

Mergers, Acquisitions and Corporate Restructurings, *Gaughan, P.*, 4th edn, J. Wiley and Sons, 2007, chapters 1–2 and 4–6.

Corporate Finance, *Brealey, B., Myers, S. and Allen, F.*, 9th edn, McGraw-Hill, 2008, chapters 32 and 33.

Stock Valuation: An Essential Guide to Wall Street's Most Popular Valuation Models, *Hoover, S.*, McGraw Hill, 2006.

REVIEW QUESTIONS

Answers to these questions can be found at the back of the book on p. 548.

12.1 Distinguish between a merger and a takeover.

12.2 Identify and discuss four reasons why a business may undertake divestment of part of its operations.

12.3 Identify four reasons why a business seeking to maximise the wealth of its shareholders may wish to take over another business.

12.4 Identify four tactics the directors of a target business might employ to resist an unwelcome bid.

EXERCISES

Exercises 12.4 to 12.7 are more advanced than 12.1 to 12.3. Those with coloured numbers have answers at the back of the book starting on p. 571.

 If you wish to try more exercises, visit the students' side of this book's Companion Website.

12.1 When a business wishes to acquire another, it may make a bid in the form of cash, a share-for-share exchange, or loan capital-for-share exchange.

Required:

Discuss the advantages and disadvantages of each form of consideration from the viewpoint of:

(a) The bidding business's shareholders
(b) The target business's shareholders.

12.2 Dawn Raider plc has just offered one of its shares for two shares in Sleepy Giant plc, a business in the same industry as itself. Extracts from the financial statements of each business for the year ended 31 May Year 8 appear below:

	Dawn Raider £m	Sleepy Giant £m
Income statements		
Sales revenue	150	360
Profits for the year	18	16
Statement of financial position (balance sheet) data		
Non-current assets	150	304
Net current assets (Note 1)	48	182
	198	486
Loans	(80)	(40)
	118	446
Share capital (Note 2)	50	100
Reserves	68	346
	118	446

Notes

		Dawn Raider	*Sleepy Giant*
1	Includes cash/(overdrafts):	(£60m)	£90m
2	Shares	25p	50p
3	Dividends paid and proposed	4	14

Stock market data for each business is as follows:

	31 May *Year 6*	*31 May* *Year 7*	*31 May* *Year 8*
Dawn Raider plc			
Share price (pence)	120.0	144.0	198.0
Earnings per share (pence)	5.3	6.9	9.0
Dividends per share (pence)	2.0	2.0	2.0
Sleepy Giant plc			
Share price (pence)	45.0	43.0	72.0
Earnings per share (pence)	8.4	7.4	8.0
Dividends per share (pence)	8.0	7.0	7.0

If the takeover succeeds, Dawn Raider plans to combine Sleepy Giant's marketing and distribution channels with its own, with a post-tax saving of £1 million a year. In addition it expects to be able to increase Sleepy Giant's profits after tax by at least £5 million a year by better management. Dawn Raider's own profits after tax are expected to be £23 million (excluding the £1 million saving already mentioned), in the year ended 31 May Year 9.

One of the shareholders of Sleepy Giant has written to its chairman arguing that the bid should not be accepted. The following is an extract from his letter: 'The bid considerably undervalues Sleepy Giant since it is below Sleepy Giant's net assets per share. Furthermore, if Dawn Raider continues its existing policy of paying only 2p a share as a dividend, Sleepy Giant's shareholders will be considerably worse off'.

Required:

(a) Calculate:
  (i) The total value of the bid and the bid premium.
  (ii) Sleepy Giant's net assets per share at 31 May Year 8.
  (iii) The dividends the holder of 100 shares in Sleepy Giant would receive in the year before and the year after the takeover.
  (iv) The earnings per share for Dawn Raider in the year after the takeover.
  (v) The share price of Dawn Raider after the takeover assuming that it maintains its existing price/earnings ratio.

(b) Comment on:
  (i) The points that the shareholder in Sleepy Giant raises in his letter.
  (ii) The amount of the bid consideration.

12.3 An investment business is considering taking a minority stake in two businesses, Monaghan plc and Cavan plc. Both are in the same line of business and both are listed on the London Stock Exchange.

Monaghan plc has had a stable dividend policy over the years. In the financial reports for the current year, the chairman stated that a dividend of 30p a share would be paid in one year's time and financial analysts employed by the investment business expect dividends to grow at an annual compound rate of 10 per cent for the indefinite future.

Cavan plc has had an erratic dividend pattern over the years and future dividends have been difficult to predict. However, to defend itself successfully against an unwelcome takeover, the business recently announced that dividends for the next three years were expected to be as follows:

Year	Dividend per share (pence)
1	20
2	32
3	36

Financial analysts working for the investment business believe that, after Year 3, Cavan plc would enjoy a smooth pattern of growth, and dividends would be expected to grow at a compound rate of 8 per cent for the indefinite future.

The investment business believes that a return of 14 per cent is required to compensate for the risks associated with the type of business in which the two businesses are engaged. Ignore taxation.

Required:

(a) State the arguments for and against valuing a share on the basis of its future dividends.

(b) Calculate the value of a share in:
   (i) Monaghan plc, and
   (ii) Cavan plc
   based on the expected future dividends of each business.

12.4 The directors of Simat plc have adopted a policy of expansion based on the acquisition of other businesses. The special projects division of Simat has been given the task of identifying suitable businesses for takeover.

Stidwell Ltd has been identified as being a suitable business and negotiations between the board of directors of each business have begun. Information relating to Stidwell Ltd is set out below:

Statement of financial position (balance sheet) as at 31 May Year 9

	£
Non-current assets (at cost less depreciation)	
Property	180,000
Plant and machinery	90,000
Motor vehicles	19,000
	289,000
Current assets	
Inventories	84,000
Receivables	49,000
Cash	24,000
	157,000
Total assets	446,000
Equity	
Ordinary £0.50 shares	150,000
Retained earnings	114,000
	264,000
Non-current liabilities	
10% loan notes	140,000
Current liabilities	
Payables and accruals	42,000
Total equity and liabilities	446,000

The profit for the year of Stidwell Ltd for the year ended 31 May Year 9 was £48,500 and the dividend paid for the year £18,000. Profits and dividends of the business have shown little change over the past five years.

The realisable values of the assets of Stidwell Ltd, at the end of the year, were estimated to be as follows:

	£
Property	285,000
Plant and machinery	72,000
Motor vehicles	15,000

For the remaining assets, the values as per the statement of financial position were considered to reflect current realisable values.

The special projects division of Simat plc has also identified another business, Asgard plc, which is listed on the Stock Exchange and which is broadly similar to Stidwell Ltd. The following details were taken from a recent copy of a financial newspaper:

Years 8–9		Stock	Price	± or	Dividend	Cover	Yield	P/E
High	Low				(net)	(times)	(gross %)	(times)
560p	480p	Asgard plc	500p	+4p	10.33p	4.4	2.76	11

Assume a lower rate of tax of 10 per cent.

Required:

(a) Calculate the value of an ordinary share of Stidwell Ltd using each of the following valuation methods:
  (i) Net assets (liquidation) basis
  (ii) Dividend yield
  (iii) Price/earnings ratio.

(b) Critically evaluate each of the valuation methods identified in (a) above.

12.5 Alpha plc, a dynamic, fast-growing business in microelectronics, has just made a bid of 17 of its own shares for every 20 shares of Beta plc, which manufactures a range of electric motors. Financial statements for the two businesses are as follows:

Income statements for the year ended 31 March Year 9

	Alpha plc	Beta plc
	£000	£000
Sales revenue	3,000	2,000
Operating profit	300	140
Interest	(100)	(10)
Profit before tax	200	130
Tax	(100)	(65)
Profit for the year	100	65
Other information:		
	Alpha plc	Beta plc
Number of issued shares (million)	1.0	0.5
Earnings per share	10p	13p
Price/earnings ratio	20	10
Market price per share	200p	130p
Capitalisation (that is, market price per share × number of shares)	£2m	£0.65m
Dividend per share	2p	6p
Dividends paid and proposed	20,000	30,000

Historical share prices (in pence) at 31 March each year have been:

	Year 4	Year 5	Year 6	Year 7	Year 8
Alpha plc	60	90	150	160	200
Beta plc	90	80	120	140	130

Statements of financial position (balance sheets) at 31 March Year 9

	Alpha plc £000	Beta plc £000
Non-current assets	1,200	900
Current assets	900	700
Total assets	2,100	1,600
Equity		
Share capital £0.25 ordinary shares	250	125
Retained earnings	750	755
	1,000	880
Non-current liabilities – loans	800	120
Current liabilities	300	600
Total equity and liabilities	2,100	1,600

The merger of the two businesses will result in post-tax savings of £15,000 per year to be made in the distribution system of Alpha.

One of the shareholders of Beta has queried the bid and has raised the following points. First, he understands that Alpha normally pays only small dividends and that his dividend per share will decrease. Secondly, he is concerned that the bid undervalues Beta since the current value of the bid is less than the figure for shareholders' funds in Beta's balance sheet.

Required:
(a) Calculate the bid consideration.
(b) Calculate the earnings per share for the combined group.
(c) Calculate the theoretical post-acquisition price of Alpha shares assuming that the price/earnings ratio stays the same.
(d) Comment on the shareholder's two points.

(*Hint*: In order to answer this question you need to calculate the number of shares to be issued by Alpha and the total profit after tax following the merger. The market value of the shares following the merger can be found by rearranging the P/E ratio equation and inserting the relevant figures.)

12.6   Larkin Conglomerates plc owns a subsidiary, Hughes Ltd, which sells office equipment. Recently, Larkin Conglomerates plc has been reconsidering its future strategy and has decided that Hughes Ltd should be sold off. The proposed divestment of Hughes Ltd has attracted considerable interest from other businesses wishing to acquire this type of business. The most recent financial statements of Hughes Ltd are as follows:

Statement of financial position (balance sheet) as at 31 May Year 5

	£000
Non-current assets (cost less depreciation)	
Property	200
Motor vans	11
Fixtures and fittings	8
	219
Current assets	
Inventories	34
Receivables	22
Cash at bank	20
	76
Total assets	295
Equity	
£1 ordinary shares	60
General reserve	14
Retained earnings	55
	129
Non-current liabilities	
12% loan: Cirencester bank	100
Current liabilities	
Trade payables	52
Tax and accruals	14
	66
Total equity and liabilities	295

Income statement for the year ended 31 May Year 5

	£000
Sales revenue	352.0
Profit before interest and taxation	34.8
Interest charges	(12.0)
Profit before taxation	22.8
Tax	(6.4)
Profit for the year	16.4

A dividend of £4,000 was proposed and paid during the year.

The subsidiary has shown a stable level of sales and profits over the past three years. An independent valuer has estimated the current realisable values of the assets of the business as follows:

	£000
Property	235
Motor vans	8
Fixtures and fittings	5
Inventories	36

For the remaining assets, the statement of financial position (balance sheet) values were considered to reflect their current realisable values.

Another business in the same industry, which is listed on the Stock Exchange, has a gross dividend yield of 5 per cent and a price/earnings ratio of 12. Assume a tax rate of 25 per cent.

Required:

(a) Calculate the value of an ordinary share in Hughes Ltd using the following methods:
   (i) Net assets (liquidation) basis
   (ii) Dividend yield
   (iii) Price/earnings ratio.

(b) Briefly state what other information, besides the information provided above, would be useful to prospective buyers in deciding on a suitable value to place on the shares of Hughes Ltd.

12.7 The senior management of Galbraith Ltd is negotiating a management buy-out of the business from the existing shareholders. The most recent financial statements of Galbraith Ltd are as follows:

Statement of financial position (balance sheet) as at 30 November Year 6

	£
Non-current assets (cost less depreciation)	
Property	292,000
Plant and machinery	145,000
Motor vehicles	42,000
	479,000
Current assets	
Inventories	128,000
Trade receivables	146,000
	274,000
Total assets	753,000
Equity	
£0.50 ordinary shares	100,000
General reserve	85,000
Retained earnings	169,000
	354,000
Non-current liabilities	
13% loan notes (secured)	180,000
Current liabilities	
Trade payables	147,000
Tax	19,000
Bank overdraft	53,000
	219,000
Total equity and liabilities	753,000

Income statement for the year ended 30 November Year 6

	£
Sales revenue	1,430,000
Cost of sales	(870,000)
Gross profit	560,000
Less Selling and distribution expenses	(253,000)
Administration expenses	(167,000)
Operating profit	140,000
Finance expenses	(35,000)
Profit before taxation	105,000
Tax	(38,000)
Profit for the year	67,000

The following additional information is available:

1 Dividends of £5,000 were proposed and paid during the year.
2 A professional surveyor has recently established the current realisable value of the business's assets as being:

	£
Property	365,000
Plant and machinery	84,000
Motor vehicles	32,000
Inventories	145,000

The current realisable value of trade receivables was considered to be the same as their statement of financial position (balance sheet) values.

3 The free cash flows of the business over the next ten years are estimated as follows:

	£
Year 7	97,000
Year 8	105,000
Years 9–16	150,000

4 The cost of capital for the business is 10 per cent.
5 A similar business which is listed on the Stock Exchange has a price/earnings ratio of 8 and a gross dividend yield of 2.2 per cent.

Assume a 20 per cent rate of tax.

Required:

(a) Calculate the value of a share in Galbraith Ltd using the following valuation methods:
   (i) Liquidation basis
   (ii) Price/earnings basis
   (iii) Dividend yield basis
   (iv) Free cash flow basis (assuming a ten-year life for the business).
(b) Briefly evaluate each of the share valuation methods set out in (a) above.
(c) Which share valuation method, if any, do you consider to be most valid as a basis for nego-tiation and why?
(d) What potential problems will a management buy-out proposal pose for the shareholders of Galbraith Ltd?

Appendix A

Present value table

Present value of 1, that is, $(1 + r)^{-n}$
where: r = discount rate
n = number of periods until payment.

Discount rate (r)

Period (n)	1%	2%	3%	4%	5%	6%	7%	8%	9%	10%	Period (n)
1	0.990	0.980	0.971	0.962	0.952	0.943	0.935	0.926	0.917	0.909	1
2	0.980	0.961	0.943	0.925	0.907	0.890	0.873	0.857	0.842	0.826	2
3	0.971	0.942	0.915	0.889	0.864	0.840	0.816	0.794	0.772	0.751	3
4	0.961	0.924	0.888	0.855	0.823	0.792	0.763	0.735	0.708	0.683	4
5	0.951	0.906	0.863	0.822	0.784	0.747	0.713	0.681	0.650	0.621	5
6	0.942	0.888	0.837	0.790	0.746	0.705	0.666	0.630	0.596	0.564	6
7	0.933	0.871	0.813	0.760	0.711	0.665	0.623	0.583	0.547	0.513	7
8	0.923	0.853	0.789	0.731	0.677	0.627	0.582	0.540	0.502	0.467	8
9	0.914	0.837	0.766	0.703	0.645	0.592	0.544	0.500	0.460	0.424	9
10	0.905	0.820	0.744	0.676	0.614	0.558	0.508	0.463	0.422	0.386	10
11	0.896	0.804	0.722	0.650	0.585	0.527	0.475	0.429	0.388	0.350	11
12	0.887	0.788	0.701	0.625	0.557	0.497	0.444	0.397	0.356	0.319	12
13	0.879	0.773	0.681	0.601	0.530	0.469	0.415	0.368	0.326	0.290	13
14	0.870	0.758	0.661	0.577	0.505	0.442	0.388	0.340	0.299	0.263	14
15	0.861	0.743	0.642	0.555	0.481	0.417	0.362	0.315	0.275	0.239	15

	11%	12%	13%	14%	15%	16%	17%	18%	19%	20%	
1	0.901	0.893	0.885	0.877	0.870	0.862	0.855	0.847	0.840	0.833	1
2	0.812	0.797	0.783	0.769	0.756	0.743	0.731	0.718	0.706	0.694	2
3	0.731	0.712	0.693	0.675	0.658	0.641	0.624	0.609	0.593	0.579	3
4	0.659	0.636	0.613	0.592	0.572	0.552	0.534	0.516	0.499	0.482	4
5	0.593	0.567	0.543	0.519	0.497	0.476	0.456	0.437	0.419	0.402	5
6	0.535	0.507	0.480	0.456	0.432	0.410	0.390	0.370	0.352	0.335	6
7	0.482	0.452	0.425	0.400	0.376	0.354	0.333	0.314	0.296	0.279	7
8	0.434	0.404	0.376	0.351	0.327	0.305	0.285	0.266	0.249	0.233	8
9	0.391	0.361	0.333	0.308	0.284	0.263	0.243	0.225	0.209	0.194	9
10	0.352	0.322	0.295	0.270	0.247	0.227	0.208	0.191	0.176	0.162	10
11	0.317	0.287	0.261	0.237	0.215	0.195	0.178	0.162	0.148	0.135	11
12	0.286	0.257	0.231	0.208	0.187	0.168	0.152	0.137	0.124	0.112	12
13	0.258	0.229	0.204	0.182	0.163	0.145	0.130	0.116	0.104	0.093	13
14	0.232	0.205	0.181	0.160	0.141	0.125	0.111	0.099	0.088	0.078	14
15	0.209	0.183	0.160	0.140	0.123	0.108	0.095	0.084	0.074	0.065	15

Appendix B
Annual equivalent factor table

Annual equivalent factor $A_{N,i}^{-1}$

	i	0.04	0.06	0.08	0.10	0.12	0.14	0.16	0.18	0.20
N	1	1.0400	1.0600	1.0800	1.1000	1.1200	1.1400	1.1600	1.1800	1.2000
	2	0.5302	0.5454	0.5608	0.5762	0.5917	0.6073	0.6230	0.6387	0.6545
	3	0.3603	0.3741	0.3880	0.4021	0.4163	0.4307	0.4453	0.4599	0.4747
	4	0.2755	0.2886	0.3019	0.3155	0.3292	0.3432	0.3574	0.3717	0.3863
	5	0.2246	0.2374	0.2505	0.2638	0.2774	0.2913	0.3054	0.3198	0.3344
	6	0.1908	0.2034	0.2163	0.2296	0.2432	0.2572	0.2714	0.2859	0.3007
	7	0.1666	0.1791	0.1921	0.2054	0.2191	0.2332	0.2476	0.2624	0.2774
	8	0.1485	0.1610	0.1740	0.1874	0.2013	0.2156	0.2302	0.2452	0.2606
	9	0.1345	0.1470	0.1601	0.1736	0.1877	0.2022	0.2171	0.2324	0.2481
	10	0.1233	0.1359	0.1490	0.1627	0.1770	0.1917	0.2069	0.2225	0.2385
	11	0.1141	0.1268	0.1401	0.1540	0.1684	0.1834	0.1989	0.2148	0.2311
	12	0.1066	0.1193	0.1327	0.1468	0.1614	0.1767	0.1924	0.2086	0.2253
	13	0.1001	0.1130	0.1265	0.1408	0.1557	0.1712	0.1872	0.2037	0.2206
	14	0.0947	0.1076	0.1213	0.1357	0.1509	0.1666	0.1829	0.1997	0.2169
	15	0.0899	0.1030	0.1168	0.1315	0.1468	0.1628	0.1794	0.1964	0.2139

Appendix C
Solutions to self-assessment questions

Chapter 2

2.1 Quardis Ltd

(a) The projected income statement for the year ended 31 May 2009 is:

	£000	£000
Sales revenue		280
Cost of sales		
Opening inventory	24	
Purchases	186	
	210	
Closing inventory	30	(180)
Gross profit		100
Wages		(34)
Other overhead expenses		(21)
Depreciation – Premises		(9)
Fixtures		(6)
Operating profit		30
Interest payable		(12)
Profit before tax		18
Tax (35%)		(6)
Profit for the year		12

(b) Projected statement of financial position (balance sheet) as at 31 May 2009:

	£000	£000
Non-current assets		
Premises	460	
Accumulated depreciation	(39)	421
Fixtures and fittings	60	
Accumulated depreciation	(16)	44
		465
Current assets		
Inventory		30
Trade receivables (60% × £280 × 3/12)		42
		72
Total assets		537
Equity		
£1 ordinary shares		200
Retained earnings [144 + (12 − 10)]		146
		346

	£000	£000
Non-current liabilities		
Borrowings – Loan		95
Current liabilities		
Trade payables (£186 × 2/12)	31	
Accrued expenses (3 + 4)	7	
Bank overdraft (balancing figure)	55	
Tax due (50% × 6)	3	
		96
Total equity and liabilities		537

(c) The projected statements reveal a poor profitability and liquidity position for the business. The liquidity position at 31 May 2009 reveals a serious deterioration when compared with the previous year.

 As a result of preparing these projected statements the management of Quardis Ltd may wish to make certain changes to their original plans. For example, the repayment of part of the loan may be deferred or the dividend may be reduced in order to improve liquidity. Similarly, the pricing policy of the business and the level of expenses proposed may be reviewed in order to improve profitability.

Chapter 3

3.1 **Ali plc and Bhaskar plc**

To answer this question you may have used the following ratios:

	Ali plc	Bhaskar plc
Current ratio	$\dfrac{853.0}{422.4} = 2.0$	$\dfrac{816.5}{293.1} = 2.8$
Acid test ratio	$\dfrac{(853.0 - 592.0)}{422.4} = 0.6$	$\dfrac{(816.5 - 403.0)}{293.1} = 1.4$
Gearing ratio	$\dfrac{190}{(687.6 + 190)} \times 100 = 21.6\%$	$\dfrac{250}{(874.6 + 250)} \times 100 = 22.2\%$
Interest cover ratio	$\dfrac{(131.9 + 19.4)}{19.4} = 7.8$ times	$\dfrac{(139.4 + 27.5)}{27.5} = 6.1$ times
Dividend payout ratio	$\dfrac{135.0}{99.9} \times 100 = 135\%$	$\dfrac{95.0}{104.6} \times 100 = 91\%$
Price/earnings ratio	$\dfrac{£6.50}{31.2p} = 20.8$ times	$\dfrac{£8.20}{41.8p} = 19.6$ times

 Ali plc has a much lower current ratio and acid test ratio than Bhaskar plc. This may be partly because Ali plc has a lower average settlement period for receivables. The acid test ratio of Ali plc is substantially below 1.0: this may suggest a liquidity problem.

 The gearing ratios of the two businesses are quite similar. Neither business seems to have excessive borrowing. The interest cover ratios for the two businesses are also similar. The ratios indicate that both businesses have good profit coverage for their interest charges.

The dividend payout ratios for the two businesses seem very high. In the case of Ali plc, the dividends announced for the year are considerably higher than the profit for the year that is available for dividend. As a result, part of the dividend was paid out of retained profits from previous years. This is an unusual occurrence; although it is quite legitimate, such action may nevertheless suggest a lack of prudence on the part of the directors.

The P/E ratios for both businesses seem high, which indicates market confidence in their future prospects.

Chapter 4

4.1   Beacon Chemicals plc

(a) Relevant cash flows are as follows:

	Year 0 £000	Year 1 £000	Year 2 £000	Year 3 £000	Year 4 £000	Year 5 £000
Sales	–	80	120	144	100	64
Loss of contribution		(15)	(15)	(15)	(15)	(15)
Variable costs		(40)	(50)	(48)	(30)	(32)
Fixed costs (Note 1)		(8)	(8)	(8)	(8)	(8)
Operating cash flows		17	47	73	47	9
Working capital	(30)					30
Capital cost	(100)					
Net relevant cash flows	(130)	17	47	73	47	39

Notes:

1 Only the fixed costs that are incremental to the project (existing only because of the project) are relevant. Depreciation is irrelevant because it is not a cash flow.

2 The research and development cost is irrelevant since it has been spent irrespective of the decision on X14 production.

(b) The payback period is as follows:

	Year 0 £000	Year 1 £000	Year 2 £000	Year 3 £000
Cumulative cash flows	(130)	(113)	(66)	7

Thus the equipment will have repaid the initial investment by the end of the third year of operations.

(c) The net present value is as follows:

	Year 0 £000	Year 1 £000	Year 2 £000	Year 3 £000	Year 4 £000	Year 5 £000
Discount factor	1.00	0.926	0.857	0.794	0.735	0.681
Present value	(130)	15.74	40.28	57.96	34.55	26.56
NPV	45.09 (that is, the sum of the present values for years 0 to 5)					

Chapter 5

5.1 **Choi Ltd**

(a) In evaluating the two machines, the first step is to calculate the NPV of each project over their respective time periods:

Lo-tek

	Cash flows £	Discount rate 12%	Present value £
Initial outlay	(10,000)	1.00	(10,000)
1 year's time	4,000	0.89	3,560
2 years' time	5,000	0.80	4,000
3 years' time	5,000	0.71	3,550
		NPV	1,110

Hi-tek

	Cash flows £	Discount rate 12%	Present value £
Initial outlay	(15,000)	1.00	(15,000)
1 year's time	5,000	0.89	4,450
2 years' time	6,000	0.80	4,800
3 years' time	6,000	0.71	4,260
4 years' time	5,000	0.64	3,200
		NPV	1,710

The shortest common period of time over which the machines can be compared is 12 years (that is, 3×4). This means that Lo-tek will be repeated four times and Hi-tek will be repeated three times during the 12-year period.

The NPV for Lo-tek will be:

$$\text{Total NPV} = £1,110 + \frac{£1,110}{(1+0.12)^6} + \frac{£1,110}{(1+0.12)^9} + \frac{£1,110}{(1+0.12)^{12}}$$

$$= £2,358.8$$

The NPV for Hi-tek will be:

$$\text{Total NPV} = £1,710 + \frac{£1,710}{(1+0.12)^8} + \frac{£1,710}{(1+0.12)^{12}}$$

$$= £2,840.3$$

The equivalent-annual-annuity approach will provide the following results for Lo-tek:

$$£1,110 \times 0.4163 = £462.09$$

and the following results for Hi-tek:

$$£1,710 \times 0.3292 = £562.93$$

(b) Hi-tek is the better buy because calculations show that it has the higher NPV over the shortest common period of time and provides the higher equivalent-annual-annuity value.

Chapter 6

6.1   Helsim Ltd

(a) The liquidity position may be assessed by using the liquidity ratios discussed in Chapter 3:

$$\text{Current ratio} = \frac{\text{Current assets}}{\text{Current liabilities}}$$

$$= \frac{£7.5\text{m}}{£5.4\text{m}}$$

$$= 1.4$$

$$\text{Acid test ratio} = \frac{\text{Current assets (excluding inventories)}}{\text{Current liabilities}}$$

$$= \frac{£3.7\text{m}}{£5.4\text{m}}$$

$$= 0.7$$

These ratios reveal a fairly weak liquidity position. The current ratio seems quite low and the acid test ratio very low. This latter ratio suggests that the business does not have sufficient liquid assets to meet its maturing obligations. It would, however, be useful to have details of the liquidity ratios of similar businesses in the same industry in order to make a more informed judgement. The bank overdraft represents 67% of the current liabilities and 40% of the total liabilities of the business. The continuing support of the bank is therefore important to the ability of the business to meet its commitments.

(b) The finance required to reduce trade payables to an average of 40 days outstanding is calculated as follows:

	£m
Trade payables at balance sheet date	1.80
Trade payables outstanding based on 40 days' credit 40/365 × £8.4m (that is, credit purchases)	(0.92)
Finance required	0.88 (say £0.9m)

(c) The bank may not wish to provide further finance to the business. The increase in overdraft will reduce the level of trade payables but will increase the risk exposure of the bank. The additional finance invested by the bank will not generate further funds and will not therefore be self-liquidating. The question does not make it clear whether the business has sufficient security to offer the bank for the increase in overdraft facility. The profits of the business will be reduced and the interest cover ratio, based on the profits generated last year, would reduce to about 1.6* times if the additional overdraft were granted (based on interest charged at 10% each year). This is very low and means that only a small decline in profits would leave interest charges uncovered.

* Existing bank overdraft (3.6) + extension of overdraft to cover reduction in trade payables (0.9) + loan notes (3.5) = £8.0m. Assuming a 10% interest rate means a yearly interest payment of £0.8m. The operating profit was £1.3m (that is, 6.4 − 3.0 − 2.1). Interest cover would be 1.63 (that is, 1.3/0.8).

(d) A number of possible sources of finance might be considered. Four possible sources are as follows:

- *Issue ordinary (equity) shares.* This option may be unattractive to investors. The return on shareholders' funds is fairly low at 7.9% (that is, profit for the year

(0.3)/equity (3.8)) and there is no evidence that the profitability of the business will improve. If profits remain at their current level the effect of issuing more equity will be to reduce further the returns to equity.

- *Make other borrowings*. This option may also prove unattractive to investors. The effect of making further borrowings will have a similar effect to that of increasing the overdraft. The profits of the business will be reduced and the interest cover ratio will decrease to a low level. The gearing ratio of the business is already quite high at 48% (that is, loan notes (3.5)/(loan notes + equity (3.5 + 3.8)) and it is not clear what security would be available for the loan. The gearing ratio would be much higher if the overdraft were to be included.

- *Chase trade receivables*. It may be possible to improve cash flows by reducing the level of credit outstanding from trade receivables. At present, the average settlement period is 93 days (that is, (trade receivables (3.6)/sales revenue (14.2)) × 365), which seems quite high. A reduction in the average settlement period by approximately one-quarter would generate the funds required. However, it is not clear what effect this would have on sales.

- *Reduce inventories*. This appears to be the most attractive of the four options. At present, the average inventories holding period is 178 days (that is, (closing inventories (3.8)/cost of sales (7.8)) × 365), which seems very high. A reduction in this period by less than one-quarter would generate the funds required. However, if the business holds a large amount of slow-moving and obsolete items, it may be difficult to reduce inventories levels.

Chapter 7

7.1 **Ceres plc**

(a) (i) Preliminary calculations

Annual depreciation is £4m [that is, property (£40m × 2$\frac{1}{2}$%) and plant (£20m × 15%)].

Cost of acquiring the business is £120m (that is, £10m × 12).

Loan finance required is £70m (that is, £120m − £50m).

Loan outstanding at 31 May Year 10

Year to 31 May	Yr 7	Yr 8	Yr 9	Yr 10
	£m	£m	£m	£m
Operating profit	10.0	11.0	10.5	13.5
Add Annual depr'n	4.0	4.0	4.0	4.0
	14.0	15.0	14.5	17.5
Less Working capital	–	(1.0)	–	–
Loan interest	(7.0)	(6.3)	(5.5)	(4.6)
Cash to repay loan	7.0	7.7	9.0	12.9
Loan at start of year	70.0	63.0	55.3	46.3
Cash to repay loan	7.0	7.7	9.0	12.9
Loan at end of year	63.0	55.3	46.3	33.4

(ii) Internal rate of return (IRR)

The net amount to be received in Year 10 by the private equity firm is calculated as follows:

	£m
Sale proceeds (12 × £13.5m)	162.0
Loan repayment	(33.4)
Proceeds to shareholders	128.6
Less	
Amount to shareholder/managers (10%)	(12.9)
For private equity firm	115.7

Trial 1 – Discount rate 24%
NPV is:

$$(£115.7m × 0.42) – £45m = £3.6m$$

As it is positive, the IRR is higher.

Trial 2 – Discount rate 28%
NPV is:

$$(£115.7m × 0.37) – £45m = (£2.2m)$$

As it is negative, the IRR is lower.

A 4% change in the discount rate leads to a £5.8m (£3.6m + £2.2m) change in the NPV. Thus, a 1% change in the discount rate results in a £1.45m change in NPV. The IRR is:

$$24\% + \left(\frac{£3.6m}{1.45} \right)\% = \underline{26.5\%}$$

(b) The IRR exceeds the cost of capital and so the investment should go ahead. However, the calculations are likely to be sensitive to forecast inaccuracies. The forecast inputs should be re-examined, particularly the anticipated profit in the year of sale. It is much higher than in previous years and forms the basis for calculating the sale price.

Chapter 8

8.1 Russell Ltd

(a) (i) The projected income statements are:

Projected income statements for the year ended 31 May Year 5

	Shares	Loan notes
	£000	£000
Profit before interest and tax	662.0	662.0
Interest	(30.0)	(90.0)
Profit before taxation	632.0	572.0
Tax (25%)	(158.0)	(143.0)
Profit for the year	474.0	429.0

(ii) The earnings per share (EPS) are:

	Shares	Loan notes
$EPS = \dfrac{\text{Profit available to ordinary shareholders}}{\text{No. of ordinary shares}}$	$\dfrac{474}{(400 + 150)}$	$\dfrac{429}{400}$
	£0.86	£1.07

(iii) Gearing ratio

	Shares	Loan notes
$\dfrac{\text{Loan capital}}{\text{Share capital + Reserves + Loan capital}} \times 100\%$	$\dfrac{250}{(832.4 + 284.4 + 600.0 + 250)} \times 100\%$	$\dfrac{850}{(832.4 + 257.4) + 850} \times 100\%$
(See note below)	12.7%	43.8%

Note: The retained earnings for the year are calculated as follows:

	Shares £000	Loan notes £000
Profit for the year (see above)	474.0	429.0
Dividend proposed and paid (40% payout ratio)	(189.6)	(171.6)
Retained earnings	284.4	257.4

(b) The loan notes option provides a significantly higher EPS figure than the share option. The EPS for the most recent year is £0.96 (384/400) and this lies between the two options being considered. On the basis of the EPS figures, it seems that the loan notes option is the more attractive. Pursuing the share option will lower EPS compared with the current year, and will result in a single shareholder obtaining 25 per cent of the voting share capital. As a result, this option is unlikely to be attractive. However, the gearing ratio under the loan notes option is significantly higher than under the share option. This ratio is also much higher than the current gearing ratio of the business of 23.1 per cent (250/1,082.4). The investor must balance the significant increase in financial risk with the additional returns that are generated.

(c) The level of operating profit (profit before interest and taxation) at which EPS under each option is the same will be:

$$\text{Ordinary shares} \qquad \text{Ordinary shares plus loan notes}$$

$$\frac{(x - 30.0)(1 - 0.25)}{(400.0 + 150.0)} = \frac{(x - 90.0)(1 - 0.25)}{400.0}$$

$$400(0.75x - 22.5) = 550(0.75x - 67.5)$$
$$300x - 9,000 = 412.5x - 37,125$$
$$112.5x = 28,125$$
$$x = \underline{250(000)}$$

The above figure could also have been calculated using a PBIT-EPS indifference chart as shown in the chapter.

Chapter 9

9.1 Sandarajan plc

(a) The dividend per share and dividend payout ratio over the five-year period under review is as follows:

Year	Dividend per share	Dividend payout %
1	22.0p	52.4
2	14.0p	26.4
3	17.3p	40.0
4	7.3p	14.9
5	30.7p	52.3

The figures above show an erratic pattern of dividends over the five years. Such a pattern is unlikely to be welcomed by investors. In an imperfect market, dividends may be important to investors because of taxation policy and information signalling.

(b) Managers should, therefore, decide on a payout policy and then make every effort to stick with this policy. This will ensure that dividends are predictable and contain no 'surprises' for investors. Any reduction in the dividend is likely to be seen as a sign of financial weakness and the share price is likely to fall. If a reduction in dividends cannot be avoided, the managers should make clear the change in policy and the reasons for the change.

Chapter 10

10.1 Williams Wholesalers Ltd

	£	£
Existing level of trade receivables (£4m × 70/365)		767,123
New level of trade receivables: £2m × 80/365	438,356	
£2m × 30/365	164,384	602,740
Reduction in trade receivables		164,383
Costs and benefits of policy		
Cost of discount (£2m × 2%)		40,000
Less Savings		
Interest payable (£164,384* × 13%)	21,370	
Administration costs	6,000	
Bad debts (20,000 − 10,000)	10,000	37,370
Net cost of policy		2,630

* It could be argued that the interest should be based on the amount expected to be received, that is, the value of the trade receivables *after* taking account of the discount.

The above calculations reveal that the business will be worse off by offering the discounts.

Chapter 11

11.1 Cupid plc

Adjusted net assets (capital invested)

	£m	£m
Total assets less		231.0
current liabilities as		
per the statement of financial position		
Add Property (£200m − £60m)	140.0	
R&D (9/10 × £10m)	9.0	149.0
Adjusted total assets less current liabilities		380.0*

* This figure represents the adjusted figure for share and loan capital.

Market value added calculation

	£m
Market value of shares (60m × £8.50)	510.0
Less Capital invested (see above)	(380.0)
MVA	130.0

Chapter 12

12.1 **Miocene plc**

(a) (i) The statement of financial position (balance sheet) basis is:

$$\text{Price of an ordinary share } (P_0) = \frac{\text{Net assets at statement of financial position values}}{\text{Number of ordinary shares}}$$

$$= \frac{£60.1\text{m}}{40\text{m}} = £1.50$$

(ii) Liquidation basis

$$= \frac{\text{Net assets * at current realisable values}}{\text{Number of ordinary shares}}$$

$$= \frac{85.1\text{m}}{40\text{m}} = £2.13$$

* The net assets figure is derived as follows:

	£m	£m
Assets		
Property		65.4
Plant and equipment		18.8
Fixtures and fittings		4.6
Inventories		38.9
Trade receivables		29.6
		157.3
Less **Liabilities**		
Current	51.2	
Non-current	21.0	72.2
Net assets		85.1

(iii) The price/earnings basis is:

$$P_0 = \frac{\text{Price/earnings ratio} \times \text{Profit for the year}}{\text{Number of ordinary shares}}$$

$$= \frac{11 \times £17.2\text{m}}{40\text{m}}$$

$$= \frac{£189.2\text{m}}{40\text{m}} = £4.73$$

(iv) The dividend growth basis is:

$$P_0 = \frac{D_1}{K_0 - g}$$

$$= \frac{[(£17.2\text{m} \times 40\%)/40\text{m}]}{(0.10 - 0.04)} = £2.87$$

(b) This topic is covered in the chapter. Refer as necessary.

Appendix D
Solutions to review questions

Chapter 1

1.1 The key tasks of the finance function are:

- financial planning and forecasting
- investment appraisal
- financing decisions
- capital market operations
- financial control.

1.2 Wealth maximisation is considered to be superior to profit maximisation for the following reasons:

- The term 'profit' is ambiguous. Different measures of profit can lead to different decisions being made, as we saw in the chapter.
- Profit maximisation in the short term may be at the expense of profit maximisation in the long term.
- Profit maximisation ignores the issue of risk. This may lead to decisions that result in investments in risky projects in order to gain higher returns. However, this may not meet with shareholders' needs.

Wealth maximisation takes both risk and long-run returns into account.

1.3 Survival is a basic objective for a business. However, shareholders will expect to receive returns from their investment and will not be interested in businesses that see this as their primary objective. Nevertheless, there may be difficult times when survival becomes the main objective. In a highly competitive economy, a business has to pursue shareholder wealth maximisation in order to survive. Under such circumstances, wealth maximisation and survival become different sides of the same coin.

1.4 Various problems are associated with such an incentive plan. These include:

- It is a 'one-way bet'. There are no penalties if the managers fail to deliver.
- It fails to take risk into account. One way of increasing profits is to increase the investment risks.
- The profits generated may not be entirely due to the actions of managers. Other factors (for example, general economic conditions) may have an important influence.

Chapter 2

2.1 When a business is growing fast, it is vitally important that managers maintain a balance between increases in the level of sales and the finance available to sustain this increase. The business must not pursue sales growth to the point where it becomes financially over-stretched and then collapses. Projected financial statements will show the impact of future changes in sales on the profitability, liquidity and financing requirements of the business. If the business shows signs of being unable to sustain the level of sales growth in the future, corrective action can be taken.

2.2 It is true that the future is uncertain. It is also probably true that projected financial statements will prove to be inaccurate. Most businesses, however, find that, despite the inaccuracies inherent in forecasting, it is better to produce these statements than not to do so. The question to be asked is: can a business function if no projections are made available to managers? The problem of uncertainty should not prevent some form of financial planning. It is far better to deal with uncertainty through such techniques as sensitivity analysis and scenario analysis.

2.3 An existing business may find it easier than a new business to prepare projected financial statements, for several reasons. These include:

- Past data concerning sales, overheads and so on for a number of years may be available and used for comparison and extrapolation.
- Close links with customers, suppliers and so on which will help to identify likely future changes within the industry and future price changes.
- A management team that is experienced in producing forecasts and that has an understanding of the impact of competition on the business.

2.4 The sales forecast is of critical importance because it will determine the overall level of operations of the business. Thus, the future levels of investment, financing and overheads will be influenced by the level of sales. The cash received from sales will be an important factor in deriving the projected cash flows, and the sales revenue will be an important factor in deriving the projected profits. The projected cash flows and profits will, in turn, be important factors in preparing the projected statement of financial position (balance sheet). For these reasons, care must be taken in deriving a sales forecast for the business.

Chapter 3

3.1 The fact that a business operates on a low operating profit margin indicates that a small operating profit is being produced for each £1 of sales revenue generated. However, this does not mean necessarily that the return on capital employed will be low as a result. If the business is able to generate a large amount of sales revenue during a period, the operating profit may be very high even though the operating profit per £1 of sales revenue is low. If the overall operating profit is high, this can lead, in turn, to a high return on capital employed, since it is the total operating profit that is used as the numerator (top part of the fraction) in this ratio. Many businesses (including supermarkets) pursue a strategy of 'low margin, high sales turnover'.

3.2 The statement of financial position (balance sheet) is drawn up at a single point in time – the end of the financial period. As a result, the figures shown may not be representative of the position during the period. Wherever possible, average figures (perhaps based on monthly figures) should be used. However, an external user may only have access to the opening and closing statements of financial position (balance sheets) for the year and so a simple average based on these figures may be all that it is possible to calculate. Where a business is seasonal in nature, or is subject to cyclical changes, this simple averaging may not be sufficient.

3.3 In view of the fact that *Z*-scores are derived from information that is published by the businesses themselves, it is difficult to say that *Z*-scores should not be made publicly available. Indeed, many of those connected with a business – shareholders, lenders, employees, and so on – may find this information extremely valuable for decision making. However, there is a risk that a poor *Z*-score will lead to a loss of confidence in the business among investors and suppliers, which will, in turn, prevent the business from taking corrective action as lines of credit and investment will be withdrawn.

3.4 The P/E ratio may vary between businesses within the same industry for the following reasons.

- *Accounting conventions.* Differences in the methods used to compute profit (for example, inventory valuation, depreciation, and so on) can lead to different profit figures and, therefore, different P/E ratios.
- *Different prospects.* One business may be regarded as having a much brighter future owing to factors such as the quality of management, the quality of products, location and so on. This will affect the market price that investors are prepared to pay for the share and, hence, the P/E ratio.
- *Different asset structure.* The underlying asset base of one business may be much higher and this may affect the market price of the shares.

Chapter 4

4.1 NPV is usually considered the best method of assessing investment opportunities because it takes account of:

- *The timing of the cash flows.* Discounting the various cash flows associated with each project, according to when they are expected to arise, it recognises the fact that cash flows do not all occur simultaneously. Associated with this is the fact that, discounting, using the opportunity cost of finance (that is, the return that the next best alternative opportunity would generate), enables the net benefit after financing costs have been met to be identified (as the NPV).
- *The whole of the relevant cash flows.* NPV includes all of the relevant cash flows irrespective of when they are expected to occur. It treats them differently according to their date of occurrence, but they are all taken into account in the NPV and they all have, or can have, an influence on the decision.
- *The objectives of the business.* NPV is the only method of appraisal where the output of the analysis has a direct bearing on the wealth of the business. (Positive NPVs enhance wealth, negative ones reduce it.) Since most businesses seek to increase their value and wealth, NPV clearly is the best approach to use.

NPV provides clear decision rules concerning acceptance/rejection of projects and the ranking of projects. It is fairly simple to use, particularly with the availability of modern computer software.

4.2 The payback method, in its original form, does not take account of the time value of money. However, it would be possible to modify the payback method to accommodate this requirement. Cash flows arising from a project could be discounted, using the cost of finance as the appropriate discount rate, in the same way as in the NPV and IRR methods. This discounted payback approach is used by some businesses and represents an improvement on the original approach described in the chapter. However, it still has the other flaws of the payback approach that were discussed: for example, it ignores relevant data after the payback period. Thus, even in its modified form, the PP method cannot be regarded as superior to NPV.

4.3   The IRR method may be preferred to the NPV method for the following reasons:

- A preference for a percentage return rather than an absolute figure as a means of express-ing the outcome of a project. This preference may reflect the fact that other financial goals of the business are often set in terms of percentage returns: for example, return on capital employed.
- A preference for ranking projects in terms of their percentage return. Managers feel it is easier to rank projects on the basis of percentage returns (although NPV outcomes should be just as easy for them). We saw in the chapter that the IRR method could provide mis-leading advice on the ranking of projects and the NPV method was preferable for this purpose.

4.4   Cash flows are preferred to profit flows because cash is the ultimate measure of economic wealth. Cash is used to acquire resources and for distribution to shareholders. When cash is invested in an investment project, an opportunity cost is incurred as the cash cannot be used in other investment projects. Similarly, when positive cash flows are generated by the project they can be used to reinvest in other investment projects.

Profit, on the other hand, is relevant to reporting the productive effort for a period. This measure of effort may have only a tenuous relationship to cash flows for a particular period. The conventions of accounting may lead to the recognition of gains and losses in one period and the relevant cash inflows and outflows occurring in another period.

Chapter 5

5.1   Although inflation rates have been quite low in recent years, the effect of inflation on invest-ments should be taken into account. Investments are often made over a long time period and even quite low rates of inflation can have a significant effect on cash flows over time.

(a) The effect of discounting nominal cash flows at real discount rates will be to over-state the NPV calculations, as the cash flows will be increased in line with inflation whereas the discount rate will not.
(b) The effect of discounting real cash flows at a nominal discount rate will be to understate the NPV, as the discount rate will be increased in line with inflation whereas the cash flows will not.

5.2   It has been suggested that risk arises when more things can happen than will happen. In other words, the future is unclear and there is a chance that estimates made concerning the future may not necessarily occur. Risk is important in the context of investment decisions for two reasons:

- Investment projects often have long timescales and so there is a greater opportunity for things to go wrong.
- If things go wrong, there can be serious consequences because of the size of the investment.

5.3   The risk-adjusted discount rate suffers from three major problems:

- Subjective judgement is required in assigning projects to particular risk categories.
- The risk premium will reflect the views of the managers rather than those of the investors. Any difference between the attitudes of investors and the interpretation of these attitudes by managers can have an effect on the accept/reject decision.

● It assumes that risk increases over time. The further into the future the cash flows arise, the more heavily they are discounted. However, risk may not necessarily increase with time. It will be determined by the nature of the product or service being offered, and so on.

5.4   Risk arises when there is more than one possible outcome for a project. The standard deviation measures the variability of returns and can provide a useful measure of risk. Generally speaking, the higher the standard deviation, the higher the level of risk associated with a project. However, when the distribution of possible outcomes is skewed, the standard deviation may not provide a reliable measure of risk as it fails to distinguish between 'downside' and 'upside' risk.

Chapter 6

6.1   Share warrants may be particularly useful for young, expanding businesses wishing to attract new investors. They can help provide a 'sweetener' for the issue of loan notes. Attaching warrants may make it possible to agree a lower rate of interest and/or less restrictive loan covenants. If the business is successful, the warrants will provide a further source of finance. Investors will exercise their option to acquire shares if the market price of the shares exceeds the exercise price of the warrant. However, this will have the effect of diluting the control of existing shareholders.

6.2   A convertible loan gives an investor the right to convert a loan into ordinary shares at a given future date and at a specified price. The investor is not, however, obliged to convert. This will be done only if the market price of the shares at the conversion date exceeds the agreed conversion price. The conversion price is usually higher than the market price at the time the convertible loans are issued and so the market price of the shares will usually have to rise over time in order for the lender to exercise the option to convert. During a period of stagnant or falling market prices, the lender is unlikely to exercise the option and so no conversion will take place. Hence, it cannot be assumed that there is an automatic conversion from loan capital to ordinary (equity) share capital.

6.3   A swap agreement can be a useful hedging device. A business with a floating rate loan agreement, for example, may believe that interest rates are going to rise, whereas a business with a fixed rate agreement may believe that interest rates are going to fall. By entering into a swap agreement, they can both hedge against risk. Swap agreements may also be used to exploit capital market imperfections, such as where one business has an advantage over another when negotiating interest rates.

A swap arrangement involves two businesses agreeing to assume responsibility for the other's interest payments (although, in some cases, a bank may act as counterparty to a swap agreement). Typically, a business with a floating interest rate loan will swap interest payment obligations with a business with a fixed interest rate loan. The arrangement is usually negotiated through a bank. Legal responsibility for interest payments still rests with the business that entered into the original loan agreement. Thus, the borrowing business may continue to make interest payments to the lender in line with the loan agreement. However, at the end of an agreed period, a compensating cash adjustment between the two swap parties will be made.

6.4   Invoice discounting is a service offered to businesses whereby a financial institution is prepared to advance a sum equivalent to 80 per cent (or perhaps more) of outstanding trade receivables. The amount advanced is usually payable within 60 to 90 days. The business will retain responsibility for collecting the amounts owing from customers and the advance must be repaid irrespective of whether the receivables have been collected. Factoring is a service whereby a financial institution (factor) takes over the receivables collection of the client business. The factor will also be prepared to make an advance of 80 per cent of approved debts, which is repayable from the amounts received from customers. Businesses have shown a preference for invoice discounting rather than factoring in recent years, because it is a cheaper and more flexible form of finance.

Chapter 7

7.1   Various reasons have been put forward to explain the difference in the proportion of total investment made in business start-ups by UK and US private equity firms. These include:

- UK firms are more cautious than their US counterparts. Start-ups are more risky and UK private equity firms may be less willing to take on these risks.
- UK firms have a shorter-term investment perspective that makes them prefer financing existing businesses.
- There is greater competition among US private equity firms for good investment opportunities, which leads them to invest in business start-ups to achieve the required returns.

7.2   A listed business may wish to revert to unlisted status for a number of possible reasons. These include:

- *Cost*. A stock exchange listing can be costly as the business must adhere to certain administrative regulations and requirements for financial disclosures.
- *Scrutiny*. Listed businesses are subject to close scrutiny by analysts and this may not be welcome if the business is engaged in sensitive negotiations or controversial activities.
- *Takeover risk*. The shares of the business may be purchased by an unwelcome bidder and this may result in a takeover.
- *Investor profile*. If the business is dominated by a few investors who wish to retain their interest in the business and do not wish to raise further capital by public issues, the benefits of a listing are few.

7.3   An offer for sale involves an issuing house buying the shares in the business and then, in turn, selling the shares to the public. The issue will be advertised by the publication of a prospectus that will set out details of the business and the issue price of the shares (or reserve price if a tender issue is being made). The shares issued by the issuing house may be either new shares or shares that have been purchased from existing shareholders.

A public issue is one where the business undertakes direct responsibility for issuing shares to the public. If an issuing house is employed it will usually be in the role of adviser and administrator of the issue. However, the issuing house may also underwrite the issue. A public issue runs the risk that the shares will not be taken up and is a less popular form of issue for businesses.

7.4   A business should have owners who are:

- committed to realising the growth potential of the business
- prepared to sell some of the ordinary shares in the business
- comfortable with the financing arrangements that private equity firms usually employ.

A business should have a management team that is:

- ambitious
- experienced
- capable
- well balanced.

Chapter 8

8.1 To find out whether or not a planned level of gearing is likely to be acceptable to investors, the managers of a business could look at the levels of gearing in similar businesses operating within the same industry. If the business adopts a much higher level of gearing than these businesses, there may be problems in raising long-term funds. The managers could also discuss the proposed level of gearing with prospective investors such as banks and financial institutions to see whether they regard the level of gearing as being acceptable.

8.2 The lender may consider the following factors:

- The security for the loan.
- The performance record of the business.
- Likely future prospects of the business and the industry.
- The existing level of gearing for the business.
- Likely interest cover for the loan.
- The purpose of the loan.
- The expected level of return compared with other investment opportunities of the same level of risk.
- Restrictive loan covenants in place from existing lenders.

8.3 It would not be appropriate to employ the specific cost of raising capital for an investment project as the appropriate discount rate. The use of such an approach could result in bizarre decisions being made. Projects with an identical return may be treated differently according to the particular cost of raising finance for each project. It is better to view the individual elements of capital as entering a pool of funds and thereby losing their separate identity. The cost of capital used for investment decisions will represent the average cost of the pool of funds. It should also be remembered that individual elements of capital are interrelated. It would not be possible, for example, to raise debt unless the business had a reasonable level of ordinary share capital. To treat each source of capital as being quite separate is therefore incorrect.

8.4 An important implication of (a), the traditional approach, is that financial managers should try to establish that mix of loan/share finance that will minimise the overall cost of capital. At this point, the business will be said to achieve an optimal capital structure. Minimising the overall cost of capital in this way will maximise the value of the business. An important implication of (b), the MM (excluding tax effects) approach, is that the financing decision is not really important. As the overall cost of capital remains constant, a business does not have an optimal capital structure as suggested by the traditionalists. This means that one particular capital structure is no better or worse than any other and so managers should not spend time evaluating different forms of financing the business. Instead, they should concentrate their efforts on evaluating and managing the investments of the business. However, (c), the MM (including tax effects) approach, recognises that the tax shield on loan capital benefits the ordinary shareholders and the higher the level of interest payments, the greater the benefits. The implications of this approach are that there is an optimal capital structure (and in that sense it is similar to the traditional approach), and that the optimal structure is a gearing ratio of 100 per cent.

Chapter 9

9.1 A business may decide to repurchase shares in order to:

- return surplus cash to shareholders
- adjust its capital structure.

9.2 The residual theory of dividends states that dividends can be regarded as a residual amount arising when the business does not have enough profitable opportunities in which to invest. The argument assumes that shareholders will prefer the business to reinvest earnings rather than pay dividends, as long as the returns earned by the business exceed the returns that could be achieved by shareholders investing in similar projects. However, when all the profitable projects that meet this criterion have been taken up, any surplus remaining should be distributed to shareholders. Thus, dividends will be, in effect, a by-product of the investment decision as stated.

9.3 The type of distribution policy adopted may not be critical because of the clientele effect. The particular distribution policy will attract a certain type of investor depending on his or her cash needs and taxation position. Thus, investors who rely on dividend income to meet living expenses may prefer a high payout policy whereas investors with high marginal tax rates may prefer a low (or zero) payout policy.

9.4 Agency theory is based on the idea that the business is a coalition of interest groups, with each group seeking to maximise its own welfare. This behaviour is often at the expense of the other groups, and so 'agency costs' arise. In order to minimise these agency costs, the particular group bearing the costs may seek to restrain the actions of others through contractual or other arrangements. Thus, in order to prevent managers from awarding themselves various perks, the shareholders may insist that all surplus cash is returned to them in the form of a dividend. Similarly, in order to prevent shareholders from withdrawing their investment in the business and allowing lenders to bear all, or the majority of, the risks of the business, the lenders may seek to limit the amount that can be declared in the form of a dividend.

Chapter 10

10.1 Although the credit manager is responsible for ensuring that receivables pay on time, Tariq may be right in denying blame. Various factors may be responsible for the situation described which are beyond the control of the credit manager. These include:

- a downturn in the economy leading to financial difficulties among trade receivables;
- decisions by other managers within the business to liberalise credit policy in order to stimulate sales;
- an increase in competition among suppliers offering credit, which is being exploited by customers;
- disputes with customers over the quality of goods or services supplied;
- problems in the delivery of goods leading to delays.

You may have thought of others.

10.2 The level of inventories held will be affected in the following ways.

(a) An increase in production bottlenecks is likely to result in an increase in raw materials and work in progress being processed within the plant. Therefore, inventory levels should rise.

(b) A rise in interest rates will make holding inventories more expensive (if they are financed by debt). This may, in turn, lead to a decision to reduce inventory levels.

(c) The decision to reduce the range of products should result in fewer inventories being held. It would no longer be necessary to hold certain items in order to meet customer demand.

(d) Switching to a local supplier may reduce the lead time between ordering an item and receiving it. This should, in turn, reduce the need to carry such high levels of the particular item.

(e) A deterioration in the quality of bought-in items may result in the purchase of higher quantities of inventories in order to take account of the defective element in inventories acquired and, perhaps, an increase in the inspection time for items received. This would lead to a rise in inventory levels.

10.3 Inventories are held to meet customer demand, to avoid the problems of running out of inventories and to take advantage of profitable opportunities (for example, buying a product that is expected to rise steeply in price in the future). These reasons are similar to the transactionary, precautionary and speculative motives that were used to explain why cash is held by a business.

10.4 (a) The costs of holding too little cash are:

- failure to meet obligations when they fall due which can damage the reputation of the business and may, in the extreme, lead to the business being wound up;
- having to borrow and thereby incur interest charges;
- an inability to take advantage of profitable opportunities.

(b) The costs of holding too much cash are:

- failure to use the funds available for more profitable purposes;
- loss of value during a period of inflation.

Chapter 11

11.1 Some believe that it is difficult for the stakeholder approach and the shareholder value approach to coexist. It has been suggested, for example, that in the USA the stakeholder approach has been seriously affected by the pursuit of shareholder value. The application of various techniques to improve shareholder value, such as hostile takeovers, cost cutting and large management incentive bonuses, have badly damaged the interests of certain stakeholders such as employees and local communities. However, others argue that the shareholder value approach must consider the interests of other stakeholders in order to achieve its objectives.

11.2 Two problems with the use of MVA as a tool for internal management purposes were identified in the text. First, MVA depends on establishing a market price for shares and so only businesses listed on the Stock Exchange can use this technique. Secondly, MVA cannot be used to evaluate the performance of strategic business units as there is no market share price for each unit. However, there is also a third reason why it is inappropriate for management purposes. Share prices may fluctuate significantly over the short term and this could obscure the performance of managers.

11.3 The problem with taking changes in the market value of the shares as an indicator of shareholder value created (or lost) is that it does not take account of capital required to generate that market value.

Let us assume there are two companies, A and B, which each start with £100 million capital invested. After two years, let us assume that the market value of A is £250 million and the market value of B is £300 million. However, B raised £80 million in additional capital to finance the business. Although B has a higher market value after two years, it has been achieved through a much higher level of capital invested. MVA takes the difference between the market value and the capital invested and so avoids this problem.

11.4 If businesses are overcapitalised it is probably because insufficient attention is given to the amount of capital that is required. Management incentive schemes that are geared towards generating a particular level of profits or achieving a particular market share without specifying the level of capital invested can help create such a problem. EVA® can help avoid the problem by focusing on the need to obtain a profitable return on capital invested.

Chapter 12

12.1 A merger involves a combination of two (or more) businesses of roughly equal size. The combination involves the creation of a new business and does not involve the purchase of the shares of one of the existing businesses by the other business. The merger is undertaken with the agreement of the managers and shareholders of each business and there is continuity of ownership of the resources. A takeover involves one business acquiring the shares of another business in order to gain control of the resources of that business. This may lead to a change of ownership and the takeover may be resisted by the managers of the target business.

12.2 Reasons for divestment may include the following:

- A business may decide to focus on its core activities. Any activities that are not regarded as core activities may be sold following such a review. In recent years, a number of businesses have decided, often as a result of bitter experience, that it is better for them to 'stick to their knitting'.
- A business may receive an unwelcome takeover bid because it has particular operations that are of interest to the predator business. The target business may, therefore, try to sell off these operations in order to protect the rest of its operations from takeover.
- A business may decide that in order to improve its overall profitability, poorly performing operations should be sold. The business may not feel it is worth investing time and resources in trying to improve the level of performance achieved by these poorly performing operations.
- A business may require funds for investment purposes or to deal with cash flow problems. The disposal of certain business operations may be the most feasible solution to these problems.

12.3 Four reasons for taking over another business are:

- To exploit underutilised resources.
- To acquire complementary resources.
- To achieve benefits of scale.
- To eliminate competition and increase market share.

12.4 Four methods of resisting a takeover bid are:

- Find a white knight to take over the business instead.
- Refer the bid to the Competition Commission in the hope that this will result in a bid withdrawal.
- Become less attractive to the predator business by selling valuable assets.
- Issue information to shareholders indicating that it is not in their long-term interest to support the takeover.

Other reasons could have been cited.

Appendix E
Solutions to selected exercises

Chapter 2

2.1   Choice Designs Ltd

(a) The projected income statement is:

Projected income statement for the year to 31 May 2009

	£000
Sales revenue	1,400
Cost of sales (70%)	(980)
Gross profit (30%)	420
Admin. expenses	(225)
Selling expenses	(85)
Profit before taxation	110
Tax	(34)
Profit for the year	76

(b) The projected balance sheet is:

Projected statement of financial position (balance sheet) as at 31 May 2009

	£000	£000
Non-current assets		
Premises	600	
Depreciation	(112)	488
Fixtures and fittings	140	
Depreciation	(118)	22
Motor vehicles	40	
Depreciation	(10)	30
		540
Current assets		
Inventory [240 + (25% × 240)]		300
Trade receivables [8/52 × (80% × 1,400)]		172
Bank (balancing figure)		42
		514
Total assets		1,054
Equity		
Ordinary £1 shares		500
Retained earnings		297
		797
Current liabilities		
Trade payables [12/52 × 1,040*]		240
Tax due (50% × 34)		17
		257
Total equity and liabilities		1,054

* Purchases = Cost of sales + Closing inventories − Opening inventories
= 980 + 300 − 240 = 1,040

2.2 Prolog Ltd

(a) The cash flow projection is:

Projected cash flow statement for the six months to 30 June Year 6

	Jan £000	Feb £000	Mar £000	Apr £000	May £000	June £000
Receipts						
Credit sales	100	100	140	180	220	260
Payments						
Trade payables	(112)	(144)	(176)	(208)	(240)	(272)
Operating expenses	(4)	(6)	(8)	(10)	(10)	(10)
Shelving				(12)		
Taxation			(25)			
	(116)	(150)	(209)	(230)	(250)	(282)
Cash flow	(16)	(50)	(69)	(50)	(30)	(22)
Opening balance	(68)	(84)	(134)	(203)	(253)	(283)
Closing balance	(84)	(134)	(203)	(253)	(283)	(305)

(b) A banker may require various pieces of information before granting additional overdraft facilities. These may include the following:

- Security available for the loan.
- Details of past profit performance.
- Profit projections for the next 12 months.
- Cash flow projections beyond the next six months to help assess the prospects of repayment.
- Details of the assumptions underlying the projected figures supplied.
- Details of the contractual commitment between Prolog Ltd and its supplier.
- Details of management expertise. Can they manage the expansion programme?
- Details of the new machine and its performance in relation to competing models.
- Details of funds available from the owners to finance the expansion.

2.5 Kwaysar Ltd

(a) The projected income statement is:

Projected income statement for the six months to 30 November 2008

	£000	£000
Sales revenue		
Retailers [(£90 × 3,000) + (£90 × 3,600)]		594.0
Public [(£90 × 900) + (£90 × 1,200)]		189.0
		783.0
Opening inventory	44.0	
Purchases [(£50 × 6,600) + (2,100 × £50)]	435.0	
	479.0	
Less Closing inventory	44.0	(435.0)
Gross profit		348.0
Wages		(108.0)
Advertising expenses		(72.0)
Discount allowed [($\frac{1}{2}$ × 594) × 2%]		(5.9)
Depreciation		
Property		(3.5)
Fixtures		(6.0)
Motor vehicles		(12.0)
Misc. overheads		(84.0)
Profit for the period		56.6

(b) The projected cash flow statement is:

Projected cash flow statement for the six months to 30 November 2008

	£000
Cash receipts	
Trade receivables and cash sales	
Retailers – 1 month	290.1
3 months	135.0
Public – cash	189.0
	614.1
Cash payments	
Trade payables	(387.0)
Advertising costs	(72.0)
Motor vehicles	(80.0)
Loan repaid	(48.0)
Wages	(108.0)
Misc. overheads	(82.0)
	(777.0)
Cash deficit	(162.9)
Opening balance	120.0
Closing balance	(42.9)

(c) We can see from the projected income statement for the six-month period a 9 per cent decline in profit as compared to the previous six-month period. The profit per £1 of sales generated has declined from 11.9p in the previous period to 7.2p in the forecast period.

Implementing the new marketing strategy will mean that there will be additional expenditure on such items as motor vehicles and marketing costs, and receipts from customers will be slower. These factors will combine to produce a cash deficit for the six-month period which will have to be financed in some way.

The decline in profitability and liquidity in return for an increase in market share indicates that the new strategy has little to commend it – at least in the short term. However, it is possible that over the longer term a large market share will allow the business to increase profits and improve its cash flows to compensate for the short-term problems.

Chapter 3

3.1 **Three businesses**

A plc operates a supermarket chain. The grocery business is highly competitive and to generate high sales volumes it is usually necessary to accept low operating profit margins. Thus, we can see that the operating profit margin of A plc is the lowest of the three businesses. The inventory turnover periods of supermarket chains also tend to be quite low. They are often efficient in managing inventory and most supermarket chains have invested heavily in inventory control and logistical systems over the years. The average collection period for receivables is very low as most sales are for cash: although where a customer pays by credit card, there is usually a small delay before the supermarket receives the amount due. A low inventory turnover period and a low average collection period for receivables usually mean that the investment in current assets is low. Hence, the current ratio (current assets/current liabilities) is also low.

B plc is the holiday tour operator. We can see that the sales to capital employed ratio is the highest of the three businesses. This is because tour operators do not usually require a large investment of capital: they do not need a large asset base in order to conduct their operations. The inventory turnover period ratio does not apply to B plc. It is a service business, which does not hold inventories for resale. We can see that the average collection period for receivables is low. This may be because customers are invoiced near to the holiday date for any amounts outstanding and must pay before going on holiday. The lack of inventories held and low average collection period for receivables leads to a very low current ratio.

C plc is the food manufacturing business. We can see that the sales to capital employed ratio is the lowest of the three businesses. This is because manufacturers tend to invest heavily in both current and non-current assets. The inventory turnover period is the highest of the three businesses. Three different kinds of inventories – raw materials, work in progress and finished goods – are held by manufacturers. The average receivables' collection period is also the highest of the three businesses. Manufacturers tend to sell to other businesses rather than to the public and their customers will normally demand credit. A one-month credit period for customers is fairly common for manufacturing businesses, although customers may receive a discount for prompt payment. The relatively high investment in inventories and receivables usually results in a high current ratio.

3.2 Amsterdam Ltd and Berlin Ltd

The ratios reveal that the average settlement period for trade receivables for Amsterdam Ltd is three times higher than that for Berlin Ltd. Berlin Ltd is therefore much quicker in collecting amounts outstanding from customers. On the other hand, there is not much difference between the two businesses in the time taken to pay trade payables.

It is interesting to compare the differences between the trade receivables and payables collection periods for each business. As Amsterdam Ltd allows an average of 63 days' credit to its customers, yet pays suppliers within 50 days, it will require greater investment in working capital than Berlin Ltd, which allows an average of only 21 days to its customers but takes 45 days to pay its suppliers.

Amsterdam Ltd has a much higher gross profit percentage than Berlin Ltd. However, the operating profit margin for the two businesses is identical. This suggests that Amsterdam Ltd has much higher overheads (as a percentage of sales revenue) than Berlin Ltd. The inventories turnover period for Amsterdam Ltd is more than twice that of Berlin Ltd. This may be due to the fact that Amsterdam Ltd maintains a wider range of inventories in an attempt to meet customer requirements. The evidence therefore suggests that Amsterdam Ltd is the one that prides itself on personal service. The higher average settlement period for trade receivables is consistent with a more relaxed attitude to credit collection (thereby maintaining customer goodwill) and the high overheads are consistent with incurring the additional costs of satisfying customers' requirements. Amsterdam Ltd's high inventories levels are consistent with maintaining a wide range of inventories, with the aim of satisfying a range of customer needs.

Berlin Ltd has the characteristics of a more price-competitive business. Its gross profit margin is much lower than that of Amsterdam Ltd, that is, a much lower gross profit for each £1 of sales revenue. However, overheads have been kept low, the effect being that the operating percentage is the same as that of Amsterdam Ltd. The low inventories turnover period and low average collection period for trade receivables are consistent with a business that wishes to minimise investment in current assets, thereby reducing costs.

3.6 Harridges Limited

(a) Eight ratios for assessing the performance of Harridges Ltd are:

	2007	2008
ROCE	$\dfrac{310}{1,600} = 19.4\%$	$\dfrac{350}{1,700} = 20.6\%$
ROSF	$\dfrac{155}{1,100} = 14.1\%$	$\dfrac{175}{1,200} = 14.6\%$
Gross profit margin	$\dfrac{1,040}{2,600} = 40\%$	$\dfrac{1,150}{3,500} = 32.9\%$
Operating profit margin	$\dfrac{310}{2,600} = 11.9\%$	$\dfrac{350}{3,500} = 10\%$
Current ratio	$\dfrac{735}{400} = 1.8$	$\dfrac{660}{485} = 1.4$
Acid test ratio	$\dfrac{485}{400} = 1.2$	$\dfrac{260}{485} = 0.5$
Settlement period – trade receivables	$\dfrac{105}{2,600} \times 365 = 15$ days	$\dfrac{145}{3,500} \times 365 = 15$ days
Settlement period – trade payables	$\dfrac{300}{1,560} \times 365 = 70$ days	$\dfrac{375}{2,350^{*}} \times 365 = 58$ days
Inventories turnover period	$\dfrac{250}{1,560} \times 365 = 58$ days	$\dfrac{400}{2,350} \times 365 = 62$ days
Gearing ratio	$\dfrac{500}{1,600} = 31.3\%$	$\dfrac{500}{1,700} = 29.4\%$
EPS	$\dfrac{155}{490} = 31.6\text{p}$	$\dfrac{175}{490} = 35.7\text{p}$

* Cost of sales used because the credit purchases figure is not available.

(b) There has been a considerable decline in the gross profit margin during 2008. This fact, combined with the increase in sales revenue by more than one-third, suggests that a price-cutting policy has been adopted in an attempt to stimulate sales. The resulting increase in sales revenue, however, has led to only a small improvement in ROCE and ROSF. Similarly, there has only been a small improvement in EPS.

Despite a large cut in the gross profit margin, the operating profit margin has fallen by less than 2%. This suggests that overheads have been tightly controlled during 2008. Certainly, overheads have not risen in proportion to sales revenue.

The current ratio has fallen and the acid test ratio has fallen by more than half. Even though liquidity ratios are lower in retailing than in manufacturing, the liquidity of the business should now be a cause for concern. However, this may be a passing problem. The business is investing heavily in non-current assets and is relying on internal funds to finance this growth. When this investment ends, the liquidity position may improve quickly.

The trade receivables period has remained unchanged over the two years, and there has been no significant change in the inventories turnover period in 2008. The gearing ratio seems quite low and provides no cause for concern given the profitability of the business.

Overall, the business appears to be financially sound. Though there has been rapid growth during 2008, there is no real cause for alarm provided that the liquidity of the business can be improved in the near future. In the absence of information concerning share price, it is not possible to say whether or not an investment should be made.

Chapter 4

4.1 **Mylo Ltd**

(a) The annual depreciation of the two projects is:

$$\text{Project 1: } \frac{(£100,000 - £7,000)}{3} = £31,000$$

$$\text{Project 2: } \frac{(£60,000 - £6,000)}{3} = £18,000$$

Project 1

(i) Net present value is:

	Year 0 £000	Year 1 £000	Year 2 £000	Year 3 £000
Operating profit/(loss)		29	(1)	2
Depreciation		31	31	31
Capital cost	(100)			
Residual value				7
Net cash flows	(100)	60	30	40
10% discount factor	1.000	0.909	0.826	0.751
Present value	(100.00)	54.54	24.78	30.04
NPV	9.36			

(ii) Clearly the IRR lies above 10%. Try 15%:

15% discount factor	1.000	0.870	0.756	0.658
Present value	(100.00)	52.20	22.68	26.32
NPV	1.20			

Thus the IRR lies a little above 15%, perhaps around 16%.

(iii) To find the payback period, the cumulative cash flows are calculated:

Cumulative cash flows	(100)	(40)	(10)	30

Thus the payback will occur within three years.

Project 2

(i) Net present value is:

	Year 0 £000	Year 1 £000	Year 2 £000	Year 3 £000
Operating profit/(loss)		18	(2)	4
Depreciation		18	18	18
Capital cost	(60)			
Residual value				6
Net cash flows	(60)	36	16	28
10% discount factor	1.000	0.909	0.826	0.751
Present value	(60.00)	32.72	13.22	21.03
NPV	6.97			

(ii) Clearly the IRR lies above 10%. Try 15%:

15% discount factor	1.000	0.870	0.756	0.658
Present value	(60.00)	31.32	12.10	18.42
NPV	1.84			

Thus the IRR lies a little above 15%, perhaps around 17%.

(iii) The cumulative cash flows are:

Cumulative cash flows	(60)	(24)	(8)	20

Thus, the payback will occur within three years.

(b) Assuming that Mylo Ltd is pursuing a wealth maximisation objective, Project 1 is preferable since it has the higher NPV. The difference between the two NPVs is not significant, however.

(c) The NPV is the preferred method of assessing investment opportunities because it fully addresses each of the following:

- *The timing of the cash flows*. Discounting the various cash flows associated with each project, according to when they are expected to arise, takes account of the fact that cash flows do not all occur simultaneously. Associated with this is the fact that by discounting, using the opportunity cost of finance (namely the return that the next-best alternative opportunity would generate), it is possible to identify the net benefit, after financing costs have been met, as the NPV.
- *The whole of the relevant cash flows*. The NPV includes all of the relevant cash flows irrespective of when they are expected to occur. It treats them differently according to their date of occurrence, but they are all taken into account in the calculation of the NPV and they all have, or can have, an influence on the decision.
- *The objectives of the business*. The NPV is the only method of appraisal where the output of the analysis has a direct bearing on the wealth of the owners of the business. (Positive NPVs enhance wealth; negative NPVs reduce it.) Since most businesses seek to increase their owners' wealth, the NPV clearly is the best approach to use.

4.5 **Newton Electronics Ltd**

(a) (i) Option 1

	Year 0 £m	Year 1 £m	Year 2 £m	Year 3 £m	Year 4 £m	Year 5 £m
Plant and equipment	(9.0)					1.0
Sales revenue		24.0	30.8	39.6	26.4	10.0
Variable costs		(11.2)	(19.6)	(25.2)	(16.8)	(7.0)
Fixed costs (ex. dep'n)		(0.8)	(0.8)	(0.8)	(0.8)	(0.8)
Working capital	(3.0)					3.0
Marketing costs		(2.0)	(2.0)	(2.0)	(2.0)	(2.0)
Opportunity costs		(0.1)	(0.1)	(0.1)	(0.1)	(0.1)
	(12.0)	9.9	8.3	11.5	6.7	4.1
Discount factor 10%	1.000	0.909	0.826	0.751	0.683	0.621
Present value	12.0	9.0	6.9	8.6	4.6	2.5
NPV	(19.6)					

(ii) Option 2

	Year 0 £m	Year 1 £m	Year 2 £m	Year 3 £m	Year 4 £m	Year 5 £m
Royalties	–	4.4	7.7	9.9	6.6	2.8
Discount factor 10%	1.000	0.909	0.826	0.751	0.683	0.621
Present value	–	4.0	6.4	7.4	4.5	1.7
NPV	24.0					

(iii) Option 3

	Year 0	Year 2
Instalments	12.0	12.0
Discount factor 10%	1.000	0.826
Present value	12.0	9.9
NPV	21.9	

(b) Before making a final decision, the board should consider the following factors:

- The long-term competitiveness of the business may be affected by the sale of the patents.
- At present, the business is not involved in manufacturing and marketing products. Would a change in direction be desirable?
- The business will probably have to buy in the skills necessary to produce the product itself. This will involve costs, and problems will be incurred. Has this been taken into account?
- How accurate are the forecasts made and how valid are the assumptions on which they are based?

(c) Option 2 has the highest NPV and is therefore the most attractive to shareholders. However, the accuracy of the forecasts should be checked before a final decision is made.

4.6 Chesterfield Wanderers

(a) and (b) Incremental cash flows

(i) Player option

	Year 0 £000	Year 1 £000	Year 2 £000	Year 3 £000	Year 4 £000	Year 5 £000
Sale of player	2,200					1,000
Purchase of Bazza	(10,000)					
Sponsorship and so on		1,200	1,200	1,200	1,200	1,200
Gate receipts		2,500	1,300	1,300	1,300	1,300
Salaries paid		(800)	(800)	(800)	(800)	(1,200)
Salaries saved		400	400	400	400	600
Net cash received (paid)	(7,800)	3,300	2,100	2,100	2,100	2,900
Discount factor 10%	1.000	0.909	0.826	0.751	0.683	0.621
Present values	(7,800)	3,000	1,735	1,577	1,434	1,801
NPV	1,747					

(ii) Ground improvement option

	Year 1 £000	Year 2 £000	Year 3 £000	Year 4 £000	Year 5 £000
Ground improvements	(10,000)				
Increased gate receipts	(1,800)	4,400	4,400	4,400	4,400
	(11,800)	4,400	4,400	4,400	4,400
Discount factor 10%	0.909	0.826	0.751	0.683	0.621
Present values	(10,726)	3,634	3,304	3,005	2,732
NPV	1,949				

(c) The ground improvement option provides the higher NPV and is therefore the preferable option, based on the objective of shareholder wealth maximisation.

(d) A professional football club may not wish to pursue an objective of shareholder wealth enhancement. It may prefer to invest in quality players in an attempt to enjoy future sporting success. If this is the case, the NPV approach will be less appropriate because the club is not pursuing a strict wealth-related objective.

Chapter 5

5.1 Lee Caterers Ltd

The first step is to establish the NPV for each project:

(a) Cook/chill project

	Cash flows £000	Discount rate 10%	Present value £000
Initial outlay	(200)	1.00	(200)
1 year's time	85	0.91	77.4
2 years' time	94	0.83	78.0
3 years' time	86	0.75	64.5
4 years' time	62	0.68	42.2
		NPV	62.1

(b) Cook/freeze project

	Cash flows £000	Discount rate 10%	Present value £000
Initial outlay	(390)	1.00	(390)
1 year's time	88	0.91	80.1
2 years' time	102	0.83	84.7
3 years' time	110	0.75	82.5
4 years' time	110	0.68	74.8
5 years' time	110	0.62	68.2
6 years' time	90	0.56	50.4
7 years' time	85	0.51	43.4
8 years' time	60	0.47	28.2
			NPV 122.3

Eight years is the minimum period over which the two projects can be compared. The cook/chill will provide the following NPV over this period:

$$NPV = £62.1 + \frac{£62.1}{(1 + 0.1)^4} = £104.5$$

This NPV of £104,500 is lower than the NPV for the cook/freeze project of £122,300 (see above). Hence, the cook/freeze project should be accepted.

Using the equivalent-annual-annuity approach we derive the following:

$$Cook/chill: £62.1 \times 0.3155 = £19.59$$

$$Cook/freeze: £122.3 \times 0.1874 = £22.92$$

This approach leads to the same conclusion as the earlier approach.

5.3 Simonson Engineers plc

(a) The steps in calculating the expected net present value of the proposed plant are as follows:

	(a) Estimated cash flows £m	(b) Probability of occurrence	(a) × (b) Expected value £m
Year 2	2.0	0.2	0.4
	3.5	0.6	2.1
	4.0	0.2	0.8
			3.3
Year 3	2.5	0.2	0.5
	3.0	0.4	1.2
	5.0	0.4	2.0
			3.7
Year 4	3.0	0.2	0.6
	4.0	0.7	2.8
	5.0	0.1	0.5
			3.9
Year 5	2.5	0.2	0.5
	3.0	0.5	1.5
	6.0	0.3	1.8
			3.8

Taking the expected cash flows for each year into account:

	Year 1 £m	Year 2 £m	Year 3 £m	Year 4 £m	Year 5 £m
Expected cash flows	(9.0)	3.3	3.7	3.9	3.8
Discount factor	0.909	0.826	0.751	0.683	0.621
Expected present values	(8.18)	2.73	2.78	2.66	2.36
	ENPV 2.35				

The expected net present value is £2.35 million.

(b) To find the NPV of the worst possible outcome and the probability of its occurrence:

	Year 1 £m	Year 2 £m	Year 3 £m	Year 4 £m	Year 5 £m
Cash flows	(9.0)	2.0	2.5	3.0	2.5
Discount factor	0.909	0.826	0.751	0.683	0.621
Present values	(8.18)	1.65	1.88	2.05	1.55
	NPV (1.05)				

Probability of occurrence $0.2 \times 0.2 \times 0.2 \times 0.2 \times$ 0.0016

(c) The ENPV of the project is positive and so acceptance will increase the wealth of shareholders.

5.4   Helena Chocolate Products Ltd

(a) The first step is to calculate expected sales (units) for each year:

	Sales (units)	Probability	Expected sales
Year 1	100,000	0.2	20,000
	120,000	0.4	48,000
	125,000	0.3	37,500
	130,000	0.1	13,000
			118,500
Year 2	140,000	0.3	42,000
	150,000	0.3	45,000
	160,000	0.2	32,000
	200,000	0.2	40,000
			159,000
Year 3	180,000	0.5	90,000
	160,000	0.3	48,000
	120,000	0.1	12,000
	100,000	0.1	10,000
			160,000

Then the expected net present value can be arrived at:

Expected demand (units)	Incremental cash flow per unit	Total cash flow	Discount rate 10%	ENPV
	£	£		£
118,500	0.38	45,030	0.909	40,932
159,000	0.38	60,420	0.826	49,907
160,000	0.38	60,800	0.751	45,661
				136,500
Less				
Initial outlay				(30,000)
Opportunity costs				(100,000)
ENPV				6,500

Note: Interest charges should be ignored as the cost of capital is reflected in the discount factor.

The expected net present value is £6,500.

(b) As the ENPV is positive, the wealth of shareholders should be increased as a result of taking on the project. However, the ENPV is quite small and so careful checking of the underlying figures and assumptions is essential. The business has the option to sell the new product for an amount that is certain, but this option may have associated risks. The effect of selling the product on the long-term competitiveness of the business must be carefully considered.

Chapter 6

6.1 (a) This topic is dealt with in the chapter. The main benefits of leasing include ease of borrowing, reasonable cost, flexibility and avoidance of large cash outflows.

(b) This topic is also dealt with in the chapter. The main benefits of using retained profits include no dilution of control, no share issue costs, no delay in receiving funds and the tax benefits of capital appreciation over dividends.

(c) A business may decide to repay a loan earlier than required for various reasons including:

- A fall in interest rates may make the existing loan interest rates higher than current loan interest rates. Thus, the business may decide to repay the existing loan using finance from a cheaper loan.
- A rise in interest rates or changes in taxation policy may make loan financing more expensive than other forms of financing. This may make the business decide to repay the loan using another form of finance.
- The business may have surplus cash and may have no other profitable uses for the cash.
- The business may wish to reduce the level of financial risk by reducing the level of gearing.

6.5 Cybele Technology Ltd

(a) Cost of current policies

	£
Cost of financing receivables (60/365 × £4m × 14%)	92,055
Bad debts	20,000
	112,055
Cost of using a factor	
Factor service charge (2% × £4m)	80,000
Finance charges [40/365 × (85% × £4m) × 12%]	44,712
Bank overdraft charges [40/365 × (15% × £4m) × 14%]	9,205
	133,917
Less Administration cost savings	(26,000)
	107,917

The expected increase in profits arising from using a factor is:

$$£112,055 - £107,917 = \underline{£4,138}$$

Thus it would be more profitable to employ a factor. However, the difference between the two options is fairly small and other considerations, such as the need to control all aspects of customer relationships, may have a decisive influence on the final outcome.

(b) This topic is dealt with in the chapter. The main benefits include savings in credit management, releasing key individuals for other tasks, cash advances linked to sales activity and greater certainty in cash flows.

6.6 Telford Engineers plc

(a) Projected income statement for the year ending 31 December Year 10

	Loan notes £m		Shares £m
Operating profit	21.00		21.00
Interest payable	(7.80)	[(20 × 14%) + £5m]	(5.00)
Profit before taxation	13.20		16.00
Tax (30%)	(3.96)		(4.80)
Profit for the year	9.24		11.20
Dividends payable	4.00		5.00

	Loan notes £m	Shares £m	
Equity			
Share capital 25p shares	20.00	25.00	(20m + (20m × 0.25))
Share premium	–	15.00	(20 × (1.00 − 0.25))
Reserves*	48.24	49.20	
	68.24	89.20	
Non-current liabilities	50.00	30.00	
	118.24	119.20	

* The reserves figures are the Year 9 reserves *plus* the Year 10 (after taxation) profit *less* dividend paid. The Year 9 figure for share capital and reserves was 63, of which 20 (that is, 80 × 0.25) was share capital, leaving 43 as reserves. Add to that the retained profit for Year 10 (that is, 5.24 (debt) or 6.20 (shares)).

(b) The projected earnings per share are:

Loan notes (9.24/80)	11.55p
Shares (11.20/100)	11.20p

(c) The loan notes option will raise the gearing ratio and lower the interest cover of the business. This should not provide any real problems for the business as long as profits reach the expected level for Year 9 and remain at that level. However, there is an increased financial risk as a result of higher gearing and shareholders must carefully consider the adequacy of the additional returns to compensate for this higher risk. This appears to be a particular problem since profit levels seem to have been variable over recent years. The figures above suggest only a marginal increase in EPS compared with the equity alternative at the expected level of profit for Year 9.

The share alternative will have the effect of reducing the gearing ratio and is less risky. However, there may be a danger of dilution of control by existing shareholders under this alternative and it may, therefore, prove unacceptable to them. An issue of equity shares may, however, provide greater opportunity for flexibility in financing future projects. Information concerning current loan repayment terms and the attitude of shareholders and existing lenders towards the alternative financing methods would be useful.

Chapter 7

7.1 The answer to this question is covered in the chapter. Refer as necessary.

7.2 The answer to this question is covered in the chapter. Refer as necessary.

7.7 **Carpets Direct plc**

(a) The stages in calculating the theoretical ex-rights price of an ordinary share are as follows:

   (i) Earnings per share

$$\frac{\text{Profit for the year}}{\text{No. of ordinary shares}} = \frac{£4.5m}{120m} = \underline{£0.0375}$$

   (ii) Market value per share

$$\text{Earnings per share} \times \text{P/E ratio} = £0.0375 \times 22 = \underline{£0.825}$$

   (iii) For the theoretical ex-rights price:

	£
Original shares (4 × £0.825)	3.30
Rights share (1 × £0.66)	0.66
Value of five shares following rights issue	3.96
Value of one share following the rights issue	$\dfrac{£3.96}{5}$
Theoretical ex-rights price	= 79.2p

(b) The price at which the rights are likely to be traded is derived as below:

Value of one share after rights issue	79.2p
Less Cost of a rights share	(66.0p)
Value of rights to shareholder	13.2p

(c) Comparing the three options open to the investor:

    (i)   Option 1: Taking up rights issue

	£
Shareholding following rights issue [(4,000 + 1,000) × 79.2p]	3,960
Less Cost of rights shares (1,000 × 66p)	(660)
Shareholder wealth	3,300

    (ii) Option 2: Selling the rights

Shareholding following rights issue (4,000 × 79.2p)	3,168
Add Proceeds from sale of rights (1,000 × 13.2p)	132
Shareholder wealth	3,300

   (iii) Option 3: Doing nothing

As the rights are neither purchased nor sold, the shareholder wealth following the rights issue will be:

Shareholding (4,000 × 79.2p)	3,168

We can see that the investor will have the same wealth under the first two options. However, if the investor does nothing the rights issue will lapse and so the investor will lose the value of the rights and will be worse off.

Chapter 8

8.2   Celtor plc

(a) The cost of capital is important in the appraisal of investment projects as it represents the return required by investors. Incorrect calculation of the cost of capital can lead to incorrect investment decisions. Too high a cost of capital figure may lead to the rejection of profitable opportunities whereas too low a figure may lead to the acceptance of unprofitable opportunities.

(b) The first step in calculating the weighted average cost of capital is to arrive at the cost of ordinary shares:

$$K_0 = \frac{d_1}{P_0} + g$$

$$= \frac{(20 \times 1.04)}{390} + 0.04$$

$$= 9.3\%$$

Then the cost of loan capital:

$$K_d = \frac{I}{P_d}$$

$$= \frac{9(1 - 0.25)}{80} \times 100$$

$$= 8.4\%$$

The WACC can now be calculated:

	Cost	Target structure (weights)	Proportion	Contribution to WACC
	%		%	%
Cost of ordinary shares	9.3	100	58.8	5.5
Cost of loan capital	8.4	70	41.2	3.5
WACC				9.0

The weighted average cost of capital to use for future investment decisions is 9 per cent.

8.3 Grenache plc

(a) (i) Loan notes issue

Projected income statement for the year ended 30 April Year 8

	Optimistic	Most likely	Pessimistic
	£m	£m	£m
Profit before interest and taxation	22.0	18.1	11.8
Interest payable (£55m × 10%)	(5.5)	(5.5)	(5.5)
Profit before taxation	16.5	12.6	6.3
Tax (25%)	(4.1)	(3.2)	(1.6)
Profit for the year	12.4	9.4	4.7

(ii) Rights issue

Projected income statement for the year ended 30 April Year 8

	Optimistic	Most likely	Pessimistic
	£m	£m	£m
Profit before interest and taxation	22.0	18.1	11.8
Interest payable (10% × £25m)	(2.5)	(2.5)	(2.5)
Profit before taxation	19.5	15.6	9.3
Tax (25%)	(4.9)	(3.9)	(2.3)
Profit for the year	14.6	11.7	7.0

(b) (i) Earnings per share (EPS)
   ● Loan notes option

$$EPS = \frac{\text{Profit available for ordinary shareholders}}{\text{No. of ordinary shares in issue}}$$

		Optimistic	Most likely	Pessimistic
EPS	=	$\frac{£12.4m}{25m}$	$\frac{£9.4m}{25m}$	$\frac{£4.7m}{25m}$
	=	£0.50	£0.39	£0.19

● Rights option

		Optimistic	Most likely	Pessimistic
EPS	=	$\frac{£14.6m}{30m}$	$\frac{£11.7m}{30m}$	$\frac{£7.0m}{30m}$
	=	£0.49	£0.39	£0.23

(ii) Gearing ratio
 • Loan notes option

$$\text{Gearing ratio} = \frac{\text{Loan capital}}{\text{Ordinary share capital} + \text{Reserves} + \text{Loan}}$$

Optimistic	Most likely	Pessimistic
$= \dfrac{£55m}{£(55.0 + 43.6 + 6.7)m} \times 100\%$	$\dfrac{£55m}{£(55.0 + 43.6 + 3.7)m} \times 100\%$	$\dfrac{£55m}{£(55.0 + 43.6 + 0.5)m} \times 100\%$
$= \underline{52.2\%}$	53.8%	55.5%

Note: The retained profit for the year, which appears in the lower part of the fraction, is calculated as follows:

	Optimistic £m	Most likely £m	Pessimistic £m
Profit for the year	12.4	9.4	4.7
Dividends proposed and paid	(5.7)	(5.7)	(4.2)
Retained profit for the year	6.7	3.7	0.5

 • Rights option

Optimistic	Most likely	Pessimistic
$= \dfrac{£25m}{£(25.0 + 43.6 + 30.0 + 7.7)m} \times 100\%$	$\dfrac{£25m}{£(25.0 + 43.6 + 30.0 + 4.8)m} \times 100\%$	$\dfrac{£25m}{£(25.0 + 43.6 + 30.0 + 2.0m)} \times 100\%$
$= \underline{23.5\%}$	$\underline{24.2\%}$	$\underline{24.9\%}$

Note: The retained profit for the year, which appears in the lower part of the fraction, is calculated as follows:

	Optimistic £m	Most likely £m	Pessimistic £m
Profit for the year	14.6	11.7	7.0
Dividends proposed and paid	(6.9)	(6.9)	(5.0)
Retained profit	7.7	4.8	2.0

(c) The above calculations do not reveal any major differences in EPS between the two financing options. The optimistic and most likely options are almost identical. The pessimistic option favours the rights issue. The differences in the gearing ratios, however, are much more pronounced. Under each scenario the gearing ratio for the loan notes option is more than double that under the rights option. The loan notes option involves a significant increase in the level of financial risk for the business as the existing gearing ratio is 36.4 per cent (£25m/£68.6m).

The existing EPS is £0.40 (£9.9m/25m) and so the returns offered under the most likely and pessimistic scenarios do not compare favourably. This may make it difficult to persuade ordinary share investors that additional ordinary share finance should be provided. It may also mean that existing shareholders would resist any increase in gearing in order to finance the venture.

In order to produce a more considered assessment, it would be useful to attach probabilities to each of the three scenarios. An assessment of the likely implications of not undertaking a proposed change should also be provided. Finally, all investments undertaken by the business should be subject to proper investment appraisal using NPV analysis.

8.5   Ashcroft plc

(a) The earnings per share for Year 4 for the loan notes and ordinary share alternatives are computed as follows:

	Loan notes £m	Shares £m
Profit before interest and taxation	1.80	1.80
Interest payable	(0.30)	(–)
Profit before taxation	1.50	1.80
Tax	(0.75)	(0.90)
Profit for the year	0.75	0.90
Shares issues	4.0m	5.3m
EPS	18.75p	17.0p

(b) Let X = the operating profit (profit before interest and taxation) at which the two schemes have equal EPS.

$$\text{Loan notes} \qquad\qquad \text{Shares}$$

$$\frac{(X - £0.3m)(1 - 0.5)}{4.0m} = \frac{X(1 - 0.5)}{5.3m}$$

$$(5.3m\ X - £1.59m)(1 - 0.5) = 4.0m\ X(1 - 0.5)$$
$$0.65m\ X = £0.795m$$
$$X = £1.223m$$

This could also be solved graphically as described in the chapter.

(c) The following factors should be taken into account:

- stability of sales and profits
- stability of cash flows
- interest cover and gearing levels
- ordinary share investors' attitude towards risk
- dilution of control caused by new share issue
- security available to offer lenders
- effect on earnings per share and future cash flows.

Chapter 9

9.1   These factors are discussed in the chapter. Review as necessary.

9.4   Fellingham plc

The dividends over the period indicate a 9 per cent compound growth rate and so the chairman has kept to his commitment made in Year 1. This has meant that there has been a predictable stream of income for shareholders. However, during the period, inflation reached quite high levels and in order to maintain purchasing power the shareholders would have had to receive dividends adjusted in line with the general price index. These dividends would be as follows:

Year 2	$10.00 \times 1.11 = 11.10$p
Year 3	$11.10 \times 1.10 = 12.21$p
Year 4	$12.21 \times 1.08 = 13.19$p

We can see the actual dividends (Year 2, 10.90p; Year 3, 11.88p; Year 4, 12.95p) have fallen below these figures and so there has been a decline in real terms in the dividend income received by shareholders. Clearly, the 9 per cent growth rate did not achieve the anticipated maintenance of purchasing power plus a growth in real income which was anticipated.

However, the 9 per cent dividend growth rate is already high in relation to the earnings of the business, and a higher level of dividend to reflect changes in the general price index may have been impossible to achieve. The dividend coverage ratios for each of the years is:

Dividend coverage (EPS/DPS)

Year 1	1.1
Year 2	1.1
Year 3	0.9
Year 4	1.3

We can see that the earnings barely cover the dividend in the first two years and, in the third year, earnings fail to cover the dividend. The existing policy seems to be causing some difficulties for the business and can only be maintained if earnings grow at a satisfactory rate.

9.6   Traminer plc

(a) This part is dealt with in the chapter. Review as necessary.
(b) This part is also dealt with in the chapter. Review as necessary.
(c) The dividend payout ratio and dividend per share of the business over the past five years are:

Year	Dividend payout %	Dividend per share £
2004	50.0	0.84
2005	48.7	1.16
2006	23.9	0.43
2007	23.2	0.45
2008	37.9	0.97

We can see from this table that there is no stable dividend policy. The payout ratio fluctuated between 50 per cent and 23.2 per cent. The dividend per share has also fluctuated significantly over the period. This suggests that dividends are viewed simply as a residual, that is, dividends will only be paid when the business has no profitable opportunities in which to invest its earnings.

A fluctuating dividend policy is unlikely to be popular with shareholders. The evidence suggests that a policy that is predictable and contains no surprises is likely to be much more welcome. The signalling effect of dividends must also be borne in mind. Sudden changes in payout ratios may result in the market interpreting these changes incorrectly.

Thus, the chairman is probably wrong to suggest that the dividend policy need not be changed, and the view of the chief executive seems more sensible.

Chapter 10

10.1 Hercules Wholesalers Ltd

(a) The liquidity ratios of the business seem low. The current ratio is only 1.1 : 1 (that is, 306/285) and its acid test ratio is 0.6 : 1 (that is, 163/285). This latter ratio suggests that the business has insufficient liquid assets to pay its short-term obligations. A cash flow projection for the next period would provide a better insight to the liquidity position of the business. The bank overdraft seems high and it would be useful to know whether the bank is pressing for a reduction and what overdraft limit has been established for the business.

(b) The operating cash cycle can be calculated as follows:

	Number of days
Average inventories holding period:	
$\dfrac{[(\text{Opening inventories} + \text{Closing inventories})/2] \times 360}{\text{Cost of sales}} = \dfrac{[(125 + 143)/2] \times 360}{323}$	149
Add Average settlement period for trade receivables:	
$\dfrac{\text{Trade receivables} \times 360}{\text{Credit sales revenue}} = \dfrac{163}{452} \times 360$	130
	279
Less Average settlement period for trade payables:	
$\dfrac{\text{Trade payables} \times 360}{\text{Credit purchases}} = \dfrac{145}{341} \times 360$	153
Operating cash cycle	126

(c) The business can reduce the operating cash cycle in a number of ways. The average inventories holding period seems quite long. At present, average inventories held represent almost five months' sales needs. This period can be shortened by reducing the level of inventories held. Similarly, the average settlement period for trade receivables seems long at more than four months' sales revenue. This may be shortened by imposing tighter credit control, offering discounts, charging interest on overdue accounts and so on. However, any policy decisions concerning inventories and trade receivables must take account of current trading conditions. The operating cash cycle would also be reduced by extending the period of credit taken to pay suppliers. However, for the reasons mentioned in the chapter, this option must be given careful consideration.

10.5 Mayo Computers Ltd

New proposals from credit control department

	£000	£000
Current level of investment in trade receivables		
[£20m × (60/365)]		3,288
Proposed level of investment in trade receivables		
[(£20m × 60%) × (30/365)]	(986)	
[(£20m × 40%) × (50/365)]	(1,096)	(2,082)
Reduction in level of investment		1,206

The reduction in overdraft interest as a result of the reduction in the level of investment will be

$$£1,206,000 \times 14\% = £169,000.$$

	£000	£000
Cost of cash discounts offered (£20m × 60% × 2½%)		300
Additional cost of credit administration		20
		320
Bad debt savings	(100)	
Interest charge savings (see above)	(169)	(269)
Net cost of policy each year		51

These calculations show that the business would incur additional annual costs if it implemented this proposal. It would therefore be cheaper to stay with the existing credit policy.

10.6 Boswell Enterprises Ltd

(a) The investment in working capital will be:

	Current policy		New policy	
	£000	£000	£000	£000
Trade receivables				
[(£3m × ¹/₁₂ × 30%) + (£3m × ²/₁₂ × 70%)]		425.0		
[(£3.15m × ¹/₁₂ × 60%) + (£3.15m × ²/₁₂ × 40%)]				367.5
Inventories				
[[£3m − (£3m × 20%)] × ³/₁₂]		600.0		
{[£3.15m − (£3.15m × 20%)] × ³/₁₂}				630.0
Cash (fixed)		140.0		140.0
		1,165.0		1,137.5
Trade payables				
[[£3m − (£3m × 20%)] × ²/₁₂]	(400.0)			
{[£3.15m − (£3.15m × 20%)] × ²/₁₂}			(420.0)	
Accrued variable expenses				
[£3m × ¹/₁₂ × 10%]	(25.0)			
[£3.15m × ¹/₁₂ × 10%]			(26.3)	
Accrued fixed expenses	(15.0)	(440.0)	(15.0)	(461.3)
Investment in working capital		725.0		676.2

(b) The expected profit for the year will be:

	Current policy		New policy	
	£000	£000	£000	£000
Sales revenue		3,000.0		3,150.0
Cost of goods sold		(2,400.0)		(2,520.0)
Gross profit (20%)		600.0		630.0
Variable expenses (10%)	(300.0)		(315.0)	
Fixed expenses	(180.0)		(180.0)	
Discounts	–	(480.0)	(47.3)	(542.3)
Profit for the year		120.0		87.7

(c) We can see that the investment in working capital will be slightly lower under the proposed policy than under the current policy. However, profit will be substantially lower as a result of offering discounts. The increase in sales revenue resulting from the discounts will not be sufficient to offset the additional costs of making the discounts to customers. It seems that the business should, therefore, stick with its current policy.

Chapter 11

11.1 Aquarius plc

There are a number of ways in which the accuracy of the predicted free cash flow figures may be checked. These include:

- *Internal*
  - *Past results*. These may be used to see whether the future projections are in line with past achievements.
  - *Strategy*. The future free cash flows for the business should reflect the strategies that have been put in place over the planning period.
  - *Capacity*. The ability of the business to generate the free cash flows from the resources available over the planning period should be considered.
  - *Market research*. The evidence from any market research carried out by the business should be consistent with the estimates made.
- *External*
  - *Industry forecasts*. Forecasts for the industry as a whole may be examined to see whether the predicted sales and profits for the business are in line with industry forecasts.
  - *External commentators*. Stockbrokers and financial journalists may have made predictions about the likely future performance of the business and so may provide an external (and perhaps more objective) view of likely future prospects.
  - *Technology*. The likely impact of technological change on free cash flows may be assessed using technology forecasts.
  - *Competitor analysis*. The performance of competitors may be used to help assess likely future market share.

This is not an exhaustive list. You may have thought of others.

11.3 Virgo plc

There is no single correct answer to this problem. The suggestions set out below are based on experiences that some businesses have had in implementing a management bonus system based on EVA® performance.

In order to get the divisional managers to think and act like the owners of the business, it is recommended that divisional performance, as measured by EVA®, should form a significant part of their total rewards. Thus, around 50 per cent of the total rewards paid to managers could be related to the EVA® that has been generated for a period. (In the case of very senior managers it could be more, and for junior managers less.)

The target for managers to achieve could be a particular level of improvement in EVA® for their division over a year. A target bonus can then be set for achievement of the target level of improvement. If this target level of improvement is achieved, 100 per cent of the bonus should be paid. If the target is not achieved, an agreed percentage (below 100 per cent) could be paid according to the amount of shortfall. If, on the other hand, the target is exceeded, an agreed percentage (with no upper limits) may be paid.

The timing of the payment of management bonuses is important. In the question it was mentioned that Virgo plc wishes to encourage a longer-term view among its managers. One approach is to use a 'bonus bank' system whereby the bonus for a period is placed in a bank and a certain proportion (usually one-third) can be drawn in the period in which it is earned. If the target for the following period is not met, there can be a charge against the bonus bank and so the total amount available for withdrawal is reduced. This will ensure that the managers try to maintain improvements in EVA® consistently over the years.

In some cases, the amount of bonus is determined by three factors: the performance of the business as a whole (as measured by EVA®), the performance of the division (as measured by EVA®) and the performance of the particular manager (using agreed indicators of performance). Performance for the business as a whole is often given the highest weighting and individual performance the lowest weighting. Thus, 50 per cent of the bonus may be for corporate performance, 30 per cent for divisional performance and 20 per cent for individual performance.

11.5 Pisces plc

Adjusted NOPAT

	£m	£m
Operating loss		(20.5)
EVA® adjustments		
R&D costs [40 – (1/16 × 80)] (Note 1)	35.0	
Excess allowance	6.5	41.5
Adjusted NOPAT		21.0

Adjusted net assets (or capital invested)

	£m	£m
Net assets per statement of financial position		196.5
Add		
R&D costs (Note 1)	70.0	
Allowance for trade receivables	6.5	
Restructuring costs (Note 2)	6.0	82.5
		279.0
Less Marketable investments		(9.0)
Adjusted net assets		270.0

Notes

1 The R&D costs represent a writing back of £40 million and a writing off of 1/16 of the total cost of the R&D as the benefits are expected to last 16 years.

2 The restructuring costs are added back to the net assets as they provide benefits over an infinite period.

EVA® can be calculated as follows:

$$EVA® = NOPAT - (R \times C)$$
$$= £21m - (7\% \times £270m)$$
$$= £2.1m$$

Thus, the EVA® for the period is positive even though an operating loss was recorded. This means that shareholder wealth increased during the third year.

Chapter 12

12.2 Dawn Raider plc

(a)

	£m
(i) The bid consideration is [(200m shares/2) × 198p]	198
The market value of the shares in Sleepy Giant is (£100m × 2 × 72p)	(144)
The bid premium is therefore	54

(ii) Sleepy Giant's net assets per share are £446m/200m = £2.23

(iii) Dividends from Sleepy Giant before the takeover are 100 × 7p = £7.00

Dividends from Dawn Raider after takeover are 50 × 2p = £1.00

(iv) Earnings per share after takeover:

	£m
Expected post-tax profits of Dawn Raider	23
Current post-tax profits of Sleepy Giant	16
Post-tax savings	1
Improvements due to management	5
Total earnings	45
Expected EPS [£45m/(200m + 100m shares)]	15p

(v) Expected share price following takeover will be calculated as follows: P/E ratio × expected EPS.

$$\text{P/E ratio at 31 May Year 8} = \text{Share price/EPS}$$
$$= 198/9.0$$
$$= 22$$
$$\therefore \text{Expected share price} = 22 \times 15p$$
$$= £3.30$$

(b) (i) The net assets per share of the business is irrelevant. This represents a past investment that is irrelevant to future decisions. The key comparison is between the current market value of the shares of Sleepy Giant and the bid price.

The dividend received from Dawn Raider will be substantially lower than those received from Sleepy Giant. However, the share value of Dawn Raider has grown much faster than that of Sleepy Giant. The investor must consider the total returns from the investment rather than simply the dividends received.

(ii) We can see above that by accepting the bid, the shareholders of Sleepy Giant will make an immediate and substantial gain. The bid premium is more than 37 per cent higher than the current market value of the shares in Sleepy Giant. This could provide a sufficient incentive for the shareholders of Sleepy Giant to accept the offer. However, the shareholders of Dawn Raider must consider the bid carefully. Although the expected share price calculated above is much higher following the bid, it is based on the assumption that the P/E ratio of the business will not be affected by the takeover. However, this may not be the case. Sleepy Giant is a much larger business in terms of sales and net assets than Dawn Raider and has a much lower P/E ratio (nine times). The market would have to be convinced that Sleepy Giant's prospects will be substantially improved following the takeover.

12.4 **Simat plc**

(a) (i) Calculating the value per share in the consideration of Stidwell Ltd on a net assets (liquidation) basis gives:

$$P_0 = \frac{\text{Total assets at realisable values} - \text{Total liabilities}}{\text{No. of shares in issue}}$$

$$= \frac{£347,000[(285 + 72 + 15 + 157) - (42 + 140)]}{300,000}$$

$$= £1.16$$

(ii) The dividend yield method gives:

$$P_0 = \frac{\text{Gross dividend per share}}{\text{Gross dividend yield}} \times 100$$

$$= \frac{(18,000/300,000) \times 100/90}{2.76} \times 100$$

$$= £2.42$$

(iii) The P/E ratio method gives:

$$P_0 = \frac{\text{P/E ratio} \times \text{Net profit}}{\text{No. of ordinary shares in issue}}$$

$$= \frac{11 \times £48,500}{300,000}$$

$$= £1.78$$

(b) This topic is covered in the chapter. Review as necessary.

12.6 Larkin Conglomerates plc

(a) The value of an ordinary share in Hughes Ltd according to the three methods is calculated as follows:

(i) Net assets (liquidation) basis:

$$P_0 = \frac{\text{Total assets at realisable values} - \text{Total liabilities}}{\text{No. of ordinary shares}}$$

$$= \frac{£(326 - 166)}{60}$$

$$= \frac{£160}{60} = £2.67$$

(ii) Dividend yield method:

$$P_0 = \frac{(\text{Net dividend per share} \times 100/75)}{\text{Gross dividend yield}} \times 100$$

$$= \frac{(4.0/60.0) \times 100/75}{5} \times 100$$

$$= £1.78$$

(iii) Price/earnings ratio method:

$$P_0 = \frac{\text{P/E ratio} \times \text{Net profit}}{\text{No. of ordinary shares}}$$

$$= \frac{£16.4 \times 12}{60} = £3.28$$

(b) Other information might include:

- Details of relations with suppliers, employees, the community and other stakeholders should be ascertained.
- The nature and condition of the assets owned by the target business should be examined. The suitability of the assets and their ability to perform the tasks required will be vitally important.
- Key personnel will need to be identified and their intentions with regard to the business following the takeover must be ascertained.
- Onerous commitments entered into by the business (for example, capital expenditure decisions, contracts with suppliers) must be identified and evaluated.
- Details of the state of the order book, the market share of the products or services provided by the business and the loyalty of its customers should be established.
- Examination of the budgets which set out expected performance levels, output levels and future financing needs would be useful.
- Information concerning the cost structure of the business would be useful.

Glossary of key terms

ABC system of inventories control   A method of applying different levels of inventories control based on the value of each category of inventories. *p. 402*

Accounting rate of return (ARR)   The average profit from an investment, expressed as a percentage of the average investment made. *p. 125*

Acid test ratio   A liquidity ratio that relates the current assets (less inventories) to the current liabilities. *p. 87*

Ageing schedule of (trade) receivables   A report dividing receivables into categories, depending on the length of time outstanding. *p. 413*

Agency problem   The conflict of interest between shareholders (the principals) and the managers (agents) of a business which arises when the managers seek to maximise their own welfare. *p. 15*

Alternative Investment Market (AIM)   Second-tier market of the London Stock Exchange that specialises in the securities of smaller businesses. *p. 297*

Annuity   An investment that pays a constant sum each year over a period of time. *p. 177*

Arbitrage transactions   Transactions that exploit differences in price between similar shares (or other assets) and which involve selling the overpriced shares and purchasing the underpriced shares. *p. 347*

Asset-based finance   A form of finance where assets are used as security for cash advances to a business. Factoring and invoice discounting, where the security is trade receivables, are examples of asset-based finance. *p. 247*

Average inventories turnover period   An efficiency ratio that measures the average period for which inventories are held by a business. *p. 80*

Average settlement period for (trade) payables   The average time taken by a business to pay its payables. *pp. 81, 426*

Average settlement period for (trade) receivables   The average time taken for credit customers to pay the amounts owing. *pp. 80, 413*

Bank overdraft   Amount owing to a bank that is repayable on demand. The amount borrowed and the rate of interest may fluctuate over time. *p. 243*

Behavioural finance   An approach to finance that rejects the notion that investors behave in a rational manner but make systematic errors when processing information. *p. 276*

Beta (coefficient)   A measure of the extent to which the returns on a particular share vary with the market as a whole. *p. 312*

Bill of exchange   A written agreement requiring one party to the agreement to pay a particular amount at some future date. *p. 243*

Bond   *See* Loan notes. *p. 277*

Bonus issue (scrip issue)   Transfer of reserves to share capital requiring the issue of new shares to shareholders in proportion to existing shareholdings. *p. 280*

Business angels   Wealthy individuals willing to invest in businesses at an early stage in their development. *p. 296*

Capital asset pricing model (CAPM)   A method of establishing the cost of share capital that identifies two forms of risk: diversifiable risk and non-diversifiable risk. *p. 311*

Capital markets   Financial markets for long-term loans, capital and shares. *p. 5*

Capital rationing   Limiting the long-term funds available for investment during a period. Soft capital rationing is imposed by managers, and hard capital rationing is imposed by investors. *p. 156*

Cash discount   A reduction in the amount due for goods or services sold on credit in return for prompt payment. *p. 412*

Clientele effect   The phenomenon where investors seek out businesses whose dividend policies match their particular needs. *p. 373*

Coefficient of correlation   A statistical measure of association that can be used to measure the degree to which the returns from two separate projects are related. The measure ranges from +1 to −1. A measure of +1 indicates a perfect positive correlation and a measure of −1 indicates a perfect negative correlation. *p. 209*

Combined Code   A code of practice for companies listed on the London Stock Exchange which deals with corporate governance matters. *p. 16*

Competition Commission   (formerly Monopolies and Mergers Commission) A UK government regulatory body that seeks to prevent monopolies and mergers from occurring that are anti-competitive and not in the public interest. *p. 498*

Competitor profiling   Building a profile of the strengths and weaknesses of a major competitor in order to understand the threats posed. *p. 34*

Conglomerate merger   A merger between two businesses engaged in unrelated activities. *p. 474*

Convertible loan notes   Loan notes that can be converted into ordinary share capital at the option of the holders. *p. 229*

Corporate governance   Systems for directing and controlling a business. *p. 15*

Cost of capital   The rate of return required by investors in the business. The cost of capital is used as the criterion rate of return when evaluating investment proposals using the NPV and IRR methods of appraisal. *pp. 140, 308*

Creative accounting   Adopting accounting policies to achieve a particular view of performance and position that preparers would like users to see rather than what is a true and fair view. *p. 106*

Crown jewels   The most valued part of a business (which may be sold to fend off a hostile takeover bid). *p. 496*

Cum dividend   A term used to describe the price of a share that includes the right to receive a forthcoming dividend. *p. 365*

Current ratio   A liquidity ratio that relates the current assets of the business to the current liabilities. *p. 86*

Debt factoring   *See* Factoring. *p. 244*

Deep discount bonds   Redeemable bonds that are issued at a low or zero rate of interest and at a large discount to their redeemable value. *p. 238*

Degree of financial gearing   A measure of the sensitivity of earnings per share to changes in profit before interest and taxation. *p. 331*

Demerger (spin-off)   The transfer of part of the assets in an existing business to a new business. Shareholders in the existing business will be given shares, usually on a pro rata basis, in the new business. *p. 499*

Discount factor   The rate used when making investment decisions to discount future cash flows in order to arrive at their present value. *p. 139*

Discriminate function   A boundary line, produced by multiple discriminate analysis, that identifies those businesses that are likely to suffer financial distress and those that are not. *p. 104*

Diversifiable risk   That part of the total risk that is specific to an investment and which can be diversified away through combining the investment with other investments. *p. 211*

Diversification   The process of reducing risk by investing in a variety of different projects or assets. *p. 208*

Divestment   The selling off of part of the operations of a business. *p. 498*

Dividend   A transfer of assets (usually cash) made by a business to its shareholders. *p. 364*

Dividend cover ratio   The reciprocal of the dividend payout ratio (*see* below). *pp. 92, 366*

Dividend payout ratio   An investment ratio that divides the dividends announced for the period by the profit generated during the period and available for dividends. *pp. 91, 366*

Dividend per share   An investment ratio that divides the dividends announced for a period by the number of shares in issue. *p. 92*

Dividend yield ratio   An investment ratio that relates the cash return from a share to its current market value. *pp. 92, 507*

Earnings per share   An investment ratio that divides the earnings (profits) generated by a business, and available to ordinary shareholders, by the number of shares in issue. *p. 93*

Economic order quantity (EOQ)   The quantity of inventories that should be purchased in order to minimise total inventories costs. *p. 402*

Economic value added (EVA®)   The difference between the net operating profit after tax and the required returns from investors. *p. 446*

Efficient stock market   A stock market in which new information is quickly and accurately absorbed by investors, resulting in an appropriate share price adjustment. *p. 268*

Equivalent-annual-annuity approach An approach to deciding among competing investment projects with unequal lives which involves converting the NPV of each project into an annual annuity stream over the project's expected life. *p. 177*

Eurobonds Bearer bonds that are issued by listed businesses and other organisations in various countries with the finance being raised on an international basis. *p. 227*

Event tree diagram A diagram that portrays the various events or outcomes associated with a particular course of action and the probabilities associated with each event or outcome. *p. 198*

Ex dividend A term used to describe the price of a share that excludes any right to a forthcoming dividend. *p. 365*

Expected net present value (ENPV) A method of dealing with risk that involves assigning a probability of occurrence to each possible outcome. The expected net present value of the project represents a weighted average of the possible NPVs where the probabilities are used as weights. *p. 195*

Expected value A weighted average of a range of possible outcomes where the probabilities are used as weights. *p. 195*

Expected value–standard deviation rule A decision rule that can be employed to discriminate among competing investments where the possible outcomes are known and are normally distributed. *p. 216*

Factoring A method of raising short-term finance. A financial institution ('factor') will manage the credit sales records of the business and will be prepared to advance sums to the business based on the amount of trade receivables outstanding. *p. 244*

Finance lease Agreement that gives the lessee the right to use a particular asset for substantially the whole of its useful life in return for regular fixed payments. It represents an alternative to outright purchase. *p. 237*

Financial derivative Any form of financial instrument, based on share or loan capital, which can be used by investors either to increase their returns or to decrease their exposure to risk. *p. 236*

Financial gearing The existence of fixed-payment-bearing securities (for example, loans) in the capital structure of a business. *p. 88*

Five Cs of credit A checklist of factors to be taken into account when assessing the creditworthiness of a customer. *p. 407*

Fixed charge Where a specific asset is offered as security for a loan. *p. 225*

Fixed costs A cost that remains the same irrespective of the level of output. *p. 35*

Fixed interest rate A rate of return payable to lenders that will remain unchanged with rises and falls in market interest rates. *p. 236*

Floating charge Where the whole of the assets of the business is offered as security for a loan. The charge will 'crystallise' and fix on specific assets in the event of a default in loan obligations. *p. 225*

Floating interest rates A rate of return payable to lenders that will rise and fall with market rates of interest. *p. 236*

Free cash flows Cash flows available to long-term lenders and shareholders after any new investment in assets. *p. 440*

FTSE (Footsie) indices   Indices available to help monitor trends in overall share price movements of Stock Exchange listed businesses. *p. 263*

Future growth value (FGV®)   Value placed on the future growth potential of a business by investors. Equal to the market value of the business – capital invested + EVA®/r. *p. 464*

Gearing ratio   A ratio that relates the contribution of long-term lenders to the total long-term capital of the business. *p. 89*

Golden parachute   Substantial fee payable to a manager of a business in the event that the business is taken over. *p. 496*

Gross profit margin   A profitability ratio relating the gross profit for the period to the sales for that period. *p. 77*

Hedging arrangement   An attempt to reduce or eliminate the risk associated with a particular action by taking some form of counter-action. *p. 236*

Hire purchase   A method of acquiring an asset by paying the purchase price by instalments over a period. Normally, control of the asset will pass as soon as the hire purchase contract is signed and the first instalment is paid, whereas ownership will pass on payment of the final instalment. *p. 240*

Horizontal merger   A merger between two businesses in the same industry and at the same point in the production/distribution chain. *p. 474*

Indifference point   The level of profit and interest before taxation at which two, or more, financing schemes provide the same level of return to ordinary shareholders. *p. 338*

Inflation   A rise in the general price level. *p. 135*

Information asymmetry   Where the availability of information differs between groups (such as managers and shareholders). *p. 374*

Information signalling   Conveying information to shareholders through management actions (for example, increasing dividends to convey management optimism concerning the future). *p. 374*

Interest cover ratio   A gearing ratio that divides the profit before interest and taxation by the interest payable for a period. *p. 89*

Interest rate swap   An arrangement between two businesses whereby each business assumes responsibility for the other's interest payments. *p. 236*

Internal rate of return (IRR)   The discount rate for a project that has the effect of producing zero NPV. *p. 142*

Invoice discounting   A form of finance provided by a financial institution based on a proportion of the face value of the credit sales outstanding. *p. 246*

Junk (high-yield) bonds   Loan capital with a relatively high level of investment risk for which investors are compensated by relatively high levels of return. *p. 232*

Just-in-time (JIT) inventories management   A system of inventories management that aims to have supplies delivered to production just in time for their required use. *p. 405*

Lead time   The time lag between placing an order for goods or services and their delivery. *p. 400*

Linear programming A mathematical technique for rationing limited resources in such a way as to optimise the benefits. *p. 173*

Liquidation method A method of valuing the shares of a business by reference to the net realisable values of its net assets. *p. 504*

Loan covenants Conditions contained within a loan agreement that are designed to protect the lenders. *p. 226*

Loan notes Long-term borrowings usually made by limited companies. *p. 227*

Market capitalisation Total market value of the shares of a business. *p. 263*

Market value added (MVA) The difference between the market value of the business and the total investment that has been made in it. *p. 455*

Materials requirement planning (MRP) system A computer-based system of inventories control that schedules the timing of deliveries of bought-in parts and materials to coincide with production requirements to meet demand. *p. 405*

Merger When two or more businesses combine in order to form a single business. *p. 474*

Mission statement A statement setting out the purpose for which a business exists. *p. 9*

Mortgage A loan secured on property. *p. 234*

Multiple discriminate analysis A statistical technique used to predict financial distress, which involves using an index based on a combination of financial ratios. *p. 104*

Net present value (NPV) The net cash flows from a project that have been adjusted to take account of the time value of money. The NPV measure is used to evaluate investment projects. *p. 133*

Net realisable value The selling price of an asset, less any costs incurred in selling the asset. *p. 504*

Non-diversifiable risk That part of the total risk that is common to all investments and which cannot be diversified away by combining investments. *p. 211*

Normal distribution The description applied to the distribution of a set of data which, when displayed graphically, forms a symmetrical bell-shaped curve. *p. 205*

Objective probabilities Probabilities based on information gathered from past experience. *p. 206*

Offer for sale Method of selling shares to the public through the use of an issuing house which acts as an intermediary. *p. 283*

Operating cash cycle The time period between the outlay of cash to purchase goods supplied and the ultimate receipt of cash from the sale of the goods. *p. 420*

Operating lease A short-term lease where the rewards and risks of ownership stay with the owner. *p. 238*

Operating profit margin A profitability ratio relating the operating profit for the period to the sales for that period. *p. 76*

Opportunity cost The value in monetary terms of being deprived of the next best opportunity in order to pursue the particular objective. *p. 147*

Optimal capital structure   The particular mix of long-term funds employed by a business that minimises the cost of capital. *p. 342*

Overtrading   The situation arising when a business is operating at a level of activity that cannot be supported by the amount of finance which has been committed. *p. 99*

Pac-man defence   A means of defending against a hostile takeover bid, which involves launching a bid for the bidding company. *p. 496*

Payback period (PP)   The time taken for the initial investment in a project to be repaid from the net cash inflows of the project. *p. 129*

PBIT–EPS indifference chart   A chart that plots the returns to shareholders at different levels of profit before interest and taxation for different financing schemes. *p. 337*

Per-cent-of-sales method   A method of financial planning that first estimates the sales for the planning period and then estimates other financial variables as a percentage of the sales figure. *p. 49*

Placing   An issue of shares to selected investors, such as financial institutions, rather than to the public. *p. 285*

Plug   The particular form of finance used to fill a financing gap. *p. 50*

Poison pill   A defensive measure taken by a business that is designed to make it unattractive to potential acquirers. *p. 496*

Post-completion audit   A review of the performance of an investment project to see whether actual performance matched planned performance and whether any lessons can be drawn from the way in which the investment was carried out. *p. 159*

Price/earnings ratio   An investment ratio that relates the market value of a share to the earnings per share. *p. 94*

Private equity   Equity finance primarily for small and medium-sized businesses wishing to grow but which do not have ready access to stock markets. *p. 286*

Profitability index   The present value of the future cash flows from a project divided by the present value of the outlay. *p. 173*

Projected financial statements   Financial statements such as the cash flow statement, income statement and statement of financial position that have been prepared on the basis of estimates and which relate to the future. *p. 30*

Public issue   Method of issuing shares that involves a direct invitation from the business to the public to subscribe for shares. *p. 283*

Record date   A date that is set by the directors of a business to establish who is eligible to receive dividends. Those shareholders registered with the company on this date will receive any dividends announced for the period. *p. 365*

Relevant costs   Costs that are relevant to a particular decision. *p. 147*

Replacement cost   The cost of replacing an asset with an identical asset. *p. 504*

Residual theory of dividends   A theory that states that managers should only make dividend distributions where the expected returns from investment opportunities are below the required rate of return for investors. *p. 378*

Return on capital employed (ROCE)   A profitability ratio expressing the relationship between the operating profit and the long-term capital invested in the business. *p. 74*

Return on ordinary shareholders' funds (ROSF)   A profitability ratio expressing the relationship between the profit available for ordinary shareholders during the period and the ordinary shareholders' funds invested in the business. *p. 73*

Rights issue   An issue of shares to existing shareholders on the basis of the number of shares already held. *p. 278*

Risk   The likelihood that what is estimated to occur will not actually occur. *pp. 52, 134, 181*

Risk-adjusted discount rate (RADR)   A method of dealing with risk that involves adjusting the discount rate for projects according to the level of risk involved. The RADR will be the risk-free rate plus an appropriate risk premium. *p. 194*

Risk-averse investors   Investors who select the investment with the lowest risk, where the returns from different investments are equal. *p. 190*

Risk-neutral investors   Investors who are indifferent to the level of risk associated with different investments. *p. 190*

Risk premium   An extra amount of return from an investment, owing to a perceived level of risk: the greater the perceived level of risk, the larger the risk premium. *p. 135*

Risk-seeking investors   Investors who select the investment with the highest risk where the returns from different investments are equal. *p. 190*

Sale and leaseback   An agreement to sell an asset (usually property) to another party and simultaneously lease the asset back in order to continue using the asset. *p. 239*

Sales revenue per employee   An efficiency ratio that relates the sales generated during a period to the average number of employees of the business. *p. 83*

Sales revenue to capital employed   An efficiency ratio that relates the sales generated during a period to the long-term capital employed. *p. 82*

Satisficing   The idea that managers should try to provide each stakeholder group of the business with a satisfactory level of return. *p. 8*

Scenario analysis   A method of dealing with risk that involves changing a number of variables simultaneously so as to provide a particular scenario for managers to consider. *pp. 53, 189*

Scrip dividend   A dividend to shareholders consisting of additional shares rather than cash. *p. 386*

Securitisation   Bundling together illiquid financial or physical assets of the same type in order to provide backing for issuing interest-bearing securities, such as bonds. *p. 241*

Security   An asset pledged or guarantee provided against a loan. *p. 225*

Semi-variable costs   Costs that have an element of both fixed and variable costs. *p. 35*

Sensitivity analysis   An examination of the key variables affecting a project to see how changes in each variable might influence the outcome. *pp. 53, 181*

Sensitivity chart   A chart that portrays the effect of changes to key variables on the NPV of a project. *p. 187*

Share options   A scheme that allows managers and employees the right, but not the obligation, to acquire shares in the business at some future date at an agreed price. *p. 19*

Shareholder value   Putting the needs of shareholders at the heart of management decisions. *p. 436*

Shareholder value analysis (SVA)   Method of measuring and managing business value based on the long-term cash flows generated. *p. 439*

Shareholder wealth maximisation   The idea that the main purpose of a business is to maximise the wealth of its owners (shareholders). This idea underpins modern financial management. *p. 6*

Shortest-common-period-of-time approach   A method of comparing the profitability of projects with unequal lives that establishes the shortest common period of time over which the projects can be compared. *p. 175*

Simulation   A method of dealing with risk that involves calculating probability distributions from a range of possible outcomes. *pp. 54, 189*

Spin-off   *See* Demerger. *p. 499*

Standard deviation   A measure of spread that is based on deviations from the mean or expected value. *p. 202*

Statement of financial position (balance sheet) method   A method of valuing the shares of a business by reference to the value of the net assets as shown in the statement of financial position. *p. 503*

Stock Exchange   A primary and secondary market for business capital. *p. 262*

Subjective probabilities   Probabilities based on opinion rather than past data. *p. 207*

Subordinated loan   A loan that is ranked below other loan capital in the order of interest payment and capital repayment. *p. 226*

Takeover   Normally used to describe a situation where a larger business acquires control of a smaller business, which is then absorbed by the larger business. *p. 474*

Tender issue   An issue of shares to investors that requires the investors to state the amount that they are prepared to pay for the shares. *p. 283*

Term loan   A loan, usually from a bank, which is tailored specifically to the needs of the borrower. The loan contract usually specifies the repayment date, interest rate and so on. *p. 227*

Total shareholder return (TSR)   The change in share value over a period plus any dividends paid during the period. *p. 459*

Univariate analysis   A method used to help predict financial distress, which involves the use of a single ratio as a predictor. *p. 104*

Utility function   A chart that portrays the level of satisfaction or pleasure obtained from receiving additional wealth at different levels of existing wealth. *p. 191*

Value drivers   Key variables that determine business performance. *p. 441*

Variable cost   A cost that varies according to the volume of activity. *p. 35*

Venture capital   *See* Private equity. *p. 286*

Vertical merger   A merger between a supplier of goods or services and its customer. *p. 474*

Warrant   A document giving the holder the right, but not the obligation, to acquire shares in a business at an agreed price at some future date. *p. 234*

Weighted average cost of capital (WACC)   A weighted average of the post-tax costs of the forms of long-term finance employed within a business where the market value of the particular forms of finance are used as weights. *p. 322*

White knight   A potential bidder for a business that is approached by the managers of that business to make a bid. The approach is made to defend the business against a hostile bid from another business. *p. 497*

White squire   A business that is approached by the managers of another business to purchase a large block of shares in that business with the object of rescuing the business from a hostile takeover. *p. 497*

Working capital   Current assets less current liabilities. *p. 394*

Index